MW00627423

BENDING THEIR WAY ONWARD

Bending Their Way Onward

Creek Indian Removal in Documents

EDITED AND ANNOTATED BY
CHRISTOPHER D. HAVEMAN

UNIVERSITY OF NEBRASKA PRESS
Lincoln and London

Manufactured in the United States of America

Library of Congress Cataloging-in-Publication Data
Names: Haveman, Christopher D., 1976–, editor.
Title: Bending their way onward: Creek Indian removal in documents / Edited and annotated by Christopher D. Haveman.
Other titles: Creek Indian removal in documents
Description: Lincoln: University of Nebraska Press, [2017] | Includes bibliographical references and index.
Identifiers: LCCN 2017036836
ISBN 9780803296985 (cloth: alk. paper)
ISBN 9781496204141 (pdf)
Subjects: LCSH: Creek Indians—Relocation.
Creek Indians—Government relations.
Creek Indians—History—19th century—Sources.
Indian Removal, 1813–1903—Sources.
Classification: LCC E99.C9 B46 2017
DDC 975.004/97385—dc23
LC record available at https://lccn.loc.gov/2017036836

Set in Minion Pro by E. Cuddy.

CONTENTS

ILLUSTRATIONS

MAPS

ACKNOWLEDGMENTS

The origins of this project can be traced back to 2009 when I began transcribing the relocation journals for inclusion in my dissertation's appendix. Fortunately, neither the transcriptions nor the appendix materialized, and what emerged out of those ashes is the edited volume now before you. Since that time I have been helped by many kind and generous people who were instrumental in making this volume a reality. At the University of West Alabama, R. Volney Riser and Monroe C. Snider allocated funds for the purchase of microfilm; university research grants allowed me to travel to Washington DC to photocopy documents; and the UWA foundation generously purchased two *carte-de-visite* images of Lieutenant John Titcomb Sprague, one of which is included in this book. I am fortunate that Anna Bedsole continues patiently processing all my interlibrary loan requests while Christin Loehr runs interference on my myriad other library-related inquiries.

I am also lucky to have been guided by many of the best in the business. Kathryn E. Holland Braund, who has a number of edited volumes under her belt, is always my best resource. I attended the 2013 Institute for the Editing of Historical Documents in Ann Arbor, Michigan, where I learned much from Beth Luey, Mary-Jo Kline, and Daniel Feller. Steven C. Hahn and Andrew K. Frank provided many thoughtful comments and suggestions while the present work was still in the manuscript stage. At the University of Nebraska Press, Matthew Bokovoy and Sabrina Stellrecht were instrumental in bringing this project to fruition.

Countless others have contributed in all manner of ways, both large and small. As a student at Western Washington University I was fortunate to study under Laura Laffrado, who played a large role in my career development. I would also like to thank Donna Bohanan, David C. Carter, and Larry Gerber at Auburn University; Natalie Mooney, Carmen Giles, Lesa Shaul, Rich Schellhammer, and Jeff Gentsch at UWA; AnnaLee Pauls at Princeton University; Nancy Dupree at the Alabama Department of Archives and History; Jason Walker and Will Erwin at the Texas State Cemetery in Austin; and Kevin Thomas Harrell at the Historic New Orleans Collection. Finally, I want to thank especially Kiersten Fish, who patiently read through every line of every letter with me to make sure everything was where it needed to be.

Finally, I want to thank my family. My parents, Pat and Dale Haveman, my brothers Jason and Greg, and my sisters-in-law Lola and Stacy have always been an enormous source of support for me. This book is for them.

INTRODUCTION

On 15 January 1837 Captain John Stuart[1] of the 7th U.S. Infantry sat down at his desk at Fort Coffee to write to General Roger Jones, the adjutant general of the United States Army. The purpose of the letter, as Stuart quickly revealed, was to "communicate a few facts, in relation to the Emigrating Creeks." As an officer of the government, Stuart felt duty bound to report that many of the thousands of Creeks who had passed through Arkansas had fallen far behind the vanguard of their party and, having subsequently been unable to receive their food rations, had resorted to "killing a Hog" or "taking a few Baskets of Corn," from the white inhabitants. But Stuart was not writing to excoriate the Creeks; in fact, he was notifying officials that white Arkansans were likely to swindle the federal government out of money by claiming damages far in excess of what they had actually lost. Indeed, Stuart noted that there was little actual theft involved and that if whites had done the same it would "Scarcely be thought worthy of Speaking of, but those People being Indians," he predicted that locals would "make a terrible Outcry" and turn claims "of not more than a few hundred Dollars" into "the amount of many Thousands of Dollars." Then, clearly affected by what was taking place not far from his desk, Stuart noted:

> The condition of the Creeks yet on the road to Fort Gibson, is most terrible, It is said that they are Strewed along the road for a great distance, I know not how far, many of them are almost naked, and are without Shoes—The Snow for five days, has been from 4 to 8 Inches deep—and during the first and second days of the Storm, Women and children were Seen bending their way Onward, with most Piteous and

heart rending Cries, from Cold &c—I have not heard any thing from them for the last three days, and whether any of them have perrished or not, I am unable to say.[2]

The Creeks Stuart wrote about were likely members of the third detachment (out of five) that left Alabama in the heat and humidity of September 1836. The other four parties had arrived weeks earlier, in December 1836, while detachment 3—because of starting last and other delays—would not reach Fort Gibson, Indian territory until 23 January 1837. All had reached the West in their summer clothing while enduring subfreezing temperatures. Ordered west by President Andrew Jackson, who saw little use for American Indians in a white-dominated America, these Creeks made up a very small percentage of the many tens of thousands of other eastern Indians who were also moved west and suffered in a similar way. Because most Indians did not read or write, letters like Stuart's are the vital witness accounts to the sufferings of the Indian people.[3]

The abject misery of Indian removal is nearly impossible to convey in a monograph. The events are too big, and the words too small, to depict accurately the physical and emotional sufferings of those who experienced this American tragedy. In an attempt to capture the trauma of the period better, some scholars have recently moved away from the antiseptic "removal" toward more forceful terms like "ethnic cleansing" and "genocide."[4] Others have compared the treatment of the American Indians by government officials to the actions of Nazi Germany.[5] The reevaluation of language, and debates over terminology, are important and necessary and are a firm rejection of the arguments made by Andrew Jackson, as well as many twentieth-century scholars, who incorrectly believed that there was a certain benevolence to moving Indians across the Mississippi River.[6] I also struggled with terminology in *Rivers of Sand*. In an attempt to illustrate the complexity and nuance of the Creek removal story I used different words for each of the different types of migrations: "emigration" was used to classify those who went west on their own recognizance; "removal" denoted the Creeks who were shackled and forced to Indian territory against their own will; and "relocation" was used to explain the decisions of those who moved west through threats and coercion but not through direct physical force. I even contemplated using the word "dislocation" rather than "relocation" in the last moments before going to press. But "dislocation" suggests "breaking" and the over sixteen thousand Creeks (who moved west after the forced removal of the Creek prisoners) left peacefully by way of a sad, desperate, resignation. I stand by these decisions, even as I felt compelled to include the disclaimer that there is "no word or term that adequately conveys the emotional and physical horror of 'Indian removal.'" I also stand by that quote, even as scholars struggle over exactly how to characterize the uprooting of so many native peoples from their ancestral homelands.[7]

This book attempts to provide a new entry into that debate, while at the same time offering a new perspective on Indian removal. The following collection contains every significant letter and journal describing the journey of the Creek Indians as they moved from present-day Alabama to present-day Oklahoma. As the aforementioned Stuart letter exemplifies, first person accounts are more poignant, more intimate, and more insightful than anything retold in a textbook or monograph. They are the best means of humanizing characters and events while at the same time properly conveying the brutalities and hardships of removal. My hope, therefore, is that by replacing the words of the historian with those of the eyewitnesses, we will have a clearer and more unfiltered understanding of Indian removal in general and Creek removal in particular.

The data for this volume comes from any and all documents related to life in the camps and while on the journey west. This includes the official journals kept by the United States military personnel who accompanied the parties west, as well as dozens of supplemental letters written by these same military agents, along with documents from the doctors who attended to the sick, from the private contractors who were charged with conducting the Creeks to Indian territory, and (when available) from the Creeks themselves. In order to assemble this volume, I have reproduced documents from the following sources:

Microfilm

Microcopy 234—Letters Received by the Office of Indian Affairs, 1824–81, NARA, Washington DC.

Creek Agency Emigration, 1826–49, Rolls 237–40, NARA, Washington DC.

Creek Agency West, 1826–36, Roll 236, NARA, Washington DC.

Indian Removal to the West, 1832–1840, Files of the Office of the Commissary General of Subsistence, Rolls 1, 4–6, 7, 10, University Publications of America, Bethesda MD

Documents

Record Group 75, Records of the Bureau of Indian Affairs, 1793–1989, Entry 299, Emigration Lists, 1836–38, NARA, Washington DC.

Record Group 94, Records of the Adjutant General's Office, 1780s–1917, Entry 159-Q, Records of Thomas S. Jesup, NARA, Washington DC.

Record Group 217, Records of the Accounting Officers of the Department of the Treasury. Entry 525, Settled Indian Accounts and Claims, NARA, Washington DC.

In addition to these sources, a few documents have been reproduced with permission from the special collections of Indiana University, Louisiana State University, Princeton University, Vermont Historical Society, and the University of Virginia.

In addition to the letters and journals, I have included the muster rolls from the voluntary emigrations. When Coweta headman William McIntosh signed the Treaty of Indian Springs in February 1825, swapping the Creeks' Georgia land and portions of their Alabama domain "acre for acre" for territory west of the Mississippi River, he anticipated establishing a rival Creek government in the west. Although the treaty was opposed by a vast majority of the Creek people and, after an investigation, was nullified and replaced by the 1826 Treaty of Washington, the Creeks still lost their Georgia territory, and over the next decade federal agents tried to cajole the Creek population into peaceably relocating to Indian territory. Approximately 3,500 Creeks, Indian countrymen (white men married to Creek women), and slaves did move west voluntarily, despite being considered traitors by those who were committed to remaining on their ancestral homeland. These muster rolls, from the first (1827), second (1828), fourth (1834), and fifth (1835) emigrations, among others, list the name of the head-of-family;

the number of men, women, and children accompanying the head; and if applicable, the number of slaves owned by the family (the muster roll of the third voluntary emigrating party in 1829 was lost sometime around 1848 and does not appear). These rolls contain the names of many prominent Indian countrymen or Creeks of mixed parentage, which should be of interest to scholars or genealogists.

For the sake of clarity and readability, I have not reproduced the muster rolls as facsimiles. The rolls, which originally appear as long lists of the names of the heads-of-families with figures denoting the number of women, children, and slaves, have instead been typed in narrative form. Each entry contains all the relevant information from the original document with additional biographical information included when applicable (and numbered for easy cross reference). I have in most cases also standardized commonly used names or titles within these muster rolls: "Hajo" or "Hadjo" is hereafter written as "Harjo"; "Emarthlar" as "Emathla"; and "Tustunuggy" as "Tustunnuggee." In cases where the precise name of the individual is unclear, I have chosen the same spelling that appears in the documentation. For example, "Hatskee see Mauthla" could be either "Hatskee Emathla" or "Hatskee see Emathla."

In an attempt to keep these letters as true to the original as possible, I have deliberately reproduced misspelled words and names everywhere else in this volume. To reduce the use of brackets, words with one letter accidentally missing so as to render the meaning unclear have been silently emended (so "heath," for example, has been changed to "health"). Words that are so misspelled as to be unintelligible have been bracketed. When in doubt, I have erred on the side of the correct spelling.

Punctuation has also been silently emended throughout the journals and letters for clarity and consistency. I have added periods to the ends of most sentences even if not included in the original (unless the sentence ends in a dash). In some cases where there is a logical sentence break but there was no period, comma, or dash, I have simply spaced the two sentences apart for readability. I have also added a period when referring to a number (no. 1 party) to avoid suggesting that the word "no" is meant. Many of the letters have abbreviations that include superscripts. In conformity with the policies and practices of the University of Nebraska Press, I have placed these superscripts on the baseline but with an apostrophe denoting where the superscript was originally (for example, I have changed words like "recd" to "rec'd"). In cases where the contraction forms a commonly understood abbreviation, like "Doctor" to "Dr"—I have used the latter form. The layout of the letters and journals has been standardized for this volume. Finally, capitalization remains true to the original documents except in cases where lowercased letters began a paragraph. These have been capitalized for clarity.

The abbreviations list that follows reflects where the muster rolls and documents presented in this book were found. A fuller set of abbreviations appears in the notes at the back of the book, with additional sourcing details for these items and other materials consulted.

ABBREVIATIONS

CGS-IRW	Files of the Office of the Commissary General of Subsistence, Indian Removal to the West, 1832–1840, University Publications of America, Bethesda MD.
CRR-Misc.	Miscellaneous Creek Removal Records, ca. 1827–59, Record Group 75, Entry 300, NARA.
LR, CAE	Letters Received by the Office of Indian Affairs, Creek Agency Emigration.
NARA	National Archives and Records Administration.
NYPL	New York Public Library.
SFOIA	Special Files of the Office of Indian Affairs.
SIAC	Settled Indian Accounts and Claims.

BENDING THEIR WAY ONWARD

Part 1

The Voluntary Emigrations, 1827–36

1 The First McIntosh Party, 1827–28

On 12 February 1825 William McIntosh[1] and fifty of his hand-picked supporters signed the Treaty of Indian Springs, ceding the Creek domain in Georgia and a large portion of the Creeks' northern territory within Alabama to the federal government in exchange for equal parts land in Indian territory. In addition, the treaty promised to pay the transportation and subsistence of any emigrants who voluntarily emigrated across of the Mississippi River. Ceding land without the approval of the Creek National Council was illegal, however, and McIntosh had not received permission. In the darkness of 30 April 1825 McIntosh was executed at his Chattahoochee River plantation.[2]

In the fall of 1827 small parties of Creeks left their encampments at various locations around the Creek Nation and converged on Harpersville, Alabama—a site chosen because it was far removed from the Creek population, a vast majority of whom were opposed to voluntary emigration. At Harpersville a muster roll of emigrants was constructed, which showed that the party consisted of approximately seven hundred people, including Indian countrymen (whites married to Creek women) and eighty-six of the party's slaves.[3]

Once the list was finished, and their possessions were packed, the party moved out from their rendezvous in November 1827. The route was by land through Alabama to Tuscumbia, where the wet weather forced agents to purchase keelboats for the women, children, elderly, and infirm. The remainder of the party walked through Tennessee. After reuniting in Memphis the land and water parties continued toward Cantonment Gibson[4] in the Indian territory (present-day Oklahoma). Letters written by the agent

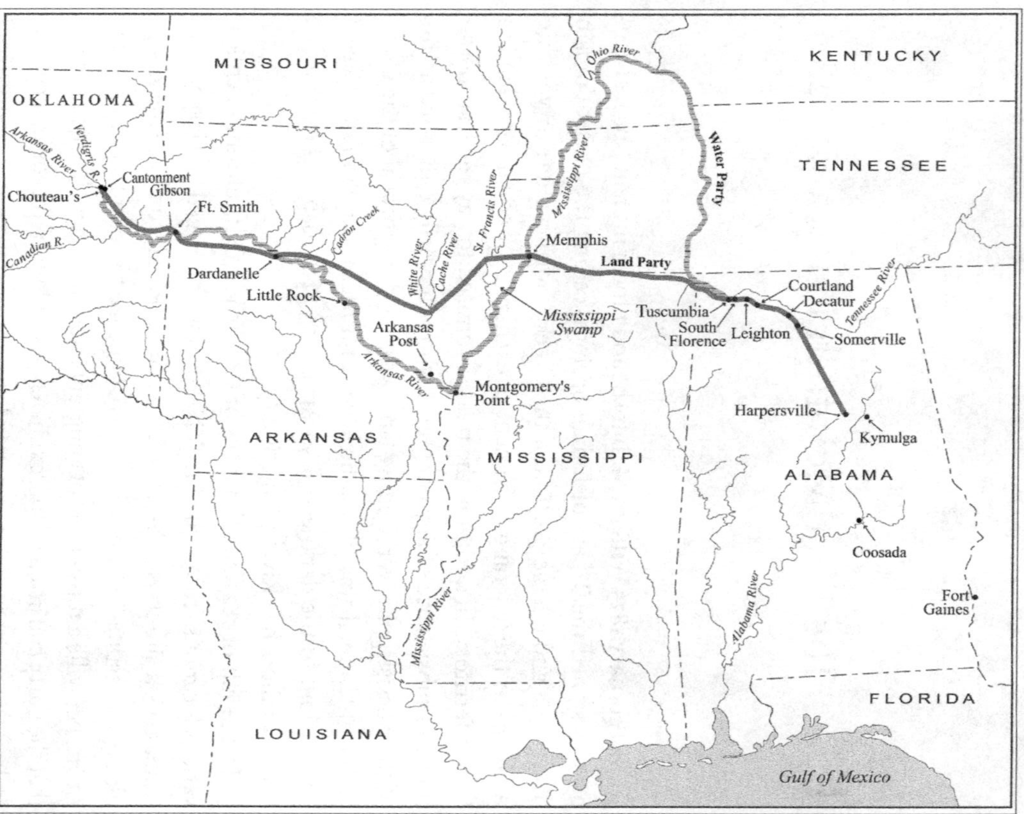

MAP 1. Route of the first McIntosh party, November 1827–March 1828. Place names correspond to stopping points or locations noted in the documentation. Route lines and locations are approximations. Cartography by Sarah Mattics and Kiersten Fish.

show the difficulty experienced by the land party as they were forced to cross swollen rivers, pass muddy roads, and endure the cold of winter. Many Creeks fell behind on the road, while over 130 Creeks became so sick that they remained behind in the western Cherokee country to rehabilitate. The party arrived at their destination during the first quarter of 1828.[5]

The first McIntosh party was conducted by New Jersey–born David Brearley,[6] who had resigned as colonel, 7th U.S. Infantry in 1820 before serving as agent to the western Cherokees and Quapaws. Also joining the party were subagents Thomas Anthony and Brearley's brother, Charles Brearley. No physicians are known to have accompanied the group; however, Dr. William L. Wharton[7] provided medical services (including the purchase of medicine for the journey) while the party was in Alabama. Dr. John W. Baylor,[8] a surgeon at Fort Gibson, tended to the sick of the party in Indian territory upon their arrival in 1828.

First McIntosh Party Muster Roll

Names listed in bold refer to the head of a family. Roll includes the number of family members traveling, the age range of the emigrants, and the number of slaves (if any). The Creek town or village is listed in parentheses. Roll found at SIAC, Agent (Brearley), Account (14,487), Year (1830), NARA.

1. **Chilly McIntosh** (Thlakatchka) 27 members consisting of 1 male over sixteen, 4 females over sixteen, 2 males under sixteen, 2 females under sixteen, and 18 slaves. Chilly McIntosh (ca. 1800–1875) was William McIntosh's oldest son by his wife, Eliza (ca. 1780–1860), and was a nephew of Roly McIntosh (William's brother, who became the principal headman of the western Creeks). He was educated at the Milledgeville Academy, was bilingual, and became the official clerk of the Creek Nation. McIntosh signed the Treaty of Indian Springs in 1825 and was in his father's plantation home as his father was executed and escaped out of the back before fleeing to Georgia's capital, Milledgeville, disguised as a traveling white man. In the east Chilly McIntosh was considered "no chief, a Clerk; had been dismissed before as Clerk of the Nation," but in the West, McIntosh became a principal chief in the western Creek government and served as a judge. He was also

FIG. 1. Chilly McIntosh (ca. 1800–1875) of Thlakatchka. Courtesy of the Research Division of the Oklahoma Historical Society.

chosen by the chiefs and warriors in full council in 1834 to be one of several principal headmen who were empowered to transact all the business of the nation, including concerning the rights and privileges of its citizens, recovering monies from the federal government, and negotiating treaties. McIntosh also was a signatory to two additional federal treaties, signed in 1838 and 1856. McIntosh was survived by three sons: William Frederick (born in 1824 to Chilly McIntosh's white Pennsylvania-born wife), John M. (born in 1833), and Luke G.; and two daughters, (Mildred and Martha) with his wives. McIntosh became a Baptist preacher in the Indian territory and commanded a regiment of Confederate Creeks during the American Civil War. On McIntosh's decision to emigrate from the land of his ancestors, Auguste Levasseur, who accompanied the Marquis de Lafayette during his tour of the United States in 1824–25, gives some insight. Levasseur met McIntosh in the eastern Creek Nation and noted: "He appreciated the real situation of his nation, he saw it gradually becoming weaker, and foresaw its speedy destruction; he felt how much it was inferior to those which surrounded it, and was perfectly aware that it was impossible to overcome the wandering mode of life of his people. Their vicinity to civilization had been of no service to them; on the contrary, it had only been the means of introducing vices to which they had hitherto been strangers; he appeared to hope that the treaty [Treaty of Indian Springs] which removed them to another and a desert country, would re-establish the ancient organization of the tribes, or at least preserve them in the state in which they now were." Chilly McIntosh died in October 1875.[9]

2. **Alexander Berryhill** (Sand Town) 5 members consisting of 1 male over sixteen, 1 female over sixteen, and 3 males under sixteen. Alexander "Alec" Berryhill was born around 1793 to John and Elizabeth (Derrisaw) Berryhill (no. 50 on second McIntosh party roll). He married Huldey Willson in 1819.[10]
3. **William Miller** (Thlakatchka) 13 members consisting of 1 male over sixteen, 1 female over sixteen, 2 males under sixteen, 2 females under sixteen, and 7 slaves. A law mender[11] and signer of the Treaty of Indian Springs. Miller remained in exile for a time in Pike County,

Georgia, in the aftermath of William McIntosh's execution in 1825. He was considered a "4th grade" chief in the eastern Creek Nation.[12]

4. **Moha pochu chee** (Thlakatchka) 1 member consisting of 1 male over sixteen.
5. **O he ta** (Coweta) 2 members consisting of 1 male over sixteen and 1 female over sixteen. Listed as "deserted" on a copy of this roll.
6. **Tallassee Harjo** (Coweta) 6 members consisting of 1 male over sixteen, 1 female over sixteen, 2 males under sixteen, and 2 females under sixteen.
7. **Okfuskee Tustunnuggee** (Thlakatchka) 1 member consisting of 1 male over sixteen.
8. **Itch has Fixico** (Thlakatchka) 1 member consisting of 1 male over sixteen.
9. **Eneha Fixico** (Coweta) 9 members consisting of 1 male over sixteen, 1 female over sixteen, 5 males under sixteen, and 2 females under sixteen.
10. **Car lis ta** (Coweta) 1 member consisting of 1 male over sixteen.
11. **George Colbert, or Golfin** (Thlakatchka) 6 members consisting of 1 male over sixteen, 1 female over sixteen, and 4 males under sixteen.
12. **Arbeka Tustunnuggee** (Thlakatchka) 7 members consisting of 1 male over sixteen, 1 female over sixteen, 1 male under sixteen, 1 female under sixteen, and 3 slaves. A law mender and signer of the Treaty of Indian Springs. Led the five-person delegation to explore the Indian territory (March–July 1827). Under Article 4 of the Treaty of Indian Springs and Article 6 of the 1826 Treaty of Washington, five members of the McIntosh party were authorized to select a piece of land in Indian territory to settle.[13]
13. **John C. Wynn** (Coweta) 4 members consisting of 1 male over sixteen, 1 female over sixteen, 1 male under sixteen, and 1 slave. Wynn was the son of Green Wynn, formerly of Hancock, Georgia, but the family was originally from Virginia. John Wynn married a Creek woman of mixed ancestry. Wynn and his family did not emigrate with the first McIntosh party, and their names were redacted from this muster roll. The family emigrated with the second McIntosh party in 1828.[14]
14. **John Harrod** (Thlakatchka) 15 members consisting of 1 male over

sixteen, 1 female over sixteen, 4 males under sixteen, 2 females under sixteen, and 7 slaves. A McIntosh party member who remained in exile for a time in Pike County, Georgia, in the aftermath of William McIntosh's execution in 1825.[15]

15. **Lar mar lee, or Boatswin** (Thlakatchka) 1 member consisting of 1 male over sixteen. Listed as "absconded" on a copy of this roll. Remained behind and enrolled briefly with the second McIntosh Party (no. 32 on second McIntosh party roll, chap. 2).
16. **Ochee Harjo** (Coweta) 7 members consisting of 1 male over sixteen, 1 female over sixteen, 2 males under sixteen, and 3 females under sixteen.
17. **Hatskee see Mauthla** (Thlakatchka) 1 member consisting of 1 male over sixteen.
18. **William Berryhill** (Sand Town) 8 members consisting of 1 male over sixteen, 1 female over sixteen, 3 males under sixteen, and 3 females under sixteen. One muster roll shows Berryhill's party consisting of 5 members without the 3 females under sixteen.
19. **Eneha Tustunnuggee** (Coweta) 1 member consisting of 1 male over sixteen.
20. **Hillis Harjo** (Coweta) 4 members consisting of 1 male over sixteen, 1 female over sixteen, and two females under sixteen.
21. **Choc chart he ne ha** (Coweta) 1 member consisting of 1 male over sixteen.
22. **Carth lo nee** (Coweta) 1 member consisting of 1 male over sixteen.
23. **Fick her mi kee** (Coweta) 5 members consisting of 1 male over sixteen, 1 female over sixteen, 1 male under sixteen, and 2 females under sixteen.
24. **Ar chu lee Harjo** (Coweta) 1 member consisting of 1 male over sixteen.
25. **Cotsa Emathla** (Coweta) 9 members consisting of 1 male over sixteen, 1 female over sixteen, 3 males under sixteen, and 4 females under sixteen. A copy of this roll shows 9 members with 1 male over sixteen, 1 male under sixteen, 3 females under sixteen, and 4 slaves.
26. **Hos pi tack Emathla** (Coweta) 7 members consisting of 1 male over sixteen, 2 females over sixteen, 1 male under sixteen, and 3 females under sixteen.

27. **Chee no la** (Coweta) 4 members consisting of 1 male over sixteen, 1 female over sixteen, and 2 females under sixteen.
28. **Nitto chee** (Coweta) 1 member consisting of 1 male over sixteen.
29. **Hothlee martee Harjo** (Coweta) 1 member consisting of 1 male over sixteen.
30. **No co see illee Tustunnuggee** (Coweta) 1 member consisting of 1 male over sixteen.
31. **Tallip Harjo** (Coweta) 7 members consisting of 1 male over sixteen, 2 females over sixteen, and 4 females under sixteen.
32. **Che pon Harjo** (Coweta) 1 member consisting of 1 male over sixteen.
33. **Lemuel B. Nichols** (Thlakatchka) 3 members consisting of 1 male over sixteen, 1 female over sixteen, and 1 female under sixteen. Listed as white on the muster roll. Nichols was an Indian countryman who had resided in the Creek Nation for only about eight years at the time of emigrating west. Was one of the five members of the March–July 1827 exploratory party to Indian territory.[16]
34. **Ock ka lee chee** (Thlakatchka) 1 member consisting of 1 male over sixteen.
35. **As a pu chee** (Hitchiti) 1 member consisting of 1 male over sixteen.
36. **Sa na wee** (Hitchiti) 6 members consisting of 2 females over sixteen, 3 males under sixteen, and 1 female under sixteen. Sa na wee is listed as a woman.
37. **Saffa mok kee** (Coweta) 1 member consisting of 1 male over sixteen.
38. **Ah har lar kee, or Jacob** (Coweta) 1 member consisting of 1 male over sixteen.
39. **A see mee, or Friday** (Hitchiti) 8 members consisting of 1 male over sixteen, 3 females over sixteen, 3 males under sixteen, and 1 female under sixteen. Was one of the five members of the March–July 1827 exploratory party to Indian territory.[17]
40. **Ka na nachee** (Hitchiti) 1 member consisting of 1 male over sixteen.
41. **Law ha way** (Hitchiti) 3 members consisting of 1 male over sixteen, 1 female over sixteen, and 1 female under sixteen.
42. **Daniel Miller** (Thlakatchka) 4 members consisting of 1 male over sixteen, 1 female over sixteen, and 2 females under sixteen.

43. **Tommy Emathla** (Coweta) 5 members consisting of 1 male over sixteen, 2 females over sixteen, and 2 females under sixteen.
44. **James W. Rogers** (Yuchi) 4 members consisting of 1 male over sixteen, 1 female over sixteen, 1 male under sixteen, and 1 female under sixteen. Listed as white on the muster roll.
45. **Samuel Miller** (Thlakatchka) 4 members consisting of 1 male over sixteen, 2 females over sixteen, and 1 female under sixteen. A Creek man of mixed ancestry, Miller was a signer of the Treaty of Indian Springs, although the headmen in full council noted that he was "no Chief; an Indian merely." Miller remained in exile for a time in Pike County, Georgia, in the aftermath of William McIntosh's execution in 1825.[18]
46. **Sack ke kee** (Hitchiti) 1 member consisting of 1 male over sixteen.
47. **Daniel Perryman** (We ky wa thlocco) 3 members consisting of 1 male over sixteen, 1 female over sixteen, and 1 female under sixteen. A McIntosh associate who supported (but did not sign) the Treaty of Indian Springs. As negotiations bogged down in the weeks leading up to the signing, Perryman was offered a $1,000 bribe by an employee of the commissioners to use his influence to effect the treaty signing. For his part, in an affidavit it was revealed that Perryman was receptive to the idea but "wanted the offer to come from the Commissioners." Perryman may have emigrated and returned to the eastern Creek Nation or may not have emigrated at all. In 1829 a number of Creeks emigrating with the third voluntary party, including Perryman, wrote from Little Rock, while on the march west. Moreover, Perryman was compensated for serving as interpreter for this party.[19]
48. **John Hambly** (We ky wa thlocco) 1 member consisting of 1 male over sixteen.
49. **Hos pi tack Harjo** (Char kee thlocco) 5 members consisting of 1 male over sixteen, 3 females over sixteen, and 1 male under sixteen.
50. **Slack kee** (Char kee thlocco) 1 member consisting of 1 male over sixteen. The son of Hos pi tack Harjo.

51. **U pack a lack kee** (Char kee thlocco) 1 member consisting of 1 male over sixteen.
52. **Spoke Harjo** (Che ah har haw) 11 members consisting of 1 male over sixteen, 3 females over sixteen, 5 males under sixteen, and 2 females under sixteen.
53. **Austis Hopoie** (Char kee thlocco) 9 members consisting of 1 male over sixteen, 3 females over sixteen, 4 males under sixteen, and 1 female under sixteen.
54. **Coosa Hopoie** (Char kee thlocco) 6 members consisting of 1 male over sixteen, 1 female over sixteen, and 4 males under sixteen.
55. **Contallee Emathla** (Char kee thlocco) 1 member consisting of 1 male over sixteen.
56. **Stick a funnee Harjo** (Char kee thlocco) 1 member consisting of 1 male over sixteen.
57. **Daniel Lashley** (Char kee thlocco) 5 members consisting of 1 male over sixteen and 4 females over sixteen. Brother of Alexander Lashley (no. 98 on first McIntosh party roll).
58. **Chock to bee** (Char kee thlocco) 1 member consisting of 1 male over sixteen.
59. **Fire hola** (Char kee thlocco) 9 members consisting of 1 male over sixteen, 3 females over sixteen, 2 males under sixteen, and 3 females under sixteen.
60. **Con chat Hopoie** (Char kee thlocco) 1 member consisting of 1 male over sixteen.
61. **Pen Harjo** (Char kee thlocco) 1 member consisting of 1 male over sixteen.
62. **Pen Harjo** (Char kee thlocco) 1 member consisting of 1 male over sixteen. There are two Pen Harjos listed next to each other.
63. **Tus co no Harjo** (Kymulga) 2 members consisting of 1 male over sixteen and 1 female over sixteen.
64. **Mutt mi ee** (Char kee thlocco) 1 member consisting of 1 male over sixteen.
65. **Benjamin Hawkins** (Hillabee) 24 members consisting of 1 male over sixteen and 23 slaves. Son-in-law of William McIntosh and interpreter for the McIntosh party. Son of Stephen Hawkins (no. 66

on first McIntosh party roll). Hawkins (d. ca. 1836) was targeted for execution after the Treaty of Indian Springs was signed. Although he was not a signer, Hawkins induced other Creeks to sign the accord. Hawkins escaped with a gunshot wound while his brother, Samuel, was executed by hanging and his body was thrown into the river. Hawkins emigrated with his slaves in 1827, only to return to the eastern Creek Nation in 1828. He self-emigrated—moved west with his own resources and was later compensated by the federal government—in August or September 1828. Hawkins initially settled on the Verdigris River in Indian territory and constructed a number of houses, including one that was described as a "Double House, Floored, Hewed, &c.," along with a kitchen, smokehouse, corn crib, and stable. Hawkins had to relocate when his land was accidentally ceded to the Cherokees in 1828. Hawkins's relationship with the McIntosh party grew strained in the west. He was accused on a number of occasions of illegally smuggling alcohol into the western Creek Nation. He was a member of a group of speculators who tried to colonize Creek families onto a piece of land in the Mexican province of Texas. Sometime before 1838 Hawkins fled the western Creek Nation and settled in Texas, where he was later murdered.[20]

66. **Stephen Hawkins** (Hillabee) 14 members consisting of 1 male over sixteen, 1 female over sixteen, 1 female under sixteen, and 11 slaves. Listed as white on the muster roll. The husband of Sarah Grayson (daughter of son of Robert Grierson and his wife Sinnugee) and the father of Eliza (wife of William McIntosh), Benjamin (no. 65 on first McIntosh party roll), and Samuel Hawkins (executed in 1825 by the Creeks over his support for the Treaty of Indian Springs). Stephen Hawkins (b. ca. 1766) became a resident of the Creek Nation around 1787 and was a trader among the Creeks. In 1797 he was described as being "an active man of weak mind; fond of drink, and much of a savage when drunk." He was accused of having a bad character by other McIntosh emigrants.[21]
67. **O yat ke tee Emathla, or Sam** (O chock o la) 1 member consisting of 1 male over sixteen.

68. **Sa dick kee, or Tom** (O chock o la) 1 member consisting of 1 male over sixteen.
69. **Thomas Miller** (Thlakatchka) 8 members consisting of 1 male over sixteen, 2 females over sixteen, 3 males under sixteen, 1 female under sixteen, and 1 slave.
70. **Richard Miller** (Thlakatchka) 1 member consisting of 1 male over sixteen.
71. **Affobo Harjo** (Coweta) 2 members consisting of 1 male over sixteen and 1 female under sixteen.
72. **Spanna Harjo** (Coweta) 2 members consisting of 1 male over sixteen and 1 female over sixteen.
73. **Sath lee kee** (Thlakatchka) 1 member consisting of 1 male over sixteen.
74. **Joc see na** (Coweta) 1 member consisting of 1 male over sixteen.
75. **William Emanuel** (Cusseta) 1 member consisting of 1 male over sixteen.
76. **Talladega Harjo** (Cusseta) 1 member consisting of 1 male over sixteen.
77. **Hospee Emathla** (Coweta) 1 member consisting of 1 male over sixteen.
78. **Fuck tee lustee** (Coweta) 5 members consisting of 1 male over sixteen, one female over sixteen, and 3 males under sixteen.
79. **Nitee** (Coweta) 1 member consisting of 1 male over sixteen.
80. **Thla hopoie** (Coweta) 1 member consisting of 1 male over sixteen.
81. **Sa watch chee** (Coweta) 4 members consisting of 3 females over sixteen and 1 male under sixteen. Sa watch chee is listed as a woman.
82. **Hy atch ee** (Wacoochee) 1 member consisting of 1 male over sixteen.
83. **Ky yoke nichee** (Thlakatchka) 1 member consisting of 1 male over sixteen.
84. **Thlock poli kee** (Thlakatchka) 1 member consisting of 1 male over sixteen.
85. **Eick kee** (Coweta) 1 member consisting of 1 male over sixteen.
86. **Billy** (Coweta) 1 member consisting of 1 male over sixteen. The brother of Eick kee.
87. **Se co po chee** (Char kee thlocco) 1 member consisting of 1 male over sixteen.
88. **Low bitch chee** (Coweta) 1 member consisting of 1 male over sixteen.

89. **O chun Yoholo** (Coosada) 6 members consisting of 1 male over sixteen, 3 females over sixteen, and 2 males under sixteen.
90. **Billy star o luccar** (Coosada) 5 members consisting of 1 male over sixteen, 2 females over sixteen, and 2 females under sixteen.
91. **John McIntosh** (Coweta) 1 member consisting of 1 male over sixteen. There are many Johns in the McIntosh family, but according to Richard A. Blount, a member of the Georgia-Alabama Boundary Survey Commission, this was William McIntosh's son, who remained in exile for a time at Indian Springs with Chilly McIntosh in the aftermath of his father's execution. Blount encountered John McIntosh on 4 July 1826 and wrote that he "took John McIntosh down to the farry [the ferry near William McIntosh's house] where we had considerable conversation about his fathers death."[22]
92. **Matawa Harjo** (Talladega) 1 member consisting of 1 male over sixteen.
93. **Echo Yoholo** (Talladega) 1 member consisting of 1 male over sixteen.
94. **You pus a ho kee** (Talladega) 1 member consisting of 1 female over sixteen.
95. **Interlifkee** (Coweta) 12 members consisting of 1 male over sixteen, 3 females over sixteen, 3 males under sixteen, 4 females under sixteen, and 1 slave. He was considered a "4th grade" chief in the eastern Creek Nation. Richard A. Blount of the Georgia-Alabama Boundary Survey Commission encountered Interlifkee in July 1826. After meeting with John McIntosh (no. 91 on first McIntosh party roll) Blount wrote in his diary that he "had a considerable interview with an intelligent Indian Ente lif ka on their present state and relative to removing over the Mississippi—He appear'd to wish Counsel." Interlifkee was a McIntosh party member who remained for a time in exile with Chilly McIntosh at Indian Springs in the aftermath of William McIntosh's execution.[23]
96. **Tallassee Micco** (Newyaucau) 6 members consisting of 1 male over sixteen, 3 females over sixteen, and 2 females under sixteen.
97. **Sa py e chee** (Talladega) 1 member consisting of 1 male over sixteen.
98. **Alexander Lashley** (Che ha haw) 4 members consisting of 1 male over sixteen, 1 female over sixteen, and 2 males under sixteen. Lashley was the son of a Scotsman of the same name, served in the first Creek War (1813–14) with William McIntosh, and signed the Treaty

of Indian Springs. Lashley was one of 133 other Creeks who were forced to stop at the homestead of John Rogers on Skin Bayou in February 1828 due to sickness. Although Lashley was identified as a "dismissed or broken Chief" in the east, he became a prominent member of the McIntosh-led government in the west and served on the western Creek council.[24]

99. **Carwarpee** (Che ha haw) 1 member consisting of 1 male over sixteen. The son of Alexander Lashley.
100. **Kadeegee** (Che ha haw) 3 members consisting of 1 male over sixteen, 1 female over sixteen, and 1 male under sixteen.
101. **Stip a la tee** (Che ha haw) 2 members consisting of 1 male over sixteen and 1 female over sixteen.
102. **Chock chartee Emathla** (Che ha haw) 4 members consisting of 1 male over sixteen, 2 females over sixteen, and 1 male under sixteen.
103. **Cotsa Emathla** (Che ha haw) 1 member consisting of 1 male over sixteen.
104. **O tal gee Harjo** (Che ha haw) 10 members consisting of 1 male over sixteen, 3 females over sixteen, 4 males under sixteen, and 2 females under sixteen.
105. **Moultee Kennard** (Che ha haw) 1 member consisting of 1 male over sixteen.
106. **Cho e ka Harjo** (Char kee thlocco) 1 member consisting of 1 male over sixteen.
107. **Tom Derasaw** (no town listed) 1 member consisting of 1 male over sixteen.
108. **Samuel Perryman** (Big Spring) 10 members consisting of 1 male over sixteen, 4 females over sixteen, 3 males under sixteen, and 2 slaves. Samuel Perryman (Thenahta Tustennuggee) was the son of Benjamin Perryman (who served as second chief of the western Creeks in Indian territory until his death in 1835 or 1836), and brother of James Perryman (no. 115 on first McIntosh party roll), Lewis Perryman (no. 118 on this roll), Henry Perryman (no. 125 on this roll), and Moses Perryman (no. 34 on second McIntosh party roll, chap. 2). Perryman served with Andrew Jackson in the Creek War (1813–14). Painter George Csatlin described Samuel Perryman as "a jolly companionable man." He died ca. 1880.[25]

FIG. 2. Sam Perryman (Hol-te-mal-te-tez-te-neehk-ee), by George Catlin, nineteenth century. Gilcrease Museum, Tulsa, Oklahoma.

109. **Tustunnuggee chee** (Big Spring) 1 member consisting of 1 male over sixteen.
110. **Chittenee Yoholo** (Big Spring) 1 member consisting of 1 male over sixteen.
111. **Okchoiee Fixico** (Big Spring) 1 member consisting of 1 male over sixteen.
112. **John Burford** (Big Spring) 11 members consisting of 1 male over sixteen, 3 females over sixteen, 6 males under sixteen, and 1 female under sixteen. Burford was possibly the same Creek interpreter of

mixed parentage who, according to Thomas S. Woodward, had been a partner in a trading house with Colonel Samuel Dale in Georgia. Dale (1772–1841) was a Virginia-born frontiersman and trader who famously fought in the Battle of Burnt Corn (July 1813) and in the "Canoe Fight" (November 1813) during the first Creek War (1813–14).[26]

113. **William Tooly** (Big Spring) 2 members consisting of 1 male over sixteen and one slave.

114. **Gristy Perryman** (Big Spring) 5 members consisting of 1 male over sixteen, 2 females over sixteen, 1 male under sixteen, and 1 slave.

115. **James Perryman** (Big Spring) 7 members consisting of 1 male over sixteen, 3 females over sixteen, 1 male under sixteen, 1 female under sixteen, and 1 slave. Perryman (Pahos Harjo) was the son of Benjamin Perryman (who served as second chief of the western Creeks in Indian territory until his death in 1835 or 1836), and brother of Samuel Perryman (no. 108, this roll), Lewis Perryman (no. 118, this roll), Henry Perryman (no. 125, this roll), and Moses Perryman (number 34 on second McIntosh party roll, chap. 2). Perryman served with the Confederate Creeks in the American Civil War. He died at Coweta around 1882.[27]

116. **So kos kee Harjo** (Big Spring) 3 members consisting of 1 male over sixteen and 2 females over sixteen.

117. **Tusakie Harjo** (Big Spring) 1 member consisting of 1 male over sixteen.

118. **Lewis Perryman** (Big Spring) 5 members consisting of 1 male over sixteen, 2 females over sixteen, 1 male under sixteen, 1 female under sixteen. Born near Fort Mitchell, Lewis Perryman (Kochukua Micco, 1787–1862) was the son of Benjamin Perryman (who served as second chief of the western Creeks in Indian territory until his death in 1835 or 1836) and brother of Samuel Perryman (no. 108 on this roll), James Perryman (no. 115 on this roll), Henry Perryman (no. 125 on this roll), and Moses Perryman (no. 34 on second McIntosh party roll, chap. 2). After arriving in Indian territory Perryman established his homestead at the falls of the Verdigris before relocating to Big Spring on Adams Creek near the present-day town of Broken Arrow, Oklahoma. In 1833 he married Hattie Winslett (née Ward, d. 1866) as well as her daughters, Befeeny (d. 1877) and Ellen (d. 1854). Perryman

had a number of children, including Andrew, Mahala, and Nancy (with his first wife); Sanford Ward, Thomas Ward, John W., Kizzie, and Phoebe (with Hattie); Alexander, David, Hattie, Ellen, and Lewis (with Befeeny); and Legus C., Josiah C., China, Henry W., George B., and Lydia (with Ellen). In 1849 a survey team visited Perryman's homestead on Adam's Creek and described the headman as "a tall man about 6 feet high very dark with a long straight nose black mustachoe. . . . he was dressed in a blue and White cotton hunting shirt with a blue and red fringe with a turban on his head. his pants were black & white cassimere with straps and bare footed. his air was a commanding one." Claudio Saunt notes that the ellipses refer to a passage in Samuel Washington Woodhouse's original diary that states, "'he showed evidently that he had considerable negro blood in him.'" Perryman's homestead was considered one of the best in the country and he had "numerous" black slaves and an extensive peach orchard. Later in life he ran a trading store near Tulsa and engaged in the cattle business along the Arkansas River. Perryman's sons enlisted in the Confederate Army but later resigned and joined the Union army in 1862. Perryman and a number of family members accompanied the refugee Creeks to Kansas, where he died in 1862.[28]

119. **Nee har Harjo** (Big Spring) 1 member consisting of 1 male over sixteen.
120. **Ista charco Micco** (Big Spring) 1 member consisting of 1 male over sixteen.
121. **John Perryman** (Big Spring) 4 members consisting of 1 male over sixteen, 1 female over sixteen, 1 male under sixteen, and 1 female under sixteen.
122. **Thli kee** (Big Spring) 3 members consisting of 1 male over sixteen, 1 female over sixteen, and 1 female under sixteen.
123. **Chula Yoholo** (Big Spring) 1 member consisting of 1 male over sixteen.
124. **Marta** (Big Spring) 1 member consisting of 1 male over sixteen.
125. **Henry Perryman** (Big Spring) 5 members consisting of 1 male over sixteen and 4 females over sixteen. Perryman (Efold Harjo) was the son of Benjamin Perryman (who served as second chief of the western Creeks in Indian territory until his death in 1835 or 1836), and brother to Samuel Perryman (no. 108, this roll), James Perryman (no. 115, this

roll), Lewis Perryman (no. 118, this roll), and Moses Perryman (no. 34 on second McIntosh party roll, chap. 2). He served as a pastor in Indian territory and helped translate portions of the Bible into the Muskogean language. He died at Choska in 1876.[29]

126. **Cho no te Harjo** (Big Spring) 5 members consisting of 1 male over sixteen, 2 females over sixteen, 1 male under sixteen, and 1 female under sixteen.
127. **Eech was wa Harjo** (Big Spring) 1 member consisting of 1 male over sixteen.
128. **Richard Robinson** (Big Spring) 5 members consisting of 1 male over sixteen, 1 female over sixteen, and 3 females under sixteen. Listed as white on the muster roll.
129. **David McKillop** (Big Spring) 6 members consisting of 1 male over sixteen, 1 female over sixteen, 1 male under sixteen, and 3 females under sixteen. Listed as white on the muster roll.
130. **Polly Brinton** (Tuckabatchee) 8 members consisting of 2 females over sixteen, 3 males under sixteen, 2 females under sixteen, and 1 slave.
131. **Thloc poswa** (Coweta) 1 member consisting of 1 male over sixteen.
132. **Andrew Lovett** (Coweta) 3 members consisting of 1 male over sixteen, 1 female over sixteen, and 1 slave. McIntosh party member who fled to Pike County, Georgia.[30]
133. **Monkee** (Coweta) 4 members consisting of 1 male over sixteen, 1 female over sixteen, and 2 males under sixteen.
134. **Tar ko see Harjo** (Talladega) 6 members consisting of 1 male over sixteen, 1 female over sixteen, 3 males under sixteen, and 1 female under sixteen.
135. **Nick Marshall** (Coweta) 2 members consisting of 1 male over sixteen and 1 female over sixteen.
136. **Wee furh wa** (Coweta) 1 member consisting of 1 male over sixteen.
137. **Charles Miller** (Coweta) 7 members consisting of 1 male over sixteen, 1 female over sixteen, 1 male under sixteen, 1 female under sixteen, and 3 slaves. A law mender and signer of the Treaty of Indian Springs who fled to Pike County, Georgia, for safety with other McIntosh party members. He was considered a "4th grade" chief in the eastern Creek Nation.[31]

138. **Is po ho gee Emathla** (Coweta) 8 members consisting of 1 male over sixteen, 3 females over sixteen, 3 males under sixteen, and 1 female under sixteen.
139. **In char kee** (Coweta) 1 member consisting of 1 male over sixteen.
140. **Sa ly par** (Coweta) 1 member consisting of 1 male over sixteen.
141. **Yar yo** (Coweta) 1 member consisting of 1 male over sixteen.
142. **Phillemee** (Coweta) 1 member consisting of 1 male over sixteen.
143. **Im par lat kee** (Coweta) 1 member consisting of 1 male over sixteen.
144. **Fixico Chopco** (Coweta) 5 members consisting of 1 male over sixteen, 1 female over sixteen, and 3 males under sixteen.
145. **Cho wash ta Uchee** (Coweta) 1 member consisting of 1 male over sixteen.
146. **Pol hom echee** (Coweta) 2 members consisting of 1 male over sixteen and 1 female over sixteen.
147. **Ka nee ta** (Coweta) 1 member consisting of 1 male over sixteen.
148. **George** (Coweta) 1 member consisting of 1 male over sixteen.
149. **Sath harth lee** (Coweta) 1 member consisting of 1 male over sixteen.
150. **Sa lis kar pee** (Coweta) 2 members consisting of 1 male over sixteen and 1 female over sixteen.
151. **Fush hatchee Micco** (Coweta) 7 members consisting of 1 male over sixteen, 3 females over sixteen, 1 male under sixteen, and 2 slaves. Became a prominent member of the McIntosh-led government in the west serving as commanding general of the militia. Fush hatchee Micco became one of the western Creek Nation's principal headmen and was empowered by the town miccos to transact all the business of the nation, including concerning the rights and privileges of its citizens, recovering monies from the federal government, and negotiating treaties.[32]
152. **Hy yar hatchee** (Coweta) 1 member consisting of 1 male over sixteen.
153. **In clennis Harjo** (Coweta) 1 member consisting of 1 male over sixteen.
154. **Emarth Uchee** (Coweta) 6 members consisting of 1 male over sixteen, 2 females over sixteen, 1 male under sixteen, and 2 slaves.
155. **No go chee** (Coweta) 1 member consisting of 1 male over sixteen.
156. **See puck har gee** (Coweta) 1 member consisting of 1 male over sixteen.
157. **Thla kee tar** (Coweta) 1 member consisting of 1 male over sixteen.

158. **Haga McIntosh** (Coweta) 9 members consisting of 1 male over sixteen, 5 females over sixteen, 2 males under sixteen, and 1 female under sixteen.

159. **Qua ho thlocco Harjo** (Newyaucau) 5 members consisting of 1 male over sixteen, 1 female over sixteen, and 3 males under sixteen.

160. **Locha Tustunnuggee** (Newyaucau) 5 members consisting of 1 male over sixteen, 1 female over sixteen, 2 males under sixteen, and 1 female under sixteen.

161. **Ninnee hanar Uchee** (Newyaucau) 10 members consisting of 1 male over sixteen, 4 females over sixteen, 4 males under sixteen, and 1 female under sixteen.

162. **E fine nee Emathla** (Newyaucau) 1 member consisting of 1 male over sixteen.

163. **Tommy Harjo** (Newyaucau) 3 members consisting of 1 male over sixteen, 1 female over sixteen, and 1 male under sixteen.

164. **Eufaula Tuskenehaw** (Newyaucau) 11 members consisting of 1 male over sixteen, 2 females over sixteen, 7 males under sixteen, and 1 female under sixteen.

165. **Chee na wa** (Newyaucau) 8 members consisting of 1 male over sixteen, 2 females over sixteen, 2 males under sixteen, and 3 females under sixteen.

166. **Co war cuchee Harjo** (Newyaucau) 4 members consisting of 1 male over sixteen, 1 female over sixteen, 1 male under sixteen, and 1 female under sixteen.

167. **Ene ha thlocco Harjo** (Newyaucau) 4 members consisting of 1 male over sixteen, 1 female over sixteen, 1 male under sixteen, 1 female under sixteen.

168. **Miss ho ee** (Newyaucau) 5 members consisting of 1 male over sixteen, 1 female over sixteen, and 3 females under sixteen.

169. **No co see ekar** (Newyaucau) 2 members consisting of 1 male over sixteen and 1 female over sixteen.

170. **Oh high at kee** (Newyaucau) 5 members consisting of 1 male over sixteen, 2 females over sixteen, 1 male under sixteen, and 1 female under sixteen.

171. **Conchartee** (Sand Town) 2 members consisting of 1 male over sixteen and 1 female over sixteen.
172. **Ar see** (Sand Town) 7 members consisting of 1 male over sixteen, 2 females over sixteen, 2 males under sixteen, and 2 females under sixteen.
173. **Tim so nee** (Sand Town) 1 member consisting of 1 male over sixteen.
174. **Colonel Bushyhead** (Sand Town) 8 members consisting of 1 male over sixteen, 3 females over sixteen, 3 males under sixteen, and 1 female under sixteen.
175. **Sow wee** (Sand Town) 1 member consisting of 1 male over sixteen.
176. **John Randall** (Sand Town) 3 members consisting of 1 male over sixteen, 1 female over sixteen, and 1 male under sixteen. McIntosh party member who remained in exile for a time at DeKalb County, Georgia, in the aftermath of William McIntosh's execution. Randall became a prominent member of the McIntosh-led government and served as a town chief.[33]
177. **George Randall** (Sand Town) 1 member consisting of 1 male over sixteen. McIntosh party member who remained in exile for a time in DeKalb County, Georgia, in the aftermath of William McIntosh's execution in 1825.[34]
178. **Con tallee** (Sand Town) 6 members consisting of 1 male over sixteen, 2 females over sixteen, 1 male under sixteen, and 2 females under sixteen.
179. **Tacco see Harjo** (Sand Town) 3 members consisting of 1 male over sixteen, 1 female over sixteen, 1 male under sixteen.
180. **Jack Randall** (Sand Town) 2 members consisting of 1 male over sixteen and one female over sixteen. McIntosh party member who remained in exile for a time in DeKalb County, Georgia, in the aftermath of William McIntosh's execution in 1825.[35]
181. **Sam** (Sand Town) 3 members consisting of 1 male over sixteen, 1 female over sixteen, and 1 male under sixteen.
182. **Succa tharhar** (Sand Town) 5 members consisting of 1 male over sixteen, 1 female over sixteen, 2 males under sixteen, and 1 female under sixteen.

183. **U hi ker** (Sand Town) 2 members consisting of 1 male over sixteen and 1 female over sixteen.

184. **Tu sa kia chartee** (Sand Town) 9 members consisting of 1 male over sixteen, 2 females over sixteen, 5 males under sixteen, and 1 female under sixteen.

185. **Lie lar kar** (Sand Town) 1 member consisting of 1 male over sixteen.

186. **Fos Harjo** (Sand Town) 5 members consisting of 1 male over sixteen, 1 female over sixteen, and 3 males under sixteen.

187. **Tomma dee kee** (Sand Town) 3 members consisting of 2 females over sixteen and 1 male under sixteen. Tomma dee kee is listed as a woman.

188. **Chock to bee** (Che ah har) 5 members consisting of 1 male over sixteen, 2 females over sixteen, 1 male under sixteen, and 1 female under sixteen.

189. **William Walker** (Tuckabatchee) 1 member consisting of 1 male over sixteen. Listed as white on the muster roll. The son-in-law of Tuckabatchee headman Big Warrior. Walker did not move with the first McIntosh party, but he was a subagent to David Brearley and aided in the logistics of emigration. As the party moved out of Harpersville sometime around 8 November 1827, Walker remained behind and established a second rendezvous camp at Fort Strother per Brearley's orders.

190. **Benjamin Derasaw** (Coweta) 2 members consisting of 1 male over sixteen and 1 female over sixteen. McIntosh party member who remained in exile for a time at Indian Springs with Chilly McIntosh in the aftermath of William McIntosh's execution in 1825. He was considered a "4th grade" chief in the eastern Creek Nation.[36]

191. **Jacob Derasaw** (Coweta) 1 member consisting of 1 male over sixteen. He was a judge and a pro-Confederate headman in the Indian territory.[37]

192. **James Derasaw** (Coweta) 4 members consisting of 1 male over sixteen and 3 females over sixteen. Sometime around 1830 James Derasaw accompanied a band of Cherokees to Texas on a retributive attack against the Tawakoni Indians, who had killed and scalped three Cherokees attempting to steal horses. The war party took the Tawakoni village by surprise, and in his recollections a warrior who participated in the attack noted that "Scarcely any guns were fired,

but the Tomahawk drank human gore." Women and children were not spared, and neither were the fleeing survivors, who were "cut down as fast as overtaken."[38]

193. **Somo kee** (Coweta) 1 member consisting of 1 male over sixteen.
194. **Co e Emathla** (Coweta) 1 member consisting of 1 male over sixteen.
195. **Charles** (Talladega) 1 member consisting of 1 male over sixteen. The son of Tar ko see Harjo (no. 134 on first McIntosh party roll).
196. **Chitto kee michee** (Talladega) 1 member consisting of 1 male over sixteen.

Supplemental Letters of the First McIntosh Party

Colonel David Brearley reports to Secretary of War James Barbour[39] that the party has completed explorations of that portion of Indian territory allotted to the Creeks, and has chosen for their settlement a piece of land west of the Arkansas Territory's boundary line, on the north side of the Arkansas River. Letter found at LR, CAE, Roll 237, 29.

Fort Gibson May 28th 1827

Sir,

I have the honor to inform you, that the exploring party of creek Indians, under my direction completed their examination of the country offered by the Government of the United States for their future residence, on the 27 Ins't.

The result of their views are to, commence their location, on the north bank of the Arkansas river immediately west of the Territorial line[40]—Their limits of course will be governed by their numbers—

We shall with the least possible delay, return to the Creek Nation, where I have reason to expect a portion of the emigrating party in readiness to remoove, which operation will immediately commence—The road and necessary provisions, will be established, & provided on my return, a more detailed view of which will be furnished on my arrival in the nation.

I have the honor to be
with great respect

Your Ob't Ser't
D. Brearley
ag't In. affs.[41]

Hon James Barbour

☾

Colonel David Brearley provides a detailed account of the exploratory party's travels and offers an assessment of the quality and condition of the Indian territory land set aside for the western Creeks. Letter found at LR, CAE, Roll 237, 33–35.

Montgomery July 20th 1827

Hon'ble James Barbour
Sec'y of War

Sir

I have the honor of reporting to you the return of the party who accompanied me from the Creek Nation, for the purpose of exploreing the Country offered for their future residence West of the mississippi. The Season We left this place (15th of March) would not justify Our proceeding by land, We therefore availed Ourselves of a Steam Boat[42] Conveyance by the Way of Orleans[43] up the Arkansas river to the Dardanells;[44] from thence by land We proceeded to Fort Gibson On the Grand River where it became necessary to procure an Interpreter, guides, and additional horses, and an Outfit for Our excurtion beyond the line. Through the Kindness of Col'n Arbuckle[45] together With the other officers of the Station Who afforded every facility in their power, We proceeded On the 11th With a View to examine the north Side of the Arkansas River about 100 Miles or rather as far as good lands might extend up it, but from excessive rains the ground became So Soft that On the 15th We Were Compelled to Cross the Arkansas before We had reached Our intended destination; from Whence We proceeded a South West Course

Crossing the Several minor branches untill We Struck the main Canadian River On the 23d, from Whence by an East and North East Course We made the mouth of Grand River and arrived at Fort Gibson On the 27th. On the 5th of June We reached the Dardanells from Whence We decended in an open boat to the mouth of White River Which We reached On the night of the 18th and immediately embarked On board a Steam Boat[46] for Waterloo On the Tennessee River in this State from Whence by land We arrived at this place On the 14th Ins't.

From the opportunity We had of Seeing, and information obtained, I have reason to believe that the rich bottom lands extend On the north Side of the Arkansas about 75 or 80 Miles averageing from 3 to 5 Miles in Wedth; It is also my impression that nearly that quantity of Similar land may be found On the Verdigris River, Within the Osage Cession.[47]

The Prairies in this region are also rich and the Country tolerably Supplied With Springs and is by far the best We met With. South of the Arkansas, barren, Sterril Prairies form the general Character of the Country; there are however partial bottoms On the intermediate Streams which may at an advanced period afford locations for a few Indians.

We did not find the bottoms or Prairies On the Canadian equal in quantity or quality to those described, it is however represented and I have no doubt Correctly, to afford a greater portion of good land near its junction With the Territorial line, Which time did not permit us to explore, it Was also Stated that there is Some good land at the mouth of the Red fork about 100 Miles up the South Side of the Arkansas.

From all the observations I have been able to make, I am inclined to believe that On the north Side of Arkansas is to be found the greatest portion of unappropriated lands Suitable for Indian location.

In the Selection of a Spot the One which Seems most to attract the attention of the party is evidently <u>that</u> Which Will afford the government the greatest facilities in furnishing the necessary aid and protection during the infant Stage of their Settlement, Which they propose to make about Eight Miles West of Fort Gibson being about half that distance from the Territorial line On the north Side of Arkansas.[48] We Were received With great attention On Our passage through the Cherokee nation between Whom and our party Beads and Tobacco the usual tokens of friendship On Such occasions, Were reciprocaly pledged, I am Sure With the utmost affection and friendship.

We also had an interview With the principal chiefs of Clermor[49] & Talleys[50] Band of Osages[51] from whom We received Similar pledges of friendship Which We hope may be as lasting With them as it Will be desireable to us.[52]

The 29th of this month has been fixt by the party to assemble at the falls of the Chatahoochy, for the purpose of makeing their report to those who may Choose to listen to them; Immediately after which you Shall be furnished With the estimates and reports required of me to enable the department to Carry into effect the Wishes of the government.

I have the honor to be
Very Respectfully Y'r Ob't S't
D. Brearley
ag't In. affs

☾

Writing from Harpersville, the site of the general rendezvous, Brearley notifies Secretary of War James Barbour of the completed muster roll, which shows approximately seven hundred people enrolled. Letter found at LR, CAE, Roll 237, 67–68.

State of Alabama.
Harpersville Nov 8th 1827

Sir

I have the honor to inform you that we have this day completed the enrollment of the Indians, who offer for emigration at this time amounting to about 700. Notwithstanding the 15th September was the time fixed for them to convene, it has been out of my power with the aid of the most efficient men I could employ, to effect their assemblage at an earlier period.

We shall make a final movement tomorrow, and no time will be lost in the completion of our journey; which being an experiment, will subject us to many difficulties.

I contemplate as you will perceive by my instructions to Capt. Walker (a copy of which are herewith enclosed) to move the next party (which I shall return in time to superintend) by water; confident it will be attended with much less expense than the present mode.[53]

There is no doubt but the disposition to emigrate is daily increasing, and by the influence of Captain Walker, there is every reason to believe, that several thousands will go in the spring, which will have the effect to break up the Nation.

I have as yet no offer for a contract for their supplies, within double the amount that it costs to purchase and issue. I therefore cannot feel at liberty to make one under such circumstances, particularly as every Kind of provision is to be found cheapre on the road, than at this place.

I have the honor to be
Very respectfully
Your Obed't Serv't
D. Brearley
ag't In. affs

Hon James Barbour
Secretary of War

☾

This letter, written to William Walker, a white man who married one of the daughters of Big Warrior (a prominent Tuckabatchee headman who was the ranking chief of the Upper Creeks), serves as notice of employment for the job of subagent for the McIntosh party. Brearley directs Walker to "reconcile the parties to each other"—in other words, find a way to convince those Creeks who opposed moving to Indian territory to join their McIntosh countrymen—and to "augment the number of emigrants" by collecting and enrolling any Creeks who may be willing to go west with the second party. Letter found at LR, CAE, Roll 237, 69–70.

Copy

Harpersville Nov 8th 1827

Sir

The Hon. Secretary of War has authorized me to employ your services, to aid me in effecting the movements of the Creek Indians, west of the Mississippi.

It is therefore expected that you will use all your influence, by every proper means, to reconcile the parties to each other, and to augment the number of emigrants, which it is believed you have it greatly in your power to do.

I have also to request that you will commence, and continue your operations, during my absence, from the nation, and on your first visit to the several towns, point out the time, and place of our next rendezvous, and urge upon them by timely notice the necessity of punctuality in their assemblage.[54]

You will also commence and continue an enrollment according to the form in the possession of Col. Crowell,[55] who will cordially cooperate in the execution of the duties assigned you, I also refer you to him for advice and any explanation you may require with regard to the Treaty;[56] or law, relative to the emigration of said Indians.

You will be allowed for your services five dollars per day and reasonable expenses when thus employed. Economy and vigilence will be expected in all your operations.

With an ardent wish for your success.

I am very respectfully
Your Ob't Sev't
D. Brearley (Signed)

Ag't In. affs.

Capt William Walker

☾

In this letter, also written on 8 November, Brearley provides additional instructions for Walker while the agent is off conducting the first McIntosh party west. Specifically, Brearley directs Walker to find a new general rendezvous closer to the Tennessee River so that the second McIntosh party can use water conveyance, which the agent believes will be cheaper than traveling by land. Walker subsequently chose the old Creek War garrison Fort Strother as the general rendezvous. Letter found at LR, CAE, Roll 237, 71.

Copy

Harpersville alabama Nov 8th 27

Sir

In addition to the instructions furnished you this day, which commits to your care the entire management of the emigrating Indians in the Creek Nation, during my absence. I have to request, that you select for the general rendezvous, a place on the northern boundary of the nation, most contiguous to the Tennesee river by a good road where it will be understood they are to embark on board of boats suitable for their transport, to the arkansas—

You will be furnished with advice relative to the procurement of their provisions, and presents[57] as it is desirable that the movement should commence in the early part of March next.[58] I leave it to the sound discretion of yourself, and Col Crowell to fix the time for the assemblage of this party.

I am very respectfully
Your obed't Serv't
D. Brearley (Signed)
Agt In. aff

Capt. William Walker

In this letter, Brearley announces his arrival in the north Alabama city of Tuscumbia and his decision to employ keelboats to take the women, children, and elderly by water, thereby avoiding the bad road from Tuscumbia to Memphis. Those accompanying the horses went by land. Letter found at LR, CAE, Roll 237, 73.

Tuscumbia alabama Dec. 1st 1827

Sir

I have the honor to inform you, that the party of emigrating creek Indians under my charge arrived at this place on the 25th ult'o.

Finding that the difficulties and expense attending their transportation by land, could not be with propriety further sustained, as soon as the weather would permit 28th those possessing horses and others relying on the public teams[59] amounting to upwards of three hundred proceeded by land, the balance nearly four hundred and fifty, for whom boats and provissions are furnished will embark tomorrow morning—

I have the honor to be
With great respect
Your ob't Servant
D. Brearley
ag't In. affs

Hon James Barbour
Secretary of War

Writing from Little Rock, Brearley describes the "tedious" journey the land party encountered through the Mississippi Swamp west of Memphis. This stretch, inundated with water for most of the year, was made worse by the fact that it had rained for most of the journey. Brearley accompanied the land party from Memphis to Arkansas Territory before leaving that group to join the water party in Little Rock (the land party bypassed Little Rock to the north); the water party had been detained by the high water and swift current of the Arkansas River. Brearley subsequently employed the steamboat *Facility* to tow the keels. Letter found at SIAC, Agent (Brearley), Account (14,487), Year (1830), NARA.

Little Rock Arkansas Terr'y Jan'y 26 1828

Sir

I have the honor to inform you that the emigrateing party of Creek Indians under my charge moveing by land and Water have progressed thus far. We left Memphis On the 25th Dec'r about 255 On board of Keel boats, the balance about 475 I accompanyed by land which from the excessive rains and unusual rise of Waters for the Season rendered Our route tedious and distressing to the Indians. I reached White River by Way of the new road On the 6th Ins't Completed With great difficulty and labour the Crossing of the party 22d whom I left On the 24th and met the Keels (which had been detained in Consequence of high Water) at this place On the 25th they proceeded immediately, and a Steam Boat[60] is now in the act of moveing to take them in tow. I expect to join the land party by the 28th a more full report of our movement Will be furnished On Our arrival from whence I Shall proceed immediately for the General rendevous in the Creek Nation—

I have herewith transmitted you an account of disbursements for improvements amounting to 4911 Dollars—In Consequence of not effecting a Contract for the Supply of rations to the party I have used and Continue to do So the balance of that fund I therefore request.

I may be Charged with $15,089 On account of the provisioning and Contingent expences of the Indians and that the Sum of $15,089 may be placed as Soon as possible to my Order in the Bank of milledgeville Georgia to reimburse the fund for improvements Which Will be requisit On my return to the nation.

I have the honor to be
Very restpectfully
Y'r Ob't S't
D. Brearley
ag't In. affs

To the H'ble
James Barbour
Sec'y of War

(

After accompanying the water party to their destination through the use of the steamboat *Facility*, Brearley delayed his return trip to help the land party (which was still on the road) in order to attend an impromptu meeting with the Osages, whose land had been ceded to make way for the McIntosh party. Brearley then traveled eastward to pick up members of the land party, many of whom had not yet reached Dardanelle, Arkansas Territory. Letter found at LR, CAE, Roll 237, 105–7.

Dardanells Feb'y 16th 1828

Sir,

After I had the honor of writing you from the little Rock, an opportunity offerred by which a Steam boat was procured to transport the water party to the falls of the Verdigris—which induced me to abandon my intention of rejoining the land party & we arrived at the falls, Chautaus trading house,[61] on the 30th ult.

I remained two days, in order to secure the Stores, and to reconcile our party with the Osages, whom we found at the place, (the whole of Clermore & Talleys band) although the Osages were some what sour at first—and ours from their diminutive number say two hundred and fifty chiefly noneffectives were not without their fears. Col. Arbuckle acted with his usual promptness, and gave the Osages distinctly to understand that our party was under his immediate protection, and that any offence committed by them, would be followed by the severest punishment; he recommend confining themselves to their own section of the country, and not attempt to pass through our location which lays on their direct road to war, as it would be productive of mischief on boath sides;

Clermore solicited a council with me the next night in owr camp where he manifested a great desire, not only to be on friendly terms with us—but that the bonds might be streanthened by intermarriage of the nations and expressed a willingness that some of our people who understood farming might settle among them—also proposed that his favorite Son,[62] one of finest young men in the nation, should reside with me, which offer I readily accepted—how far he is sincere in those pretentions time will soon demonstrate. Cap't Pryor[63] their sub ag't and Col. Chautau[64] gentlemen whose opinions are entitled to great weight believe them to be in earnest, and I assure you, that nothing shall be omitted on my part which will aid in cherishing that disposition.

Having returned thus far, in order to bring up the land party, the rear of which has not yet reached this place—desirable as it would be, to see them all on their own ground before I leave the Territory, it will not be compatible with my other views[65]—the weather and roads we have had to encounter, have so completely worn down our people and horses that much patience is required.

I shall leave this tomorrow for the Verdigris and as soon, as the necessary arraingments can be made, for their supplies of provisions &c. I shall set out for the creek nation, where I have reason to believe my presents are now required.[66]

I have the honor to be
With the highest respect
Your Ob't Ser't
D. Brearley
Ag't In. affs

Hon. James Barbour

John Rogers, a western Cherokee Indian living on Skin Bayou reports on 134 Creeks of the McIntosh party who were forced to stop at his homestead in February 1828 due to sickness. They remained for five weeks while Rogers issued them food and even horses for the last leg of their journey. Rogers seeks compensation from the Secretary of War. Letter found at SIAC, Agent (John Rogers), Account (14,999), Year (1831), NARA.

Cherokee Nation Skin Baiew,
February 27th 1829.

To the Honerable the Secretary of War,
For the U States.—

The undersigned would respectfully represent that, in the latter part of February last (1828), a party of the Emigrating Creek Indians, consisting of one hundred and thirty four persons, among whom were Ose-po-kajo,[67] Ose-pot-ok-hajo,[68] and Alex Ashley,[69] Chiefs in the Creek Nation, came to his residence in the Cherokee Nation, on Skin Bayou, in great distress; being on their way to their new homes, at what is called the western Creek Agency, destitute of provisions, or comforts of any Kind; a considerable number of them Sick and altogether without the means of proceeding to their destination without assistance and supplies to subsist on.—They stated to the undersigned that unless he would take pity on them and relieve their wants, that some of them must inevitably perish, as they would be compelled to throw away and abandon their sick.

The undersigned after hearing their complaints and witnessing their suffering condition could not hesitate to do what the feelings & obligations of humanity required, and therefore, supplied them with Beef & Corn for nearly five weeks, during which time they were detained in and about the premises of the undersigned, by the sickness which prevailed among them; and finally, when they had sufficiently recovered, he supplied them with horses to proceed to their destination. For the use and service of the horses & for the provisions furnished them to subsist from the time they left his house untill they arrived at the agency, their sub agent, Mr

Anthony,[70] paid the undersigned; but for the provisions furnished them from the time they reached the residence of the undersigned untill they departed from it, the sub agent said he had no authority to pay the undersigned, but did not doubt, that Col'o David Brearley, the agent, who was then absent, would pay him on his return.—accordingly, on the return of the agent the undersigned presented his account, amounting to one hundred & nine and eighty seven and a half dollars for said provisions, but the said agent refused to pay him, observing that, he, the undersigned, having furnished the provisions of his own accord, it was at his own risk and responsibility, and that he, the agent, did not conceive himself bound to pay for them, and has not, nor has any other person paid for them. The undersigned therefore, seems to have no other resort, or alternative but to appeal, through you, to the justice of the government, or relinquish a claim, the amount of which he is not able to loose.—

With great respect, the undersigned has the honor to be, your Ob. Servant.—

John Rogers

We the undersigned Chiefs of the western Creek Nation do hereby certify that the Supplies mentioned in the foregoing Petition, were furnished to the Party of Emegrating Creeks of which we were then chiefs in company as mentioned therein to the best of our Knowledge and belief—Signed Sealed this 8th Day of Nov. 1829

Alex Ashley
Osepokogo

in presence of
Benjamin Hawkins

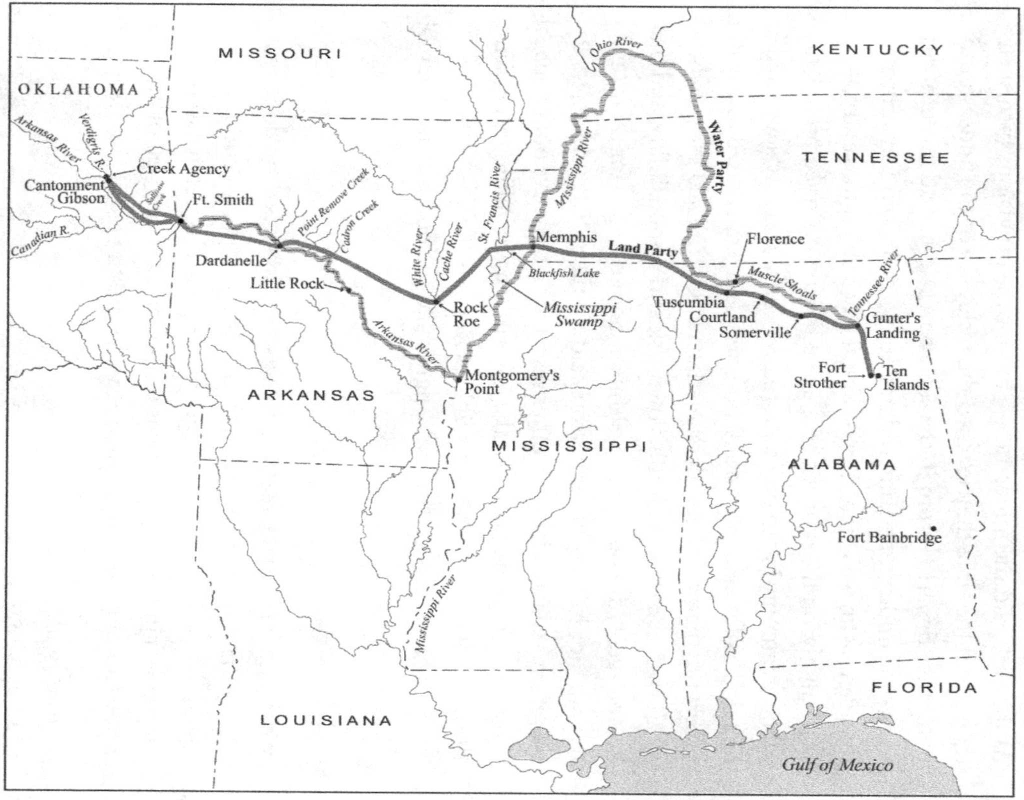

MAP 2. Route of the second McIntosh party, ca. October 1828–ca. January 1829. Place names correspond to stopping points or locations noted in the documentation. Route lines and locations are approximations. Cartography by Sarah Mattics and Kiersten Fish.

2 The Second McIntosh Party, 1828–29

In the fall of 1828 a second, smaller McIntosh party, also conducted by David Brearley, left the Creek Nation for the west. Many of these emigrants were being collected even as the first party was still marching through Alabama. Just prior to leaving Harpersville in November 1827, Brearley sent orders to his subagents to establish a new rendezvous point closer to the Tennessee River in order to take advantage of water conveyance. The site chosen for the second party was Fort Strother, a Creek War fort on the Coosa River, and emigrants began arriving at the rendezvous site while the first party was still en route.

By all accounts this party likely would have been much larger had powerful headmen not threatened would-be emigrants with death and driven others from the enrollment camps. Fifty Yuchis, for example, were physically driven from Fort Strother by orders of a headman, and there were estimates that perhaps two hundred Creeks had abandoned the site and returned home. Only "a few mulattoes" remained, and when Brearley went to the camp to see how enrollment was coming along, he found those who were still there to be "wavering." At Fort Bainbridge a child was kidnapped from an emigrating mother, the victim of an apparent clan attack. The camp at Ten Islands (at or near Fort Strother) was in a "mutaneous and disorderly Situation" due to threats made against enrollees.[1]

When the party commenced its march from Fort Strother, the *Alabama Journal* reported that it consisted of only 518 people. Many of the emigrants were Indian countrymen—whites married to Indian women—or Creeks of mixed parentage. This was not lost on the *Cherokee Phoenix* newspaper, which noted of this party that they "are called Creeks, though we are credibly informed that there were but few full Indians, most of the party being white men, half breeds, and mulattoes."[2]

The second McIntosh party did not encounter many of the problems that plagued the first emigration. The weather was dry and warm, and the land party moved swiftly. In contrast, the water party was delayed because of the low stages of the western rivers. The land party arrived at the newly built western Creek Agency on the Verdigris River in late November 1828. The water party arrived about a month later.

The Second McIntosh Party was conducted by Colonel David Brearley, with the aid of his clerk, Samuel DeWheat.

Second McIntosh Party Muster Roll

Names listed in bold refer to the head of a family. Roll includes the number of family members traveling, the age range of the emigrants, and the number of slaves (if any). The Creek town or village is listed in parentheses. Roll found at SIAC, Agent (Brearley), Account (14,487), Year (1830), NARA.

1. **Kendall Lewis** (Thlakatchka) 16 members consisting of 1 male over sixteen, 1 female over sixteen, 1 male under sixteen, and 13 slaves. Roll lists Lewis as white. An accused murderer who escaped charges in Hancock, Georgia, in 1808 after allegedly killing a man over a card game. He sought refuge in the Creek Nation and married one of Big Warrior's daughters. Lewis (b. 1789), a native of Maryland, became a valuable member of the Creek Nation because of his bilingualism and was used often to negotiate with federal agents. Forty years old at the time of his voluntary emigration, Lewis was a trader whose license had been granted by John Crowell. Served in the First Seminole War with William McIntosh. While never a headman in the east, Lewis became a principal chief in the western Creek nation and was given authority to conduct official business and negotiate treaties with the federal government. Had a stand at Fort Bainbridge on the Federal Road. Irish traveler Adam Hodgson, who visited the Creek Nation in 1820, noted that Lewis had "contracted so ardent a love of solitude, by living in the woods, that he lately removed his stand from the most profitable situation, because there was a neighbour or two within four

miles." This, and the fact that Lewis "regretted, in the most feeling terms, the injury which the morals of the Indians have sustained from intercourse with the whites; and especially from the introduction of whiskey, which has been their bane," may help explain Lewis's decision to emigrate with this party. Once in Indian territory Lewis settled for a time on the Canadian River, establishing a homestead complete with a dwelling house, a store house (with cellar, a "Passage," and shed), a corn crib, hen house, kitchen, surrounded by four acres of cleared land, 2,648 rails, and 54 peach trees. He was forced to move when his farm was accidentally ceded to the Cherokees in 1828. While waiting in camp at Fort Bainbridge in preparation for his emigration west, Lewis had a number of horses stolen as punishment for his decision to leave the Creek Nation.[3]

2. **John Lewis** (Thlakatchka) 4 members consisting of 1 male over sixteen, 1 female over sixteen, 1 female under sixteen, and 1 slave. Roll lists Lewis as white.
3. **Samuel Sells** (Thlakatchka) 11 members consisting of 1 male over sixteen, 1 female over sixteen, 1 male under sixteen, 1 female under sixteen, and 7 slaves. Roll lists Sells as white. Sells was an Indian countryman who had resided in the Creek Nation for about twenty years at the time of the Treaty of Indian Springs signing. Bilingual, Sells was adopted into the Creek Nation and appears to have found the favor of William McIntosh. Sells fought with McIntosh during the First Creek War. Although he emigrated with the second party in 1828, Sells returned to the eastern Creek Nation and self-emigrated approximately twenty members of his family in 1830 (see no. 74 on G. W. Stidham's roll, chap. 17).[4]
4. **Daniel Sells** (Yuchi) 3 members consisting of 1 male over sixteen and two slaves.
5. **James Randall** (Thlakatchka) 7 members consisting of 1 male over sixteen, 1 female over sixteen, and 5 slaves. Roll lists Randall as white.
6. **David Carr** (Thlakatchka) 4 members consisting of 1 male over sixteen, 1 female over sixteen, and 2 slaves.
7. **William Carr** (Thlakatchka) 2 members consisting of 1 male over sixteen and 1 female over sixteen.

8. **Saw nor way** (Thlakatchka) 5 members consisting of 2 males over sixteen, 2 females over sixteen, and 1 female under sixteen.
9. **Co Emathla** (Thlakatchka) 8 members consisting of 1 male over sixteen, 4 females over sixteen, and 3 males under sixteen.
10. **Okmulgee Micco** (Thlakatchka) 9 members consisting of 2 males over sixteen, 2 females over sixteen, 4 males under sixteen, and 1 female under sixteen. Listed as "dead" in muster roll margin.
11. **Tommy Harjo** (Thlakatchka) 7 members consisting of 4 males over sixteen, 2 females over sixteen, and 1 female under sixteen.
12. **Toney** (Thlakatchka) 9 members consisting of 3 males over sixteen, 2 females over sixteen, 2 males under sixteen, and 2 females under sixteen. A copy of this muster roll lists one member as white.
13. **Co nub bee Emathla** (Thlakatchka) 6 members consisting of 2 males over sixteen, 3 females over sixteen, and 1 male under sixteen.
14. **Pol hom mitchee** (Thlakatchka) 5 members consisting of 2 males over sixteen, 1 female over sixteen, 1 male under sixteen, and 1 female under sixteen.
15. **Francisco** (Thlakatchka) 4 members consisting of 1 male over sixteen, 2 females over sixteen, and 1 female under sixteen.
16. **Con chat Harjo** (Thlakatchka) 1 member consisting of 1 male over sixteen.
17. **Us cee hah** or **Mus cee hah** (Oswitchee) 1 member consisting of 1 male over sixteen.
18. **Pows Harjo** (Chowokolo Tallahassee) 7 members consisting of 2 males over sixteen, 2 females over sixteen, 2 males under sixteen, and 1 slave. Complained of having one of his riding horses stolen while in the enrollment camp at Fort Bainbridge in June 1828 while preparing to emigrate west.[5]
19. **Thlath lo Harjo** (Chowokolo Tallahassee) 6 members consisting of 2 males over sixteen, 2 females over sixteen, 1 male under sixteen, and 1 female under sixteen. Possibly the same "Thla Tho Hajo" who signed the Treaty of Indian Springs. Listed as "a broken or dismissed Chief."[6]
20. **Tuskenehaw** (Chowokolo Tallahassee) 8 members consisting of 1 male over sixteen, 3 females over sixteen, 3 males under sixteen, and 1 female under sixteen.

21. **Tustunnuggee Emathla** (Chowokolo Tallahassee) 6 members consisting of 4 males over sixteen and 2 females over sixteen.
22. **Liftiff Harjo** (Chowokolo Tallahassee) 4 members consisting of 1 male over sixteen, 1 female over sixteen, 1 male under sixteen, and 1 female under sixteen.
23. **Daniel Christa** or **Daniel Christie** (Chowokolo Tallahassee) 2 members consisting of 1 male over sixteen and 1 female over sixteen. Roll lists Christa as white.
24. **Co so Yoholo** (Coosada) 8 members consisting of 3 males over sixteen, 1 female over sixteen, 2 males under sixteen, and 2 females under sixteen.
25. **Os potock Harjo** (Coosada) 7 members consisting of 1 male over sixteen, 1 female over sixteen, 2 males under sixteen, and 3 females under sixteen.
26. **Ta lo bee** (Coosada) 2 members consisting of 1 male over sixteen and 1 female over sixteen.
27. **Yoholo Fixico** (Coosada) 2 members consisting of 1 male over sixteen and 1 female over sixteen.
28. **Hillabee Harjo** (Coosada) 7 members consisting of 1 male over sixteen, 5 females over sixteen, and 1 male under sixteen.
29. **Benjamin McGahee** (Thlakatchka) 2 members consisting of 1 male over sixteen and 1 female over sixteen. Roll notes that all members of party were white. McGahee married Martha "Patsy" Berryhill (b. 1785), the daughter of John and Elizabeth (Derrisaw) Berryhill (see no. 50 on this roll).[7]
30. **Nancy Posey** (Thlakatchka) 7 members consisting of 1 male over sixteen, 2 females over sixteen, and 4 males under sixteen. Roll notes that all seven members of party were white. Nancy Posey (née Berryhill) was born in 1784 to John and Elizabeth (Derrisaw) Berryhill (no. 50 on this roll) She married a member of the Posey family around 1800. She is the mother-in-law of Samuel H. Hopwood (no. 45 on this roll), who married Nancy's daughter Sarah Posey (b. 1801); and the mother of Thomas Posey (no. 64 on this roll).[8]
31. **Benjamin Lott** (Hitchiti) 8 members consisting of 2 males over sixteen, 2 females over sixteen, 1 male under sixteen, and 3 females under

sixteen. Lott (b. 1775) was an Indian countryman and licensed trader in the eastern Creek Nation.[9]

32. **Lar mar bee, or Boatswain** (Hitchiti) 1 member consisting of 1 male over sixteen. The same person that appears on the first McIntosh party roll (no. 15, although listed there as from Thlakatchka). "Returned" is written in the "remarks" section of the second party muster roll.
33. **Oak chun Harjo** (Hitchiti) 13 members consisting of 7 males over sixteen, 3 females over sixteen, 2 males under sixteen, and 1 female under sixteen.
34. **Moses Perryman** (Hitchiti) 7 members consisting of 2 males over sixteen, 2 females over sixteen, 2 males under sixteen, and 1 female under sixteen. Moses Perryman (Aktayahehe) was the son of Benjamin Perryman (who served as second chief of the western Creeks in Indian territory until his death in 1835 or 1836), and brother of Samuel Perryman (no. 108 on first McIntosh party roll, chap. 1), James Perryman (no. 115 on first McIntosh party roll, chap. 1), Lewis Perryman (no. 115 on first McIntosh party roll, chap. 1) and Henry Perryman (no. 125 on first McIntosh party roll, chap. 1). He died in 1866.[10]
35. **Lewis Milford** (Hitchiti) 6 members consisting of 1 male over sixteen, 2 females over sixteen, 1 male under sixteen, and 2 females under sixteen.
36. **Nulcupper Emathla** (Hitchiti) 5 members consisting of 1 male over sixteen, 1 female over sixteen, 1 male under sixteen, and 2 females under sixteen.
37. **Lewe** (Hitchiti) 3 members consisting of 1 male over sixteen, 1 female over sixteen, and 1 slave.
38. **Ar pah lit chee** (Hitchiti) 2 members consisting of 1 male over sixteen and 1 female over sixteen.
39. **Chehaw Harjo** (Hitchiti) 2 members consisting of 1 male over sixteen and 1 female over sixteen.
40. **Lum he Emathla** (Hitchiti) 1 member consisting of 1 male over sixteen.
41. **David Pidgeon** (Tuckabatchee) 3 members consisting of 1 male over sixteen, 1 female over sixteen, and 1 female under sixteen. David Pidgeon's name is crossed out on another muster roll and "not gone" is scribbled, meaning he enrolled but later changed his mind and stayed behind. "Returned" is written in the "remarks" section of muster roll.

42. **Thomas Pidgeon** (Tuckabatchee) 8 members consisting of 2 males over sixteen, 2 females over sixteen, 1 male under sixteen, and 3 females under sixteen. Thomas Pidgeon was a Catholic Indian countryman who married a Creek woman. Thomas Pidgeon's name is crossed out on one muster roll and "not gone" is scribbled, meaning he enrolled but later changed his mind and stayed behind. Thomas S. Woodward notes in his *Reminiscences* that Pidgeon "stopped at Pass Christian, and never went with the Indians to Arkansas." Indeed, an 1839 letter, written from Pass Christian, Mississippi, reports that "Tom Pigeon and family are at Wolf River—consisting of himself and four others." Pidgeon was a part of detachment 6 and relocated to the Gulf of Mexico in 1837 but never followed the rest of the detachment to Indian territory. In the "remarks" section of one of the muster rolls, "Joseph P run off" is written. Joseph Pidgeon, Thomas Pidgeon's son, was a student at Withington, a Baptist mission school operated by Lee Compere in the 1820s. Joseph Pidgeon absconded from the rendezvous site at Fort Strother and appears on the 1832 Creek census from the town of Cubihatchee. According to Thomas S. Woodward, Joseph Pidgeon was later hanged in Mobile for killing a "cab-man" during a robbery.[11]
43. **John Reed** (Clewalla) 14 members consisting of 1 male over sixteen, 5 females over sixteen, 4 males under sixteen, and 4 females under sixteen. John Reed was one of many Creeks whose life was threatened over their decision to enroll with the second McIntosh party. Sometime in the spring of 1828 Tuckabatchee headman Tuskenehaw (along with Clewalla headman Jim Boy) drew a sword and threatened to kill William J. Wills (no. 61, this roll) while he was at Reed's mother's house near Line Creek. On another occasion Reed testified that these two headmen threatened him, saying he "was Rong for going" and that he "aught not to go" to Indian territory. The threats appear to have worked; next to Reed's name is written "one not gone," although Reed's name is not crossed out. It appears he did remain in the Creek Nation, however, and was killed sometime in 1834.[12]
44. **Vardy Jolly** (Tuckabatchee) 4 members consisting of 1 male over sixteen, 1 female over sixteen, and 2 females under sixteen. Roll lists

Jolly as white. Next to Jolly's name "not gone" is written, meaning he enrolled but later changed his mind and stayed behind.

45. **Samuel Hopwood** (Tallassee) 2 members consisting of 1 male over sixteen and 1 female over sixteen. Roll lists Hopwood as white. Around 1820 Samuel H. Hopwood (b. 1795 in Virginia) married Sarah Posey (b. 1801), who was the daughter of Nancy Posey (no. 30 on this roll). Hopwood was compensated for steering a boat from the Tennessee River to Fort Smith, Arkansas Territory, and for issuing provisions to the Creeks during their journey west.[13]
46. **James Edwards** (Tallassee) 3 members consisting of 1 male over sixteen and 2 females under sixteen. Roll lists Edwards as white.
47. **Is ful leach cah hiar** (Clewalla) 1 member consisting of 1 male over sixteen. One roll lists Is ful leach cah hiar as white. Next to Is ful leach cah hiar's name "not gone" is written, meaning he enrolled but later changed his mind and stayed behind.
48. **Ottus Harjo** (Cusseta) 1 member consisting of 1 male over sixteen.
49. **John Berryhill Jr.** (Thlakatchka) 11 members consisting of 3 males over sixteen, 2 females over sixteen, 4 males under sixteen, and 2 females under sixteen. Both rolls list all eleven members as white. John Dallas Berryhill was born around 1789 to John and Elizabeth (Derrisaw) Berryhill (no. 50 on this roll) and married Mary Rutledge in 1809. Berryhill enrolled for emigration at the Line Creek encampment and was threatened by Tuskenehaw for his decision to move west. According to testimony, Berryhill reported that Tuskenehaw used "Insulting languige" and "for a trifle he would Cut our throats" for emigrating.[14]
50. **John Berryhill Sr.** (Thlakatchka) 4 members consisting of 1 male over sixteen, 1 female over sixteen, 1 male under sixteen, and 1 slave. Roll lists Berryhill Sr. as white. Berryhill was born in the 1750s or 1760s in either the Carolinas or Georgia. Around 1781 he married Elizabeth Derrisaw (sometimes Martha Elizabeth Derrisaw), the daughter of interpreter James Durouzeaux and his Creek wife. Berryhill camped at Line Creek with his son, John Jr., before rendezvousing with the party at Fort Strother. Berryhill appears not necessarily to have seen eye-to-eye with all the members of the McIntosh-led government in

the west on every issue. When the western Creeks wrote a memorial accusing Creek agent David Brearley of a number of offenses, it was noted that "old John Berryhill opposed the memorial in Council but was forced to Sign it by the chiefs."[15]

51. **Andrew Berryhill** (Thlakatchka) 2 members consisting of 1 male over sixteen and 1 female over sixteen. Possibly the brother of John Berryhill (no. 50 on this roll).[16]
52. **Oc ta lee gee** (Thlakatchka) 1 member consisting of 1 male over sixteen.
53. **Samuel Berryhill** (Thlakatchka) 9 members consisting of 2 males over sixteen, 3 females over sixteen, 3 females under sixteen, and 1 slave. Samuel Berryhill was born around 1798 to John and Elizabeth (Derrisaw) Berryhill (no. 50 on this roll). Berryhill also refused to sign as a witness to the signatures opposing Brearley (see no. 50 this roll).[17]
54. **Daniel Kennard** (Thlakatchka) 4 members consisting of 1 male over sixteen, 1 female over sixteen, 1 female under sixteen, and 1 slave. A member of the March–July 1827 exploratory delegation who selected land for the initial western Creek settlements in the Indian territory.[18]
55. **Chu lee ti lee Emathla** (Thlakatchka) 4 members consisting of 1 male over sixteen, 2 females over sixteen, and 1 female under sixteen.
56. **Sparny cloc co** (Hitchiti) 1 member consisting of 1 male over sixteen.
57. **Thomas Berryhill** (Thlakatchka) 3 members consisting of 1 male over sixteen, 1 female over sixteen, and 1 male under sixteen. Thomas S. Berryhill was born in 1782 to John and Elizabeth (Derrisaw) Berryhill (no. 50 on second McIntosh party roll). Thomas married Sarah Deacle in 1804.[19]
58. **Baxter Self** (Thlakatchka) 6 members consisting of 1 male over sixteen, 1 female over sixteen, 2 males under sixteen, and 2 females under sixteen. Both rolls list all six members as white. Baxter Self was the brother of John Self (no. 59 on this roll). In 1819 or 1820 Self married Susanna "Sukey" Berryhill (b. 1802), who was the daughter of John and Elizabeth (Derrisaw) Berryhill (no. 50 on this roll). Their sons were named John B. Self and William Baxter "Buck" Self.[20]
59. **John Self** (Thlakatchka) 6 members consisting of 1 male over sixteen, 1 female over sixteen, 2 males under sixteen, and 2 females under sixteen. Both rolls list all six members as white. John Self was the

brother of Baxter Self (no. 58 on this roll). In 1820 John Self married Catherine "Katy" Berryhill (b. 1795), who was the daughter of John and Elizabeth (Derrisaw) Berryhill (no. 50 on this roll).[21]

60. **Pleasant Berryhill** (Thlakatchka) 3 members consisting of 1 male over sixteen, 1 female over sixteen, and 1 female under sixteen. Both rolls list all three members as white. Pleasant Berryhill was born in 1800 to John and Elizabeth (Derrisaw) Berryhill (no. 50 on this roll). He married Martha Right in 1823, before marrying a young Creek woman named Winnie. He received federal compensation for working as a flatboat hand on the Tennessee River from Gunter's Landing to the bottom of the Muscle Shoals during the emigration.[22]
61. **William J. Wills** (Thlakatchka) 4 members consisting of 1 male over sixteen, 1 female over sixteen, and 2 males under sixteen. Both rolls list all four members as white. Around 1804 William J. Wills married Elizabeth "Betsy" Berryhill (b. 1787), the daughter of John and Elizabeth (Derrisaw) Berryhill (no. 50 on this roll). Next to Wills's name is written "his wife not gone," meaning Betsy Berryhill enrolled but later appears to have changed her mind and stayed behind. Her decision to stay in the Creek Nation may have been related to the threats William Wills received for choosing to leave for Indian territory. Wills was with John Reed (no. 43 on this roll) at Reed's mother's house at Line Creek when Tuckabatchee headman Tuskenehaw, along with Jim Boy, threatened the men for emigrating.[23]
62. **John Winslett** (Hitchiti) 10 members consisting of 4 males over sixteen, 3 females over sixteen, 1 male under sixteen, and 2 females under sixteen. Winslett was a white man who served in the first Creek War (1813–14). Winslett traveled west with his Creek wife, Hattie Ward (d. 1866), and their young daughters, Befeeny (d. 1877) and Ellen (d. 1854). In the early 1830s Winslett, serving as attorney for the western Creek Nation, traveled to Florida to negotiate the return of a number of slaves who were in the possession of the Seminoles.[24]
63. **See tim part lee** (Hitchiti) 4 members consisting of 2 females over sixteen and 2 males under sixteen.
64. **Thomas Posey** (Thlakatchka) 3 members consisting of 1 male over sixteen, 1 female over sixteen, and 1 male under sixteen. Both rolls list

all three members as white. Born in 1803, Thomas Posey was the son of Nancy Posey (no. 30 on this roll). In 1827 Posey married Elenore Mayhew of Georgia. Posey received federal compensation for working as a flatboat hand on the Tennessee River from Gunter's Landing to the bottom of the Muscle Shoals during the emigration.[25]

65. **Co e Harjo** (Chowokolo Tallahassee) 1 member consisting of 1 male over sixteen.
66. **Pi yock Harjo** (Chowokolo Tallahassee) 1 member consisting of 1 male over sixteen.
67. **Joseph Gooldsby** (Tuckabatchee) 1 member consisting of 1 male over sixteen. Joseph Gooldsby's name is redacted on one muster roll and absent on another. Almost certainly did not emigrate with this party.
68. **John Wynn** (Thlakatchka) 7 members consisting of 3 males over sixteen, 2 females over sixteen, and 2 slaves. Both rolls list Wynn as white. Wynn originally enrolled to move with the first McIntosh party in 1827 (no. 13, first McIntosh party roll, chap. 1), only to remain behind and emigrate with the second party in 1828.[26]
69. **William Lott** (Thlakatchka) 1 member consisting of 1 male over sixteen. Both rolls list Lott as white. Lott, who was born around 1783, noted in an affidavit that he "was raised in the Creek nation, and is acquainted with the Indian character, customs, laws, and language." Lott accused Stephen Hawkins (no. 66 on first McIntosh party roll, chap. 1) of bad character and declared that he "would not believe him upon oath or in any other way." This statement was given after disputes arose regarding the amount of money and property claimed to have been lost by the McIntosh and Hawkins families during the raids that occurred as punishment for the Treaty of Indian Springs signing in 1825. Former Creek agent David B. Mitchell, a close McIntosh ally, countered Lott by testifying that "the character of William Lott is notoriously bad, and I would not believe him on oath if unsupported by other credible testimony."[27]
70. **Co wock co chee Emathla** (Thlakatchka) 8 members consisting of 2 males over sixteen, 2 females over sixteen, 1 male under sixteen, and 3 females under sixteen. Became a second judge in the western Creek Nation by 1834.[28]

71. **Ar cher hatchee Tustunnuggee** (Thlakatchka) 14 members consisting of 4 males over sixteen, 4 females over sixteen, 1 male under sixteen, and 5 slaves.
72. **O ful chee Emathla** (Thlakatchka) 8 members consisting of 2 males over sixteen, 2 females over sixteen, 3 males under sixteen, and 1 female under sixteen.
73. **David McIntosh** (Thlakatchka) 11 members consisting of 1 male over sixteen, 2 females over sixteen, 4 males under sixteen, 1 female under sixteen, and 3 slaves.
74. **O cos co Harjo** (Thlakatchka) 6 members consisting of 1 male over sixteen, 2 females over sixteen, 1 male under sixteen, and 2 females under sixteen.
75. **Al butter Harjo** (Thlakatchka) 1 member consisting of 1 male over sixteen.
76. **Bob Tiger** (Thlakatchka) 7 members consisting of 1 male over sixteen, 1 female over sixteen, 1 female under sixteen, and 4 slaves. A close McIntosh associate. In 1832 Tiger and Chilly McIntosh returned to the eastern Creek Nation with powers-of-attorney to sell the five full sections of land granted by the eastern Creeks to the western Creeks under the 1832 Treaty of Washington.[29]
77. **Sin lit ho chee** (Thlakatchka) 4 members consisting of 1 male over sixteen, 2 females over sixteen, and 1 female under sixteen. This family appears on only one muster roll and is redacted, meaning they almost certainly did not emigrate with this party.
78. **John Owen** (Thlakatchka) 1 member consisting of 1 male over sixteen. Both rolls list Owen as white. On 4 March 1825 John Owen (or Owens) transcribed a letter that was dictated by Thlakatchka headman Little Prince (the principal chief of the Lower Creeks and a staunch opponent of the Treaty of Indian Springs and emigration), in which Little Prince invited Chilly McIntosh to return safely from exile to the Creek Nation. The letter was signed by Lemuel B. Nichols (no. 33 on the first McIntosh party roll, chap. 1) as a witness and was carried to Chilly McIntosh by Samuel Sells (no. 3 on this roll).[30]
79. **David Colvin** (Tallassee) 2 members consisting of 1 male over sixteen and 1 female over sixteen. Both rolls list Colvin as white.

80. **William Alfred** (Tuckabatchee) 1 member consisting of 1 male over sixteen. Both rolls list Alfred as white.
81. **Benjamin Jolly** (Tuckabatchee) 1 member consisting of 1 male over sixteen. Both rolls list Jolly as white. Next to Jolly's name "not gone" is written, meaning he enrolled but later changed his mind and stayed behind.
82. **William G. Jacobs** (Tuckabatchee) 1 member consisting of 1 male over sixteen. Both rolls list Jacobs as white.
83. **Pleasant Austin** (Tuckabatchee) 1 member consisting of 1 male over sixteen. Both rolls list Austin as white. Austin traveled alone and was even compensated by the federal government for helping to pole and steer one of the flatboats from Gunter's Landing to the Ohio River during this emigration. He later returned to the eastern Creek Nation and self-emigrated his wife Polly Austin and son Daniel Austin to Indian territory in 1830.[31]
84. **James Moore** (Weogufka) 9 members consisting of 1 male over sixteen and 8 slaves. Both rolls list Moore as white. Born in Pennsylvania ca. 1771 or 1772, Moore was an Indian countryman who came to the Creek Nation sometime around 1796. He was the father of John P. Moore (see 1835–36 voluntary self-emigrations, chap. 17), Jackson Moore (who died at Shreveport, Louisiana, while on his way to Texas), Peggy (who moved to Texas), Catherine (who moved to Texas), and Nancy Hutton (no. 23, Stidham roll, chap. 17). Moore was threatened over his decision to emigrate west with his Creek family. Sometime in late February or early March 1828, Opothle Yoholo, and possibly others, confronted Moore and confiscated his property, including a letter written by William Walker in which Walker counseled the Creeks to emigrate west. Opothle Yoholo took the letter and presented it to the Cherokees during his visit to their northern neighbors. The Creeks also threatened to whip Moore's wife and "take her away from him" if he followed through on his decision to move west. While Moore appears to have emigrated with this party (there is no "not gone" written by his name), he returned to Alabama and was living in Tallapoosa County, Alabama, by 1837.[32]

85. **Sei ee** (Thlakatchka) 1 member consisting of 1 male over sixteen.
86. **David M. Mordecai** (Okfuskee) 1 member consisting of 1 male over sixteen. Next to Mordecai's name "not gone" is written, meaning he enrolled but later changed his mind and stayed behind. A Creek man of Jewish and African descent, Mordecai appears in the West by 1832, when he was hired at St. Louis by the delegation that included Washington Irving, Henry Leavitt Ellsworth, Charles Latrobe, and Count Albert-Alexandre de Pourtlès to explore the Indian territory in 1832.[33]
87. **Nelson Kent** (Hitchiti) 1 member consisting of 1 male over sixteen. Both rolls list Kent as white.
88. **Tuscoona Fixico** (Weogufka) 1 member consisting of 1 male over sixteen.
89. **Tuffo Fixico** (Tallasseehatchee) 1 member consisting of 1 male over sixteen.
90. **Tallassee Harjo** (Coosada) 1 member consisting of 1 male over sixteen.
91. **E fi Yoholo** (Ottissee) 1 member consisting of 1 male over sixteen. Next to E fi Yoholo's name "not gone" is written, meaning he enrolled but later changed his mind and stayed behind.
92. **Pah fot chee** (Weahgoafcoochee) 1 member consisting of 1 male over sixteen.
93. **Fee kee thla** (Cusseta) 1 member consisting of 1 male over sixteen.
94. **Woy ey Harjo** (Chowokolo Tallahassee) 1 member consisting of 1 male over sixteen.
95. **Itch hars Harjo** (Wockocoy) 8 members consisting of 3 males over sixteen, 3 females over sixteen, 1 male under sixteen, and 1 female under sixteen.
96. **Pompey Grant** (Hillabee) 1 member consisting of 1 male over sixteen. Listed as a free black.
97. **Ne hi Yoholo** (Coweta) 9 members consisting of 1 male over sixteen, 3 females over sixteen, 2 males under sixteen, and 3 slaves.
98. **Co sattee Chopco** (Coweta) 1 member consisting of 1 male over sixteen.
99. **Spo coak Harjo** (Emarhee) 1 member consisting of 1 male over sixteen.

100. **James Parker** (Coweta) 1 member consisting of 1 male over sixteen. Both rolls list Parker as white.

101. **Walter Grayson** (Hillabee) 15 members consisting of 4 males over sixteen, 2 females over sixteen, 3 males under sixteen, 2 females under sixteen, and 4 slaves. Walter Grayson (b. 1781) was the son of Robert Grierson and his wife Sinnugee; brother of Thomas and William Grayson (nos. 102 and 103, this roll), and Sandy Grayson (Grieson, no. 44 on fourth voluntary emigrating party roll, chap.5), and uncle of Sampson Grayson (Grieson, no. 1 on fourth voluntary emigrating party roll, chap. 5). Next to Grayson's name "not gone" is written, meaning he enrolled but later changed his mind and stayed behind.[34]

102. **Thomas Grayson** (Hillabee) 8 members consisting of 1 male over sixteen, 1 female over sixteen, 3 males under sixteen, 1 female under sixteen, and 2 slaves. Thomas Grayson was the son of Robert Grierson and Sinnugee; brother of Walter Grayson (no. 101, this roll) and William Grayson (no. 103, this roll), and Sandy Grayson (no. 44 on fourth voluntary emigrating party roll, chap. 5); and father of Sampson Grayson (Grieson, no. 1 on fourth voluntary emigrating roll, chap. 5). Next to Grayson's name "not gone" is written, meaning he enrolled but later changed his mind and stayed behind.[35]

103. **William Grayson** (Hillabee) 8 members consisting of 1 male over sixteen, 1 female over sixteen, 3 males under sixteen, and 3 females under sixteen. William Grayson (1787– ca. 1860) was the son of Robert Grierson and Sinnugee; brother of Walter and Thomas Grayson (nos. 101 and 102, this roll), and Sandy Grayson (Grieson, no. 44 on fourth voluntary emigrating party roll, chap. 5); and uncle of Sampson Grayson (Grieson, no. 1 on fourth voluntary emigrating party roll, chap. 5). Next to Grayson's name "not gone" is written, meaning he enrolled, but later changed his mind and stayed behind.[36]

104. **Wah lock Emathla** (Coweta) 7 members consisting of 3 males over sixteen, 3 females over sixteen, and 1 slave.

105. **Po ilth Harjo** (Coweta) 2 members consisting of 1 male over sixteen and 1 female over sixteen.

106. **Cot chee Harjo** (Coweta), 3 members consisting of 2 males over sixteen and 1 female over sixteen.
107. **Ha lee** (Coweta) 1 member consisting of 1 male over sixteen.
108. **Sup peet hoe** (Coweta) 3 members consisting of 2 females over sixteen and 1 male under sixteen.
109. **Roly McIntosh** (Coweta) 14 members consisting of 14 slaves. Also known as Artris Micco, Roly McIntosh (ca. 1790–1863) was the brother of William McIntosh and became the leader of the McIntosh party after the Coweta headman's death in 1825. Although described as "an underling Chief, inferior degree" in the East, once in Indian territory, Roly McIntosh became the principal chief of the western Creek Nation, a position he held until his retirement in 1859. He then moved to Texas, where he died in 1863. McIntosh maintained his rank even after prominent members of the National Council were forced west in 1836–37. He did not emigrate with a government-sponsored emigration but on his own with his own resources. Here he is having the government move his slaves west.[37]
110. **Mrs. Stinson** (Coweta) 5 members consisting 1 female over sixteen, 2 males under sixteen, 1 female under sixteen, and 1 slave. "Mrs. Stinson" was probably the ex-wife of George Stinson, a white man. George Stinson later abandoned his wife, moved to Georgia, and married a white woman. He had been arrested by Creek agent John Crowell for violating intercourse laws (trading without a license) and hauled off to Savannah at least once for trial.[38]
111. **Polly Kennard** (Coweta) 4 members consisting of 2 females over sixteen and 2 males under sixteen.
112. **El lee kee** (Coweta) 1 member consisting of 1 female over sixteen.

Supplemental Letters of the Second McIntosh Party

William Walker reports on the threats of death for any person who enrolls for emigration. Letter found at LR, CAE, Roll 237, 181–84.

Fort Hull Creek nation
March 3d 1828

The Hon'l
Thomas L. McKenney[39]

Sir

In Case of Improper interfearance on the part of the Indians opposed to emigration I deem it my duty to Report—they Chiefs having Just Returned from the agency from drawing Some goods—I am told that they have made a Regulation to Kill any man who will Enrole for the arkensaws—this day the Big Warriors Son[40] Came to my hous as he said to see some young men who had Just Signed for Emigration—and on one of the young men approching nere to the Big fellow he the Big fellow Seased one of the guns that one of the young men had Recd as a present—and told the young man I have come to Kill you and now I will do it—and turned the loded gun to the young man and snapt the Rifle at him—then an other Indian and a black man Seased the gun and prevented him from making an other attempt untill the young man mounted a horse and made his ascape—two white men who was present took out the flint from the gun and attempted to take her away the Big Warrior son Seased the gun and had a Concederable Scuffle for hir and was perfectly and [illegible]. I saw the hole transaction and Can procure the affedavids of the white men if Required—Hopoethleyohola has lately been to the Cherokees of which mentioned in my last letter to you—as he past through John Davis's town[41]—he said and don Every thing in his power to defeate the Emigration—I Rote a letter to an old Indian Cuntriman who is a Residenter of Johns town and is friendly to John and the Emigration. Hopoethley hola went to Moores[42] the Indian Cuntreyman with an angry and [illegible] and demanded the letter he had Recd from me—Moore was Compeld to deliver it—having no protection—he Hopoethley hola Carreyed it to the Cherokees there was nothing in the letter—only my friendly advice to Moore and the Indians to Emigrate—as I past last up to the upper towns I went through the nabourhood of Tuckbachee and Inrolled between 25 and 30 in a place of a day as I past along—one Indian of which had been badly beten the night before becaus he was disposed to Emigrate—and a fiew days after

I had past by they Collected at Tuckebachee and the Kings directed that the heads of the differant famileys—should meet and bind the differant famileys up aganst the Emigration, the Tiger—the wind—and Patotes familey met in the nabourhood of my old place where Capt Triplet[43] now lives—this proceding produced such a state of things as to make those who I had Inroled to retrait—and but one of the 25 or 30 got on that day will now agree to go. When John was In the upper towns he was threated to be Kild if he had any thing to do with the Emigration. I have thought this was a violation of the treaty—and if we are thus to be anoyed—and they views of the Goverment fore-stald—we may as well yeld the point at once—and Every person that has been Ingaged Either direct or Indirect to get away—for here they Can not stay—there is a Remedy and it aught I think to be applyed—for the Intentions of the Goverment is good to the Indians—if I have said more to the department then I aught—I hope I will be Excused—I Intend nothing only for good.

I am yours yours with Interests of high [esteem]
Wm Walker

P.S. John Davis says that James Moore the Indian Cuntreyman Spoken of in the letter—that his property it is said will perhaps be taken a way from him unless some protection given him—do let me here from you

Wm W

☾

The Creeks of the second McIntosh party complain of harassment and the stealing of horses while waiting in camp by those opposed to emigration. Letter found at LR, CAE, Roll 237, 154–56.

Indian Camp near
Fort Bainbridge Creek Nation
June 3rd 1828

Col'o D. Brearley

Sir

We the under Signed persons being acquainted with the Indian Language and having a better opportunity of Knowing the extent of the opposition to the emegration than those who may not understand the tongue—we do without hesitation say that every exertion is used by the chiefs and those under their influence to prevent the people from emegrating, chiefs has visited the camp and applyed every argument in their power to get them to return and not to go—and have resorted to the creation of the most foul falshoods about the country on the arkensaw and even stated that the people has not got to the Country they started for—they are now as we are informed in council not far from hear—and what may be the deliberations of their council we Know not—but would not be surprised if they were of a more serious Charactor than ever—the time for emegration has as they think expired and they now think they will be at Liberty to do allmost anything they have come to the camp and arrested the child from the Mother and bare it off. two Horses has been taken from the camp last Night Kendal Lewis Gray horse and Powes Hargo Riding horse and a number of K. Lewis' out horses driven off or at least Missing so that they cannot be found—we have been told by Indians repeatedly that the Publick Interpreter Paddy Car has used continual opposition and advised to the people not to go—and some of us knows this to be the facts from his own statements.

we are yours with Sentiments of
high Respects &c.

Powes Hargo
Samuel Sells
James Randle
John Berryhill
Benj'm Lott
K. Lewis
Jno Hambly
John Winslett

Tuskeni Hargo
Thlath lo Hargo
Lif tiff Hargo
Cot chee Fixico
Francis Lovett
Tallom Har chee
Hose pi tock Hargo

☾

The Creeks reiterate their complaints about their horses being stolen by Creeks opposed to emigration and note that they will adjudicate their claims through the federal government and not by Creek custom. Letter found at LR, CAE, Roll 237, 158–59.

Indian Camp Creek nation
July 18th 1828.

The Hon'r
Thomas L McKenney—

Sir

We the undersigned being a part of the Emegrating party of Indians now on our way for the arkensaw—deem it our duty to state to the goverment of the united States the facts in rolation to the treatment of the Indians who is opposed to Emegration—dureing the time we were in camp near Lewis stand Horses were stolen from us of which we made complaint to Col'o Brearley who was then in washington City—the Horses we then complained of was actuly stolen of which fact we have the proof but they have been recovered—but when we left that camp allmost every night we have had some taken more or less seventeen in one night—in the morning they were persued and a part off them recovered when they were found the Bells were taken off with some hickry bark a flap string and ropes a round their necks, the whole we have lost and we made the complaint above mentioned is twenty seven ten of which is entirely gone unless we fortune than we expect the chief of this party has come this conclusion not to take any from the other party as is Indian custom but to rely on the government for a fair Investigation and make the nation accountable for the horses we are the people that is in accordance with the views of the Government and therefore do Expect and hope that you will see that we have Justice done us it is useless for us to call on the chiefs for Justice, for they are offended with us for doing as the Government desires—you are our dependence we remain your children &c.

Different Towns	
Hitcheta	Benj'm Lott
	John Winslett
Coweta	K. Lewis
	Samuel Sells
	Senorway
Chiwackley	Powes Hargo
Coweta	Coe Marthley
	Oak Mulgee Mico
Chiwackley	Tuskenehah
	Thlatch Le Hargo
Coosawda	Potock Hargo
	Co se yoholo
Cuseta	Artis Hargo
	Thlock Quee chee
Tuckabatchee	David Pigeon
	Wm J Wills

☾

Emigration subagent William Walker reports on the headmen's attempts to stop emigration through threats and fear. Letter found at RG 75, NARA,

Letters Received by the Office of Indian Affairs, 1824–81, Microcopy 234, Creek Agency West, 1826–36, Roll 236, 33–35.

Indian Camp near Ten Islands Sept'm 8th 1828.

Col'o David Brearley

Sir

Your Letter of late date has been received in camp with grate acclamation of Joy—it has produced the gratest change imaginable—I must confess that the camp was in a mutaneous and disorderly Situation without my having the means of controling it but now I hope for the better behavour of the people—you say you wish to know my opinion with regard to the disposition of the Troops in the nation and if any would be wanted near the principal Randezvous I am clearley of the opinion that they will do but little good at Fort Mitchell there ought to be some at Tuckabatchee—the seat of diseffection—and some near the heart of the upper creeks Perhaps Hillabee—and march them from place to place as occasion may require—if the officers should be directed by the Secritary of war to be governed by your Requesitions and to receive your directions in relation to their opposition—then you may expect to be benefited by their comeing to the nation, but if they are to remain at Fort Mitchell and then Publick councils to be held to investigate the charges made against them you might as well send them back at onst for they will not answer the purpose for which they have been brought—if the officers will be friendley and march from place to place as might be required on Proof punish a few then the object will be affected—if not the object will be lost—a grate deal will depend on the officers vegilence in the business at this time there is a fit Subject for chastisement at Hatchett creek—A man by the name of Red Mouth who has been the means of preventing the wife & family of James Moore from going to the arkensaw—that family came to me and enroled and the old man is gone and the family was to follow—as soon as he started Red Mouth came to Mrs Moore & prevented her from going. John Davis is knowing to the facts—he has done every thing in his power to prevent Emegration—and even to stop those that had consented to go if that old Rascall could get a good scare all things will go on well there and that family will go immediately—I hope you will have an order to cause all persons who has enroled or drawn rations to be compeled to go—and In perticular Lamarlee[44] and Spanish Tom Son Joe[45] who run away from hear and stole two horses—a good number has gone back from hear and it Seemed that they thought they would enrole draw provisions and return Just when they saw cause this must be put down—and in the most rash way would please me the best—Old Cap't McGirth[46] near where I live has been much opposed and made Every statement in his power to prevent Emegration, which is Supported by the Evidence forwarded you—the people in this nabourhood has been so far friendly more so than any part of the nation—with Regards to the Evidence aganst Mr McGirth—Joseph Goldsbay[47] who was at his hous doing some Carpenters work stats that he heard McGirth say to the Big Warriors son[48] that he aught to stop the people from Emegrating and that he had given them his best advice not to go—and that he was frequently at it in his [illegible] in the [illegible] of the last Spring I have an acquantance with Goldsbay and satisfied he tells the trooth—there are many in the Cunterey who heard him say and do Every thing in his power to prevent the Indians from Emegrating.

I am yours Respefely
Wm Walker

☾

Announcing the arrival of the land party, which he accompanied, Brearley notes a relatively easy and dry journey west. At the agency Brearley met with a three-person delegation of Creek Indians visiting the western Creek Nation in possible anticipation of their own emigration. Letter found at LR, CAE, Roll 237, 136.[49]

Western Camp Agency,[50]
Dec. 12, 1828.

Sir,

I have the honor to inform you that the land party of emigrating, Creeks consisting of two hundred and thirty six arrived at this place on the 28th of November being fifty-four days on the road from the Creek Nation in Alabama.

The water party I have not heard from since they passed Memphis in the early part of this month I presume they are detained at the mouth of White River on account of the low state of the water.

I am using every exertion to close the payment of provisions, immediately after which I shall return to the old nation.

The exploring delegation of Creeks under Mr. L. Blake came here and were kindly received by the emigrants who express a great desire for a reunion of the parties which there is no difficulty in effecting and a general produced if improper interference be prevented.[51]

It is also my duty to mention to you that a modification of the late Cherokee Treaty or a definite construction of that under which the emigration together with the promises made them (which seems to be provided for in the passage of the Cherokee Treaty will be requisite to continue the emigration.[52]

You will be furnished with a map of this section of country by Colonel Arbuckle together with his views and knowledge on the subject to which I humbly offer to add mine when I reach the city which of course will be before the movement of another party could take place.

I have the honor to be
Very respectfully
Your Obedt. Servt.
D. Brearly Agt. Ind. Aff.

To the
Honorable Peter B. Porter[53]
Secretary of War.

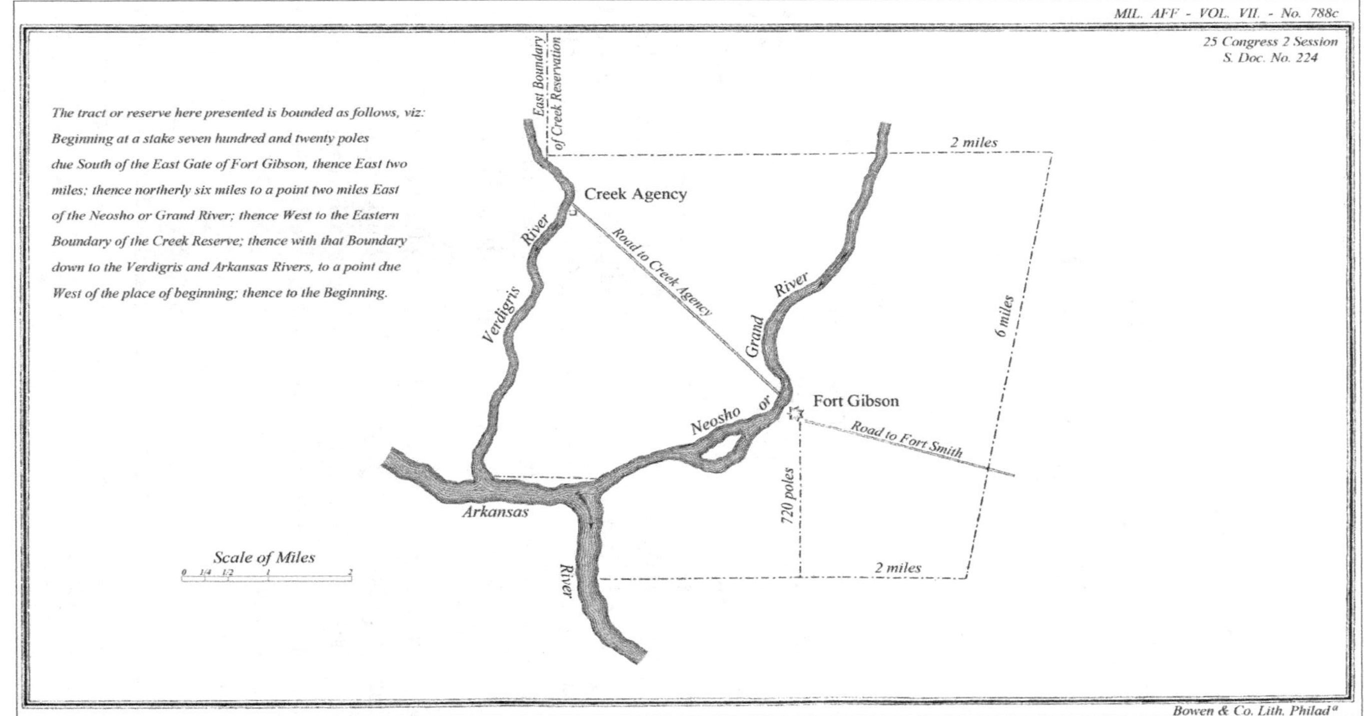
MIL. AFF - VOL. VII. - No. 788c
25 Congress 2 Session
S. Doc. No. 224
The tract or reserve here presented is bounded as follows, viz:
Beginning at a stake seven hundred and twenty poles
due South of the East Gate of Fort Gibson, thence East two
miles; thence northerly six miles to a point two miles East
of the Neosho or Grand River; thence West to the Eastern
Boundary of the Creek Reserve; thence with that Boundary
down to the Verdigris and Arkansas Rivers, to a point due
West of the place of beginning; thence to the Beginning.
East Boundary
of Creek Reservation
Creek Agency
Road to Creek Agency
Verdigris
River
Grand
River
Neosho
or
Fort Gibson
Road to Fort Smith
2 miles
6 miles
720 poles
2 miles
Arkansas
River
Scale of Miles
0
1/4
1/2
1
2
Bowen & Co. Lith. Philad[a]

MAP 3. Fort Gibson and the Western Creek Agency. American State Papers, Military Affairs, vol. 7, 788c. Cartography by Sarah Mattics and Kiersten Fish.

3 The Third Voluntary Emigrating Party, 1829

By 1829 the exigencies of the loss of the Creeks' Georgia land from the Treaties of Indian Springs and Washington had taken its toll. Many Creeks were unable to find quality soil within the limits of Alabama after being forced from Georgia in 1826, and they began a long period of transience and starvation. As a result, large numbers of people—almost 1,300—decided to take their chances in the West. Only a small number of this party, however, considered themselves members of the McIntosh party. Indeed, while members of the Perryman (Benjamin), Stidham (G. W.), Bruner, and Reed (Vicey) families fancied themselves members of the "third and last part of the McIntosh party," most had no connection to the late William McIntosh. While some Creeks accompanied this party because, in their words "it was impossible for us to [live] while we were sorrounded by the whites," other Creeks left because they felt that their children's future was at stake. A group of emigrants wrote to Andrew Jackson and stated as much, declaring that "we old men did not come to this country for our own good but for our children who loves to hunt we find plenty of game more than we can destroy."[1]

No muster roll is known to have survived, but receipts for improvements show that in addition to the Perrymans, Bruners, Stidhams, and Reeds, a number of other prominent Creeks also emigrated in 1829. Among them was John Davis, a Creek man of African ancestry and Baptist minister who was educated at the Withington Mission School in the Creek Nation.

Daniel N. McIntosh—William McIntosh's son (1822–1895, by McIntosh's Creek wife, Susannah) and Chilly McIntosh's half-brother—also may have emigrated with this party.[2] Ten-year-old Samuel Checote, who would go on to become the first elected principal chief of the Creek Nation in 1867, emigrated with his family in 1829.[3] Other receipts show that Creeks from the towns of Hitchiti, Okteyoconnee, Yuchi, Big Spring, Cowyka (a *talofa* of Sawokli), and Eufaula, among others, accompanied this group west.[4]

There is no journal describing the events of the journey, nor have many letters written along the route survived. Instead, much of what we know about the party comes from disbursement receipts and newspaper articles. From this evidence, it is clear that the party struggled with bad weather, sickness, and death. While there is evidence that few Creeks died during the first two emigrations, a number of Creeks died during the third. Receipts were issued for making coffins and burying the dead. Some black slaves were compensated for cutting a road through the Mississippi Swamp, which inundated the western side of the Mississippi River from Memphis. A number of Creek emigrants wrote to President Jackson from Little Rock, lamenting that he had "lost some of [his] red children by sickness." Indeed, as the Creeks arrived in the Indian territory in September 1829, former Tennessee governor Sam Houston observed the haggard condition of the emigrants and noted that their condition was

> enough to shock humanity. . . . Between fifty and a hundred Uchees were left in the swamps of Mississippi and I believe have not arrived. A considerable number of the emigrating party I heard of on the Illinois River about eighteen miles east of Cantonment Gibson; they were nearly all sick, famished, and most of them unable to turn themselves on their blankets. They subsisted principally upon what fish they could catch, and Mr. Flowers, a Cherokee Indian countryman, furnished them some provisions on his own responsibility.[5]

The third voluntary emigrating party was conducted west by Thomas Crowell[6] (Creek agent John Crowell's brother), William Walker, and Luther Blake.[7] Dr. Alexander J. Robison[8] served as physician to the western Creeks in Indian territory.

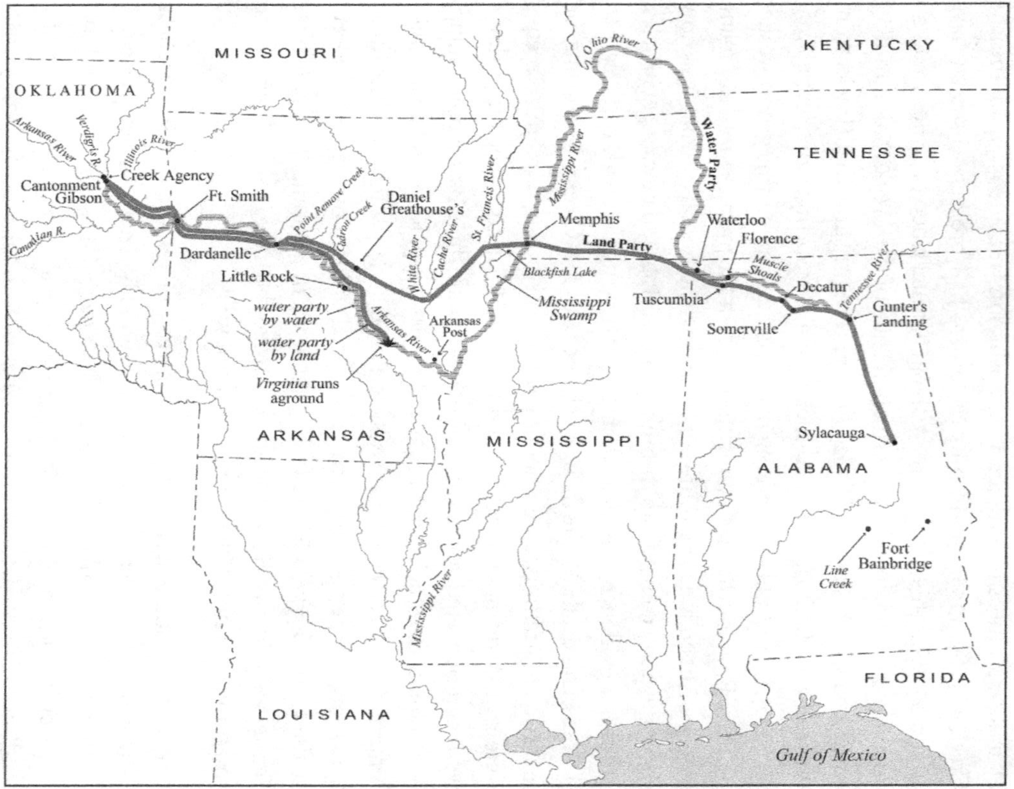

MAP 4. Route of the third voluntary emigrating party, June–September 1829. Place names correspond to stopping points or locations noted in the documentation. Route lines and locations are approximations. Cartography by Sarah Mattics and Kiersten Fish.

Supplemental Letters of the Third Voluntary Party

The members of the 1828 exploratory delegation (the same that encountered the land party of the second McIntosh party at Fort Gibson, chap. 2) request of President Andrew Jackson that he appoint Luther Blake to conduct the third voluntary emigrating party to Indian territory. Their wish was granted: Blake served as a subagent on the journey west in 1829. Letter found at LR, CAE, Roll 237, 260–61.

Columbus Jan'y 22—1829

Our Great Father

We have written on to you by Mr Blake who carried us on as an exploring party to examine the country west of the Mississippi. We have travelled a great way with Mr Blake and are glad to find him our friend who has studied our interest & has been friendly in supplying our wants—we have Known him long & have ever found him a friend to our people & we had the utmost confidence in our Great Father when he appointed Mr Blake to accompany us. We love him & we wish our Great Father to appoint him to carry our people west of the Mississippi—we have now arrived among our people & given them the talk and they are willing to go with Mr Blake for we have Known him long and he has always been our friend & the friend of our people—we Know he would take care of our women & orphan children & they have confidence in more than they have in strangers. Our great Father has appointed the best man to go with his children (because they Knew him & they have been with him on a long journey & they have not been decieved in him). We like the country & want our Great Father to appoint him to go with our people & settle the country that our Great Father has given us on the west of the Mississippi—When we arrived home a great many of our friends came to see us & we told them it was a fine country a plenty of Buffalo Elk Deer Bear & Turkeys & that your red children should remove there & they have listened to our talk and are willing to go if our friend Mr Blake go with us & see us justice done. We the delegation arrived at the Chatahoochy in good health.

Coe Martla Head Chief
Tuscemeha
Choeste

Daniel Perryman Interp'r

I certify that this is an exact representation of the Chiefs as Interpreted to me in the absence of any person but themselves.

N. F. Collins[9]

☾

Five Creek emigrants complain to the secretary of war that Hitchiti headman Neah Emathla, a staunch opponent of voluntary emigration, has visited their emigration camp with his warriors and attacked some members of the party. While the man and woman who were targeted had their ears cropped—a traditional punishment for adultery—this appears also to be a statement attack against the federal emigration program, signaling that these camps were not places of refuge. Letter found at LR, CAE, Roll 237, 263–64.

Fort Bainbridge Creek Nation
Apl. 12th. 1829.

Hon. John H. Eaton[10]
Secretary of War

Friend & Brother,

We communicate to you for the information of our great father the President that always putting confidence in whatever he tells us to do, and knowing that he is fully powerful and able to do what he says, and that he would not give bad talks to his red children, but would certainly do every thing in his power for their future welfare, and knowing it to be the wish of our white brethen at large that we should live, well but that it was impossible for us to do so while we were sorrounded by the whites, to remidy which, our great father gave us a country across the great waters of the Mississippi, promising protection and support to those that would go. This talk, of our father made our hearts glad, and a great many of our people embraced the happy opportunity, and went over, and their safe arrival there, and the good description that they gave of the Country, induced others to go. A party of us that were willing to go, collected and took our encampment at this place. When we were leaving our homes, our people that were not going exerted their utmost endeavors to prevent us from leaving this country, but placing a fierce reliance in the promised protection from our father, we paid but little attention to their menaces, being confident that it would please our father to learn that his children had taken hold on his talk. This so exasperated them, that they set no bounds to their resentment, and accordingly a party of desperadoes, headed by their chief, old He, ne, he, maltha[11] who was one of the most inveterate enimy that the United States had, in the last war,[12] attacted our Camps, and after most barberously beating two of our people, a man and a woman, they wantonly took off their ears, the said old chief, He, ne, he, maltha, exclaiming that if the United States had promised them protection, he would see whether they would be protected or not. We earnestly beg that our great father, send immediate assistance, or otherwise we will be exposed to the fury of our countrymen, and may eventually be all masacred, as we are informed that they are again threatining us—

your children
Co, we, Maltha
Pose, Harjoe
Holatu, Thlocoe
chocote, Yahola
Co, we, Harjoe

Witness
John Hambly

☾

This letter, one of the few written or dictated by Creek Indians while on the route, was addressed to new president Andrew Jackson, acknowledging that a number of the third voluntary party had died from sickness. Note the letter references the grounding of the steamboat *Virginia*, which occurred near Pine Bluff, Arkansas. Letter found at LR, CAE, Roll 237, 267–68.

Little Rock A Territory August 14 1829

Dear Father

We have the Pleasure to wright you a few lines this day our agent Capt walker who you authorise to take us to our new country has treated us well gave us a plenty to eat and we are sorry he is going to Leave us this day[13] he has used us all well one know better than another he holds the orphan child by the hand he has brought us in boats we came down the rivers in flat boats to the mouth of white river he there got a steam boat[14] to take us up the arkansaws river it could not go far the warter was so low he then got boats and horses for the sick people and fetched us this far we have lost some of your red children by sickness but if we where at home the almightty would take some of us away we had some of our freinds that went to our new country and came back to us and told us it was a good country we took there talk for we beliefd them to be straight men we have not got there yet but as far as we have come we have seen good Land and are much pleased with the country this far dear father we old men did not come to this country for our own good but for our children who loves to hunt we find plenty of game more than we can destroy. we have not got all our Rifles yet but have every reason to belief we will get them soon. Great Father we hope you will be pleased with few Lines about our agent capt walker for we are well pleased him.

Easter Charco mickco
Tustenuge Thlockco
Easter Charco Hargo
Powes mickco
Tuskenahah

Holatter mickco
Coe Marthler
Hollatter Thlockco
Tustenuge Chopco
Daniel Perriman
Coe Hargo

To
Andrew Jackson
President of the
united States

4 Chilly McIntosh's and Benjamin Hawkins's Emigrating Parties, 1833

By the early 1830s white encroachment (and the starvation resulting from land expropriation) had created such desperation that headmen took repeated trips to Washington DC in hopes of making face-to-face appeals for help. In each instance the Jackson administration told the Creeks that only emigrating across the Mississippi River would save them. With a majority of the Creek people unwilling to move west, the two sides appeared to be at a stalemate. In 1832 federal officials switched tactics. Convinced that the Creek National Council would never cede their land (because of the death penalty incurred by any headman who did so), Creek agent John Crowell proposed that the Creeks take their land in individual, privately owned reserves. Crowell presented this proposal to the headmen in council, and although opposed, after six tense days of "exertions and management," they finally relented. The Treaty of Washington, signed on 24 March 1832, ceded to the United States the entire five million acres that remained of the Creek domain, while retaining just over two million acres that were divided into 6,557 half-sections (320 acres), which were given to each head-of-family. Ninety of the principal headmen (called "mile chiefs") were given a full section (640 acres).

Although it cost the Creeks much, the 1832 Treaty of Washington appealed to the headmen in a number of ways. First, it promised to evict all white squatters from Creek land and guaranteed legal protections over the reserves (although how thoroughly federal and state officials would enforce these protections is subject to debate). Indeed, Crowell told the Creeks that the treaty was "the only mode by which they could be protected where they now are." The other aspect of the treaty that appealed to the headmen was that it was not a removal document (although it continued unabated the government's emigration program). By agreeing to terms, the Creeks no doubt expected that they would be allowed to remain indefinitely on their reserve, free from the harassment of emigration agents or white squatters.

The Treaty of Washington, however, proved to be an unmitigated disaster. By dividing the former Creek Nation into individual parts, whites no longer had to confront a united National Council; they could purchase directly from Creek land owners. Large numbers of hungry Creeks sold their reserve for life-saving cash, while others who were unfamiliar with private ownership did so without quite realizing that the sale was permanent. Many more were cheated out of their half-sections by white land speculators. Far from solving their problems, the treaty pushed the Creeks closer to the edge of despair.[1]

In September 1832 Chilly McIntosh (no. 1 on first McIntosh party roll) and Bob Tiger (no. 76 on second McIntosh party roll) returned to Alabama from the Indian territory. Granted powers of attorney to sell five 640-acre sections of land given to the western Creeks by the eastern headmen, McIntosh planned to dispose of the land and then conduct a small party of friends and family to Indian territory. In his letter to Elbert Herring, apprising the commissioner of Indian affairs of his plan, McIntosh also offered his services to the federal government in collecting any other Creeks who might want to move west. McIntosh's application to serve as emigration agent was endorsed by a number of prominent people, including his paternal relative George M. Troup, U.S. senator and former Georgia governor, as well as Columbus land speculator John Milton, who had purchased the five sections from Chilly McIntosh.[2]

There is very little documentation related to the 1833 emigration, although it is clear that it was a disaster. McIntosh hired land buyers as emigration subagents, who then tried to gain power of attorney over the emigrants' allotments. Although the reserves had not yet been assigned in May 1833, emigrant heads-of-families were entitled to half-sections under the 1832 Treaty of Washington, and speculators were interested in their claims. Some suggested that McIntosh was the "dupe" or the "tool" of "heartless speculators" who used every argument to convince the Creeks to emigrate in order to acquire their land. Moreover, a reputed gambler loitered about the enrollment camp trying to swindle the Creeks out of their money. McIntosh allegedly went on a two-day drinking and gambling binge, and witnesses noted that he "and all the Indians, men, women [and] children, were drunk." The western headman subsequently ran out of money, which delayed the commencement of the journey and left his provision-starved emigrants "in a state of suffering." Only the arrest of the gambler and the relocation of the encampment across the Alabama River prevented the Creeks from losing all their funds. Many of the approximately three hundred Creeks who originally enrolled subsequently had second thoughts and abandoned the encampment.

Only about sixty emigrants (twenty-one of whom were slaves) ultimately moved west. The emigrants left in the summer and arrived in August or September 1833, although approximately twenty people (mostly slaves) belonging to McIntosh's party were conducted by Benjamin Hawkins (no. 65 on first McIntosh party muster roll) and had arrived the previous spring. Their exact route remains unclear, although a Grayson family slave who emigrated with his (or his owner's) own resources overtook the party at the White River and accompanied them for two weeks before reaching Dardanelle and going off on his own. Eight people died during the forty-two-day journey or shortly after arriving in the West, and the emigrants told officials at Fort Gibson that they were "in a starving condition."[3]

Chilly McIntosh and Benjamin Hawkins Party Muster Roll

Names listed in bold refer to the head of a family. Roll includes number of family members traveling, age range, and number of slaves (if any). Roll found at CGS-IRW, Roll 4, 934.

1. **Sally Harrod** 26 members consisting of 3 females over sixteen, 3 males under sixteen, and 20 slaves.
2. **Woc see Harjo** 7 members consisting of 1 male over sixteen, 2 females over sixteen, and 4 males under sixteen.
3. **Talmus Harjo** 4 members consisting of 1 male over sixteen, 2 females over sixteen, and 1 female under sixteen.

4. **Tusti chee** 3 members consisting of 1 male over sixteen, 1 female over sixteen, and 1 female under sixteen.
5. **Marnar chee cha** 2 members consisting of 1 male over sixteen and 1 female over sixteen.
6. **Top ler** 1 member consisting of 1 male over sixteen.
7. **Chit ta** 3 members consisting of 1 male over sixteen, 1 female over sixteen, and 1 male under sixteen.
8. **Ni tee** 2 members consisting of 1 male over sixteen and 1 female under sixteen.
9. **Cholar Fixico** 1 member consisting of 1 male over sixteen.
10. **Billy Williams** 1 member consisting of 1 male over sixteen.
11. **Auson lah** 3 members consisting of 1 male over sixteen, 1 female over sixteen, and 1 male under sixteen.
12. **Sin thee key** 3 members consisting of 1 male over sixteen, 1 female over sixteen, and 1 male under sixteen.
13. **Hallis Fixico** 3 members consisting of 1 male over sixteen and 2 females over sixteen.
14. **Sally Grayson's Black Boy** 1 member consisting of 1 slave.

Supplemental Letters of Chilly McIntosh's Party

Chilly McIntosh reports that he is planning to emigrate thirty or forty friends and family to Indian territory but offers his services to the United States government to act as emigrating agent to move any Creek person west. Letter found at LR, CAE, Roll 237, 390–91.

Creek agency 28th Jan'y 1833

Sir

I have been here since September last and engaged in persuading my red brothers of this part of the nation and particularly my kin, to remove west of the Mississippi. A considerable difficulty was in the way to [heal] the ill feelings occasioned by my Fathers death and the transactions about them or yet has not subsided and the heart could never be healed until we upon both sides called in the mediation of the commissioners, which happily succeeded.

Now I can take thirty or forty families of my connection off with me, provided you will advance the fifteen dollars per head, and promise the other benefits allowed by the Treaty, and pay to each head of a family the fair value of his reservation when he reaches his home. To prevent fraud you may appoint if you please an agent here to see the number I have upon my roll, & take a list of their names and take deeds of relinquishment to the United States from those entitled to reservations and their names and towns, and forward to you and then let the number be taken & names be taken by our agent when I reach home and by this means fraud cannot be committed. If you will approve my plan please to write to me at this place, and as soon as I have arrived at home I will return and gather more.

Your ob't Serv't
Chilly McIntosh

P.S. I will chearfully render any assistance in my power in removing the Indians if the government will allow me fair compensation.

Chilly McIntosh

☾

John Milton reports that he has purchased the five sections of land given to the western Creeks as well as the land claims of the emigrants. He also notes the difficulties of getting Chilly McIntosh's emigrating party prepared for their journey to Indian territory due to drunkenness and gambling and notes that he has lost faith in McIntosh's ability to lead the party west. Letter found at LR, CAE, Roll 237, 397–99.

Columbus June 18th 1833—

Sir,

On yesterday I received yours of the 8th ult in which you informed me that Col'o Abert[4] was instructed to supply Gen'l McIntosh with the necessary means of completing his engagements. Previously to the receipt of your letter McIntosh and his company having despaired of the aid solicited from the Government applied to me to purchase their claims under the treaty—so that they should be enabled to Emigrate, and realize at once the advantage, of the treaty.—After conversation with Col'o Abert as to their probable value, and the character of their claims—I purchased.—I have also purchased the five sections, obtained by the western Creeks from the Eastern.—I purchased from McIntosh & Tiger who were appointed with full powers by the western Creeks in the General council, agents—for the purposes of sale.—which power of attr'y, was attested by Gen'l Campbell, the agent, the Clerk of the council—the interpreter & others.—In these transactions I have been chiefly influenced by an anxiety to promote the welfare of the Indians & give success to the policy of the government relative to them.—Of these matters, however, a more correct judgement Can be formed from an inspection of the Exhibits and propositions which will be forwarded by Gen'l Parsons[5] and Col'o Abert, than from naked assertions—

Within the last three days I have been convinced that I was deceived in the character of McIntosh and I avail myself of the earliest opportunity to convey, thro, you, my beleif, that he is not qualified to conduct the Indians in their Emigration. From the following facts you may derive the causes of this beleif.—After I had furnished them with the money to defray the Expences,—paid him for the five sections & the Indians for their claims—& furnished the tents & in fact prepared them for the route.—instead of moving off with the promptitude, rendered necessary by a long delay, to inspire the Indians with confidence in his management—and hopes of success in their emigration, he became intoxicated and spent two days in drunkenness and gambling &c.—Having received information of his condition and that it was the result of the manouevering of an artful gamester who had formed plans by which to win from him the Indians their money, I employed an individual to inform against the Gambler, & to have him arrested and punished according to the laws of Alabama, and to accompany the Indians beyond the Alabama river and prevent them from drinking to Excess— &, gambling.—

—These means only saved the money, which otherwise they would have lost by gambling: they could not be prevented from drinking and when I last heard from them, McIntosh and all the Indians, men, women & children, were drunk—

Many of them have deserted and returned—These facts I have communicated from a sense of duty to the Government, because of the assistance, (if for nothing else) that I gave by recommendation—for the appointment—

At that time I had many reasons to beleive him qualified to discharge the duties of an enroling & emigrating agent & none to doubt his abilities to do so.

I was not alone deceived in his character—Gen'l. Parsons the US agent—and others, who were better acquainted with him, also recommended him, and perhaps their recommendations alone, had any influence in procuring him the appointment.

But on my communication relative to him may have had a proportional influence, I have availed myself of the Earliest, to inform you that my opinions relative to him have changed & have assigned the causes of the change.—

Very Respectfully
Your most ob't sv't
Jno Milton, purchased by

Hon'l Lewis Cass—
Sec'y of War Department

☾

Lieutenant Jefferson Van Horne[6] reports on the manner in which Chilly McIntosh subsisted (or failed to subsist) his party during their 1833 voluntary emigration. Van Horne notes that due bills (a promise to pay), rather than actual rations, were often issued to the emigrants. Letter found at CGS-IRW, Roll 5, 186–87.

Rec'd 9 June

Fort Gibson 7th May 1834.

Sir

Since my last, I have ascertained the following additional circumstances relative to the subsistence of McIntosh's party.

Helis Fexico says that it was at Love's store, where he was induced by Brown to sign recepts for the whole party. That none were present except Love, Brown & himself.[7]

The principal men of the party say that Aham, (Sally Grayson's black man,) emigrated on his own resources: He overtook McIntosh's party at White river, Ark Ter. and left them at the Dardenou, (or Dardenelles). He rode Sally Grayson's horse. They say McIntosh never supplied him with any provisions, either while emigrating or since; except for about two weeks while he travelled with the party as above stated. They say that McIntosh paid none of his expenses while emigrating.

Cholar Fexico[8] states that he never received any rations, during the whole year; and that McIntosh gave him a due bill for $25.12½ for his years subsistence. He states that he has traded the whole amount of this due bill at Love's store.

Soh-ho-pi-a-che traded to the full amount of his due bill at Love's store also. Billy Williams[9] received a due bill for $15.12½ for part of the first and the last six months subsistence. For this I now learn he received a Cow and calf, valued at $10; and traded for the balance at Love's store.

McIntosh's due bills are of the following form.

$36.75 Due Sintherkey[10] Thirty-six dollars and seventy-five cents, balance for the term of twelve months.

24 Feb. 1834.
(Signed) Chilly McIntosh

This is for a family of three. It is marked on the face, Paid $2-$6.75-$3-$1.62½ $2 & $1. On the 5th May, it appears Love's clerk, (Pennington,)[11] takes up this due-bill; and gives Sintherkey another as follows,

Due the Barer fifteen dollars in goods.

5th May 1834.

(signed) H. Love
By Pennington

In this manner many of the original due-bills of Chilly McIntosh are taken up by Love, and made payable at Love's store in goods. Some of these are signed by Love, others by Pennington for him.

These emigrants also traded at Hills store to the amount of $20 a head on Chilly McIntosh's orders.

Very respectfully
Sir Your obt servt.
J. Van Horne 2 Lieut 3 Inf.
Disb'g. Agent Creeks

Gen. Geo. Gibson
Com. Gen. Sub.

5 The Fourth Voluntary Emigrating Party, 1834–35

In response to the large number of reserves being transferred to white ownership (either through sale or fraud), federal officials decided the time was right to renew voluntary emigration, which had been halted on Jackson's orders in 1830.[1] Colonel Alexander Hill, a resident of Bibb County, Alabama, and former Alabama senator (1832–34), was appointed special agent to superintend the Creek emigration and oversaw the entire operation.[2] With the expectation that large numbers of landless Creeks would choose to move west, administration officials ordered Hill not to move the party until he had enrolled at least two thousand people. Hill subsequently established enrollment camps throughout the Creek country (including at Fort Hull and Fort Mitchell) and a rendezvous site at Centreville, Alabama. Hill was aided by Captain John Page,[3] a Maine-born soldier with the 4th U.S. Infantry, who would tragically have his lower jaw blown off by Mexican artillery fire while standing next to Lieutenant Ulysses S. Grant at the 1846 Battle of Palo Alto in Texas (he died from his wounds two months later).

The 1834 voluntary party was hampered by a number of problems from the start. Page, who was a veteran of the Choctaw removals, was frustrated by the incompetence of Hill, who spent a lot of money without much to show for it. In fact, one acquaintance of Hill's, shocked that the government would appoint him superintendent, noted of the former senator that he was "a good old man, but stupidly ignorant of every discription of business, except that of making corn & fodder."[4] Indeed, Page visited the

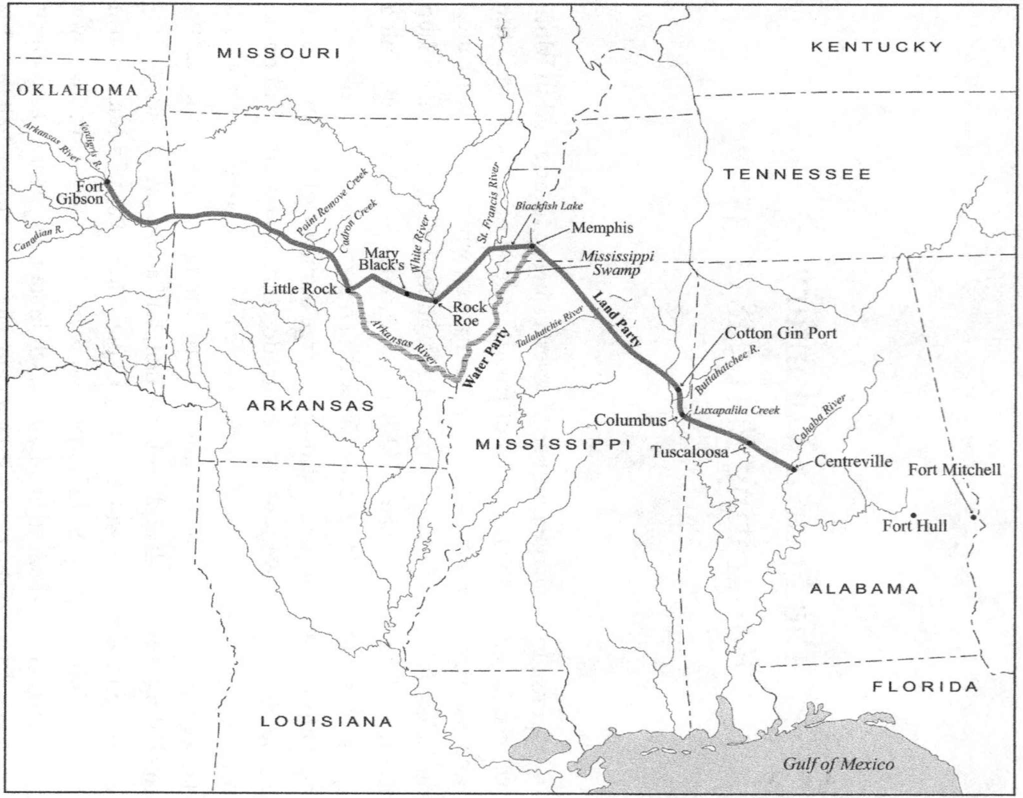

MAP 5. Route of the fourth voluntary emigrating party, December 1834–March 1835. Place names correspond to stopping points or locations noted in the documentation. Route lines and locations are approximations. Cartography by Sarah Mattics and Kiersten Fish.

camp at Fort Hull, Alabama, and discovered enrolling agents and horse-drawn wagons, but only one person signed up to move west. Moreover, with the requirement that each party have between two thousand and five thousand emigrants, Hill was forced to delay the commencement as he was left scurrying to find more people. But as summer turned to fall and then winter, many of those who had signed up to move west changed their minds and went home. As a result, when the party left Centreville in late December 1834, only 630 Creeks and their slaves made the journey to Indian territory. The party suffered terribly from the extreme cold, which was compounded by rain, hail, and snow. The Arkansas Territory, through which the Creeks passed, also suffered from an influenza epidemic.

John Page conducted the party west, while William J. Beattie,[5] a native of Ryegate, Vermont, who had moved to Alabama looking for opportunity, served as his subagent. Beattie's decision to accompany the Creeks west reportedly was "more for the novelty of the thing" and he did not request a salary but "said if he could claim his expenses it was all he wished."[6]

Fourth Voluntary Party Muster Roll

Names listed in bold refer to the head of a family. Roll includes the number of family members traveling, the age range of the emigrants, and the number of slaves (if any). No town affiliations are noted on this muster roll. Roll found at Record Group 75, Records of the Bureau of Indian Affairs, Creek Removal Records, Entry 299, Emigration Lists, 1836–1838, Box 2, Volume 8, NARA.

1. **Sampson Grieson** 35 members consisting of 1 male of twenty-five and under fifty, 18 male slaves, and 16 female slaves. Grayson (b. 1804) was the grandson of Robert Grierson and his wife Sinnugee; the son of Thomas Grayson (no. 102 on second McIntosh party roll, chap. 2); and nephew of Sandy Grayson (Grieson, no. 44, this roll), Walter Grayson (no. 101 on second McIntosh party roll, chap. 2), and William Grayson (no. 103 on second McIntosh party roll; no. 150 on this roll). Sampson Grayson returned to Alabama soon after arriving in the Indian territory and began spreading rumors about the terrible journey of the fourth voluntary party. He alleged that

during the emigration the agents had only enough provisions for half of the journey, so the emigrants were forced to pay $100 for adults and $50 for children or "be made slaves to the sugar plantations of Mississippi." Grayson also noted that many Creeks died along the route as a result of the "cruel neglect" of the agents and—"that their dead bodies were denied the right of sepulture." Grayson advocated for a move to Texas but remained in Alabama until the Creeks were relocated west in the mid-1830s.[7]

2. **Charles** 3 members consisting of 1 male under ten, 1 male of ten and under twenty-five, and 1 female of ten and under twenty-five. Listed as a "Mulatto."
3. **Eufaula Harjo** 4 members consisting of 1 male under ten, 1 male of ten and under twenty-five, 1 male of twenty-five and under fifty, and 1 female of twenty-five and under fifty. As the party passed through Alabama's state capital, Tuscaloosa, the Creeks were invited into the state house. Headman Eufaula Harjo addressed both chambers of the legislature. His speech, translated into English and subsequently reprinted in newspapers, went as follows: "I come brothers to see the great house of Alabama, and the men that make the laws, and tell them farewell in brotherly kindness before I go to the far west, where my people are now going. I did think at one time that the white man wanted to oppress my people and drive them from their homes by compelling them to obey the laws that they did not understand—but I have now become satisfied that they are not unfriendly towards us, but that they wish us well. In these lands of Alabama, which have been my forefather's, where their bones lie buried, I see that the Indian fires are going out—they must soon be extinguished. New fires are lighting in the west—and we will go there. I do now believe that our great father, the president, intends no harm to the red men—but wishes them well. He has promised us homes and hunting ground in the far west, where he tells us the red men shall be protected. We will go. We leave behind our good will to the people of Alabama, who build the great houses, and to the men who make the laws. This is all I have to say—I came to say farewell to the wise men who make the laws, and to wish them

peace and happiness in the country which my forefathers owned and which I now leave to go to other homes in the west. I leave the graves of my fathers—but the Indian fires are going out—almost clean gone—and new fires are lighted there for us. There are two houses of the men who make the laws—I have already bid farewell to the other house—I now bid farewell to you, and wish not only you but all the people of Alabama, to be happy and prosperous. I leave you in friendship and good will. I have nothing more to say."[8]

4. **Nar both che Emathla** 6 members consisting of 2 males of ten and under twenty-five, 1 male of twenty-five and under fifty, 1 female of ten and under twenty-five, and 2 females of twenty-five and under fifty.
5. **Har lok Fixico** 6 members consisting of 1 male under ten, 1 male of ten and under twenty-five, 1 male of twenty-five and under fifty, 2 females under ten, and 1 female of ten and under twenty-five.
6. **Har le Emathla** 6 members consisting of 1 male under ten, 1 male of ten and under twenty-five, 1 male of twenty-five and under fifty, 2 females under ten, and 1 female of ten and under twenty-five.
7. **Mon clar we** 2 members consisting of 1 female under ten and one female of ten and under twenty-five.
8. **Okfuskee Yoholo** 7 members consisting of 1 male under ten, 2 males of twenty-five and under fifty, 1 male over fifty, 1 female under ten, 1 female of ten and under twenty-five, and 1 female over fifty.
9. **Nor thlar gee** 1 member consisting of 1 female of twenty-five and under fifty.
10. **Ar chu le Emathla** 3 members consisting of 1 male under ten, 1 male of twenty-five and under fifty, and 1 female of ten and under twenty-five.
11. **Har lok Harjo** 2 members consisting of 1 male under ten and 1 female of ten and under twenty-five.
12. **Ne har Fixico** 5 members consisting of 1 male under ten, 1 male of twenty-five and under fifty, 1 female under ten, 1 female of ten and under twenty-five, and 1 female of twenty-five and under fifty.
13. **Kith lok engee** 5 members consisting of 1 male under ten, 2 females under ten, 1 female of ten and under twenty-five, and 1 female of twenty-five and under fifty.

14. **Ene ho gee** 4 members consisting of 1 male under ten, 1 male of ten and under twenty-five, 1 male of twenty-five and under fifty, and 1 female of ten and under twenty-five.
15. **Lutchar kee** 1 member consisting of 1 male of twenty-five and under fifty.
16. **Tuskenehaw** 2 members consisting of 1 male of twenty-five and under fifty and 1 female of twenty-five and under fifty.
17. **Chok sar Fixico** 5 members consisting of 1 male of ten and under twenty-five, 1 male of twenty-five and under fifty, 2 females under ten, and 1 female of twenty-five and under fifty.
18. **Yar gin Harjo** 4 members consisting of 1 male of ten and under twenty-five, 1 male over fifty, 1 female of ten and under twenty-five, and 1 female of twenty-five and under fifty.
19. **Nar both che Emathla** 9 members consisting of 2 males under ten, 1 male of ten and under twenty-five, 1 male of twenty-five and under fifty, 1 male over fifty, 2 females under ten, and 2 females of twenty-five and under fifty.
20. **Par has Yoholo** 1 member consisting of 1 male of twenty-five and under fifty.
21. **Echo Yoholo** 2 members consisting of 1 male of ten and under twenty-five and 1 female of ten and under twenty-five.
22. **Mar he thle gee** 4 members consisting of 2 males under ten, 1 female of twenty-five and under fifty, and 1 female over fifty.
23. **Nar both che Harjo** 4 members consisting of 1 male of twenty-five and under fifty, 2 females under ten, and 1 female of ten and under twenty-five.
24. **Sin ta hope kee** 4 members consisting of 1 male under ten, 1 female under ten, 1 female of ten and under twenty-five, and 1 female of twenty-five and under fifty.
25. **Tin ar lut ho ge** 2 members consisting of 1 male under ten and 1 female of ten and under twenty-five.
26. **Pin Harjo** 6 members consisting of 2 males under ten, 1 male of ten and under twenty-five, 1 male of twenty-five and under fifty, 1 female under ten, and 1 female of twenty-five and under fifty.
27. **Tustunnuggee** 7 members consisting of 1 male of twenty-five and

under fifty, 1 male over fifty, 2 females under ten, 1 female of ten and under twenty-five, and 2 females of twenty-five and under fifty.

28. **Muffo gee chee** 1 member consisting of 1 male of twenty-five and under fifty.
29. **Barney** 1 member consisting of 1 male of twenty-five and under fifty.
30. **Tallowar Harjo** 5 members consisting of 2 males under ten, 1 male of twenty-five and under fifty, 1 female of ten and under twenty-five, and 1 female of twenty-five and under fifty.
31. **Kotchar Fixico** 6 members consisting of 2 males under ten, 1 male of twenty-five and under fifty, 2 females under ten, and 1 female of ten and under twenty-five.
32. **Echo Harjo** 4 members consisting of 1 male of twenty-five and under fifty, 2 females under ten, and 1 female of ten and under twenty-five.
33. **Kon chart Fixico** 5 members consisting of 2 males of ten and under twenty-five, 1 male over fifty, 1 female under ten, and 1 female of twenty-five and under fifty.
34. **On talla Harjo** 7 members consisting of 2 males under ten, 1 male of twenty-five and under fifty, 2 females under ten, 1 female of ten and under twenty-five, and 1 female of twenty-five and under fifty.
35. **Par he lustie Fixico** 1 member consisting of 1 male of twenty-five and under fifty.
36. **Har lok Fixico** 7 members consisting of 2 males under ten, 1 male of ten and under twenty-five, 1 male of twenty-five and under fifty, 1 female of ten and under twenty-five, and 2 females of twenty-five and under fifty.
37. **Spoak Yoholo** 3 members consisting of 1 male of under ten, 1 male of twenty-five and under fifty, and 1 female of ten and under twenty-five.
38. **Osooch Harjo** 5 members consisting of 1 male of ten and under twenty-five, 2 males of twenty-five and under fifty, and 2 females of ten and under twenty-five.
39. **Echo Emathla** 7 members consisting of 2 males under ten, 1 male of ten and under twenty-five, 1 male of twenty-five and under fifty, 1 female under ten, 1 female of ten and under twenty-five, and 1 female of twenty-five and under fifty. "Deserted" noted in the margin.

40. **Ogee de Yoholo** 5 members consisting of 1 male under ten, 1 male of ten and under twenty-five, 1 male of twenty-five and under fifty, 1 female under ten, and 1 female of twenty-five and under fifty.
41. **Ko no Fixico** 1 member consisting of 1 male of twenty-five and under fifty.
42. **Chor kar Harjo** 1 member consisting of 1 male of twenty-five and under fifty.
43. **Ko nip Harjo** 4 members consisting of 1 male under ten, 2 males of ten and under twenty-five, and 1 female under ten. "Deserted" noted in the margin.
44. **Sandy Grieson** 7 members consisting of 1 male under ten, 1 male of ten and under twenty-five, 1 male of twenty-five and under fifty, 1 female under ten, 2 females of ten and under twenty-five, and 1 female of twenty-five and under fifty. Sandy Grayson was the son of Robert Grierson and his wife Sinnugee, brother of Thomas (no. 102 on second McIntosh party roll, chap. 2), Walter (no. 101 on second McIntosh party roll, chap. 2), and William (no. 103 on second McIntosh party roll), and uncle to Sampson Grayson (Grieson, no. 1, this roll).[9]
45. **Irwin B. Haney** 3 members consisting of 1 male under ten, 1 male of twenty-five and under fifty, and 1 female of ten and under twenty-five.
46. **Che waste Harjo** 5 members consisting of 2 males under ten, 1 male of twenty-five and under fifty, 1 female of ten and under twenty-five, and 1 female of twenty-five and under fifty.
47. **Niggy** 1 member consisting of 1 male of twenty-five and under fifty.
48. **Ne har Harjo** 4 members consisting of 1 male under ten, 1 male of twenty-five and under fifty, 1 female under ten, and 1 female of twenty-five and under fifty.
49. **Me ho gee** 1 member consisting of 1 female of ten and under twenty-five.
50. **Le tif Harjo** 4 members consisting of 2 males under ten, 1 male of twenty-five and under fifty, and 1 female of ten and under twenty-five.
51. **Co as sart Harjo** 2 members consisting of 1 male of twenty-five and under fifty and 1 female of twenty-five and under fifty.
52. **Echo Fixico** 4 members consisting of 1 male under ten, 1 male of

twenty-five and under fifty, 1 female under ten, and 1 female of ten and under twenty-five.

53. **Fi elustie Harjo** 5 members consisting of 1 male under ten, 2 males of ten and under twenty-five, 1 male of twenty-five and under fifty, and 1 female over fifty.
54. **Tim ho lartie** 4 members consisting of 2 males under ten, 1 male of ten and under twenty-five, and 1 male of twenty-five and under fifty.
55. **Hillabee Harjo** 1 member consisting of 1 male of twenty-five and under fifty.
56. **Archula Harjo** 6 members consisting of 1 male under ten, 2 males of ten and under twenty-five, 1 male of twenty-five and under fifty, 1 female under ten, and 1 female of twenty-five and under fifty.
57. **Mikee** 1 member consisting of 1 male of twenty-five and under fifty.
58. **Sow ump kee** 5 members consisting of 1 male under ten, 1 male of twenty-five and under fifty, 2 females under ten, and 1 female of ten and under twenty-five.
59. **Tar so** 2 members consisting of 1 male of twenty-five and under fifty and 1 female of twenty-five and under fifty.
60. **To we lip kee** 1 member consisting of 1 male of twenty-five and under fifty.
61. **Tal wy kee** 2 members consisting of 1 male of twenty-five and under fifty and 1 female of twenty-five and under fifty.
62. **No cos eaker chopco** 1 member consisting of 1 male over fifty.
63. **Neathlar** 2 members consisting of 1 male of twenty-five and under fifty and 1 female of twenty-five and under fifty.
64. **Tippee** 2 members consisting of 1 male of twenty-five and under fifty and 1 female of twenty-five and under fifty.
65. **Bevers** 9 members consisting of 2 males under ten, 1 male of twenty-five and under fifty, 1 male over fifty, 3 females of ten and under twenty-five, 1 female of twenty-five and under fifty, and 1 female over fifty. "Deserted Near Memphis Ten" noted in the margin.
66. **Thlar bas kee** 1 member consisting of 1 male of twenty-five and under fifty.
67. **Suck ar gee** 1 member consisting of 1 male of twenty-five and under fifty.

68. **Sinne** 5 members consisting of 1 male under ten, 1 male of twenty-five and under fifty, 2 females under ten, and 1 female of ten and under twenty-five. "Deserted Near Memphis Ten" noted in the margin.
69. **Daniel Asbury** 1 member consisting of 1 male of twenty-five and under fifty.
70. **Echo Yoholo** 5 members consisting of 2 males under ten, 1 male of ten and under twenty-five, 1 male of twenty-five and under fifty, and 1 female of twenty-five and under fifty. "Deserted" noted in the margin.
71. **Ar ko poye** 1 member consisting of 1 male of twenty-five and under fifty.
72. **Yar ton echee** 2 members consisting of 1 female of twenty-five and under fifty and 1 female over fifty.
73. **Lar bo ti chee** 3 members consisting of 2 males of ten and under twenty-five and 1 female of twenty-five and under fifty.
74. **Nel lup Harjo** 5 members consisting of 1 male under ten, 1 male of ten and under twenty-five, 1 male of twenty-five and under fifty, 1 female under ten, and 1 female of twenty-five and under fifty. "Deserted" noted in the margin.
75. **Soweer** 3 members consisting of 1 female under ten, 1 female of twenty-five and under fifty, and 1 female over fifty.
76. **Mutkee** 10 members consisting of 2 males under ten, 3 males of ten and under twenty-five, 1 male of twenty-five and under fifty, 1 male over fifty, 1 female under ten, 1 female of twenty-five and under fifty, and 1 female over fifty. "Deserted Near Memphis Ten" noted in the margin.
77. **Ar ho wepee** 8 members consisting of 2 males under ten, 1 male of ten and under twenty-five, 1 male of twenty-five and under fifty, 1 female under ten, 2 females of ten and under twenty-five, and 1 female of twenty-five and under fifty. "Desert'd" noted in the margin.
78. **Lucy** 2 members consisting of 1 female under ten and 1 female of twenty-five and under fifty. "Desert'd" noted in the margin.
79. **Hopoye** 1 member consisting of 1 male of twenty-five and under fifty. Hopoye died on 12 March 1835 en route to western Creek Nation.
80. **John Stidham** 28 members consisting of 1 male over fifty, 1 female

over fifty, 12 male slaves, and 14 female slaves. A once-powerful headman from Sawokli (Raccoon Town) and member of the National Council. Stidham publicly opposed William McIntosh at Indian Springs in 1825 and signed the 1826 Treaty of Washington. Stidham was denied the right to acquire a full section of land under the 1832 Treaty of Washington for his advocacy of voluntary emigration. Stidham, however, appears to be emigrating only his slaves with the fifth voluntary party, because he was in Alabama when the Second Creek War broke out in 1836.[10]

81. **William Stidham** 1 member consisting of 1 male of twenty-five and under fifty.
82. **Michael Stidham** 1 member consisting of 1 male of twenty-five and under fifty.
83. **Hannah Gray** 2 members consisting of 1 male under ten and 1 female of ten and under twenty-five.
84. **Jack Stidham** 2 members consisting of 1 male of twenty-five and under fifty and 1 female of ten and under twenty-five. Listed number 4 on 1832 Sawokli census.
85. **Ok pir Harjo** 1 member consisting of 1 male of twenty-five and under fifty.
86. **Fi its hoye** 5 members consisting of 1 male of ten and under twenty-five, 1 female of ten and under twenty-five, 1 female of twenty-five and under fifty, and 2 female slaves. "2 Taken Back, Negroes Claimed by other Indians" noted in the margin.
87. **Ko wok ko ge Emathla** 3 members consisting of 1 male under ten, 1 male of twenty-five and under fifty, and 1 female under ten.
88. **Major Hardage** 1 member consisting of 1 male of twenty-five and under fifty. Hardage died on 7 March 1835 en route to the western Creek Nation. Hardage's wife (Stemonarke, number 224 on the 1832 Lower Eufaula census) remained behind in Alabama.
89. **Charlo Harjo** 7 members consisting of 2 males under ten, 1 male of ten and under twenty-five, 1 male of twenty-five and under fifty, 2 females of ten and under twenty-five, and 1 female of twenty-five and under fifty. "Deserted" noted in the margin.
90. **Thlath lo Harjo** 4 members consisting of 1 male of twenty-five and

under fifty, 1 female under ten, 1 female of ten and under twenty-five, and 1 female of twenty-five and under fifty.

91. **Sally Stidham** 22 members consisting of 1 female over fifty, 9 male slaves, and 12 female slaves. Listed number 2 on 1832 Sawokli census.
92. **Hillabee Tustunnuggee** 1 member consisting of 1 male over fifty. Hillabee Tustunnuggee died on 28 December 1834 en route to the western Creek Nation.
93. **Walker Pochassee** 1 member consisting of 1 female over fifty. "Deserted" noted in the margin.
94. **Yar har Tustunnuggee** 7 members consisting of 1 male under ten, 2 males of ten and under twenty-five, 1 male of twenty-five and under fifty, 1 female under ten, 1 female of ten and under twenty-five, and 1 female of twenty-five and under fifty. "Deserted" noted in the margin.
95. **Othle walle Tustunnuggee** 1 member consisting of 1 male over fifty.
96. **David Hardage** 2 members consisting of 1 male of twenty-five and under fifty and 1 female of twenty-five and under fifty. "1 Deserted" noted in the margin.
97. **Yoholo Micco** 12 members consisting of 1 male under ten, 4 males of ten and under twenty-five, 1 male over fifty, 2 females under ten, 3 females of ten and under twenty-five, and 1 female of twenty-five and under fifty.
98. **To for ta** 3 members consisting of 1 male of twenty-five and under fifty, 1 female under ten, and 1 female of ten and under twenty-five.
99. **Koy ey gee** 3 members consisting of 1 male of ten and under twenty-five, 1 male of twenty-five and under fifty, and 1 female under ten.
100. **Isip ye gee** 6 members consisting of 1 male of ten and under twenty-five, 1 male of twenty-five and under fifty, 3 females of ten and under twenty-five, and 1 female of twenty-five and under fifty.
101. **To koth lie gee** 1 member consisting of 1 male of twenty-five and under fifty. To koth lie gee died on 9 March 1835 en route to the western Creek Nation.
102. **Te wassar kee** 3 members consisting of 2 males under ten and 1 female over fifty. "1 Died" on 9 March 1835 noted in the margin.
103. **Kar poy ea** 3 members consisting of 1 male of twenty-five and under fifty, 1 female under ten, and 1 female of ten and under twenty-five.

104. **George Hatkin** 4 members consisting of 1 male under ten, 1 male of twenty-five and under fifty, 1 female under ten, and 1 female of ten and under twenty-five. "Deserted" noted in the margin.
105. **Billy ump kar** 4 members consisting of 1 male under ten, 1 male of twenty-five and under fifty, 1 female under ten, and 1 female of ten and under twenty-five. "Deserted" noted in the margin.
106. **Thlar pie** 3 members consisting of 1 female under ten and 2 females of ten and under twenty-five.
107. **Mattar hie** 1 member consisting of 1 female over fifty.
108. **Yar har lar nie** 4 members consisting of 2 males under ten, 1 male of ten and under twenty-five, and 1 female of ten and under twenty-five. "1 Died" on 3 March 1835 noted in the margin.
109. **Kotchar Fixico** 2 members consisting of 1 male of twenty-five and under fifty and 1 female of twenty-five and under fifty.
110. **Ule tin gee** 1 member consisting of 1 female of twenty-five and under fifty.
111. **Kotchar Micco** 4 members consisting of 2 males of ten and under twenty-five, 1 male of twenty-five and under fifty, and 1 female of ten and under twenty-five.
112. **Par has Emathla** 5 members consisting of 1 male under ten, 1 male of ten and under twenty-five, 1 male of twenty-five and under fifty, 1 female under ten, and 1 female of ten and under twenty-five.
113. **Ochoty** 2 members consisting of 1 male of ten and under twenty-five and 1 female of ten and under twenty-five. "1 Died" noted in the margin.
114. **Nochky** 2 members consisting of 1 male of ten and under twenty-five and 1 female of ten and under twenty-five. "1 Died" noted in the margin.
115. **Lubucto Harjo** 1 member consisting of 1 male of twenty-five and under fifty.
116. **Tuckose Yoholo** 1 member consisting of 1 male of twenty-five and under fifty.
117. **Tla par ke** 5 members consisting of 1 male under ten, 1 male of twenty-five and under fifty, 2 females under ten, and 1 female of twenty-five and under fifty.

118. **Tommy Yoholo** 6 members consisting of 2 males under ten, 1 male of ten and under twenty-five, 1 male of twenty-five and under fifty, 1 female under ten, and 1 female of twenty-five and under fifty.
119. **Tuck kosar Harjo** 1 member consisting of 1 male of twenty-five and under fifty.
120. **Tustenug Harjo** 4 members consisting of 2 males of ten and under twenty-five, 1 male of twenty-five and under fifty, and 1 female of ten and under twenty-five.
121. **Chow e hoc** 6 members consisting of 1 female over fifty, 3 male slaves, and 2 female slaves.
122. **Honso gee** 2 members consisting of 1 male of ten and under twenty-five and 1 female of ten and under twenty-five.
123. **Yelkey Harjo** 1 member consisting of 1 male of twenty-five and under fifty.
124. **Tim fie ker kee** 1 member consisting of 1 female of ten and under twenty-five.
125. **Talladega** 3 members consisting of 1 male of twenty-five and under fifty, 1 female of ten and under twenty-five, and 1 female of twenty-five and under fifty.
126. **Lummanly** 1 member consisting of 1 male of twenty-five and under fifty.
127. **John Oponey (Negroes)** 16 members consisting of 6 male slaves and 10 female slaves. Oponey (or Oponee) was a once-powerful headman who was broken (removed) as chief for his support of voluntary emigration. For this he was denied a square-mile reserve under the 1832 Treaty of Washington. Here he appears to have been preparing for a voluntary emigration to Indian territory by first sending his slaves west. Oponee did not emigrate west, however. Oponee denounced the rebels of the Second Creek War and volunteered for service in Florida to fight the Seminoles during the Second Seminole War. After his service Oponee joined the sixth detachment of Creeks waiting on the Gulf of Mexico before commencing their voyage up the Mississippi River in October–November 1836. Oponee died at the mouth of the Arkansas River in 1837 before reaching Indian territory.[11]

128. **McIntosh (Negroes)** 4 members consisting of 2 male slaves and 2 female slaves.
129. **Thomas Marshall** 10 members consisting of 2 males under ten, 1 male of twenty-five and under fifty, 3 females under ten, 1 female of twenty-five and under fifty, 1 male slave, and 2 female slaves. "1 Deserted" noted in the margin. Listed as number 8 on 1832 Coweta census (Toosilkstookee Hatchee Town).
130. **Yan ko na** 1 member consisting of 1 female under ten.
131. **David Marshall** 7 members consisting of 1 male under ten, 1 male of twenty-five and under fifty, 1 female under ten, 1 female of twenty-five and under fifty, 2 male slaves, and 1 female slave. "1 Died" noted in the margin. Listed as number 18 on 1832 Coweta census (Koochkalecha Town). Was also known as "Ko we Emathla."
132. **Simmons** 2 members consisting of 1 male of twenty-five and under fifty and 1 female of ten and under twenty-five.
133. **Mathew Marshall** 6 members consisting of 2 males under ten, 1 male of twenty-five and under fifty, 2 females under ten, and 1 female of twenty-five and under fifty. Listed as number 2 on 1832 Coweta census (Toosilkstookee Hatchee Town).
134. **Cusseta** 1 member consisting of 1 male of twenty-five and under fifty.
135. **Ko wok ko ge Yoholo** 3 members consisting of 1 male of ten and under twenty-five, 1 male of twenty-five and under fifty, and 1 female of twenty-five and under fifty.
136. **Ulon ho aky** 12 members consisting of 2 males under ten, 1 male of ten and under twenty-five, 4 females under ten, 2 females of ten and under twenty-five, 2 females of twenty-five and under fifty, and 1 female slave.
137. **Tallasee Harjo** 7 members consisting of 1 male under ten, 1 male of twenty-five and under fifty, 3 females of ten and under twenty-five, 1 female of twenty-five and under fifty, and 1 female over fifty.
138. **She me he is kar** 5 members consisting of 3 males of ten and under twenty-five, 1 female of ten and under twenty-five, and 1 female of twenty-five and under fifty.
139. **Pah lot ka** 3 members consisting of 2 males of ten and under twenty-five and 1 female of twenty-five and under fifty.

140. **So le ather** 2 members consisting of 1 male of twenty-five and under fifty and 1 female of ten and under twenty-five.

141. **Tallona** 1 member consisting of 1 male of ten and under twenty-five.

142. **Wok ie ka** 4 members consisting of 2 males under ten, 1 male of ten and under twenty-five, and 1 female of ten and under twenty-five. "Deserted" noted in the margin.

143. **Che ful war** 3 members consisting of 1 male of ten and under twenty-five, 1 male of twenty-five and under fifty, and 1 female of ten and under twenty-five. "1 Died" noted in the margin.

144. **Yar ke na** 2 members consisting of 1 male of twenty-five and under fifty and 1 female of ten and under twenty-five.

145. **Lum pie ka** 7 members consisting of 1 male under ten, 1 male of ten and under twenty-five, 1 male of twenty-five and under fifty, 2 females under ten, 1 female of ten and under twenty-five, and 1 female of twenty-five and under fifty. "Deserted" noted in the margin.

146. **Echo Fixico** 4 members consisting of 1 male of ten and under twenty-five, 1 male of twenty-five and under fifty, 1 female under ten, and 1 female of twenty-five and under fifty. "Deserted" noted in the margin.

147. **Jacob Beavers** 7 members consisting of 1 male of ten and under twenty-five, 1 male of twenty-five and under fifty, 3 females under ten, 1 female of ten and under twenty-five, and 1 female of twenty-five and under fifty. McIntosh party member who remained in exile for a time in Pike County, Georgia, in the aftermath of William McIntosh's execution. In 1829 Beavers visited the western Creek Nation to explore the country for possible resettlement. Beavers remained in the Creek Nation through the 1820s and was chosen as one of the ninety principal headmen who received a full section of land under the 1832 Treaty of Washington. He was from Coweta.[12]

148. **Eastibuggy** 2 members consisting of 1 female of ten and under twenty-five and 1 female of twenty-five and under fifty.

149. **William Shirley** 5 members consisting of 2 males under ten, 1 male of ten and under twenty-five, 1 male of twenty-five and under fifty, and 1 female of twenty-five and under fifty.

150. **William Grieson** 9 members consisting of 1 male under ten, 1 male of ten and under twenty-five, 1 male of twenty-five and under fifty,

2 females under ten, 3 females of ten and under twenty-five, and 1 female of twenty-five and under fifty. The same William Grieson enrolled earlier (Grayson, no. 103 on second McIntosh party roll, chap. 2). Although enrolled again here, Claudio Saunt notes that William Grayson, his wife Judah (1800–1860s), and their children emigrated with their own resources, separate from this party.[13]

Supplemental Letters of the Fourth Voluntary Party

In this letter to Bvt. Brigadier General George Gibson,[14] the commissary general of subsistence, Captain John Page complains of the incompetence of Alexander Hill and reports that he has paid this year's annuity to the Creek Nation. Letter found at CGS-IRW, Roll 5, 99–101.

Rec'd 25 Octr

Fort Mitchell Ala
14th October 1834.

Sir

I have the honor to acknowledge the receipt of Your Letter of the 24th September and 2d October last the blank spoken of in my Letter were only ruled for the purpose of Entering the heads of families and the number without specifying the age this to be done when we were holding talks with them and no Extra Expence incured by so doing the object was merely for me to predicate my Estimate upon the mode pointed out in the instructions is decidedly the best mode for Enrolling for when an Indian breaks up at home and leaves to the rendezveaus for the purpose of Enrolling he brings his property with him as also his family and there is no doubt about his intentions but if they are Enrolled at their homes Every thing is uncertain.

I have not Seen Col. Hill for two or three weeks he went to Centerville and he writes me he was detained there Longer than he Expected his son Came here Yesterday with a Letter to report to me for duty he also says his father has got several Encampments & made some Contracts all of which I Know nothing about I had no idea of his rendezveausing them and Enrolling them at their own Towns for it is much more Expensive and verry uncertain whether they will go after their names are Enrolled. two places to Called all that are going this Year are sufficient and this place will be the most important there being more Indians in the vicinity of this place that Calculates to go than in any other part of the nation but he has been off so long I have been unable to Know his intentions he has got his Wife with him and it appears he Cannot Leave her his son is quite incompetent for this business Col Hill writes me he had brought some people from Centerville to Emigrate the Upper Creeks I sent his son back to tell him I had provided Teams and would Call them in service when they were wanted I done this because I understood he had also ordered some Teams all of which was contrary to my Knowledge and in fact I enjoined on him not to Engage any that I would make the nesessary arrangements the number of persons he has got employed in these Encampments & what they are doing I do not Know but I have sent for him to Come here that I Can have some understanding with him—The fact is Col Hill is too ignorant a man for this business and if he does wrong it is through ignorance he has not appointed the propper persons to assist him Sommerville is the only one that Knows any thing Col H thinks a man that Can drive Cattle Can make a good agent what Indians are in this vicinity will Come in when they are Called for I Leave here to day for Mobile after funds the Annuity was paid on the 7th but it was only divided into two parcels one part of the Nation took $20,000 & the other took the other $20,000 one thousand Dollars reserved so there is to be another meeting on the 26th this month to distribute it again and it appears to me nothing Can be done untill the money is disposed of this Annuity has injured our Cause Verry much so soon as I return from Mobile I will give You all the information [of] our prospects &c.

With respect
I have the honor to be
Your Ob't Servt
John Page
Capt & Disbur'g Agent

Brig Gen'l Ge'o Gibson
Com'y Gen'l of Sub't
Washington City

☾

Alexander Hill reports on the progress of the enrollment and details some of the obstacles he has faced. Letter found at CGS-IRW, Roll 5, 163–64.

Rec'd 3 Nov

Coweta, Chambers County
Octo. 18th 1834—

To Geo. Gibson
Emigration of Indians
Commissary General of
Subsistence—
Washington City

Sir,

I have received your letter of the 19th of Sept, and agreable to your request shall give you a brief account of my movements & prospects. I attended the meeting of the Indians at their council to receive their annuity, this was later than I had expected, I there explained to the chiefs & Head men of the nation, my motives & plan for their Emmigration, together with the wishes & good feelings of the Goverment in regard to their removal; The annuity was but partially paid, the upper Creeks received their Dividend, but the lower Creeks was undivided untill the 26th of this Inst. when I expect again to attend in person. I have found it necessary to appoint several Enrolling Clerks, and stationed them at the several Towns, which I conceived to be the best means to hasten the Emmigration.

Coln. William Hunter one of my assistants is in the upper Towns from whom I expect you have heard. Many difficulties present themselves which operate to retard the Enrolment, some of the chiefs, particularly Tuckabatchee Hajo[15] the Head of the Cussitahs, and whose influence extends in a great degree over the Lower Indians, laboring Incessanly, using every exertion to prevent & procrastinate the Emmigration, presenting to the Indians terrors, which have no existence, this is more or less the case with most of the chiefs.

The arrival of the Rectifying agent (Coln Meigs)[16] has had a prejudicial effect upon the minds of the Indians, it is rumored among them, that he is authorised by the Goverment to restore to the Indians who have sold their Lands, I find this also a great check, but I am in hopes this in a few days will be removed.

The Enrolment progresses much slower than I had anticipated, but I am & shall labour dilligently to remove all difficulties, & meet the wishes & expectations of the Goverment, with a view particularly to Economy.

Respectfully
yo Obt Servt.
Alex. Hill S. C. R.

☾

Page reports on the delay caused by Hill, the status of the enrollment camps, and feeding 170 poor Creeks. Letter found at CGS-IRW, Roll 5, 114–16.

Rec'd Nov. 22d

Fort Mitchell (Ala)
7th November 1834

Sir

When I left this place for Mobile after Funds I was in hopes on my return I should be able to give you a correct account of the number of Indians that would Emigrate this year and the exact time we should start, but every thing appears to be about the same as before I left.— Co'l Hill has been very unsuccessful in the upper-part of the nation where he has been operating, not-withstanding it is in that section of country where he lives.

I have been decieved by his calculations; he told me he had five encampments and things looked very prosperous, but I believe he has only collected about four hundred; it is possible he may get some few more but I think the prospect a bad one.

I have just returned from among those Towns that I had been visiting previous to my going to Mobile they are all willing to go and are getting ready; so soon as I can see Co'l Hill I shall rendezvous them, which I can do, in a very short time.—

I have sent for him and requested him to come and decide upon something at once. I think I have enough to make a party sufficiently large to start with.—

I could have collected mine three weeks ago if he had been ready.— I have never till yesterday called a Team into service, but I engaged them the first thing I done and they have at all times been ready when called for. I told Co'l Hill particularly that I had engaged Teams and that they were ready when they were wanted, but he has brought into service several Teams long before he got any Indians and they have been under pay and subsistence ever since; they are none of those that I engaged, I believe he took them from Centreville, my accounts will show what were employed by him. I have incured no expense myself of any consequence. The Co'l has had all the ass't Agents with him six or seven I have understood.

I have had one man as ass't Comy at $2.50 per day and an Interpreter, that is all.

On my way to Mobile the stage turned over and crippled'd me but in a few days I got so I could ride about and attend to business.

As I passed by a place (called Fort Hull) I see one of the Encampments Co'l Hill had made and there was an Enrolling agent and an ass't agent, an Interpreter and two five horse Teams and they had been there about three weeks they told me & had enrolled but one Indian; I immediately wrote to Co'l Hill the unnecessary expense he was incuring without any prospect and he told me he would break it up immediately. I advised with the agent the best mode of collecting them but he got these

Encampments in his head and established them and appointed agents to them before he got any Indians. They have appeared to me, to adopt the same plan they would to enlist soldiers.

I have had to feed about 170 Indians for about two or three weeks; they were some poor families that were scattered a long ways apart and had no means of subsisting and teams could not get to them, they said they were ready and I told them to pack their own plunder to this place and I would give them rations till the Emigration was ready to start, this is all the subsistence I have paid for on account of my own movements. When Co'l Hill and myself seperated, he went into one part of the nation and I the other and I did not see him for three or four weeks, he had some business at Centreville that detained him there and before he returned he had adopted the plan of encampments and from what he told me I thought he was going to succeed very well, but he was led away by taking the advise of people who wanted employ and had corn to sell, and when he stated to me what people in the nation had told him, I requested him not to pay any attention to their plans but adopt the ones laid down in our instructions which were the most equinomical and sure of success.

Co'l Hill will be here in a couple of days and in my next communication I shall endeavor, if possible, to give you the number that will Emigrate this year, if any.

I have apprised William Armstrong[17] at different times of our success so he may know what to depend on.

With respect
I have the honor to be
Your Obt Servt
John Page
Capt & Disbursing Agent

Brig Gen'l Ge'o Gibson
Com'y Gen'l Sub't
Washington

☾

Writing a couple of weeks before the commencement of the party, Captain John Page reports to Commissary General of Subsistence George Gibson that the party will be small. This is due, according to Page, to the ineffectiveness of Alexander Hill in collecting emigrants. As winter set in, Page suggested that the agents abandon the emigration until the spring of 1835. Hill, however, believed it was too late to turn back. This letter notes that Hill has 286 Creeks at Centreville, Alabama, waiting for their journey to commence. Letter found at CGS-IRW, Roll 5, 118–19.

Rec'd 13 Decr

Fort Mitchell, Ala
3d December 1834

Sir

I have the honor to report to You that the whole number of Indians we shall Emigrate this fall will not Exceed six or seven hundred   Col. Hill arrived here on the 10th Nove. after an absence of four weeks in the upper part of the nation and sent about two hundred & Eighty six at or near Centerville Ala. there to remain untill what few in this vicinity could join them   I had never rendezveaused them and of Course they had to be collected after his return   our prospect being dull and I presumed unless he met with better success than he had that he would give it up for the present time as our instructions say from two to five Thousand   I could not tell or Know whether it was his intention to start with so small a party which are now nearly all collected & will start in two or three days   he had no reason to depend on me to make up a party sufficient to make it an object to Emigrate this fall; one month ago I could have started from this place a much Larger number than I now shall. I told him they were strongly opposed to Emigrating this fall as the season was so far advanced   what <u>few</u> are going are generally verry poor and destitute of clothing and it would be a prudent and humane act to give it up untill spring when if the <u>propper measures</u> are taken they would Emigrate verry willingly   I Knew 6 or seven hundred out of twenty odd thousand was no object. I believe he has appointed ass't agents Enough and had them stationed in the upper part of the nation to have Emigrated ten Thousand and all they have collected from what I can Learn are 286   I do not Know what number of assis't agents he has got but I Know of Eight or nine & they are all with his small party at or near centerville unless he has discharged them Except Mr Sommerville[18] who is bringing in camp those I have ben amongs't, Col Hill is also with him; I returned from the nation a few days since and Expected Col Hill would have been here before this   we shall not get to Tuscaloosa till Jan'y probably the 20th.

with respect I am

Your most ob't ser't
John Page
Capt & Disbur'g Agent

Brig Gen'l Geo Gibson
Com'y Gen'l Subsis't

☾

Page again complains of the incompetence of Alexander Hill and reports on the need to move the party as soon as possible as winter was setting in. Letter found at CGS-IRW, Roll 5, 124–25.

Rec'd Dec. 16.

Fort Mitchell Ala
5th December 1834

Sir

I have the honor to acknowledge the receipt this day of Yours of the 19th and 20th November Last   Col. Hill is not here although in my Last communication I Expected him here Every hour but still he does not come   I have sent the communication to him.

As the business now stands I am unable to prolong the Emigration any Longer for the sake of getting a few more at this time as the party I spoke of that Col Hill had Sent to Centerville there to wait till the party goes from this place could join them and having already brought into Camps nearly all that will go from this point it is practicable to start with what we have as soon as possible I know not the number of teams &c. he has got Employed with that party I have asked him but he did not appear to Know himself it is two Hundred miles from this where the advance party is I shall pay them off on his certificate of the hire &c all the teams previous to the 14th or 15 of Nov'r. were ordered into service by him and contrary to my Knowledge or wish for I told him Several times that I had made Every arrangement for teams when they were wanted and were at my Command without any Expence to the Government Whenever I had a Chance to see Col Hill I told him he was not aware of the Expence he was incurring without any prospect and I at all times told him our instructions enjoined it on us to try the Experiment Without incurring unnecessary Expence and if the Indians would not Emigrate this fall to report our progress as it was and give it up or start with what we had but his answer was never mind I will take it all on my shoulder nothing more at this Late period Can be done toward Emigration than take what few we have got One month ago we could have got off with a much Larger party many who were disposed to go this fall have given it up in Consequence of the Cold weather I shall take on with as Little Expence as possible the small party I have in Charge as I pass through Montgomery I will Look at the Public Property Your Letter of the 19th speaks of and act accordingly.

I have the honor to be
Verry Respectfully
Your Ob't Ser't
John Page
Capt & Disb'g agent

Brig Gen'l Geo Gibson
Com Genl Subsist
Washington D.C.

(

Writing during the first stage of the journey west, Page describes how the cold weather, coupled with rain and hail, had already strained the party as they reached Columbus, Mississippi, via Tuscaloosa, Alabama. Although Page opposed commencing the journey so late in the year when the winter months made travel difficult and expensive, he was overruled by Alexander Hill, who superintended the emigration. Page's letter notes the firing of Hill in the second sentence. Letter found at CGS-IRW, Roll 5, 134–37.

Rec'd Jany 23d

Columbus Missippi
6th January 1835

Sir

I have the honor to acknowledge the riciept of your letter dated the 13th of last month. Your letter apprising me of the discontinuance of Co'l Hill was acknowledged immediately on the riciept of it, but I discovered it must have laid in the Post office two or three days before I got it, notwithstanding I sent to the office every day the Post Master had left his business with a clerk who probably did not know where to look for them. I dispatched the communications immediately to Co'l Hill as directed and on his arrival started the Indians the next day. the cold weather caused many of those who assembled for the purpose of Emigrating to leave us and return to their town again, Co'l Hill put off the time for starting so long, they were getting impatient; and on the receipt of your letter I started fourth with. I have only 590 and a great many of them are in a dreadful situation to move in the cold weather. I have found it almost impossible to get along, the roads are almost impassible, we have labored from day light till long after dark to get some days 6 miles, the waters are up and the bridges swept off, and it has rained and hailed almost every day since I left Fort Mitchell the only thing I have to console me is that we may have some fair weather after a while All the asst. agents were discharged agreeable to your instructions I continued Mr Sommervill till I got to this place as I could not be with the party for many days having to settle the debts Co'l Hill contracted through the nation, I think I have paid as many as 14 Enrolling Agents and a great many teams and other persons Employed, I knew he had been extravagant but had no idea to what amount till I arrived at Centrevill, and the accounts I had to settle were more trouble than the whole Choctaw Emigration and all were accumulated by Co'l Hill as you will see when my accounts are rendered.—I shall continue Mr Sommervill at $2,50 per day. All the persons I shall have to assist me will be at that price. It is possible Co'l Hunter may continue with me till I get to Memphis.—I shall incur as little expense as possible, but the cold weather is so severe on the little children and old persons and some of them nearly naked that they would perish if they were not attended to. we have to stop the waggons to take the children out and warm them and put them back again 6 or 7 times in a day, I send a head and have fires built for this purpose, I wrap them in tents and any thing I can get hold of to keep them from freezing; five or six in each waggon constantly crying in consequence of suffering with cold. I am some times at a stand to know how to get along under existing circumstances.—When I get to Memphis I shall adopt some plan to get them on board of steam boats and send their horses through the swamp.[19]—what number I can get on board of the boats I do not know as yet not having named it to them, but I think they will suffer so much before they get to Memphis they will be willing to take the boats.

Agreeable to instructions I examined the Public property stored in Montgomery, 30 Boxes of Rifles all in good order I examined two boxes and found they did not want any cleaning, they were as bright as when they were put up. One box had been opened the rifles taken out, I requested the owner of the building to account for them and he said he would, the balance of the boxes were in good order. There was also a very large bale of blankets well put up also two Boxes I presumed contained domesticks[20] they were so well packed I did not open them as I was convinced they were in good order and better secured from the moths than they could, if they were repacked.

I enclose you a Bill of the storeage as rendered. They are in good order, but to sell them at auction they would bring but little. I think they would well pay the government to ship the articles to any point they may be wanted.

With respect
I have the honor to be
your ob't sev't
John Page
D. Agent[21]

Brig Gen'l Ge'o Gibson
Com'y Gen'l Sub
Washington

☾

This letter, written by federal disbursing agent Jacob Brown[22] who was based at Little Rock, notes the departure of the party from that city. Brown records that the cold weather had not abated, and with ice on the Arkansas River, the entire group was forced to travel by land during the final stage of their journey. Letter found at CGS-IRW, Roll 5, 249–50.

Rec'd 26 March

Little Rock, A.T.
March 1st 1835.

Sir:

The Party of Creek Emigrants—over 500 in number = under the direction of Cap't. Page, broke up Camp this morning, and commenced their March, for their New Country, which they will reach, if not greatly impeded by high Waters and bad Roads, on or about the 20th inst. The Emigrants have with them several small Wagons, and about 160 Ponies.

Owing to the long and continued exposure of these Emigrants, embracing the whole of an unusually cold winter, and being destitute of clothing, many of them at this time are sick. I have kept a

Physician[23] in their camp since they reached this. Two or three have died. The four or five days rest, however, together with the attentions of Agents and the Physician, they appear to be getting better—are evidently more cheerful; and as the morning is mild, being the first indications of the approach of spring, hopes are entertained that their sufferings hence forward, will be greatly ameliorated.

These Emigrants were 20 days getting from Memphis to this place. The Boat was compelled to ly-too some two or three days in the Mississippi, in consequence of high winds; and in the Arkansas, several days, from Ice and sand Bars. They reached this on the 24th ulto. and were immediately encamped. The River not being in a stage to justify further attempts to ascend it; and no probability of its being in a better condition for some time, I directed the Boat to be discharged, and procured the necessary number of Teams to make the balance of the journey by land.

I have received from Capt. Page, $2.500. All the Funds he could spare.

Very Respectfully,
Your Obt. Servt.
J Brown Capt. U.S.A.
Pr Dis Agt Ind Rem'l;

Genl. Geo. Gibson,
Com'y. Genl. of Subs.
Washington, D.C.

☾

After conducting the fourth voluntary party west, Page traveled back via New Orleans and Mobile to Fort Mitchell, where he wrote the following three letters (25 and 27 April and 1 May), summarizing the problems he faced along the route. Page's repeated complaints about Alexander Hill's competency as well as his acknowledgment that it may have cost the federal government upward of sixty dollars to get one Creek emigrant only as far as Little Rock, was the final straw for a cost-conscious administration gearing up for the massive removal and relocation of tens of thousands of eastern Indians. Capitalization has been emended for consistency. Letter found at CGS-IRW, Roll 5, 140–46.

Rec'd 8 May

Fort Mitchell Ala
25th April 1835

Sir

I have the honor to report my arrival at this place Last Evening after a journey of Twenty Eight days from Fort Gibson. I should have reported my arrival at that place but there was no mail & I started the next day in a flat Boat as it was the only Conveyance, the Low stage of the water prevented steam Boats from assending the river; I was thirteen days getting to Little Rock where I met with a steam Boat, I Brought the mail with me to New Orleans, I did not stop an hour there but proceeded to Mobile where I Consulted with Maj'r Hogan,[24] not finding any instructions for me at that place he thought it advisable for me to proceed to this place as he was about Leaving there himself & I Could not render my accounts in Season to accompany him and this was the place where he wished to Consult me, at the same Time I was making up my accounts;—they shall be forwarded as Soon as I Can possibly make them out. We suffered verry much in Consequence of the severity of the winter the people of Arkansas admit they never witnessed anything like it before. I never Layed by one day unless it was in Consequence of high water where it Could not be Bridged, places where people moving with large numbers of Slaves had been Laying by for Seven or Eight days in Consequence of high water and Cold weather I passed through without any detention there was one days march of 17 miles we had to make with the Choctaws[25] in Consequence of the Secarsity of water and Could not find any place short of that distance where we Could Encamp, this Year we were three days going it & had to build two Bridges, So You Can See the impropriety of moving Indians in the winter season and I assure You that we were up Every morning by 4 Ock. Let the weather be what it would prepairing for a start and worked hard and suffered much from day Light untill sun down to get six and sometimes ten Miles, it rained snowed or hailed almost Every day and freezing at the same time. We were Compelled to thaw the Tents & Blankets before we Could roll them up to put them in the waggons in the morning, the Indian Children and sick Indians had to go in the waggons on top of their Baggage and to prevent them from freezing we were Compelled to have fires along the road and take them out and warm them, dry their blankets that were wrapped round them and replace them again in the waggons strict attention had to be paid to this or some must inevitably have perished and there was a Continual Crying from morning untill night with the children I used to Encourage them by saying that the weather would moderate in a few days and it would be warm but it never happened during the whole trip on the 9th March, where we were about one hundred & fifty miles from Fort Gibson we had a verry severe snow storm and the roads were impassable for all Carriges of Every description Except those Employed in the Emigration I do not recollect of Meeting any thing but one or two horse Carts and they gave it up, when they struck the road that we Came over, there was nothing but prying out waggons from morning untill night. I am well aware it was not the intention of the Gov't. the Emigration should take place in the winter season but the delay of Co'l Hill Caused it to be so I Endeavoured to get him to suspend it untill spring as he was deviating from his instructions by starting with so few, but he had started two hundred & Thirty or forty and directed them to stop at Centerville Consequently it was too Late to suspend the Emigration. I sent the Indian horses through the Miss Swamp with seventy two Indians in Charge of Mr Beattie, some places he Cut the ice sufficiently wide to drive them through other places was so wide they had to tie [the horses'] Legs and pull them over, this was the only way they Could get through unless they Layed by some ten or fifteen days till the ice might thaw I started in the SBoat and when I got into the arkansas River it was frozen over and detained me some days there was only about five miles the river was frozen so the ice entirely stopped I went to work & fell trees in the river to start the ice and run the Boat into it and Cut off Cake at a time and in two days and a half we worked our way through and with much difficulty assended as far as Little Rock. I should have returned back immediately and gone up White River and Landed at Rock Roe but I ascertained that was frozen up also Consequently there was but one plan to adopt that was to go through the ice the best way I Could. There was not one Indian frozen to death but a Considerable number Chill blane[26] and I had to have them Carried the whole distance after it occured. They were all getting well when I Left them. The influenza was prevailing in Arkansas Tery and as many as six or seven in a family died it soon got amongst the Indians but we Lost but three or four of that Complaint and in fact the whole party was remarkably healthie Considering our situation. I am well Convinced if we had attempted to have Laid by in Consequence of the severity of the weather that one half would have died of that Complaint it proved so fatal with the inhabitants when I Called at a house and found almost Every member of the family down with this disease I was Convinced nothing kept it from us but being Constantly on the move and Exposed to the Severity of the Winter The Expences of this Emigration has been Enormous. I got fifty Thousand Dollars out of Bank in Mobile and when I arrived at Tuscaloosa I did not Like to Carry so much mony the risk was too great so I deposited in the Bank in that place $20,000, as Co'l Hill told me the debts were not much but when I Came to pay off I found Them Enormous I thought with thirty Thousand Dollars I Could turn over to Capt Brown the am't directed and have a Considerable Sum Left but all I Could Spare was $2500 or 3000$ I do not reccollect & I was Compelled to draw on the $20,000 that I Left in the bank I think it has Cost the rise of $60 a head to get to Little Rock so soon as I render my accounts You will see how the mony is Expended.[27] I Shall have the am't transfered from Tuscaloosa to Montgomery where I Can draw for the money as I want it I will send in a day or two the Muster roll & shall Loose no time in rendering my accounts. I have received Your Circular of 21st March at Mobile.

With Respect
I have the honor to be
Your Obt Serv't
John Page Capt &
Disburg Agent
Creek Removal

Brig Gen'l Geo Gibson
Com'y Gen'l Subst
Washington City

☾

Writing to notify the commissary general of subsistence that he is forwarding the muster roll, Page provides additional information about the problems he encountered during the journey west. He notes the problems he had with desertion—both before the journey commenced and while in the Chickasaw country. He also reports widespread dissatisfaction by the emigrants when they did not receive their rifles and blankets at Memphis, as promised by Alexander Hill. Page blames the muster roll form, which did not contain a column for warriors (who were to receive the presents), and the difficulty in ascertaining who was a warrior and therefore eligible for a rifle and blanket. Capitalization has been emended for consistency. Letter found at CGS-IRW, Roll 5, 151–54.

Rec'd 8 May

Fort Mitchell Ala
27th April 1835

Sir

I have the honor to Enclose herewith a muster roll of the Creek Emigrants of Last Years I have marked a number as deserted, some Left before the Emigration started, they were Encamped so Long and cold weather approaching they determined to suspend their movements untill another Year. I Lost a considerable number in the Chickasaw Nation the interpreter informed me a number of

Emigrants were about to Leave the party. I called them together and had a talk with them, they stated that they had agreed to go with Co'l Hill as far as the Chickasaw Nation and that they had fulfilled their contract and Co'l Hill told them they need not go any farther they called up Several Indians to prove their assertions I Explained to them the injury they would sustain by remaining in the Chickasaw Nation and that the Chickasaws were in great trouble themselves they continued to go on but in a day or two slip'd off in the night.— Several others Left when they found they were not to receive their Rifles & Blankets at Memphis Eufauley Hajo (their chief) said Co'l Hill promised them they should receive them at Memphis as also Co'l Hills Interpreter stated the same thing and a great many other promises they said he made them—and what they colled on me for repeatedly I told them what they might depend on and what they would receive when they got to their new country—some of them appeared to be much dissatisfied that the promises made to them were not fulfilled. after I arrived at Centerville I Enrolled the Indians, Co'l Hill had there as he never had done it, he had no roll to turn over to me but said there they are and I have counted them and they are all present but when I Enrolled them I could not find the number and I think I paid from thirteen to fifteen Enrolling agts. I was directed to state or disignate in the muster roll the warriors. there is no column for the warriors, and again if I had done it according to my Judgement probably the agents who Issue the Rifles might disagree with my Judgement, it requires a Considerable investigation to ascertain who are actually Entitled to Rifles and who are not, if I had disignated them on the rolls I am Convinced many would have been presented that in my apinion were not Entitled to Rifles probably they would make such statements the persons Issuing the Rifles as to convince them they were Entitled to receive them agreeable to the treaty.[28] I assisted in Issuing the Rifles to the Choctaw and two or three persons were selected as judges and many Young men that we rejected the Chiefs and their relatives proved to our Satisfaction that they were entitled to a rifle and others who we thought were Entitled to a rifle they proved that they were not, this was come at by their being a Little jealous at the time and Exposed Each other there is no place or time the different ages of the Warriors Can be had so Correctly as when they Come forward to receive them.

I have the honor to be
Very Respectfully
Your most ob't sert
John Page Capt & Disbur'g Agent

Brig Gen'l Geo Gibson
Com'y Gen'l Sub'st
Washington City

☾

Writing to notify the commissary general of subsistence that he is forwarding his disbursement accounts, Page once again attempts to pin the blame for the high cost of the emigration on Alexander Hill. Letter found at CGS-IRW, Roll 5, 147–50.

Rec'd 21 May.

Fort Mitchell Ala
1st May 1835

Sir

I have the honor to Enclose herewith my accounts for Expenditures in the Last Creek Emigration the Expenditures are Enormous, but You will perceive it is by the missmanagement of the Superintendant (Col Hill) the vouchers will show for themselves, I was issuing to Teams and Teamsters as also Indians nearly two months Longer than was nesessary. Col Hill sent Three Teams here to report to me and requested me to Forage them I of cource agreeable to instructions done it; the regulations compelled me to do it. I supposed he had it in contemplation [to] a move in the Cource of Ten days, he went off to Centervill & I did not see him again for about a month & then I wrote to him it was necessary to Come to some Conclusion either to suspend the operations untill Spring or make a move as I was Convinced he Could not Comply with his instructions to move a party not Less than Two Thousand I Collected two hundred & sixty Indians myself the ballance with all the assistance of his agents he Collected which were Enough to make the rise of five hundred. You Can readily see what measures he took to Collect this small number and the Expence he incured in doing it; he had teams & agents scattered all through the Country, I told him it was Contrary to all rules and regulations and that I did not believe he would be sustained in it, but he told me that Gen'l Gibson understood his plans and that he would stand the test for all his own acts I reported from time to time about his movements and it was all I Could do about it the Length of time I was performing the journey after I got under way was much greater than it would have been at any other season of the Year Consequently the subsistance and Transportation was much more Expensive. I Laboured Early and Late to get them to their new-Country I never did witness or Experience any thing to Equel the scenes of the trip in my Life and hope it will never be my Lot to do it again. Many persons pronounced it murder in the highest degree for me to move Indians or Compell them to march in such severe weather when they* were dying Every day with the influenza; but I am well Convinced it was the only thing that Kept them alive not withstanding their Exposure. I hope my accounts will be taken up soon as practicoble as I am anxious to Know the result—Col. Hills accounts gave a great deal of trouble. I worked night and day at Centervielle and at Tuscaloosa, the persons he imployed followed me to the Latter place before I got through with them I Left numerous accounts behind that I positively refused and would have nothing to do with them and stated to Col Hill it was useless to follow me any further as I would pay no more I Kept paying when he told me I was most through I presume Such as I rejected will never be presented.

with respect
I have the honor to be
Your Ob't Servt
John Page
Disbur'g Agent
Creek Rem'l

Brig Gen'l Geo Gibson
Com'y Gen'l Subs't
Washington City

* the people, not the indians—see Capt P's ultimo 25 Ap'l &c)[29]

6 The Fifth Voluntary Emigrating Party, 1835–36

As the letters in the previous chapter show, the 1834 voluntary emigrating party was a disaster. Hill's unfamiliarity with the business of emigration had cost the government money and the Creeks their health. Making matters worse, Sampson Grayson (Grieson, no. 1 on the fourth voluntary party muster roll, chap. 5) returned to Alabama in 1835 and began telling would-be emigrants that the government did not have enough provisions to feed the 1834 party the entire way. He claimed that during the journey west, the agents began charging the emigrants for food—$100 for adults and $50 for children—and those who failed to pay would be "made slaves to the sugar plantations in Mississippi." He also reported that those who died were denied a proper Creek burial. Although there is no evidence to back up Grayson's claims, enrolling agents in the field reported that these rumors had their desired effect, and many people simply refused to move west.[1]

In an attempt to salvage the emigration program, federal officials made a number of changes. First, Hill was fired and replaced by Colonel John B. Hogan. The Virginia-born Hogan was a War of 1812 veteran who helped capture Fort George in Upper Canada in 1813, was in Fort Erie during the siege in 1814, and served under Andrew Jackson in Florida in 1818. Hogan had actually been tapped by Alexander Hill a year earlier to serve with the fourth voluntary party but had declined, declaring that working under Hill was "too humble" a position for him. This is not surprising, considering that Hogan was the very person who had called Hill "stupidly ignorant" (see chapter 5; they knew each other in the Alabama Senate). Captain John Page, however, was retained as disbursing agent.[2]

Federal officials then moved to rein in the enormous expenditures associated with moving the Creeks west. The cost to transport one person from the Creek Nation to Indian territory during David Brearley's two emigrations averaged $43.58, while in Crowell's 1829 party it cost $21.22. Because of the repeated delays and the higher prices associated with winter travel, the expense to transport one Creek Indian only as far as Little Rock in 1834–35 ran as high as $60. Desperate to shift the financial burden away from the Treasury Department, federal officials decided to hire a private contracting firm; on 17 September 1835 the United States agreed to terms on a no-bid contract with the John W.A. (William Augustine) Sanford and Company for the removal of five thousand Creeks at twenty dollars per person. If this was completed by 1 July 1836, Sanford and Company would have rights to conduct the remainder of the Creeks west. Although contracting for removal had first been proposed as early as 1830, Sanford and Company was not formed until sometime around 1834, in response to the struggle Hill was having recruiting emigrants. Indeed, in November 1834 company partner Alfred Iverson told his father-in-law John Forsyth, the U.S. secretary of state and a former Georgia governor, that Hill was "wholly unqualified to conduct this business to a successful issue."[3]

The switch to private contractors was extremely controversial, however. Many of the members of John W.A. Sanford and Company were the very land speculators who had stolen the Creeks' reserves. Many Creeks, even those not particularly interested in emigrating, came out against the company. John B. Hogan, who in addition to his role as superintendent of Creek emigration also investigated the land frauds, reported that "the change is obnoxious to the Indians" and that the contractors were "unpopular with the Indians, who know them." One prominent Creek headman, who had no desire to leave the land of his ancestors, weighed in on the controversy by declaring that "the Indians will not go with them; they are the very men, who have cheated the Indians out of their lands, and they now want to cheat them out of what little they have left, and

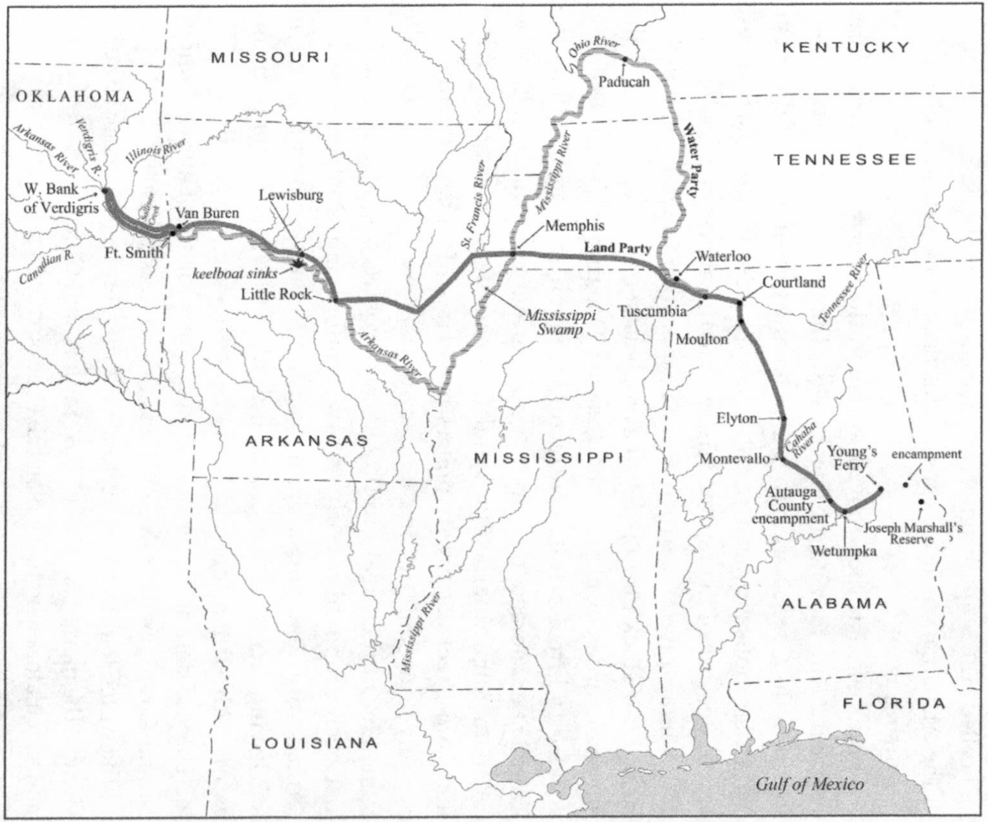

MAP 6. Route of the fifth voluntary emigrating party, December 1835–February 1836. Place names correspond to stopping points or locations noted in the documentation. Route lines and locations are approximations. Cartography by Sarah Mattics and Kiersten Fish.

while on the march, they will be drove like a parcel of pigs to market." Similarly, other Creeks declared that they would refuse to emigrate with Sanford and Company because they believed some company members had stolen their lands and "would abuse them" along the journey. In fact, the fear of abuse by the contractors concerned many Creeks, who worried that the contractors placed profit above their welfare. Creek headmen said as much in a letter to President Andrew Jackson when they wrote that "we believe the health comfort and interest of the Indian will never be consulted but that all their arrangements will be conducted for their own good and pecuniary benefit."[4]

Not surprisingly, the John W.A. Sanford and Company had great difficulty attracting emigrants. Most Creeks were committed to remaining in Alabama, and those who were wavering simply refused to be conducted by the very people who stolen their land. To facilitate enrollment the company brought on board Benjamin Marshall, a signer of the Treaty of Indian Springs, to replace an original member who withdrew because of illness. Marshall did not invest in the company but was hired because he had "extensive connexions" among the Creek people. For his part, Marshall offered his services in order to "'get his negroes removed'" to the Indian territory, and his slaves appear on the list (no. 73 on the fifth voluntary muster roll). He apparently planned on removing his family sometime later. But the Sanford company overestimated Marshall's connections. When asked whether the company would reach their required number of one thousand emigrants, Marshall stated that "'he did not think the party would be over a few hundred.'"[5]

The fifth voluntary emigrating party was conducted west by Dr. Stephen Miles Ingersoll, a founding member of John W.A. Sanford and Company, and William J. Beattie, a veteran of the fourth voluntary emigrating party, who was also a silent partner in the organization. South Carolina–born Lieutenant Edward Deas[6] of the 4th U.S. Artillery (and West Point graduate) was appointed military oversight in accordance with Article 10 of the contract. Dr. Burton Randall,[7] who at the time of his appointment was serving on hospital duty at Bay St. Louis, Mississippi, accompanied the party as surgeon.[8]

FIG. 3. Stephen Miles Ingersoll (1792–1872), portrait by John Maier, *Dr. Stephen Miles Ingersoll*, 1847, oil on canvas, 30¼ x 25¼ inches. Courtesy of the Collections of the Columbus Museum, Georgia; museum purchase G.1995.11. Image © The Columbus Museum.

Contract between the United States and John W.A. Sanford and Company

The following is an agreement between the United States and a private contracting firm called John W.A. Sanford and Company. It specifies the obligations and liabilities for each side as well as what the Creeks are entitled to on the journey west. Contract found in Records of the Adjutant General's Office, 1780s–1917, Entry 159-Q, Records of Major General Thomas S. Jesup, Container 31, Folder: "Various reports, returns, and papers 1836 (2 of 5)," NARA.

Articles of Agreement entered into this seventeenth day of September One Thousand Eight Hundred and Thirty five between George Gibson Commissary General of Subsistence under the authority of the President of the United States on the part of the United States and John W.A. Sanford,[9] Alfred Iverson,[10] John D Howell,[11] Benjamin Marshall,[12] Luther Blake[13] and Stephen M Ingersoll[14] of Georgia to be known in said articles as, and acting under the firm of John W.A. Sanford and Company.

This Agreement witnesseth that the said George Gibson, for and on behalf of the United States and the said John W.A. Sanford and Company, their Heirs Executors and Administrators have agreed and by these presents do mutually covenant and agree.

I. That the said John W.A. Sanford and Company their Heirs &c shall remove the Creek Indians occupants of the Creek Nation in the State of Alabama from said nation to a point in the new Country alloted to the Creeks West of the Territory of Arkansas, and within Twenty miles of Fort Gibson, to wit, men, women and children, with their slaves and their goods and chattels as herein after provided, in manner and form, and for the consideration specified in these articles of agreement.

II. That the said John W.A. Sanford and Company their Heirs &c shall collect the Indians together at convenient times and places, and that the Indians shall be subsisted by them from the day that they commence to march to the place of assemblage.

III. That the said John W.A. Sanford and Company, their Heirs &c, will dispatch to the new country aforesaid, parties of One Thousand Indians, or more, under the conduct of such agents as the said John W.A. Sanford and Company their Heirs &c may deem it proper to appoint, the Indians having been first carefully enrolled.

IV. That the following shall be the rations, and the kind and quantity of Transportation to which the Indians &c shall be entitled: The ration of Bread shall be one pound of wheat flour, indian meal or hard bread, or three fourths of a quart of Corn. The meat ration shall be one pound of fresh, or three fourths of a pound of salt, meat or bacon; and with fresh meat, two quarts of salt to every hundred rations. The Transportation shall be one six horse waggon and fifteen hundred pounds of baggage, to from fifty to Eighty persons. The provisions and transportation shall be the best of the kind. The average daily travel shall not exceed twelve miles.

V. That the provisions shall be issued daily if practicable, and not less frequently than every other day, as well whilst at rest as during the travel, until the day, inclusive, of arrival at the point of destination west; and that there shall be established, within three months, points upon the entire route westward, at which the provisions are to be issued.

VI. That the sick, those enfeebled from age or other cause, and young children, shall be transported in waggons or on horseback. That those who may be pronounced unable to proceed may be left on the route at some proper place, and under the care of some proper person, at the expence of the United States.

VII. That the Indian ponies[15] shall be given from the day of starting west one half gallon of corn Each; provided such disposition in the active operations of the removal may be made of them, (not to include the hauling of the waggons before mentioned) as the said John W.A. Sanford and Company their Heirs &c may deem proper; but that they will not be separated from the company to which their owners respectively are attached, nor compelled to carry other baggage or persons than those belonging to the family of their owners.

VIII. That the said John W.A. Sanford and Company their Heirs &c shall be entitled to Twenty dollars a head for each person transported from the Creek Nation to the place of delivery before mentioned; and for all persons who may die or be necessarily left on the way as authorized by article VI of this contract an amount in proportion to the distance travelled; provided that the evidence herein required in such cases, of arrival westward &c be furnished to the proper Department. The amount due to the said John W.A. Sanford and Company their Heirs &c to be paid promptly at such points as may be previously indicated by them and under instructions hereafter to be given by the War Department.

IX. That said John W.A. Sanford and Company their Heirs &c shall not coerce the Indians to remove; all threats and violence towards them being prohibited; and that they shall be treated by the said John W.A. Sanford and Company their Heirs &c, and by the Agents of the same with lenity, forbearance, and humanity.

X. That the United States will furnish the following Agents

1st A Superintendent whose duty it shall be to remain within the limits of the Creek Nation during the proper season for operations under this Contract, for the purpose of seeing that its stipulations are fulfilled by the parties thereto. He shall receive his instructions from the Commissary General of Subsistence and will not be accountable in any way for his Acts to the said John W.A. Sanford and Company their Heirs &c; and that such Superintendent shall decide whether fifty or Eighty or any intermediate number of Indians ought consistent with the health and comfort of the Indians to be assigned to Each waggon.

2d Two or more military agents one of whom shall accompany Each party west. The duties of these Agents shall be to attend particularly to the treatment received by the Indians; their Rations, Transportation; to remonstrate against any course of conduct on the part of the agents of the said John W.A. Sanford and Company, their Heirs &c, inconsistent with the letter and spirit of this contract; and to protest to the proper Department, and if a remedy can be found in a pecuniary expenditure to make it, which, if approved by the Secretary of War shall be deducted from the payments to be made under this contract to the said John W.A. Sanford and Company their Heirs &c.

3d A Surgeon for Each Emigrating party, whose duty shall be to attend to the sick thereof. He shall also be the arbiter in cases of differences of opinion between the Agents of the United States and of the said John W.A. Sanford and Company, relative to the quality of provisions, the time and place of issueing the same, and the time of starting and stoping on the daily travel; and he shall also decide whether invalids may be left on the way and take care that they are provided for agreeable to Article VI of this Contract; and enter upon the Roll the time and place of such occurrence with the date of decease of all Indians who may die on the route.

4th A Disbursing agent[16] in the new Creek country West of the Mississippi whose duty it shall (be) to receive the Indians as they arrive, to muster them and to certify upon the Roll presented to him by the agent of the said John W.A. Sanford and Company their Heirs &c, the result of that muster. Said muster to take place on the day of arrival, if practicable, at the point of destination. And that the said John W.A. Sanford and Company their Heirs &c shall render every facility to the aforesaid Superintendent, military, medical and Disbursing agents that may be necessary to enable them freely to attend to the duties of their several offices.

XI. That the said John W.A. Sanford and Company their Heirs &c will without delay, and within Sixty days from the date of this contract, commence active operations in the Creek Nation, Alabama: and by or before the first day of July next remove, to within the limits of the Creek Nation West, Five Thousand persons. And it is expressly understood that the rights of the said Sanford and Company their Heirs &c under this contract, so far as regards the removal of Indians from Alabama cease after the removal of Five Thousand Indians, or on the first day of July One Thousand Eight Hundred and Thirty Six; allowing afterwards due time for Indians, moved prior to that date, to reach the new country West.

XII. And it is further agreed that within the period specified in Article XI for the termination of this contract, whatever expence per head, in addition to that stipulated to be paid to said John W.A. Sanford and Company their Heirs &c, may be incurred by the United States shall be repaid to the United States by the said John W.A. Sanford and Company their Heirs &c and be recoverable by suit at law. And it is also hereby reserved to the United States to annul this contract to all intents at any time the aforesaid George Gibson may deem proper. But it is understood that the privilege guarantied in Section XI to the said John W.A. Sanford and Company their Heirs &c of time for the removal of those who start before the termination of the contract shall be extended to this case:

Provided and it is hereby understood by the contracting parties that all such matters as are merely in the nature of Regulations, and do not effect the pecuniary interest of the said John W.A. Sanford and Company their Heirs &c are saved to the United States; and that under all circumstances the United States have complete controul of their own officers and agents. And further that where infractions of this contract exist, they must be alledged by Either party at the time of their occurrence, and that no effect whatever is to be given hereafter to allegations not thus brought forward.

Geo Gibson C G S

Witnesses to the signature of George Gibson, Commissary General of Subsistence.
Wm. C. Easton. principal clk Ind Emg'rn[17]
Wm Brown, clk[18]

J.W.A. Sanford
Alfred Iverson
Jno D Howell
B. Marshall
Luther Blake

Stephen M Ingersoll

Witnesses to the signatures of

Edw'd Barnard
D Hudson Notary public.

(Copy)

Fifth Voluntary Party Muster Roll

Names listed in bold refer to the head of a family. Roll includes the number of family members traveling, the age range of the emigrants, and the number of slaves (if any). No town affiliations are noted on this muster roll. Roll found at SIAC, Agent (Page), Account (220), Year (1837), NARA; copy of roll found at LR, CAE, Roll 237, 655–57.

Osenubba Indians[19]

1. **Kotchar Tustunnuggee** 11 members consisting of 1 male of ten and under twenty-five, 1 male over fifty, 1 female of ten and under twenty-five, 1 female of twenty-five and under fifty, 4 male slaves, and 3 female slaves. In "remarks" section of muster roll is written "one born 2 miles [above] Fort Smith 29 Jany" 1836. Was a mile chief from Coweta (at Choloseparpkar or Kotchar Tustunnuggee's Town) who was granted a full reserve under the 1832 Treaty of Washington.[20]
2. **Che pi chee** 3 members consisting of 2 females under ten and 1 female of ten and under twenty-five.
3. **Tuskenehaw** 4 members consisting of 1 male over fifty, 2 females of ten and under twenty-five, and 1 female over fifty.
4. **Spar ne Fixico** 5 members consisting of 1 male under ten, 1 male of twenty-five and under fifty, 2 females under ten, and 1 female of ten and under twenty-five.
5. **McInia** 14 members consisting of 4 males under ten, 1 male of ten and under twenty-five, 1 male over fifty, 1 female of ten and under twenty-five, 1 female of twenty-five and under fifty, 2 male slaves, and 4 female slaves.
6. **Ko nip Harjo** 4 members consisting of 1 male of ten and under twenty-five, 1 male of twenty-five and under fifty, 1 female under ten, and 1 female of twenty-five and under fifty.
7. **Fixio lichee** 3 members consisting of 1 male of twenty-five and under fifty, 1 female of ten and under twenty-five, and 1 female over fifty.
8. **Fix Yoholo** 5 members consisting of 2 males under ten, 1 male of ten

and under twenty-five, 1 male of twenty-five and under fifty, and 1 female of twenty-five and under fifty.

9. **Cas iste Emathla** 6 members consisting of 1 male under ten, 1 male over fifty, 3 females under ten, and 1 female of twenty-five and under fifty.
10. **Whorth ligee** 1 member consisting of 1 male of twenty-five and under fifty.
11. **No coos Harjo** 7 members consisting of 1 male under ten, 1 male of twenty-five and under fifty, 1 male over fifty, 2 females under ten, 1 female of ten and under twenty-five, and 1 female of twenty-five and under fifty.
12. **Ar lok Emathla** 3 members consisting of 1 male over fifty, 1 female of ten and under twenty-five, and 1 female of twenty-five and under fifty.
13. **Lizzy Kennard** 12 members consisting of 1 female of ten and under twenty-five, 6 male slaves, and 5 female slaves. In "remarks" section of muster roll is written "1 Left for Ft. Gibson 230 miles from starting point." Deas's journal notes that Kennard left the party on 19 December 1835 and joined some of her friends who were traveling separately from the government-sponsored emigration.[21]
14. **Joseph Carr** 13 members consisting of 1 male under ten, 1 male of twenty-five and under fifty, 2 females under ten, 1 female of ten and under twenty-five, 4 male slaves, and 4 female slaves. Listed number 38 on 1832 Cusseta census (on Little Euchee Creek).
15. **Hannah Carr** 6 members consisting of 1 male under ten, 1 female of ten and under twenty-five, 1 male slave, and 3 female slaves.
16. **Paddy Carr's Negroes** 4 members consisting of 3 male slaves and 1 female slave. Born at Fort Mitchell, Alabama, in March 1807 (according to Harry F. O'Beirne and Edward S. O'Beirne), Carr was the son of an Irishman and a Cusseta woman but was raised by former Creek agent John Crowell. Carr was a controversial figure in the Creek Nation, and was noted for his "natural sagacity and shrewdness," which "was such that he obtained a great control over the Indian

people while yet a young man. Before he was thirty years of age, he had seventy or eighty negro slaves, besides landed property and a large stock of cattle and horses; especially race horses, for which he had a great partiality, frequently riding his own racers." Removal agent John B. Hogan, who later investigated the land frauds under the 1832 Treaty of Washington, noted that he was "as great a rogue as any in the nation." He worked as a land purchaser for the notorious Michael W. Perry & Company based in Columbus, Georgia, and no doubt, worked with other land speculators as well. Neah Emathla, a prominent Hitchiti headman and veteran of the First Seminole War and Second Creek War, claimed that Carr had personally stolen his reserve. Carr volunteered to fight alongside the Americans in the Second Seminole War and served with other the Creek volunteers under Captain John F. Lane. Of his service in Florida it was noted that he "fought well—He has generally headed the scouting parties, and has performed those laborious and dangerous duties with great promptitude and cheerfulness." He was discharged in 1837 and returned to Alabama, before voluntarily emigrating to Indian Territory in 1847. On his physical appearance and demeanor, Jacob Rhett Motte, an army surgeon who served in the Second Creek and Second Seminole Wars, wrote that "Paddy Carr is a half-breed Indian of dark complexion, about forty years of age [in 1836], five feet eight or nine inches, handsomely proportioned, and muscular in his person, very intelligent in conversation, and has no doubt received a good education. He speaks our language with fluency, is correct in his deportment, and rather polished in his manners."[22]

17. **Osia Harjo** 7 members consisting of 2 males of ten and under twenty-five, 1 male of twenty-five and under fifty, 1 male over fifty, 2 females under ten, and 1 female of twenty-five and under fifty.
18. **Ceezupee** 6 members consisting of 2 males under ten, 1 male of twenty-five and under fifty, 2 females under ten, and 1 female of ten and under twenty-five.
19. **Pin Harjo** 5 members consisting of 1 male of ten and under twenty-five, 1 male of twenty-five and under fifty, 2 females under ten, and 1 female of ten and under twenty-five.

20. **Corne Yoholo** 8 members consisting of 3 males under ten, 1 male of twenty-five and under fifty, 2 females under ten, 1 female of ten and under twenty-five, and 1 female of twenty-five and under fifty.

21. **So yar kar pee** 6 members consisting of 2 males under ten, 1 male of twenty-five and under fifty, 2 females under ten, and 1 female of twenty-five and under fifty.

22. **In clanis Harjo** 9 members consisting of 2 males under ten, 1 male of ten and under twenty-five, 2 males of twenty-five and under fifty, 1 male over fifty, 1 female of ten and under twenty-five, and 2 females of twenty-five and under fifty.

23. **Lin ti chee** 3 members consisting of 1 male of twenty-five and under fifty, 1 female under ten, and 1 female of ten and under twenty-five.

24. **Hie ker** 6 members consisting of 1 male of ten and under twenty-five, 1 male of twenty-five and under fifty, 2 females under ten, 1 female of ten and under twenty-five, and 1 female over fifty.

25. **Te ho po ye** 10 members consisting of 2 males under ten, 2 males of ten and under twenty-five, 3 males of twenty-five and under fifty, 1 female under ten, 1 female of twenty-five and under fifty, and 1 female over fifty.

26. **Capt. Tim ar lee** 6 members consisting of 1 male under ten, 1 male of twenty-five and under fifty, 1 female under ten, 1 female of ten and under twenty-five, and 2 females of twenty-five and under fifty.

27. **Otulkee Yoholo** 12 members consisting of 2 males under ten, 1 male of ten and under twenty-five, 2 males of twenty-five and under fifty, 1 male over fifty, 2 females under ten, 2 females of ten and under twenty-five, and 2 females over fifty.

28. **Chesser Harjo** 2 members consisting of 1 male of twenty-five and under fifty and 1 female of twenty-five and under fifty. In "remarks" section next to Otulke Yoholo (no. 27) is written "one born 50 miles below Little Rock A Ty 7th Jany" 1836, but the agents probably intended it for this family as the Indian territory muster roll shows 3 members with 1 male under ten added. Indian territory muster roll also shows 1 female over fifty and no female of twenty-five and under fifty.

29. **Fas hach Emathla** 5 members consisting of 1 male under ten, 1 male of twenty-five and under fifty, 2 females under ten, and 1 female of

twenty-five and under fifty. Indian territory muster roll shows 1 female over fifty and no female of twenty-five and under fifty.

30. **Che ban lustee** 4 members consisting of 1 male under ten, 1 male of ten and under twenty-five, 1 male of twenty-five and under fifty, and 1 female of ten and under twenty-five.
31. **Kowak ko gee Harjo** 1 member consisting of 1 male over fifty.
32. **Fas Harjo** 3 members consisting of 1 male of twenty-five and under fifty, 1 female under ten, and 1 female of twenty-five and under fifty.
33. **Miche kee** 6 members consisting of 1 male under ten, 2 males of twenty-five and under fifty, 1 female of ten and under twenty-five, 1 female of twenty-five and under fifty, and 1 female over fifty. Indian territory muster roll shows 1 female under ten and no female over fifty.
34. **Chofolwar** 3 members consisting of 1 male over fifty and 2 females of ten and under twenty-five. Indian territory muster roll shows one female over fifty, 2 male slaves, and no male over fifty or females of ten or under twenty-five.
35. **Sal ar yee** 4 members consisting of 1 male of twenty-five and under fifty, 1 female of twenty-five and under fifty, 1 female over fifty, and 1 male slave.
36. **Capt. Che was tie Micco** 6 members consisting of 1 male under ten, 1 male of ten and under twenty-five, 2 males of twenty-five and under fifty, 1 male over fifty, and 1 female of twenty-five and under fifty.
37. **Tim i lum ha** 4 members consisting of 2 males of ten and under twenty-five and 2 females of ten and under twenty-five.
38. **Yoholo gee** 5 members consisting of 1 male under ten, 1 male over fifty, 2 females of ten and under twenty-five, and 1 female over fifty.
39. **Yar top Harjo** 7 members consisting of 2 males under ten, 1 male of twenty-five and under fifty, 2 females under ten, 1 female of twenty-five and under fifty, and 1 female over fifty.
40. **Ene he Emathla** 4 members consisting of 1 male of ten and under twenty-five, 1 male over fifty, 1 female of ten and under twenty-five, and 1 female over fifty.
41. **Lucy Chatly** 3 members consisting of 1 male of ten and under twenty-five and 2 females of ten and under twenty-five.

42. **Viney Scott** 8 members consisting of 1 male under ten, 1 male of ten and under twenty-five, 1 male of twenty-five and under fifty, 2 females under ten, 1 female of ten and under twenty-five, 1 male slave, and 1 female slave.
43. **Capt. Charles Miller** 5 members consisting of 1 male under ten, 1 male of ten and under twenty-five, 1 male of twenty-five and under fifty, 1 female of twenty-five and under fifty, and 1 female over fifty. Possibly the husband of Nanny Miller, number 86 on the Thlakatchka (Horse Path Town) census. In "remarks" section of muster roll is written "19th Decr . . . an Indian woman joined 230 miles from her home Creek Nation" and "19th Decr Negro Woman the Slave of Nanny Miller Indian Joined 230 miles from" her home, Creek Nation.
44. **Cho bof Micco** 6 members consisting of 2 males under ten, 1 male of twenty-five and under fifty, 2 females under ten, and 1 female of twenty-five and under fifty.
45. **Tow ye hie per** 5 members consisting of 2 females under ten, 2 females of ten and under twenty-five, and 1 female over fifty.
46. **Cho kart kie** 6 members consisting of 1 male under ten, 1 male over fifty, 2 females under ten, 1 female of ten and under twenty-five, and 1 female over fifty.
47. **Hasper** 4 members consisting of 1 male of twenty-five and under fifty, 1 female under ten, 1 female of ten and under twenty-five, and 1 female over fifty.
48. **Fossee Emathla** 7 members consisting of 2 males under ten, 2 males of ten and under twenty-five, 1 male of twenty-five and under fifty, 1 female under ten, and 1 female of twenty-five and under fifty.
49. **No cos e ker** 7 members consisting of 1 male under ten, 2 males of ten and under twenty-five, 1 male over fifty, 2 females under ten, 1 female of twenty-five and under fifty.
50. **Tallassee Harjo** 3 members consisting of 1 male of twenty-five and under fifty, 1 male over fifty, and 1 female of ten and under twenty-five. A copy of the muster roll shows three members with 1 female under ten and no male over fifty.
51. **Tezikiah Harjo** 7 members consisting of 1 male under ten, 2 males of ten and under twenty-five, 1 male of twenty-five and under fifty,

1 male over fifty, 1 female of ten and under twenty-five, and 1 female over fifty.

52. **Ce ho ye** 4 members consisting of 2 males under ten, 1 male of twenty-five and under fifty, and 1 female of ten and under twenty-five.
53. **Wox e Harjo** 8 members consisting of 2 males under ten, 1 male of twenty-five and under fifty, 1 male over fifty, 2 females of ten and under twenty-five, 1 female of twenty-five and under fifty, and 1 female over fifty.
54. **Lime tut gar** 7 members consisting of 2 males under ten, 1 male of twenty-five and under fifty, 2 females under ten, 1 female of ten and under twenty-five, and 1 female of twenty-five and under fifty.
55. **Capt. No e tie** 6 members consisting of 1 male under ten, 1 male of ten and under twenty-five, 1 male over fifty, 2 females under ten, and 1 female of twenty-five and under fifty.
56. **Chobof Harjo** 7 members consisting of 1 male under ten, 2 males of twenty-five and under fifty, 3 females under ten, and 1 female of ten and under twenty-five.
57. **Holcobichee** 4 members consisting of 1 male under ten, 1 male of twenty-five and under fifty, 1 female under ten, and 1 female of ten and under twenty-five.
58. **Colloza** 2 members consisting of 1 female of ten and under twenty-five and 1 female over fifty.
59. **As ko yo ho gar** 6 members consisting of 1 male under ten, 1 male of ten and under twenty-five, 3 females under ten, and 1 female of ten and under twenty-five.
60. **Chiker** 3 members consisting of 1 male over fifty, 1 female of ten and under twenty-five, and 1 female over fifty.
61. **Thlock par ligee** 5 members consisting of 1 male of twenty-five and under fifty, 3 females under ten, and 1 female of ten and under twenty-five.
62. **Co chees Harjo** 8 members consisting of 1 male under ten, 2 males of ten and under twenty-five, 2 males of twenty-five and under fifty, 1 female under ten, 1 female of twenty-five and under fifty, and 1 female over fifty.
63. **Si ki as tee** 5 members consisting of 1 male under ten, 1 male of

twenty-five and under fifty, 1 female under ten, 1 female of ten and under twenty-five, and 1 female over fifty. In remarks section of muster roll is written "1 Killed on the 7th Decr 85 Miles from home." Deas's journal notes that on the morning of December 7 "a drunken quarrel took place among some of the Indians, when one of them, (Sikeastic) received a blow upon the head which fractured his scull & caused his death." He died that evening.[23]

64. **Chastie** 7 members consisting of 2 males under ten, 1 male of twenty-five and under fifty, 2 females under ten, 1 female of ten and under twenty-five, and 1 female of twenty-five and under fifty. Indian territory muster roll shows two males over fifty and no females under ten.
65. **Big Boy** 8 members consisting of 2 males under ten, 2 males of twenty-five and under fifty, 1 male over fifty, 1 female under ten, 1 female of ten and under twenty-five, 1 female of twenty-five and under fifty.
66. **Black Dirt** 5 members consisting of 1 male of ten and under twenty-five, 2 females under ten, 1 female of ten and under twenty-five, and 1 female over fifty. Also known as Fuckte Lustee, number 50 on the Thlakatchka or Broken Arrow/Wetumpka census (on Euchee Hatchee).
67. **Scott** 10 members consisting of 3 males under ten, 1 male of ten and under twenty-five, 2 males of twenty-five and under fifty, 2 females of ten and under twenty-five, 1 female of twenty-five and under fifty, and 1 female over fifty.
68. **Sparney Micco** 8 members consisting of 1 male under ten, 1 male of ten and under twenty-five, 4 males of twenty-five and under fifty, 1 female of ten and under twenty-five, and 1 female of twenty-five and under fifty.
69. **James Marshall** 14 members consisting of 1 male of ten and under twenty-five, 1 male over fifty, 1 female of ten and under twenty-five, 1 female of twenty-five and under fifty, 4 male slaves, and 6 female slaves. Listed as number 5 on 1832 Coweta census (Toosilkstookee Hatchee Town) census.
70. **Billy** 1 member consisting of 1 male over fifty.
71. **William Marshall** 27 members consisting of 2 males of ten and under twenty-five, 1 male of twenty-five and under fifty, 12 male slaves, and 12 female slaves. Listed as number 3 on 1832 Coweta census (Toosilk-stookee Hatchee Town).

72. **David Derisaw Sr.** 5 members consisting of 2 males under ten, 1 male of twenty-five and under fifty, 1 male over fifty, and 1 female of ten and under twenty-five. Father of David Derasaw Jr. (no. 76, this roll). In "remarks" section of muster roll is written "one born on 1st Feby 5½ miles from Ft. Gibson."
73. **Benjamin Marshall** 36 members consisting of 1 male of twenty-five and under fifty, 17 male slaves, and 18 female slaves. In "remarks" section of muster roll is written "one male Slave died 22 Decr 280 miles from starting Point, C Nation."[24]
74. **Lucy** 1 member consisting of 1 female of twenty-five and under fifty.
75. **Paskofar** 8 members consisting of 2 males of ten and under twenty-five,1 male of twenty-five and under fifty, 1 male over fifty, 1 female under ten, 2 females of ten and under twenty-five, and 1 female over fifty.
76. **David Derisaw Jr.** 16 members consisting of 4 males under ten, 1 male of ten and under twenty-five, 2 males of twenty-five and under fifty, 1 male over fifty, 2 females under ten, 4 females of ten and under twenty-five, 1 female of twenty-five and under fifty, and 1 female over fifty. Son of David Derasaw Sr. (no. 72, this roll).
77. **Kar pitch Yoholo** 6 members consisting of 1 male over fifty, 4 females under ten, and 1 female of twenty-five and under fifty.
78. **Oke chun Harjo** 1 member consisting of 1 male of twenty-five and under fifty.
79. **Ewoddy** 2 members consisting of 1 female of ten and under twenty-five and 1 female slave.

Daily Journal of the Fifth Voluntary Party

This is a journal kept by Lieutenant Edward Deas describing the daily progress of the party. It was the first journal of the Creek removal era and would be a standard practice for military agents going forward. Journal found at CGS-IRW, Roll 6, 33–55.

Rec'd March 25

Journal of Occurrences on the route of a Party of Emigrating Creek Indians, kept by Lieut. Edw Deas Disbursing Agent in the Creek Emigration.

6th December 1835.

The first Party of Indians about to Emigrate to Arkansaw under the direction of J.W.A. Sanford and Co'y were to-day mustered & Enrolled at the Encampment 4 miles N.W. from Wetumpka Alabama, in the presence of Major Blue[25] the Acting Superintendent of the Removal, & myself and their numbers found to be Five hundred and Eleven. In consequence of this, and the Contractors having to make some arrangements for the necessary means of Transportation no progress has been made upon the route to-day.

7th December

The Party started this morning at 8 o'clock & has come to-day about 17 miles upon the road leading in the direction of Montevallo Alaba'a. The means of Transportation provided is of such quality, & in the quantity required by the Contract.

Before starting this morning a drunken quarrel took place among some of the Indians, when one of them, (Sikiastic)[26] received a blow upon the head which fractured his scull & caused his death this evening after the Party had encamped. It is thought that the man who struck him had no intention of killing him and will probably be pardoned.[27] Nothing else of importance has occurred through the day, the weather has been fine & the roads are now in very good order.

8th December

We have come to-day 16 miles without any occurrence worthy of notice. The Party started about 8 o'clock & stopped for the night a little after 4. P.M. The weather still fine and the roads very good. This being the case we are able to travel rather more than the avarage of 12 miles a day, but it is understood that when the weather becomes bad & the roads muddy the rate of travelling will be diminished accordingly. Since I have joined the Indians I have carefully attended to the quantity & quality of the Rations and have seen them issued agreeably to the Contract. The provisions so far have consisted of Corn & Fresh Beef.

9th December

We started this morning about 8 o'clock as usual & stopped for the night and encamped between 4 & 5 P.M. after travelling about 16 miles. The weather and roads still good. Nothing of consequence has occurred through the day.

10th December

The Party started this morning between 8 & 9 o'clock and passed through Montevallo in the forenoon. After travelling about 18 miles without any occurrence of importance we stopped & encamped between 4 & 5 o'clock P.M., about 8 miles north of Montevallo.

11th December

It rained last night and the roads to-day have not been so good as heretofore. The Party started between 8 & 9 o'clock this morning and encamped this afternoon between 4 & 5 after travelling about eleven miles. Forded the Cahawba River in the forenoon.

12th December

The Party started at ½ past 8 o'clock this morning, the weather rainy and the roads muddy. Passed through Elyton in the middle of the day and encamped in the afternoon three miles further on at 4 o'clock after travelling about 13 miles in all. Up to this time the Party has been healthy and nothing of consequence has occurred upon our route besides what has been mentioned.

13th December

No progress has been made to-day in consequence of delay upon the part of some of the Wagoners who remained at Elyton yesterday for repairs, & were expected to come up this morning early. They have been discharged by the Agent and others engaged in their stead.

14th December

The Party started this morning at ½ past 8 o'clock and has travelled about

16 miles to the south bank of the Black Warrior River and encamped about 4 in the afternoon. The weather still fine & the roads good.

15th December

The Party started to-day at ½ past 8 o'clock A.M. crossed the Mulberry fork of the Black Warrior & travelled about 15 miles further and crossed another fork of the same stream.[28] The roads were in good order but hilly. Encamped between 4 & 5 o'clock in the afternoon, without any occurrence worthy of notice.

16th December

We started this morning at the usual hour between 8 & 9 o'clock and travelled about 15 miles to Harris' on another Fork of the Black Warrior, crossed it and encamped for the night about 4 o'clock P.M. The roads to-day were hard and good and tolerably level.

The Route selected by the Contractors for the Emigration of this Party is somewhat longer than that passing lower down through Tuscaloosa.

This has been preferred in consequence of its being generally in better order at this season of the year than the lower route.

17th December

There was a little delay in starting this morning in consequence of engaging another six horse team of Mr. Harris, which required some preparation. The Party started about ½ past 9 o'clock and travelled over level and good roads 17 miles to Day's. Encamped about ½ past 4 P.M. Thus far the progress of the Party has met with no impediment. The weather has been fine the roads good & the people healthy. Provisions of proper quality and quantity have been issued regularly agreeably to the Contract for removing the Indians, under my observation.

18th December

The Party left Day's this morning about 8 o'clock and proceeded 12 miles to the west Fork of Flint Creek and encamped at 4 o'clock in the afternoon. The roads were muddy having passed through low swampy ground. Meal was issued to-day for the first time, this being the only opportunity of procuring it since starting. Two days issue was procured at a mill in the neighbourhood of the Camp.

19th December

The Party started from Flint Creek this morning about 8 o'clock & has since come 18 miles and encamped between 4 & 5 o'clock P.M.

We passed through Moulton in the middle of the day which is ten miles back. The distance travelled to-day has been rather greater than was intended but after leaving the neighbourhood of Moulton, no water was met with until reaching the present place of Encamping. The roads were fine and level. An Indian woman named Ewoddy and one female Slave joined the Party to-day. Lizzy Connard also left the Party and proceeded with some of her friends who passed on their way to Arkansaw.[29]

20th December

The Party left the Encampment this morning at ½ past 8 o'clock a good deal of rain fell last night and the roads to-day have been muddy. It rained also through the day.

The direct road from Moulton to Tuscumbia being impossible[30] at present, we have been obliged to take that through Courtland which place we passed in the middle of the day.[31]

After travelling 12 miles encamped for the night. One of Ben Marshall's negro boys is very ill, but not much sickness otherwise up to this time.

21st December

Left the Encampment about 8 o'clock this morning & travelled about 14 miles to within one mile of Tuscumbia & encamped. The roads through the first part of the day were muddy but afterwards were much better.

Provisions have still been issued regularly and I hear of no complaints among the People upon any subject.

22nd December

The Party has not left the vicinity of Tuscumbia to-day. The Contractors having heard very unfavourable accounts of the state of the roads from this to Memphis and west of the Mississippi have determined to take water from this place and have made arrangements for suitable Boats for that purpose.

The state of the water in the Tennessee and other intermediate rivers is said to be good at present and it is probable we shall get through the journey sooner and more to the comfort of the Indians in this manner than by continueing to travel by land. The Party has been moved to-day to the Steam Boat landing ready to start tomorrow. Ben Marshall's negro boy who has been sick for some time back died to-day.

23rd December

The People during the fore part of the day were engaged in putting their baggage and small wagons on board the Boats, a Steam Boat and two Keels which are to convey them to Waterloo thirty miles below at the foot of the shoals where an exchange of boats is to take place. The Indian Ponies & Horses were also collected and a sufficient number of volenteers from the Party to take charge of them set out about noon for Memphis by land, accompanied by two Agents of the Company. In the afternoon the Boats left the wharf with the remainder of the Party and came twenty miles down the Tennessee River where we are now encamped for the night.

24th December

The Party started again this morning at 9 o'clock on board the two Keel Boats and came down to Waterloo by noon, where we expected to find the Steam Boat Wheeling which was supposed at Tuscumbia to be at this place. The Party is now encamped just above the town and the Agents are making arrangements to proceed as speedily as possible.

25th December

The Agents of the Company made arrangements with the Steam Boat Alpha[32] to convey the Party from Waterloo to Fort Gibson in case the water in the intermediate Rivers will permit. The Party accordingly came on board in the forenoon and about 12 o'clock we proceeded on our way. Two Keel boats of nearly the largest size are also employed and have been put in good order for the comfort and health of the Indians. It is intended to stop at night allowing the People time for Encamping, preparing their food &c. We have come to day about 30 miles below Waterloo and landed accordingly. The Indians appear well pleased so far with this mode of travelling and appear to be well satisfied in all respects.

26th December

The Boats with the Party on board started this morning at 8 o'clock and have come to-day about 60 miles and encamped for the night between 4 & 5 P.M.

The Contractors have been engaged in putting up temporary Cooking Hearths on the decks of the Keel Boats to enable the people to prepare their food through the day, and keep themselves warm when the weather requires it. This has not been the case as yet the weather having been remarkably mild. Other necessary fixtures have also been constructed to preserve cleanliness and pure air in the interior of the Boats.

27th December

The Party came on board the Boats this morning after day light and we are still running and shall do so through the night in order to reach Paduca at the mouth of the Tennessee River tomorrow morning. I have consulted the surgeon upon the propriety of running through the night, who has no objection and the Indians have also expressed to me their satisfaction with the arrangement, all appearing desirous of getting on as speedily as possible when the health and comfort of none is interfered with.

Provisions of Fresh Beef and Corn meal have been issued since leaving Tuscumbia.

28th December

The Boats arrived near Paduca at the mouth of the Tennessee River this morning at 9 o' clock and the greater part of the Indians were landed on an Island in the vicinity of the town.[33] During the day the contractors have been engaged in procuring provisions, & the Captain of the S. Boat in making preparations to proceed. It being nearly dark before these were compleated, we have decided not to move the Indians from their camps until tomorrow morning. The Steam Boat has been brought over to the Island the Keels lashed and every thing put in readiness to make an early start.

29th December

The Boats with the Party on board started this morning shortly after day light and have come to-day about 75 miles and have stopped for the night about 20 miles below the mouth of the Ohio River. The Contractors purchased to-day a few issues of Salt Pork which will be issued with the Fresh Beef the Indians preferring it so. The Party still continues healthy and the weather up to this time has been mild for the season.

30th December

The Party came on board the Boats this morning at ½ past 8 o'clock since when we have travelled without interruption. The weather to day has been remarkably fine and mild so that we have determined to run through the night and expect to reach Memphis in the morning.

31st December

We reached Memphis this morning about 9 o'clock, and landed the Party opposite the town, to prevent the Indians if possible from having access to liquor which always creates more difficulty amongst them than any other cause.

The Party having charge of the Ponies has also arrived and the operation of bringing them across the Mississippi was finished this afternoon near dark. All the People who accompanied them have arrived without accident, but the case is different with regard to the Horses and Ponies. One hundred & fifty-four of these started from Tuscumbia and only one hundred & thirty-two have crossed the Mississippi.

This loss the Agent who accompanied them informed me was owing to a want of sufficient Forage, the allowance of two quarts of corn each not being enough to support them. I found however that the rate of travelling from Tuscumbia to Memphis had more than doubled that laid down in the Contract, and I therfore stated to the Agent of the

Company, that it was my opinion that when the avarage rate of travelling was exceeded, the amount of Forage should be increased by them in proportion and that unless it was their intention to do so, I objected to the Ponies being obliged to travel more than an avarage of 12 miles a day. After some discussion my proposition was acceeded to and directions were accordingly given that for the future four quarts of corn should be issued instead of two, as it is expected they will probably travel between 20 & 30 miles a day. Nothing else of importance has occurred through the day & every thing is in readiness to start as usual in the morning.

1st January 1836.

We left our stopping place opposite Memphis this morning at 9 o'clock and have since run without interruption and shall continue to do so through the night. The Party with the Ponies were also assembled opposite the town at the same time ready to proceed west through the Mississippi Swamp.

2nd January

We reached the mouth of White River this morning about 6 o'clock and stopped a short time to procure Provisions Wood &c.[34] The Boats then entered the mouth of White River passed through the cut-off into the Arkansas and are now lying by for the night about 40 miles above its mouth. The Boats stopped between 4 & 5 o'clock in the afternoon and the weather being rainy many of the People prefer remaining on board to going on shore and encamping.

3rd January

The Party started this morning shortly after day light and has since come about 40 miles and stopped for the night between 4 & 5 o'clock P.M. Nothing of importance has occurred through the day.

4th January 1836.

The Boats were got under way this morning between 6 & 7 o'clock and nothing of consequence has since occurred. We stopped in the afternoon near 5 o'clock having come about 40 miles and some of the People have gone on shore and made their Camps the others prefer remaining on board. The weather has been remarkably mild since leaving Memphis and only one day of rain. Provisions have been issued regularly and the Party is still healthy.

5th January

The Party started this morning about 7 o'clock since when we have come something over 40 miles and stopped for the night at 5 o'clock, nothing of consequence has occurred through the day.

6th January

We started this morning between 6 & 7 o'clock as usual and nothing of consequence has since occurred. After coming between 40 & 50 miles the boats were landed at 5 o'clock for the night. There has been a little rain at intervals through the day, but the weather is at present good and remarkably mild for the season, as it has been since leaving Tuscumbia.

7th January

The Party started as usual this morning between 6 & 7 o'clock and has since come about 40 miles and stopped for the night at 5 o'clock. A Child was born to-day 50 miles below Little Rock but nothing else of any consequence has occurred.

8th January

The Boats got under way this morning about 7 o'clock, and we have come to-day between 30 & 40 miles. We passed Little Rock in the afternoon without stopping and are now a few miles above that place.

The small Boat was sent on shore at the town for a few minutes, but it is always a disadvantage to allow the Indians to stop at any place where they can obtain liquor.[35]

The most peaceable and apparently well disposed when sober sometimes become the most refractory and troublesome when intoxicated. There are some examples of this with the present Party.

9th January

The Boats started as usual this morning after day light, and in the middle of the day it was necessary to stop several hours for the purpose of cutting wood which could not be found at the landings. In consequence we have come only about 22 or 23 miles. The Party was landed for the night between 4 & 5 o'clock this afternoon.

10th January

We got under way this morning about 7 o'clock and have since come between 30 & 40 miles and stopped for the night.

In the afternoon a Pilot was taken on board with wose assistance it was thought we should be able to run in the night without any risk but after doing so a short time after dark one of the Keels struck a snag[36] and sprung a leak in consequence of which it was found necessary to land for the night.

11th January

The Party did not start this morning until 11 o'clock in consequence of delay occasioned by having to leave the Boat which last night sprung a leak. We have since come between 20 & 30 miles and stopped for the night before dark. There was hard rain last night, but the weather is still very mild for the season of the year.

12th January

The Boats were got under way this morning shortly after day light as usual & have since come between 40 & 50 miles without any occurrence of importance and stopped for the night before dark. It is impossible to tell the exact distance travelled upon this river as no two persons agree upon this point. The weather is still mild and very fine and the People continue healthy. Provisions have also been issued regularly up to this time under my observation.

13th January

We started this morning as usual shortly after day light but after running six miles were so unfortunate as to run upon a sand-bar which extended across the river. They were unable to get the Boats off until near dark when the Party was landed and encamped for the night. The Party with the Ponies also arrived within a quarter of a mile of this place this afternoon in good condition. This is the first time we have heard of them since leaving Memphis. Nothing worthy of notice has occurred upon their way here and it has only been necessary to leave three of the Ponies upon the road, which were placed in charge of persons who will take care of them until the next Party passes.

14th January

The Boats started this morning about 7 o'clock and we have since come 40 miles without interruption. We stopped a short time in the forenoon to take in Fresh Beef & stores and landed a little before dark for the night.

15th January

The Boats started again this morning as usual about 7 o'clock but after running ten miles struck a Sand-Bar which detained us until near dark when the Boats were seperated and thus enabled to reach the shore, and the Party was encamped for the night. The weather still continues fine & mild and the People healthy.

16th January

A new Pilot was taken on Board this morning but we were not able to get fairly started until 11 o'clock on account of the Sand-Bars and have since come about 25 or 30 miles and stopped for the night before dark.[37]

17th January

We have been very unfortunate for the last week in running upon Sand-bars in consequence of the low state of the water. No accident however affecting the Indians has occurred. The Party has only come 5 or 6 miles to-day on account of the Rapids in the neighbourhood though it was found necessary to tow the Boats after seperating them, all the People who could walk without injury were landed for this purpose.

18th January

The Party has made no progress to-day in consequence of the difficulty of getting the Boats through the shoals. The Steam-Boat was unlashed from the Keel this morning & passed through the Rapids, but the Keel was not got through until near dark when all the People were carried to the north bank of the river and encamped for the night. There has been no regular issue of corn to-day. I spoke to the Agent upon the subject, who said it was impossible to obtain it to-night there being none in the neighbourhood but that he can obtain a supply in the morning a few miles above.[38] Had the proper means been made use of through the day it might have been obtained before night. I have spoken to the Chief Cotchy-tustenugga[39] upon the subject, who thinks there is enough surplus among the Indians to keep them from suffering until to-morrow.

19th January

The Boats started this morning after day light and after running two hours came to a wood landing where corn was obtained for two days and some surplus to make up for the deficientcy of yesterday. We have since only come between 20 & 30 miles in consequence of running upon another Sand-Bar this afternoon at 3 o'clock. Every exertion was made to get off until dark without unlashing the Keel but failed. This has since been done at 8 o'clock and carried to the north bank of the river and landed with nearly the whole of the Party. The Steam-Boat still remains fast upon the Bar with some of the People on Board.

20th January

We have made no progress to-day the whole of the time having been employed until dark in getting the S-Boat off the Sand-bar which at last was done. We progress but slowly on our way, but there is no remedy at present and provisions being plentiful and the weather fine, the Indians appear comfortable and satisfied. This River at low water is obstructed by numerous Bars which are constantly changing and without an experienced Pilot the navigation of it is extremely uncertain.

21st January

We have only come 12 miles to-day and are now in the vicinity of the small town of Van Buren. It was necessary to stop several hours in the middle of the day to procure provisions of Corn & Fresh Beef. The Boats started at 9 o'clock A.M. and stopped a short time before dark.

22nd January

The Boats left the neighbourhood of Van Buren this morning about ½ past 7 o'clock and passed Fort Smith about eleven.[40] After proceeding about 2½ miles above the latter place we were stopped by another Sand-Bar which it was found impossible to pass. The People were therefore landed and Encamped about two miles above Fort Smith, on the north Bank of the River. The weather to-day for the first time has been tolerably cold.

23rd January

As it is impossible to go any further up the Arkansas by Steam, the Agent of the Contractors is now making preparations to proceed by land. The Party still remains encamped as yesterday. It was acertained at Fort Smith that the Party with the Ponies and horses had passed on up towards Fort Gibson about a week ago. A messenger was therfore sent for them to-day to return to this place. There has been some misunderstanding upon this point. The Agent informed me that he had given directions for them to encamp near Fort Smith until the Boats arrived there fearing as has been the case that we should be unable to go the whole distance by water. They are also making arrangements for Wagons in the neighbourhood to proceed as speedily as possible. The weather still continues cold though not very severe.

24th January

Another messenger was despatched to day for the return of the Ponies in order to prevent mistakes and as soon as they arrive and the wagons are procured the Party will proceed. Nothing of consequence has occurred through the day, the People continue healthy and Provisions have been issued regularly up to this time. The weather is still cold but dry.

25th January

The Party remains encamped as yesterday. Wagons have been engaged and are expected in, tomorrow or the day after. Nothing of consequence has occurred through the day. The weather is still cold.

26th January

Five ox-wagons arrived at the Camp to-day and the others will be in tomorrow. The first messenger that was despatched to Fort Gibson returned this afternoon, having seen the Agent in charge of the Ponies. They had crossed over into the Creek nation but will be here by day after to-morrow when we shall be able to proceed on our journey.

27th January

The Party is still encamped near Fort Smith awaiting the return of the Horses from Fort Gibson. The remaining Wagons have arrived at the Camp and every thing is in readiness to proceed as soon as the Ponies and horses get back.

28th January

The Horses & Ponies arrived this afternoon & the Party will proceed in the morning. The weather is fine but cold. A child was born in Cotchy-tustynugga's family. Nothing else of any consequence has occurred through the day.

29th January

The Party started this morning between 9 & 10 o'clock. Ten Wagons are engaged as follows—Three with six oxen; Four with four oxen, one with four oxen & one horse, one with four horses, and one with six mules besides the small wagons belonging to the Indians. One light four-horse wagon was also engaged after the Party had started to convey the family & baggage of a sick woman who was unable to set out; on her account with the rest of the Party. This wagon overturned in the course of the day, but no serious injury was done. We are now encamped Eight miles from Fort Smith. The Party stopped at 5 o'clock.

30th January

The Party started this morning at 8 o'clock, and has come without interruption or any occurrence of consequence to within one mile of Salasaw Creek. The weather is still fine but cold. The Party continues healthy and Provisions have been issued agreeably to the Contract up to this time.

31st January

The Party started this morning at ½ past 8 o'clock and has come 16 miles & is now encamped at Mackey's 18 miles from Fort Gibson. The weather to-day for the first time has been severely cold, but the roads since leaving Fort Smith have been in very good order. The Party stopped this afternoon at 4 o'clock.

1st February 1836.

The Party left Mackey's this morning at ½ past 8' o'clock and crossed the Illinois R. by fording. They are now encamped 3½ miles east of Fort Gibson, having come 14½ miles to-day, and stopped in the afternoon between 3 & 4 o'clock. A child was born this afternoon at the Encampment nothing else of any consequence has occurred. The weather is still very fine and not so cold as yesterday.

2nd February

The Party started this morning at 9 o'clock and reached Fort Gibson between 10 & 11. There being but one Flat at the Garrison Ferry, it was near dark before the whole were crossed over the Grand River. They are now encamped on the east bank of the Verdigris River, one of the boundaries of the Creek Nation, four miles west of Fort Gibson.

3rd February

The Party was to-day mustered in the presence of Capt J. R. Stephenson,[41] the Agent of the Company, and myself and the greater part of them crossed over the Verdigris River. The Indians have stated that they do not wish to be taken any further than the west bank of the Verdigris, at which point Capt— Stephenson accordingly receives them.

4th February 1836.

The remainder of the Party was put over the Verdigris River to-day and Captain Stephenson has commenced subsisting them from this date. The Rolls have been signed agreeably to instructions and that of the Contractors and my own were found to agree in all respects.

In the foregoing Journal every occurrence of any importance has been mentioned that has taken place under my observation upon the Route, from the time the Party of Indians left the Creek Nation Alabama, until they were to-day received by Capt— J. R. Stephenson in the new Country west of Fort Gibson, the 4th February 1836.

Edw— Deas
2nd Lieut. and
Disb'g Agent in the Creek Emigration

Supplemental Letters of the Fifth Voluntary Party

In this letter to President Andrew Jackson, Eufaula headman Yoholo Micco (one of the ninety principal chiefs of the Creek Nation) and several lesser leaders lament the loss of their sovereignty and request of the president that Dr. John Scott (a notorious land speculator) conduct their party west in 1835. Letter found at CGS-IRW, Roll 5, 782.

Referred by War Dpt:
21st Sept.

State of alabama August 27th 1835

To our father the President

We as a Nation and a people that have once enjoyed our own laws and privileges, and who could once meet at our own town houses and there settle our own business and no man there to disturb us.

Our [illegible] were then our own, our [illegible] were then our own, and our children obedient to our commands.

But these days are now gone. Our privileges as a nation in this country forever lost and we as a people in great trouble. Our country is now full of bad white men. Our property we dare not call our own. The land we had given us by the last treaty though unwilling to Sell it ourselves, is often stolen from us by bad white men and bad indians while we are at home with our little families, and before we know it our homes are taken from us and we left to sufer. Now convinced that we must go to the new home provided for us in the west by our father the President. Our last petition is, that our father the President will give Dr John S. Scott[42] for our agent to see us safe to our western homes, as we all know him, and have long known him to take a deep interest in our welfare. Your compliance with our last request will be thankfully received and the request of our father the president faithfully complied with.

Yoholo Micco	Eufawlee town	Tommy Yoholo	Oaktarsarsey
John Smith	Hillabee	Fe go cithly	Fish Pond
Cle Chum hadjo	Fish Pond	Charley	Fish Pond
Sandy Greison	Oakfusky	Osar hadjo	Fish Pond
Jim Lurney	Fish Pond	Rachael Spiller	Oakfusky
Hillabbee Hadjo	Fish Pond	Walter Greison Senr[43]	Oakfusky

☾

Major Uriah Blue reports on the consolidation of some of the emigrating camps and that only about 500 Creeks will make the trip to Indian territory. Letter found at CGS-IRW, Roll 5, 239.

Rec'd 11 Decr

Tuskeegee Dec'r 1st 1835
Genl. Geo. Gibson

Sir,

When Col. Hogan left the nation, he left me as his representative, and I have been making my regular reports to him; but it was his intention that I should make them until his return direct to your Department, and sent me written instruction to that effect, but in consequence, of my being up in the Cusetaw Town attending to the Indian encampment there, and out of the way of any Post office;—I never received his instructions until my arrival at this place yesterday—under those instructions, I make this my first report.—

Ben. Marshall, started from Joe Marshall's old place on the 24th of last month to the encampment in Tallapoosa County, in the vicinity of the Fish Ponds, Kialijah, Hilabies; and Osolonimie[44] Towns there, to await until the Cusetaws come up;—I left them on Sunday morning last and they were to strike tents that afternoon, and be off—I am now on my way to the Tallapoosa encampment and shall await, there until they all get together and have them properly enrolled and turn them over to Lieut. Deas who will have charge of them on the march—I am looking for Col. Hogan every day;—If he does not arrive by the time I get the Indians enrolled, I shall then make a full report of the party;—Ben Marshall's party amounts to about 160.—one half blacks—The Cusetaw to 200—and I think the party in Tallapoosa will not exceed 150 or 200—I think 500—will be a fair estimate of the party that will emigrate this winter.—

Respectfully Y'r Ob't Serv't
U. Blue
Ass't Emg't Agent

☾

Major Uriah Blue reports that he had to move the emigrating party out of

Tallapoosa County and into Autauga County, Alabama, in order to avoid the whiskey shops nearby. Blue also seeks clarity on whether Dr. Burton Randall will accompany the party or not. Letter found at CGS-IRW, Roll 5, 236–37.

Rec'd 21 Dec

Tuskeegee Dec'b 6th 1835

Gen'l George Gibson

Sir

In my last report I calculated on enrolling the emigrating party of Indians in Tallapoosa County, where all the parties were to Join but I found it impossible to get a correct roll while in the nation in the vicinity of so many grog shops, & as they expected more to join near Wetumpka, I determined to accompany them out of the nation and get them out of the way of those grog shops, then halt & Enroll them, which I did after crossing the Coosa at Wetumpka, and going about four miles in Autaugua County; I stood by and Counted the number in each family as they was brought up and enroll'd the whole party amounting to 511—The party is conducted by Doc'tr Ingersol on the part of the Contractors & Lieu't Deas as the Agent of the Government, they appear to be well supplied with Transportation and goes on well. Doc'tr Ingersol shews every disposition to fullfill the contract. Doc'tr Randol shew'd me a letter from your department refering him to Co'lo Hogan as to the propriety of his being permited not to accompany the present Emigrating party. The Contract requires that the goverment should furnish a Doc'tr to each party, and if any differance should arrise between the Contractor & the goverment agent as to the provisions, the Doc'tr is made the arbitrator I therefore thought it proper he should continue—Co'lo Hogan has not yet joined but is looked for daily—The muster roll will shew the number in each family.—

Verry respectfully
Y'r ob't Serv't

U. Blue ass't agent
& act'g Super Intendant

☾

Writing from the new general rendezvous site in Autauga County, Alabama, near Wetumpka, Lieutenant Edward Deas updates the commissary general of subsistence on the progress of enrolling the Creeks and other clerical matters. Letter found at CGS-IRW, Roll 5, 318–20.

Rec'd 21 Decr

Encampment of Indians, four
miles N. West of Wetumpka Aa.
6th December 1835.

To, General George Gibson
Commissary Gen'l of Subsis.

General,

I have the honor herewith to forward a Statement of Letters received & written on the Indian Emigration for the month of November last made out as near the form as I remember, having by mistake left the Blanks furnished me at Fort Mitchell. This is the earliest opportunity, I have had of doing so since the first of the month not before having been in the vicinity of a Post office.

On the 11th of last month I received a letter from the Superintendent of the Removal Col. Hogan assigning me to the first party of the Emigrants that should go west as military Agent on the part of the Government. About the same time I was informed by the Contractors at Columbus that a Party was in preparation to move & would probably assemble at Young's Ferry[45] on the Talapoosa River about the 22nd of last month. On the 13th therefore I left Fort Mitchell for the purpose of joining them proceeding first to Montgomery to obtain the Funds turned over to me by Capt. Page that might become necessary on the route West. On the 23rd of last month I reached one of the points of Assembling the Indians and have accompanied them since that time. On the 2nd of this month about Five hundred coming from different points met near Young's Ferry on the Talapoosa which is about thirty miles from this place & on the next day the whole under the direction of the Agent of the Contractors proceeded on their way to Wetumpka which place we passed through yesterday & encamped here in the afternoon. As the Contractors expected that the number of Indians would increase until the Party left the nation the enrollment of them did not take place until to day. Major Blue has been directed by the Superintendent to see this properly attended to, & will I presume Sign & forward the Roll to-morrow. Since joining the party of Emigrants I have carefully attended to the Issue of Provisions, the comfort & proper treatment of the Indians, & such other duties as have been assigned to me. Thus far nothing of particular importance has occurred upon the route the Indians appear well satisfied & every disposition has been evinced upon the part of the Company to comply with the Conditions of the Contract.

When any thing of interest occurs upon the way I will of course communicate it by the earliest opportunity.

My Instructions direct that the Abstracts for any Disbursements I may have occasion to make, shall be signed by the Superintendent & by Capt. Page. I therefore request to be informed whether my Accounts shall be forwarded at the end of the Quarter or whether I shall await until my return from the West, to submit my Accounts for the signatures of those officers.

A letter directed to me at Memphis, after the receipt of this will have time to reach there before our arrival at that place.

I am Sir, Respectfully
Your Obe't Servant
Edw— Deas
2nd Lieut &
Disbur'g Agent
Creek Emigration

(

Deas reports that the party has arrived near Tuscumbia, Alabama, by the "northern route"—through Elyton and Moulton—rather than through Tuscaloosa. Deas also acknowledges that one Creek man died during a drunken fight with other members of the party. Letter found at CGS-IRW, Roll 5, 307–09.

Rec'd 6 Jany

Encampment of Indians one mile west
of Tuscumbia Alaba'a 21st Dec'r 1835.

To,
General George Gibson
Commissary Gen'l of Subsis'ce

General,

I have the honour to state that the Party of Emigrating Creek Indians to which I am attached, arrived & encamped at this place this afternoon. On the 6th of this month I had the honour to address you from near Wetumpka, giving an account of the progress of the Party up to that time. On the 7th ins't the Indians having been mustered & enrolled proceeded on the way to Memphis in the direction of Montevallo, the contractors preferring what is called the northern route through Elyton, Moulton, & Tuscumbia, on account of the roads being generally at this season, better than that which was taken last year through Tuscaloosa, although the latter is somewhat shorter. up to this time nothing of particular importance has occurred upon our way—the weather has been uncommonly fine & the roads consequently very good. This being the case the party has been enabled to travel rather more than the avarage of 12 miles a day, but of course when the weather becomes bad & the roads muddy, the rate of travelling will be diminished accordingly.

As yet I have had no occasion to remonstrate upon any subject with the Agent of the Contractors. The means of Transportation & subsistence have been of the proper kind, & in the quantity required by the Contract. The rations have been issued regularly under my observation, and have consisted of Beef & Corn with the exception of three days, when meal was issued instead of the latter. I purchased before starting such medicines as Dr. Randall required, but up to this time few cases of sickness have occurred & it has not been necessary to leave any upon the route from that cause.

An unfortunate quarrel took place upon the 7th ins't amongst some of the Indians whilst intoxicated, which resulted in the death of one of them. This however was supposed to be accidental, or rather unintentional, in consequence of which the friends of the man killed have taken no steps to punish his death in the usual manner, according to their laws.

No other difficulties have occurred and as far as I am able to judge the removal of the Party has been well conducted according to the Contract.

I have nothing further of interest to communicate at present upon the subject of the Emigration.

I am Sir, very
Respectfully
Your Obed't Servant
Edw Deas
2nd Lieut &
Disb'g Agent in the
Creek Emigration

☾

Writing to John D. Howell, a fellow John W.A. Sanford & Company partner, Stephen Miles Ingersoll reports that the party will embark on a steamboat from Tuscumbia, Alabama. Ingersoll also reports on the poor condition of the Mississippi Swamp, which will have to be traversed by those Creeks accompanying the horses. Letter found at CGS-IRW, Roll 5, 979.

(Copy)

Tuscumbia 22nd Dec'r 1835

Dear sir,

It is night and we have just finished getting on board of boats, the Indian waggons and our beef and corn—we go in the morning on board, bag and baggage save the horse party which has to try the swamp and the deep roads. we have most appaling accounts of the Mississippi swamp, it is said that hundreds of people are in the mire without a prospect of getting out and it is believed it will be very difficult to get the horses through, if not impossible, their bones may be found one thousand years hence by a different race of men than white men—If the Arkansaw river should favour us we shall make a short trip of it, if it should not we shall yet have to plod our way through a little mud—the Indians are pleased with the plan of going by water and entered into it with spirit, so soon as we declared to them the necessity of it—the roads we are informed are almost impassable between this and Memphis.—I should like to have you here just that you might be able to judge between a camp life and the enjoyments of a warm parlour and a pretty wife.

Yours &c.—
S. M. Ingersoll

Maj. John D Howell

☾

Dr. Burton Randall discusses his journey to Tuscumbia as "disagreable" and notes the freezing temperatures and the sufferings of the poorer class of Creek emigrants. Letter found at Papers of Burton Randall [manuscript] 1827–1865, University of Virginia Special Collections, Charlottesville.

Tuscumbia Alabama Decr 22nd 1835

My dear Brother

We arrived here yesterday after a tedious and disagreable journey having to camp out every night whilst the water would freese in our tents, but here we take steam as far as Little Rock, when our exposure

FIG. 4. Dr. Burton Randall (1806–1886), the attending physician for the fifth voluntary emigrating party. From *Army Medical Department Album, Volume 1*, National Library of Medicine, Bethesda, Maryland.

commences again, but this kind of Life agrees very well with me I never for a number of years enjoyed more robust health. I must have gained 10 or 15 pounds of flesh by the trip the regular exercise coarse plain food and living in the open air has given me a wolfish appetite, the most disagreable part of the trip is that you are so much occupied in keeping yourself warm and comfortable that you cant read. when we stop for the night we are always turning to warm both sides and avoid the smoke I often think of my dear Mothers warm rooms the chinks covered with cloth. I have no doubt I should become attatched to this mode of life If I continued on it much longer but the sufferings of some of the poorer class of Indians we have along rather mars our pleasures, one of which is the windward side a hickory fire made of logs twice as large as your body. as this is a borrowd pen I must conclude with my best love to all.

Yours
B Randall

☾

Deas reports that due to the poor condition of the roads from Tuscumbia, Alabama, to Memphis, Tennessee, the party (except those accompanying the horses) has taken steamboats and descended the Tennessee River to Paducah, Kentucky. Deas also acknowledges that a slave child died during the passage. Letter found at CGS-IRW, Roll 5, 304–6.

Rec'd 14 Jany

Paduca Ky. Mouth of Tennesse River
28th December 1835.

To,
General George Gibson
Commissary General of Subsistence

General,

On the 21st ins't I had the honour to address you from Tuscumbia Alaba. on the subject of Emigrating Party of Creek Indians, now on their way to the West.

At the time I wrote it was intended to proceed at least as far as Memphis by land, but the day after, travellers arriving from that direction, gave such extremely unfavourable accounts of the state of the roads, that it was decided to take water at Tuscumbia; which was done accordingly.

The Indian Ponies were as usual, sent on by land under charge of Agents and a sufficient number of volunteers from the Indians to take proper care of them.

The Party arrived at this place to-day at 9 o'clock A.M. on board the S'm Boat Alpha and two Keels, & landed, & will proceed this afternoon, as soon as the necessary provisions can be procured and placed on board. Nothing of particular importance has occurred since I last wrote.

One Negro Boy died at Tuscumbia on the 22nd but thus far but little sickness has occurred. We left Tuscumbia on the afternoon of the 23rd & since that time the mode of travelling has been to stop before dark & allow the Party to encamp & start again the next morning after daylight. In this way the Indians prefer this mode of conveyance to travelling by land, & appear well satisfied in all respects. The same plan is intended to be pursued until we arrive at Fort Gibson, unless circumstances should make it preferable on all accounts to continue to run at night. Fresh Beef & meal have been regularly issued since we left Tuscumbia, and temporary Hearths have been constructed on the decks of the two Keel-Boats by which the people are enabled to prepare their food & keep themselves warm through the day.

The Boats are also cleaned out every night after stopping, & I shall continue to see that all proper precautions are taken to insure the health & comfort of the Emigrants.

There is nothing further to communicate upon this subject at present, but I hope that in a short time I shall be enabled to inform you from Memphis, that the Party is still progressing upon its route in good condition.

I am Sir Respectfully

Your Obed't Servant
Edw— Deas
2nd Lieut &
Disb'g Agent in the
Creek Emigration

☾

Deas updates George Gibson on the progress of the party as it arrives in Memphis, Tennessee, and reports that no deaths have occurred since leaving Tuscumbia, Alabama. Letter found at CGS-IRW, Roll5, 301–2.

Rec'd 18 Jany

Memphis Tenn'e 31st Dec'r 1835—

To,
General George Gibson
Commissary General of Subsistence

General

I have the honour to report that the Emigrating Party of Creek Indians arrived near this place to day. I had the honour to address you from Tuscumbia Alaba. on the 21st ins't & from Paduca on the 28th giving an account of our progress up to that time, & also the mode of proceeding intended to be pursued until our arrival at Fort Gibson. Nothing of particular consequence has since occurred. The Boats were landed this morning on the opposite bank of the river to prevent the Indians having access to the whiskey shops of the town, and it is intended to proceed this afternoon. The Party having charge of the Ponies also arrived this morning & will proceed without delay through the Mississippi Swamp towards their destination.

Thus far there has been but little sickness on our route, and no deaths since we left Tuscumbia.

I have nothing further of interest to communicate at present.

I am sir

Respectfully
Your Obed't Servant,
Edw— Deas
2nd Lieut. &
Disb'g Agent in the
Creek Emigration

☾

Captain Jacob Brown, the government's principal disbursing agent at Little Rock, reports on the departure of the party for Indian territory. Letter found at CGS-IRW, Roll 5, 874.

Rec'd 1 Febr'y

Little Rock, A.T.
Jan'y 9th 1836.

Sir—

A party of Creek Emigrants, in number 511, passed this last evening for their new country West. They were in charge of Mr. Beattie, accompanied by Lieut. Deas and Dr. Randall, U.S.A.—

Should the River continue at its present stage, they will be able to get up as far as Dardanell—from thence by land, they will reach the Creek Agency between the 20th and 25th inst.—should the Boat not be able to pass the bar at Palarm, 20 miles from this, the party will then, by land, from that place be enabled to reach its destination by the close of this month.

Dr. Randall informed me that the Emigrants were very healthy, not a single individual was sick or in any way indisposed.

The Weather is now, as it has been for the last 30 days, remarkably warm and fine for the season.

Very Respectfully
Your Obt. Svt.
J Brown Capt. U.S.A.
Pr Dis Agt Ind Rem'l

Gen'l Geo. Gibson
Com'y Gen'l of Sub.
Washington D.C.

☾

Deas reports on the progress of the party from aboard the steamboat *Alpha*. Deas notes that because the contractors had marched the Creeks' horses farther than the twelve miles per day as required in the contract (while not increasing the amount of forage), approximately twenty of the animals became ill and were "disposed of." Letter found at CGS-IRW, Roll 5, 932–34.

Rec'd 8 Feb'y

Steam Boat Alpha 20 miles above Little
Rock Arkansas, 9th January 1836.

To
General George Gibson
Commissary General of Subsistence

General

It was my intention to have written yesterday from Little Rock, but after reaching that place it was found expedient to make our time of stopping so short as not to admit of my doing so properly. There is a small town a short distance above us where I shall have an opportunity of mailing this. I had the honour last to address you from Memphis on the 31st ult'o reporting the progress of the Party now emigrating up to that time. We did not leave that place until the next morning, the 1st ins't, about 9 o' clock at which time also, the Ponies were assembled on the west bank of the river, ready to proceed towards Fort Gibson through the Mississippi Swamp.

Since that time nothing of consequence has occurred to the Party on board of the Boats. The Arkansas is not high, but is on the rise, and we hope to reach the end of our journey without being again obliged to travel by land. The Boats have stopped every night since entering this river, and we have avaraged about 40 miles a day. The weather has been remarkably mild & favourable to our progress, and the Indians are healthy & apparently well satisfied.

The Horses & Ponies were not all ferried over the Mississippi at Memphis until the evening of the 31st ult'o, & until this was done their numbers could not be acertained. I then found that out of 154 that had left Tuscumbia on the 23rd ult., upwards of twenty had not crossed the Mississippi. They had been disposed of on the way with the exception of two, which were lost. This sacrafice of property the Agent who accompanied them informed me was owing to a want of sufficient Foriage, the allowance of two quarts of corn not being sufficient to support them. I acertained the above facts from the Agent who had charge of the Ponies and as soon as I had done so, (finding that the avarage rate at which they had travelled from Tuscumbia to Memphis had more than doubled that laid down in the Contract), I stated to the Agent of the Company, that it was my opinion that when the avarage rate exceeded that laid down, the amount of Foriage should be increased by them in proportion, and that unless it was their intention to do so, I explicitly objected to the Ponies being obliged to travel more than an avarage of 12 miles a day. After some discussion my proposition was acceeded to, and directions were accordingly given that for the future four quarts of corn should be issued, as it was expected they would probably travel between 20 & 30 miles a day. We hoped to hear from them yesterday at Little Rock but did not. We shall probably do so at Dardanell's, about 100 miles above. The above embraces all the facts of interest that have occurred since I last wrote & I have nothing further at present to communicate upon the subject of the Emigration.

I am Sir, Respectfully
Your Obed't Servant
Edw Deas
2nd Lieut &
Disb'g Agent in the
Creek Emigration

☾

Deas reports that the party has been detained for some time because of the low state of the Arkansas River and the delay in procuring land transportation. Letter found at CGS-IRW, Roll 5, 310–11.

Rec'd Feb 26

Encampment of Indians 2 miles
west of Fort Smith Arkansas Ty.
28th January 1836.

To,
General George Gibson
Commissary General of Subsistence

General

On the 9th ult'o I had the honour to address you from near Little Rock upon the subject of the Party of Creek Indians now Emigrating. Since that time we have met with much detention from the low state of the water in the Arkansas River. On the 22nd ins. we reached this place, and it was found impossible to proceed further by water.

The Party was therefore encamped at this place on the north bank of the river, and the Agents of the Contractors proceeded to provide the necessary means of Transportation by land.

Messengers were also sent on to Fort Gibson for the return of the Indian Ponies & wagon Horses, which by some mistake had gone on there instead of encamping near Fort Smith as was directed, until the arrival of the Boats.

Those that were fit for use returned this afternoon, and the requisite number of Wagons having been procured every thing is in readiness to proceed to morrow morning.

The weather & roads being good at present, the Party will probably reach Fort Gibson within five days.

The Indians have remained healthy & nothing else of particular importance relative to them has occurred since I last had the honour to address you upon this subject.

I am Sir, Respectfully
Your Obed't Servant
Edw— Deas
2nd Lieut &
Disbur'g Agent in the
Creek Emigration

☾

Deas reports on the party's arrival in Indian territory and the Creeks' desire to stop at the Verdigris River, rather than Fort Gibson. Letter found at CGS-IRW, Roll 5, 940.

Rec'd 10 March

Fort Gibson Arkansas Ty.
5th February 1836.

To,
General George Gibson,
Commissary Gen'l of Subsis'ce

General,

I have the honour to state that the Party of Emigrating Creeks which I have accompanied from Alabama, arrived at their destination near this place on the 2nd inst. On the 3rd they were mustered in the presence of Captain Stephenson, the Agent of the Contractors, & myself, as directed, & the Rolls have been signed accordingly. The Indians expressed their wish to be carried no further than the western bank of the Verdigris River, where they were received by Capt. Stephenson, who commenced issuing provisions to them yesterday. Dr. Randall and myself having no further business here will return to the Creek Nation, East, as soon as possible. Nothing else of particular importance has occurred in relation to the Indians since I had the honour to address you upon the 28th ultimo. My journal exhibits in detail all occurrences upon the route, and will be forwarded as directed upon my return to Alabama.

I am Sir, Respectfully
Your Obed't Servant
Edw— Deas
2nd Lieut. & Disbur'g Agent
in the Creek Emigration

☾

Captain James R. Stephenson, a disbursing agent at Fort Gibson, reports on the arrival of the fifth voluntary party, their mustering into the western Creek Nation, and the issuing of provisions. Letter found at CGS-IRW, Roll 6, 433.

Rec'd 15 March

Fort Gibson
February 16. 1836.

Sir

Your communication of 2nd January 1836, has been received.

A party of Emigrant Creeks consisting of 513, and conducted by an Agent of J.W. Sandford & Co. and accompanied by Lieut E. Deas of the Army Disbursing Agent, arrived in their new Country on the 3d Inst. and were mustered in my presence; provisions were furnished to them for a few days, and preparations made to continue the supply.

Very Respectfully
Your Obedt. Servt.
Ja's. R. Stephenson
Capt. U.S. Army
Disbg. agt. (Creeks)

Emigration of Indians
Com. Gen'l Subs'e
Washington
D.C.

☾

Dr. Burton Randall reports on the arrival of the party of Creeks and notes that two perished during the journey. Letter found at CGS-IRW, Roll 6, 295.

Rec'd 29 March

Mobile March 15th 1836

Sir

I have the honor to inform you that I accompanied the Party of Creek Emigrants under the charge of Sandford & co, as far as the Verdigris River, where they were turned over to Capt Stephenson. You will observe that Lieut Deas Journal includes every incident of importance that occurred during the Journey, I am happy to inform you that but two deaths occurred, the one, an Indian who was killed, the other, a negro Boy who did not come under my charge; the Emigrants suffered most from Inflamation of the Bowels & Lungs from the unavoidable exposure to cold in travelling in winter. I arrived here on the 12th and in compliance with your order reported myself to Col'n Hogan, and shall proceed with him to the Creek Nation.

Your obt Servt
B Randall
Asst Surgeon
U S Army

Emigration of Indians
Commisary Gen'l of Subsistance
Washington City

☾

Excerpt from the Autobiography of John Hewitt Jones,[46] part owner of the steamboat *Alpha*, who accompanied the fifth voluntary emigrating party from Waterloo, Alabama, to Fort Smith, Arkansas, in 1835–36. Autobiography found at Lilly Library, Indiana University, Bloomington.

Moses Turner, who built the flouring mill and run it several years, now went into the dry goods business and offered me better wages so I set in with him, during which time there was a Steam Boat Company formed.

It was in December, 1834, (a book with the articles of agreement &c I keep as a relic) I had saved every year from my wages and now having a surplus thought it a fine chance to invest in a Steam Boat and was urged in it by older men, supposing it would pay. I took a share—$100.00 stock—but the company departed from the first calculation, which was to build a little flat boat like for $1800.00. It was enlarged on, from time to time, until it cost about $5000.00. Finally in the wind-up it took all the money I had made, say $500.00, to pay up.

I run on the boat, which was called the "Alpha", as clerk. First in the Cincinnati and Rising Sun trade and then in the Cincinnati and Portsmouth trade, say in 1836, for then goods from New York was sent by canal to Buffalo and then across the Lake (Erie), by canal to Portsmouth and by Steam Boat to Cincinnati &c.

We left Rising Sun on Sunday the 13th of December, 1835, on board the Steam Boat "Alpha" for Florence, Alabama. The river full of ice when we left.

Saturday, the 19th, found us about 100 miles up the Tennessee River, we laid at Paducah at the mouth of the Tennessee to repair wheels &c damaged by ice. After turning up the Tennessee we saw no more ice.

December 20th, '35, we saw the wreck of the old "Rising Sun" Steam Boat converted into a house 150 miles up from the mouth of the river.

The morning of the 22nd found us at Waterloo, a town without houses at the foot of Muscle Shoals, a sorry set of steam boat men. We had to reship freight in keels to Florence, above, which delayed us some days. (1)

While there Beatty and Ingersoll, Govt. Agents, came in with about 511 Creek Indians to be removed to the Indian Territory up the Arkansas River to Fort Gibson. We bought two [keel] boats and took the Indians aboard, a Keel boat on each side, and started on our trip. Was getting $2200.00 for the trip and were to stop and lay up nights for the Indians to camp out and do their cooking &c.

The Indians had slaves and they said they were better treated—in fact look up to—and learned them agriculture and domestic work. The names of monies then in circulation and use were

Dollahumpkin—$1.00
Nulcupachee—12½ ¢
Calloxogee—6¼ ¢

They wore turbans instead of hats. A group of little Indians 6 to 8 years old sat on the forecastle flat on deck playing cards.

We happened to make Memphis just in the evening and so had to land on the opposite side of the river. Next morning the party who went by land to take the ponies thru were crossing the river so it was impossible to get away for the Indians must see their ponies and would bring them into camp and make a terrible fuss over them and were very loth to part with them. Some offered to sell a nice little pony for 5$ for fear they would not go through the trip.

Some of the Indians went over to Memphis to buy saddles, gears, clothes &c.

We entered the mouth of White River and went through a cut-off into the Arkansas River on the morning of the 2nd of January 1836.

We anchored out in the river at Little Rock—the agents and the Boat having some business to transact. We had to use this precaution to keep the Indians from getting in to town and getting whiskey, for when they did there was a tear round among the Indians. The women (squaws) would down a fellow and tie his legs and tie his arms and let him lay till he got sober.

Little Rock was of about 1000 inhabitants, a very pretty place.

We had lost time and the agents agreed we might run some of nights to make up. (2) The first night, the river being very snaggy, we stove one of the keel boats and made a terrible rumpus among the Indians, again having to lay up of nights and leave the sunken keel boat at Lewisville.[47] It was a very dark night, the stove keel boat sinking fast with about 250 Indians on board, caused great confusion and such a time to get them and their baggage on the Steam Boat. The yelling of the yellow skins, big and little, old and young was not easily forgotten.

The keel was run aground as soon as possible on a sand bar (for they are plenty in that river) got all save and then laid up for the night.

It was a fine sight to see the camping of the Indians on the trip. As soon as the Boat was tied to the shore and a plank out the first to leave was the squaws, who gathered up their kit, which was usually tied up by the corners in a blanket in which was their tents, blankets, cook articles &c. They would throw it over their backs and let the tie come across their forheads, resting on their backs and in one hand take an axe and in the other and under their arm a little papoose and run ashore and up the bank.

They would chop trees and make a fire and prepare supper. I often used to walk through the camp of pleasant evenings. It looked like a little village. They parched corn in a kettle and then would pound it in a mortar or deep cut trough in a log and then boil it up and make a very fine dish which they called "sophka" and would broil their meat stuck on a stick before the fire.

This was played on the violin by a half-breed Indian (Creek) on the Steam Boat "Alpha" which was removing them from their old home in Georgia, in the winter of 1835, to their new home in the Indian Territory.

"Indians"

Alas! For them—their day is o'er
Their fires are out from hill and shore:
No more for them the wild deer bounds;
The pale man's axe rings through their woods,
Their pleasant springs are dry.
Their children—look! by power oppressed,
Beyond the mountains of the west,
Their children go—to die,
By foes alone their death song must be sung."

We only got a few miles above Fort Smith, the water being too low, and had to give up the trip and return. We bought 25 Bbls. Pecans at Fort Smith for 5$ per Bbl. and started back. We had to check up near Van Buren and stay there two weeks, when the river rose and we left and got back to Rising Sun in March, all safe.

It was not long till we sold the "Alpha". It proved to be poor stock—my last dollar was gone—so I had to start again. I got a letter from McDowell & Davis of Portsmouth, O., commission merchants who I got acquainted with while running on the "Alpha". They wished me to go on a new boat they were building, the "Home", as clerk—which I did. I was with them some months until I got sick and had to quit the river.

(1) Memorandum of the Tennessee River

Started up the Tennessee River the 18th day of December, 1835. Very few and poor settlements for about 30 miles up. The first place is Sandy, at the Mouth of Sandy.[48] On the right Carrollsville, on the left Perrysville, on the left Waterloo, on the left Culberts' (?) Shoals; 10 miles above Waterloo is Muscle Shoals and, above, Florence.[49]

(2) Memorandum of the Arkansas River

Entered the mouth of White River (a cut off into the Arkansas) on the 2nd day of January, 1836. Very few settlements for some distance up the river. The first place we find is the Posts of Arkansaw, we begin to find some fine cotton plantations and the Posts in 45 miles from the mouth.

The next place is Little Rock, about 300 miles from the mouth, a very handsome place of about 1000 inhabitants. Next a little village called Louisburgh and the next is a military [crossing] called the Dardinells, a small chain of mountains. A very high cliff just at the [crossing].

On Sunday the 10th day of January, 1836, we got a pilot that pretended to know the river and run us aground before he got out of sight of home. We calculated to run all night, as we had a pilot, but about 9 o'clock we run over a breaker[50] with one of the keels that caused her to leak very fast, the boat sinking with about 200 Indians in and on it, which caused great confusion.

We finally got on a sand bar and lay there until we got things regulated. Discharged the pilot.

The 13th we lost a day by getting aground at Jesse May's Wood Yard (first mountains wore the Little Johns). The next place is Spadra, situated on a rock.

Ended our trip four or five miles above Fort Smith on the 24th day of January, 1836, and started back, grounding four times in running five miles below Fort Smith.

Lay up for a rise on the 29th of January, Friday, on Lee's Creek Bar in the Arkansas River, 600 miles from the mouth. In that distance there is 300 bends and a bar in every bend, or rather under the points. The bends are all full of snags, almost, as a cornfield is of stalks. In coming from Lee's Creek to the mouth of White River we grounded about one dozen times.

* * * * *

Portsmouth, June 12th, 1836. Steam Boat Rufus Putnam lay at the wharf the better part of the day (having on board a number of Preachers) while they preached two sermons on the boat and one on shore. Something uncommon.

* * * * *

Ohio River, Diamond Island, March 6th, 1836.[51]

S.B. "Alpha"[52]
Capt.—I.C. Waggener
Mate—James Read
Pilot—Zeke Hewitt
Engineer—Wm. Gouldson
Engineer—Elijah Towner
Steward—N. Greene
Barkeeper—L. Clark
Cabin Boy—Jno. Vannader
Cook—Isaac Delenna
Dock hands—W. Artkins, W. Walker, Jno. Bays, Smith Soldier, Fin McBeth, Sam Blair.
Jno. H. Jones, Clerk, 1836.

Part 2

The Forced Removals, 1836

7 First Detachment of Creek Prisoners, July–August 1836

The failure of the 1832 Treaty of Washington was a devastating blow for the Creeks, who had hoped that the agreement would preserve their rights to remain on their land. Instead the document was a wedge that allowed speculators to pry reserves from unsuspecting landowners. As the land frauds got worse into 1835, and starvation continued unabated, a small group of Lower Creeks felt they had little choice but to lash out at white encroachment. The Second Creek War, as it came to be called, began in May 1836 and soon spread throughout east Alabama and into Georgia and Florida. The war gave Andrew Jackson the excuse he needed to remove the entire Creek people west of the Mississippi River. As the Creek prisoners were captured they were placed in chains at Fort Mitchell and Montgomery. In July 1836 a detachment of prisoners, shackled double-file by the ankles, marched from Fort Mitchell to Montgomery, where they were placed on steamboats for the west. Wagons carrying weeping women and children followed in their wake. Some Creeks continued to fight even after capture, and were able to escape into the Alabama and Georgia swamps, while others, with little to lose, tried to overthrow their captors violently. One father and son tandem, both of whom were due to face capital charges in Georgia, were determined to escape or die trying. According to witnesses, the son grabbed a hatchet as his handcuffs were being taken off by a guard and "struck him a violent blow upon the head which came near killing him upon the spot." The son ran a hundred yards before he was shot, while the father grabbed the same hatchet and was bayonetted before he could render the same blow. Other Creeks simply committed suicide rather than face the uncertainty of restarting life in a strange land. An elderly man was found hanging by the neck at Fort Mitchell on the eve of his march to Montgomery, while another prisoner drew a knife and slit his throat as he was being wheeled down the street.[1]

The Creek prisoners were transported to Indian territory by John W.A. Sanford and Company under the guidance of partner John D. Howell. Although the original contract had ended on 30 June 1836, Captain John Page and the contractors entered into a handshake agreement that allowed the company to continue operations. Twenty-six-year-old Lieutenant John Waller Barry[2] of Kentucky, who was the son of William T. Barry, the former U.S. postmaster general and minister to Spain, served as the military oversight. French-born Dr. Eugene Hilarian Abadie[3] accompanied the party as surgeon. Due to the large number of prisoners and the prevalence of sickness along the journey, Barry hired a second physician—Dr. William Stout Chipley,[4] who would later become an early pioneer in the diagnosis of *anorexia nervosa*.

Supplemental Letters of the First Detachment of Creek Prisoners

Captain John Archer Elmore, Jr.[5] reports that three Creek prisoners escaped at Calebee Swamp before they could be transported to the west. Letter found at Record Group 94, Records of the Adjutant General's Office, 1780s–1917, Entry 159-Q, Records of Major General Thomas S. Jesup, Container 8, Folder: "Letters Received from Officers, Captain John Elmore," NARA.

Polecat Springs
July 10th 1836

Sir,

To day at 12 oclock I met the two companies from Lowndes in charge of the prisoners under the command of Capt Gaffney[6]—I regret to communicate to you the loss of three prisoners in crossing the Calebah Swamp—Their names were Weiky, Keheartla, and Sakoye as

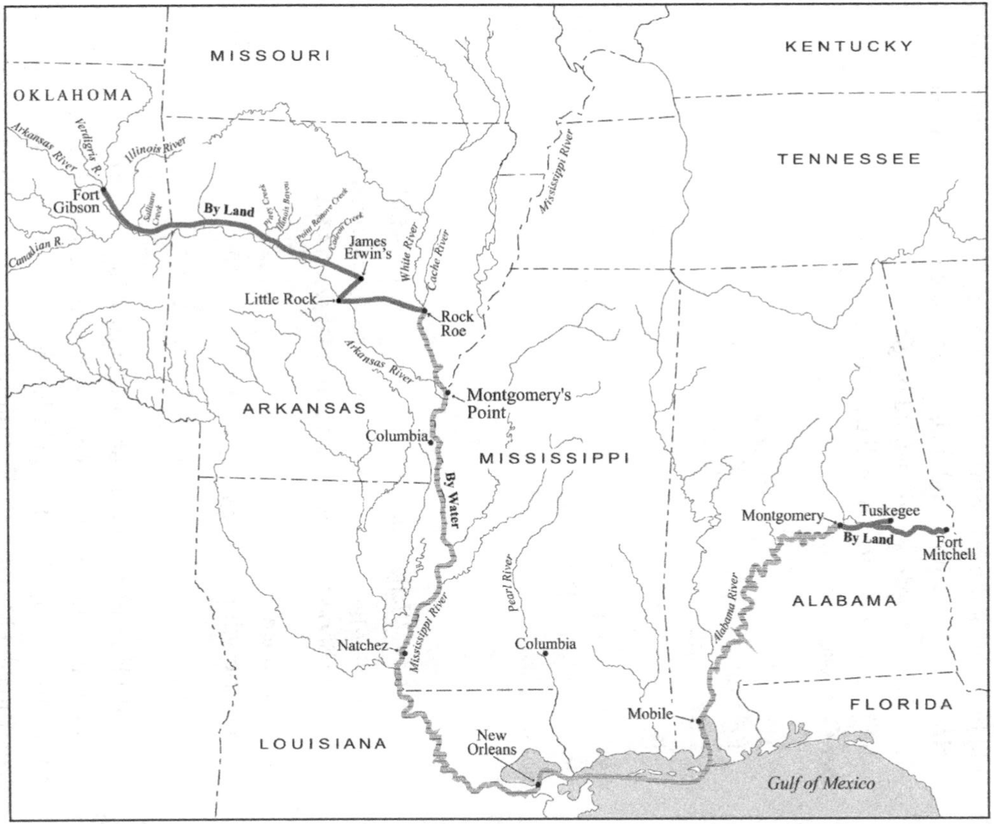

MAP 7. Route of the first detachment of Creek prisoners, July–September 1836. Place names correspond to stopping points or locations noted in the documentation. Route lines and locations are approximations. Cartography by Sarah Mattics and Kiersten Fish.

told by some of the other prisoners. They say that those who made their escape had left behind their wives and children. Capt Gaffney has no written orders and I would be glad if I could receive some from your [Excellency]. I shall take the command and proceed as per Capt Gaffneys order—

Yrs Resptly
J A Elmore
Capt Com. A
1st Bat. Ala. Vol.

Maj Genl. Jesup
Commanding—Division
South—Army

☾

Lieutenant John Waller Barry reports on his arrival at Montgomery, Alabama, and the impending arrival of the Creek prisoners. Letter found at SIAC, Agent (Barry), Account (507), Year (1837), NARA.

Q'r M'rs Office
Montgomery July 11th 1836.

General,

I reached here yesterday about 6 P.M. Cap't Page arrived this morning, & the Indians will be here in a few hours—three of them, I am informed by Cap't Page, made their escape at Calebee Swamp. I have directed Mr Howell, the Contractor or agent, to hasten as much as possible, the preparations for their departure; & have made a requisition upon the Q'r M'rs Dep't for the necessary transportation for Cap't Miltons[7] company.[8]

I do not apprehend any difficulty in taking the Indian prisoners to their destination, & shall, unless circumstances, now unforeseen, should arise dispense with Cap't Milton's escort at Mobile. Cap't Page is busily engaged in completing the rolls, & I hope, that day after tomorrow, will find me on my way to Arkansas.

I am, General, most resp'y
Your Ob't Ser't
J Waller Barry
L't & ass't Q'r Master

Maj Gen'l Thos: S Jesup
Comm'g Southern Army
Tuskegee Ala:

☾

In this letter to the commissary general of subsistence, Barry reports on the delay caused by the approximately six hundred captives who had not yet arrived at Montgomery. Barry also reports on the deaths of a father and son who attempted to escape. Both were due to face charges in Georgia for crimes they allegedly committed during the Second Creek War. Letter found at SIAC, Agent (Barry), Account (507), Year (1837), NARA.

Rec'd 27 July

Montgomery July 12th 1836.

General,

Orders have been received from Gen'l Jesup[9] directing that the Indians at this place (about two thousand) should remain here until another body of them (600) should arrive from Tuskegee—This will delay their embarkation for two days at least.[10]

To-day, a circumstance much to be regretted, occurred in the Indian Camp. a small company of men from Georgia came in, for the purpose of claiming some Indians against whom they had made charges for capital offences. They were delivered to them by order of Gen'l Jesup—two of them father & son, while the handcuffs were preparing to fasten them, determined to escape or be Killed—The son took the opportunity to seize upon the hatchet of the man engaged in remitting the handcuffs, & struck him a violent blow upon the head which came near Killing him upon the spot—he then started & run about a hundred yards, when he was shot—The father, picked up the hatchet, & was in the act of repeating the blow, when he was bayonetted by one of the guard.[11] This circumstance has created much excitement amongst the Indians; & I fear will be followed by further difficulty.—

I am, Sir, very resp'y, Y'r Ob't Ser't
J. Waller Barry
L't & Ass't Q'r Master

Brig: Gen'l Geo: Gibson
Comm'y Gen'l Sub'e
Washington City.

☾

Barry wrote two letters notifying his superiors of his arrival at Mobile, Alabama, on 16 July. The first, to Commissary General of Subsistence George Gibson, notifies the brigadier general of the agent's decision (while at Montgomery) to hire a second physician to take care of the increasing number of sick. Letter found at CGS-IRW, Roll 5, 829–30.

Rec'd 1 Aug't
& An'd 2 Aug't

Mobile Ala July 16th 1836.

General,

I have the honor to report to you my arrival at this place, with the emigrating Creek Indians, on their way to Arkansas. They left Montgomery, in two Steam boats, each having two barges in tow, on the 14th ins't, & reached here this morning about day.[12] No difficulty has occurred since their departure, & although the most of them were hostile, not the slightest disposition to escape has been evinced. They are cheerful & better contented with their situation than I expected them to be.

The contractors have been very active, & very attentive to the wants of the Indians—they have not suffered them to want in any one particular, that I can ascertain. Mr. Howell, one of the contractors, is with me, & appears anxious to discharge faithfully, & in a manner which shall be entirely satisfactory to the Gov't, the obligations of his contract.

I have found it absolutely necessary to employ some person to assist Dr Abadie in the discharge of his duties; it is not practicable for one physician to superintend & prescribe for some twenty three hundred Indians, especially when the number is divided between two boats, which are very often not even within hail of each other. Believing that the Department would sanction an act which humanity required, I have employed Dr Chipley to take charge of one of the boats & her crew. We have to take on water, & subsistence stores for the Indians at this place, & shall probably be detained all day. The weather is exceedingly warm & unpleasant, & the Indians are most comfortable when in motion. I shall write again by the first opportunity.

I am very resp'y, General
your most Ob't Ser't
J. Waller Barry
L't & Ass't Q'r Master

Brig Gen'l
Geo: Gibson
Comm'y Gen'l Sub'e
Washington City
D.C.

☾

In Barry's second letter written from Mobile—this one to Brevet Major General Thomas S. Jesup—Barry paints a rosy picture of the journey from Montgomery. There is no mention of the attempted escape attempt from the steamer *Meridian* (as recorded by Captain John Milton in his 18 July letter, following), and Barry incorrectly portrays the captive Creeks as "cheerful, & contented with their situation." Letter found at Record Group 94, Records of the Adjutant General's Office, 1780s–1917, Entry 159-Q, Records of Major General Thomas S. Jesup, Container 4, Folder: "Letters Received from Officers, Lieutenant J. Waller Barry," NARA.

Mobile July 16th 1836.

General

On the 14th Ins't the Steam Boats Lewis Cass & Meridian left Montgomery with two barges each, freighted with Indians. The whole number amounts to about 2300—they were divided between the boats in such manner that all the Creeks should be together, as it was found next to impossible to prevent strife between the Creek & Uchee women.[13] I apprehended when the Indians were allowed to land for the first time, that some might attempt to escape, & took accordingly such precautions as seemed to me most proper; but my mind was relieved from all doubt afterwards—They not only had no design, but, I really believe, no wish to get away—They appeared convinced that though they might retard they could not alter the fate which awaits them; & they become every day more & more reconciled to it. So far, every thing has proceeded remarkably well; the Indians are cheerful, & contented with their situation, which has been made as comfortable as possible—they are necessarily much crowded, but no ill effect has as yet resulted from this cause.

It will require nearly the whole day to supply the boat with fresh water for N, orleans, & the subsistence stores for the Indians. Cap't Milton's company, although not found necessary to suppress any disturbances, has been of much assistance, & deserves together with its Captain,[14] the highest credit for prompt & soldierlike conduct during the trip. Their services will no longer be required, & I shall accordingly dispense with the company. I have not been able to ascertain the state of the Arkansas River, & shall not probably, until we reach it—should it be low, the land trip will be exceedingly long & tedious.

I am, General, very resp'y
your Ob't Ser't
J. Waller Barry
L't & Ass't Q'r Master

Major Gen'l Thos: S Jesup
Comm'g Southern Army
Tuskegee, Ala:

☾

Barry sent this communiqué to Captain John Milton at Mobile, Alabama, notifying him that the services of the Alabama Artillery Number 1 will no longer be needed. Letter found at Record Group 94, Records of the Adjutant General's Office, 1780s–1917, Entry 159-Q, Records of Major General Thomas S. Jesup, Container 4, Folder: "Letters Received from Officers, Lieutenant J. Waller Barry," NARA.

Mobile
Steamboat Lewis Cass
July 16. 1836.

Capt J. Milton
Commanding Company Mobile Artillery
in the service of the United States

Sir,

In obedience to instructions from Major General Jessup, leaving the necessity of taking on your command to New Orleans to be decided by my judgment, I have the honor to inform you that the services of the troops will no longer be required.—

The conduct of the Indians since their departure from Montgomery has been perfectly peaceable and orderly—For this we are greatly indebted to the efficient guard afforded by your command on board the Boats; and the no less efficient disposition made for the security of the Indians while on shore.—

In taking leave I return to you, and beg you will for me, to your Officers and Company my sincere thanks for the courtesy extended me during our brief intercourse.

I am sir most resp'lly
Yr Obt servant

Signed— J Waller Barry
Lt & asst. Q'r Master.

☾

In this letter to Brevet Major General Thomas S. Jesup, future Florida governor John Milton, the commanding officer of the Alabama Artillery Number 1, reports on his journey on board the steamboat *Meridian* while accompanying the Creek prisoners to Mobile. The journey was not without incident, as Milton discovered an attempt by perhaps thirty Indians to escape in the middle of the night. Once the plot was foiled, Milton notes that the Creeks became reconciled to their situation and no other problems occurred. The Alabama Artillery accompanied the party only as far as Mobile. Letter found at Record Group 94, Records of the Adjutant General's Office, 1780s–1917, Entry 159-Q, Records of Major General Thomas S. Jesup, Container 13, Folder: "Letters Received from Officers, Captain John Milton," NARA.

Camp Jesup 18th July 1836

Sir

In obedience to your orders of the 10th inst I marched "The Alabama Artillery No. 1" to Montgomery and relieved Major Churchill[15] from his charge of the advance detachment of prisoners.

With them and the prisoners accompanied from Tuskeege to Montgomery, by the commands of Captains Elmore,[16] Gayson[17] & Robertson[18]—the aggregate number exceeding twenty three hundred Indians, I departed from that place on the night of the 13th instant.[19] Fifteen hundred were placed in the Steamer Meridian & the two barges attached—and the others were put aboard the Steamer Lewis Cass and one barge.[20]

Having discoverd a restive spirit among them I declined descending the river with the company in a seperate boat—and placed a platoon of forty men, on each of the boats—the meridian & Lewis Cass, with orders to have no intercourse with the Indians—to watch them closely, & to shoot any who might evince a hostile spirit, or attempt to escape.

At Montgomery one was shot dead and another bayoneted (who has since died) because of an effort by them with axes to Kill one of the guard and a Mr Bender while examineing the Hand Cuffs on other Indians.[21]

I placed Lt Erwin[22] in command of the Lewis Cass, and accompanied in person the platoon on the meridian, and about 3 O clock A.M., discovered arrangements in progress among upwards of thirty of the Indians to escape—but could not ascertain from their conversation, whether it was to be with, or without force.

I retired, unobserved, from the position I had occupied and they were not apprized of their design having been made Known, until they discovered the entire guard, on the hurricane deck[23] in readiness to fire upon them—They then became quiet.

The next morning He-ne Emathla[24] the chief told them it was useless for any of them to attempt to escape, that they could not escape, and if any other was made that they all would be shot.—He urged upon them the necessity of their becoming reconciled to their situation, and they soon afterwards became cheerful.

On several occasions while the boats were detained to procure Wood I allowed all of them to go ashore, and none evinced a disposition to escape—but on the contrary, all were playful, in fishing swimming &c. and at the sound of the bell came aboard without delay.

We arrived here on the morning of the 15th without having lost one, by an escape or sickness.

Soon after our arrival, I rec'd from Lt Barry, a letter of which the enclosed is a copy, and on yesterday morning, the boats having been cleansed, and the necessary provision procured, he departed with them for New Orleans.[25]

I enquired of them frequently, whether they had enough to eat—and was always answered in the affirmative. They left here in good health and fine spirits—were comfortably situated, and I do not hesitate to say that the agents with them are worthy, in their trust of the utmost confidence.

The last party of Indians arrived at Montgomery too late to dispose of their horses, except at considerable sacrifice—and Capt

Walker by my request, agreed to take charge of them, and will no doubt do justice to the owners.

I shall respectfully await your orders at this place.—

Very respectfully
Yr. Obt. Svt.
Jno Milton Com'g
"The Alabama Artillery No. 1"

Major General Thomas Jesup
Com'g the army of the South

P.S. our camp is near the City.[26]

☾

Notifying the commissary general of subsistence of his party's arrival at New Orleans, Barry writes of the treacherous passage across the Gulf of Mexico. Barry also reports on a number of sick Creeks and the death of one child. Letter found at CGS-IRW, Roll 5, 820–21.

Rec'd 2 Aug't
& an'd 2 Aug't

New Orleans
July 19th 1836.

General,

I had the honor to inform you in my last letter that we should probably be detained at Mobile for one day: in consequence however, of the activity of the agents & captains of S. Boats we succeeded in getting under way at 6 P.M. the day that letter was written.

About 12 O'Clock on the night of the 17th we had a very severe gale, & although every precaution had been taken, I was for some time apprehensive lest we should lose some of the Indians overboard. They were frightened, & consequently submissive & obedient—As many as could be, were stowed away in the holds of the barges & the remainder Kept in the center. Not a single Indian was lost—one, a child, died on the passage. We landed yesterday morning at the new canal & put the Indians on shore.[27] One of the barges was retained, for the purpose of taking the sick-infirm-children & luggage up the canal, & was towed up by the Indians themselves to their present encampment near the basin.[28] The situation is by no means a good one for a camp,—the ground being low & wet, but, it is the best to be had in the neighbourhood of the City.

It is possible we may be able to ascend the Arkansas River, & the contractors are now engaged looking up boats for the purpose. We shall leave to-morrow.

I am Sir very Resp'y
your Ob't Ser't
J. Waller Barry
L't & Ass't Q'r Master

Brig'r Gen'l
Geo: Gibson
Comm'y Gen'l Sub'e
Washington City,
D.C.

☾

Reporting on the delay caused by the unavailability of suitable water transportation, Barry notifies George Gibson of his desire to reach Fort Gibson solely by boat. Barry again mischaracterizes the Creeks as "cheerful & contented." Letter found at CGS-IRW, Roll 5, 834.

Rec'd 5 Aug't

New Orleans
July 20th 1836.

General,

The Indians have been detained here for the last two days, in consequence of the difficulty of procuring suitable boats for their transportation. As I informed you in my last letter, there is a great probability of our being able to ascend the Arkansas river as high up as Fort Gibson, & I have insisted upon having such boats procured as would be able to perform the whole distance. This has been accomplished, & we shall leave here to-morrow as early as practicable. Of the 2300 Indians landed at this place only one (a small child) has died. The Indians are cheerful & contented, &, I think, will proceed to their destination without creating any unusual difficulty or opposition.

I am Sir very resp'y
Your Ob't Ser't
J. Waller Barry
L't & Ass't Q'r M'sr

Brig'r Gen'l
Geo: Gibson
Comm'y Gen'l Sub'e
Washington City

☾

Barry reports that the Creek Indian (Mo-git-har) who led a small group of men who stopped and robbed the mail stage is at Fort Mitchell and not among his party. Letter found at Records of the Adjutant General's Office, 1780s–1917, Entry 159-Q, Records of Major General Thomas S. Jesup, Container 19, Folder: "Letters Received Relating to Creek and Seminole Affairs, July 1836 (1 of 3)," NARA.

New Orleans
July 20th 1836.

Sir

I had the honor to receive this morning your communication addressed to me at Montgomery, in relation to Mo-git-har—a supposed mail robber.[29] An examination was immediately made among the Indians, & from all I could ascertain the Indian above named was left at Fort Mitchell—I inspected the rolls submitted to me by Cap't Page myself & there is no such name to be found upon them.

As requested I return you herewith the enclosed papers; & am very respy.

Sir, your Ob't Srv't
J. Waller Barry
<u>L't & Ass't Q'r Master</u>

Cap't J. F. Lane[30]
Ac'g Adj't Gen'l
Southern Army
Tuskegee Ala:

☾

Dr. Eugene Abadie reports that the party has experienced several instances of bowel complaints (diarrhea) and fever, which has been particularly hard on the children. Abadie also notes that the party will leave the city in three steamboats. Letter found at CGS-IRW, Roll 5, 804–5.

New-Orleans July the 21st 1836

General,

Having reported repeatedly to Lt Barry that he might inform you of the health of the Indians under his charge, and the mortality among them, I cannot but express my satisfaction at the few deaths that have occured, and although there has been much sickness, Bowel complaints and fever, particularly among the children, we have lost but six since we left Fort Mitchel.

The manner in which the contractors have so far fulfilled their contract deserves praise particularly in furnishing at my request to the sick such articles of food as were necessary for them, besides their receiving the usual rations allowed by government.

Their care also in providing them with proper shelter when unavoidably detained on shore must be mentioned; the day of our arrival at N. Orleans through the Canal we encamped the Indians on the basin the highest and dryest spot that could be found, in the course of the night a heavy rain having come on the camp became very wet as the soil was of a clayey nature the water was not absorbed; the following morning the rain continuing the contractors immediately went in search of some good shelter, and finally they obtained an old rope walk,[31] to which the Indians were immediately removed and where they had every comfort.

This morning the Indians have embarked on three good and large Steam-Boats one of which has a barge in tow. If the variety of fruit the indians have been eating since they have been at N. Orleans does not increase the sickness and mortality I think we shall be able to reach our destination with comparatively few deaths when the number of people is taken into consideration, and if it is in the power of men to obviate it, all will be done that can be devised, to insure such a state of things as may best comport with the health of our charge.

I have the honour to be, General
with respect your ob't Serv't
E.H. Abadie M.D.

☾

Writing on board the steamboat *Lamplighter* south of Natchez, Barry updates George Gibson on the party's progress. Letter found at CGS-IRW, Roll 5, 836–37.

Rec'd 16 Aug't
ans'd 18th

Steam Boat Lamplighter
Mississippi River
July 23rd 1836.

General,

The Indians were embarked on the 21st inst. on board the Steam Boats Majestic, Lamplighter, & Revenue.[32] The Majestic took

FIG. 5. Dr. Eugene Hilarian Abadie (1810–1874). From *Army Medical Department Album, Volume 1*, National Library of Medicine, Bethesda, Maryland.

the Coseteas,[33] about five hundred in number, & will probably reach Montgomery Point[34] two days before the other Boats. I have endeavoured to Keep the boats as near together as possible, but find it utterly impracticable. I have on this boat nearly eight hundred Creeks, with their Chiefs Neah Emathla, Neah Micco[35] & Choctnalla. So far I have had no difficulty with them—they are well satisfied with their provisions, &, with the exception of the summer complaint[36] hereabout among the children, have no disease or sickness among them. One man died yesterday—he was very old had no complaint—no pain—his physical powers were almost entirely destroyed, so much so, that the pang of death itself passed without causing a struggle.

It is intended to remain a few hours, at some suitable place this side of Natchez, for the purpose of letting the Indians go on shore & having the boat cleansed.

In my communications to the Department, I have found it impossible to conform strictly to the forms prescribed in the order from Head Quarters. It is my wish, & shall be my endeavour, to Keep you informed of every imminent & important occurrence which takes place among the party under my charge & should any informality be noticed in my reports, I beg it may be ascribed to any cause other than a desire to avoid or evade the operation of a general order.

I am, Sir, very resp'y
Your Ob't Svt
J. Waller Barry
L't & Ass't Q'r Master

Brig'r Gen'l
Geo Gibson
Comm'y Gen'l Sub'e
Washington City
D.C.

☾

FIG. 6. Neah Emathla of Hitchiti. From McKenney and Hall, *History of the Indian Tribes of North America* (1842). Courtesy of the Archives and Rare Books Library, University of Cincinnati.

Disbursing agent Captain Jacob Brown reports on the arrival of 2,300 Creek Indians at Rock Roe and the difficulty they had in procuring wagons. Letter found at CGS-IRW, Roll 5, 876–77.

Rec'd 24 Aug't

Little Rock
July 31. 1836.

Sir—

By Express from Rock Roe I am informed that 2300 emigrating Creeks were landed at that place on the 29th inst. They are represented to be in good health, subordinate, and evince much anxiety to reach their new country.—

Assistance has been asked to procure Teams, which has been rendered so far as was practicable, & necessary to establish confidence on the part of owners by an assurance that they would be promptly paid by the Contractors engaged in removing those Indians.

How far I shall be justified in meeting a Contingence by guaranteeing payments under the Contract system of movement, is wholly conjectural; inasmuch as I have not received any instructions touching these points. But there was a case when the government was concerned—Teams were wanted, people were unacquainted with the parties—and that there should be no delay by doubts, &c. I did not hesitate, but at once fixed the compensation they should receive for the service of their Teams, and pledged that the same should be promptly paid to them.

I am not acquainted with the fact, yet I do not doubt but the Contractors are prepared to meet expenses accruing in the movements of the Emigrants. Yet a contingence might occur wherein pecuniary aid might be of importance to them. I am therefore desirous of receiving some instructions on the subject.

I have the honor to be
Very respectfully
Your Obt. Sr't
J Brown Capt U.S.A.

Pr Dis Agt Ind Rem'l

Genl. Geo. Gibson
Com'y Gen'l of Sub.
Washington D.C.

☾

Captain John Page recalls the five- to six-day detention of the party in order to wait for more prisoners, notes the high cost of corn and water transportation, and expresses his intent to sign a new agreement with a contracting firm to relocate the entire Creek population west. Letter found at SIAC, Agent (J.W.A. Sanford), Account (66), Year (1837), NARA.

Rec'd 19 Aug't

Tuskegee Alabama
8th August 1836

Sir

I have the honor to Enclose here-with a Muster Roll of a party of hostile Indians turned over to the contractors for transportation to their country. Lieu't Barry has charge of the party and I presume (agreeable to his instructions) has made his reports.—

After the contractors had started on march with the Indians I received an order from the commanding officer to detain the party five or six days untill other hostile Indians were collected, this order operated very severe on the contractors, as they had fifteen hundred in charge that I turned over to them and they were paying Eight and ten dollars per day for each five horse team and finding them, corn at two dollars per bushel delivered, and previous to the war $3.50 was the usual price for a team per day. Their steamboats were on heavy demurage. The usual price for Steamboats from Montgomery to New Orleans was $2000, and the contractors had to pay $4000, the great demand for boats on the Alabama river at that time to transport Public supplies and troops is the cause of transportation being so high. I feel bound to state these facts in justice to the old contractors[37] as they have at all times been prompt and ready when called on to fulfill the obligation they had entered into with the Dept, and as far as they have come under my observation, done justice to the Emigrants.—

I shall close a new contract on the 12th Ins't when I will give the earliest inteligence.[38]

With respect
I have the honor to be
Your ob't Seve't
John Page Capt &
Supt Creek Rem'l

Bri'g Gen'l George Gibson
Com, Gen'l Sub't
Washington City

☾

Barry, writing from the neighborhood of Little Rock, reports on the delay at Rock Roe while waiting for wagons and teams to transport baggage and sick Creeks overland and that the party has recently been traveling at night in order to avoid the excessive heat of the prairie. He also notes an act of resistance by a number of Yuchis, who rolled the barrels containing the handcuffs and chains into the river. Also of note: Barry writes that the Creeks engaged in ball plays and dances. These dances, coupled with the Creeks eating large amounts of green corn and fruit, may have been an abbreviated Green Corn Ceremony held on the route west (see Abadie's 14 August 1836 letter, following). Letter found at CGS-IRW, Roll 5, 823–24.

Rec'd 5 Sept.

Near Little Rock
Arkansas, Aug't 10th 1836

General,

The party of emigrating Indians landed at Racrot[39] on the 30th Ult'o, were detained there in consequence of the impracticability of procuring teams until the 8th Inst. The conduct of the Indians, while in camp, was perfectly peaceable & orderly—they had their dances & ball plays, for amusement, fishing & hunting for occupation.[40] Some apprehension was entertained that Neo Micco's people would refuse to move; & indeed they had threatened to do so, but, when the waggons arrived they offered no opposition, & started off with apparent cheerfulness. The situation at Racrot was very unfavorable for an encampment, no water fit for drinking, could be procured, & there was no protection from the heat which was most excessive—notwithstanding these disadvantages the health of the party continued good, very few died & a very small proportion of the whole number suffered from sickness. The Chains & handcuffs taken off the Ind. were packed up in barrels & brought up to Racrot on board the Revenue Steam Boat—They were put on shore with some thirty or forty barrels of meat & provisions & during the night, rolled into the river by the Uchee Indians, the barrels containing them were not headed up & the chains are lost irrecoverarly.

The party left on the night of the 8th Ins't; it being impossible to proceed with the teams through the prairie during the day time. We have reached this point without accident & shall go on ten mile to night, making for the three nights' journies forty miles.

I shall write again from Irwin's[41] settlement, & cater more fully into details of some matters which at present I feel too much indisposed to take up.

I am, Sir, very resp'y
your Ob't Ser't
J. Waller Barry
L't & A Q'r Master
in charge of Emig'g Ind'ns

Brig'r Gen'l
Geo: Gibson
Comm'y Gen'l Sub
Washington City
D.C.

☾

Writing from James Erwin's settlement near present-day Cabot, Arkansas, Barry complains of the lack of suitable wagons to convey the sick and infirm overland and the corruption of local Arkansans, who offered to help the agents control the use of alcohol in camp while at the same time selling whiskey to the Creeks behind their backs. Barry also reports that it became necessary for the headmen to create a law against raiding the orchards and cornfields of white settlers along the route. Letter found at CGS-IRW, Roll 5, 816–17.

Rec'd & ans'd 13th Sep't

Irwin's Settlement
Aug't 14th 1836.

General,

There were only twenty waggons ready for the transportation of the Indians at RacRot on the 8th Inst—these I did not consider sufficient for the purpose, but consented to start upon the assurance of the Agents that more would be procured after the second days travel. One waggon gave out at the Grue[42]—the termination of the first days march—& two have since been obtained, making twenty one in all. These are still insufficient. It is true that the baggage, & sick, with many of the children can be transported, but, there are still many that should be transported who are compelled to walk. These teams will meet the party ten miles from this place & we shall then have enough.

The Contractors have been very active, & have, I believe, used every effort to procure waggons. They were not to be procured nearer than sixty or a hundred miles, & had I waited until the number required by the Contract arrived, we could not possibly have got off till late in the month. The Uchees, about nine hundred in number, have very little baggage; & among the Creeks, the waggons are loaded up in a great measure with old women & children.

The party has progressed so far extremely well. The Indians enjoy good health, are satisfied with the manner in which they are treated, & appear cheerful & well disposed. When the party first moved, they committed depredations on orchards & corn fields, & it was impossible either to restrain or punish them; but a law has now been established by all the chiefs, inflicting the punishment of fifty lashes upon any person who shall be found guilty of theft. The day after the promulgation of the law, two Uchee girls suffered the penalty of its violation—they were whipped before the whole camp. This has already operated beneficially, & I trust that its influence will last throughout the trip.

We have experienced more trouble & difficulty from the few white men in this part of the Country, than from all the Indians—they are the most depraved, lying, cut-throat scoundrels I ever met with. They would come into camp with offers of service to assist us, in seizing whiskey & other liquors; & at the same time, be selling it to the Indians behind our backs. No serious difficulty occurred, but the people of the neighbourhood when we landed, are entitled to all the credit of having done every thing in their power to bring it about. I have permitted several of the Indians to purchase rifles—the country through which they pass abounds in game of every description, & the young men can easily hunt through the woods all day & be up with the party in time to camp. They have Killed a great many deer since we started.

I shall write again as soon as an opportunity presents itself.

I am, Sir, very resp'y
your Ob't Ser't
J. Waller Barry
L't & Ass't Q'r Master
in charge of Emig'g Indians

To.
Brig'r Gen'l
Geo: Gibson
Comm'y Gen'l Sub'e

Washington City
D.C.

☾

Writing from James Erwin's settlement, Dr. Eugene Abadie reports that the party has had "only" between forty and fifty deaths, primarily from dysentery and cholera. The cause, Abadie believes, was from the Creeks "eating every thing green they can find on the road." What Abadie was likely witnessing here, was a Creek Green Corn Ceremony, or Busk. The Busk was the most important celebration of the year and ushered in the new harvest. The ceremony was so important that attendance was mandatory. And yet, because of the Second Creek War, most combatants and prisoners were unable to celebrate the Busk. Subsequently, it is very probable that they held an abbreviated Green Corn Ceremony while on their way to Fort Gibson.[43] Letter found at CGS-IRW, Roll 5, 807–8.

Rec'd 13. Sep't

Erwin's Settlement August the 14th
1836

To Gen'l Gibson Commiss. Gen'l of Subs.

General,

I take pleasure in informing you of our arrival so far, with comparatively few losses by death among the Indians, although we layed eight days at Racrot waiting untill the waggons could be collected, where they obtained a great deal of green fruit and corn, which I could not prevent their purchasing, and which occasioned much Dysentary[44] & cholera amongst them, I have had only between 40 and fifty deaths since we left Fort Mitchel and those among the very young or very old. The proportion is 35 children the balance old people and a few men—Much sickness still prevails from their eating every thing green they can find on the road, but fortunately it is not of a very fatal character, and yeilds to remedial means—

I can but ascribe the success of our remedies to the dietetic means furnished by the agents of the contractors, the sick being supplied with rice through the entire course of the disease if necessary, and by my preventing that any thing injurious should be given them, in which I encountered much opposition and difficulty. I had the satisfaction of seeing many bad cases recover.

The transportation for the sick has been satisfactory to me, and the size of the party, as well as the time of the year being taken in consideration, we have been much favored in having so few deaths—

Doubtless Lieut. Barry has informed you that an assistant[45] has been furnished me at Montgomery which was then very necessary two boats being required to cary the party to New Orleans; he has been continued in the service from the many sick and the great labour attending our attendance upon them, the camp being extensive, and the necessity we are under of visiting every tent to find the sick—

Early this morning we broke up our camp, with the hope of experiencing no more delays, if so the party will enjoy good health from the constant excitement of motion and from their inability of obtaining articles of food that may be [hurtful] to them—

I have the honour to be with respect
Your ob't Serv't
E.H. Abadie M.D.

☾

Written by John D. Howell on behalf of J.W.A Sanford & Company, this letter reports on the party's arrival at James Erwin's settlement, the difficulty in procuring wagons, and the number of deaths to that point in the journey. Letter found at CGS-IRW, Roll 6, 386–88.

Rec'd & ans'd 13th Sep't

Arkansaw— Pulaski cty
August 14 1836

Gen'l Geo Gibson
C.G.S.

Dear Sir

The party of hostile Creek Indians under our charge arrived at this place (Ervine's settlement 50 miles from Rock Roe, on White River) on the 12th inst; & left this morning for their place of destination.—

Before the Creek disturbances commenced we were satisfied that no party of any considerable size would likely emigrate before the fall: we, therefore, instructed the Contractor for supplies in Arkansas to sell out his Corn &c but to hold himself in readiness for an early fall supply—this was done: & the consequence was a great scarcity of provisions for this party.—The rapid movements of the party from Fort Mitchell to Rock Roe rendered it impossible for our agents in this part of the country to get advices of our movements & the size of the party so as to enable them to prepare for us.—We have, however, done all which the party required.—after laying at Rock Roe for ten days.—Our supplies of provisions had to be drawn from a great distance & at a verry great advance on their prices—to get wagons two prices was paid & even then could not get as many as we wanted—we started from Rock Roe with twenty wagons—at Mrs Black's we got one more from Little Rock & tomorrow we shall get three more from the river; which will make the number twenty four wagons—another wagon cannot be got short of One Hundred miles above—but we do not think that the party requires even that number as many of the wagons have not more than from 1500lbs to 2000lbs of baggage, childr & sick—Altho' provisions have been extremly scarce up to this point we have every assurance of getting supplies beyond the Cadron in greater abundance. We hope to arrive at Fort Gibson in twenty days from this date.—

Greater exertions could not have been made to comply with the letter of our agreement with Government & we hope our efforts have given satisfaction to your officer accompaning the party.[46]

From the time we left Fort Mitchell & Tuskega to this place we have lost forty two by deaths of this number thirty five were small children & infants; the others verry old women—The party under all the circumstances under which they started from the nation, may be considered verry healthy.

We have regularly corresponded with the Superintendent of Emigration Capt Page since we left & duly advised him of our movements.

With much Respect
Yr M'o Ob St,
Jno W A Sanford & Co

☾

William Armstrong reports on the impending arrival of the first detachment of Creek prisoners, the threats against the new arrivals by the McIntosh party, and Roly McIntosh's fear of being "superseded" or "abridged" by Neah Emathla. Letter found at Letters Received by the Office of Indian Affairs, 1824–81, Microcopy 234, Creek Agency West, 1826–36 (hereafter LR, CAW), Roll 236, 675.

Choctaw Agency Augst 31, 1836

C. A. Harris Esqr
Comr of Ind Affairs

Sir

The first party of emigrating Creeks are now on the opposite side of the river Arkansas, on their way up. I shall leave to-morrow so as to meet them at Gibson; while there, I will see the McIntosh party and endeavor to learn the state of feeling amongst the several parties. Many threats have been made; and much dissatisfaction manifested by both Chilly & Rolly McIntosh, the latter has sworn to kill A-po-the-holo who was concerned in taking the life of his Father.[47] Rolly McIntosh and the other Chiefs now over, are opposed to Ne-a-math-la the Chief who is with the party emigrating upon the ground mainly that they may probably be superseded, or their authority abridged. I will however report to you, fully, after I shall have informed myself of the state of feeling &c, and will endeavor with Genl Arbuckle, to bring about a reconciliation.

Respectfully
Your Ob't Serv't
Wm Armstrong
Act Supt West'r Ter'y

☾

Barry reports on the arrival of the first detachment of Creek prisoners on 3 September 1836 at their destination. In perhaps their final act of resistance, the Creeks refused the order of the commanding officer at Fort Gibson, General Arbuckle, to relocate ten miles beyond their encampment on the west bank of the Veridigris River. Barry notes that after crossing the river, the Creeks "concluded they would stop there." Letter found at CGS-IRW, Roll 5, 814.

Rec'd 4 Oct

Fort Gibson Ark's
Sep't 4th 1836

General

I have the satisfaction to inform you that the party of Emigrating Creek Indians accompanied by me from Montgomery Ala, arrived safely at this place on yesterday, & on the evening of the same day encamped on the western bank of the Verdigris & were turned over to Cap't Stephenson this morning.

The Indians were advised by Gen'l Arbuckle to proceed ten miles beyond the river & consented to do so; but on getting over the river concluded they would stop there. The total number of deaths amount to eighty, which is a very small proportion, considering the season & the quantity of green fruit eaten on the way.

I am now labouring under a slight attack of intermittent fever, which I beg may excuse the brevity of this communication.

I am, Sir, very resp'y y'r Ob Ser't
J. Waller Barry

L't & Ass't Q'r m. Emi'g In'ds

Brig Gen'l
Geo. Gibson
Comm'y Gen'l Sub'e
Washington City D.C.

☾

William Armstrong reports that the first detachment of Creek prisoners passed Fort Gibson and arrived at the Verdigris River. He also notes that Roly McIntosh was meeting with Neah Micco and Neah Emathla in order to settle differences. Letter found at LR, CAW, Roll 236, 679.

Fort Gibson
7th Sept 1836.

C.A. Harris Esq'r
Comm'r of Ind. Affr's

Sir,

The emigrating Creeks about twenty three hundred in number passed here on the 5 Inst—and are now at the Verdigris in their own Country—. I visited them to day—and have seen the chiefs Nea Math la, Neo Micco, with Roly McIntosh—they are to meet, Genl. Arbuckle & myself to morrow after which I will advise the Dept—of the result of our interview—

Respectfully,
Your Obt. Servt.
Wm Armstrong
Act Supt West'r Ter'y

☾

Stephenson reports on the arrival of 2,159 Creek prisoners at Fort Gibson. Letter found at SIAC, Agent (J.W.A. Sanford), Account (66), Year (1837), NARA.

Rec'd 26 Octo

Fort Gibson, Sept. 20th 1836.

Sir,

A party of Emigrant Creeks consisting of 2159 souls and conducted by an agent of J. W. Sanford & Co. and accompanied by Lieut. J. W. Barry A.Q.M. U.S. Army arrived in their new country on the 5th inst.—Provisions of good quality have been furnished them, and in sufficient quantity to enable them to select sites for their residences—They are apparently well satisfied with their reception, and so far as my duties are connected with them, I anticipate no cause for complaint.

Very Respectfully
your Obt. Servt.
Ja's R. Stephenson
Capt. U.S. Army
Disbg. Agt. (Creeks)

Emigration of Indians
Comg. Gen'l of Sub's
Washington

8 Second Detachment of Creek Prisoners, August–October 1836

On 2 August 1836 a second party of 193 Creeks, consisting primarily of women and children, began their journey down the Alabama River. The party included eighty Creek prisoners who had been marched to Montgomery after the departure of the first detachment. While in town, the Creeks were "threatened with death" by local whites, so Jesup hastily arranged for their removal westward.[1]

The second detachment of Creek prisoners was conducted to Indian territory by Captain Francis Smith Belton,[2] a Baltimore-born veteran of the War of 1812. Assisting him was Hiram W. Cooke,[3] a young Tennessee volunteer. A doctor by the name of Brown accompanied the party. While in New Orleans, Belton hired Dr. James Jones,[4] possibly the same chair of obstetrics at the Medical College of Louisiana in New Orleans (now Tulane University School of Medicine) to accompany the party.

Daily Journal of the Second Detachment

This is a journal kept by Francis Smith Belton describing the daily progress of the party. Journal found at LR, CAE, Roll 237, 520–26.

Journal of the removal of a party of hostile Creek Indians from the vicinity of Montgomery Alabama to the new Creek Country west of Fort Gibson Captain F.S. Belton Cond & disbursing Agent, agreably to orders from Major General Jesup comm'g Army of the South &c.

Montgy ala. aug 1, 1836 Pursuant to orders from Maj'r Gen'l Jesup,

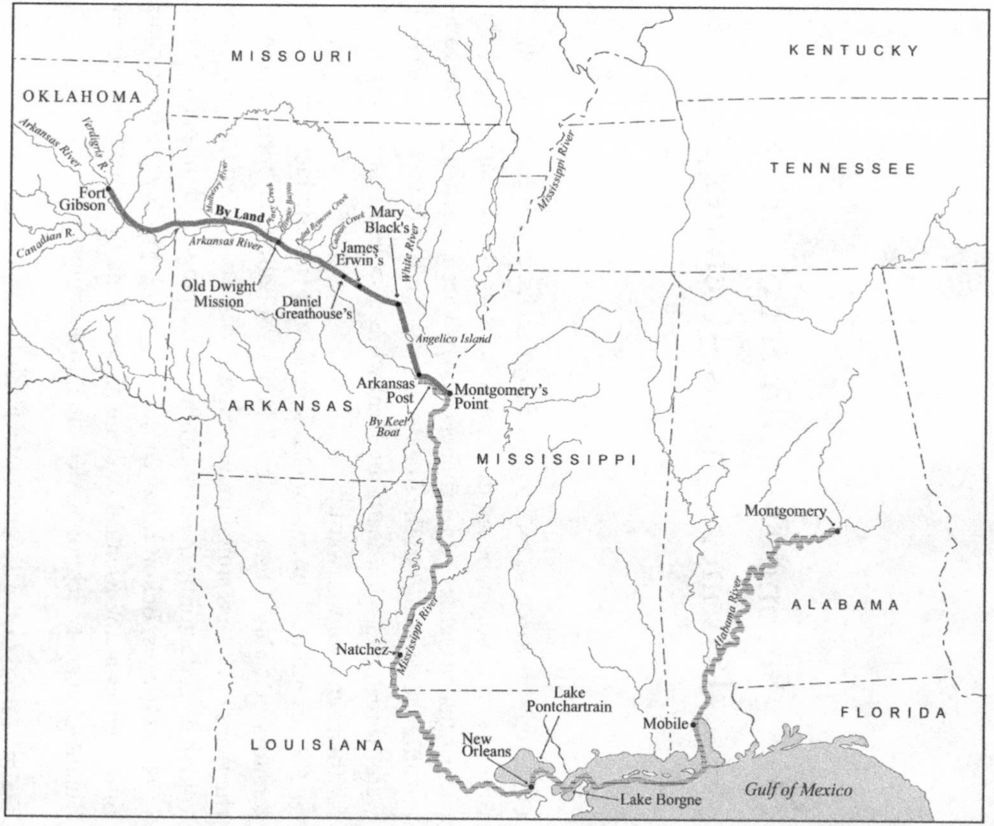

MAP 8. Route of the second detachment of Creek prisoners, August–October 1836. Place names correspond to stopping points or locations noted in the documentation. Route lines and locations are approximations. Cartography by Sarah Mattics and Kiersten Fish.

through Major Brant[5] QMUSA[6] the Conductor & ag't appointed[7] by said order received the muster rolls of the Creeks lately hostile & encamped in charge of a Tennessee Co'y[8] near Montgomery—A muster of the party was forthwith made, of this party an unknown and undefined[9] number were stated to be in the hands of the civil authority for trial & Private H W Cook of the Tennessee Vol's joins as Act'g Commissary Sup't.[10]

August 2d 1836. Embarked @ 9 AM on board steamer Lewis Cass, Capt Frye[11] for Mobile The Indians baggage &c in a Lighter.[12]

From 3rd to 6th Aug't 1836. nothing [illegible] Two Indian children died.

Mobile 6th Aug't arrived at 3 a.m. Transferred Indian party to Steamboat Mazeppa[13] Capt Sutton.[14] Left Mobile at noon. Passage outside of Key's[15] and through Lake Borgne very rough.

Aug 7. arrived at Lake end of Pontchartrain R Road; Engaged Cars for baggage sick Infirm &c of the Emigration party weather rainy & very Sultry. obtained Q'rs for party in old Barracks[16] Doct Brown attends. Sick &c increase in number. For transportation up the river enormous prices are asked Viz. 400 per day.—

Aug 8–9 & 10th aug't. This 10th inst Transportation was furnished by Maj Clark QM'r[17] and the party embarked on board Steam Boat Moine[18] Capt [illegible] bound to St. Louis: health of the party very bad. Made purchases of provisions—Dr James Jones of New Orleans engaged[19] to accompany party—Drew On Comm'y Gen'l at washington at sight & for $1000 favor of Cash of Comm'l Bank N Orl's.

Aug 10th. Tranp'a being ready The party embarked at 7 PM.

11th 12th 13th & 14th Aug. On the Mississippi River—Nothing important touching the party addressed the Comm'y Gen'l of Subsistence Via Memphis.

Aug 15. Mouth of white river 15 Aug. Landed at the Mouth @ 8 am. The Arkansas river is said to be high and in fine boating order, but all the boats are withdrawn but one a very small one boiler boat the Eagle[20] said to be up White river. If the party could be landed at Rock Row the passage of the prairie might be expected with some delay to meet which the supplies of salt pork & corn meal laid in at New Orleans were intended.

Aug 23d. Montgomery's Point the Indian Party have become very unhealthy and several have died. Indeed all the inhabitants here are down with Congestive & Intermittent fever. The cond'r & agent succeeds at last in obtaining a Keel boat & hands & contracts with Mr Wm Mahon[21] to take the sick Infirm, &c. all who are unable to march through the swamp, provisions &c. under charge of Doctor Jones to Post Arkansas where it is hoped some transportation can be procured, and health reestablished accordingly, this morning; the embarkation is made in the Keel Boat and they are moved off, with great reluctance however, as families are divided, and they are very suspicious of evil intended them.

24th August—an Indianna flat boat stopped in the night and sold quantity of whiskey to the Indians the whole marching party are drunk, what liquor they had concealed, was taken from them & destroyed, not however without some bad feelings and threats. Crossed White river ferry and Cutt off.—buried a dead man left by the Keel boat party and passed the heaviest part of the swamp & camped at Menard[22] 18 miles.

25th Aug. arrived at the Post Arkansas—Met Mr Chase[23] of the Emig'n Ind Dep't sent on by Capt'n Brown,[24] immediate measures taken to procure transportation, but every thing indicates difficulty & delay. The business of the Country is done in miserable ox (cotton) carts, many without tired wheels or indeed, without Iron of any kind—The wagons at remoter points are all away with the volunteers[25] on the road to Fort Towson,[26] Red River, and the same Cause has made drivers [scarce] of teams & [no] wagons could be procured; the sickness abates somewhat.

28. The Keel Boat arrives from Mouth of white river. Sick of the party are improving—

Sept 3rd. Several Carts came in, and are detained there Seems no choice, and we must wait to get all in & select from them the best—. This is the best that can be done though it incurs some expense without service; but the lazy & independent population see our extremity, and conduct themselves accordingly.—

Sept 4th. The party would have started but for incessant & heavy rain, two of the principal Carts most relied on for strength & Capacity have not come in.—

Sept 5. Moved the party & reached Williams Grande Prairie 12 miles.

Sept 6th. Moved early and reached Robins 15 miles. The flies are most distressing, a horse can hardly be controlled from lying down to roll; such is the torment & The heat is excessive and water of the worst description Some forty five sick, and constantly dropping, the ox teams breaking, and Carts tumbling to pieces.

Sept 7th. Reached angelico Island,[27] a timber Island in the midst of the prairie—the want of water further on, obliges us to halt here.—10 miles.—

Sep 8: Grande Prairie:—halt at Stilwells[28] 15 miles

Sep 9. Halt at Mrs Blacks.[29] 10 miles, Bakers[30] two wagons engaged, for the timbered part of the road.

Sep 10. Halt at bayou Pond, 11 miles, the rocks & roots of the timber here break down our Carts, and without Baker's wagons the party could not have proceeded.

Sep't 11. Halt at Irwin's—20 miles.[31] During the passage of the prairie, it has, with the exception of two days of scorching Sun, rained almost all day and night the situation of the Indians is deplorable the sick exceed fifty of the small party, and death occasionally carries off the weakest, the wagons or Carts have been overloaded & great difficulties surmounted, to reach Settlements forced marches have been necessary paid off & discharged the Carts engaged at Post Arkansas. Three additional wagons are engaged for Indians & one for officers' transportation—These are miserable small & old vehicles, poor teams and harness but better cannot be done. The Charges too are high indeed the people taking advantage of an Obvious necessity, & having heard of larger partyes in the rear, very indifferent about engaging at all—what better can be done—The sick require attention to their situation & weakness: & the very elements are against us. There is nothing better in prospect, the best wagons being with the large hostile party in charge of L't Barry and the Volunteers marching from the neighbouring settlements for Fort Towson have engaged every good thing of the kind at enormous prices. The Country is sparsely settled; we are at the mercy of circumstances. Mr. Chase delivers $1750 from Capt. Brown.[32]

14 Sept. 1836. The party moved over a very rocky rough road to Greathouse's[33] 12 miles; high water, nearly swimming at an intervening creek, rain in torrents.—one wagon wheel shattered.

15 Sept. 1836. a new wheel was required nearly out & out the broken wagon was refitted & party moves a long & late march to Newells[34] 15 miles rain incessant the Country inundated, and every little rill a torrent the banks of the water courses are generally steep & rocky, the road, mere cut out without draining or causeways.—

16 Sept 36. Left Newells & moved to Cadron, the Cadron bottom the worst possible, passed Ferry & Camped at Mather's.[35] 15 Miles = 30.

17 Sep't 36. Left mather's & passed P Remove Creek by Fletchers Toll Bridge,[36] the bottom is probably the worst on the road and nearly impassable. Halted at Blounts[37] old place 4 miles beyond Pt. Remove—12 miles.

18th Sep't 36. The Party reached Potts[38]—road very bad and rain in heavy torrents. 12 miles:—The state of the wagons here requires a days work at the blacksmith shop, distance 12 miles.

19 Sept. a Teamster taken violently ill place supplied by Indian Ben;[39] as he must be left.—The Cond & agent is also taken sick.[40] Meet Lt Barry on his return from F't Gibson.

20 Sep't. Rain—Party moved early & reached Lovely's place;[41] passed Illinois Bayou by Ferry below old Dwight[42] rain in drenching torrents and waters very high & rapid.

21 Sept. Reached Piney Creek. 7 miles passed the very rapid ferry with great difficulty & halted 3 miles further at May's[43] prairie = 10 miles a glimpse of sunshine, the first for three weeks—

22d Sept 36. Reached Judge Garretts[44] crossing Spadra Creek rains all day and night. 18 miles.

23 Sept 36. Reached Morrisons. 15 miles—

24 Sep't 36. Reached Rolling's. 13 Miles.

25th Sep't 36. Reached Mulberry & encamped at the Bank one mile from Lassiters.[45] 12 miles. The Stream is a wild torrent now impassable at best a rocky rapid ford. detained next day by high waters.

26. Impossible to cross Mulberry. Indian party very sickly say 37.—

27th. The Conductor & ag't is now obliged in consequence of a fever of seven days continuance to give up & turn over the party &c. to Doctor J Jones, to conduct &c to the Agency, his hope was to continue on, relying on a vigorous constitution but weakness prevents his mounting a horse; and this measure is reluctantly adopted. He hopes however that a few days rest medicine &c. may enable him to overtake the party—In this he was dissappointed, and the return of Doctor Jones, found me just able to resume the return movement—on the 15th Oct. The Indian party were delivered on 3d Oct to Capt Stephenson. 165 strong—The Muster Roll rec'd with them were very imperfect but of those embraced on the original roll 210. 17 were detained by Civil authority in alabama. = 193 died on the march. 19 = 174—and nine, missing from some unaccountable cause, probably on the road in the Cherokee Country—number delivered 165.—

The Cond & agent made every endeavour as stated in the remarks <u>on Mahon's Contract</u> to obtain the desirable Voucher on his return to White river, where he was delayed as also at Memphis, by a recurrence or relapse of fever. This disease only enabled him to move by stages & finally to report at Mobile & to proceed to this place to close his accounts &c touching this Service, completed he trusts satisfactorily to the Dep't of Emigration but, with sacrafices of health & constitution to all employed & particularly to the Journalist.

Respectfully Submitted
F. S. Belton
Capt 2nd Art

New Orleans, La
28th Nov'r 1836—

Supplemental Letters of the Second Detachment of Creek Prisoners

Captain Francis S. Belton reports on the party's impending arrival at the mouth of the White River and the uncertainty over whether the state of the Arkansas River will allow for water transportation. Belton also notes a number of sick people in the party, including Belton's assistant, Hiram W. Cooke, a Tennessee Volunteer. Letter found at CGS-IRW, Roll 5, 870–71.

Rec'd Sep't 2d

Steam Boat Moyne, below mouth
of white River ark's Aug. 1836.

Sir:

On my arrival at New Orleans with a party of Creek Indians, on their way to their allotted region, in Arkansas, I expected to be relieved in the charge of the party. I met however Maj. General Jesups order, to proceed with them to their destination, and after five days halt in New Orleans a passage has been procured in the Steam Boat Moyne, by a contract with the Quartermaster's Department, to the mouth of White River, and twenty days provisions were laid in by me. It seemed clearly to be foreseen, in N Orl's that this party would, from the low stage of the water in the Arkansas, be obliged to march the whole distance, which operation seems yet to threaten us. To meet that operation and the Subsistence and contingencies of the party for the Land Route of near 400 miles, I have received funds to the am't of one thousand dollars by a draft on you in favor of the Commercial Bank of New Orl's in addition to three hundred dollars received from Major Brant Q Master Montgomery. The party comprehends some very infirm and aged as well as some very young and there exists at this time considerable sickness among them. My Assistant, a Tennessee Volunteer and unacclimated is also down with the fever since leaving New Orl's—To guard against reasonable apprehensions from the season &c. on the score of health I have engaged at New Orleans a physician Doctor Jones, for the whole route at the rate of $150 monthly compensation.

I am unable to say from the uncertainty of things what will be my course on arriving at White River, but will of course advise the Dep't of every important act in a service in which I am without instructions and experience and for my conduct of which I request your favorable consideration.

I have the honor to be
Your very Ob't Servant
F. S. Belton.
Capt 2nd Reg Arty
Cond'r & agent Emi'gr Creeks.

To,
B'r Gen'l Geo Gibson
Comm'y General of Subs'e

☾

Disbursing agent Jacob Brown reports on the arrival of the second detachment of prisoners at the mouth of White River and his decision to send Luther Chase, who was acquainted with the region, to help Captain Belton procure land transportation. Letter found at CGS-IRW, Roll 5, 879.

Rec'd 13 Sept & an'd 13th

Little Rock
Aug 22d 1836.

Sir—

I am informed that a small party of about 200 Creek Emigrants were landed at the Mouth of White River on the 10th inst.—

Capt. Belton who has charge, informs me that the party is composed of women and children, aged and infirm, and many sick;—That he has procured a Keel boat and shall make an effort to get to the Post of Arkansas.—

As Capt. Belton is unacquainted with this section of the country, its resources, &c.—and knowing as I do, the slim—as well as very indifferent means of Transport to be found at the Post, I have deemed it proper in order to facilitate the movement as much as possible, to send a person well acquainted with that section of the country, with instructions to aid in procuring Teams, should assistance for that purpose be required; if not—being the bearer of Letters—to return to this place.

Very respectfully
Your obt. Svt.
J. Brown Capt U.S.A.
Pr Dis Agt Ind Removal

Gen'l. Geo. Gibson
Com'y. Gen'l. of Sub.
Washington D.C.

☾

Captain Francis S. Belton reports that the second detachment of Creek prisoners arrived at Fort Gibson on 3 October 1836 and that he is on his way to join his detachment fighting the Seminoles in Florida. Letter found at LR, CAE, Roll 237, 507.

Mobile Nov'r 10—1836

Sir

I have the honor to report from this place; the party of Creek Indians lately under my command, having been delivered at Fort Gibson on the 3rd ult'o.

Two severe attacks of the fever which has prevailed in the country I had traversed has caused some delay. I shall however be able to send on my journal in a few days and my accounts very soon after, which being accomplished I shall join my regiment for duty in Florida.[46]

Respectfully, I have the honor
to be Yr Ob't Servant
F. S. Belton
Capt 2nd Art

To
B'r Gen Gibson
C Gen. of Sub.
&c. &c. &c.

Part 3

The Coerced Relocations, 1836–37

9 Detachments 1–6

Despite the fact that a minority of Creek Indians participated in the Second Creek War, and many had helped the United States capture the rebels, Andrew Jackson ordered the relocation of the remaining Creeks from the east. He justified his decision by stating that peaceful Creeks might later turn "hostile." Although Creek headmen were probably not surprised at Jackson's decision, they were "astonished" at the rapidity with which they were ordered to leave Alabama. The Creeks were organized into five detachments with camps at Tallassee, Wetumpka, Chambers County, and two camps located near Talladega. As the most powerful headman, Opothle Yoholo[1] was assigned to detachment 1 and ordered to leave on August 25, 1836. Detachment 2, which contained Creeks from towns affiliated with Tuckabatchee, were ordered to leave the following day. Opothle Yoholo directed these Creeks to follow in his footsteps. As the Creeks prepared for removal they were bombarded by creditors who seized the Creeks' money, slaves, horses, and other property. Many other Creeks worried that if they left Alabama they would never see the money from their land fraud claims. Jesup subsequently delayed the movement by five days. During this detention, several Upper Creek headmen signed a contract with James C. Watson & Company for the sale of 656 reserves that had been purchased earlier but set aside by investigators under the suspicion of fraud. On 31 August 1836 Opothle Yoholo's detachment number 1 commenced their journey to Indian territory. The party was led by nine Creek men who were in charge of the Tuckabatchee town's sacred brass plates.[2]

The Creeks were relocated by a company called the Alabama Emigrating Company—essentially a reorganized John W.A. Sanford and

Company—which had been renamed after J.W.A. Sanford pulled out of the partnership for good in 1836. And, just like its predecessor, the Alabama Emigrating Company was composed largely of land speculators, many of whom had cheated the Creeks out of their reserves. Indeed, Watson, the same man who led a group of speculators that purchased the 656 reserves, was a founding partner of the Alabama Emigrating Company. Some of the contractors were even members of two different land companies. The Creeks had always feared that private contractors would be less attentive to their safety and comfort than the government military agents. They were correct. Provision stands were not established to the military personnel's satisfaction; some Creeks who went by land through the Mississippi Swamp were abandoned by company employees; and the contractors tried to cram as many people onto steamboats as possible. Moreover, winter clothing—unnecessary in the August heat of Alabama—was stored away and remained inaccessible as the Creeks passed through Indian territory in December in four to eight inches of snow.

As the five detachments made their way from Alabama to Fort Gibson over the course of the late summer, fall, and winter of 1836–37, detachment 6 remained in Alabama. Prior to leaving the East, military personnel had visited each detachment and asked if any Creeks would be willing to serve against the Seminoles in Florida. The Second Seminole War began in 1835 and continued through 1836 as the Creeks were forced from Alabama. Some Creeks fled to Florida to aid the Seminoles, while the Creeks participating in the Second Creek War eventually merged the two conflicts as the theatre of operations moved to southern Georgia and north Florida. While most Creeks were uninterested in helping the U.S. government, as many as 776 agreed to serve. Incentives such as money, a promise to discharge them from duty prior to 1 February 1837, and a quick settlement to their land fraud claims were among the promises made to the Creeks. The warriors also demanded that their families be allowed to remain in east Alabama until their tour of duty was over so that they could travel westward together. Subsequently, three encampments were established to house the warriors' families.[3]

Despite the assurances given, the headmen had actually obligated their warriors contractually for an indefinite term in Florida, and the government eventually reneged on its promise to discharge them by the 1 February deadline. Subsequently their tour of duty was extended through the summer of 1837. Brevet Major General Thomas S. Jesup, who oversaw the war with the Seminoles, gave his rationale for extending the deployment of the warriors by noting "had [the Creeks] left me on the 1st of February according to the assurances given to them, I must have called into service at least two regiments of militia or volunteers to have taken their places, at a heavy expense." The extended service strained the capabilities of the Creeks, and many were worn down by the hard service. To make matters worse, the Creek families in Alabama also suffered from the warriors' extended tour of duty. Local whites in Alabama grew impatient with the presence of large numbers of Creeks near their settlements, especially after the resumption of violence of the Second Creek War in 1837. Local militias descended on the camps and stole property and tried to arrest Creeks they believed were complicit in the violence. The whites, however, also turned violent. A ninety-year-old man was beaten to death, and whites attempted to rape a fifteen-year-old Creek girl.

In order to prevent more assault, federal agents moved the Creek families to Mobile Point, where it was thought the Creeks would be safe. Instead, the Creeks became violently ill and died of yellow fever in the encampments. Agents searched for better land, and in July 1837 moved the camp to Pass Christian, Mississippi. The Creek warriors were not happy about the move to the Gulf, however. News probably spread from the warriors who returned to Mobile Point or Pass Christian to convalesce and then returned to Florida with news that their families had been moved south. Jesup noticed a decisive change in the attitude of many of the warriors after learning of the depredations committed on their families and their movement to the Gulf. The general observed that "if not disposed to favour the Seminoles are at least not very zealous in our cause. With the exception of a very small portion of them they were zealous and true until they received information of the removal of their families from Alabama, and the outrages committed upon them there."

In October 1837 up to seven steamboats ascended the Mississippi River from New Orleans carrying the warriors and their families. As one of the boats—the *Monmouth*—ascended the river on 31 October, it passed Profit Island as did all boats traveling north on the Mississippi River. Instead of passing the island on the side reserved for northbound travel, however, the *Monmouth* ascended on the opposite side, leaving it vulnerable to collision from boats descending the river. While the *Monmouth* traveled this dangerous route at night in a drizzling rain, it was cut in two by the steamboat *Trenton*, which was being towed by the *Warren*. The *Monmouth*'s cabin detached from its hull and drifted for a period in two pieces, before sinking. Approximately three hundred people died. The Creek warriors and their families arrived at Fort Gibson in late December 1837.[4]

Contract with the Alabama Emigrating Company, 13 August 1836

This contract, like the John W.A. Sanford and Company contract before it, is an agreement between the United States and a private contracting firm called the Alabama Emigrating Company. It specifies the liabilities for each side as well as what the Creeks are entitled to on the journey west. Contract found at Henry J. Wilson Papers, 1779–1885, Louisiana State University Special Collections, Baton Rouge.

Articles of agreement entered into this thirteenth day of august Eighteen hundred and thirty six between Capt John Page U.S. army, and Superintendant of Creek Removal under the authority of the President of the United States; and James C. Watson,[5] Edward Hanrick,[6] Felix G. Gibson, R. W. Williams, S. M. Ingersoll, James Abercrombie,[7] William A. Campbell,[8] William J. Beattie, John D. Howell, William Walker, T. Gilman.[9]

To be known in said articles as, and acting under the firm and style of the alabama Emigrating Company.

This Agreement Witnesseth that the said Capt. John Page, U.S. army for and on behalf of the United States of America, and the said Alabama Emigrating Company their Heirs, Executors, & Administrators have agreed and by these Presents do mutually covenant and agree.

1st That the said Alabama Emigrating Company, their Heirs &c. shall remove the Creek Indians, Occupants of the Creek Nation in the State of alabama from said Nation to a point in the New Country allotted to the Creeks West of the Territory of Arkansas, and within twenty miles of Fort Gibson—To Wit: Men, Women and children, & their slaves, and their goods and chattels as herein after provided in manner and form, and for the consideration specified in these articles of agreement.

2d That the said Alabama Emigrating Company their Heirs &c shall collect the Indians together at such times and places as the Superintendant, under the orders of the Commanding General shall direct: and said Indians shall be subsis by them from the day of Assembly designated by said Superintendant.

3d That the said alabama Emigrating Company their Heirs &c will dispatch to the New Country aforesaid by such routes as the Superintendant shall point out—parties of one thousand Indians, or more, under the Conduct of such Agents as the said Alabama Emigrating Company their Heirs &c may appoint the Indians having been first carefully enrolled.

4th That the following shall be the Rations and the kind and quantity of Transportation to which the Indians &c shall be entitled: Viz't the ration of Bread shall be one pound of Wheat flour, Indian Meal, or hard bread—or three fourths of a quart of Corn: the Meat ration shall be one pound of fresh or three quarters of a pound of Salt Meat or Bacon, and with fresh meat—two quarts of Salt to every hundred rations. The transportation shall be one five Horse waggon and fifteen hundred pounds of Baggage to-from Seventy to Eighty persons. The provisions and transportation shall be the best of their kind.

The average daily travel shall not exceed from twelve to fifteen Miles to be determined by the Officer and Surgeon.

5th That the provisions shall be issued daily (if practicable) and not less frequently than every other day as well whilst a rest as during the travel untill the day inclusive of arrival at the point of destination West, and that there shall be established, immediately, points upon the entire route Westward at which the provisions are to be issued.

6th That the Sick, those enfeebled from age or Other cause, and young children shall be transported in Wagons or on Horseback, that those who may be pronounced unable to proceed, may be left on the way at some proper place and under the care of some person at the expence of the United States.

7th That the Indian Ponies shall be given from the day of starting Westward, one half gallon of Corn each—provided such disposition in the active operations of the removal may be made of them, not to include the hauling of Wagons before mentioned, as the said Alabama Emigrating Company and their Heirs &c may deem proper, but that they will not be seperated from the Company to which the owners are respectively attached, nor compelled to carry other baggage or persons than those belonging to the family of their owners.

8th That the said alabama Emigrating Company their Heirs &c shall be entitled to Twenty Eight Dollars and fifty cents a head for each person transported from the Creek Nation to the place of delivery before mentioned: and for all persons who may die or be necessarily left on the way as authorized by article 6th of this contract, an amount in proportion to the distance travelled: provided that the evidence herein required in such cases of arrival Westward &c is furnished to the proper department. The amount due to the said Alabama Emigrating Company, their Heirs &c to be promptly paid at such points as may be previously indicated by them and under instructions to be hereafter given by the War department.

9th The removal of the Indians being a Military operation, and under the direction of the military authorities the said Alabama Emigrating Company their Heirs &c shall not correct them; and all threats and violence toward them are prohibited; and they (the Indians) shall be treated by the said Alabama Emigrating Company their Heirs &c and by the Agents of the same with lenity, forbearance and humanity.

10th That the said United States will furnish the following Agents Viz't

> 1st A Superintendant whose duty it shall be to remain within the limits of the Creek Nation during the proper season for operations under this Contract for the purpose of seeing that its stipulations are fulfilled by the parties thereto. He will not be accountable in any way for his acts to the said alabama Emigrating Company their Heirs &c. and that such Superintendant shall decide whether Seventy or Eighty or any intermediate number of Indians ought, consistently with the health and comfort of them, to be assigned to each Wagon.
>
> 2d Two or more Military or other Agents One or more of whom shall accompany each party West.
>
> The duties of these Agents shall be to attend particularly to the

treatment received by the Indians, their rations and transportation, to remonstrate against any course of conduct on the part of the agents of the said alabama Emigrating Company their Heirs &c inconsistent with the letter and spirit of this Contract and if a remedy can be found in a pecuniary Expenditure, to make it, which said expenditure shall (if approved of by the Superintendant) be deducted from the payments to be made under this Contract to the said Alabama Emigrating Company their Heirs &c.

3d A Surgeon for each Emigrating party whose duty it shall be to attend to the Sick thereof. He shall also be the arbiter in cases of difference of opinion between the agents of the United States and of the said Alabama Emigrating Company relative to the quality of provisions the time and place of issuing the same, and the time of starting and stopping on the daily travel; and he shall also decide whether invalids may be left on the way, and take care that they are provided for agreeable to article 6th of this contract, and enter upon the roll the time and place of such occurrence with the date of decease of all Indians who may die on the route.

4th A Disbursing Agent in the New Creek Country West of the Mississippi, whose duty it shall be to receive the Indians as they arrive, to muster them and to certify upon the roll presented to him by the Agent of the said Alabama Emigrating Company their Heirs &c the result of that muster; said muster to take place on the day of arrival (if practicable) at the point of destination.

And the said Alabama Emigrating Company their Heirs &c shall render every facility to the aforesaid Superintendant, Military, Medical, and Disbursing Agents, that may be necessary to enable them freely to attend to the duties of their Several offices.

11th That the said Alabama Emigrating Company shall hold themselves in readiness at all times to proceed in the discharge of their duties under this contract and are to commence the removal of such parties and at such times and places as may be designated by the Superintendant of Creek Removal upon notice being given of time and place of starting and the number of the party to be removed.

12th And it is also hereby reserved the United States to annul this Contract to all intents at any time the aforesaid Superintendant under the orders of the Genl. or officer Commanding in the Creek Country may deem proper—upon a non-compliance therewith on the part of the said Alabama Emigrating Company.

Provided; and it is hereby understood by the Contracting parties, that all such matters as are merely in the nature of regulations, and do not effect the pecuniary interest of the Said Alabama Emigrating Company their Heirs &c.—are saved to the United States and that under all circumstances the United States have complete control of their own officers and Agents.

And further that where infractions of this contract exist, they must be alleged by either party at the time of their occurrence and that no effect whatever is to be given here after to allegations not thus brought forward.

Witness (as on the other side)[10] our hands and seals this the 13th day of august Eighteen hundred and thirty six.

Signed
John Page Capt'n
Sup't Creek Removal
J.C. Watson
Edward Hanrick
Felix G. Gibson
R. W. Williams
A. Abercrombie[11]
Alfred Iverson
Geo. Whitman[12]
S. M. Ingersoll
James Abercrombie
Wm A. Campbell
Wm J. Beattie by his atty[13] *Alfred Iverson*
John D. Howell by his atty A Iverson
William Walker
T. Gilman

Signed, Sealed & Duplicates delivered & exchanged in presence of
Signed

M. W. Bateman
1st Lt. 6th Infantry &c

☾

The following order (no. 63), issued by Thomas S. Jesup on 17 August 1836, organized the first two detachments of Creek Indians. Orders found at SIAC, Agent (Reynolds), Account (1687), Year (1838), NARA.

Head Quarters Army of the South
Tuskeegee 17th Aug; 1836.

Orders
No 63.

Par: 1. The Indians under the chief Opoth le yohola ordered to rendezvous near Tallassee will form detachment No. 1 and will move westward on the 25th inst.

Par 2. The Indians ordered to rendezvous near Wetumpka will form detachment No. 2 and will move westward one days march after detachment No. 1.

Par. 3. The superintendant of Creek emigration[14] will cause detachments Nos. 1 & 2 to be immediately enrolled and organised into parties: will notify the Alabama Emigration Company of the order for removal and that issues of rations by them will begin on the 25th inst:—will require them to consult the wishes of the Indian chiefs in reference to the Agents selected, and the arrangements adopted in so far as it can be done without affecting the pecuniary interests of the Company—and will promptly report any anticipation or actual failure on their part.

Par. 4. To facilitate the adjustment of unfinished land business the Superintendant in conjunction with the certifying Agents will cause descriptive lists to be made out of the Indians, the lands in question—the present position and desired arrangement of the points in issue and will assure the Indians that measures are taken to do them justice, that the lands shall be disposed of at their fair value and the proceeds paid them at their western homes.

Par. 5. Lieut. Bateman is assigned as principal military agent to detachment No. 1. and will forthwith enter upon duty and assume the direction of the preparatory arrangements, subject to the orders of the Superintendant.

Par 6. Lieut. Reynalds[15] of the U.S. Marine Corps is with the approbation of Colonel Henderson[16] appointed military Agent, will report to Lieut. Bateman at Tallassee and act under his orders.

Par 7. Mr. Dubois[17] is appointed assistant agent and will report to Lieut. Bateman.

Par 8. Dr. J. B. Busby[18] is appointed Surgeon to Detachment No. 1. will report to Lieut. Bateman at Tallassee and enter upon duty.

Par 9. Lieut. Screven[19] is assigned to detachment No. 2. as principal military Agent and will forthwith join Lieut. Simpson[20] at Wetumka and assume the direction of the preparatory arrangements subject to the orders of the Superintendant.

Par 10. Lieut. Simpson[21] at present on duty at Wetumka will continue to act as Military Agent, subject to the orders of Lieut. Screven.[22]

Par 11. Lieut. Screven will provide a Surgeon for Detachment No. 2.

Par. 12. The Superintendant will forthwith take measures for the enrollment and organization into parties of the Creek Indians not included in detachments Nos. 1 & 2—and for obtaining the descriptive lists mentioned in Par. No. 4. He will report the number of parties—and will notify the Alabama Emigration company to be in readiness to charge of detachments 3 & 4 by the 28th August.

By order of Majr. Gen'l Jesup
{Signed} Henry Stanton[23]
& Adjt. Gen'l
Army of the South

True copy
M. W. Bateman
1st Lieut 6th Infantry
P. M. Agent &c.

Order no. 67, issued by Thomas S. Jesup on 22 August 1836, organized detachments 3 through 6. Because the order was given prior to the raising of a Creek volunteer force to Florida, it was never implemented. Jim Boy and Echo Harjo, among others, ultimately agreed to fight the Seminoles, and after subsequent reorganization, five detachments left Alabama in the summer of 1836. The sixth (comprising the Creek volunteers and their family members), remained in the east until relocating in 1837. Order found at SIAC, Agent (Reynolds), Account (1687), Year (1838), NARA.

Head Quarters Army of the South
Tuskegee august 22. 1836.

Order
No. 67.

Par. 1. The band of Jim Boy[24] & Yee ho-Harjo will constitute the third detachment for emigration. They will be organised into parties, and on the first of Septr will be turned over to the alabama Emigration company, and on that day issues of rations by the Company and the movement westward will begin.

Par. 2. Echo-Harjos band with such other Indians as the Superintendant of emigration may assign thereto, will be organised into parties and turned over to the Alabama Emigration Company on the 5th Septr; and on that day issues of rations by the Company and the movement westward will begin.

Par. 3. Tuski batchi Harjos band, with such Indians as the Superintendant of Emigration may assign thereto, will constitute the fifth detachment, they will be organised into parties and on the 29th of august will be turned over to the Alabama Emigration Company and on that day Issues of Rations and the movement westward will begin.

Par. 4. The Talladega Indians will constitute the sixth detachment, they will be organised into parties and turned over to the Alabama Emigration Company, at such times between the twenty third and the thirty first of August as Lieu't Deas under the orders of the superintendant, shall designate. The issues of rations by the company, and the movements of the several parties westward will commence on the days designated.

Par. 5. In addition to the prescribed Reports through the Superintendant of Emigration, the senior Military agents with the several detachments will report by express direct to the commanding General, at least once in two days, the progress of the preparations, the necessity for the presence of Military force, and such incidents as may impede the prompt fulfilment of the orders for emigration.

Par. 6. Doctor McKnight[25] of the U.S. Marine Corps. is with the approbation of Co'l Henderson temporarily relieved from duty with the Marine Corps. He will report to Major Lomax and relieve ass't Surgeon M Mills now on duty with Major Lomax's[26] Battalion, ass't Surgeon Mills, in pursuance of orders from the war Department is assigned to duty in the emigration of Indians and attached to the second detachment. He will repair to Wetumpka and report to Lieu't Screven principal Military Agent of the detachment.

Par. 7. Doctor G. W. Hills is appointed Surgeon to the fifth detachment, and will report for duty to Lieu't Sprague Military Agent of Detachment No. 5.

Par. 8. Lieu't Reynolds of the U.S. Marine Corps is relieved from duty in the Detachment No. 1; is appointed principal Military Agent to detachment No. 2 and will report in person to the superintendant of Emigration.

Par. 9. Lieu't Sloan of the U S Marine Corps, is with the approbation of Co'l Henderson, assigned to duty in the Emigration of Indians; he is appointed principal Military Agent to Detachment No. 4 and will report in person to the superintendant of emigration.[27]

By order of Major Gen'l Jesup—
Henry Stanton
Lt Co'l & Adj Gen'l
army of the south

10 Detachment 1

The first detachment was based three miles west of Tallassee and consisted of Indians from the town of Tuckabatchee (and its affiliates), who were led by the powerful chief Opothle Yoholo. The party was conducted to Indian territory by Stephen Miles Ingersoll on behalf of the Alabama Emigrating Company. Pennsylvania-born Mark W. Bateman (sometimes Batman)[1] of the 6th U.S. Infantry served as military oversight, and Dr. John B. Bussy of Tallassee, Alabama, accompanied the party as physician.[2]

Orders from Jesup

Thomas S. Jesup advises Opothle Yoholo that he has been assigned to the first detachment and that his relocation is imminent. Letter found at SIAC, Agent (Reynolds), Account (1687), Year (1838), NARA.

> Head Quarters army of the South
> Tuskegee Ala. 17th Aug. 1836.
>
> The Creek Chief
> Opothleyohola
>
> Brothers,
>
> I send you the orders I have this day given providing for the removal of yourself and your people.
>
> Mr Bateman of the army is an excellent officer and to him you can always apply.
>
> As you are the leading chief I have made your party the first detachment—and your people at Wetumka the second detachment.

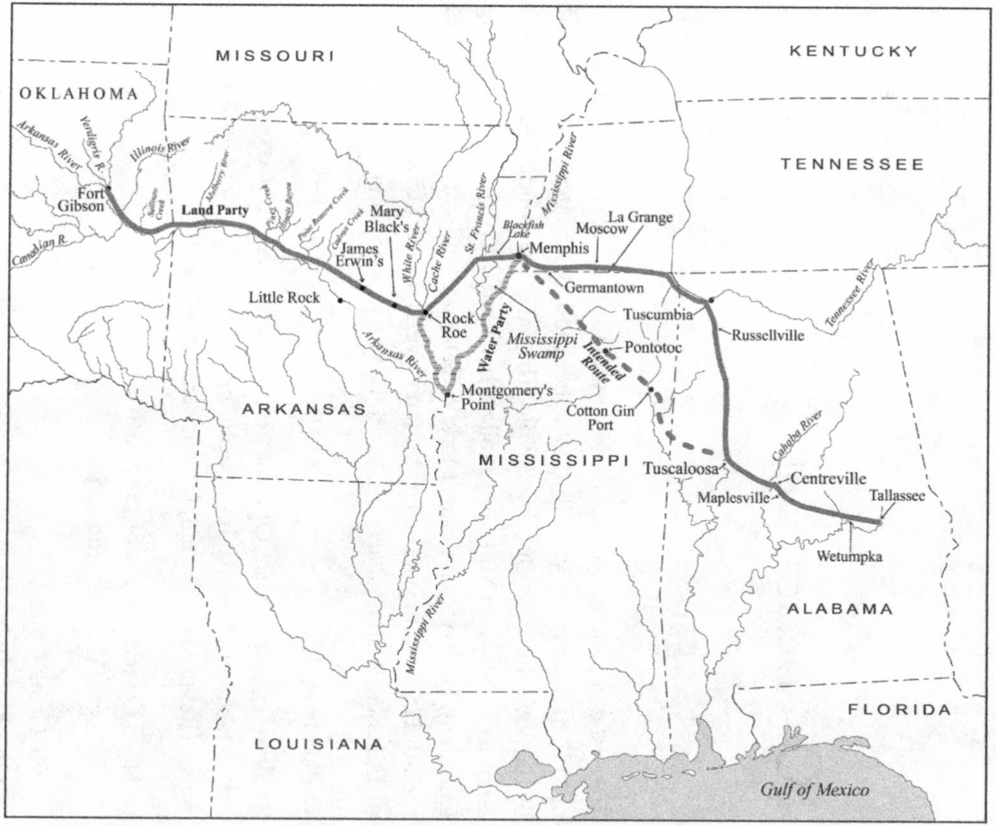

MAP 9. Route of detachment 1, August–December 1836. Place names correspond to stopping points or locations noted in the documentation. Route lines and locations are approximations. Cartography by Sarah Mattics and Kiersten Fish.

I have done every thing that can be done to procure you good means of getting to your homes, and I rely upon you to have every thing ready on your part.

Those of your people who have unfinished land business need not fear to leave—full justice will be done to them and the fair proceeds be paid over to them at the West, by the Government.

I shall see you on Saturday and hope to find that some of your young Warriors have come forward to receive the favors and perform the service assigned them by their Great father the President—They will gain honor and profit to themselves and do honor to your people.

I give my best wishes to yourself and your people.

I am your friend and Brother
{Signed} Th. S. Jesup
Major Gen'l Comdg.
Army of the South

This will be handed to you by Lieut. Reynolds of the U.S. service and by Dr. Busby both of whom are appointed to go with you to the west.

True copy
M. W. Bateman
1st Lieut. 6th Infy
Disbg Agent

Journal of Detachment 1

Capitalization and punctuation emended for clarity. Journal found at SIAC, Agent (Reynolds), Account (1687), Year (1838), NARA.

A journal of Events, kept by Lieut M. W. Bateman U.S. Army, conducting Detachment No. 1, Creek Emigration, from Tallassee Alabama, to Fort Gibson Arkansas, pursuant to the following orders Viz.

Head Quarts Army of the South
Tuskeegee 17th August 1836

Orders
No. 63 "Extract"

Par 1. The Indians under the Chief Opoth lo yo holo ordered to rendezvous near Tallassee will form detachment No. 1, and will move westward on the 25th Inst.

Par 5. Lieut Bateman is assigned as principle Military agent to detachment No. 1, and will forth with enter upon duty, and assume the direction of the preparatory arrangements, Subject to the orders of the Supperintendant.

Par 6. Lieut Reynolds of the U.S. marine Corps is with the approbation of Col Henderson appointed Military Agent, will report to Lieut Bateman at Tallassee and act under his orders.

Par 7. Mr. Dubois is appointed assistant agent & will report to Lieut Bateman.

Par 8. Dr. J. B. Bussy is appointed Surgeon to Det. No. 1, will report to Lieut Bateman at Tallassee, and enter upon duty.

By Order of Majr Genl Jesup
Signed Henry Stanton
Qr Ma & Adjt Gen'l
Army of the South

Tallassee Alab
17th August 1836

This day Mr. Dubois and Dr. Bussy reported for duty, and were ordered into camp.

Camp near Tallassee A 25 August 1836. This being the day fixed upon and designated for the movement to commence. Every thing was in readiness on part of the agents for the U States and that of the contractors, when on the application of the Chiefs to Major Genl Jesup the movement was postponed untill 30th August 1836.[3]

August 26th 27th 28th and 29th spent in camp at near Tallassee.

Thursday 30th Augt. Every effort was made to put the party in motion. The day however was spent in fruitless harangs and vexcatious delays, toward evening we succeeded in moving a portion of the Indians from the lower to the upper part of the Encampment. Exceedingly anoyed by Sheriffs and Constables, who detained the Chiefs on writs for debt.

Wednesday 31st. At an early hour every means within our reach was put in requisition to induce the Indians to pack up. To day as yesterday, several of the chiefs were arrested for debt. At 1 Oclk P.M. a detachment of U.S. Troops visited camp which was productive of much good. The white people left camp and the Indians commenced to pack up, and we succeeded in getting on 6 miles when we Encamped for the night, Indians generally sober.

Thursday 1st September 1836. Got under way at 7 Oclk A.M. progressed 10 miles. Encamped at 2 P.M. 1 mile East of Wetumpka. Four wagons broken party much scatered. Continue to be annoyed by sheriffs & constables.

Friday 2d Sept. This day spent in camp near Wetumpka at the request of Capt Lane[4] U.S.A. for the purpose of organizing a war party for service in Florada. Organized the party. Compleat the muster Rolls. Forty warriors taken from the party for service in Florada.

Saturday 3d Sept. Party in motion at 9 Oclk a.m. passed through Wetumpka. Horses, Blankets, sadles, &c taken by the Bailiffs, from the Indians. Six horses taken from one Indian. A great portion of the party drunk. Spony Fixico[5] shot by his brother, died in a few hours. Encamped at 6 Oclk P.M. ten miles west of Wetumpka, progressed 12 miles. Almost every Indian in camp drunk. The weather fine and the roads good.

Sunday 4th Sept. Party in motion at 5 Oclk. a.m. progressed 13 miles. Encamped at 12 N. Indians continue drunk, cant prevent the Grog shops from selling Liquor to the Indians.

Monday 5 Sept. Got under way at 7 a.m. halted at 1 Oclk P.M. progressed 14 miles. Rains fell last night—Roads hilly—weather fine. Indians apperantly contented, much troubled last night by white people (drunken white people). The Chiefs at my request, plan a guard of forty Indians arround our Camp.

Tuesday 6th Sept. Party in motion at 5 Oclk. A.M. halted at 4 Oclk P.M. six miles west of Maplesville, Bibb County, Ala. progressed 15 miles.

Wednesday 7th Sept. Left our Encampment at ½ past 6 Oclk a.m. halted at 3—10 miles East of Centrevile, progressed 10 miles. Rains fell in torrents throughout the day.

Thursday 8th Sept. Party in motion at 7 passed through Centrevile. Crossed the Cahawbe River[6] and Encamped on its right bank at 7 Oclock (evening). Sick report increasing.

Friday 9th Sept. Party in motion at 9. Encamp at 3, progress 13 miles. Weather very warm. Indians suffer from the want of water.

Saturday 10th Sept. Party in motion at 7, halt at 2, 12 miles East of Tuscaloosa, progres 13 miles. Country rough, roads bad, rains fell at intravells throughout the day. Indians appear contented.

Sunday 11th Sept. Got under way at 7, reach Tuscaloosa at 12 N. crossed the Black Warrior. Encamped at 6 Oclk 2 miles west of Tuscaloosa, progressed 14 miles.

Monday 12th Sept. This day spent in camp in order to repair wagons, shoe horses, and to give the Indians an opportunity to wash their clothes &c. one half of the Indians drunk.

Tuesday 13th Sept. Commenced packing up at 5 Oclk, got a portion of the party under way at 12 halted at 5 P.M. progressed 6 miles, one half of the Indians drunk. The Chiefs with many of their people in the rear, rains fall in torrents during the whole day. The Indians less manageable than usual.

Wednesday 14 Sept. Party in motion at 6 Oclk a.m. halted at 2, progressed 14 miles, roads tolerable, weather fine. Many of the party still in the rear.

Thursday 15th Sept. Party in motion at 5 Oclk halt at 1 Oclk P.M. progressed 13 miles, passed through the town of Lexington. The Chiefs with their people all up, weather & roads good. Sick report increasing.

Friday 16th Sept. Party in motion at ½ past 6 oclk, halt at 3, progress 15 miles, roads bad, weather fine party all up, all in fine spirits.

Saturday 17th Sept. Party in motion at 8, halt at 2, progress 12 miles. Crossed Sipsy River, roads bad Sick report increasing.

Sunday 18th Sept. party in motion at 7, halted at 2, progressed 15 miles, roads & weather good.

Monday 19th Sept. This day spent in camp to enable the Indians to wash and police.

Tuesday 20 Sept. party in motion at 7. Encamped at 2, at Bear Creek Marion County Alaba. progressed 14 miles. Country rough, roads bad, rains fell in torrents last night, Indians in good spirits.

Wednesday 21st Sept. Party in motion at 8, halted 4 miles South of

Russelville, Franklin County Ala. progressed 13 miles, day hot. Thermometer 96°.

Thursday 22d Sept. Party in motion at 8., passed through Russelville, halted at 5, progressed 12 miles, roads bad, weather hot.

Friday 23 Sept. Party under way at 8, halted at 2, progressed 14 miles, roads very bad, weather fine but hot, party halted at Cany Creek, 10 miles west of Tuscumbia.

Saturday 24th Sept. Party in motion at 8, halted at 4, on Bear Creek Chickasaw nation, progressed 15 miles, roads bad, weather warm. The Indians and the ponies lame, their feet being worn out traveling over the Gravel roads. Many of the Indians drunk and behind. This day the following note was addressed to the Contractors.

Camp on Bear Creek Chicaw Nation
24th Sept 1836 (10 Oclk night)

Dr Ingersoll
Contractor & agent
Alabama Emigrating Company

Sir

I have the honor most respectfuly to call your attention to articles 4, 5, 7 and 9 of a contract made and Entered into between the U States and the Alabama Emigrating Company dated 13 August 1836, and under which we are now acting. Circumstances must be peculiar indeed to justify irregularity in the issues, & curtailment in the quantity, or a deficiency in the meat part of the Indian ration. That such a state of things does now Exist, and will exist tomorrow I have too much reason to fear. I have therefore most earnestly to request that you will apply a remedy, which will superceed the necessity of my having recourse to the remedy pointed out in section 2nd article 10th of your contract.

I have also to request that you will afford me the facilities contemplated in article 10th of said contract.

I am Sir very
Respectfully

your O St
M. W. Bateman
Pr Military agent Dt [1]

Sunday 25th Sept. Party in motion at 9, halted at 6 progressed 18 miles. Crossed Bear Creek. Encamped on Yellow Creek state of Mississippi. Indians generally drunk, got their Liquor from the Chickasaw Indians. Roads bad, Indians feet sore. Ponies giving out. Chiefs cross. Evils complained of yesterday remedyed.

Monday 26th Sept. This day spent in camp for the Indians to wash, police &c.

Tuesday 27th Sept. Party set in motion at 7 halted at 1, progressed 13 miles, roads bad, rains fell in torrents.

Wednesday 28th Sept. Party in motion at 10 halted at 6, on Muddy Creek in McNairy County Tennessee, progressed 14½ miles, roads bad, Indians discontented, complain of the distance travelled per day. Every effort made to concentrate them. Frost this morning.

Thursday 29th Sept. Party in motion at 7, halted at 4, progressed 15 miles, roads horridly bad. The contractors very indiscreet, (halt on Cypress Creek).

Friday 30th Sept. Party in motion at 7, halt at 12 progress 10½ miles, weather fine roads good. Country broken & poor. Crossed Hatchee river. Enter Hardeman County Ten.

Saturday 1st October 1836. Party in motion at 10 halted at 12 progressed 4½ miles. The Indians very discontented. Every thing appears to go wrong. I am disgusted with Indian Emigration.

Sunday 2nd Oct. Party in motion at 7 halted at 2 progressed 15 miles, roads tolerable, weather cool. Frost this morning.

Monday 3 Oct. Party in motion at 7, halted at 1, 3 miles East of La Grange, progressed 13 miles roads good, party all up. Indians becoming contented.

Tuesday 4 Oct. Party in motion at 7, halted at 1, progressed 12 miles. Encamped 4 miles west of Moscow, a town filled with grog shops. Indians drunk. Crossed Wolf River, roads & weather fine.

Wednesday 5 Oct. Party in motion at 7, halted at 11, 27 miles East of Memphis, roads & weather good number of deaths increasing, old men & women & children dropping off.

Thursday 6th Oct. Party in motion at 7, halted at 2, progressed 14½ miles, passed through Germantown. Compelled to go 2 miles from the road to find water.

Friday 7th Oct. Party in motion at 6, halt at 2, progressed 16½ miles, 2 miles East of Memphis. Indians becoming more healthy.

Saturday 8th Oct. This day spent in camp, no provision having been made to cross the river.

Sunday, Monday & Tuesday 9, 10 and 11th Oct. spent in camp, waiting for Steam Boat Transportation. Indians Sober, healthy, and contented.

Wednesday 12th Oct. Party in motion at 9, proceed to Memphis, pass some of the Ponies over the Mississippi River. Some delay occasioned, owing to a misunderstanding with the Chiefs.

Thursday 13th Oct. The whole of our party together with the ponies, cross over the river, and 10 or 1200 Indians Embarque on board the S Boat Farmer[7] for Rock Row on White River. The ponies of the whole party sent through the Mississippi Swamp, via St Francisville, in charge of some 500 Indians. Leave Memphis at 1 Oclk decend the river 40 miles. Encamp at 5. The Indians appear pleased with water transportation.

Friday 15 Oct.[8] Embarque at 6, debarque at 5, 35 miles above the mouth of White River. Indians comfortable & contented.

Saturday 16 Oct. Embarque at 6, pass Montgomerys Point at 11. Enter White River at 12, progress 45 miles up White River and Encamp at 5 on the right bank of the river.

Sunday 17th Oct. Embarque at 6, all in good health, reach the Mouth of Cashe River at dark, where we halted. White river very high, banks over flowed, cant land on the west bank, determine to drop down to Rock Row.

Monday 18th Oct. Embarqued at 5, dropped down to Rock Row (8 miles) and debarqued, and pitched our tents on Rock Row Blufs. The ponies still in the Swamp, weather fine but cold.

Monday 31st October.[9] Still in camp at Rock Row, rains have been falling in torrents for the last five days, weather cold, camp very disagreeable. The Indians have been hitherto healthy, two cases of sickness arrises which smack of cholera, determine to remove the camp imediately. The Indian ponies arrive, determine to resume our march tomorrow.

Tuesday 1st November 1836. At 3 Oclk A.M. I am on horse back, at

11 a.m. get a portion of our camp in motion, roads most horrid. Thirty wagons bogged down within 2 miles of our old camp, progressed 3 miles.

Wednesday 2d Nov. All the agents on horse back at 4 Oclk a.m. impossible to get the Indians to stir. Some of the party in motion at 8, roads indescribably bad. Sleep on the prairie without any comforts.

Thursday 3 Nov. Every effort made to get the party together (I ride 47 miles to day) party Scattered 15 miles along the road. Despair of getting to Arkansas. Sick report large and increasing. The Surgeon sick, progress 10 miles.

Friday 4th Nov'r. Some of the party in motion at 8 Oclk. Mr Dubois asst conductor behind endeavouring to bring up the party, halt at Mrs Blacks, progress 12 miles. Many of our people in the rear roads in a horrid condition, Chiefs all ahead.

Saturday 5th Nov'r. Some of the party in motion at 8, halt at 4, progress 14 miles. A great portion of our party still in the rear. Determine to halt tomorrow-evening untill all the party get up.

Sunday 6th Nov'r. In motion at 8, halt at 12 at Mr Irwins[10] 25 miles north of Little Rock progress 7 miles. Here I determine to remain untill the whole of the party get up, one third of which have been behind since we left Rock Row on White River. Here I leave the party for Little Rock, with a view to consult His Excellency, the Gov of Arkansas, in relation to the expediency of the Indians making a tempory halt in the state of Arkansas, and turned over the charge of the party to Major B. Dubois asst military agent with the following instructions Viz.

Camp near Irwins, 25 miles north
of Little Rock 6th Nov'r 1836

Special Instructions

During the absence of the undersigned Major B. Dubois asst agent will act as Principle Conductor to Det No. 1, all entrusted are required to recognize him as such.

M. W. Bateman
U.S.A. Principle Military
Agent Det No. 1—

Previous to Capt Batemans leaving Camp he addressed to the Contractor the following note.

Camp near Irwins Pulasky County
Arkansas, 7th Nov'r 1836

Doct. Ingersoll
Contractor for Det No. 1
Creek Emigration

Sir

The party has been separated since we left Rock Row, White River. I deem it of the utmost importance that they should be united. I have therefore to request that you will remain on this ground untill the rear is brot up.

I have no wish to delay the party, but the party must be concentrated and travel together.

I am Sir very
Respectfully
your O St
M. W. Bateman
U.S. Military agent &c

Monday 7th Nov'r. This day spent in camp near Irwins.

Tuesday 8th Nov'r. Still in Camp, the party in the rear came up after dark this day, having travelled 21 miles during the day.

Wednesday 9th Nov'r. Party in motion at 9 Oclk, the advance party travelled 13 miles. Two thirds of the waggons not up, roads very bad rains fell throughout the day.

Thursday 10th. Party in motion at 8 Oclk halted after dark, travelled 13 miles, roads very bad, more than one half of the party behind rains fell throughout the day.

Friday 11th Nov'r. This day spent in camp, for the rear to come up, roads most horriblably bad.

Saturday 12th Nov'r. Party in motion at an early hour. Travelled 7 miles. Party much scatered, roads very bad.

Sunday 13th Nov'r. Party in motion at 8, halted at 3, progressed 8 miles, roads bad, waggons not all up. Fine weather. Here M. W. Bateman joined us from Little Rock, he held a talk with the Chiefs, told us that we should have progressed more rapidly. Told us that we must rush ahead, that winter would soon set in, and left us for Fort Gibson.[11]

Monday 14th Nov'r. Party in motion at 8 halted at 5 three miles west of the Cadron River, progressed 5½ miles. Much time lost, and dificulty Experienced in crossing the Cadron River, roads bad, weather fine.

Tuesday 15th Nov'r. Party under way at an Early hour, travelled 4 miles and halted, for the rear to join us, roads very bad.

Wednesday 16, Nov'r. Party in motion at 6 Oclk. Crossed Point Remove Swamp, and Encamped 3 miles west of Point Remove River. The advance of the party travelled 14 miles. Two thirds of the waggons not up, roads horrid.

Thursday 17th Nov'r. Party in motion at 8 Oclk, travelled 12 miles. Roads very boggy and covered with water, rains fell in torrents throughout the day, but five of the waggons got up to camp.

Friday 18th Nov'r. This day we do not move, waiting for the rear to come up, 12 waggons in the rear. We are within 1 mile of Lieut Spragues party.[12] The rains continue to fall in torrents.

Saturday 19th Nov'r. This day spent in camp waiting for the rear & to repair waggons &c. Teamsters horses and mules all worn out, and sick. Some of the wagons still in the rear, and many of the Indians still behind.

Sunday 20th Nov'r. Party in motion at 12 N. crossed a very bad creek and Encamp at 5, progress 4 miles. The road is very bad, being principly Post oak bottoms.[13]

Monday 21st Nov. Left camp at 7 proceeded to the ford on Illinois Creek, found it too deep to ford. Turned down the creek to an old Missionary Establishment[14] where we crossed in a small Flat Boat. The waggons broken, one teamster ran off leaving his waggon in the mud. Party much scattered. Horses mules and oxen failing very fast, not being able to hawl half loads. I made a request of the contractor to halt here untill the rear, sick &c could be brot up, which he willingly acceeded to—Doctor Bussy sent back to bring up the rear, weather clear & cold, travelled 10 miles this day.

Tuesday 22d Nov'r. This day spent in camp Indians & waggons continue to arrive untill late at night, hungry, cold and cross. Many waggons still in the rear.

Wednesday 23rd Nov'r. Party in motion at 7 Oclk, many of the Indians in the rear. Sent Doctor Bussy back as far as Point Remove, to ascertain the number in the rear, and to take measures to bring them up. Many of the Chiefs in the rear. Crossed little Piney Creek, and halt 3 miles west of Saxe Creek. Travelled 13 miles to day with a tolerable good road.

Thursday 24th Nov'r. This day the advance part of the party did not move, waiting for the rear waggons to come up. All got up this day for the first time since leaving Irwins. Had a talk with the Chiefs on the Subject of their people remaining behind. The Chief give out a strong talk to their people requiring them to close up to camp every night. Got some new teams. Every prospect of a fine start in the morning, weather clear and cold.

Friday 25th Nov'r. Party in motion at 7, traveled 9 miles, roads good, all the waggons and Indians in camp at an early hour in the evening, being the first time that the Indians & waggons got up to the regular Encamping ground before night since we left Rock Row.

Saturday 26th Nov'r. Left Camp at an Early hour. Travelled 11 miles. Some of the waggons did not get up till after dark. Weather cold and clear. The roads good. The Indians in fine spirits, believing they will soon arrive in their new country. This evening Lieut MW Bateman joined us and took charge of the party.

B. Dubois
Actg Prin: Conducting
Agent Det No. 1

Sunday 27th Nov'r. Party in motion at 7, halted at 4, on White Oak Creek Crawfort County Arkansas progressed 14 miles, roads tolerable, weather fine but cold.

Monday 28th Nov'r. Party in motion at 6 halted at 4, on Mulberry Creek, progressed 15 miles, roads good, weather cold, Indians contented.

Tuesday 29th Nov'r. Party in motion at ½ past 6: halt at 3 on Frogg Bouyeo, progress 16 miles, party scatered. Ox teams unable to keep up with the party.

Wednesday 30th. Party in motion at 7, halt at 6, on Lees Creek, progress 8 miles, we had much dificulty in crossing Lee's Creek.[15]

Thursday 1st December 1836. Party in motion at ½ past 6 Oclk, pass out of the State of Arkansas halt at 4, near the Military road in the Cherokee Nation, progress 9 miles, roads good.

Friday 2nd Dec'r. Party in motion before sun rise, halt at 3, progress 12 miles, roads bad, night cold. Indians suffer.

Saturday 3rd Dec'r. Party in motion before the dawn of day, halt at 4 on the Sallisaw Creek   Cherokee Nation, progress 14 miles, morning very cold. Indians suffer much.

Sunday 4th Dec'r. In motion at the dawn of day, halted at dark on the Illinois River, which is very dificult to cross, progress 18 miles, weather very cold. Indians suffer.

Monday 5th Dec'r. Party in motion before day light, halt at 4 on Bouyeu Menard progress 17 miles, weather very cold. Some of our party behind.

Tuesday 6th Dec'r. This day we remained in camp for the rear to close up.

Wednesday 7th Dec'r. Party in motion at 11 Oclk, proceed to Fort Gibson (4 miles) with a portion of our party, and turn them over to Genl M. Arbuckle U.S. Army.

Thursday 8th Dec'r. Remain in camp waiting for about 300 of our party who are still in the rear.

Friday 9th Dec'r. 300 of our party still in the rear, take measures to get them up.

Saturday 10, Dec'r. Rear party not yet up.

Sunday 11th Dec'r. The party get up and turned over. Major B. Dubois Asst Conductor, and the attending Surgeon Dr J. B. Bussy, discharged the Service.

M. W. Bateman
1st Lieut 6th Infantry
Prin. Military agent
Det no. 1
Creek Emigration

Note—The correspondence hereunto appended is to show the steps I have taken in relation to certain promises made by Major Genl Jesup to Opothlo yo. ho. lo. pursuant to his leaving his old country.

M. W. Bateman
1st Lieut 6th Infantry
P. M. agent.[16]
& Disbursing Agent
Creek Removal

Supplemental Letters of Detachment 1

Several Upper Creek headmen complain that those appointed to relocate them to Indian territory are strangers to them or have defrauded them out of their land. They request that they be allowed to choose people whom they trust to move them to the West. Letter found at Records of the Adjutant General's Office, 1780s-1917, Entry 159-Q, Records of Major General Thomas S. Jesup, Container 24, Folder: "Letters Received regarding Creek and Seminole Affairs, August 1836," NARA.

Tuckabatchie Square August 15th 1836.

To, Maj. Gen'l Jesup

D'r Sir,

We the undersigned Chiefs of the Tuckabatchies—would respectfully request, that you would inform us before you leave this place, if possible, whether it is not in your power to give us the persons of our own choice to Emigrate us to our new homes in the far west, instead of the persons who have been appointed.—We have had several talks together upon this subject & to us it is a subject upon which we feel a deep interest, & one upon which much of our comfort depends. It is well Known to you and all of our white Brethren in this vicinity that we & our people have been on the most friendly terms with our white brethren—that we have never been guilty of any depredations upon their property—& that we have in this late war taken an active part in favour of our white Brethren against our red brethren—amongst which—many of us had near family relations—does not our conduct deserve some return on your part? we have been promised that we should be emigrated by the Agents of our Great Father the President and this is what we should still wish, but as that cannot be—Ought we not to be allowed to have a choice in the persons to remove us—when those persons are willing to carry us at as low a price as any others—The men who we are in formed have been appointed to remove us are some of them well Known to us & others are entire strangers—most of those whom we do Know have been engaged in defrauding us of our Lands & we Know they are not our friends & doubt much whether they will treat us well in removing us—There are men here with whom we have had dealings & found them to treat us well—we have always been friends with them & have been with them in the late war—we have every confidence in them & believe they will treat us well & make us as comfortable as possible on our journey & as we shall probably not have many more requests to make before we leave the Land of our Fathers never to see it again—we earnestly request that you will endeavour if it is possible to allow us to be carried to our new homes by messrs Gerald, &, Russell, &, Hagerty[17] as we are informed they will carry us as cheap as the other people who we do not have any Confidence in—we are anxious to be gone soon & if you will grant this request, we will try & be ready to start as soon as they are ready to go with us.

We remain Your friends & Brothers

Hopoethle	Yoholo
Mad	Blue
Little	Doctor
Young	King
Ar le coo chie	Emathlee
Micco	Poe ka
Osooch	Micco
Ho-pealth	ho poie
Tomath	E Micco

Witnesses
J. A. Chambers[18]

L't. U.S. Army
Tho's J. Abbott[19]

☾

Fifteen prominent Upper and Lower Creek headmen notify Jesup that it is unlikely they can raise a force to fight the Seminoles in Florida. They also report that they will do all they can to entice those Creeks participating in the Second Creek War to go peaceably to Indian territory and request payment of their annuity in order to pay off their debts. Letter found at Records of the Adjutant General's Office, 1780s–1917, Entry 159-Q, Records of Major General Thomas S. Jesup, Container 20, Folder: "Letters Received, 1836–1838, From Camps and Forts during the Creek War," NARA.

Hopothle Yohele's Camp of
Friendly Indians
21st August 1836

To
Maj'r Gen'l Thomas S. Jesup
Commanding Army of the South

Sir

Yours of this day has been receaved and read in General Council. True it is that previous to your arrival among us the war of the hostiles was waging hot against our white breathren, but our Exertions was Ever to the utmost used to put it to an End, and after your arrival we succeede in putting an End to this war, upon the call made through Col Hogan we most cheerfully call'd the young warriors into the field and under your direction soon Succeeded in taking the hostiles and prevented the further Spilling of our white brothers blood, this war being now Ended, by the taking of the hostiles and Sending them off we hoped there would have been no more service for our young warriors.

Upon the Subject of calling the young warriors out and Sending them into Florida to fight the Simanoles we must Say that upon the

Ending of this war, and while the <u>hostile</u> red men were in our hands, had you at that time intimated a wish that, our young warriors should have joined you to go & fight the Simanoles, & you would at that time have placed under our command the hostiles taken, we would then have gone with you, as these hostiles were well acquainted with the Country and could have been our guides & of much Service in this war,—but we are Strangers in that country & Know not the land—or the places of those people, therefore fear it is now too late for the people to join you to go into Florida—

When you talked to us on this Subject but a few days ago, we then told you we would lay the Subject before the young warriors; we have done so, & told them that if they wish'd to go down & have a frolick with the Simenoles we should be pleased to have them Say so & that they could make ready and join you & that you had asked them to go & have frolic with the Simenoles, but they have not replyed to your request as you could have wished, they Say had they been before asked to go down to Florida against the Red Sticks where they had time for Some war they would have done so with their full heart, but they have now turned their thoughts upon another Subject, <u>near & dear</u> to them their home, their new home, their home in the far west,—that they have short time Enough to get there & plant themselves in a Strange country that they cannot think of going upon a hunting party while their fathers & mothers & brothers & Sisters are journeying through the land of Strangers to Settle themselves beyond the great River;—As our young warriors have made the answer to your request, we must Say to you our Brother, that as our young men look up to us for council & advise we cannot in justice to them and their families & friends advise them to a course against their wishes, they are now ready to move & to advise them another course when they look up to us for the best is what we cannot do—Upon the Subject of the few Skulking Hostiles that are Still out the talk has been given out but as yet nothing has been heard of them or where they are, all means will be used in our power to Entice them in & to go to our new homes with us in a friendly manner, but if they cannot be Enticed to come in before we leave, and they have to be taken by our white Brethren in arms, they must be sent to their new homes or dealt with in Such manner as the President our Great Father may think best—

As the president our Great Father has by his advise thought it best for his Red Children to remove immediately to their new homes in the west, and as we have taken his good council & are ready to remove, we have asked that our annuity might be paid us to Enable us to pay off some of our just debts as far as it may go to Enable us to do justly by our white brothers that we are leaving & to Enable us to go without being troubled with our white Brothers law, we thank our Father the President that he is going to give us our annuity that we may in Some part pay our just debts before we leave, but our Brother, we fear that our young warriors are so much in debt to our white Brothers that they will not have the means from the annuity to pay all, and when all is gone & nothing to pay with that they will then be harrass'd by our white Brothers Law, and unless you our Brother can render us Some council & assistance on this Subject we fear we Shall have much trouble & difficulty before we can be able to leave for our new homes, but we shall do all we can to pay our just debts, leave this our old homes for our new, but we fear much trouble before we can effect it, but we trust that you our Brother will do all in your power to advise & council & assist us paying our just debts & prepaireing us to leave this the land of the graves of our Fathers—

On the Subject of the fraudulint Land contracts that you have mentioned, it has been talked in council, but as that is a Subject of much interest to our people we decline Saying any thing upon it in this, but will defer it for a Special letter or council, as we are aware that our Father the President will do his Red children ample justice in this matter—as to the other parts of your letter they meet the wishes & views of your Red Brethren, and we herewith close this with our best wishes and [illegible] ourselves.

Your Brothers[20]

This done & Signed in council
in our presince as witness
our Signatures—

D. Carpenter
Barent Dubois

Hopothle	Yohela
Mad	Blue
Little	doctor
Jim	Islands
Tuskalaha	Micco
Tuskona	Hargo
Manarwa	
Kotche	Martha
Hachechuby	Tom
Yohola	Micco
Horby	Fixico
Tallassee	Fixico
Tustenuge	Chopco
Conip	Nehe Lamatha
Spokoke	Micco[21]

☾

With only a few days until he begins his march to Indian territory, Opothle Yoholo writes to Jesup with requests about the adjudication of the Indians' land fraud claims, payment of their 1837 annuity, the return of their slaves and horses taken by creditors, and other matters related to their relocation west. Letter found at Letters Received by the Office of Indian Affairs, 1824–81, Creek Agency Reserves, 1832–1850, Roll 243, 1067-1 (hereafter LR, CAR).

Indian Camp

26 August 1836

Major Gnl Jesup

In conference with you on yesterday I am induced to believe we did not fully understand each other on several points. I will therefore endeavour to explain myself fully by writing.—at the time the Indian frauds commenced in the Nation by the Indians personating[22] each other there were a great many Indians who did not intend to sell their reservations—but intended to remain in the country and raise their families and become citizens of the state.[23]

The first thing we knew our lands were sold from under us, the white man had fraudalently purchased it from a rougish Indian and we required to leave it. We complained to the Government and an Investigation was ordered by our father the President. The agent Doct. McHenry[24] examined into the cases of frauds, which it appears was not approved by the president. Col. Hogan then Succeeded him & made examination into such cases as were presented to him—and we thought matters would have soon been closed—the true Indian would get his land—& the fraud exposed—But it appears his reports were not received—Now we are promised that two more Agents[25] have been appointed who will examine the matter west of the Mississippi and that every justice will be done us.

During the Red Stick war when Gen'l Jackson was in this country, we united with him and the Georgia General[26] and put down all the Hostile Indians—The Genl. then stated to us to make out our accounts of our losses during the war and they should be paid—We done so—half the amount was paid to us—the agent then stated the other half was in Bank and would be paid us at some other time—we have not heard of it since, and when I tell our chiefs and men they will get the money west of the Mississippi they say we shall not hear from it any more.

The Speculators have come amongst my people and say to them—that had their lands fraudulently taken from them—that they will purchase them with all their encumbrances—that they will risk all the consequences—and gave the value therefor.

In many cases Individuals have purchased from the true Indian and made advances there for upon the faith of an examination into the frauds and when the lands should be certified to—the full value would be paid.

Now I wish to know of you what is best for me to do under these difficulties—to go west as we are, or suffer my people to make the best arraingements they can with the land buyers?

You told me the other day the President had sent our Annuity to us—that you had it. We want it to pay our debts, and will then fall far short in effecting that object—and I wish to know if arraingements cannot be made through you with the Government or some persons in the neighbourhood to pay us the amount of the next years annuity so as to settle our debts.—In many cases fraudulent debts have been raised against Indians—and the Negroes & horses have been taken from our camp to pay them—and in other cases—the shop Keeper has sold goods and whiskey to the poor Indians, knowing that he could never pay for them, they are now taken them with writs—and they say they must go to jail—Can you not arrainge all the matters for us—relieve our men from debt by giving us the next years Annuity, Let our negroes & horses be brought back to our camp—and then all will be pleased—the young men will go freely to Florida the women & children will go in peace to the far west.

The council requested me to ask of you what disposition had been made with the money arising from the sale & rent of the orphan lands,[27] and what had become of the rent of the chiefs lands which have been sold—all of which we need at this trying time.—

We must all leave here in a few days and my object is fully to understand these matters that there may be no difficulty hereafter.—I expect to take up the line of march & to continue to the Cherokee line in Arkansas—then I wish to go down & visit Genl. Gaines, who is a friend of mine & see if arrangements cannot be made with him, for myself and such of my people as may not be pleased in the arkansas, to settle on the Saline—

When I made the treaty with the President he promised me a Blanket, Kettle & Rifle for each warrior. Two Blacksmiths with all the Iron we wanted when we went west of the Mississippi. I wish to know when & where these things are placed for us.—

There are a portion of Chatahoochee, Alabama, Coosauda, and some of Seminole Indians who have gone to Texas who I wish to visit—According to our custom when we are about to take a long journey, we are fasting to day and will dance all night to night, and I should like to have an answer from you this evening if possible, while we are altogether that the talk may go out—that our difficulties may be removed—the necessary arrangements for the Florida War—and all be prepared at a short time to quit this place for our home in the far west.

your friend & brother
(Signed) Hopoethleyoholo

Witnesses

(Sig) Ja's L. alexander[28]
(Sig) Barent Dubois

ℭ

The following is a statement made by Alfred Balch, one of two commissioners sent by the federal government to investigate the causes of the land frauds (associated with the 1832 Treaty of Washington) and the Second Creek War. On 28 August 1836 several Upper Creek headmen signed a contract with a land company headed by James C. Watson (an Alabama Emigrating Company partner) for the sale of 656 reserves that had previously been sold under the suspicion of fraud. Because of the desire to settle their land-fraud claims, and due simply to the exigencies of relocation, most of the camps were in a state of "chaos." This statement underlines the general confusion of the situation at the very moment when detachment 1 began their journey west. Statement found at LR, CAR, Roll 243, 293–95.

J. S. [Julian S.] Devereux a witness says he was at the square of O-poth-le-holos camp on the day that the first party of Indians started to Arkansas. Tucka-batchee-Micco[29] was there. The white men were ordered to go away unless they had business. Witness said he could not know whether he had business or not unless he could know what the Indians were assembled there for. It was said they were going to enrol the Indians to go to Florida, and that they were going to pay the annuity to the Indians. Two or three Indians were called up whose reserves had been purchased by deponent and one [Wildridge] Thompson. The witness rose and told them that if they were going to pay <u>those</u> Indians any money for their lands, he wished them to ask them if they had not sold to the witness and Thompson.

Dubois then rose and said it would take a week to go through the business. He went off one way and Tucka-batch-ee Micco another & the Indians generally dispersed. Tucka-batchee-Micco had bank notes in his hat but witness does not Know how much. Some one said the Indians were assembled to pay them for their lands. Edward Hanrick one of the purchasers with Watson was there and was engaged in making calculations to see how much each Indian would be entitled to out of the money.

All this happened late in the evening. The waggons of the emigrating party had started. Deponent remained till dark but saw no money paid to the Indians.

The witness is interested in eighteen reserves all of which were purchased subsequent to the reversal of them and before the contract with Watson & others was made.

☾

Lieutenant Mark W. Bateman reports on his party's slow progress due to the arrest of a number of Creeks for debt and in order to raise a party to fight the Seminoles in Florida. Letter found at CGS-IRW, Roll 5, 840.

Ans'd 14. Sep't.

In Camp near Wetumpka Ala
2d Sept 1836

Commissary Genl of Sub.
Washington city

Sir

In obedience to Genl Jesups orders I left Tallassee on the 31st ult. with Opothle yo. ho. lo's party of Creek Indians amounting to from 2 to 3,000 Souls, destined for their new homes west of the Mississippi. Thus far we have progressed slowly, owing to the difficulty of collecting the Indians, and a number of the principle men—having been arrested by the Civil authority for debt &c. We have spent this day at this place at the request of Capt Lane (under the orders of Genl Jesup) to enable him to organize a War party of Creeks for Florada.

Respectfully y ob s[30]
M. W. Bateman
1 Lt 6th Infantry
in charge of party

☾

Worried about the bad roads and scarcity of provisions (especially after receiving word of the decision of detachment 2 to follow in the footsteps of Opothle Yoholo, see Screven's journal, chap. 11), Bateman notifies Thomas Jesup that he has decided to avoid Cotton Gin Port, Mississippi, and travel instead through Moulton, Alabama. Letter found at Records of the Adjutant General's Office, 1780s–1917, Entry 159-Q, Records of Major General Thomas S. Jesup, Container 4, Folder: "Letters Received from Officers, Lieutenant M. W. Bateman," NARA.

In Camp 2 miles west of
Tuskaloosa Alabama
12th Sept 1836

Genl T. S. Jesup
Comg South Army

Sir

I have the honor to report that the party of Creek Indians under my charge arrived at this place yesterday. This day has been spent in camp repairing waggons shoeing horses &c we will leave tomorrow.

So many reports have reached us this day in relation to the secarcity of provisions, bad roads &c on the rout by Cotton gin port and through the Chickasaw nation that I am inclined to think we will Change our rout & go by way of Moulton. Opothlo yo ho lo, will be much oposed to this rout. I believe it is his wish to unite as many parties as possible at an early day. I have just learned that the party under Lt Screvan have refused to go by way of Elytown, they will suffer for want of provisions on this rout.

Respectfully your
ob st
M. W. Bateman
1st Lieut 6 Infantry

☾

In addition to writing Jesup, Bateman sent a communiqué to Commissary General of Subsistence George Gibson notifying him that there had been five deaths by the time the party reached Tuscaloosa, Alabama. Letter found at CGS-IRW, Roll 5, 859.

Rec'd 26 Sept

In Camp 2 miles west of
Tuskaloosa Alabama
12th Sept 1836

Commissary General of Subsistence
Washington City

Sir

I have the honor to report that the party of Creek Indians under my charge arrived at this place yesterday. Thus far nothing has arisen to interrupt our progress. The Indians get drunk at every Town or village we pass through. We have lost five by death. The Indians are only tolerably healthy.

I am Sir Respectfully
your O St
M. W. Bateman
1st Lieut 6th Infantry

☾

Jesup notifies Bateman that Opothle Yoholo requested permission to stop in Arkansas for a time in order to confer with General Edmund P. Gaines and that it is his responsibility to make that happen. Letter found at SIAC, Agent (Reynolds), Account (1687), Year (1838), NARA.

Head Quarters, Army of the South,
Fort Mitchell, Alabama Oct. 3d 1836.

Sir,

One of the Stipulations made by Hopoeth le yo holo, when he consented to put his band in motion towards the West, and to furnish Warriors for service in Florida, was that he should be allowed to halt somewhere within the Arkansas Territory with his people, until he should have time to confer with General Gaines, or the officer commanding on the South Western frontier, and to visit certain Creek and Cherokee chiefs who had emigrated some time ago.— as there was no legal right under the treaty to remove the Creeks, but their movements was necessarily voluntary, I acceded to his wish, and assured him that he would be permitted to halt any where west of Little Rock that might be most agreeable to himself, provided a place should be selected where supplies could be readily obtained, and provided also that no objection be made by the authorities of Arkansas.

My object in now addressing you is to apprise you of the Stipulation and to desire you to cause it to be carried into effect.— I consider it a solemn contract by which my honor as well as the faith of the Government is bound. I desire you to see the Superintendant of Indian Affairs West of the Mississippi, and state to him the importance of carrying this Stipulation into effect and the injurious effect which a disregard of it would probably have on the Indian Corps serving in Florida, should they by any means learn that it has not been complied with.

I am Sir
Respectfully
Your Obt. Servt.
{Signed} Th. S. Jesup

Lieut. M. G. Bateman
Agent for Creek Emigration
conducting Ho poth le yo hola's Band
Memphis Tennessee

True copy.
M. W. Bateman
1st Lieut 6th Infantry

☾

Bateman reports on the progress of the party and its arrival near Memphis, Tennessee. Letter found at CGS-IRW, Roll 5, 861.

Rec'd 21 Oct'r.

Camp 2 miles East of Memphis
7th Oct 1836

Commissary Genl of Sub
Washington City

Sir

I have the honor to report that Detachment of Creek Indians in my charge arrived at this place this day. These other Detachments are within 10 or 15 miles of us, and will be down upon us in two days. We will have from 10 to 12,000 Indians, here together.

Respectfully
your O St
M. W. Bateman
1st Lieut 6th Infantry

☾

This letter, dictated by four prominent Tuckabatchee headmen (and intended to be read aloud to their warriors fighting in Florida) reports on the party's arrival at Memphis and provides a list of the names of those who had died since leaving Tallassee. The letter also urges the warriors to do their duty and fight honorably. Letter found at Records of the Adjutant General's Office, 1780s–1917, Entry 159-Q, Records of Major General Thomas S. Jesup, Container 19, Folder: "Letters Received Relating to Creek and Seminole Affairs, September–December 1836," NARA.

Camp 2 miles West of Memphis
9th October 1836

Major Gnl T. S. Jesup
Comg. Army of the South
Florada

Friend

I am glad to inform you that we arrived at Memphis on the 7th Inst. after travelling 38 days.

I view you as my friend and brother and now send you a strait talk which I wish you to give to our Warriors who are with you.

The understanding before we started was, that we were to have straight talks, before we started I did not Know how many of our Warriors would go with you to Florada. On our arrival at Wetumpka, I met a man[31] attending to that business, I then found out how many Warriors went.

When a man is sent to do his duty, he is under his head men, and should do his duty. You have been sent by the President to fight, and I wish you may conquer. Our Warriors are under your command

and I wish that you and them may conquer. Some of them may be Killed, but warriors are made for that: yet I hope that all or most of them may return. Save as many of them as you can, so that we may see them again.

All the head Chiefs from Taladega, Kialega &c are to meet Opothlo yo ho lo, here to day to hold a general Council, to tell how they have been treated on the road and to consult on other maters.

We have had much sickness among our people. I do not Know how many have died, but will find out and put it down, our party will commence crossing the river to day, we will cross very slow as the boats are small. All the other parties are close by us, and cross over, so soon as we get over, how long it will take us to cross over I do not Know, perhaps it will be more than ten days. We hear that Swamp is very bad.[32]

your friends & Brothers
Opothlo yo ho lo
Tuckabatcha Micco
or Young King
Mad Blue
To Mathla Micco

To be read to
Te pha Tuska Nugga
or The Dog Warrior

List of Deaths in the Tuckabatcha Town

1. Osa Hadgo
2. Thlethe a Nee Hadgo's Son
3. Charley E mathla's (Daughter)
4. Hillis Fixico's (Daughter)
5. Hillis Fixico
6. A Thlipth pe's son, a large boy
7. Che O Hadgo's 2 Sons
8. Ne ha Hadgo an old man, lived with Cotche Fixico
9. Coosa opo ehethlo's Daughter

10. Oche Yoholo's Son (a little boy)
11. Tome Yo ho lo's son a little boy
12. Gin luck O Hadgo
13. Che Was le E mathla's son (a large boy)
14. Yo ho lo Micco's Daughter
15. Fe lit Hadgo's Daughter
16. E. Na he na ho's (Daughter)

The above is a list of names of those who have died since we started, we send it so that you may Know how many have died. Some have died absent from their friends and we are sorry. Their friends will be sorry when they hear it, but we must all die some time, we must listen to all talks, some times they bring good news and some times bad news.

☾

Bateman reports that he has convinced a majority of detachment 1 to take water transportation around the Mississippi Swamp despite the fact that the Creeks were typically averse to water travel. Letter found at LR, CAE, Roll 237, 498–99.

Steam Boat Farmer
35 miles above White River
15th Oct 1836

Commissary General of Subsistence
Washington City

Sir

I have the honor to inform you that 12 or 1300 of Detatchment No. 1 Emigrating Creek Indians under my charge are thus far on their way to their new homes west of the Mississippi. We left Memphis yesterday on board the S.B. Farmer. The Indians were averse to water transportation, but on a proper representation of the horrid condition of the roads through the Miss Swamp they consented to go on board the Boats thus far they appear satisfied. Nothing shall be wanting on my part to make them comfortable, and to guard against accident. We left in the vicinity of Memphis three Detachments (say 8,000 Indians) who will follow us so soon as the Boats (3 in number) can convey them from that place to Rock row on White River, where we intend to debarque and resume our march by land. The health of the Indians comprising the different Detachments is generally good, and I hope that nothing will occur to retard or prevent the full and final accomplishment of the views of the Govt. in relation to these people.

Thus far we have been Successfull, and I think, that with prudence and care we will be able to get all these people to their new homes.

I am Sir very
Respectfully
your o st
M. W. Bateman
1 Lieut 6 Infantry
Military agent
1st Det. &c

Camp Rock Row White River Arkansas
18th Oct 1836

We arrived at this place last night, all in good health. The White River is over its banks, we will have much trouble in crossing the ponies over it.[33]

M.W.B.

☾

In this talk, written in Bateman's handwriting, the headmen of Tuckabatchee petition Arkansas governor James Conway for permission to stop in the state in order to settle matters with the headmen who participated in the Second Creek War. Letter found at Records of the Adjutant General's Office, 1780s–1917, Entry 159-Q, Records of Major General Thomas S. Jesup, Container 21, Folder: "Indian Affairs and Correspondence," NARA.

Camp near Irwins
Pulaski County Arkansa
7th November 1836

To His Excellency
James S. Conway[34]
Gov of Arkansas

Brother

Myself with 10 or 12,000 of my people are now within the limits of your state, you will see from the letter of Major Genl Jesup which accompanys this, that I have been promised permission to make a halt in your state untill I could visit Genl Gains and transact other business for my people.

Myself and my people visit your state with the most friendly feellings towards your people. In the late Creek disturbances we assisted the whites in suppressing hostilities a larger portion of the Creek Nation we sent to Arkansas by our orders, where they now are with bad feellings towards us, and should we go directly into the Creek Country, they would doubtless try to revenge themselves upon us. A large number of our warriors are now in Florada assisting the whites to suppress Seminole hostilities Under all these Circumstances we have to request that you will permit us to halt at some suittable point within your state, untill we can settle our difficulties. We have always been friends to the whites, and wish to continue the friends, and in becoming your neighbors we wish to cultivate the most friendly feellings towards you and your people.

This letter will be handed you by our friend Capt Bateman of the Army, who has been sent with us by the Government, to see that justice is done us. This talk is our talk, when you see his face you see ours.

your Brothers
Opothlo yo ho lo
Principle Chief Creek Nation

Little Doctor
Mad Blue Chiefs
Tuckabatch Micco

Ned
Interpreter

Witness
B. Dubois
Asst Military Agent

A true Copy
M. W. Bateman
USA

☾

Bateman reports to Gibson that he has left his party for Little Rock to deliver letters to Governor Conway requesting permission to halt for a time in the state of Arkansas. Letter found at LR, CAE, Roll 237, 509–10.

Little Rock Arkansas
9th Nov'r 1836

Commissary Genl of Sub.
Washington City

Sir

I have the honor to report that I left my party of Creek Indians, yesterday morning at a place called Irwins Stand, about 20 miles north of this place on their way to the mouth of the Cadron where I expect to join them tomorrow evening. The roads are most horridly bad. Rains have been falling almost every day.

I was fearfull at one time that we would not get these people to their new homes without some serious dificulty, owing to causes which I deem unnecessary here to state, but I now hope that [a] brighter sun is about to dawn upon us. Nothing has been wanting on my part to concentrate the Indians and to land them in their new country with Kind feellings towards the Whites, to affect this most desirable object, I have dificulties of almost every Kind to encounter.

Previous to the Indians leaving their old homes they were promised by Genl Jesup that they should be permitted to halt within the limits of the state of Arkansas, provided the authorities of the state made no objections. Yesterday I put into the hands of the Governor letters from Genl Jesup, and the chiefs in relation to this subject. I will receive his answer to day, when I will write you more fully.

Respectfully
your ObSt
M. W. Bateman
1st Lieut 6th Infantry
Prin Military agent
Creek Removal

Note—The Indians are generaly healthey

☾

Bateman officially delivers two letters to Arkansas governor James S. Conway requesting that the Creeks be allowed to halt within the state's limits for a time. Letter found at Records of the Adjutant General's Office, 1780s–1917, Entry 159-Q, Records of Major General Thomas S. Jesup, Container 21, Folder: "Indian Affairs and Correspondence," NARA.

Little Rock Arkansas
9th Nov'r 1836

His Excelency
James S. Conway
Gov of Arkansas

Sir

Enclosed herewith I have the honor to hand you two Communications, one from Major Genl T. S. Jesup, Comg the Army of the South. The other from the principle Chiefs of the Creek Nation in relation to Creek Indian affairs, and have respectfully to request that you will be pleased to give to them that consideration which their importance may seem to require.

These Indians left their Eastern homes under assurances that they would be permited to halt for a limited period, within the State of Arkansas. Under these Circumstances I hope your Excellency will pardon me when I request that the promises of the Commanding General and the wishes of the Indians may be complyed with.

Respectfully
Your O St
M. W. Bateman
1 Lieut 6th Infantry
Prinl Military Agt Creek Removal

☾

This letter was delivered to William Armstrong by Bateman on his short visit to Fort Gibson in November 1836 (and referenced in Armstrong's 24 November 1836 letter) requests Armstrong's presence upon the arrival of detachment 1 in order to ensure peace upon the frontier. Letter found at LR, CAW, Roll 236, 699.

(Copy)

Little Rock, Nov 9th 1836

Capt Wm Armstrong
Supt Indian Affrs
South Western Territory

Sir

I have the honor to inform you that 13,000 Creek Indians are now west of the Mississippi, on their way to their new country, some of these people are as far advanced as the Cadron. I enclose for your information, a copy of a letter from Gen'l Jessup, I have respectfully to request that you will meet us with as little delay as possible. The interest of the Indians requires it. They will not enter their new country without arms, rumour (Indian rumour) says there are but few arms at your disposal, and those have recently been siezed by the hostile Indians, don't fail to meet us as early as possible. The safety of the frontier may depend on it.

I am Sir, very respectfully
Your Obt Servant
(Signed) M. W. Bateman,
1st Lt 6 Infantry
Prin Military agent
Creek Removal

☾

This is Arkansas governor James Conway's response to the Tuckabatchee leaders who requested time to stop in the state's limits and confer with the western headmen. Conway, citing the need to have the assent of his people (white Arkansans), refuses to allow the Creeks to stop and instead requests that they proceed to the military reservation at Fort Gibson. Letter found at SIAC, Agent (Reynolds), Account (1687), Year (1838), NARA.

Executive Office
Little Rock arkansas
10th November 1836.

To Opothlo yo ho la
Principal chief of the Creek Nation,

Friend & Brother,

Your letter of the 7th Inst. written at camp near Irvans[35] was received two days ago by your friend Capt. Bateman together with a letter from Maj'r. Gen'l Jessup—each informing me that one of the stipulations made by you, when you consented to remove with your people to the West and furnish warriors for the service in Florida, was that you should be allowed to halt somewhere within the limits of arkansas with your people until you should have time to confer with Gen'l. Gaines[36] or the officer commanding on the South Western Frontier, and to visit certain creek and cherokee chiefs, who emigrated some time ago.—I feel every wish and anxiety to have that stipulation complied with, but am not authorized to do so, except with the approbation of my people in the part of the country which you might select for the purpose.—The assurance which is given in your letter of the friendly feelings you entertain towards your white breathern is highly appriciated and confided in to the utmost extent.—your white Brother wants no greater proof of your friendship to the people of your great father the President, than you have given by sending your warriors to assist us in suppressing hostilities in Florida. I much regret that the creeks who emigrated some time since have unkind and probably hostile feelings towards you and your people now with you.—and I will do all in my power to secure to you and your people protection and security, until you will have ample time to settle all your difficulties: and now inform you of the place which I deem best to adopt for the accomplishment of the object which you have in view, and to enable me to give you assistance, viz: I recommend that you continue your march towards your country until you arrive at Fort Gibson, there the United States have a reservation of ten miles square including the Fort: and I have no doubt but General Arbuckle, the commanding officer will give you permission to halt at some suitable situation within that reservation, until you accomplish the objects you desire; Should you think proper to adopt this course, I will immediately order two companies composed of 120 mounted men, to that Garrison as a means of protection to you: there are now there, two hundred men and about 400 mounted men now stationed on Red River, which Gen'l Arbuckle will no doubt order without delay to Fort Gibson—this will make an efficient force of about 720 men principally mounted and well armed which force together with any further number that General Arbuckle may think necessary to call on me for to be raised and ordered there without delay will ensure you protection.—This place seems to me to be a better one, to give you and your people protection, security and comfort than any that can be adopted, and I hope it will meet your approbation and that of your people.

Your friend and
Brother
{Signed} J. S. Conway

True copy
M. W. Bateman
1 Lieut 6th Infantry

☾

In this short, hastily written letter Bateman notifies Jesup that he is waiting on Governor Conway's response to the headmen's request to stop in the state of Arkansas. Conway's response (the preceding letter), dated the day prior, had not yet reached the agent. Letter found at Records of the Adjutant General's Office, 1780s–1917, Entry 159-Q, Records of Major General Thomas S. Jesup, Container 20, Folder: "Letters Received 1836–1838, From Camps and Forts during the Creek War," NARA.

Cadron Arkansas
11th November 1836

Major Genl T. S. Jesup
U.S. Army Comg &c

Sir

Yours dated 3rd Oct last was received on the 3rd Inst at Rock Row, White River. I have the honor to Enclose herewith for your information a Correspondence between Opothlo yo ho lo, and the Governor of Arkansas. I have not as yet received the answer of the latter as to what course he will adopt. We have been much delayed. Bad weather, and most horrid roads. The weather is very cold, and the Indians must suffer much, before they reach their destination.

In haste
your O St

M. W. Bateman
1st Lieut 6th Infantry
&c

☾

After his request to stop in the state of Arkansas was denied by Governor James Conway, Opothle Yoholo turned to General Matthew Arbuckle, the commander of Fort Gibson, with a similar request. Letter found at SIAC, Agent (Reynolds), Account (1687), Year (1838), NARA.

Cadron Arkansas
14th November 1836.

Gen'l Mathew Arbuckle
Comd'g. S. Westn. Frontier
Fort Gibson

Friend,

I take the liberty of addressing you on the subject of creek Indian affairs. You have doubtless been apprized of some of the conditions and Stipulations under which I left my country East of the Mississippi.—One of these Stipulations was that Neomicco's party should be disfranchized, receive no part of the creek annuity, and be placed at such point within the creek country west, as I might designate.—Another Stipulation was, that I should be permitted to halt with my people, at some point within the State of arkansas until I could visit General Gaines or the officer commanding on the South Western Frontier, and settle other business for my people. Gen'l Gaines being absent, and you being in command of his department, together with the advice of the Governor of arkansas as contained in his letter, which will be shown you by Mr. Bateman, I have thought it best to proceed on to the Military reservation at your post. I visit your part with the most friendly feelings.—I wish to select a suitable place on which to locate my people, and to visit and consult with certain creek and cherokee chiefs who have emigrated some time ago, which will require some time.

I have been and still am recognized by the Government as the principle chief of the creek nation, and should any of the creeks West object to me as such, I wish time to consult, and arrange all our difficulties which I hope we can do in a friendly way.—During the time we are arrangeing our difficulties, and while I remain on the Military reservation, I will consider myself and my people under the protection of the Troops subject to your orders, and have respectfully to request that you will be pleased to take such measures as will secure to me and my people perfect protection from all harm.—Many of our warriors are now in Florida, assisting the whites to suppress Seminole hostilities, and their wives and children are with us.[37] I ask for their women and children, protection in the absence of their husbands and fathers.—You must excuse me for making these requests, as all were promised me before I left my old country.

I am your friend
and Brother
his
{Signed} Opothlo-yo-ho-lo

Witness.
{Signed} B. Dubois.

True copy
M. W. Bateman
1st Lieut 6th Infantry

☾

William Armstrong reports to the commissioner of Indian affairs on Bateman's visit to Fort Gibson and the news that Opothle Yoholo expects to become the principal headman of the Creek Nation upon his arrival. Armstrong counsels that it should remain up to the Creek people to decide who leads them. Letter found at Letters Received by the Office of Indian

Affairs, 1824–1881, Creek Agency West (hereafter LR, CAW), Roll 236, 697–98, NARA.

Choctaw Agency
Nov 24th, 1836

C A Harris Esqr
Com'r of Ind affr's

Sir

In order that you may understand the difficulties that is to be encountered with the Creeks, I enclose for your information a letter from Gen'l Jessup to Lieu't Bateman, and also one from Lieut Bateman to myself.

Since the receipt of these letters Mr Bateman has been here; and has returned to the party, of which O pothle yo ho lo is Chief. Mr B. has also seen Gen'l Arbuckle; and it is understood that the Creeks will halt upon the Garrison reserve at Fort Gibson, until McIntosh and other leading Creeks can be seen, I shall be there although much engaged in preparing for the annuity payments, as Capt Brown has just arrived, I shall be compelled to be with him on Red river to witness the payment there.

I will advise you immediately of the result of the expected meeting of the Creeks. I am informed by Lieut Bateman, that the Creeks now emigrating with O pothle yo ho lo as their Chief, say they have the nation and government with them—that they hold councils and pass laws on the way; and that upon their arrival, they contend for, and will expect immediate submission, to their laws and Chief, of the party now in the nation, they say they have been promised so by those who controled their movements last. I have informed Mr Bateman that I had nothing to do with making Chiefs, neither had any other person, except the Creeks themselves, that I should take the case of the Choctaws, that I considered in point, when they removed, the Secretary of War directed the then Agent F W Armstrong[38] to recognise the Chiefs then in power, until the nation emigrated and chosed others that as the principal part of the nation were near, close at hand, the Creeks could also be brought together; and then settle who shall be Chief; and form their own mode of Government. The prevailing opinion is that we must have a rupture, I yet hope that with Gen'l Arbuckle's experience and my own humble efforts, we may be able to check it, but it cannot be disguised that the present prospect is gloomy, but as before stated, I will Keep you advised of what we do. As to the rumour about the arms being Seized as mentioned in Mr Bateman's letter, it is all without the shadow of foundation.

Respectfully
Your Ob't Serv't
Wm Armstrong
Act Sup't West'n Ter'y

☾

William Armstrong reports on the arrival of detachment 1. Letter found at LR, CAW, Roll 236, 703.

Choctaw Agency
7 Dec 1836

C. A. Harris Esq'r
Commr. of Ind. affr's

Sir

I have just learned that A poth le ho lo has reached Fort Gibson the main body of the emigrants are now near this on the opposite side of the river on their way up—I leave in the morning for Gibson to meet the Creeks—the Commissioners Col. Kearney[39] and others have also reached Gibson. I will advise you from there of the meeting and of the manner the two parties McIntosh & A poth le ho lo receive each other.

Respectfully
your Obt Serv't

Wm Armstrong
act Supt West Ter'y

☾

Bateman reports on the partial arrival of his party, with about six thousand yet to arrive. Interestingly, Bateman signs his letter as a lieutenant, unaware that he had been promoted to captain in November 1836, in the midst of conducting detachment 1 west. Letter found at LR, CAE, Roll 238, 43–44.

Fort Gibson
12th December 1836

C. A. Harris Esq'r.
Commissioner of Indian Affairs
Washington City

Sir

I have the honor to report that a portion of Detachment No. 1 Creek Emigration under my charge arrived at this post on the 7th Inst. and the balance of the party on the 11th Inst. and were turned over to the authorities of this post, and the agents &c Employed by the U States discharged on that day (11th Inst). The march has been long, laborious, and tedious. The roads and weather have been indescribaly bad. The Indians have suffered much, [especially] the old and infirm and children. Two of the rear parties (say about 5,000 souls) arrived within the last two days. Two parties are still in the rear (say about 6,000). I am fearfull they are detained by high water, and so soon as my health will permit (which is now bad) I will go back and make every exertion to get them up. I am extreamly anxious they should get up before the winter sets in. So soon as I can make a copy of my journal, I will transmit it to you together with a general report.

Major B. Dubois my asst Military Agent has rendered important services to the Indians and our Country. Permit me to recommend him to the favourable consideration of the Department.

I am Sir verry
Respectfully
your Obt Svt
M. W. Bateman
1 Lieut 6th Infantry
Principle Military Agent
Det No. 1 Creek Emigtg

☾

Arbuckle reports that the Creeks under Opothle Yoholo arrived in a wretched condition and are in need of blankets to protect them from the cold weather. He also notes that Opothle Yoholo and his party will not be able to move to the Canadian River for a number of months due to the scarcity of provisions. Letter found at LR, CAE, Roll 238, 9–10.

Head Qrs SW Frontier
Fort Gibson Dec 18th 1836

Sir

The Creek chief Opoth yo ho la is encamped in the vicinity of this post with about six thousand of his people who have arrived here in a wretched condition in consequence of their want of blankets and clothing to protect them from the cold. He requests me to inform you that the contractors in order to prevent their waggons being heavily loaded on the journey had entered into an agreement with him and his people to transport by water their baggage which was not necassary on the march consisting of farming utensils, clothing, bedding &c. The truth of this statement is confirmed by the contractors now here and that about twenty tons of Creek baggage was boxed up and placed in a store house at Wetumpka Alabama which the contractors promised should be here by the time they arrived. We have no information of the property here and therefore Opoth yo ho la and his people are apprehensive that the contractors have failed to forward it in accordance with their voluntary agreement to do so and that unless some agent of the Government is required to give particular attention to this matter that they will probably lose their property. I therefore in justice to them hope you will adopt such measures as may be necassary to ensure the certain and early arrival here of the property referred to.

Subsistence for the Creek Emigrants cannot be furnished by the portion of our country for more than two or three months and therefore the meat part of the ration and probably corn will have to be procured from the Mississippi for several months and in consequence of the inability of the contractor to furnish subsistence on the Canadian Opoth yo ho la and about ten or eleven thousand Creeks who design settling there will be compelled to encamp on the South bank of the Arkansas river (in the Creek country) until Feb'y or March next or longer—I much regret this, as the early departure of Opoth yo ho la and his party to the Canadian is necassary to ensure the continuance of peace in the Creek nation and is also very material to these emigrants to enable them to make corn the next season.

I am Sir
Very Respectfully
Your obdt Servant
M. Arbuckle
Brev't Brig'dr Gen'l Commd'g

To

C. A. Harris Esqr
Commiss'r of Indian affairs
Washington City

☾

Bateman reports on the imminent arrival of a portion of detachment 1; his ill health (a condition that will contribute to his death seven months later); and the increasingly cold weather. Letter found at LR, CAE, Roll 237, 532.

Fort Gibson Aks
20th Dec'r 1836

C A Harris Esq'r
Commissioner of Indian Affairs
Washington City

Sir

I have the honor to report that I am still at this place in bad health. One of the two rear parties referred to in my last* is within four miles of this place, the other still back, I know not how far. The ground is covered with snow and ice, the Thermometer stands at Zero. The winter has set in with great severity. The Indians must suffer much, but I hope they will all be up in a few days.

I am Sir very
Respectfully
your Ob St
M. W. Bateman
U.S. Military agent
Creek Emigration

*dated 12th Inst.

☾

Bateman forwards his journal and accompanying letters to Commissioner of Indian Affairs Carey A. Harris. Letter found at LR, CAE, Roll 238, 87–88.

Fort Gibson arks
25 Dec'r 1836

C. A. Harris Esquire
Commissioner of Indian Affairs
Washington City

Sir

I have the honor to Enclose you herewith a journal kept by me while conducting Det No. 1 Creek Indians from Tallassee Alabama to Fort Gibson Arks. togeather with sundry letters in relation to Indian Affairs, thereunto appended. The bad state of my health (I being compleatly worn out and broken down) precluded the possibility of my transmitting them to you at an earlier period.

You will percive on refference to the journal, that the 25 August was the day designated for the movement to commence, we did not however move untill the 30 or 31st of said month, for reasons fully explained in the journal.

The journey was long laborious and tedious. The Indians occasionally suffered much, owing to the inclemency of the weather, and the bad condition of the roads. On my part no effort was wanting to place these people in their new homes with the most Kind feellings towards the Whites, and I hope I have been successfull.

You will percive on refference to the correspondence attached to the journal, that my party were promised permission to halt within the State of Arkansas; this not meeting with the approbation of the Executive of the State. I succeeded in bringing them to this place, where they were received with great kindness by Genl Mathew Arbuckle U.S. Army: and were Encamped within one mile of the Fort.

The apprehend difficulties between Opothlo yo-ho-lo and the McIntosh parties, can I believe with proper care, be amicably adjusted.

I am Sir very
Respectfully
your Ob St
M. W. Bateman
1st Lieut 6th Infantry
P. Military Agt &
Disbg Agent.

P.S. I will leave in a few days for Fort Mitchell Alabama, unless detained by Genl Arbuckle to assist in bringing up the rear party, where please address me.

M.W.B.

☾

Bateman reports on his departure from Fort Gibson. He notes that there are approximately ten thousand Creeks encamped near the mouth of Grand River. Letter found at LR, CAE, Roll 238, 47–48.

Little Rock Arkansas
8th January 1837

C. A. Harris Esq'r
Commissioner of Indian Affairs
Washington City

Sir

I have the honor to report that I left Fort Gibson on the 31st Ult. and reached this place yesterday. Previous to my leaving Fort Gibson about 10,000 Indians had arrived. They had been halted on the Military Reservation at that post, where they were met in a friendly manner by the McIntoshe's, and on the 28th   29th and 30th Dec'r crossed over the arkansas river into their new country, near the mouth of Grand river, where they will remain a few days, when they will proceed out to the Canadian river, where tis their intention to locate. Lieut Deas's party had not reached its destination, but were near the Cherokee country, all well.

The appointment of Capt Jacob Brown to the Presidency[40] of the Bank of Arkansas,[41] will make a vacancy in the Office of the Pri Disbg[42] agent Indian removal. I would be pleased to be appointed his successor, as to my qualifications, capability &c. I beg leave to refer you to Gen'l G. Gibson Commissary Genl. USA, Washington City.

I will leave tomorrow for Fort Mitchell Alabama, where he's pleased to address me.

I am Sir very
Respectfully
your OSt
M. W. Bateman
U.S.A. Disbursing

Agent Creek Rem'l

P.S. All fears on the subject of Indian dificulties on the Arkansas frontier at the present, have subsided.

M.W.B.

☾

Commissioner of Indian Affairs Carey A. Harris asks Captain John Page to investigate reports that the Creeks of detachment 1 left approximately twenty tons of excess baggage at Wetumpka, Alabama. Rather than being forwarded to Fort Gibson as the party left in 1836, these items were discovered rotting on a steamboat on the Gulf of Mexico in 1837. Letter found at SIAC, Agent (Reynolds), Account (1687), Year (1838), NARA.

Copy—

War Department
Office Indian Affairs
Feb'y 6. 1837.

Capt John Page.

Sir,

By a letter this day received from Brig: Gen'l Arbuckle dated the 18th Dec'r last, I am informed that the Emigrating party of O-poth-le-yoholo left at Wetumpka a large quantity of baggage consisting of blankets, clothing and other articles necessary for protection from the severity of the season & amounting to about 20 tons; that the contractors received this property which was boxed up and left in stores for their accommodation in order to prevent over loading the wagons, and upon assurances that it should be immediately forwarded. The emigrants have arrived at Fort Gibson and are now in a suffering condition for want of these articles which there is reason to fear have been entirely neglected by the Contractors. I have to request that you will immediately attend to this matter & ascertain whether the property has been forwarded or not and if not that you will take measures to have it sent on with the utmost possible despatch. If on enquiry you find that the property is such as the contractors were required by contract to carry you will Keep an account of the expenses incurred by you in forwarding it that they may be deducted on settlement.

Gen'l Watson,[43] one of the Contractors & who is now in this city informs me that Mr Edward Hanrick of Montgomery County, Al'a made the arrangement with the Indians as the agent of the Company; & feel their expresses his apprehension that the delay in forwarding the goods has been occasioned by the low state of the water in the Arkansas and consequent difficulty of navigation. Your first application will be to Mr Hanrick and your subsequent measures will depend upon the information obtained from him.

Very &c
C A Harris.[44]

☾

Bateman reports that he has returned to Alabama, after waiting for four of the detachments to reach Fort Gibson. Detachment 3, which had not yet arrived, Bateman passed some seventy or more miles east of the garrison. Letter found at Records of the Adjutant General's Office, 1780s–1917, Entry 159-Q, Records of Major General Thomas S. Jesup, Container 19, Folder: "Letters Received Relating to Creek and Seminole Affairs, 1837," NARA.

Fort Mitchell Ala
10th February 1837

Major Gen'l T. S. Jesup
Comg Southern Army
Florada

Sir

I have the honor to report that I returned to this place on the 4th Inst. We had a long and tedious march, having been 109 days from Tallassee to Fort Gibson. The weather was bad, and the roads were in a most horrid condition. I remained at Fort Gibson untill all the companies had reached there, except Lieut Deas's party from Taladega. I passed this party some 70 or 80 miles East of Fort Gibson. They were progressing slowly, winter having set in, and the weather very cold. They must have, most certainly reached their destination by the 20th Jany.[45]

The apprehended difficulties between the McIntosh and Opoth lo-ho-lo parties were peacebly arranged (for the present).

The Indians were better pleased with their new Country than I had expected [they] would have been. I left them in good health, and appearantly contented. I received the most efficient Services from Major Dubois.

I am Sir very
Respectfully
Your O St
M. W. Bateman
Captain 6th U.S. Infantry
Disb'g Agent Creeks

☾

Bateman reports on the circumstances that led him to change the route of detachment 1 from Pontotoc, Mississippi, to Russellville, Alabama. Letter found at SIAC, Agent (Reynolds), Account (1687), Year (1838), NARA.

Mobile Alabama
28th June 1837

W. J. Beattie Esq'r
M. A. Em Company[46]

Sir

I have the honor to acknowledge the receipt of your letter of yesterdays date, in which you state that the "Alabama Emigrating Company have suffered pecuniary losses in the removal of the Creek Indians &c" with a request that I would give you a statement containing my views in relation thereunto. I am compelled to be very brief owing to the fact that I have to write from memory, not having my Journal of occurrences; or memoranda within my reach or at hand, and to the fact that my opperations were generally confined to Det no. 1 or what was commonly called Opoth lo yo. ho-lo's party.

The rout designated for Det no. 1 (or my party) was by Tuscaloosa Ala, Cotton gin Port & to Memphis. That designated for Det. no. 2. (or Lt Screvens party) was by Ealyton &c to Memphis.

Along each of these routs I understood that depots of provisions were placed for the subsistence of the Indians. On my arrival at Tuscaloosa with Det. no. 1, I learned with regret that Det. no. 2, had refused to go by the Ealyton rout, and had determined to follow the rout traveled by Det. no. 1. On enquiry & from such information as I could obtain, I was clearly of opinion that the two Detachments could not be subsisted on the Pontetock and Cotton gin Port rout. I therefore determined to change the rout of Det no. 1, believing it the only means of procuring Subsistence for Det no. 2, it therefore follows that what ever of subsistence   Forage &c were prepared on the Ealyton and Pontetock routs, was unavailable to the Company, as both parties travelled by the rout of Russellville &c.

There were doubtless other delays, but where and when they arrived I can not now state. I therefore beg leave to refer you to the reports &c of Conductors & Disbursing Agents for information therein.

In haste I am Sir very
Respectfully
your Obt Srt
M. W. Bateman
Capt 6th U.S. Infty
D.A.C. Reml[47]

11 Detachment 2

The second detachment was based at Wetumpka, Alabama, and consisted of Indians from the affiliated towns of Tuckabatchee who were loyal to Opothle Yoholo. The party was conducted to Indian territory by Thomas M. Martin on behalf of the Alabama Emigrating Company. South Carolina–born Lieutenant Richard Bedon Screven of the 4th U.S. Infantry served as military oversight. Dr. Madison Mills[1] of New York City, aided by Dr. Eugene B. Hutchinson[2] of Montgomery, Alabama, accompanied the party as physicians.

Journal of Detachment 2

Journal found at SIAC, Agent (Reynolds), Account (1687), Year (1838), NARA.

Fort Gibson Indian Territory Jan'y 9th 1837

Sir,

I have the honor to inform you that on the 6th of Sept. last Detachment No: 2 of Emigrating Creek Indians consisting of about three thousand one hundred and forty-two, under my direction crossed the Coosa River at Wetumpka Al. and after a march of four miles encamped. On the morning of the 7th resumed the march and after making a distance of 14 miles encamped. Here the roads forked—the right hand leading through Elyton and the left through Tuscaloosa, the former being the route designated for this party and upon which arrangements had been made to meet its coming.

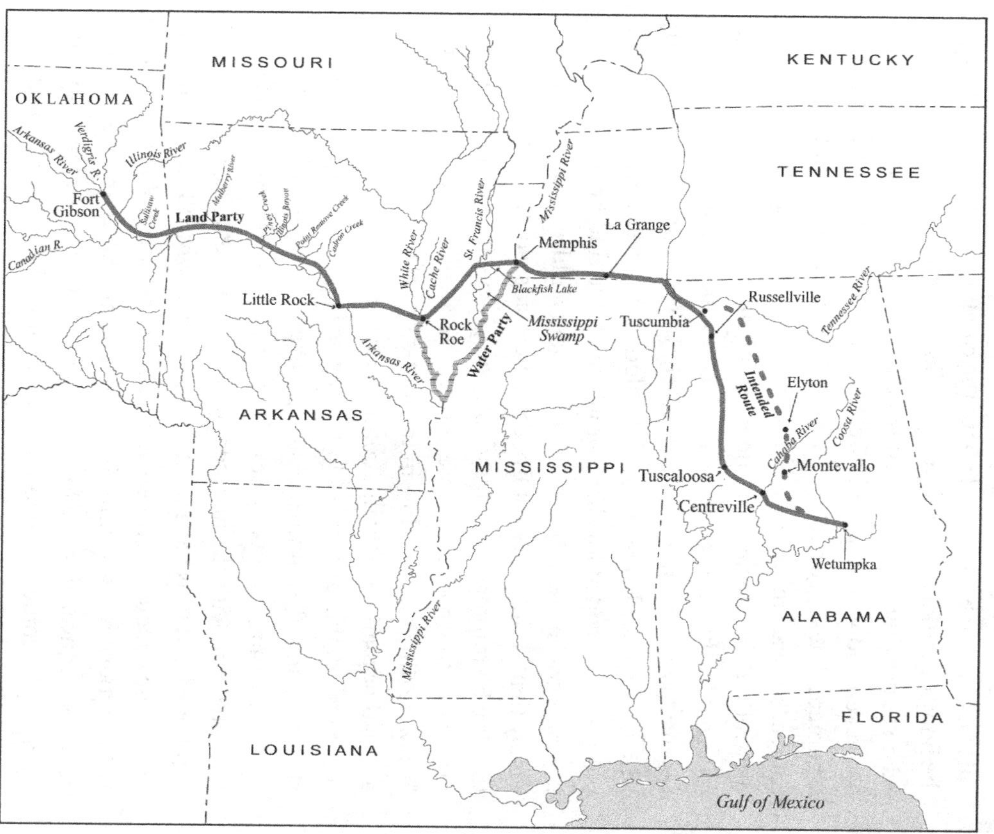

MAP 10. Route of detachment 2, September–December 1836. Place names correspond to stopping points or locations noted in the documentation. Route lines and locations are approximations. Cartography by Sarah Mattics and Kiersten Fish.

This fact having been hinted about the camp I received a visit from the body of Indian chiefs about 9-O'clk. at night who remonstrated against diverting from the road which their chief Opoth-lo-yo-holo had taken and which he had directed them to follow also. Every argument that suggested itself was used to dissuade them from this course, but was unheeded and finding that I also, was unyielding they retired dissatisfied. On the morning of the 9th this visit was repeated by the same body, where their former arguments were renewed and the same responses given. In vain I urged that the party which had preceded us on the Tuscaloosa road had destroyed all the provisions provided for them—that we should find none and that it would grieve me to see their women and children starving—and finally that in the course of five days the roads would reunite—that the Elyton road was abundantly supplied with Every article of provisions to which they were entitled. To all of which they replied "we were directed to follow in the foot-steps of Opoth-lo-yoholo and rather than disobey this command we are willing to starve the five days." In this dilemma I found my-self constrained Either to stop the party at an immense and perhaps unwarrantable expense to the Al. Emig. Company or order them to take the road which I pointed out, with the firm conviction that it would have been disobeyed and thus have what little influence which I might possess over these people prostrated at the commencement of a long and tedious journey. I was unwilling to hazard the latter and was equally solicitous concerning the former course. At this critical juncture the agent of the company, who was present at both interviews yielded—I offerred no further opposition and the Indians were indulged. By great exertions on the part of the agents of the company I am pleased to inform you that a supply of provisions was procured. After this our journey progressed without interruption and on the 12th passing through Centreville forded the Cahawba and encamped on its right bank. Night of the 15th encamped two miles S. and East of Tuscaloosa and on the morning of the 16th passing through the city, crossed the Black Warrior and encamped six miles to the N. & west of this river. Thence taking a course due North crossed the Sipsey river and on the 25th passed through Russellville and encamped on Rocky Branch—distant about seven miles. Directing our course more westerly left Tuscumbia and Florence about 8 miles to the right and passing through the N. Eastern corner of the Chickasaw Nation reached La Grange on the 6th of October and encamped in its vicinity.[3] Continueing the westerly course crossed the Chickasaw Line into Tennessee and on the 9th Struck Wolf river at a point distant about 16 miles East of Memphis and encamped. Here learning that the party under Lieut. Bateman 6th Inf. was detained in the immediate vicinity of Memphis for the want of water transportation I determined to tarry until he might vacate his position, when I should reoccupy it. Remained in camp 10th and 11th and on the 12th marched 13 miles and took up the old position of Lt. Bateman distant 3 miles East of Memphis. Remained in camp 13th and on the 14th marched to Memphis and commenced crossing and on the 21st completed the passage of the Mississippi river. The Indians consenting to take water transportation, it became necessary to divide the party—accordingly on the 22d a portion under charge of Mr. A. H. Sommerville[4] asst. agent & actg. asst. surgeon E. B. Hutchinson embarked for Rock Roe—a portion with the horses took the road through the mississippi swamp and the remainder, Estimated at 1300 souls under charge of Dr. & asst. Surgeon Madison Mills and my-self embarked on the afternoon of the 22d on board the Steamer John Nelson[5]—having two well covered Substantial "Flat boats" in tow—descended the river 25 miles and encamped. Morning of the 23d got under weigh at 7–a.m. and descended the river 60 miles and encamped an hour by sun. Morning of the 24th got under weigh at 7–a.m. and descended to the mouth of white river and encamped at 4–P.M. Morning of the 25th ascended white river 15 miles and encamped at 3–P.M. having started at 8–a.m. Got under weigh on the 26th at 8–a.m. and made about 40 miles and encamped at 5–P.M. Got under weigh at ½ after 6–a.m. on the 27 and encamped at 5–P.M. having made 40 miles. morning of the 28th started at 6–a.m. and having made 48 miles arrived at Rock-Roe bayou at 4–P.M. and encamped—

FIG. 7. Lt. Richard Bedon Screven (1808–1851), military oversight of detachment 2. Reprinted with permission of Indiana University Press.

This position is on the right bank of White river—is estimated at 143 miles above its mouth and about 6 miles below the mouth of the Cache where the military road crosses the white river. From the 29th of Oct. to the 8th of November inclusive detained in camp waiting the arrival of the party who had taken the swamp road, crossing the waggons and teams over the river &c &c &c— The weather during this period was generally cold and rainy which greatly retarded the business. On the 9th made a slight start and taking a N. west course passed through the Prairies and on the 20th struck the Arkansas river opposite the city of Little Rock.[6] During the greater part of this time the weather continued cold and mirky & the prairies rendered thereby almost impracticable for loaded waggons—wood and water were scarse and the party suffered exceedingly from cold. Distance between these two points estimated at 65 miles. On the morning of the 21st continued the journey westward and crossed in succession Palerm creek, Cadron, Point Remove, Illinois bayou, Pine, Horse-head, Mulberry, Frogg-bayou, Lee's creek, Salisa and Vian creek and on the 17th December arrived on the banks of the Illinois river—distant from Fort Gibson 18 miles. This River was found to be much swollen and the current rapid.

One of our best teams made an ineffectual effort to cross, which produced a consternation amongst the waggoners and in a body declared their determination not to risk their property in the river.—seeing this state of things I directed the driver of our private mess waggon to cross the river at all hazards. The attempt proved vain—the waggon was upset and one horse drowned. For a while the whole business seemed paralized, but fortunately one or two proving bolder than the rest successfully crossed and the balance followed in succession without further accident.

Between this point and Little Rock difficulties of a serious and unforseen nature arose to retard the progress of the party; the road through "Point Remove bottom" would appear impassable for any wheel carriage and in extent is about 4 miles—rising thence on the high land the road traverses a "Hurricane"[7] which if any thing is worse than the bottom. The weather was excessively cold and the Indians positively refused to travel—added to this the abundance of game attracted the hunters from their camps and at the point of renewing the march they were found unprepared and would not move Either for threat or persuasion. Hence the party straggled many miles asunder. On the 22d of December the main body arrived at this place and took up a position one mile below the Fort and on the 26th I certified to the rolls exhibiting an aggregate of three thousand and ninety five souls turned over to Capt. J. R. Stephenson 7th Inf. at this place by order of Bvt. Brig. Genl. M. Arbuckle.

By reference to a memorandum of daily travel the distance from Wetumpka al. to Fort Gibson, including the water route, is estimated at 1039 miles. The whole time employed is 110 days—number of travelling days is 75—number of days of detention and resting days 35. This by calculation gives a daily average travel of little more than 13 miles. The ordinary time of starting varied from 5 to 8–O'clk. A.M. and that of halting from 12 noon to 3–O'clk. P.M.

In taking a retrospect of events as connected with this emigration it is painful to reflect that, at the very moment of leaving their old homes peaceably in search of new ones, the Indians should have had their camps beset by a gang [of] swindlers, horse theives and whiskey-traders, practising every species of fraud that is calculated to disgrace the human character. The route has been anticipated and an abundant supply of whiskey furnished on the road-side—hence the source of more than one half the trouble I have had to encounter.

It is the firm conviction of its necessity alone, that induces me to intrude the opinion that in all future Emigrations a show at least, of mil. force is absolutely required to protect the Indians in their property and to scourge from camps a class of men who are nothing loth to pilfer the last penny from a starving Indian.

It is a subject of peculiar congratulation to my-self, that notwithstanding the delicate relation in which I have stood to the Gentlemen of the Alabama Emig. co. with whom I have been associated, no unpleasant collision has taken place between us.

Holding a just regard for the interests of the Comp'y I have seen them humane and indulgent to the Indians and were mindful of the obligations of their contract.

I beg leave to recommend to your especial consideration Mr. A. H. Sommerville asst. agent by whose experience, great zeal and untiring perseverance in the discharge of his duties the Emigration has been materially forwarded. It is proper to state that oweing to a protracted indisposition I was necessarily absent much of the latter part of the journey from camp and a continuation of this indisposition detains me at this Post. In due season a certificate to this effect will be presented from Drs: DeCamp[8] & Mills U.S.A.

At as early a date as practicable an acct. of my disbursements &c &c shall be forwarded.

In conclusion, I am happy to inform you that almost universally a spirit of cheerfulness and contentment prevailed amongst the Indians—considering the number they were healthy—having been able to ascertain only 37 deaths and 18 births, 'tho I freely confess that these numbers are liable to great Error. Expressions of an unfriendly character have sometimes escaped them and Even personal threats have been made, to which I have attached no importance at the time, yet is it not improbable that they were the overflow of feeling that sooner or later is destined to show itself in a more tangible form on this frontier.

I have the honor
to be
Yr. obt. svt.
R. B. Screven
1st Lieut. 4th Inf.
Mil. & Disbursing agent Creek removal.

C.S. Harris Esqr.[9]
Commissioner Indian affairs
Washington
D.C.

Supplemental Letters of Detachment 2

Lieutenant Richard Bedon Screven reports on the difficulty of keeping the Creeks in camp and getting them to assemble. Letter found at Records of the Adjutant General's Office, 1780s–1917, Entry 159-Q, Records of Major General Thomas S. Jesup, Container 20, Folder: "Letters Received, 1836, Montgomery, Alabama during the Creek War," NARA.

Wetumka Ala. August 27th 1836

General,

In compliance with the 11th Par. of Order no: 63 dated "Head Qrs Army of the South Tuskegee 17th August 1836", I had contracted with Dr. E. B. Hutchinson of Montgomery to accompany detachment no: 2 of Emigrating Indians, when through the politeness of Lieut. Simpson[10] I was furnished with a perusal of order no: 67 dated "Head Qrs. Army of the South Tallassee 22d August 1836", by the 6th Par. of which I perceive that Asst. Surgeon M. Mills has been ordered to report to me at this place—under these circumstances I request to be informed what disposition shall be made of Doct. Hutchinson.

I have the honor to inform you that in consequence of the protracted absence of the chiefs of the Indians ordered to rendezvous at this place the warriors are under no control—day after day the Town is filled with Indians and very often they are seen returning in a state of intoxication and independent of this I have good reason to believe that the sale of whiskey is carried on extensively by hangers-on in and about their camps and I am very sure that nothing can so effectually eradicate this Evil as the presence of a Military force in this quarter. On the 25th inst. I made a statement to this effect to the Supt. of Emigration.

Yesterday I rode to the Hickory Ground with the view of witnessing the issue by the Contractors and was much disappointed in not finding the Indians ready to receive their rations—comparatively but few had assembled and these very soon began to skulk away. Seeing this embarrassment I determined to go into their camps and ascertain the cause of delay and to the enquiry why they had not come after their rations? I was answered in some cases that they did not Know the day for issueing, in others that their chiefs being absent they could receive nothing and again that they had left the ground because some white-men had told them that the waggons there had been sent to transport them to Arkansas immediately.—To such trifling excuses sir you will give their just weight but it is proper that I should say that the general listlessness which discovers itself upon making a circuit of their camps looks but little like people who should be engaged in making active preparations to Emigrate to a distant and new home. The business of emigration in this quarter appears to be backward—but two-thousand five hundred and Eighty-nine of those enrolled have come into camps & are now being rationed by the contractors—a number falling far short of that which has been anticipated—others have been enrolled but have not yet come in.

I despatched a runner yesterday calling upon the chiefs to meet me at 11—O'clk. this morning with the view of telling them of the necessity of remaining at home and Keeping their men under subjection and to warn them for the last time to be in readiness to move when called upon. What may be the result I am unable to say.

By return of Express I have just received an extract from order no: _____ delaying the movement of the several detachments.[11]

I have the honor
to be
Yr. obt. srt.
R. B. Screven
1st Lieut: 4th Inf.
Prin'le Mil. Agent. 2d Det.

Majr: Gen'l. T. S. Jesup
Comd'g. Army of the South

☾

Screven reports on the necessity of supplying a military force in order to protect the Creeks of his party from whites peddling whiskey and as a means of cajoling the Indians to prepare for their movement west. Letter found at Records of the Adjutant General's Office, 1780s–1917, Entry 159-Q, Records of Major General Thomas S. Jesup, Container 20, Folder: "Letters Received during the Creek War, Headquarters, Columbus, Georgia 1836," NARA.

Wetumka Alabama Aug. 29th 1836—

Sir,

Your note of yesterday's date reached me last Evening by return Express and in reply have to inform you that I Know of no just grounds to believe that the Indians Encamped in this vicinity will offer any active opposition to the order for Emigration, but I regret to inform you that their encampments exhibit a want of preparation from which I fear delay. I have ordered the chiefs to meet me with the view of informing them finally that the Comdg-General will allow no further procrastination and that it behooves them and their people to be in readiness to move at a moment's notice. The rumor that the Wetumka Indians had "refused to receive rations and dispersed" taken in its broad sense is not true.

On the morning of the 26th inst. I repaired to the Encampment with the view of witnessing the issue by the contractors—on my way there I met a great many Indians coming in to Town and upon my arrival at the store-house I found comparatively but a small number assembled to receive their rations. Seeing this state of things I resolved to make the circuit of their encampments and ascertain the true cause for this disappointment. To the enquiry, why they had not gone for their rations? I was answered by some that they did not Know the day for drawing and by others that they had gone to the store-house but having been informed by some of the white men that the waggons present had been sent there to convey them off to Arkansas immediately, they had left the ground fearing that such was actually the case. Upon my return to the store house I was informed that in one or two cases the Indians had said that their chiefs being absent they were not authorized to receive rations, but as there was nothing general in these excuses, I could see no concert and have there fore attached but little importance to the affair.

In obedience to my orders they came in next morning and received their rations and since then there has been no difficulty.

I request that you will urge to the Comdg. Genl. the necessity of haveing a military force quartered at this place, not from any fear of an outbreak amongst the Indians, but for the purpose of patrolling their encampments and ferreting out a set of white-men who are hanging about the Indians, trafficking in whiskey, and poisoning their minds with forged stories. As your note calls for information upon the very subjects which I had already deemed of sufficient importance to lay before the General in my letter of the 27th inst. directed to Col. Stanton and forwarded by express I am to conclude that it had not reached its destination, accompanying is a copy of a letter which I have this day forwarded to Genl. Armstrong.

I have the honor
to be
Yr. obt. svt.
R. B. Screven
1st Lieut. 4th Inf.
Mil. agent Creek removal.

Capt. J. F. Lane
2d Dragoons
A. M. Camp
Tallassee Alabama.

☾

The following is the accompanying letter (addressed to General Robert Armstrong[12] of the Tennessee volunteers) mentioned in Screven's 29 August letter (preceding). Letter found at Records of the Adjutant General's Office, 1780s–1917, Entry 159-Q, Records of Major General Thomas

S. Jesup, Container 19, Folder: "Letters Received Relating to Creek and Seminole Affairs, August 1836," NARA.

Copy—

Wetumka Ala. August 29th 1836—

General,

In compliance with the 10th Par—of order no: 67 dated "Head Qrs—Army of the South Tallassee 22d August 1836" I have the honor to in form you that I have no just ground to apprehend any active oppositions on the part of the Indians rendez-voused in this vicinity to the fulfilment of the orders for emigration—Yet deem the presence of a military force necessary for the purpose of patroling their encampments and ferreting out a set of white-men who are hanging about the Indians, trafficking in whiskey and poisoning their minds with forged stories.

In addition, I believe that the moral tendency of this force would bring more strongly to the minds of these people the fact that the time for emigration had actually arrived and thus induse them to prepare seriously for a movement at the appointed time.

With this view of the subject I submit to you the propriety—of ordering one or more companies of your command to take position at this place.

I have the honor to be
Yr. obt. svt. R B Screven
1st Lt. 4th Inf. mil. agent

Gen'l. Armstrong
Comd'g. Brigade Ten. Vol.
Camp Jordan Ala.

☾

Screven reports on his arrival at Memphis and the commencement of detachment 2's ferriage across the Mississippi River. Letter found at LR, CAE, Roll 237, 636.

Indian camp Memphis Ten.
Oct. 14th 1836

General,

I have the honor to report that on the afternoon of the 12th inst. detachment no: 2 of Emigrating Creek Indians consisting of about three thousand one hundred and forty-two under my direction arrived within two miles of this place and encamped.

On the 13th remained inactive in order that the party under Lieut. Bateman 6th Inf. should Effect the passage of the river—he has done so and I am now Engaged in the same operation and will probably be embarked in the course of two days. The Mississippi swamp having been ascertained to be impracticable for loaded waggons the Indians have consented to take water as far as Rock-rowe and their horses are to be taken to this place by a party detailed for this purpose.

It affords me great pleasure to inform you, that as far as my observation has been able to extend over a body so large, the contract has been faithfully complied with and that cheerfulness and contentment appear to prevail amongst the Indians.

I have the honor
to be
Yr obt. svt.
R. B. Screven
1st Lieut. 4th Inf
Mil. agent Creek Removal

Genl. George Gibson
C. G. S.[13]
U.S. Army
Washington D.C.

12 Detachment 3

The third detachment was based four miles east of Talladega and consisted of the Upper Creeks living along the Tallapoosa River from Horseshoe Bend to Tallassee. The two most prominent chiefs of this party were Menawa of Okfuskee and Tuscoona Harjo of Fish Pond. The party was conducted to Indian territory by Dr. R. W. Williams on behalf of the Alabama Emigrating Company. Lieutenant Edward Deas, who had previously conducted the fifth voluntary emigrating party in 1835, accompanied as military oversight. Dr. James W. Townsend[1] of Talladega, Alabama, served as physician until he became ill and Dr. James G. Morrow[2] of Somerville, Alabama, took his place until reaching Memphis.

Journal of Detachment 3

Found at SIAC, Agent (Reynolds), Account (1687), Year (1838), NARA.

Journal of Occurrences—on the Route of a Party of Emigrating Creek Indians, kept by Lieut. Edw. Deas Disbur'g Agent in the Creek Emigration.

17th September 1836.

The Party of Indians under my charge, about to emigrate to the new country west of the Mississippi River under the contract with the Alabama Emigrating Company, left the point of assembly, 4 miles east of Taladega Alaba'a., to-day about noon. The number enrolled is 2420. These Indians have come into camp without the necessity of using force & appear to be well disposed towards the Agents employed to remove them, & at present

MAP 11. Route of detachment 3, September 1836–January 1837. Place names correspond to stopping points or locations noted in the documentation. Route lines and locations are approximations. Cartography by Sarah Mattics and Kiersten Fish.

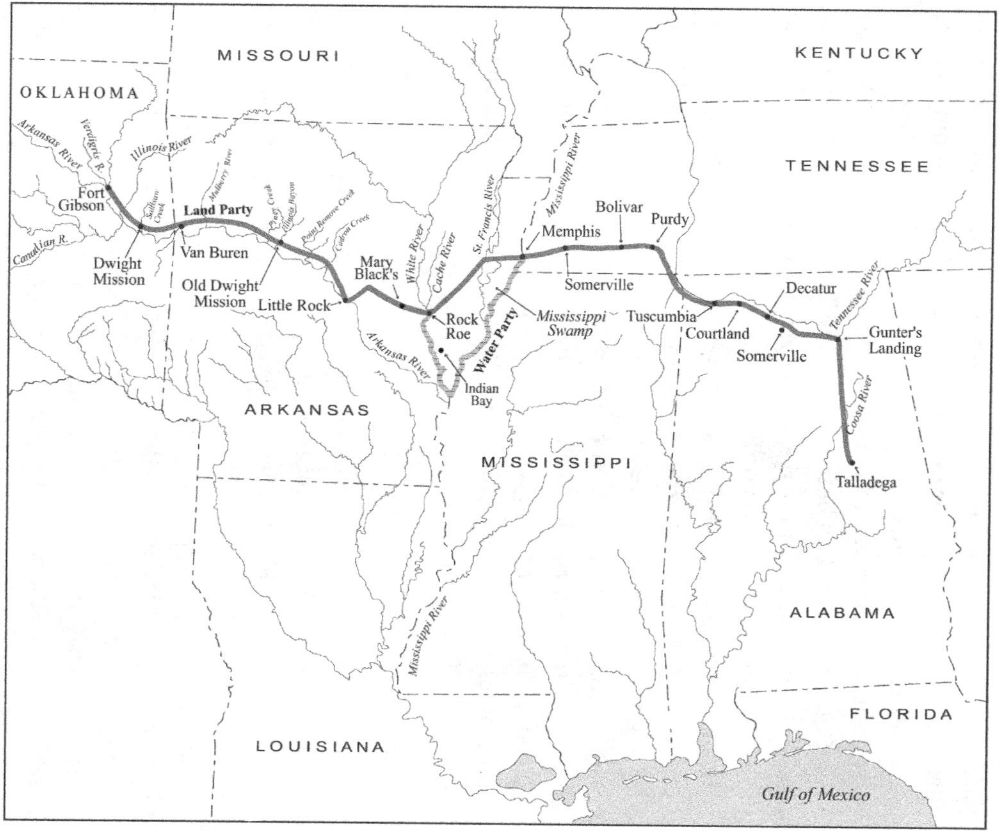

evince a disposition to proceed on their journey to the West, with cheerfulness & friendly feelings towards the White people with whom they are necessarily thrown in contact.

The Indians constituting this Party, have inhabited that portion of the Creek Country situated on both banks of the Talapoosa River, near that stream, and that part of it intercepted between the Horse Shoe Bend to the north, and the small town of Tallassee to the south.[3]

The muster Rolls of the Party which will be forwarded to the Department, shew the respective names & numbers of Each of the Towns composing the Party. It is therefore unnecessary to insert them here.

The means of Transportation & Subsistence are at present supplied agreeably to the Contract for the Removal, and thus far all things therewith connected appear to be going on well. The Party to-day has travelled about 7 miles & is now encamped near Riddle & Walkers Store about 6 miles north of Taladega.[4]

18th September

The Party started this morning about 8 o'clock—has travelled to-day 12 miles & is now encamped 18 miles north of Taladega. Nothing worthy of notice has occurred thro' the day, the weather is good but the Roads are unpleasantly dusty.

The Indians appear in good Spirits & well satisfied in all respects. The route selected for this Party and that which went over the same road about 10 days since,[5] is to go in a direction a few degrees west of north about 80 miles from Taladega, & within a few miles of Gunter's Landing, which is near the most southern point of the Tennessee River; and then to take the most direct course to Memphis, either by crossing the Tennessee or passing thro' it's valley on its south bank.

It would be much shorter to go direct to Tuscumbia, but the roads would be extremely bad & mountainous & the country thinly settled & provisions scarce. Moreover the large Parties that crossed the Coosa River lower down than Taladega will pass over the roads in the interior.

As the hours at which the Party starts & stops each day will be mentioned so freequently, it is proper here to remark that in mooving a Party of the present size a space of time of more than an hour generally elapses, between the starting of the first of the Indians & the Baggage Wagons, and the time at which the whole body has left the last nights encampment & is fairly on the road. In stopping also the interval between the arrival of the first of the Indians & their wagons, at the new place of Encampment, and the time at which the whole party comes up, is generally from one to two hours & sometimes more than that space of time. When it is here in mentioned, therefore, that the Party started at a certain hour, it will be understood that at the hour mentioned, a majority of the Wagons & Indians had set out.

In like manner the period mentioned as the hour of stopping or encamping, will be understood that point of time at which about half the number of Wagons & Indians have reached the new Encamping ground.

19th September.

The Party started this morning at the usual hour about 8 o'clock & has since come about 9 miles to Drivers ferry[6] on the Coosa R., which point was reached about noon and the operation of crossing immediately commenced & several hundreds of the Party are now encamped upon the north bank. Much the greater part still remain upon the south bank yet to be ferried over. Nothing of importance has occurred through the day, the weather is fine, & the people generally healthy.

The Physician employed by me under authority from the Superintendent of the Emigration to attend the present Party, is Doctor Townsend of Taladega.

20th September.

The whole of the day has been occupied in crossing the Coosa River and most of the Party is now encamp'd one mile north of the Ferry.

Nothing of consequence has occurred through the day. a small number of the Indians remain on the south side of the River but will cross in the morning before the Party starts.

21st September.

The Party started this morning about 8 o'clock & has since come 9 miles to Conoe Creek, the day's travel made short as some of the Party still remained to cross the Coosa River before starting. We stopped in the afternoon about 2 o'clock & nothing of particular consequence has occurred.

The means of subsistence & Transporta'n furnished is such as the Contract requires, & the Agents of the Emigrating company with the present Party appear well qualified to assist in the business of the removal.

22nd September.

We left the encampment at Conoe Creek this morning at the usual hour about 8 o'clock, & proceeded thro' the Pine swamp, 7 miles across, and stopped in the afternoon at Walkers, at 2 P.M. after having travelled 13 miles from last nights encampment. The weather is still fine & the Indians generally healthy.

Nothing of importance has yet occurred upon our Route, every thing in regard to the progress of the Party is going on well and the Indians express themselves well satisfied.

23rd September.

The Party started this morning as usual & has since ascended the Mountains forming the dividing Ridge between the tributaries of the Coosa & Black Warrior Rivers on the south, and the Tennessee River on the north.

The distance travelled was about 12 miles, and the Party is now encamp'd on the mountain 4 miles south of Coxe's Stand.[7] The Party reached the camping ground about 3. P.M.

24th September.

The Party started this morning as usual and after travelling over good level roads about 11 miles decended the mountain and encamped at its foot near Ramsay's, the whole distance travelled to-day being about 13 miles. The present encampment is about 4 miles south of Gunter's Landing which is near the southernmost point of the Tennessee River. There was a little rain in the forenoon to-day for the first time since leaving Taladega. Nothing of importance has occurred through the day.

25th September.

Since starting from Taladega up to yesterday the general direction of our

Route was a little west of north. To-day we have travelled in a direction nearly western-ly on the road leading towards Sommerville & Decatur.

We have determined to take the road on the south side of the Tennessee River, as it will not take so long to reach Memphis by this route, and will be in conformity with the wishes of the Indians who are much opposed to crossing the River.

The Party started and stopped to-day at the usual hours, & has travelled about 12 miles.

26th September.

Last night about 10 o'clock information was brought to me at the camp that an Indian named No-cose-yoholer who had remained behind the Party at a store upon the road with a few companions, had got drunk and had some disagreement with a White man named Burns, who drew a Pistol and shot the Indian.

I returned immediately & found the man about six miles back still very drunk but as I thought not dangerously wounded.

I immediately had him conveyed to the Camp, and as Burns had made his escape I wrote to General Moore[8] an assistant Agent in the Creek Emigration, at Claysville a few miles off, giving him information of their circumstances, that he might have the outrage duly punished.

The Party started this morning as usual and has travelled over good roads about 12 miles & encamp'd in the afternoon at the usual hour between 2 & 4 o'clock. Nothing of importance has occurred through the day.

The friends of the man who was shot last night were much incensed & wished to return to do mischief. I assured them that General Moore would take the necessary measures to have justice done in the case, which appears to have satisfied them.

27th September.

The Party started this morning about 8 o'clock & after travelling over rough roads about 10— miles, encamped for the night at the usual hour in the afternoon about 4 miles east of the small town of Sommerville.

Nothing of importance has occurred to-day.

It should have been mentioned that before the present Party left the limits of the Creek country a number of Indians from various Towns came into camp & joined the Party for Emigration.

This took place after the original Roll of the Party had been signed & forwarded. Their names were therefore entered only upon the Roll which accompanies the Party. The number that joined in this manner was two hundred & seventy-five.

2420
275
———
2696

28th September.

The Party to-day has travelled over very good roads about 14 miles. We started at the usual hours & passed thro' Sommerville a little country town, in the forenoon & stopped for the day at the usual hours between 2 & 4 P.M. 6 miles east of Decatur.

Nothing of consequence has taken place to-day in reference to the progress of the Party.

Up to this time the Rations have been regularly issued of such quality & in such quantity as the Contract requires & the means of Transportation is also such as specified. Since leaving Taladega the roads have generally been mountainous, but we are now getting into a more level and fertile tract of country in the valley of the Tennessee River.

29th September.

It is customary amongst Indians when performing long journeys, to stop a day occasionally for the purposes of resting and allowing the women an opportunity of washing &c.

To day therefore has been appropriated to these occupations & no progress has consequently been made.

30th September.

The Party started this morning about 8 o'clock passed thro' Decatur in the middle of the day, and encamped in the afternoon about 9 miles west of that place at 4 o'clock P.M. Nothing of importance has occurred through the day. The country for the last 20 or 30 miles has been level & fertile & well cultivated, for the most part in cotton. The roads are good but at present unpleasantly dusty, the weather having been dry for some time back.

1st October 1836.

The Party started this morning at the usual hour and encamped this afternoon about 5 o'clock.

The distance travelled to-day was too great being 19 miles, but was necessarily so, in consequence of the impossibility of obtaining water at a nearer point than the present encampment on Town Creek. Nothing of importance has taken place. We passed thro' the small town of Courtland in the middle of the day; the weather is still very dry & the roads excessively dusty.

2nd October.

The Party left Town Cr. this morning at the usual hour & is now encamp'd half a mile from Tuscumbia on the Road towards Memphis, leading thro' the Chik-a-saw country, having travelled to-day about 16 miles.

The weather still continues remarkably fine & the roads level but dusty & consequently extremely unpleasant to travel.

3rd October.

The Indians have been remarkably sober yesterday & to-day, when it is considered that the Party has been nearly 24 hours in the vicinity of a Town. We left the Camp this forenoon about 10 o'clock a late start being caused by the Indian's remaining in Tuscumbia for the purpose of trading &c.

The distance travelled to-day was nine miles and the Party encamped in the afternoon at Cane Creek at 5 o'clock without any circumstance having occurred thro' the day worthy of notice.

Dr. Townsend the Physician employed to attend this party was obliged to stop near Sommerville on the 27th ultimo from indisposition, expecting to over-take us in a few days.

Dr. Williams[9] the Agent of the Contractors with the Party has agreed with him to perform his duties during his absence.

4th October

The roads still continue tolerably good and the distance travelled to-day was 15 miles. The Party started at the usual hour about 8, P.M. and encamped in the afternoon between 2 & 4. Nothing of consequence has occurred thro' the day, the Indians continue healthy & appear well satisfied.

5th October

The Party started this morning between 8 & 9 o'clock & after travelling 8 miles encamp'd at 2, P.M. The roads to-day were hilly & dusty as the weather is still dry.

It has been rather cold since yesterday morning, at which time a considerable change took place in the temperature.

We crossed the Mississippi line to-day three miles back and are now in the Chick-a-saw country and on the most direct road from Tuscumbia to Memphis. Corn is scarce at present, but the Rations have been regularly issued up to this time.

6th October.

The Party started and stopped to day at the usual hours having travelled 10 miles.

We are now encamp'd on the banks of Little Yellow Creek. The weather still continues dry & cold. The roads to-day were hilly and somewhat rough.

7th October.

The Party left Yellow Cr. this morning about the usual hour & after travelling 12 miles over tolerably good roads encamp'd between 2 & 4 P.M. at Hindman's.

There has been some rain to-day for the first time since leaving Gunter's Landing. Nothing of importance has occurred.

8th October.

We started to-day at 9 o'clock P.M. & encamp'd in the afternoon between 3, & 4.

The distance travelled was 12 miles & we crossed the Tennessee line 8 miles back and are now about 8 miles S.E. of Purdy a small town.

The roads to-day were good & not so dusty as heretofore. The Party continues healthy & the People still seem well satisfied in all respects.

The Rations have been regularly issued up to this time.

9th October.

The Party started this morning about 9, & has come about Eleven miles to a point 3 miles west of the small town Purdy which place most of the Indians passed thro' in the middle of the day. a few loitered behind until near dark for the purpose of obtaining Liquor. The sale of this article to Indians travelling, is the cause of more disturbances & difficulties in the camp, than all others put together.

There are almost always persons at every small town or Settelment who are base enough to persist in selling it to them, even after the evil consequences have been fully explained & they requested to refrain from doing so. The influence of gain is all powerful. No serious difficulty has yet taken place from this cause upon the present journey other than has been herein mentioned.

The roads to-day were very good & the weather remarkably fine.

10th October.

No progress has been made to-day as the Party has been again allowed to rest, in conformity with the wishes of the people.

Nothing of consequence has occurred through the day and the weather continues fine.

I have to-day received information that Doctor Townsend still remains sick at Sommerville.

I have therefore engaged Dr. J. G. Morrow to supply his place until he overtakes the Party.

Dr. Morrow resides at Sommerville and has come on to join the Party, knowing that a Physician would be required. He left his house on the 6th ins't & his appointment takes affect consequently from that day. It is lucky that he has joined us as I have been unable to provide a Physician on the road at any price.

11th October.

Since leaving Purdy the Party has travelled on the direct mail Route from Florence Alaba'a. to Memphis.

The first Party which left Taladega, & which crossed the Tennessee River at Deposit ferry,[10] & re-crossed it at Savannah, passed over the same road about a week ago.

We started to-day about 8 o'clock A.M. and after travelling about 13 miles encamp'd in the afternoon between 2 & 4. Nothing of importance has taken place to-day. The Party is now encamp'd on Little Hatchee about 15 miles east of Bolivar.

12th October.

We have travelled to-day about 15 miles & are now encamped a quarter of a mile east of Bolivar.

The Indians have been a little troublesome to-day in consequence of getting drunk. Some fighting took place, but none were killed although several were wounded.

Nothing else of consequence has occurred.

13th October.

The Party started this morning between 8 & 9 o'clock & encamped in the afternoon 10 miles west of Bolivar.

The weather continues fine & the roads very good.

We hear from Memphis that all the large Parties of Creeks, four in number, that have gone in advance of the present, are now in the neighbourhood of that place & will probably be detained there some time. It is therefore better for us to make our rate of travelling slow for the present.

Since we left the Chickasaw country & have been in the State of Tennessee the country has been rather thickly settled & provisions plenty.

The rations have been regularly issued to the Indians up to this time, and the Party generally, continues healthy.

14th October.

The Party started this morning between 8 & 9 o'clock & has come about

11 miles to-day & encamped about a mile east of the town of Sommerville at 3 o'clock P.M. Nothing of importance has taken place thro' the day. There was a little rain last night which served to lay the dust which had become excessive.

15th October.

The Party to-day has travelled about 7 miles & encamped about one o'clock 6 miles west of Sommerville. The hour of starting was as usual & the distance has been made short as there is no water to be obtained nearer than 10 miles west of the present encampment.

The roads since we have been in the State of Tennessee have been very good & the country remarkably level. We have crossed no mountains & scarcely a hill of any size.

16th October.

I have to-day received information from Memphis that there will be some delay at that point owing to the bad state of the roads west of the Mississippi & the impossibility of passing them with heavy loaded wagons.

As the other large Parties are now near Memphis, we have determined not to approach nearer that place at present. No progress has therefore been made to-day.

17th October.

The Party was mooved to-day to the present encampment about 4 miles north of that occupied last night.

This change has been made for the purpose of obtaining a better supply of water. No thing of consequence has taken place through the day.

The present place of Encamp't is about 40 miles to the Eastward of Memphis.

20th October

For the last three days the Party has remained encamped on the Loosahatchy Creek waiting for the departure of the others to take place from the neighbourhood of Memphis.

Nothing of importance has taken place at the present encampment.

The Party continues healthy & the Rations have been regularly issued up to this time.

21st October

As one of the large Parties in advance has now been removed from Memphis and arrangements being made for the others to set out speedily, we shall approach that place slowly.

The Party left the encampment on the Loosahatchy Creek this morning between 8 & 9 o'clock & has come to-day about 5 miles to a point on the mail route towards Memphis.

A good deal of rain has fallen in the last two or three days which served to lay the excessive dust and the roads are now in good travelling condition.

22nd October.

We came to-day 9 miles to Cypress Creek, so called, but is at present nothing but a succession of Ponds now stagnant.

The hours of Starting & stopping were as usual & nothing of importance has occurred thro' the day.

23rd October.

The Party to-day has travelled 17 miles in consequence of the impossibility of procuring water at a shorter distance. We started about 8, A.M. & stopped about 3, o'clock this afternoon.

The present encampment is at Wolf River 9 miles east of Memphis.

24th October.

To day there has been hard & constant rain and the roads are consequently extremely muddy.

The Party left Wolf River this morning between 8 & 9 o'clock & stopped at noon about 2 miles east of Memphis.

Nothing of importance has taken place through the day.

Two of the large Parties that preceeded ours have left Memphis and the remainder will do so as soon as possible.

The plan proposed is to take the Indians & their baggage by Steam

Boats & to send their Horses through by land to meet them at some point west of the Swamps, that are situated between Memphis & Little Rock.

These are said to be impassible at present for loaded wagons.

25th October.

The Party was mooved to-day to the present Encampment, situated about a quarter of a mile below Memphis & near the bank of the Mississippi.

We shall be detained at this point a number of days awaiting the departure of the other Parties, which the Contractors are using exertions to hasten.

They have in employ four Steam Boats, one of which is used as a Ferry Boat, having a Flat attached to its side for the purpose of conveying the Horses across the Mississippi. Two of them are plying between this place and Rock Row on White River, and the fourth will ascend the Arkansas River with a load of Indians.

30th October

The Party under my charge has remained encamped since the 25th instant, and in that time all the Indians of the other Parties have left this neighbourhood, and proceeded westward towards their destination.

The last Boat started day before yesterday & when one of the others that went to Rock Row returns we shall also proceed in the same manner.

31st October.

The Party still remains encamped as yesterday & nothing of importance has taken place through the day.

1st November 1836.

The operation of ferrying the Indian Horses and Ponies across the Mississippi commenced to-day & upwards of a hundred were carried over. Their owners crossed with them and are now encamped on the west bank of the River. The remainder of the Party still remains stationary.

2nd November.

To-day between 3 & 4 hundred of the Indian Ponies were ferried over the

Mississippi with their owners. Nothing Else of importance has occurred through the day.

3rd November.

The main body of the Party still remains encamped and the remainder of the Ponies were ferried over the River to-day.

The Wagon horses have also been taken down to the water's edge ready to cross in the morning.

The Wagons were also taken down and some of them taken to pieces ready to be put on board of the S-Boat without delay on her arrival from Rock Row.

Some of the wagon Horses were ferried over this afternoon.

4th November.

To-day at noon the Steam Boat Farmer returned and the people & Agents have been actively employed this afternoon in placing the Wagons on board of her.

The Lady Byron has been employed as heretofore in ferrying and nearly all of the Wagon horses are now on the west bank of the River.

Nothing else of consequence has occurred to-day.

5th November.

The forenoon to-day was employed in getting the remainder of the wagons & Baggage on board of the Boats employed to carry the main Body of the Party to Rock Row. These are the Farmer and the Lady Byron, the former being of the largest class of boats & the latter of about one hundred Tons burthen.

Every thing being in readiness to start, about sunset they were got under way & have since come 12 miles below Memphis & stopped for the night.

Two of the Chiefs of the Party refused to go by water as many of the Indians have a strong prejudice against Steam Boats.

It has been decided that the Indians have the Right to go the whole journey by land, and the Chiefs referred to, insisted upon doing so, and have taken with them near 500 of their people. Their names are Tuscoona-Hadjo,[11] and Monawee,[12] the former of the Fish Pond and the latter of the

Chat-off-soph-ka Town.[13] They together with the Indians having the care of the Horses & Ponies of the rest of the Party, started westward thro' the Mississippi Swamps in the direction of Little Rock, before the Boats left Memphis. They are accompanied by an Agent of the Emigrating Company and several Assistants.

All the Creek Indians now emigrating under Contract have therefore left the eastern bank of the Mississippi.

The weather continues remarkably fine & the Indians are still generally healthy.

Up to the present time every thing in relation to the Removal of the Party under my charge has gone on well and the Agent of the Emigrating company, with it, has shewn every disposition, as far as I have been able to observe, to treat the Indians well and to comply with all the stipulations of the Emigrating Contract.

6th November.

The Boats started this morning about day light the Lady Byron taking the start. The Farmer passed her about 10 o'clock A.M., and stopped in the afternoon about half an hour before sun set, when most of the people went on shore for the night.

We are now about 140 miles below Memphis & 25 above the mouth of White River.

7th November.

The Farmer got under way this morning about day light & entered the mouth of White River in the forenoon and has since ascended that stream about 70 miles. She was landed for the night a short time before sun set, and most of the Indians have gone on shore and encamped for the night.

8th November.

We again got under way this morning about day light and after running near 65 miles reached the present stopping place two miles below Rock Row, this afternoon at 4 o'clock.

All the Indians have landed & encamped.

We find that the other parties, which preceed ours have left the

FIG. 8. Menawa. From McKenney and Hall, *History of the Indian Tribes of North America* (1842). Courtesy of the Alabama Department of Archives and History, Montgomery.

neighbourhood of this place except that under charge of Lieut. Scriven. They are encamped about two miles above us, near the junction of Rock Row Bayou with White River, and expect to start in a day or two. Nothing of any consequence but what has been mentioned has taken place to-day.

9th November.

Last night and this forenoon were employed in landing the Indian Baggage and small wagons, and the Running Gier[14] of the Large wagons that were taken to pieces at Memphis and brought [onboard] in the Farmer to this point.

A large Flat was made use of to bring the Bodies & was attached to the side of the S-Boat & towed in that manner.

The Lady Byron has not yet arrived.

10th November.

The Lady Byron arrived this afternoon a short time before sun-set, having been detained by running aground.

The People arrived in safety, with the exception of an Indian who was killed by falling into the Fly-wheel[15] of the Engine, whilst in a state of intoxication. No other accidents occurred on her trip from Memphis to this place.

All of the people that came by water are now Encamped on the west bank of White River and there is nothing to detain us, after the arrival of the Party by land, with the wagon Horses & Ponies.

11th November

A few of the land Party arrived this afternoon and think that the others will soon be up.

The roads from Memphis here, are represented as being as bad as possible & almost impassible.

12th November

The People continue to come in, in small numbers.

Nothing of consequence worthy of notice has taken place to-day.

There has been a deficientcy in the Rations since our arrival at this place. There has been no Fresh meat issued as yet since the arrival of the Party here, and only a short allowance of indifferent Bacon, brought from Memphis on board of the Boats.

This deficientcy of Provisions might easily have been prevented had the necessary means been taken to procure supplies before the arrival of the Indians.

The neighbourhood of Rock Row, our present place of encampment being one of the most important points upon the whole Route of Emigration, there should here have been established by the Agents of the company, previous to the arrival of the Indians, a large Depot of Provisions.

The Lady Byron will be dispatched to-morrow to "Indian Bay" 60 miles below this for the purpose of procuring supplies, as there are none to be had in the neighbourhood.

The country for many miles around this place is very thinly settled, but White River affords an easy means of communicating with better cultivated portions of the country.

16th November.

The Steam Boat Lady Byron returned from "Indian Bay", this afternoon loaded with about four thousand pounds of Fresh Beef & between 5 & 6 hundred Bushells of Corn.[16] Nothing of importance has occurred since the last date.

Tuscoona Hadjo and Monawee, and their people have not yet arrived.

Every thing is in readiness to proceed as soon as they do so.

18th November.

The remainder of those that left Memphis by land have not yet reached Rock Row.

The Party is now only waiting for them to set out from this place.

Nothing of particular consequence has taken place here than what has already been mentioned.

19th November.

I determined to-day to return towards Memphis to discover the cause of the detention of the Indians in the swamps.

An Agent of the Emigrating Company is with me.

I left the main body of the Party at Rock Row with every thing in readiness to set out towards Little Rock tomorrow morning.

The Indian Baggage the use of which can be dispensed with upon the road, was also to-day put on board of the Lady Byron to be transported up the Arkansas River. It is under the charge of an Agent of the company accompanied by a few of the Indians.

I am now six miles to the eastward of the "Mouth of Cache."

The Cache River empties into White River about 9 miles above Rock Row. The Government road crosses White River at Cache where there is a Post-office, and a small settlement.

20th November.

To-day I have only been able to come 15 miles to Patricks.

The roads were one continued bog greatly resembling the clay used by Brick makers, 2 or 3 or more feet deep over the whole surface of the ground and in some places covered with standing water. The Public Road is cut through this swamp by cutting two parralled Ditches, and throwing up & forming the Earth between them.

Whenever the Ditches are drained the roads are hard & very good, but to-day I have not passed over more than a mile or two of this description.

The remainder is such as I have described, with holes occasionally, where it is with some difficulty that a horse can pass.

I found Tuscoona Hadjo the Fish Pond chief about 10 miles from Cache, who says he has been detained by sickness in his family & bad roads.

21st November.

I have to-day come about 20 miles over roads like those described yesterday but in places much worse. At several of these in addition to the mud, the water was nearly up to a Horse's back.

Both to-day & yesterday I have found Indians encamped along the road, at intervals of half a mile or so, who gave the same reasons for their detention as Tuscoona Hadjo, but some also said they had got out of provisions and had to stop to hunt.

I have given them all directions to push on to Cache as soon as possible, which they seem well disposed to do.

22nd November.

This afternoon I reached Strong's[17] near Saint Francis River Ferry, having found many Indians on the road to-day under the same circumstances as those I mentioned yesterday.

From what I have seen upon the road since leaving Cache, & have acertained at this point, I have no difficulty in explaining the cause of the detention of the Indians.

This place (Strong's) is the only Stand at which Rations were issued to the land-party, after they left a point 17 miles west of Memphis, no other Depot being established between that point & Rock Row or Mouth of Cache, a distance of about 80 miles.

This failure to have Issuing Stands upon the Route, (which I find might easily have been established) at intervals of not more than 25 or 30 miles is a non-compliance with an article of the Emigrating Contract on the part of the Company, which is of essential importance at all times & particularly so when the roads are bad.

Moreover the Agent of the company sent thro' with the land Party did not accompany the Indians further than this place and issued before the whole had crossed the St. Francis River about ½ a mile to the east of this.

It therefore appears that a large number of the Indians from the negligence of the Agents did not receive Rations from the Company and were therefore compelled to shift for themselves for a distance of 80 miles if they should reach Cache before I return and overtake them.

The Agents sent thro' with the land Party should by all means have remained with the Indians for the purpose of assisting and urging them on.

It was my understanding that this was to be done when the Party set out from Memphis.

I believe that all of those Emigrating under contract are now to the west of this point and to-morrow the Agent of the Company now with me will return towards Little Rock for the purpose of taking up all stragglers and others that may be found upon the road west of this place. When I left Rock Row upon the 19th instant I gave directions that the main body of the Party should proceed towards Little Rock & when a point was reached at which the necessary supplies could be procured, then to encamp and await the arrival of that portion of the Party which was in the rear.

This arrangement was necessary as their provisions were nearly exhausted at Rock Row, and a change of position for the Party was desirable on account of health.

The Agent of the company now with me is considered a responsible man, and as I can be of no service in bringing up the stragglers I shall set out to morrow to over take the main Party.

26th November.

On the morning of the 23rd I left Strong's & to-day reached the main body of the Party where it is now encamped, 12 miles to the eastward of Little Rock.

They have come slowly from Rock Row to this point in the last six days.

The roads from that place to this a distance of about 48 miles, are mostly over extensive praries and in consequence of recent bad weather are at present in a very bad condition. The wagons cut through in many places nearly up to the hubs of the Wheels.

I find the Party at present generally healthy and am told by the government Agents with it, that there has been no scarcity of Provisions since leaving Rock Row.

27th November.

The Party started about 8 o'clock A.M. and reached the neighbourhood of Little Rock early in the afternoon and is now encamped on the north bank of the Arkansas opposite the Town.

As this location is considered healthy and affords abundance of wood and good water, and is also the most convenient point in the surrounding country for obtaining supplies, it is intended at present that the Party shall remain where it now is until those in the Rear have been brought up.

28th November.

Nothing of any importance has occurred thro' the day.

30th November.

The Party still remains encamped opposite Little Rock waiting for those behind. Many have come up & it is reasonable to expect the others in a few days. Nothing of importance has taken place since the arrival of the Party at this place.

7th December 1836.

The main Body of the Party has remained encamp'd opposite Little Rock since the last date.

A considerable number of the Indians that were behind have come up & the Agent of the Contractors whom I left at Strongs on the 23rd ultimo, has arrived in Camp and brings information that the whole of those that are still behind must be in the neighbourhood of this place by tomorrow or the day after.

At any rate we must leave this place in a day or two as provisions are becomeing very scarce and as those in the rear will probably soon over take the main Party it will be better for us to proceed slowly by which means supplies of Subsistence can be more conveniently provided.

8th December 1836.

The Party is still encamp'd. opposite Little Rock.

I received to-day a communication from the Governor of Arkansas stating that the Indians had been represented as having killed Hogs & Cattle, stolen corn & vegetables & burned fence rails.

There appears to be no just foundation for these accusations.

Since the arrival of the Party at this place subsistence has been plentiful as their Rations have been regularly issued & the Indians have besides killed a great deal of Game.

I have also examined the fences in the neighbourhood, and find that they are in as good a condition now as they were upon our arrival at the present Encampment.

Moreover it is probable that had there been any proof of the above charges, the complainants would have availed themselves of the civil authority to obtain redress as in ordinary cases of depredation.

I have no doubt that the real cause of discontent is the fact that the presence of so many Indians raises the price of Corn & other supplies and that the above charges are made a pretext for having the Indians removed from the neighbourhood.

The Governor's communication also directs that the present Party proceeds to take up the line of march without delay, but this had become unnecessary as I had determined it should do so in a day or two before the receipt of his Excellency's letter.

I have answered this and expressed my opinions upon the Charges referred to by his Excellency and also stated the causes of the detention of the Party under my charge.

I shall of course forward copies of the letters to the Department.

9th December

The Encampment opposite Little Rock was broken up to-day about noon and we are now halted about 3 miles N.W. from that place.

Nothing of importance has taken place thro' the day. The Party continues to be generally healthy & has been so since leaving Rock Row.

10th December.

A wagoner who returned to Rock Row arrived in camp to-day and brings intelligence that Monawee the Chat off soph ka Chief is still two or three days journey behind the Party with a considerable number of Indians from various Towns. Therefore the interests of the Emigration require that we should not proceed further until those Indians overtake the Party or at least until most of them arrive in its vicinity so as to communicate with the Chiefs. If we were to attempt to proceed with the main Party before those in the rear arrived the consequence would be that the whole Route would be lined with stragglers.

Two of the most important Chiefs are behind and many of their people are now in camp & if the Party was to proceed the latter would for the slightest cause fall to the rear and wait upon the road for the arrival of their head-men.

There are also others who would not start at all until they hear that their Chiefs are near them.

13th December.

The Party is still encamped 3 miles N.W. from Little Rock waiting for the Indians that have not yet come up. Nothing of importance has occurred since the 11th instant at the present Encampment.

It is impossible to procure any further supplies in this immediate neighbourhood, the Party will therefore proceed to-morrow towards the nearest point at which these can be obtained in sufficient quantity, and there again make a halt.

19th December[18]

The main Party left the Encampment 3 miles N.W. of Little Rock on the 14th instant, and at the same time I returned towards White River, accompanied by the principal Agent of the Contractors, to see to bringing up the Indians that were still in the rear, and to acertain the circumstances which have caused so much delay.

The Agents who were sent back to Rock Row with wagons & provisions from Little Rock on the 1st instant, reached White River on the 5th instant.

They there found several hundreds of the Indians on the Eastern bank of that stream, without the means of crossing.

From the 5th to the 11th December was employed in getting the Indians over White River and in bringing them out of the Swamps on its western shore. This is the statement of the Agents who were there, and it is therefore clear that all delays up to the 12th December were owing to the deficientcy of the arrangements of the Emigrating Company at White River & to the difficulty of crossing that stream.

After getting the Indians on hard ground west of White River, from the 12th until this forenoon, (the 19th) was employed in bringing them to the neighbourhood of Little Rock, and in that time, two days delay was caused by the Indians refusing to travel in consequence of the severity of the weather.

The last detachment passed Little Rock this forenoon and after travelling one mile N.W. of that place, refused to travel any further to-day. As they had only come six miles I wished them to go 8 miles further in order to procure provisions and to be able to overtake the main Party tomorrow.

They however persisted in refusing to go any further to-day and I was therefore prevented from going on to overtake the main Party which I intended to do.

25th December 1836.[19]

I last mentioned that on the 19th instant the hindmost detachment of the Indians belonging to the Party under my charge passed Little Rock & encamp'd one mile N.W. of that place.

On the 20th there was very severe cold Rain and Wind and they could not therefore be expected to travel.

On the 21st & 22nd the weather was very fine for travelling, but the Indians just refused to, still refused to proceed. Their numbers were about 400, belonging to the Fish Pond and Chat-off-soph-ka Towns.

The Principal chiefs of Each of these Towns was present, namely Tus-coo-na-Hadjo, and Mo-naw-ee. The latter was too drunk on the 22nd to attend to business, but the former evinced a stubborn obstinate disposition and every thing that could be said to persuade him to travel was in vain. There was 5 wagons with provisions ready, which had been sent back for their use. I therefore informed the Indians that we could wait for them no longer.

That there was no reason for their refusing to proceed and that on the day after the wagons must start. If they would go, we should be glad of it but if they refused it was the last assistance that would be offered them.

On the 23rd therfore the wagons started from near Little Rock bringing the Chat off soph ka people and some of the Fish Pond, but Tus coona Hadjo stated that he did not want wagons and would come on after the Party at his leasure. Upwards of a hundred of the Fish Ponds remained. As this man has a considerable sum of money & good Poneys there was no danger of his suffering on the road.

At the same time that the wagons started from near Little Rock on the 23rd ins't. I also set out from the same place and proceeded to overtake the main Party. Being detained one day on the road by business with the Agents of the Government who accompanied one of the other large Parties to Fort Gibson, I reached my own Party to-day, (the 25th December) encamped about 35 miles N. West from Little Rock, & 3 miles to the eastward of Cadron Creek.

I find that no thing of particular importance has occurred since I left it near Little Rock on the 14th instant.

26th December 1836.

The Party remained encamped to-day waiting for those still behind. Nothing of importance has occurred.

27th December.

All the Indians that were in the rear, with the exception of Tuscoona Hadjo and some of his people, came up to-day, and most of the Party removed about 3 miles to the bank of Cadron Cr. a part crossed that stream & encamped this afternoon on its western bank.

Tuscoona Hadjo has sent on word not to wait for him & that he will over take the Party before it reaches Fort Gibson.

28th December

The remainder of the Party crossed Cadron Creek to-day & about half of the number have come on 7 miles to Plummer's Stand[20] and encamped for the night. The others remained near Mather's on the west bank of the Cadron.

29th December.

That portion of the Party that encamped at Plummer's last night remained stationary to-day & the remainder of the people also reached that point this afternoon.

The roads from Little Rock thus far have been excessively bad.

The whole of my Party is at present once more collected in one body, Excepting of course Tus coon a Hadjo & about 150 of his people, who will no doubt reach the end of the journey about the same time with the rest of the Party. Nothing of importance has taken place to-day. Since I have overtaken the Party there have been no complaints on account of Provisions which have been regularly issued.

30th December.

The Party started this morning from Plummers about 8 o'clock & after travelling 9 miles encamped about noon.

The roads to-day were tolerably good & level. Nothing of importance took place. The people remain generally healthy.

31st December.

We started this morning about 8 o'clock & crossed Point Remove Bayou after travelling 2 miles.

The present encampment is about 10 miles from that of last night.

The roads to day were very bad part of the way, having come thro' a Swamp on each side of the Bayou of 5 miles in extent.

The remainder of the road was better except at a few points, where it was crossed by small streams. The Party encamped about 2. P.M.

Since I joined them on the 25th ins't. the weather has been very fine & is at present quite mild for the season.

1st January 1837.

The Party to-day started between 7 & 8 P.M.[21] and encamped early in the afternoon near and to the west of Pott's Stand having travelled about 9 miles.

The roads to-day were somewhat better than yesterday & the weather fine but cold.

We found the Cow-E-ta chief Tuck-a-bach-E-Hadjo[22] and about 200 of his people encamped in this neighbourhood where he has been since the Party of Lieut. Sprague passed this place. He says he has been detained by Sickness and that he also wished his brother to overtake him, who is with our Party, having joined us at Little Rock.

2nd January

The Party started & stopped to-day at the usual hours after travelling about 9 miles.

The present encampment is near "Old Dwight" formerly a missionary station for the Cherokee Indians.

Tuck-a-bach-e-Hadjo with his people joined my Party to-day and appears anxious to get on. The citizens in this neighbourhood have succeeded in getting up a prejudice against this chief, on the ground that he has been committing depredations on their property.

There being no proof I believe the reports to be unfounded.

Tuck a bach e Hadjo appears to be an orderly & well disposed Indian. There will no doubt be endless claims presented to government from the citizens of Arkansaw for Indian Depredations said to have been committed by the Emigrants & it is to ground these claims that various articles have made their appearance in the Papers of the county, charging these unfortunate people with various thefts which there is no evidence of their having committed.

3rd January

The Party left the neighbourhood of "Dwight" this forenoon about 8 o'clock and after travelling about 6 miles over tolerably good roads stopped about noon at the present encampment situated on the Arkansas River at May's. Nothing of importance has taken place to-day, the weather is fine & not very cold.

The Present Party travels over the road on the north bank of the Arkansas as it is equally as good as that to the South & the ferrying the River twice is avoided.

4th January 1837.

The Party started this morning about 8 o'clock and after travelling about 9 miles crossed Piney Creek by fording & stopped about 2. P.M.

We are now encamped near Maddens Mill[23] a quarter of a mile west of Piney Creek. The roads to-day were better than any we have travelled in Arkansas. Since leaving Little Rock the country we have passed thro' has been broken and Hilly & for the last two days mountainous.

The weather is still fine.

5th January 1837.

The Party to-day came 8 miles, starting about 8 o'clock P.M. and stopping this afternoon about 2. P.M.

We are now encamp'd on both banks of Spadua Creek[24] at Ward's.[25]

The roads to-day were good and the weather very fine & moderately cold.

The Spadua is a small stream, at present easily fordable. Nothing of importance has taken place thro' the day. The Party continues healthy.

6th January

We left Wards this forenoon about 8 o'clock & stopped in the afternoon about 2. on the west bank of Horse Head creek, near Pace's,[26] having come 11 miles over tolerably good roads.

The weather is fine & mild to-day. The Party continues healthy and the Rations have been regularly issued up to this time.

7th January

The Party has travelled to-day about 12 miles & is now encamped a little to the west of Russell's.[27]

The roads to-day were generally good, but there were several bad places of small extent which delayed the wagons.

The hour of starting was 8. P.M. & the whole did not reach the encampment until near dark. We are now on the west bank of the White Oak Creek a very small stream.

The people continue healthy.

8th January 1837.

The Party left the neighbourhood of Russels this morning about 8 o'clock and reached the present encampment a short time before dark having travelled 12 miles. A good deal of rain has fallen thro' the day & the roads were rather bad.

We are now half a mile east of Mulberry creek at Lasiter's Stand.

9th January.

The Party to-day has travelled about 5 miles over roads like those of yesterday. A good deal of rain fell last night, but it cleared up before the Party started this forenoon about 11 o'clock.

We are now encamped one mile west of William's.

There was no difficulty in crossing the Mulberry as the water is low at present.

The people continue healthy & the Rations have been issued in conformity with the Contract up to this time.

10th January 1837.

The Party started from near William's this forenoon about 8. & having travelled about 9 miles crossed Frog Bayou by a shallow ford, & encamped on its western bank in the afternoon at 2 o'clock.

The weather to-day is fine & the roads were tolerably good.

Nothing of consequence has occurred.

11th January.

The Party started and stopped to-day at the usual hours and is now encamped on the banks of Lees Creek having come 12 miles.

We are now at a point about 6 miles from Fort Smith & about three from the small town of Van Buren.

The roads to-day were good & the weather fine but cold.

12th January.

The Party to-day has not been able to moove in consequence of bad weather. A heavy snow storm came up last night & still continues.

I received a letter to-day from Gen'l Arbuckle at Fort Gibson by express upon the subject of the Emigration. He states that the Indians cannot be expected to travel in bad weather & that he thinks the Government will indemnify the Emigrating Company for the expense of the Detention of the Party from this cause.

15th January

The Party still remains encamped at Lee's Creek in consequence of the heavy Snow. It fell to the depth of 6 or 8 inches & has rendered the roads extremely bad. As the weather for the last 4 days has been cold it has been impossible for the Indians to travel without great suffering on their part, many of them being without shoes & badly clothed.

General Arbuckle also enclosed to me a letter from Apooth-le yohola the principle chief of the late Emigration to the Chiefs of this Party in which it is intimated to them that the people would not be required to proceed when the weather & roads are bad. As it was rather milder to-day a proposition was made to them to proceed but they refuse to do so until a thaw takes place.

Nothing of consequence affecting the Indians has taken place at the present Encampment.

16th January.

A change took place in the weather last night & to-day a good deal of the snow has melted.

The Indians agreed to start about the middle of the day & the Party has advanced about 7 miles from Lee's Creek, and is now encamped in the Cherokee country about 4 miles west of the boundary line of Arkansas.

Since the Party passed the Cadron on the 27th ultimo, the Rations have been furnished by Contracts entered into by Agents of the Emigrating company previously. As far as Mulberry creek was supplied without any failure under one Contract. Another extends from Mulberry to the end of the route.

This has not been supplied quite so punctually as the former in consequence it is said of the failure of some of the Agents owing to the great scarcity of Corn in the country.

The Indians however have not suffered for want of their Rations & the Agents of the Company with the Party have used all exertions to procure the necessary supplies in the Surrounding country.

17th January.

The Party to-day has come nine miles and is now encamp'd on the west bank of Skin Bayou, a small stream. The weather continues mild & the snow has almost entirely melted.

The roads to-day for the first 4 miles were hard & good, but hilly; the last 5 were very bad, passing thro' small prairies & Black Jack Bottoms which at present are swampy & very much cut up.

The Party started about 8. P.M. & encamp'd at 2. P.M. Nothing of consequence has occurred thro' the day.

The People continue healthy, and as they approach the end of their long journey appear more anxious to bring it to a termination.

18th January

We left Skin Bayou this morning between 8. & 9. o'clock and have come to-day 5 miles.

The Party encamped in the middle of the day half a mile or a mile west of Winter's a cherokee Indian.

There was a scarcity of corn last night, for which reason the distance to-day was made short.

A sufficient supply was obtained to-day at Winters to make up the deficientcy of yesterday.

19th January 1837.

The Party started this morning between 8. & 9. o'clock & after travelling about 9 miles encamped about 3. P.M. near a Missionary Establishment[28] on Salison Creek. The road to-day was very hilly, but hard. We might have taken a road from Winter's more to the south which passes through a prairie as far as Salison which it crosses 3 miles below this point, but that road at present is swampy & much cut up. It intersects this again 6 or 8 miles west of this & in dry weather is preferable for wagons. The road we have taken is a mile or two the shorter.

20th January 1837.

The Party started from "Dwight" the missionary Station this morning at 8 o'clock & encamped at 3. P.M. having come about 10 miles.

The road to-day was hilly & in some places very bad.

21st January

The Party started this morning about 8. P.M. and after travelling 4 miles crossed the Illinois River, which is at present easily fordable & after coming 5 miles further encamped at 3. P.M.

To-day the roads were tolerably hard but hilly. The weather continues very fine & mild and the Indians remain healthy.

22nd January

The Party again started this morning about 8 o'clock & having travelled

10 miles encamp'd early in the afternoon at Drews[29] about 3 miles east of Fort Gibson.

The roads to-day were tolerably good. Nothing of importance occurred.

23rd January 1837.

The Party under my charge reached its destination near Fort Gibson to-day.

We left Drews this morning about 9 o'clock & passing by the Fort the wagons & Indians proceeded to the present encampment near the junction of Grand River with the Arkansas. As the Indians of this Party do not wish to go over into their country further, at present they will be allowed to remain where they are now until they wish to do so.

24th January 1837.

To-day the Disbursing Agent for the Creeks (West) has commenced subsisting the Party which yesterday reached their place of Destination under my charge.

To-day they received their Baggage, which was sent from Rock Row & Little Rock by the steam Boat Lady Byron, which has been in store at Fort Gibson for some time.

It was found to be in good order, the Agent who was sent in charge of it, having faithfully discharged his duty, in having it properly taken care of.

The foregoing Journal exhibits all occurrences that I considered of any importance, which have taken place upon the Route of Emigration under my observation.

In conclusion it may perhaps be well for me to remark that the principal Agent of the Emigrating Company with the Party under my charge at all times shewed a desire to comply with the letter & spirit of the Contract for the Removal.

The only failure that I had occasion to notice & which I reported to the proper Departments at the time of occurrence was one which could not be remedied after the Indians had come upon the Route of Emigration.

The failure referred to, was the neglect to have provision Stands established west of the Mississippi, & consequently depending upon the resources of the Country at the time that the Party or Parties happened to pass thro'.

I consider this to be the principal cause of the delay of the Party under my charge upon the road & that provision of the Emigrating Contract in reference to this point, is one of the highest importance to the Rights & Interests of the Indians.

It is to be hoped that the Department will place no confidence in News Paper publications, unless authenticated by a responsible signature, upon the subject of the Emigrating Creeks.

They were written no doubt by interested individuals, & some of them tending to cast censure upon Agents employed in the business of the Emigration, I know to have been incorrect.

Edw— Deas
Lieut. U.S. Army &
Disburs'g Agent in the
Creek Emigration
Fort Gibson Ark's Ty.
24th January 1837.

Supplemental Letters of Detachment 3

Lieutenant Edward Deas orders the volunteer force under Captain William Arnold to begin assembling the Creeks at the rendezvous site six miles from Talladega, Alabama. Deas specifically orders Arnold not to use force, unless absolutely necessary, and not to compel any Creek Indians into camp who had not sold the reservations assigned to them under the 1832 Treaty of Washington. Letter found at Records of the Adjutant General's Office, 1780s–1917, Entry 159-Q, Records of Major General Thomas S. Jesup, Container 19, Folder: "Letters Received Relating to Creek and Seminole Affairs, August 1836," NARA.

(Copy)

Jacksonville, Benton County, Alabama.
August 10th 1836.

To Captain William Arnold
Comman'g the Benton Rangers

Captain,

I have just arrived in this neighbourhood with authority from the commander of the Forces in the Creek nation, to make such arrangements as may be necessary & proper, for the immediate assembling of the Creek Indians in this section of country, previous to their emigration to the west. General Patterson[30] having returned to Huntsville, and your company now acting independently and at present being unemployed at this place, I am authorized by Major General Jesup, to direct in his name, that you will proceed with the force under your command, amongst the Indians to the south-east and south of this place, who have as yet made no preparation to move, for the purpose of causing them to assemble without delay at the point that has been designated for Encampment. The Indians will be found in Benton County to the S-East & within 30 miles of this place, and also near the Boundary line between Taladega & Randolph counties, & in the eastern portion of Taladega county. The Camp that has been selected is situated about six miles north of the town of Taladega at Walkers & Riddle's Store, to which place it is desired you will cause the Indians to proceed immediately after receiving the order from you to do so. You are requested not to use force unless it be absolutely necessary, nor compell them to come in, who have not sold their Reservations of Land, without further authority than that herein given. After the Indians have been assembled, to effect which, the General desires that all exertions should be made, you can return to this place with your command until further orders—

I am Sir very Respect'y
Your Ob't Servant
Edw— Deas
Lieut U.S. Army &
Disb'g Agent in the
Creek Emigrations

☾

Writing from the rendezvous site near Talladega, Deas reports that he will consolidate the various camps—consisting of approximately 2,800 people—and then proceed with enrolling them as soon as they arrive. Deas will then send 800 or 1,000 north to Gunter's Landing to join almost a thousand Creeks who were captured in the Cherokee country and were under guard near that location. Letter found at Records of the Adjutant General's Office, 1780s–1917, Entry 159-Q, Records of Major General Thomas S. Jesup, Container 20, Folder: "Letters Received 1836–1838, From Camps and Forts during the Creek War," NARA.

Taladega Alabama
30th August 1836.

To,
Major General Tho's S. Jesup
Comman'g Army of the South

General,

In conformity with the order which I yesterday received, I write by express upon the subject of the Emigration in this section of country: There are at this time 800 Indians encamped 4 miles north of this place, & I have to-day sent an agent to bring up to the same point 400 more which are now encamped 12 miles below. I also yesterday gave directions to Mr. Winslet,[31] who has charge of a camp of 1600 to have them in this neighbourhood to-morrow evening, so that I shall then have 2800 Indians encamped 4 miles north of this place, and as soon as I can enroll them, they will be ready to take up the line of march.

We propose to start 800 on Sunday next to move on and join 800 or 1000 more now at Gunter's Landing, 80 miles above this place these to constitute the first Party. The remainder to compose the Second Party, and to leave the neighbourhood of this place a day's march after the First.

The Taladega volunteers commanded by Capt-Shelly,[32] are now employed in preventing the Indians from straggling, and in bringing in any that have not yet come to camp. I find that a military force is indispensable for this purpose and I have particularly to request that an order may be sent to Capt Shelly to accompany the Indians until they leave the limits of the Indian Country.

The time of service of his company expires on the 5th September but he informs me that a sufficient number of his men are willing to continue in service after that time, for the purpose of accompanying the Indians. I have engaged with the express that carries this to return to this place by Saturday night, so that if you will Sir, be pleased to issue the order for Capt. Shelly it will reach me in time.

There are many speculators hanging about the Camp, & various demands made upon the Indians and exertions on the part of the whites to prevent their emigration which renders the presence of the military absolutely necessary to effect a thorough removal of these people. Hoping that the above views will meet your approbation, I have the honour to remain Sir very Respectfully

your Obe't Servant
Edw— Deas
Lieut. U.S. Army &
Disb'g Agent in the
Creek Emigration

P.S. I take the liberty of writing direct, as that is the construction I put upon the order which reached me yesterday.

E Deas
&c &c

☾

Writing from the north Alabama town of Somerville, Deas reports on the splitting of Creeks under his charge into two parties (detachments 3 and 4), the hiring of personnel to accompany the parties, and the commencement of the journey from the neighborhood of Talladega to their present location. Deas notes the refusal of the Alabama Emigrating Company to provide rations in accordance with the letter of the contract and the shooting of an intoxicated Creek man. Letter found at CGS-IRW, Roll 6, 121–25.

Rec'd 10 Octr

Encampment of Indians 4 miles east of
Sommervill Alaba'a 27th Sep'r 1836.

Emigration of Indians
To,
General George Gibson
Commissary Gen'l of Subsistence

General,

Whilst I remained within the limits of the Creek Country I was directed to Report direct to the Head Qrs of the Army of the South upon the subject of the Emigration, but henceforth I take it for granted I am to make my communications direct to your office, as previous to breaking out of hostilities amongst the Creeks.

On the 2nd August I was directed to proceed from Tuskegee to the upper portion of the Creek Country, for the purpose superintending the subsisting of the friendly Indians previous to emigration, & to assembling them at suitable points for Enrollment ready for immediate removal. On my arrival in the neighbourhood of Taladega on the 7th August, I selected a central point about 4 miles north of that place, & directed that the Indians in Randolph Benton & Taladega counties, together with about 400 brought from the Cherokee Country by the Troops, should assemble at that place for the purpose of Enrollment. Towards the end of August above a thousand were there encamped and on the 6th September agreeably to the order I had received, I had enrolled & turned over to the Agent of the "Alaba'a Emigra'g Company" for Subsistence & Removal, a Party of 1169 in number. I was directed by the Superinten't of the Emigration, to appoint the necessary Agents to accompany this Party on the part of the Government. I therefore on the 7th September appointed Captain Jacob D. Shelly of Taladega to go with this Party & on the 17th Sep'r finding that the number of the Party after passing Gunter's Landing was over 2000—another Agent would be necessary to assist Capt— Shelly in the performance of his duties upon the Route, I appointed Jos'h D— McCann[33] esq. of Taladega, also an Assis't Agent to take effect from the 17th Sep'r with directions to overtake the first Party & report to Capt. Shelly for duty. Gen'l Andrew Moore stationed at Gunter's Landing an Assis't Agent in the Creek Emigration had informed me that it was not his intention to accompany a Party to Arkansaw. On the 12th Sep'r I engaged Doctor Milo Smith[34] of Jacksonville Alaba'a to accompany the Party with Capt. Shelly and about the end of August I also employed Doctor Townsend[35] of Taladega, to attend the Camp near that place & accompany the Party which I should be attached to, on its route to the west. I also Employed Jos'h D. McCann esq. as Enrolling Agent from the 27th Aug't to the 16th Sep'r inclusive. I am satisfied that the above named gentlemen are as well qualified as any that I could have employed, to perform the duties for which they were severally engaged.

As soon as the 1st Party had started from the Camp near Taladega on the 8th September, I proceeded to Gunter's Landing near the southernmost point of the Tennessee River, where a large number of Creeks had been assembled under charge of Gen'l Moore, for the purpose of having them properly Enrolled ready to join & constitute a portion of the 1st Party after it should reach that neighbourhood. As soon as I saw the Enrollment fairly commenced, I returned to Taladega to join the 2nd Party, leaving directions with Gen'l Moore to finish & certify the Books & forward one and have another ready for the Agent of the Company when it should come up. I also turned over the Indians at Gunter's Landing on my arrival there on the 10th September, to an Agent of the "Alabama Company"[36] more than 1000 in number, to be subsisted by him, as the Contract says "<u>they shall subsist the Indians from the day of assembly.</u>" The 1st Party including those from Gunter's Landing crossed the Tennessee River at Deposite Landing, about the 20th Sep'r & proceeded by the way of Huntsville their numbers exceeding 2000. This however I have not yet heard officially.

When I left Taladega the day upon which the 1st Party started (the 8th September), I had information that the Superinten't of the Emigration had directed a large number of Indians from Coosa & Talapoosa Counties to rendevous at a point I had selected near Taladega, to be enrolled at that place for Emigration. I therefore left directions with Col'l Walker[37] an Assis't Agent as soon as the Indians should come in to the place of Assembly, to require Subsistence for them; from the Agent of the Emigrating company, & to enroll them as speedily as possible. A large number of them reached the camp on the 10th ins't & Col. Walker immediately required subsistence for them, from the Agent of the Company, as directed by me.

The Agent of the Company however, refused to furnish the required subsistence, alledging that he was not obliged, under the Contract, to receive the Indians until the Government Agent had Enrolled them for Emigration. These Indians were therefore subsisted at the expense of the U. States from the 11th to the 16th September inclusive.

The copy of the Contract furnished me by Captain Page, Superinten't of the Emigra'n for my guidance, says "The Company shall assemble the Indians together" and "they shall subsist the Indians from the day of assembly."

I can conceive of but one meaning to the above words & am therfore surprised to find, that the Agent of the Contractors[38] with the 1st Party made the same objection to subsisting the Indians after the day of assembly at Gunter's Landing, alledging (though I have not heard it officially) that they should claim of the Government, all the expense of Transportation & Subsistence of the Indians removed by them from that point, until the day upon which Gen'l Moore succeeded in completing the Roll of those Indians, which I understand he did not succeed in doing, until several days after the Indians from Gunter's Landing had left that point of assembly.

As the copy of the Contract furnished me says nothing in reference to such claims, and as I have performed my duties in strict conformity to the letter & spirit of the articles of agreement, I can only suppose, there must have been some understanding with the

Company, with which I am unacquainted. The above circumstances in reference to the subsistence of Indians at the Camp near Taladega were reported by me as soon as possible to the Superinten't of the Emigration, that his decision might be had in the case as required by the Contract.

I joined the 2nd Party on the 17th & started with it on the same day on the route for Arkansaw. I have travelled with it since that time, accompanied by Col. D. S. Walker Assis't Agent, & Doctor Townsend of Taladega. The number enrolled was 2320—and copies of this, together with the Roll of the 1st Party were certified & forwarded by me to the Superintendent of the Emigration. We came as far as near Gunter's Landing, over nearly the same road, as that pursued by the Party accompanied by Captain Shelly. This route was chosen to avoid travelling over the same ground with any of the large Parties from the lower part of the nation, that crossed the Coosa River below Taladega & also to pass over a more fertile country, & better roads, than by pursuing a more direct course towards Tuscumbia. Thus far every thing, with an exception to mentioned presently, has gone on well in reference to the progress of the Party, which has commenced under very favourable auspices.

The Indians appear satisfied and disposed to proceed to their new homes, with cheerfulness & alacrity.

We shall proceed along the valley of the Tennessee River & on its south bank by the way of Decatur, Courtland, & Tuscumbia & from thence to Memphis.

An unfortunate circumstance occurred two days ago. A few Indians loitered behind the Party at a grocery upon the road, near Gunter's Landing & of course became intoxicated. Whilst in this condition one of them named <u>No cose had ja</u> of the Hillabees, had some disagreement with a white man named <u>Burns</u> who drew a pistol & shot the Indian in the side. Information was [passed] to me in the night, upon which I immediately returned to the place, 6 miles, & found the Indian very drunk but as I thouht not dangerously wounded. I had him conveyed to Camp, as speedily as possible, & as <u>Burns</u> had escaped, wrote to Gen'l Moore at Gunter's

Landing, that he might have him duly prosecuted. The Indians were much incensed & wished to return & do mischief, but were persuaded to desist, being promised that the Agent would attend to having justice done in the case. There is nothing further at present to communicate upon the subject of the emigration and I hope that I shall continue to have it in my power to report favourably of the progress of the Party which I accompany towards its destination.

I have the honour to be General
very Respectfully
your Ob't Servant
Edw— Deas
Lieut U.S. Army &
Disbur'g Agent in the
Creek Emigration

☾

Deas reports on the party's arrival near Tuscumbia along with the growing number of sick, which included the attending physician, Dr. James Townsend. Letter found at CGS-IRW, Roll 5, 945–46.

Rec'd 17 Octr

Encampment of Indians near
Tuscumbia Alabama
2nd October 1836.

To,
General George Gibson
Commissary General of Subsistence

General,

I have the honour to state that the Party of Creek Emigrants which I have accompanied from Taladega, arrived and encamped at this place this afternoon. Nothing of particular importance has occurred upon the route since I last reported the progress of the Party, on the 27th ultimo. Every thing relative thereto is still going on well, except that there has been of late, some sickness amongst the people, but not of a serious nature. The cases however are numerous & as Dr. Townsend was detained near Somerville, by indisposition & has not yet come up, I am now under the necessity of engaging a Physician to attend the Party towards Memphis, as long as may be necessary. The Contractors have thus far, shewn every disposition to conform strictly to the Contract, in the removal of the present Party, & there has as yet, been no difficulties upon the route, other than the circumstances relative to a drunken Indian's being wounded which I mentioned in my last communication.

We shall proceed from this on the most direct route towards Memphis.

I have heard occasionally from travellers very favourable accounts from the 1st Party[39] that started from Taladega under my direction, & which crossed the Tennessee River, that they also are progressing towards Memphis, by a more northern route, to the satisfaction of all concerned. There is nothing further for me to communicate at present upon the subject of the Emigration.

I have the honour to be General,
Verry Respectfully
Your Obed't Servant
Edw— Deas.
Lieut U.S. Army &
Disb'g Agent in the
Creek Emigration

☾

Deas announces his arrival near Memphis and reports that he is waiting for the other detachments to finish crossing the Mississippi River. Deas confirms that his party will be the last to cross over. Letter found at LR, CAE, Roll 237, 542–44.

Encampment of Indians
near Memphis Tenn'e
26th October 1836.

To,
General George Gibson
Commissary General of Subsistence

General,

I have the honour to state that the Party of Indians which I have accompanied from Alabama arrived at this place yesterday. The present encampment is about half a mile south of Memphis & near the bank of the Mississippi & the first Party that left Taladega under my direction is also encamped about a quarter of a mile to the south of us. Since I last had the honour to address you upon this subject, nothing of particular importance in regard to the Removal had taken place until the arrival of the Parties in the neighbourhood of this place. There has been a good deal of delay at this point, in consequence of the difficulty of crossing the Mississippi & the impossibility of getting loaded wagons through the Swamps, between this place and White River. It has therfore been determined to employ steam Boats to convey the People with their wagons and baggage to Rock Row, on the White River near the mouth of Cache and take the horses & Ponies through by land, with a sufficient number of Indians to take care of them. Two of the Five large Parties[40] that lately arrived at this place, have already gone, & the Third[41] is now about to start. The other two parties that I have mentioned above will set out as soon as the S: Boats return, & that which I accompany will be the last to leave this place. I am unable to say at present how long it will be before the last will set out, but of course the Emigrating company are endeavouring to get on with as little belay as possible. The Indians thus far appear well satisfied with the arrangements that have been made, & the Agents of the company with whom I have been associated have shewn every disposition to comply with the contract for the Removal. I shall continue to give constant information upon all subjects of interest connected with the Emigration.

I have the honour to be General
very Respectfully
your Obed't Servant
Edw— Deas
Lieut U.S. Army &
Disburs'g Agent in the
Creek Emigration

☾

Eleven days after arriving in Memphis, Deas reports that detachment 3—with steamboats almost loaded—is about to commence their journey down the Mississippi River. The horses, (accompanied by a small party of Creeks) had already left the city by land. Letter found at LR, CAE, Roll 237, 546–47.

Memphis Tenn'e
5th November 1836.

To,
General George Gibson
Commissary General of Subsistence

General,

Since I last had the honour to address you upon the subject of the Emigration, the whole of the Indians excepting the Party which I accompany, have proceeded on their journey towards the west. Our Party is now upon the point of starting. The Two Steam Boats which will convey the People with their wagons & Baggage to Rock Row are now nearly loaded, and probably by Sun-set, all of the Creek Indians now emigrating will have left the eastern bank of the Mississippi. The Horses & Ponies of course have gone through by land, with a sufficient number of Agents & Indians to take charge of them.

Nothing else of particular importance has taken place since I last wrote upon this subject. The Indians continue healthy & excepting the delay occasioned at this point, every thing in regard to the Emigration has gone on well.

I hope in a short time to be able to give satisfactory intelligence from Rock Row, of our progress towards the West.

I have the honour to be General
Very Respectfully
your Obed't Servant
Edw— Deas
Lieut. U.S. Army &
Disb'g Agent in the
Creek Emigration

☾

Writing at William Strong's place, Deas complains of negligence on the part of the Alabama Emigrating Company in not providing adequate provisions for his party. Deas was frustrated by the fact that there was no fresh meat for his detachment upon arriving by steamboat at Rock Roe, only to discover later that the company had not provided enough provision stands through the Mississippi Swamp to sustain those Creeks traveling by land. Letter found at LR, CAE, Roll 237, 553–56.

Strong's Stand at St Francis Post Office
2 miles west of St Francis River Crossings
Arkansaw 22nd November 1836.

To,
General George Gibson
Commissary General of Subsistence

General,

I take the present opportunity of detailing the operations of the Indian Removal, that have come to my knowledge, since I had the honour to address you from Memphis on the 5th instant.

On the afternoon of that day, the larger portion of the Party under my charge embarked on board of two Steam Boats & reached a point on White River, 2 miles below Rock Row; the first within four days, & the last within seven days after starting.

The latter was detained by running aground. All arrived in good condition, but on reaching Rock Row, we found to our surprise, that no adequate preparation had been made for the reception of our Party. There was Corn sufficient for the subsistence of the Indians to be had in the neighbourhood, by the use of a S-Boat, but no fresh meat had been provided & for one week after our arrival, none was issued & only a stinted allowance of Indifferent Bacon.

Before leaving Memphis a large number of our party, refused to go by Steam, & left that place by land previous to the departure of the Boats. A sub-agent of the Company was sent through to conduct them, as I understood, with several assistants, and I consequently hoped they would join the main Body of the Party, at Rock Row with out difficulty. Very different however has been the result, and I have to state that the whole of the land operations, from Memphis to Rock Row have been badly conducted, & in several respects, entirely at varience with the provisions of the Contract. In the first place, there has been an entire failure in the manner of issuing the provisions. There were but two stands established between Memphis and Cache, (which place is 8 miles above Rock Row and 95 from Memphis). One of these was 17 miles from Memphis, the other is the place at which I am now writing, and is 56 miles from Cache, & 39 from Memphis.

In the next place the Indians were not conducted from Memphis to Rock Row. The Agent sent in charge of them it seems had other matters to attend to. He accompanied a part of the land Party to this point, and waited here several days but not until all had come up.

He then issued to those present, and posted on to Rock Row, leaving most of the Indians under his charge, to shift for themselves. I waited near Rock Row until the 19th instant, hoping every day, from the statements of the above mentioned Agents, that the

Indians would all come up. My hopes however were vain, & I therefore determined to return for them, accompanied by an Agent of Company. The Roads from Rock Row, are as bad as possible & I have been 3 days in reaching this place. I found between 3 & 4 hundred Indians, encamped at intervals of a few miles, along the whole road, many of them belonging to other Parties than that under my charge, and the reasons assigned by them for their detention were fully sufficient. Some were tired & sick & had no transportation. Others had had no provisions issued to them, since leaving Memphis, and I found the whole road from Rock Row full of dead Horses and Indian Ponies. There should have been provision stands, throughout the whole route as required by the Contract, and the Agents should have remained with the Indians, and continued to urge them on, & assist & encourage them, until the whole of the Swamps had been passed. I believe that all of our Party, & in fact all those now emigrating, are now to the west of this, but it is possible that there may still be a few families to the east of the S't Francis River. I cannot however return further, with a due regard to the interest of the Party under my charge. The main body of our Indians, set out from near Rock Row, on the 20th ins't and are now probably, between that place & Little Rock.

Tomorrow I shall return & overtake them, as speedily as possible & will take the proper measures to enable the straggling Indians to overtake the main Body of the Party, without delay.

It is an unpleasant duty I have to perform, to report the neglect of others, but I shall not shrink from doing so, whenever it becomes necessary. In conclusion I have to say that unless more regard is paid by the responsible Agents of the Emigrating Company, to the requirements of the Contract; a due regard to the Rights & interests of the Indians, imperiously demands that they should be discharged from all further connection with the Emigration, of these much oppressed & unfortunate people.

I have the honour to be General
most Respectfully

your Obed't Servant
Edw— Deas
Lieut. U.S. Army &
Disb'g Agent in the
Creek Emigration

☾

This letter, transcribed in Deas's handwriting, is a copy of a letter written by Arkansas governor James S. Conway. Believing rumors that the Creeks were stealing livestock, crops, and committing acts of vandalism on Arkansans' property, Conway orders Deas to move the Creeks out of the state as soon as possible. Letter found at LR, CAE, Roll 237, 564–65.

(Copy)

Executive Office
Little Rock Arkansaw
6th December 1836.

Sir,

Representations have been made to the Executive of this State by respectable citizens, that the Party of Creek Indians, now encamped on the opposite shore of the Arkansas river, are daily and perhaps hourly committing depredations on the property of the Citizens; by killing their hogs & cattle, burning their fence rails, & stealing their Corn vegitables &c.

And the further fact is set forth that said Party of Indians, have already been there encamped a considerable number of days—

These depredations cannot be tolerated—The length of time which this Party has been halted, is evidently sufficient for every necessary arrangement to have been made for the continuation of their march to their country.

Therefore I have to inform you, as principal Government Agent in conducting said Party, that they must without delay take up the line of march—and that they be not again allowed to halt, within the limits of this state, for an unnecessary length of time.

This communication and the requisition herein contained, are intended for every Agent of the Government who now is or may be hereafter, engaged in conducting a Party of any Tribe of Indians, emigrating through the State of Arkansas.

This communication will be published in the Arkansas Gazette with orders to officers, commanding Regiments, Battallions, and Companies of the Militia of the State, requiring them to see that the requisitions therein contained are strictly observed.

The officers commanding Regiments, Battallions, and Companies of the Militia of the State of Arkansas, are required to see that the foregoing requisitions are strictly observed.

I am Sir Very Respectfully
your Obe'dt Servant
(Signed) J. S. Conway

Lieut Edw— Deas
Government Agent
Removal Creek Indians
Present.

☾

This letter is a response to Arkansas governor James S. Conway's demand that the party leave the limits of the state immediately (preceding letter). Deas reports that he found no evidence of the Creeks of his party having committed depredations or stolen livestock or crops. Letter found at LR, CAE, Roll 237, 566–69.

(Copy)

Encampment of Indians opposite Lt. Rock
Arka'w 8th December 1836.

To his Excellency,
J. S. Conway

Governor of the State of Arkansaw

Governor,

I have the honour to acknowledge the receipt of your communication of the 6th ins't, upon the subject of the Emigrating Indians, to-day handed to me by Mr Irving. From all that I can learn by inquiry & observation, I am forced to believe that the Representations which have been made to your Excellency, charging our Indians with numerous depredations, such as the killing of Hogs & cattle; the burning of fence rails; & stealing of corn & vegitables, &c, are very much exaggerated, if not in some cases, without any just foundation, or proof. Since the Party under my charge, have been encamped in this neighbourhood, their Rations have been regularly issued, & they have besides killed an abundance of game, & were therefore by no means in want of Subsistence. Also the quantity of dead timber, is so great in the surrounding woods, in which the Indians have been encamped, as to render the use of fence-rails for fuel, an act of wanton mischief, so unnecessary; & if detected so dangerous to the depredator, as scarcely to be worthy of credit, without some positive testimony, in each case. Moreover the fences in the neighbourhood, will, at this time, be found on examination to be in as good order, as when our Party arrived at its present encampment.

I mention these particulars, as I am convinced your Excellency will find, that the above charges have been made on pretext, for the removal of the Indians from the neighbourhood, & that the real cause of discontent, has not been hinted at.

It is the circumstance of the rise of the price of provisions, in the surrounding country, caused by the presence of a large number of Indians, which gives dissatisfaction to a few individuals. This partial evil however, is far more than compensated to the community, by the amount of money brought into & expended in the country, by the Emigration of the Indians, & also by the large amount of traffic carried on, between the Citizens & the Indians themselves.

The order which your Excellencie's communication contains, requiring the Indians in this neighbourhood, to take up the line of march without delay, had become unnecessary, as previous to its reception, the authority which governs the movements of the Party under my charge, had determined that the Indians should proceed upon their journey westward, in a day or two. As your Excellency also directs that the Indians be not again allowed to halt, an unnecessary length of time, within the limits of the State, a few remarks may not be improper, to shew that this has not yet taken place, in the case of the Party which I accompany, as Agent of the Government. Many of the Indians have been detained, between Memphis & this place, by sickness, the miserably wretched state of the roads, & other circumstances, which rendered it impossible for them to reach this point sooner. Amongst their number were Several of the most influential chiefs of the nation, and their people, composing this Party, would not proceed further westward in a body, unless forced to do so, unaccompanied by these leading men. Had we not encamped here, we must have selected a more unhealthy, & inconvenient situation, liable in every respect, to the same objections as those above urged. Had we attempted to remove sooner, the whole emigrating route, would have been covered with straggling Indians, having no regular means of obtaining Transportation & Subsistence, & would consequently have been much more likely to commit depredations, upon the property of the Citizens of the country, than under the present arrangement. Almost all of our people have at length reached the neighbourhood of the main Party, and to-morrow, we shall endeavour to break up our present encampment, and set out once more, upon the journey towards the new homes, of these unfortunate people.

I have the honour to be,
your Excellencie's most Obed't Servant
Edw— Deas
Lieut. U.S. Army &
Disbursing Agent in the
Creek Emigration

☾

Writing three days after Deas notified Arkansas governor James S. Conway that his party would break camp and leave the state's limits, Deas reports that because one of the principal chiefs is still three days behind, the party had only progressed three miles. Deas's 10 December 1836 journal entry states that the chief was the Chattoksofke headman Menawa. Letter found at LR, CAE, Roll 237, 571.

(Copy)

Encampment of Indians, 3 miles N.W. from

Lt. Rock Ark'w 11th December 1836.

To his Excellency,
J. S. Conway
Governor of the State of Arkansaw

Governor,

In my communication of the 8th ins't, which I had the honour to address to you, from opposite Little Rock, I stated, that almost all of our people, had at length reached the neighbourhood of the main Party, and that on the following day, we should set out once more upon our journey. We did so, and reached the present encampment; but yesterday certain information was received, that one of the principal Chiefs is still, two or three days journey behind, with a considerable number of Indians from various Towns. As this was not known when I last had the honour to address you, I now mention it, as the interests of the Emigration require, for reasons stated in my previous communication, that we should not proceed until those Indians overtake the main Party.

I have the honour to remain, your Excellencie's most Ob't Servant.
Edw— Deas
Lieut U S Army & Disbursing
Agent in the Creek Emigration

☾

Deas reports that after a number of delays most, if not all, of the Creeks of detachment 3 are to the west of Little Rock, Arkansas. Letter found at LR, CAE, Roll 237, 559–62.

Little Rock Arkansaw
19th December 1836.

To,
General George Gibson
Commissary General of Subsistence

General,

I have the honour again to address you upon the subject of the Creek Emigration. I herewith enclose the copies of three letters, from which it will be perceived that the progress of the Party of Emigrants under my charge has been very much retarded.[42] Some of the reasons for our detention upon the Route are therein mentioned, but other causes have also tended to prevent the Party from progressing, and some of these were referred to, in my last communication upon this subject, dated the 22nd ultimo.

The larger portion of our Party reached the neighbourhood of this place on the 27th of last month, but at that time there were large numbers of the Indians still behind, between Memphis and this place. I therefore directed that the Party should not proceed until these were brought up with the main Body. My reasons for doing so are mentioned in one of the enclosed letters.

I also found between Memphis and this place, many Indians that had originally belonged to other Parties, that preceeded ours, who stated that they had been left upon the road. As these Indians were willing to proceed, I have taken care to see them provided for, agreeably to the Contract for the Removal.

The main Body of the Party under my charge is at this time about 20 miles to the westward, of this place, having left this neighbourhood in consequence of the scarcity of Provisions. I did not proceed with it, having returned towards Memphis, for the purpose of attending to bringing up some of the Indians that were still behind. The last detachment passed here this morning, & I believe that all of the Indians now being removed by contract, are to the west of this place. There may however, still be a few stragglers, but if so, they have willfully remained behind, as wagons & Agents were sent back, and all exertions used to bring up those that were willing to proceed.

As I understand that members of the "Emigrating Company" have doubted the propriety of detaining the larger portion of the Party under my charge, until the Indians belonging to it, had all come up; it may perhaps be well for me here to remark, that I was guided in doing so, (in addition to reasons already referred to), by that Article of the Contract, which requires, that the Company shall remove Parties of the Indians, and not fragments of Parties.

The Contract is also for the removal of the Indians, to the new Creek Country, west of the Mississippi, and not to the State of Arkansaw, for which reason I did not conceive it proper, to leave hundreds of these people encamped along the road from Memphis to Fort Gibson.

I am well convinced, that if Provision Stands had been established upon the Emigrating Route west of Memphis, as required by the Contract, and if a sufficient number of conductors had accompanied the Indians, very little delay would have occurred.

I shall proceed to over-take my Party to-day, and hope in a short time to have the pleasure to Report, that all of the Emigrating Indians are beyond the limits of this State.

I have the honour to be, General
very Respectfully
your Obed't Servant
Edw— Deas
Lieut. U.S. Army &
Disbursing Agent in the
Creek Emigration

☾

Deas notes the 23 January arrival of his party near Fort Gibson and admonishes the newspapers of Little Rock, Arkansas, for their false and exaggerated reporting on the conduct of the party. Letter found at LR, CAE, Roll 238, 190–91.

Fort Gibson Arkansas
25th January 1837.

To,
C. A. Harris Esquire
Commissioner of Indian affairs

Sir,

I have the honour to state that the Party of Creek Indians which I accompanied from Alaba'a as principal Government Agent, arrived at their destination near this Post on the 23rd instant. Nothing of particular interest relative to the Emigration; has occurred under my observation, since I last had the honour to address the Commissary Gen'l of Subsistence, upon this subject, from Little Rock, upon the 19th ultimo. There are many statements in the news Papers of that town relating to the Emigrating Indians, a few of which are correct, some Exaggerrated, & others grossly false. Amongst the latter is the assertion that the Chief Tuck a ba chee Hadjo & his people were driven from the state of Arkansas by the militia.[43]

On the contrary he joined my Party upon its arrival near his place of Encampment, without the slightest compulsions, and as far as I have observed, the Indians have behaved towards the people of Arkansas in an orderly & friendly manner.

My Journal of Occurrences upon the Route, will exhibit in detail Every thing of interest, which took place relative to the Party under my charge, & it will be forwarded by me, agreeably to the instructions which I have received upon the subject.

I have the honour to be sir
Very Respectfully
your Obed't Servant

Edw— Deas
Lieut U S Army &
Disburs'g Agent in the
Creek Emigration

☾

Captain James R. Stephenson reports on the arrival of 2,818 Creeks from detachment 3 and 70 members of Benjamin Marshall's party (originally of detachment 5). Stephenson also laments the negligence of the contractors (referring to Samuel Mackey, a western trader, not the Alabama Emigrating Company) in provisioning to the Creeks. Letter found at LR, CAE, Roll 238, 710.

Fort Gibson
January 31. 1837.

Sir

Your communication of the 5th December 1836 has been received.

In consequence of the failure of the contractor to supply Provisions to the Emigrant Creeks, this business has necessarily fallen into my hands, the consequence is I have been [furnishing] night and day and to that extent I am unable as yet to forward my Quarterly Returns, Reports &c, even at this time, by next mail I will no doubt be able to forward them.

On the 23d January 1837, I received in their new Country 2818 Emigrant Creeks conducted by Doctor Williams as Agent for the Alabama Emigrating Company and accompanied by Lieut E. Deas of the Army—I also received on the 14th January 70 Emigrant Creeks conducted by Benjamin Marshall as Agent for the same Company. These added to the Number still to be subsisted at the close of last year will amount to about 15100 Souls.

Very Respectfully
Your Obedt Servt.
Ja's. R. Stephenson

Capt. U.S. Army
Disbg. agt. (Creeks)

To/
C. A. Harris Esqr.
Commissioner Indian Affairs
Washington
(D.C.)

13 Detachment 4

The fourth detachment was based four miles north of Talladega and consisted of the Upper Creeks living north of the Tallapoosa River to the Cherokee line. The party was conducted to Indian territory by William A. Campbell on behalf of the Alabama Emigrating Company. Lieutenant Edward Deas served as military oversight for both detachments 3 and 4. Deas accompanied detachment 3 and appointed Joseph D. McCann of Talladega County, Alabama as military oversight for detachment 4 (Jacob D. Shelly, captain of a company of Talladega Rangers and a clerk of the circuit court of Talladega County, also accompanied the party through Alabama).[1] Dr. Milo Smith of Jacksonville, Alabama accompanied the party as surgeon as far as Memphis, Tennessee.[2] Dr. James G. Morrow joined detachment 4 at Memphis.

No journal or supplemental letters have been found for detachment 4.

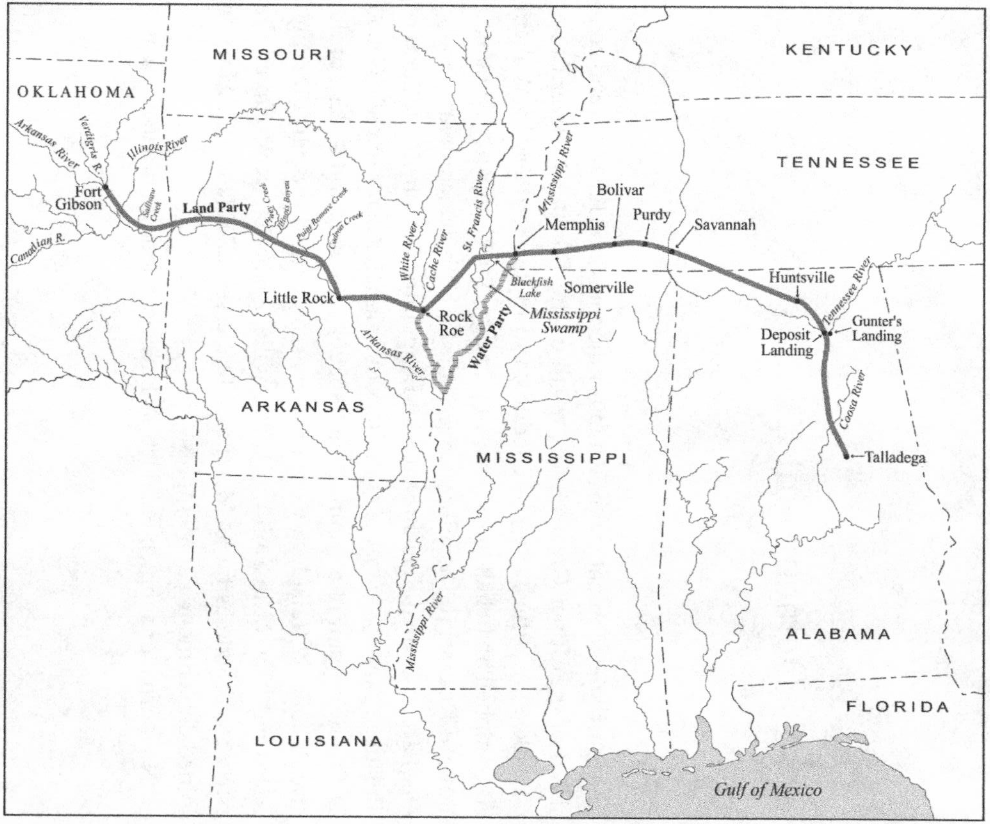

MAP 12. Route of detachment 4, September–December 1836. Place names correspond to stopping points or locations noted in the documentation. Route lines and locations are approximations. Cartography by Sarah Mattics and Kiersten Fish.

14 Detachment 5

The fifth detachment was based at LaFayette, Alabama, and consisted of the Coweta and Cusseta towns along with the rest of the Lower Creeks. The most prominent headmen associated with the party were Cusseta leaders Tuckabatchee Harjo and James Island of Coweta. The party was conducted to Indian territory by Felix G. Gibson and Charles Abercrombie[1] on behalf of the Alabama Emigrating Company. Massachusetts-born Lieutenant John Titcomb Sprague[2] of the U.S. Marine Corps accompanied the party as military oversight. Dr. G. W. Hill[3] of West Point, Georgia served as surgeon.

Journal of Detachment 5

Spelling and capitalization have been lightly emended for clarity. Journal found at SIAC, Agent (Reynolds), Account (1687), Year (1838), NARA.

Journal of my journey with two thousand Creek Indians Emigrating to Arkansas, Tuck-e-batch-e-hadjo principal Chief.

On the 3d of August I reported to General at Head Quarters, Tuskegee, Al. agreeable to his order, remained there 4th 5th 6th 7th 8th or rather made that my Head Quarters and from there visited such places as directed by the General. 9th rec'd orders to prepare Jim Islands[4] and Tuck-e-batch-e-hadjo for removal and repaired immediately to their camps; remained with them until prepared. On the 23d rec'd orders to start them on the 29th, 28th rec'd an order prolonging the time five days, to the 3d of September. 3d of September turned over to the Alabama Emigrating Co 1943 Indians as in camp—enrolled and prepared for removal in presence of a

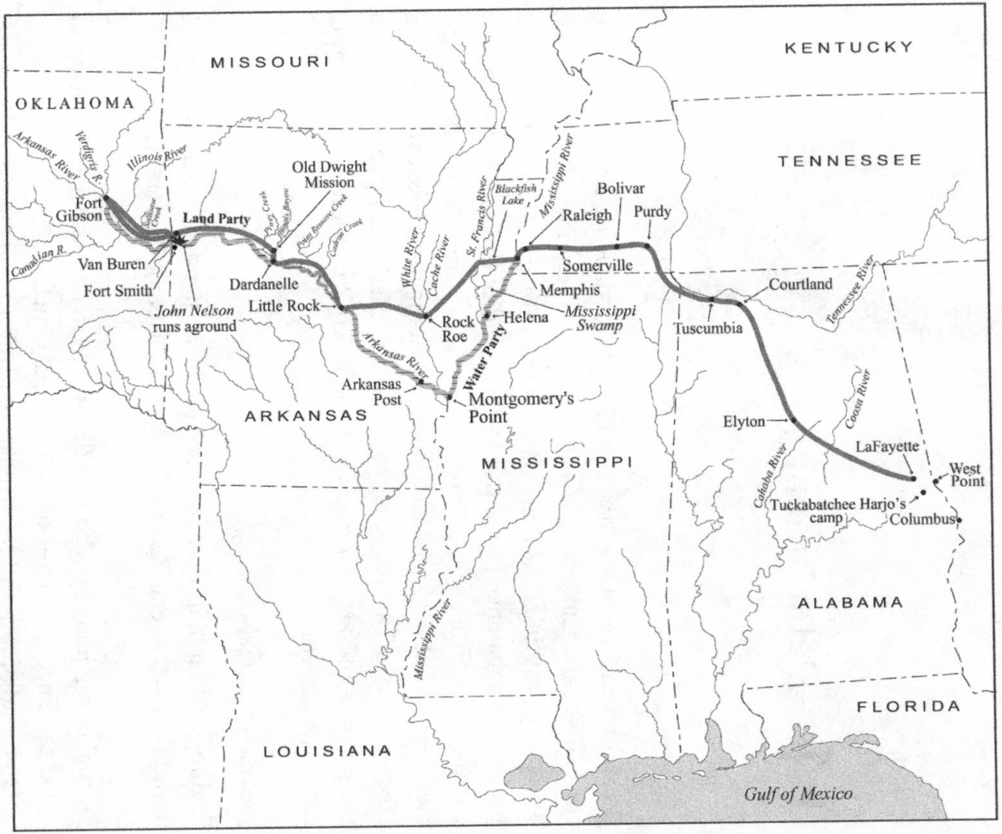

MAP 13. Route of detachment 5, September, November, and December 1836. Place names correspond to stopping points or locations noted in the documentation. Route lines and locations are approximations. Cartography by Sarah Mattics and Kiersten Fish.

large crowd, Capt Seals[5] and Lt Hill I took as witnesses. Sunday the 4th sent them the rolls complete by Lt Crabbe,[6] U.S. M Corps. 29th August Lt Hill[7] the surgeon ordered by General Jesup to accompany me reported for duty; ordered him to join the train as soon as it moved, sent an Express to General Jesup the 4th reporting my progress.

September 5th Monday. Went to Cuseter,[8] saw Tuck-e-batch-e hadjos Camp started. Early in the morning saw Jim Islands people preparing, they started in the afternoon.

Sept 6th Tuesday.—Went to columbus[9] to start Ben Marshalls Camp, they having delayed coming into Camp much longer than necessary: started them the next day.

8th. Ben Marshalls indians all gone, remained in Camp.

8th Thursday, arrived at West Point.

9th Friday. Left West Point, camped at La Fayette.

10th. Left La Fayette Camped of 12 miles.

11th, 12th. still in confusion camped 10 miles.

13th, all Came up with the train 12 M. East of the Coosa River.

14th, on the March—travelled 12 Miles roads bad.

15, on the March—travelled 10 Miles roads good.

16th. On the March, travelled 12 Miles; within 10 miles of Elyton, Indians intoxicated, weather pleasant.

17th. Passed through Elyton and camped three miles West of it; roads very good, country poor. Indians intoxicated, camped 10 miles.

18th Sunday. Travelled 14 miles—roads bad—through a very mountaneous country, country very poor, 12 Miles

19th Monday—Camped west of the Black Warrior River Country mountaneous and poor, no houses to stop in, roads very bad; Indians sober, 10 Miles.

20 Tuesday, Country more mountaneous than any portion we have passed and much less cultivated, distance travelled fifteen miles, this distance was accomplished with much fatigue to the party but the scarcity of water compelled it. The regular time of starting the days above mentioned was 7 O'clock A.M. but the party seldom got all in motion till about 8.—Camped usually about 4 P.M.—

Henry Marshall[10] with his family of twelve including himself joined the Emigrating train on the night of the 13th inst.—at the Coosa River 80 miles from La Fayette.

Sunday the 18th inst. Mr McMillen an Express sent to me by Genl Jesup & Capt Page returned. I sent Capt Page the rolls of the Party—also wrote him & Genl Jesup with the promise that I would send him the rolls of the Indians which were not enrolled through the Post office as soon as they could be finished.

21st Wednesday.—Camped at Plum Creek, Morgan Co—distance traveled to day seventeen miles. We were compelled to go this distance from the scarcity of water, arrived at the Creek at 4 A.M.[11] Indians all came up before sun down.

Col Gibson came to see soon after dark, Tuck. e. batch. e. Hadjo, had been to his tent with his principal chiefs and expressed his determination to go no further until he and all his people had rested one day; and that in the morning his sick, aged and children would remain behind agreeable to his order. The rations which had been issued to them two hours previous he declined accepting and had advised his people not to take them. He evinced much anger and left the tent saying the "word is out". This morning early I found him in conversation with the Contractors, /Gibson[12] & Abercrombie/, and found that he had been urgeing upon them the necessity of resting one day. They declined and gave their reasons. I told him that I was convinced of the propriety and of the advantages all would derive from it, but I did not think this was the proper time; we were in a very poor country, provisions were scarce, corn and fodder was diar, and that in three or four days we should be in a country better able to supply their wants and at a much cheaper rate. He left without coming to any conclusion. I sent for the Interpreter, Jesse,[13] at 10 A.M. sent word to him that I should see him early in the morning, cautined him about letting his young men go out in the morning to hunt, as he had directed them; that the people here were hostile to them and were all strangers.

22d. Saw Tuck-e-batch-e, Hadjo this morning. He concluded to go on to the Stiam Mile 14 Miles where he said he should remain one day

FIG. 9. Lt. John Titcomb Sprague (1810–1878), military agent for detachment 5. Courtesy of the University of West Alabama Special Collections.

and if his people were inclined to obey his talk they would remain also, arrived at the Stiam at 4 P.M. Camped distance 14 miles; roads bad most of the way leading through deep swamps. The county much more abundant; farms large and well cultivated.

23d Friday—Most of the Indians prepared for a start, Tuck-e-batch-e-hadjo—expressed his determination to remain to day and advised all the Cusetus[14] to remain with him, nearly all were inclined to do so, and commenced throwing out their baggage from the Waggons; this I remonstrated against and obliged many of them to put them in again. The train started at 8 O'clock A.M. Tuck-e-batch-e remained behind and about two hundred followed his example in spite of all my efforts to prevent it. Camped at McCrarys[15]—12 Miles.

Saturday 24th. Started at 7 A.M. roads good, country much better; farms large and highly cultivated, passed through a small town called Courtland. This is a village of about one thousand inhabitants, houses principally brick and has the appearance of being a place of some considerable business. Every effort was made to prevent the sale of Whiskey to the indians, but they got it and the larger portion of them were intoxicated before night. Camped at Town Creek—distance travelled to day 16 Miles.

Sunday 25th at Town Creek. The indians resting and taking a general wash. Had a talk with them, told them Tuck-e-batch-e-Hadjo was not the person for them to listen to about stopping and that what he said to them was not good unless it came first from me. Mr Gibson & Odom[16] gone to Tuscumbia to enquire about the route.—Tuck-e-batche, came up with his Indians about ten A.M. On the night of the 23d at McCrarys I waited upon the Contractors by the advice of the Doctor and by what I knew to be the state of the whole party and requested them to halt one day. They objected to it. I laid before them the fatigued state of the Indians, their sickness, the weakness of the ponies, and that in a faithful discharge of my duties I felt myself compelled to require a day for the Comfort and convenince of the Indians, and that if they would not consent I should feel myself justified in acting in Compliance with the__________Article of the

Contract;[17]—They with great confidence denied my authority to halt the party and the 25th was determined upon [by] me, to halt. I gave them an order.[18]

Monday 26th. The party left Camp at 7 A.M. arrived at Tuscumbia at 2 P.M. camped ½ mile from town: distance 15 Miles; road good.

Tuesday 27th. Left Tuscumbia ½ past 7 A.M. Camped at Caney Creek, road hilly, water scarce, distance 9 Miles.

Wednesday 28th. Left Camp at 7 A.M. roads good provisions scarce. The road to day was through the Chickasaw Nation, but few settlers. Camped at Bear Creek: distance 15 Miles.

Thursday 29th. Still in the Chickasaw Nation, roads good, Corn very scarce, but few houses upon the road. Camped at Indian Creek: distance 12 Miles. Wrote a letter to the Contractors, ordering provisions to be issued as required by the Contract.

Friday 30th. Left Camp at 7 A.M. roads very hilly and rough, provisions and settlers scarce, Country very poor, still in the Chickasaw Nation, Camped at Owens at 5 P.M. Distance 17 Miles. This distance was accomplished with great difficulty and with much fatigue to the Indians; but the scarcity of water compelled the party to go much farther than was proper for the comfort and convenience of the Indians. A large number of them arrived in Camp very late, a few as late as 9 P.M. The great scarcity of water, is the great objection to this route. Indians and horses almost suffered for water. We found the party of Indians /3000/ in charge of Lt Scriven camped here which makes our situation still more unpleasant, and O, poth-le-olos party having camped here a few days previous has been the means of draining the country of its resources. I am going to see Lt S. and to make some arrangements to separate our parties.

October 1st Saturday: Saw Lt S. last night agreed that my party should take the right hand forks of the roads seven miles distant, Lt S. the left. These roads come together within twenty miles of Memphis; the left hand fork is fifteen or twenty miles the fartherest,—Lt S. moved off early. My party at 8 A.M. Knowing that our yesterdays march was a very arduous one I concluded to make a close examination into the state of the party. I knew that from the roughness of the roads, the scarcity of water and the distance, many would be unable to proceed to day on foot, and that many would be found sick. At ½ past 9 A.M. I found in the Camp about one fourth of the party, and all the waggons belonging to the party gone; they were two miles on the road. One waggon that had been broken down the day before came up, I requested the driver to stop and take in a lame man which I had seated by the side of the road; he declined doing it and drove off. In the Camp I collected the blind, lame, and the sick who were totally unable to go on, and I also found families whose baggage had been thrown out by the waggoners without any means whatever of getting on. I endeavoured to find one of the agents or some of their assistants and found they, all of them, were four miles upon the road. Relying with confidence upon that paragraph of the Contract which says, "any pecuniary Expenditure for the Comfort and convenience of the Indians may be made" &c   I succeeded in finding a waggon sufficiently large to transport those who had no horses or any means of Conveyance. This waggon was not as large as I wished and I endeavored to find another but Could not. The Indians agreed, to pack themselves & Poneys if I would have their children put in with the sick and lame. I did so, and they left their Camp at one P.M. I remained with them until they arrived in Camp at 8 P.M. On the road I found one blind man and one in the most perfect state of decrepitude. I could not get any means of conveyance for them, the waggon having more than could be hauled, but assurd them that tomorrow they should ride, and if the waggoners would not allow them to get in to report it to me immediately and I would apply the remidy. I learnt from Dr Hill that the party camped at 5 P.M.—distance 16 Miles, roads good but water very scarce. This distance is more than should be travelled, but it could not be avoided there being not a sufficient quantity of water for the party upon the road. We left the Chickasaw Nation—the line, six miles behind, some of my party were talking of remaining in the Nation, I had a long talk with them and told them that should they remain I should send soldiers for them immediately.

I hired waggons for the purpose of bring up the lame and blind and sick which had been left through the negligence of the Agents, brought in to Camp two who were taken sick on the road, the waggoners refused to attend to them, one blind one and one feeble from old age, brought them into Camp. The Agents refused to pay for the waggon, I remonstrated with them the upon the course they were persuing, and told them that the disregard to the comfortable conveyance of the Indians I could not endure any longer.

Sunday 2d. Left Camp at 8 A.M. those that had come up were got off with some degree of comfort. I returned five miles from the Encampment and on the way counted one hundred & Ninety indians who from the distance and fatigue the day before were unable to get up, among these were many sick, feeble and the poorer class of Indians. I urged them to come up but they declared it to be impossible. The roads to day were very good the weather very pleasant, the country well settled and cultivated, passed through a small town called Purdy, Camped at McCullocks—distance travelled to day 15 Miles the Indians much fatigued. To day when remonstrating with Mr Gibson, one of the Agents, upon the course of they were persuiing I assured that I should [consider] it to be my duty to see that no Indians were left behind. He said I might, they should not. I told him that I should confine the march to twelve miles a day, hereafter, and that I should order it. He said I might he should not obey it. Great dissatisfaction in camp arising from the fatigue of the party and the disregard paid to their comfort. Wrote a letter to night to the Agents expressing my wish that some remedy should be provided for the difficulties which existed, and remonstrated strongly against their conduct and ordered them to confine the march to twelve miles a day.

Monday 3d. Sent my letter to the Agents, Mr Gibson called to see me and said my letter was a reiteration of our conversation yesterday. I asked him if I was to understand them as disregarding the Contents of my letter; He replied that they had not had time to reflect upon it. I request him to give me an answer in writing. The roads very good to day, country settled, corn scarce, with difficulty enough could be procured for the party. Tuck, e, batch-e, hadjo, with many of his chiefs stoped me to day and held a long talk. The amount of it was precisely what I had expressed in my letter this morning. He expressed his determination to halt his Indians unless something was done. I listened to him and we agreed that this evening we should wait upon the Agents and he to them should express his opinions and wishes. Camped at 4 P.M. at Webbs,[19]—distance 12¼ miles. I endeavored to find the Chief but found him intoxicated.

Tuesday 4th. Left Camp at Webbs at ½ past 7 A.M. roads very good, country well settled, passed through a small town called Bolivar, Tenn, a place of some business—took active measures to prevent the sale of Whiskey, succeeded in a measure. Camped at Hardemans Mills[20] distance travelled to 13 Miles, more attention paid to the sick & others than usual, but not enough, more men are required to attend to it. Neglect and indifference still the same. Many indians came into camp to night intoxicated, Tuck-e-batch e-hadjo very much so. Jesse, my interpreter, refused to act as such any longer, his life he said was in danger. Four indians attacked him yesterday with the determination to kill him as they said but for the timely interference of some friends who got him off. They said he was engaged with the white men in driving them on like dogs, he was against them, so was all the white men of the party, and they would kill him and the whites. The chief came to see me this morning, very much dissatisfied at the treatment he had received from the Agents, and assured me that he would go with me to them to day on our arrival in Camp. He came to camp very much intoxicated, which obliges me to postpone it. Wrote to the Contractors to move the train of Waggons at 8—clock, A.M. to commence on the morning of the 6th.

Wednesday 5th. Waggons left the Camp at 8 O' Clock, what men there were endeavoured to have things arranged but it is impossible that so few men can do so important a duty in the short time in which it must be done. Many indians refused to go on to day, saying they were fatigued and sick. I induced many to go on, and many determined to stay. Tuck-e-batch-e-hadjo with his family remained behind. I returned to Bolivar, saw Col Danlap[21] a Member of Congress, who urged the necessity of all these indians going west of the Mississippi with the best feelings towards the government. I obtained from him letters of credit at Memphis. While in Bolivar saw Mr Campbell[22] Agent of the Taledaga Party.[23] I told him all I had encountered and expressed my determination that this party should not cross the Mississippi in charge of the present Agents. I left Bolivar at 3 P.M. on my way I found many that were sick, many lame, and many children. I wrote a note back to Mr Campbell who was coming on the same road requesting him to pick up all he should find on the way. I endeavoured to find waggons, but could get none. I urged them to come on, they said they would go as far as they could. I arrived in camp at Evans Creek at 8 O' Clock distance travelled to day by the party 16 Miles. On my arrival in camp, I determined to halt the Party tomorrow the 6th and allow those belonging to the party to Come up. Being so near Memphis /45 miles/, I thought it necessary that the whole party should be together, I accordingly ordered the Agents to halt the Party.

Thursday 6th. I was up this morning before day light, orders had been given by the Agents to gear up the Waggons—for a start. I went through the camp and directed the Indians to take all they had in the Waggons out of them, that the waggons were going off, they done so. In about an hour after, the order which had been given, was ordered to be suspended. We have not moved to day and Indians are all sober. I wrote a letter to the Agents expressing my determination that the Party should not go to Arkansas in their charge. Sent an order to the Military Agent[24] of the Taledaga Party not to pass us on the road unless by a general conscensus of all concerned, rec'd for answer that they were astonished at recieving such an order. The Indians remained sober all day and conducted remarkably well. I requested them not to go into the potato & corn fields adjoining the camp, they complied strictly with my request. This Evening Mr Abercrombie called to consult me upon tomorrows march. He said there was no water for twenty miles. I told him that if this was the case we should be obliged to go it, but it was too far. Went into Camp consulted with the chief, who Expressed his willingness and promised to give his people a talk that evening upon the necessity of it. I went all through the Camp and urged them to get up Early. Mr A. consultation with me was the first during the journey.

Friday 7th. I went into camp at day-light, urged the Indians to an Early start. The indians were all prepared at ½ past 6 A.M. The train started at 20 M past 7, past through sommerville 3 M. from Camp, a very pretty and business like looking place of about one thousand inhabitants. Roads to day were remarkably good, country well cultivated. The first waggon arrived at Camp at 4 P.M. The waggons and Indians were strewn for twelve or fifteen miles. Camped at Cypress Creek distance travelled 20. Miles. No water upon the road, not enough to water the horses, all the Indians could procure was from wells, and that with difficulty.—The Indians came up better than expected at night.

Saturday 8th: The train of waggons left Camp at 8 A.M. all moved off together. The indians kept up with the waggons all day. Great scarcity of water upon the road, creeks all dry; obliged to go 17 Miles: the road was unusually good and level. The country well settled and cultivated, fine extensive cotton plantations extending for miles. Camped at 4 P.M. at Wolf River in the vicinity of a small town called Raleigh 9 miles from Memphis. Many indians did not come up till morning. I ordered the Party to halt but afterwards concluded to move two miles to a more suitable camp ground.

Sunday 9th. Moved Camp two miles to give the Taledaga Party of Indians an opportunity to camp in our rear. The train moved at 10 A.M. I started to Memphis seven miles to see the Members of the A.E. Company, took with me Tuck-e-batch-e-hadjo,=, I saw Dr Ingersole[25] and Mr Campbell two of the Contractors. I expressed to them my determination that Mr Gibson & Abercrombie should not cross the Mississippi in their charge and that their attention to the Indians had been of such a character that they had violated both the letter and spirit of the contract, go they should not, and new agents must be appointed. They said that tomorrow there should be some decisive measures taken. I remained in town in hopes of seeing all of the Agents, and getting a decisive answer. The agents were all very much engaged in getting boats to cross the Mississippi no boats are here but small ferry boats and steam Boats are required. O-pothe-le-olos party in charge of Capt Bateman I found two miles from Memphis. The Party in charge of Lt. Scriven was twelve miles from Memphis.

I represented to Capt Bateman the state of my party, that unless new agents were appointed I could not discharge my duty to the Government and that either they /the agents/ must be removed or I must be relived from the duty.

Monday 10th. In Memphis, arrangements making to go by land, through the Swamp.

Monday 10th. Still in Memphis. The Agents have not prepared to give me an answer. Saw Mr Laurence,[26] President of the Memphis Bank,[27] gave him Mr Dunlaps letter. He said he thought there would be but little difficulty in my getting what money I should want if these Indians came upon my hands. O-poth-le-o-los party began to cross the river to day in the ferry boat. Steam Boats were expected to night. I left town at 4 P.M. Came out to Camp.

Tuesday 11th. In Memphis. Steam Boat arrived at night O. poth-le-olos objects to go by water to Rock Roe, round the swamp, no answer from the Agents.[28]

Wednesday 12, Opoth. le-olos has concluded to go by water, all busy loading. Rec'd a letter from Capt Page, which completely destroyed all grounds I had taken against the Conduct of the Company, /see Letter on file/. Tuck. e. batch e. hadjo. came to see me said he must go by land and requested me to go the swamp and ascertainly correctly its state. I told him I would.

Thursday 13th, Opoth. le. olos. party left in the Steam Boat this afternoon at 5.

Had an amicable arrangement the Members of the Company. The assurances they have given me are sufficient. Mr Abercrombie has quit the party, Mr Gilman goes in his place.

Friday 14th, Still in Memphis, O. poth. le-olos party gone. Lt Scrivens party commenced crossing the river to day. I was to have gone to the Swamp to day. The Indians came in for that purpose, but we could not get a waggon. Concluded to start tomorrow morning, five Indians going.—The Party is two miles from town.

Saturday 15th. Still in Memphis   Lt Scrivens party crossing the river. I started with four Indians to look at the Swamp; we went fifteen miles, stopped at Mrs Williams' on the U.S. Road. This road for this distance is very good.

Sunday 16th. Left Mrs W at ½ past 6 A.M. The road for four miles was good. We soon after came into the swamp. The Indians soon after concluded that it was impossible to pass through with loaded waggons. We continued on five miles and found it almost impassable on horse back. The Indians wished to return, we dined at Mrs W and got back to Memphis at 7 P.M. distance 30 Miles.

Monday 17th. Lt S. Party not crossed the river, still crossing. I was in camp Tuck-e-batch hadjo and Chiefs I held a long talk with. He said he would take my advice, my talk was good he would tell his people so. The whole party concluded to go by water.—

18th Tuesday. Lt Scrivens party have all crossed the river. All waiting anxious to be moving, the Indians very impatient. The weather very pleasant. The Boat[29] which took Capt Batemans party is expected to night.—

19th. Still in Memphis. The Boat Expected last night arrived this afternoon.

20th Thursday, = Lt Scrivens Party and the remainder of O. poth-le-olos party preparing to get off.

21st Friday. The Cowetas belonging to my Party commenced crossing the river.

22d Saturday. My Party still crossing. Lt Scrivens party started this afternoon. I proposed to the Agents to purchase a Boat and take my party to Little Rock if the Chiefs would consent to it.

I saw the Chiefs, they consented, the Boat was bought, and tomorrow the Boat is to be in readiness to load.

23d Sunday. The Boat is not quite ready. Moved the Cuseter Camp within one mile of town. Tomorrow morning I fixed for them to come in and load the Boat. The horses are to go through the swamp, accompanied by as many men as are disposed to go. The waggons go in the Boat. The weather is still very fine. I have been constantly engaged the last Eight day in going with a body of Waggons to get Ponies belonging to Indians that have been stolen by other Indians and sold, and have succeeded in getting fourteen.

Monday 24th. Still in Memphis. Commenced raining this morning; the whole day was very unpleasant. The Coweta Indians all crossed to-day.

Tuesday 25th. Rained hard all day. Tuck-e-batch-e-Hadgo declined letting his Indians move from Camp. He said they should remain and cross the Mississippi tomorrow. A few however crossed the river.

Wednesday 26. Weather still unpleasant; roads very muddy. all the Caseturs crossed to day. After ascertaining correctly that none were behind I crossed in the last boat: about 5 P.M. We are making every arrangement to get off early tomorrow morning. The accommodations for the Indians is a good sized Steam Boat called the John Nelson, and two large flat boats, all of which I have ascertained from the best authority to be good, comfortable and substancial boats. A large body of Indians go through the swamp with all the Horses, all waggons are taken to pieces and put in the boat. As near as can be ascertained there will be about fifteen hundred men, women and children going in the boat, and five or six hundred go through by land. Every provision I am assured has been made on the road, and I have given Mr Freeman[30] my assistant, under whose charge the party goes, to see to it strictly.

Thursday 27th. The weather still rainy and cold. The Party to go through the Swamp left at 9 A.M. in charge of Mr Freeman.

The Party in the Steam Boat under my immediate charge left the Arkansas side at 10 A.M. We were obliged to touch on the Memphis side to take in a few of Jim Islands Indians who had come up with him the night before.[31] Here I had a long conversation with Islands. He said it was impossible for his Indians to get ready to go with us and would prefer remaining a day or two. I immediately saw Mr Gibson, Mr Hendricks,[32] Mr Campbell, and Mr Beattie[33] They were convinced that; from the great sale of whiskey it would be imprudent for our boats to remain a moment longer than possible. They all assured me the best provision should be made for all the Indians left behind. I took Islands to them and told him what arrangements had been made and that Mr Beattie and Hendricks were the Agents to whom he must make all his applications. This was perfectly understood, and I left with the most perfect confidence in their assurances.

At ½ past 12 N. we again started. The boats were very comfortable nor much crowded. at ½ past four the Boat landed for the night. Corn and Bacon was issued as usual computing the number on board at fifteen hundred, the distance to day was estemated at 16, or 18 miles.—

The weather has cleared up, bright star light, fine moon, and tomorrow bids fair to be very pleasant.

11 A.M.

Friday 28th. Up Early this morning, surrounded by a dense bank of fog. The fog came up a little about 7 A.M. Got the Indians on board, but soon found it two thick to run. at 10 A.M. the fog cleared up got started day clear. Camped four miles below Helena on the Arkansas side. Distance to day 70 Miles.

Saturday 29th. Got under way at day-light weather very unpleasant and cold and cloudy. Camped at Montgomery's Point on the Arkansas side: distance to-day called 75 Miles, but by the channel of the River I have but little doubt but that its nearer one hundred, weather very unpleasant, raining hard.

Sunday 30th: Left Montgomery Point at ½ past 7 A.M. Entered the mouth of White River at 9 A.M. camp up this river six miles and there concluded to take the principal outlet of the Arkansas, after ascertaining there was a sufficiency of water and if this should be the case, we could be confident in finding enough to ascend the Arkansas to Little Rock. The distance through this outlet is six miles. At ½ past 11 A.M. came to the mouth of the River and found water enough through the outlet. The water of the Arkansas has a most singular appearance resembling the colour of a half burnt brick. Here, is its proper termination, it then forms two arms one of them at low water empties its self into the Mississippi, and at high water the other or the most northerly arm, empties the greater portion of the waters of the Arkansas into white River and from thence into the Mississippi. This arm is the one principally navigated by steam Boats most of the year.

This morning, early, the Steam Boat Farmer with Mr Campbells Party[34] on board passed us on its way to Rock Rowe: up the White River.—Camped on the south side of the Arkansas at 5 P.M. five miles below the Post of Arkansas, distance came to day 40 Miles, weather still bad.

Monday 31st. Left Camp at 7 A.M. current very strong, river rising rapidly; it came up two feet last night. Found great difficulty in stemming the river with the two flat boats in tow. We averaged to day about one and a half miles an hour. Camped at 5 P.M. three miles above the Post of Arkansas, distance to day 13 miles,—done raining, weather clear but cold.

Tuesday November 1st. Left Camp at ¼ past 6 A.M. came up the river two miles where we concluded to leave the flat boats and equally divide the party taking on board the Steam Boat one half and leaving the other until the boat could go to Little Rock and return. Left this place at 8 A.M. boat very much crowded, river still rising. Camped at 5 P.M. distance to day 50. Miles. Placed markers upon the bank of the river to ascertain correctly the stage of the water, weather very pleasant.

Wednesday 2d. at 2 O'clock A.M. found the river had fallen two feet, and there was no time to be lost. Started the Indians in camp at ½ past 2 A.M. got them all on board at 3: and at ½ past 3 A.M. the boat got under weigh. The day remarkably fine, every thing indicating very strongly a rapid fall of the river—Camped at ¼ past 5 P.M.; the day pleasant and warm, distance to day 75 Miles.

Thursday 3d. Left Camp at 4 A.M. river still falling, morning very pleasant but cold. The Indians came on board with great reluctance. The Boat for the last three days very dirty and exceeding offensive, on the 31st ult I requested Mr Gibson, the Agent, to adopt some method to have it partially cleaned, arrived at Little Rock at ½ past 4. P.M. distance 78, weather very fine.

Friday 4th, remained at Little Rock: the Arkansas still falling, fell sixteen inches last night, undertermined whether to venture farther up by water or not. A part of the Ponies and Indians which came through the swamp joined us last evening.—

Saturday 5th. Concluded to send the S. Boat back immediately to bring up the remainder of the party from the Post of Arkansas. The boat left at 8. A.M. I proposed to Tuck-e batch-e-hadjo to start all that came up in the boat and get across a bad swamp forty five miles up the country, where there would be an abundance of game and provisions and where we would wait until the whole party could get together. This he positively declined doing. Here, there is no provisions and the quantity of whiskey sold to the Indians jeopardized the lives and property of all the citizens. I directed all the Indians that were willing to go with me to put their baggage in the waggons and start immediately; all consented but the Chief and about one hundred indians. The party started about 3 O P.M. camped at 5 = distance 5 Miles, weather very pleasant.

Sunday 6th. Left Camp at 8. A.M. roads very rough, weather pleasant, camped at 5 P.M. distance 15 Miles, at Wilsons.[35]—

Monday 7th. Left camp at 9 A.M. roads very rough and in many places very muddy, camped at 5 P.M. distance 18. Miles; ten waggons remained oweing to the bad state of the roads.

Tuesday 8th. Left Camp at 8. A.M. crossed the Cadron Creek and camped distance 3½ miles. Here we expected to meet the Party that came through the swamp. Little Rock was the place agreed upon, but unbeknown to me the Agents directed their Agent to go forty miles further up /to the cadron/ as all the Indians were going up by water. Here we could hear nothing of our Party, conclude to go on and get through the Point Remove bottom as every thing indicated rain, about noon Mr Gilman, the Agent came up with the waggons that were behind last night.

Wednesday 9th. Left camp at 8. A.M. weather very unpleasant, raining hard, roads exceedingly bad, came to Plummers. Camped at 1 P.M. distance 7 Miles.

Thursday 10th. Left Camp at 8. A.M. roads very bad, weather cold, rained most of the day very hard. Came to Mrs Slinkards camped at 1 P.M. = distance 9 Miles. =

Friday 11th. Left Camp at 9. A.M. came through the Point Remove Bottom = which was almost impassable, much worse than it has been for a year past. Camped at 2 P.M. distance 5. Miles,: at Blunts.[36]

Saturday 12th. Started at ½ Past 8 A.M. weather cleared up last night and the day is very clear but cold. The indians suffer greatly from being in their bear feet and thinly clad. Came to Potts' = Camped at 4. P.M. distance 12 Miles, roads much better, country quite hilly.— Here, I have ordered the Party to halt until the whole party can get together. The Dardinelles on the Arkansas is Eight miles from here. There we expect to meet the John Nelson, with the remainder of the Party. Sent a man there yesterday to look out for her. The Indians and Ponies that came through the Swamp are expected here tomorrow.

Sunday 13th. Still in Camp, weather very pleasant. Ponies from the swamp not arrived. They are constantly coming in in small parties. Complaints are made to me by citizens against the Indians who are left behind; that they kill their stock. Sent back Mr Freeman to urge them to come up and to collect them and keep them under his immediate charge. The agents also have gone back.

Monday 14th. Last night an express came reporting the arrival of the John Nelson at the Dardinelles. I got all the lame, sick and blind, together with those who were disposed to go, into waggons and took them to the Boat. Tuck e-batch-e-hadjo who came up in the Boat was opposed to going on board again, which detered many who came with him from going. He said a large portion of his Indians were behind with many of his family and until he could meet these he would not go on. I however succeeded in getting on board about three hundred, and placed them in charge of Doctor Hill, with instructions not to keep the Party in his charge until I should arrive at Ft Gibson. The Boat left at 5 P.M. Gibson the principal chief in camp of the Cowetas came to me this morning and requested that we might remain here until his indians could get up, that now families were separated, and those who had horses were obliged to walk, and that many children were here, and many were behind without their parents, I told him we should wait—

Tuesday 15th: The Boat came back this morning in the expectation of getting those on board who declined going yesterday, but could not succeed. When the boat landed those on board commenced bringing off their baggage and said they would not go as they had been told that they were to be taken into a distant country where they were to be placed under soldiers and their men placed in irons.—I assured them that it was false and urged them to take their baggage back, if they would do so, I would be up with them in four or five days and do as I had always done for them. To this they assented, their baggage was again taken on board and the boat started at 11 O'clock A.M. The distance from this place to Fort Gibson by water is near four hundred miles, by land one hundred and seventy. The weather the last two days has been very pleasant, the water in the Arkansas still rising. At 12 N. waggons were procured and Tuck-e-batch-e hadjo and those with him were brought to camp. He complained of being very sick.—I returned to camp this afternoon. Ponies and indians behind not arrived. Mr Odum & Mr Love,[37] two Agents, were sent back to day to bring up all behind. I told the Agents yesterday, that their entreaties, threats or representatives could not drive me from what I had promised the Indians and from what I concieved now to be my duty: the Indians should be got together and should be kept together, and that not an Indian should go from this place until I was convinced that none were behind.

Wednesday 16th. Still in Camp, weather pleasant. Waggons and Ponies not arrived. The Indians have been coming in in small parties of six, Eight and ten every day.

Thursday 17th. Ten Waggons, a large number of ponies & Indians arrived to day in charge of Mr Freeman. Mr Hudspeth, one of the sub Agents of the company arrived also. He, says that Narticker, brother of Tuck-e-batch-e Hadjo, was in the Mississippi swamp with about one hundred Indians and that they were determined to take their own time in coming. I advised Mr Gilman, the Agent, to start tomorrow, that nearly all the Indians were up Excepting those in the swamp and as they were not disposed to come up I did not think those here ought to wait for them. Every preparation is making to start tomorrow. The weather to day is very unpleasant indicating snow or rain.

Friday 18th. Rations were issued this morning for two days. Rained hard all day, with difficulty I could get the Indians to go for their rations. Finding it impossible to start to day from the violent rain, we shall endeavour to start tomorrow.

Saturday 19th. This morning there was Every indication of a pleasant day. We started from Camp, /Pott's/ at ½ past 9 A.M. a cold rain commenced this afternoon.[38] The roads were very muddy and the creeks very high, four, five and six waggons were down in the mud at once. Camped at Dwights on the Illinois B. at 5 P.M. But two waggons got to camp to night. The rest were strung upon the road for ten miles: distance to day 13 miles.—Cloudy and cold, has the appearance of snow.

Sunday 20th. Rained all day, very unpleasant and cold; remained to day at Dwights. Four of the waggons came to camp to day. Every thing indicates fair weather.

Monday 21st. Left Camp at 8 A.M. came one mile over a very bad road to a small creek, which we found very high with a bank upon the opposite side which required two hours to get our waggons up. Came on to Piney Creek, which we were obliged to cross by ferry, arrived there at 3 P.M. = Camped at Mays:[39] distance 12 Miles: weather clear but cold, six of our waggons behind.

Tuesday 22d: Remained to day at Mays for the purpose of getting all up all in the rear. all the waggons and Indians came up to night and tomorrow we intend to make a fair start. The road we are told is much better than that we have passed over. Weather very pleasant but Extremely cold.

Wednesday 23d. Left Camp at 8 A.M. Indians and waggons all started together, road good, weather very cold but pleasant. arrived at Spadra River at 1 P.M. distance 9 Miles. Here, we found Mr Gibson from the Steam Boat John Nelson which was at the mouth of the river. I directed all the waggons to go to the mouth of the river and the indians to follow, arrived there at 5 P.M. = 2. Miles. In the Evening I assembled all the chiefs and urged upon them the necessity of all the women and children going up in the boat, they very readily consented and said all would be prepared to go in the morning.

The Arkansas river is at a stand, with about six feet rise of water.—

Thursday 24th = This morning all the Indians were prepared to go in the boat most of them were on board, at 11 A.M. the boat was ready so far as the indians were conserned: = all of them that were going were on board. A difficulty occurred, however, between Mr Gibson who had been acting as Captain of the boat and all the crew, from the Pilot down; They had concluded to leave the boat to a man if he continued on board of her. They would not, they said, submit longer to his conduct towards them. Two hours elapsed, Mr Gibson was determined to remain. The indians were all on board waiting anxiously for the boat to start. I was determined that the indians should not remain in suspense any longer, and I told Mr Gibson & Gilman /the Agents/ that unless some course was determined upon and persued within one hour I should direct all the indians to come ashore, camp them and take decisive measures to take them to Fort Gibson myself. To this they replied, "there shall be no longer delay" at 1. P.M. Mr Gilman reported to me that Mr G. would go by land and he should take charge of the boat. The crew consented to this. The boat left at ½ past 1. P.M. with about as near as could be estimated, one thousand indians. All the Indians that go by land camped at Wards[40] on the Spadra, 2 Miles from the river.

Friday 25th: Left Camp at ½ past 8 A.M. = roads good, weather very pleasant, country well settled. Camped at Paces;[41] distance 12 Miles.

Saturday 26th: Started from Camp ¼ 8 A.M. roads very good, level, weather pleasant camped at Blounts: distance 23. Miles. This distance was much longer than we had ever travelled before, but the Indians being mostly mounted they were anxious to get to Fort Gibson as soon after the Steam Boat as possible. I told the Agent that if he would have a waggon expressly to carry all on foot I had no objection to the party proceeding as fast as possible. They done so, and they moved on without difficulty.

Sunday 27th. This morning I placed the Party in charge of Mr Freeman my assistant. Those on board the Steam Boat being more than those on shore, I was anxious to get to their place of destination as soon as the Boat and I according left this morning with the determination of being at Ft Gibson as soon as possible: distance 75 or 80. Miles.—came to Van Buren = distance 30 Miles.

Monday 28th. Left Van Buren at 8 A.M. roads good, but hilly, weather pleasant. Came to Mrs McCoys 30 Miles at Van Buren. I heard that the Steam Boat got aground opposite Fort Smith & remained there one day but had got off.

Tuesday 29th. arrived at Fort Gibson at sun down. Left Mrs McCoys at 8 A.M. weather pleasant, roads very rough passing over very high mountains and through quite an unsettled country, distance to day 32 Miles.

I could hear nothing of the Boat the river being from twelve to fifteen miles from the road.

Wednesday 30th. Sent a man down the river to enquire for the Boat.

Thursday December 1st: The man sent down the river not returned. A rumour was about that the Boat had gone back to Fort Smith.

Friday 2d. The man returned, ascertained that the Boat had gone back to Fort Smith, and that the Party of Indians with the horses were camped thirty miles from this, and that waggons had gone back to bring up those /Indians/, at Fort Smith, making preparations to start for that place in the morning: weather very pleasant,—water in the Arkansas low.—

Saturday 3d. Left Fort Gibson at 9 A.M. stayed at McCoys.

Sunday 4th. Left McCoys in search of the party found the party at Winters, 10 miles from McCoys.

Monday 5th. Camped with the Party at Mc weather pleasant.

Tuesday 6th. Camped at McKays distance to day 15 Miles weather pleasant.

Wednesday 7th. Remained at McKays to day for the rear of the party to get up;

Thursday 8th. Still at McKays, weather pleasant

Friday 9th. Left Camp at ½ past 8 A.M. came to Drews: camped distance 15. Miles.

Saturday 10th: Left Drews at 9 A.M. to Fort Gibson distance—4 Miles.

Here General Arbuckle ordered the Party to halt and camp within one mile of the Fort. I camped the Party in the immediate vicinity of O-poth-le-o-holos, and by order of the General informed the Agents of the company that tomorrow the Government would take charge of the Indians. I had the Indians counted, they amounted to 1605 this number together with 395 that arrived here in the Steam Boat on the 20th ult makes two thousand. A small party are left behind in charge of an Agent. This party were those who expressed a determination to remain in the swamp. I heard from this morning, they are coming on and will be here in two or three days.—

Sunday 11th: Waiting for the Party behind.

Monday 12th. Still waiting the arrival of party.

Tuesday 13th. Preparing the rolls, Party behind not arrived.

Wednesday 14. Not arrived.

Thursday 15th: Mr Odam arrived with the Party in his charge amounting to two hundred and fifty. Mr O reports, Tuckebatchehadjo behind waiting for his brother.

Friday 16th: Capt Stephenson, received them and camped them with the rest of the party.

Saturday 17th: Capt Stephenson is preparing the roll to be delivered to the Company as soon as the few behind are brought up. The number of Indians which the roll calls for have arrived.—

Sunday 18th. Capt Stephenson acknowledges the recpt of the complete roll. He gave the roll up to me for my disposal. I signed it and turned it over to the Agent Mr Gibson.—

Monday 19th. Engaged in settling up my accounts, and giving the Indians blankets according to the treaty.[42]—

Tuesday 20th. Still engaged in settling my accounts and in giving to the Indians of my party blankets, by the request of the General. Made my report to Mr Harris, put it in the office this night to go in the mail tomorrow morning,—reporting the arrival of my party the whole number after deducting ________ deaths and adding ________ births amounted to 2087. From one hundred & fifty to two hundred Indians have been counted here more than the roll. A remark respecting it made upon the muster roll.[43]

I hope no apology is necessary for the appearance of this journal. The many inconveniences attending a journey like this, and more particularly the great want of every convenience of writing, is the cause of its appearance.

I was obliged to cut it down both in matter and material sufficient to get it into my saddle bags. It was my intention to have copied it and written it out more fully, but the want of time has prevented it.

J. T. Sprague
April 6th 1837.

Supplemental Letters of Detachment 5

Lieutenant John Titcomb Sprague reports that Cusseta headman Tuckabatchee Harjo and Jim Island of Coweta are reluctant to come into camp until they sell their crops and cattle and are delaying the commencement of the detachment west. Letter found at Records of the Adjutant General's Office, 1780s–1917, Entry 159-Q, Records of Major General Thomas S. Jesup, Container 17, Folder: "Letters Received from Officers, Various USMC Officers, 1836," NARA.

Cuseter August 11th 1836.

D'r Sir,

I have been useing every exertion to get these indians into camp; not a man of Tuck-e-batch-a-hadjo's or Jim Islands have even thought of it until within the last two days. Sunday the 14th inst was the day I appointed for these two chiefs to commence their camp, and Wednesday the 17th is the day fixed for the new contractor to make the first issue, Jim Islands is to camp near his present village and Tuck-a-batch-e, near his. I have told them after the 17th, all indians that report themselves and families in camp at that time, shall be furnished with provisions, those that are out shall have none, and unless they are in immediately, efficient measures will be taken to bring them in. Their principal argument against camping so soon is, that they have crops & cattle to see to. I have avoided this by telling that when they have brought their families in the heads will be granted permission from time to time to go out and see to all they have. Tuck-a-batch-e-hadjo, after useing every arguement in his power, consented to direct his people to camp, but he done it with great reluctance. This arrangement was in full, and I think, successful operation, when to day upon my return from West Point, I learn that a long-tail-coated Lieutenant has been here, held a council—told them to disregard going into camp now, but attend to him—appoint some person to estimate land with him—and go immediately down and get their money at Tallassee. Jim Island also has shewn me a letter purporting to be written by O, Poth-le ho-lo; requesting him and the other chiefs to come to Tallassee and get their money. This arrangement seems to me to be so improbable, not only from my not receiving some information respecting it, but from the difficulties which must inevitably result, and which are certainly evident to you, all the Chiefs have been to me and say its impossible for their men to get there; their Ponies are poor and have sore backs, and by the time they are to go to Arkansas they will have no horses, and they say if they are to go there they cannot go into camp so soon. My orders have no effect with them now, nor never will have nor with any one else, unless all orders are communicated through the person who is to have the superintendence of them. Its of no use for me to talk to them, for they will always answer me as they did to day—"that what I say, don't last". The 20th they say they are directed to come for their annuities, why not postpone it untill they get in that vicinity on their way to Arkansas?

Jim Islands goes down to see you this afternoon, Tuck-a-batch-e tomorrow. I shall send this letter by him. I have visited all the towns belonging to these chiefs and told them plainly what they had to rely upon. I think its very evident that they are all positively against it, but Islands, and I doubt if any of them are removed without giving them time, unless strong measures are resorted to.—Let them sell their crops and cattle all, I think, then would go.

Your Obt Servt
J. T. Sprague

To,
Capt John Page
U.S. Army.
Superdt Creek Removal
Tallassee, Al

☾

Sprague reports delays in the formation of the Cusseta relocation camps due to Tuckabatchee Harjo's opposition to moving to Indian territory. Sprague also seeks further clarification on whether the Creeks are to receive federal money at Tallassee. Letter found at Records of the Adjutant General's Office, 1780s–1917, Entry 159-Q, Records of Major General Thomas S. Jesup, Container 17, Folder: "Letters Received from Officers, Various USMC Officers, 1836," NARA.

Cuseter, Al. August 11th 1836.

General:

Tuck-e-batch-e-hadjo's wishes to be the bearer of a letter to you. A letter has been received by him purporting to be written by O-poth-le-o-lo, requesting them to come to Tallassee and receive what is due him and his band by the United States for their services. This request seemed to them to be inconsistant, as they are required to be there on the 20th to receive their annuities; they came to me for information, but I knew nothing about it, and advised them to go to Tallassee and ascertain from you the correctness of it. There are so many designing men through the country that I do not know what to rely upon. I have directed this Chief and Jim Island to commence forming their camps on the 13th inst, and on the 17th the contractor will make the first issue of provisions. I have assured them, that after that period, those in camp shall be well supplied, and those that are out shall get none. Tuck-e-batch-e hadjo, evinced a strong inclination, the first day I talked with him, against forming a camp and with great reluctance consented to make the effort. His principal argument against it was, "that he did not wish to go to a country he knew nothing about, and that before he moved his women and children, he wished to see it". I expressed my surprise that he had not expressed it to you, and that it was a singular reason at this late period; he said, that in his last talk he told you so, and that if you did not understand him, it was the fault of the interpreter. He has, however, consented to form a camp near his own house. Jim Islands will encamp in the vicinity of West Point, ten miles from Tuck-e-batch-e-hadjos.

I should be much gratified if you could grant me the privilege of accompanying the first party of indians that start.

I am Sir, with great respect
Your obt Servt. J. T. Sprague
Lt U.S.M. Corps.

To
Major Gen'l T. S. Jesup
Tallassee, Al

P.S. Since writing this letter Tuck-e-batch-e-hadjo, says its impossible for him to [go] down, he is quite sick, and he says many of his people are.

He sends Mr Owens & Mr Freeman for the purpose of getting their money due them by the United States, these men can be relied on and have full powers from him to act. I told him I thought it quite improbable that the money would be paid them; if it was not, they must either go down or an officer would be sent up to pay them. If they go down it will be the means of keeping them out of camp longer than could be wished as they are determined to use every apology to avoid it. I have written Capt Page on the subject.

J.T.S.

☾

Sprague reports that Cusseta headman Tuckabatchee Harjo and many of his people are sick but still preparing to come into camp. He also seeks clarification on the payment of monies. Letter found at Records of the Adjutant General's Office, 1780s–1917, Entry 159-Q, Records of Major General Thomas S. Jesup, Container 17, Folder: "Letters Received from Officers, Various USMC Officers, 1836," NARA.

Cuseter August 13th 1836

D'r Sir,

Since writing the enclosed letters Tuck-e-batch e-hadjo [says] that it's impossible for him to go down; he is sick and many of his people are so. He is now (he says) preparing to go into camp and wants the money paid here. I regret that I have received no information respecting the payment of the money, consequently can give them no advice. He sends down Mr Owens and Mr Freeman whom he authorizes to draw all the money due his people for their services. If the money can be paid in this manner, all I can say is, that these gentlemen are fully authorized to act and can be relied on. I have given no advice, this course is one of his own suggestion. Write me Every opportunity and give me all the information you can.—

Yours Truly
J. T. Sprague

To
Capt Page
U.S.A.

P.S.—Inform Pothliolo[44] that Tuck-e-batch e is sick

☾

Sprague reports on the difficulty of urging the Cussetas into camp. Letter found at Records of the Adjutant General's Office, 1780s–1917, Entry 159-Q,

Records of Major General Thomas S. Jesup, Container 20, Folder: "Letters Received, 1836–1838, From Camps and Forts during the Creek War," NARA.

West Point August 28th 1836.

Sir:

Yesterday, I succeeded in finding Tuck-e-batch-e-hadjo sober after six days intoxication. He is perfectly willing to go and very readily consents to any measure proposed. None of his indians have yet been enrolled. I received instructions for the first time on the 24th inst. to have it done. I commence to day. A part of Capt Seals company will be on the ground, and those indians who are not there by the request of the chief, I have directed to be brought in by the troops. If the sale of whiskey could be prevented I could have them enrolled in three days. I have no means of suppressing this sale and the quantity sold is very great. Majr Webb[45] has been obliged to postpone the payment of their money oweing to the state they have been in. Col Miller[46] has not yet recieved orders to send a detachment of troops to Cuseter; fifty men I think will be required and nothing short of Martial Law will ever get these indians in a condition for removal. Jim Islands being absent has caused his indians to be less in a state of preparation than could be desired; they are waiting his return, none of them are in camp and like all the indians of this Detachment, none are enrolled.

I shall use every exertion to have it done immediately.

No waggons belonging to the Emigrating Company have yet arrived; none of their agents are here.

To-morrow /Monday the 29th/ I shall turn them over to the company in compliance with your order of the 22d inst. although I have no rolls, yet I can ascertain the number of rations required and before they are prepared to move I can have the rolls completed.

Getting these indians into camp, has been very much retarded by the absence of some of the principal chiefs, and the sale of whisky, but I think, from the present appearance of things, they will be ready as soon as the Company.

I am, with great respect
Your obt Servant
J. T. Sprague
Lieut & Military Agent
5th Detachment.—

To
Major General T. S. Jesup
Commanding Army of the South
Tallassee Al

P.S.—Since writing this letter Col Miller has received orders to detach thirty men from his command for White Plains; this will render me no assistance, neither will it protect those citizens of the country most exposed to the indians, White Plains is twelve miles from Tucke batch-e-hadjos camp, and West Point is ten. If these troops are sent there to render such facilities for the removal of the indians as is required, they would be quite as much so at West Point it being two miles nearer. The citizens of the country are repeatedly urging me to urge the necessity of troops being stationed in the vicinity of Cuseter, two miles from Tuck-e-batch-hadjo's; independent of this, it will be of great advantage to me to prevent the sale of whiskey. The indians in the vicinity of White Plains are now nearly all in Tuck-e-batch-e-hadjos camp and the remainder are fast coming in. If you can comply with my re-quest by having the troops stationed at Cuseter instead of White Plains, I think it would greatly facilitate the removal of the indians and give security to the citizens of the country.—

J.T.S—
Lt &c—

A report is abroad among the indians that they have been allowed ten days from the 29th to get ready. I have received no official information of it.—

☾

Sprague reports that the five days' detention ordered by Bvt. Major General Jesup has expired and notifies the Alabama Emigrating Company that he is turning control of detachment 5 over to them. Letter found at LR, CAE, Roll 238, 758.

Copy/.

Cuseter, Chambers Co. Al
September 2d 1836.

Gentlemen:

This night being the expiration of the five days granted by General Jesup after the 29th ult. for the Indians belonging to the camps of Tuck-e-batch-e-hadjo to move, I, in compliance with that order, turn them over to you as the Agents of the Alabama Emigrating Company, and expect, that tomorrow morning, the, 3d of September, you will take the entire charge and direction of them. They are now all in camp, excepting a few who have permission to see to their crops. The whole Party is enrolled, amounting to near two thousand. There may be a few not yet come in; they will be enrolled as soon as they are brought in. The rations issued by the Government are out to night. To-morrow it is expected the company will furnish them.

I am very respectfully
Your obt Servt
J. T. Sprague
Lt & Military Agt
5 Detch Em Creeks

To
Messrs Gibson & Abercrombie
Agents Al. Em. Company
Present.

☾

The contractors report that they are prepared to march and are waiting on Sprague to turn the Creeks over to them. Letter found at LR, CAE, Roll 238, 760.

Cusetau Sep't 3. 1836.

Cap't J. T. Sprague

Sir!

Yesterday evening late, your letter dated 2d Int. was handed us by [illegible] Conveying the information that Tuck-E-Batch-E-hadjo and Jim-Islands with the Indians of Both their Towns were in Camps, prepared to take up their line of march westward—and that this morning it would be Expected of the Alabama Emigrating Company to take charge of them.

In conformity with the letter and spirit of the Contract made with Gen'l Jesup, we have the pleasure of informing you that every preparation has been Completed and we now wait for you to turn the Indians over to us properly Enrolled that we may be Enabled forthwith to move forward with them to their Western Homes.

We are
Very Respectfully
Felix G. Gibson
Charly Abercrombie

☾

Sprague reports that most of the Creeks of detachment 5 have been turned over to the Alabama Emigrating Company. He notes that approximately 120 Creeks, who were secreted in the Chowokolo Swamp, wish to join the party. Sprague also seems to foreshadow the problems he will encounter with the agents of the Alabama Emigrating Company even before the party leaves Chambers County, Alabama, as they seem unwilling at first to transport the lieutenant's baggage. Letter found at Records of the Adjutant General's Office, 1780s–1917, Entry 159-Q, Records of Major General

Thomas S. Jesup, Container 17, Folder: "Letters Received from Officers, Various USMC Officers, 1836," NARA.

Cuseter September 4th 1836

Sir,

In compliance with your order of the 25th ult, granting five days permission to all the Emigrating camps from the day designated for their departure, I, yesterday morning turned over to the Agent of the Alabama Emigrating Company all the Indians in the camps of Tuck-e-batch, e, hadjo's and Jim Islands as ready for removal westward—amounting in all to about twenty two hundred. This afternoon the first waggons will start and continue to do so as fast as they fill up, the whole train will be concentrated at La Fayette—12 miles from this place. I received a message yesterday from a body of indians in the Che-war-ke-la swamp wishing to know if I would permit them to come in. I sent them word that if they came in immediately they should be received as friends and treated as other indians; they will be in tomorrow or next day: the whole body amounts to one hundred twenty as near as I could learn. I hope I shall be allowed a day or two to have them prepared for removal.—I am apprehensive that Jim Islands will cause some delay, not more than a day or two however;—his absence caused his people to remain out of camp longer than could be wished. Those that are ready will start immediately and the others will come up with them at the place of rendezvous.—But few of the Indians in the two camps were inclined to go to Florida, Tuck-e, batche—was decidedly against it but consented to hold a council with his young men upon the subject.—but the arrival of the day for their departure prevented it. I saw so little prospect of obtaining any number I could not feel myself authorized to postpone the day for their removal. I am desirous of having a waggon to transport my own baggage and Dr Hills distinct from that of the Agents. They say they are under no obligations by the contract to take it but out of <u>courtesey</u> will take it, but expect hereafter to be paid for it. From what I have seen of them I desire no such acts of kindness and if I could be allowed a waggon it would contribute much to the better discharge of my duties and much to my independence as an agent of the Government. Majr Webb is now at columbus. He wished me to say to you that he thinks the volunteers you require he can raise by the middle of next week and will be at Head Quarters as soon after as possible.—

I am with great respect
Your obt Servt
John T. Sprague
Lieut & Military Agent
5th Detachment.

To
Major Gen'l T. S. Jesup
Commanding Army of the South
Head Quarters,
Tallassee Al.

☾

Brevet Lieutenant Colonel Samuel Miller reports that Tuckabatchee Harjo was unwilling to offer any of his warriors for duty in the Florida war until he finished conducting them to Indian territory. Letter found at Records of the Adjutant General's Office, 1780s–1917, Entry 159-Q, Records of Major General Thomas S. Jesup, Container 13, Folder: "Letters Received from Officers, Colonel Samuel Miller, (1 of 3), July–September 1836," NARA.

Marine Encampment
Near Cussuta Alaba'a Sept 6th 1836

Sir

Your several orders of the 30th Ultimo did not reach me until the 1st and 2nd Inst. without delay. I marched from my position near West point, with the whole detatchment, and Encamped the same day in the vicinity of Tuckabatchee Harjo's Camp.

The public property recently in possession of Major Chambers, and Captain Still,[47] has been placed in a store at West Point, rented by a former Quarter Master attatched to the Post. The arms are in a miserable condition; and the accoutrements but little better.

Finding ten or twelve days provisions at West point, in a partial state deterioration, and impressed with the belief that a Military force would not long continue at this post, I have drawn from this source in preference to sending waggons to Columbus. By the 15th Inst we shall have Exhausted all the provisions at West point with the exception of some damaged Pork.

Captain Twiggs[48] who received orders to proceed to La Fayette, and muster out of service the four Companies of volunteers, reports that he has performed that service and delivered all the arms and accoutrements and other public property over to the Quarter Master on duty at that place. The arms are wholly unfit for use.

The Indians both at this place, and in the neighbourhood of White plains, departed for La Fayette yesterday afternoon, with the Exception of Tuckebatchee, who was permited to go to Columbus, to close some Private concerns.

On the 3d Inst I held a conversation with Tuckabatchee, through his interpretor, upon the subject refered to in your letter of the 30th Ultimo, he was most decided in having nothing to do with the Florida War, until he had first accomplished the duty of conducting his people to the west, to use his own words, he said, "he could not do but one thing at a time"—

As neither provisions or Forage can be obtained in this neighbourhood, I shall if we remain here, be compelled to obtain a supply from Columbus.

I am, With great Respect.
Your obt Servt
Sam'l Miller
L't Col. Co'y

Major General Jesup
Comm'ng Army of the South

&c. &c.
Tallassee Alabama

☾

Sprague reports on the start of Jim Island's party and the delays at Benjamin Marshall's camp. He also notes that the Creeks hiding in the swamps have not reported to detachment 5. Letter found at Records of the Adjutant General's Office, 1780s–1917, Record Group 94, Entry 159, Thomas S. Jesup, Box 19, Folder: "Letters Received From Various USMC Officers, 1836–1838."

Columbus Sept 7th 1836.

Sir:

All the Indians in the Camps of Jim Islands and Tuck-e-batch-e-hadjo are on their way to Arkansas: amounting to nineteen hundred and forty three individuals.

Ben Marshalls indians have been very dilatory in their movements and I am here to enquire the cause after sending for them four times. I find they have been relying upon the rumours put in circulation by the Carrs:[49] that the Indians were not going west for ten days, the same thing was attempted in Tuck-e-batch-e-hadjo camp. They have however, started and will be in camp this evening upon my return. Their movements has been the cause of keeping me from the party now on the march longer than could be wished, but I could not in justice leave behind, without knowing the cause, any number that belonged to my Detachment.—Those indians in the Che-war-ke-le swamp have not yet come in, and from what I learn from a Mr Coleman who lives near it, they do not intend to. He informed me yesterday, that he saw forty in the swamp on Sunday last, and they expressed to him their enmity to the whites and their determination to remain there.

I am, Respectfully
Your obt Sert
J. T. Sprague

Lt & M. Agent
5 Detch

To
Majr General T. S. Jesup
Commanding army of the South
Tuskegee, Al

☾

Samuel Miller reports on the discovery of an elderly Creek man who had been left behind by detachment 5. Letter found at Records of the Adjutant General's Office, 1780s–1917, Entry 159-Q, Records of Major General Thomas S. Jesup, Container 13, Folder: "Letters Received from Colonel Samuel Miller, (1 of 3), July–September 1836," NARA.

Marine Encampment
Near Cussuta alabama Sept 11th 1836

Sir

Since the departure of the Indians on the 5th Inst. I have been informed that an Indian upwards of one hundred years old, was left behind in the woods, about three miles from my Encampment; I immediately mounted my horse, and with a Guide discovered him Exposed to the inclemency of the weather, and wholly destitute of Provisions of any Kind; and finding he could neither rise or sit a horse, I returned, and sent a waggon for him, he now remains in an Indian house, near our Encampment, from which we furnish him with Every comfort in our power. What disposition shall be made of this apparently first of his race?

The Indians gone, our provisions short, and none to be procured at White plains, I have directed Capt Twiggs to break up his Encampment, and return to this Post, preparitory to the Execution of any orders we might receive from you.—

I am, with great Respect
Your obt Servt
Sam'l Miller

L't Col. Co'y

Major General Jesup
Comm'g Army of the South
&c. &c.
Tallassee Alabama

☾

This communiqué, forwarded to Alabama Emigrating Company employees, Felix Gibson and Charles Abercrombie (while in camp near Courtland, Alabama, ordering the party to halt for a day's rest), shows Sprague's increasing frustration with the conduct of the contractors. LR, CAE, Roll 238, 762.

Camp September 24th 1836.

Gentlemen:

You will be pleased to halt the Party of Emigrating Creek Indians in your care, tomorrow, the 25th for a days rest, and proceed the following morning the 26th. The situation of the Indians absolutely require it. You can go with your empty waggons, or remain just as you please. These being under your especial charge you of course can act your pleasure. The Indians will halt.

I am very respectfully
Your obt Sevt
J. T. Sprague
Lt & Military Agt
Emgt Creeks

Messrs Gibson & Abercrombie.
Agt Al. Emgt. Co.
Present.

☾

Writing while encamped several miles east of Purdy, Tennessee, Sprague complains that Felix Gibson and Charles Abercrombie, representatives of the Alabama Emigrating Company, are inattentive to the comfort of the party and neglectful when it comes to the weakest members. Letter found at LR, CAE, Roll 238, 764–66.

Camp October 2d 1836.

Gentlemen,

I have been engaged the last two days in picking up the lame, sick, and blind, belonging to the party of Indians which you, as Agents of the Alabama Emigrating Co, are emigrating to Arkansas. Many of these Indians from various causes I found unable to keep up with the waggons. Some of them start with them, but from fatigue, feebleness, or decrepitude they are obliged to fall behind and are left upon the road. Others are taken sick upon the road without any means of assistance or conveyance. The waggons and Agents are always ahead and no one remains to provide for them. Many I am aware are also behind from their own wilfull laziness.[50] This duty I have been engaged in, and finding the Agents of the Company out of my reach, I [relied] upon the tenth article of the Contract, which says, "If a remedy can be found in any pecuniary expenditure in contributing to their comforts & convenience to make it, which amount shall be deducted from that due them /the company/ by the United States". This remedy I applied, I saw plainly there was no one to provide for them, and I also saw, that unless they were brought up with the moving train they must be left upon the road dependent upon the charity of the country through which they passed. The scarcity of water has of late, made our daily marches much longer than they should be, and the poorer class of Indians from not having the means to get along, have been left behind. I have seen them coming into Camp late at night, loosing their rations, and totally unfit to proceed the following day. As one whose duty it is, has been left behind to see to them, and they, as well as myself, have been subject to the insolence and indifference of the waggoners in your employ. With the great inattention which has of late been paid to the proper details of the party, our marches have been too arduous, and these marches have depended too much upon the immediate resources of the Country. If corn cannot be provided at a place twelve miles distant, the indians are by the present arrangement, liable to go untill it can be found; & if it is not gathered, they are turned into a corn field after dark to gather it. The supplies of this party, excepting beef, have been obtained to much by chance; greatly to the inconvenience of the Indians. This, however, will be reported to high authority. It is now my duty to have all the Indians that fall in the rear brought up, and kept by some means with the party with which they are enrolled for Arkansas, and if you as the Agents of the company neglect doing it, the task must necessarily devolve upon me, which I shall without hesitation discharge. The fourth article of the contract says, that the average daily travel shall not exceed from twelve to fifteen miles, to be determined by the officer & Surgeon. In accordance with a faithful discharge of my duties to the Indians, you will be pleased to confine the march of the party in your charge to twelve miles pr day.

I regret, that in the unpleasant situation in which I have been placed by the Government, the discharge of my duties, should be considered by any one as the result of ungenerous or improper feelings. My uncalled for acts and ill-timed expressions as you have been pleased to [call] them, have been interpreted in an intentional design to make known my authority. This I disclaim with contempt. I deny it, and assure you that my feelings and designs are of the best kind, and assure you, that a mutual understanding I should greatly prefer, not however at the sacrifice of not discharging my duty.

I am very respectfully
Your obt Servt
J. T. Sprague
Lt & Military Agent
5th Detachment Emigr Creeks.

To

Messrs Gibson & Abercrombie
Agt Al. Em. Co.
Present

(

Writing while in camp forty-five miles east of Memphis, Sprague (with the urging of Tuckabatchee Harjo) admonishes Abercrombie and Gibson for neglecting their duties in caring for the Creeks. Letter found at LR, CAE, Roll 238, 768–69.

Copy/.

Camp, October 5th 1836.

Gentlemen:

The situation of the party of Indians in your care, requires that the hour of starting in the morning should be delayed. You will be pleased to have the waggons transporting the Party in readiness to receive the sick, lame and blind, and those enfeebled from age, or other causes and young children, at 8 o'clock A.M. and to leave the camp as soon after this time as the Indians can be arranged in a proper manner.

Tuck-e-batch-e-hadjo requested me to go with him to you, this evening. But the intoxicated state I found him prevented me. I shall coincide with him fully if he expresses the same opinion to you, that he has to me. He looks to me as the Agent of the Government for redress, and he shall have it. I shall carry out the policy of the Government to the utmost extent; that is, to concilitate and make these people believe that the Government is their friend. This man is the Chief and with him I am instructed to act. The feeling in our Camp, commencing with the Chief, is of a hostile character, now, towards you, and if I, as the Agent of the Government, do not grant them redress, the Government must meet the consequences. This party shall not cross the Mississippi with the present feelings. I owe it to myself, the Government, and the citizens of Arkansas, that these Indians should go there with the best feelings; now they do not Exist. My interpreter[51] has been attacked and threatened with his life and refuses to act for me; the indians considering him my agent and myself as yours, which is far from them the case, as you can bear testimony by my repeated acts.

I am, gentlemen very
Your obt Servt
J. T. Sprague
Lt & Military Agent
5th Detachment Emgt
Creeks.

To
Messrs Abercrombie & Gibson
Agents Al Em Co
Present

☾

Writing from at the same camp (forty-five miles east of Memphis), Sprague sends a letter to Gibson and Abercrombie expressing dissatisfaction with their performance and declaring that he will not cross the Mississippi River with them in charge. Letter found at LR, CAE, Roll 238, 771–72.

Camp, October 6th 1836.

Gentlemen:

Yesterday, I had the pleasure of seeing Mr Campbell[52] the Agent of the party in the rear. He being one of the Alabama Emigrating Company, I expressed to him what I intended should be first known to you. I endeavoured to explain to him the difficulties I had encountered in your neglecting to meet my wishes, and made known to him my determination that this party of Indians should not cross the Mississippi in your charge. The reasons I have for this conclusion are strong, I have them all in writing and shall submit them to the Department for the justification of my course. When the members of the company come together, I am willing to consent to any new arrangment which will secure the Indians their comfort and convenience—aid me in the discharge of my duties, and carry out to the extent, the policy of the Government. If they do not see fit to do this, I shall take the party into my charge, and take it to Arkansas myself. This emergency I am prepared for both in instructions and in funds. All my acts while I am with these Indians, are not the result of personal feelings. I do, and speak for a body: an authority to which I am accountable, and if any individual feels that I have personally wronged him, while acting under this authority, I will, when the duty is discharged, meet the consequences in any way or manner.

My only regret at this time is, that by your intercourse towards me and to those connected with me, you have evinced a disposition to be personally hostile. We have hostiles Enough among us, without my being one.

I did hope, that when I openly and frankly disclaimed all personalities—all ill feeling, but expressed the best, that it would lead to beneficial results, and that a mutual understanding would again be resumed and that your duties to the Indians would again be performed. But in this, I have been disappointed. My attempts were disregarded, my wishes treated with indifference, until I am now forced to the conclusion that I cannot discharge my duties in the present state of things, and to the determination that the party shall not go to Arkansas under your charge.

I am gentlemen, very Respectfully Your obt Sevt
J. T. Sprague
Lt & M. A. &c.

To
Messrs Gibson & Abercrombie.

☾

Sprague orders Gibson and Abercrombie to pick up two injured Creeks left near Raleigh, Tennessee. Letter found at LR, CAE, Roll 238, 776.

Memphis, Oct 12th 1836.

Gentlemen:

Doctor Hill, informs me that an Indian man by the name of Spiller[53] who was badly burnt is now behind a few miles beyond Raleigh and is unable to come up on foot. You will oblige me by having him brought up so that he can be taken care of. Also an Indian who was shot this side of Raleigh, is still there.

Respectfully Your obt Svt
J. T. Sprague
Lt & Military Agent
5th Decht Em Inds

To
Messrs G. & Abercrombie
Agts—

P.S. They were brought up as required

J.T.S.

☾

Noting his arrival at Memphis, Sprague reports on the bottleneck in that city as detachments 1 and 2 are encamped ahead of him. Worried about congestion on the other side of the Mississippi Swamp, Sprague writes that he has decided to bypass Rock Roe and take a steamboat to Little Rock. Sprague also reports on the negligence of the contractors in failing to transport all of the sick, blind, and infirm. Letter found at LR, CAE, Roll 237, 640–42.

Memphis, Tenn, October 16th 1836

General:

I have the honour to report to you my arrival at this place on the 9th inst in charge of Two thousand and seventy nine Emigrating Creek Indians.

We left Cuseter, Chambers County, Alabama on the 5th of September.

The health of the Party has been very good. I have had no serious difficulty, but there has been at times great dissatisfaction in the Camp, originating, I think with a party of hostile Indians who joined me from a swamp the third night on our march.[54] Finding such a feeling in the Camp I adopted the most prudent and cautious measures to allay it, and I have in a great measure succeeded.

The delay here has been much longer than could be wished. I shall leave here with my Party on the 25th or 26th inst in a Steam Boat for Little Rock. The other parties go to Rock Rowe, seventy miles this side. I found I was obliged to remain here until the two parties ahead of me were transported and the Boats returned.[55] I proposed to my chiefs to go to Little Rock to which they very readily assented. The swamp upon the Arkansas side is considered impassable otherwise I should have gone through by land.

I regret that it is not in my power to speak in terms of commendation of the course pursued by the Agents of the Alabama Emigrating Company.

If a hostile feeling existed in my camp or if any hostile acts were committed I considered myself as the person accountable to the Government for it. The contract I conceived guaranteed to me all powers necessary for a faithful discharge of my duty: not to the Company but to the Government. I made requests of them which I was convinced would contribute to the comfort and convenience of the Indians which they saw fit to disregard. The lame, sick and blind, were left behind dependent upon the charity of the country. I remonstrated against such a manifest violation of the contract; they denied all that I alleged and treated my complaints with contempt, and I accordingly relying upon the tenth Article of the Contract made such expenditures as circumstances required. I hired waggons and brought up such Indians who from various causes were unable to get up. I hope however I shall not be obliged to bring this before the Department for an official decision. A better conception of the letter and spirit of the Contract will hereafter I think remedy all evils. If my expectations should not be realized, I shall lay before you a full detail of all that has occurred accompanied by such facts as I trust will justify my course. My first step will be, to refuse giving my certificate or the Muster Roll upon which the Company draw their pay and I shall then report to you accordingly.[56]

I am, with respect
Your obt Servt
John T. Sprague
Lt & Military Agent
5th Detachment Emigrating
Creek Indians.

To
Bvt. Brig'd Gen'l G. Gibson
Commissary General of Subsistance
Washington
D.C.

☾

Captain Stephenson reports that the rolls for detachment 5 are inaccurate, and he is trying to ascertain the exact number of Creeks who joined from the swamp. Letter found at SIAC, Agent (Reynolds), Account (1687), Year (1838), NARA.

Fort Gibson 18th Dec. 1836

Sir

There is but little doubt, there were more Indians (Creeks) accompanied the party under the charge of Col. Gibson & Lieut Spraigue, than entered on the Rolls, accompanying the party.

It appears by statements of agents accompanying the party, that small bodies of Indians joined the party from the Swamps in Alabama, whose names were never entered on the Rolls. So soon as I can possibly ascertain their names & numbers I will enroll them & forward a copy to the department at Washington (D.C.)

Very Respectfully
Your Obt. Servt.
Ja's R. Stephenson
Capt. U.S. Army
Disbg. Agt. (Creeks)

Capt. John Page U.S. Army
Prin. Disbg. Agt. Ind. Rem'l East. Mississippi

☾

The following is a memorandum of remarks attached to the muster roll of detachment 5. Remarks found at LR, CAE, Roll 238, 774.

Remarks: attached to the muster roll delivered to the agents of the Alabama Emigrating Company.

The number of Creek Indians that have arrived here in the Party in my charge, is larger than the roll calls for. A few days previous to the starting of the party from Chambers Co. Ala. an express came to me from a body of Indians of about one hundred and fifty in number, who were secreted in the Chewarkeler Swamp, wishing to know if they would be received as friends should they come in. I assured them they would, I heard no more of them until the 9th or 10th day of our march, when some indians informed me that a body of hostiles had joined the train the night before. How many could not be ascertained, I believed them to be the body referred to. Every exertion was made to enroll them but without avail, and as I never could ascertain with any degree of accuracy their number, I never asked for them that which was required by the contract, as my demands could only be made under the sanction of the roll which was in the possession of the company.

Ft: Gibson, Aks. Dec 18th 1836

☾

Sprague reports on the arrival of the main body of detachment 5 at Fort Gibson, while updating Commissioner of Indian Affairs C. A. Harris on events during the last leg of their journey. Sprague also seems to ease up on his criticism of the Alabama Emigrating Company and even offers his approval of the manner in which the contractors performed their duties after their standoff at Memphis. Letter found at LR, CAE, Roll 238, 701–3.

Fort Gibson, Aks.
December 20th 1836.

Sir,

I have the honour of informing you that the whole number of the 5th Detachment of emigrating Creek Indians in my charge, amounting to two thousand and eighty seven, are here, and received by Capt Stephenson U.S. Army and are encamped within a mile of this Fort by order of General Arbuckle.

When my last communication to the Department of the 21st of October was written, arrangements were made at Memphis for all the Indians to be landed at Rock Rowe immediately west of the Mississippi swamp. Two parties were to precede mine and I saw that our detention would be longer than could be desired. The Indians being very impatient the Agents of the Company accepted my proposal to take the Party to Little Rock by water, as all reports respecting the stage of the Arkansas river were favourable. I consulted the chiefs who readily acquiesced. A good sized steam boat[57] was procured, and this, with two large flats, were found sufficient to contain all that were not going through the swamp, which were mostly women and children. On the 26th of October about six hundred men and women with all the ponies belonging to the Party started for the swamp in charge of my assistant Mr Freeman. The agents of the Company assured me that abundant provision was made for them on the route which proved to be the case. On the following morning, the 27th, the party in my immediate charge left Memphis, having on board all the boats, as near as could be estimated, fifteen hundred souls. When we arrived at the mouth of the Arkansas the waters being so high and the current so strong it was impossible to proceed with both flats in tow, and the only alternative was, to leave one and go up as fast as possible with the other. Every provision was made for the wants and comfort of the Indians that remained.

The 3d of November we arrived at Little Rock and the next day the boat returned and brought up those left behind. The indians that came through the swamp joined us sixty miles from Little Rock. I halted the Party at the Dardanelles, a point on the Arkansas river, to give all an opportunity to get up with us; while there, one of the Steam boats belonging to the Company came up bound to Fort Gibson, on board of which, I suceeded in getting the lame, sick and aged, and as many more of the Party as were disposed to go. This detachment, amounting to three hundred and ninety five arrived in their new country twelve miles from Fort Gibson, on the 21st ultimo, where they were received by Capt Stephenson.[58]

This boat on its return met us again near the river Spadra. I urged the indians to go on board as the severity of the weather and the bad state of the roads would make them suffer severely. About twelve hundred consented and the remainder continued on by land. When we arrived opposite Fort Smith we learnt that the boat had grounded oweing to the rapid fall of the river and that the indians were on shore. Waggons were immediately procured and the party were soon together and on the way to Fort Gibson, which we soon reached after a fatigueing journey of ninety five days from Chambers County, Alabama.

The health of the Party has been very good, and the feeling on the part of the indians is of the most friendly character. On our arrival here, Gen'l Arbuckle, deeming it necessary that a perfect understanding should exist between these indians and the hostiles who were emigrated last summer, ordered the Party to halt until every thing could be amicably arranged.[59] This has been done, and as soon as they receive their blankets they start for their new homes. In my letter to the Department of the 21st of October I expressed my dissatisfaction of the course persued by the Agents of the Alabama Company. The duties of the officer in charge being so much at variance with the interests of the company difference of opinion will unavoidably occur. It, however, now affords me pleasure to say that, they have adopted every measure which I deemed expedient, and done all in their power to contribute to the comfort and convenience of the indians. A stupid indifference to the stipulations of the contract, and a disposition to break down the authority of the officer, and drive the indians far beyond their powers, seemed to be the determination of these Agents; but though this did exist, I cannot now, in justice, withold from them my avowal, that they have complied with the contract and endeavoured to act up to its letter and spirit.

I am, with great respect,
Your obt Servant
J. T. Sprague,
Lt & Milty Agt 5th Detachment Emgt C. Indians

To,
C. A. Harris Esqr
Commissioner of Indian Affairs
War Department, Washington, D.C.

☾

This letter, written by the headmen of Cusseta (although not Tuckabatchee Harjo, who likely had not yet arrived at Fort Gibson), details the Creeks' hard journey west and their anger at losing their crops and being driven like "wolves." It is in stark contrast to Sprague's assertion in his letter of 20 December 1836 (preceding) that the feelings of the Indians were "of the most friendly character." Letter found at LR, CAE, Roll 238, 778.

Fort Gibson, December 21st 1836

Friend & Brother,

You have been with us many Moons—You have fought with us—You have fed us—You have taken care of us and listened to our talks and heard the cries of our women & children. We are now going from you and listen once more and the last time to the talk of your friends; it is short. Our road has been a long one—and on it we have laid the bones of our men—women & children. You were with us, you have seen and heard all—write what we now say to you.

When we left our homes the Great General Jesup told us that we should go to our Country as we wanted to go. We wanted to gather our Crops and we wanted to go in peace and friendship. Did we?! No! we were drove off like wolves—lost our crops and our peoples feet were bleeding with long marches. You listened to our talk and we rested. We are here and tell General Jackson if the white men will let us, we will leave in peace and friendship, but tell him these agents came not to treat us well, but to make money, and tell our people behind not to come and be drove like dogs. We are men—we have women and children, and why should we come like horses; We have got our Blankets and our women and children are warm—we thank you. Your road back is a long one—take our hands we will be with you. This talk is short but it's the words of our hearts.

Chiefs of the Cuseter Town of Creek Indians
Spar-ne-Mathla
Cuseter Micco
Micco Hadka

To
Lieut J. T. Sprague
5th Detachment
Emigrating Creek Indians
Fort Gibson
Aks.

☾

This lengthy letter is an extended summary of the entire journey west and serves as a supplement to Sprague's journal. In it Sprague notes the problems he had with white settlers, long marches, and the employees of the Alabama Emigrating Company. Letter found at LR, CAE, Roll 238, 739–56.

Washington City April 1st 1837.

Sir:

On the 3d of August 1836, in compliance with an order from Major General Jesup commanding the Army of the South, I reported to him in person for emigrating duty. After being engaged in the various duties connected with the large bodies of Indians in the vicinity of Tuskegee, Al. from the 3d to the 8th inst., I received a verbal order from him to repair forthwith to the Cuseter and Coweta towns of Indians, and prepare them for immediate removal.

On my arrival at these towns on the 10th, I had an interview with the principal chief, Tuck-e-batch-e-hadjo, and urged upon him the necessity of taking immediate measures to prepare his people for emigration. To this, after useing every argument against it, he reluctantly consented. His principal reasons were that his peoples crops were not gathered—their cattle were not sold, and that the time specified for their departure was earlier than he anticipated. The following day, I assembled all the chiefs, and explained to them the necessary arrangements to embody their towns, in order to transfer them to the charge of the Alabama Emigrating Company upon such a day as might be designated by the commanding General. They gave no other than a silent acquiescence to my wishes, but expressed among themselves strong feelings of dissatisfaction. I promised them every assistance in disposing of what little they had, but assured them that upon the day fixed for their departure they must be ready. The necessity of their leaving their country immediately was evident to every one; although wretchedly poor they were growing more so every day they remained. A large number of white-men were prowling about, robbing them of their horses and cattle and carrying among them liquors which kept up an alarming state of intoxication. The citizens of the country had no security, for though these Indians had professed the most friendly feelings, no confidence could be placed in them, as the best informed inhabitants of the country believed them to be allied with those who had already committed overt acts of hostility. Some families which had fled for safety were afraid to return until the country was rid of every Indian. Public indignation was strong against them, and no doubt the most serious consequences would have resulted, had not immediate measures been adopted for their removal.

In this state of things, however indignant their feelings or however great the sacrifice, it was but justice to get them out of the country as soon as possible. On the 23d inst I received orders from the commanding General to move the Party on the 29 inst. The time, however, was prolonged five days, to the 3d of September.

On the 1st of September I had in camp near two thousand ready for removal. This number comprised the whole of the two towns, excepting a few who had been secreted in a swamp from the commencement of the Creek War. These sent an express to know if I would receive them as friends should they come in. I assured them they would be treated like the rest. I heard no more from them until the ninth night of our march, when they joined the train with their women and children.[60] Their number I could never learn, as they kept themselves aloof but they might be treated as hostiles; but from other Indians, who were very silent on the subject, I learnt there were from one hundred to one hundred and fifty. The 3d of September I placed all the Indians under my charge in care of Mr Felix G. Gibson and Charles Abercrombie, members of the Alabama Emigrating Company, and on the morning of the 5th the Party started for Arkansas, arranged to waggons according to the contract. The train consisted of forty five waggons of every description, five hundred ponies and two thousand Indians. The moving of so large a body necessarily required some days to effect an arrangement to meet the comfort and convenience of all. The marches for the first four or five days were long and tedious and attended with many embarrassing circumstances. Men, who had ever had claims upon these distressed beings, now preyed upon them without mercy. Fraudulent demands were presented and unless some friend was near, they were robbed of their horses and even clothing. Violence was often resorted to to keep off these depredators to such an extent, that unless forced marches had been made to get out of this and the adjoining counties, the Indians would have been wrought to such a state of desperation that no persuasion could have detered them from wreaking their vengence upon the innocent as well as the guilty. As soon as time and circumstances would permit, proper arrangements were made to secure to the Indians, regularly, their rations and transportation. A large herd of cattle were driven ahead of the train which supplied the Party with fresh beef. Two days rations were issued every other day, while corn was issued every day. The Party moved on without any serious inconvenience, other than the bad state of the roads and frequent drunken broils, until the 22d, when from the warmth of the weather and the wearied condition of the Indians, I deemed it expedient to halt for a days rest. Tuck-e-batch-e-hadjo, the principal chief, had been desirous of stopping sooner, and had expressed his determination to do so. The situation of the Camp at the time was not a desirable one for a halt, nor was I inclined to indulge him. I ordered the train to proceed. He with reluctance came on. From the first days march, I saw a disposition in the Indians, among both old and young, to remain behind. From their natural indolence and from their utter disregard for the future, they would straggle in the rear dependent upon what they could beg, steal or find, for support. I used every entreaty to induce them to keep up, but finding this of no avail I threatened them with soldiers and confinement in irons. This had a salutary effect, and was the means of bringing most of them into Camp in good season. On the night of the 24th inst the Party encamped at Town Creek, Al. after twenty days march averaging about twelve miles a day. I waited on the contractors and requested them to halt the party the following day. To this they expressed their unqualified disapprobation and denied my authority to exercise such a power. Their expenses they said were from six to seven hundred dollars per day, and if such authority was given or implied in the contract their hopes of making any thing were gone. I assured them, that from the condition of the Indians, the common calls of humanity required it, and that one of the stipulations of the contract was, that they should treat the

Indians with humanity and forbearance. I ordered the Indians to halt, and told the contractors they could act their own pleasure; either go on with their empty waggons or remain. The Party halted and resumed the journey on the following morning, the 26th. The Indians and horses were evidently much relieved by this days rest. From this period to the fifth of October our marches were long, oweing to the great scarcity of water; no one time, however, exceeding twenty miles. The Indians in large numbers straggled behind, and many could not get to Camp till after dark. These marches would not have been so burdensome had proper attention been paid to the starting of the Party in the morning. It was necessary that their baggage as well as their children should be put in the waggons, and the sick and feeble sought out in the different parts of the Camp. But this was totally disregarded. I reminded the contractors that the party now required the utmost attention, that unless they were strictly seen to, we should not at night have more than half the Indians in Camp. To this they were indifferent, saying, that they "must keep up or be left". Early in the morning the waggons moved off, the Agents at the head, leaving those behind to take care of themselves. It's an absurdity to say, that Indians must take care of themselves; they are men it is true, but it is well known that they are totally incapable of it, and it's proverbial that they will never aid each other. To this course of proceeding I remonstrated, and the tenth article of the contract which authorizes the officer to make "any expenditure contributing to the comfort and convenience &c". I put in execution, which relieved the Indians from the destitute situation in which they would otherwise have been placed. My letters to the contractors accompanying this report embrace this period and will explain to you more fully the course I was compelled to adopt. It, however, affords me pleasure to say, that upon a better knowledge of their obligations, they very readily consented to pay the expenses which accrued in keeping up the rear. On the 5th of October I again halted the party and rested one day. To this the contractors objected and seemed determined to drive the Indians into their measures. The 7th the party again moved and on the 9th inst encamped near

Memphis, Tenn. Great inconvenience was experienced upon this entire route for the want of Depots of provisions. There was no time when the proper rations were not issued, but from the frequent necessity of gathering and hauling corn, the Indians were often obliged to take their rations after dark. This caused great confusion and many were deprived of their just share. Though the neglect of these agents in not bringing up the rear of the party deserves the severest reprehension, yet, I must in frankness acknowledge that there were many who not come up under the most favourable circumstances. This, however, was no apology for not bringing up those who would or at least making an effort. If liquor could be found upon the road, or within four or six miles of it, men and women would congregate there, and indulge in the most brutal scenes of intoxication. If any white-man broke in upon these bacchanals he did it at the imminent hazard of his life. Often in this state they would come reeling and singing into camp late at night, threatening the lives of all who came within their reach—alarming the citizens of the country, and not unfrequently creating the most indignant feelings among the sober Indians towards all the white-men who were about them. They would taunt them as cowards and dare them to join them in some nefarious act. Without the means of quelling such restless spirits by the strong arm of power, the most kind and conciliatory feelings should have been evinced towards them. But unfortunately for me, these agents entertained no such sentiments. At Memphis I met a number of the contractors and before them I laid my complaints and convinced them, that if no remedy was provided, I was determined to relieve the company of their charge of the Indians, and take the arduous responsibility of taking them to Arkansas myself. The President of the company in a highly honourable manner declared that nothing should be left undone to meet the wishes of the officers of the Government. These agents I either wanted dismissed or taught the first lesson of the obligations they had assumed. One of the agents left the party, and it was afterwards in charge of Mr Gibson and Gilman. Here, I think, Mr Gibson for the first time read the contract, and I found in him ever after a willingness to comply with what I considered expedient for the comfort and convenience of the Indians. With such indications of a proper interpretation and understanding of the contract, and upon the assurances of the most respectable men belonging to the Company, I could have no hesitation in giving them an opportunity to redeem their pledges.

At Memphis we remained from the 9th of October until the 27th. The Mississippi was here to be crossed, and the Company were much disappointed in not finding their steam boats as they anticipated. The boats, however, arrived on the 11th; Captain Batemans party were the first to cross, Lieutenant Scrivens was the second, and my own the third. Lieutenant Deas and Mr Campbells parties were in the rear. The assembling of thirteen thousand Indians at this one point, necessarily made our movements slow. This detention was of advantage to the Indians as it gave them rest and afforded the sick and feeble an opportunity to recover. The required rations were furnished them regularly within this time, and they all conducted with the greatest propriety. The common council of the city passed an ordinance prohibiting the sale of liquor, which added greatly to their comfort, and to the peace and security of the citizens. The Mississippi swamp at this season was impassable for waggons and it was agreed, that the horses should go through while the women and children with their baggage took steam boats to Rock Row. This place was attained by descending the Mississippi about one hundred miles to the mouth of White River, and ascending this river about seventy miles, and thereby avoiding a swamp about fifty miles in breadth.

Finding that the embarkation of the parties that preceeded mine would cause much delay, a mutual agreement was effected between the chiefs, the contractors and myself, to take the party up the Arkansas river to Little Rock. The advantages to be gained by this were evident; it put us ahead of all the other parties, secured us an abundant supply of provisions, and avoided a tedious journey of one hundred and fifty miles on foot. A commodious steam boat was procured and upon this and two flat boats, I put, as near as could be estimated, fifteen hundred women & children and some men, with their baggage. The men amounting to some six or seven hundred passed through the swamp with their horses, in charge of my Assistant agent Mr Freeman. I received every assurance, that upon this route, the necessary provisions was made for them. On board the boats, an abundance of corn and bacon were stored for the party to subsist upon until we should reach Little Rock. On the 27th the boat started. The Indians were comfortably accomodated, sheltered from the severity of the weather and from the many sufferings attending a journey on foot. The boats stopped at night for them to cook and sleep, and in the morning resumed the journey. The current of the Arkansas being so strong at this time, it was found expedient to leave a part of the Indians until the boat could go up and return. These were left in the care of an Agent with the necessary supplies. On the 3d of November we arrived at Little Rock. The larger portion of the party which passed through the swamp joined us the 4th. Many remained behind and sent word, that when they had got bear skins enough to cover them they would come on". Here, they felt independent, game was abundant and they were almost out of the reach of the white-men. At first, it was my determination to remain at Little Rock until the whole party should assemble. But from the scarcity of provisions and the sale of liquor, I determined to proceed up the country about fifty miles and then await the arrival of all the Indians. Tuck-e-batch-e-hadjo refused to go, "He wanted nothing from the white-men and should rest". Every resting place with him, was where he could procure a sufficiency of liquor. The petulent and vindictive feelings which this chief so often evinced, detracted very much from the authority he once exercised over his people. But few were inclined to remain with him. The 12th we encamped at Potts', the place designated for the concentration of the whole party. My assistant Agent, together with three Agents of the company, returned immediately to bring up and subsist all in the rear. Some of them went as far back as the Missisippi swamp. They collected, subsisted and transported all they could get to start by every argument and entreaty.

A body of Indians under a secondary chief Narticker-tustennugge expressed their determination to remain in the swamp in spite of every remonstrance. They evinced the most hostile feelings and cautioned the white-men to keep away from them. The 14th the Steam boat that returned from Little Rock to bring up those left on the Arkansas, arrived at our encampment with Tuck-e-batch-e-hadjo and his few adherents on board. On this boat the following day, I put all the sick, feeble and aged; placed them in charge of Doctor Hill the Surgeon of the party, with instructions to proceed to Fort Gibson, and there be governed by the proper officer at that place. This party arrived at their place of destination on the 22d inst, and were received by the officer of the proper department.[61] The Agents bringing up the rear arrived at Camp on the 17th. Those in the swamp still persisted in their determination to remain. Neither the Agents or myself had any means by which we could force them into proper measures, most conducive to their comfort and progress. The season being far advanced and the weather daily becomeing more severe, I ordered the party to proceed the following morning. The sufferings of the Indians at this period were intense. With nothing more than a cotton garment thrown over them, their feet bare, they were compelled to encounter cold sleeting storms and to travel over hard frozen ground. Frequent appeals were made to me to clothe their nakedness and to protect their lacerated feet. To these I could do no more than what came within the provisions of the contract. I ordered the party to halt on the 22d and proceeded again on the 23d. The weather was still severe, but delay only made our condition worse. The steam boat on its return from Fort Gibson, fortunately found us encamped near the river Spadra. On board of her I suceeded in getting nearly the whole party, amounting now to some sixteen hundred souls. The boat started again for Fort Gibson on the 24th. Those that determined to go up by land were all mounted or in waggons, and I directed them to proceed as fast as possible. On the 30th we learnt, that oweing to the rapid fall of the Arkansas the boat had grounded. We soon came in the vicinity of her; waggons were procured and this body from the boat soon joined those on shore. The Indians here were frequently intoxicated. They procured liquor from other Indians residents of the Country, and the artifices of both combined no man could detect. On the 7th of December, when within eighteen miles of Fort Gibson I again halted the party, and agents were sent back to bring up all that could be found in the rear. This being done we started the following morning, and arrived at Fort Gibson on the 10th inst. By the order of Brigadier General Arbuckle I encamped the party in the vicinity of the Fort. Many reports were in circulation that the Creeks settled in the country were inimical to the emigrants, and it was deemed advisable to have a perfect understanding among all parties previous to entering their new country.[62] This was effected to the satisfaction of all, but how long it will last the future can only tell. Two agents belonging to my party, who had remained behind arrived on the 15th, bringing on all they could find or all that were willing to come, a few they said were behind. As soon as I was satisfied that all were present that could be brought up, I had the number counted as correctly as circumstances would admit. The number present was twenty two hundred and thirty seven. The number, for which I required of the company rations and transportation, was two thousand and Eighty seven; leaving one hundred and fifty that were not enrolled. This number, no doubt, were the hostiles who joined the train on the march. I could never obtain from the Indians, nor from any one identified with them, any satisfactory information respecting their number or how they subsisted. Their friends, doubtless, shared their rations with them, to prevent their being enrolled lest they might be treated with severity. I gave them every assurance of friendship, but it had no avail. On the 20th inst, the officer of the Government appointed to receive the Emigrating Creeks, acknowledged the receipt of my entire party. To Captain Stephenson of the Army who performed this task, I am greatly indebted for the many facilities he granted me in the performance of my duties. He is untireing in the department assigned to him and discharges his obligations with promptness and fidelity. After the Indians had received their blankets in compliance with the treaty, I proceeded with the larger portion of them to their country assigned them. Thirty five miles beyond Fort Gibson I encamped them upon a prarie and they soon after scattered in every direction, seeking a desirable location for their new homes. The better understanding of the contract by these Agents, and the establishment of depots of provisions on the route from the Mississippi, contributed greatly to facilitate our progress, and to the "comfort and convenience" of the Indians. The duties of the officers in charge of these parties being so much at variance with the interests of the company, difference of opinion will unavoidably occur. The requirements of the Indian are against the interests of the company, one party is actuated by interest, the other by humanity. I was there to protect the rights of the Indian; the course was a straight one and I persued it. But though these misunderstandings did occur, the agents accompany the parties deserve great credit for their perseverance. The ready acquiescence of the agents of my detachment to all my wishes, after crossing the Mississippi, deserves my decided approbation; they were unremitting in every emergency.

The excessive bad state of the roads, the high waters, and the extreme cold and wet weather, was enough to embarrass the strongest minds. The distance travelled by the Party from Chambers County, Alabama to their last encampment, was Eight hundred miles by land, and four hundred & twenty five by water; occupying ninety six days. The health of the Indians upon the entire route was much better than might been anticipated.

Twenty nine deaths were all that occurred; fourteen of these were children and the others were the aged, feeble and intemperate.[63] The unfriendly disposition of the Indians towards the whites from the earliest history of our country, is known to every one. To what an extent this feeling existed in the party under my charge, I cannot with confidence say, for it was seldom expressed but when in a state of intoxication. But if this be a fair criterion, I have no hesitation in saying it was of the most vindictive and malignant kind. To say they were not in a distressd and wretched condition, would be in contradiction to the well known history of the Creeks for the last two years. They were poor, wretchedly and depravedly poor, many of them without a garment to cover their nakedness. To this there was some exceptions, but this was the condition of a larger portion of them. They left their country at a warm season of the year, thinly clad, and characteristically indifferent to their rapid approach to the rigours of a climate to which they were unaccustomed, they expended what little they had for intoxicating drinks or for some gaudy article of jewelry.

So long a journey under the most favourable auspices must necessarily be attended with suffering and fatigue. They were in a deplorable condition when they left their homes, and a journey of upwards of a thousand miles could not certainly have improved it. There was nothing within the provisions of the contract by which the Alabama Emigrating Company could contribute to their wants, other than the furnishing of rations and transportation, and a strict compliance with the demands of the officer of the Government; these demands unquestionably, must come within the letter and spirit of the contract. All these they complied with. The situation of the officers of the Government at the head of these parties was peculiarly responsible and embarrassing. They were there to protect the rights of the Indians, and to secure to them all the Government designed for them. These Indians looking up to the officers as a part of the Government, not only appealed for their rights, but their wants. They could sympathize with them, as every one must who saw their condition, but could not relieve them. They had nothing within their power, for in a pecuniary point they were scarcely better off than those they were willing to assist. All that the contract granted was secured to them. But all this, could not shield them from the severity of the weather, cold sleeting storms, and hard frozen ground.

Had a few thousand dollars been placed at the disposal of the officer which he could have expended at his discretion, the great sufferings which all ages, particularly the young, were subjected to, might have been in a measure avoided. But as it was, the officer was obliged to listen to their complaints without any means of redress. Captain Batemans was the first party to arrive at Fort Gibson, my own was the second Mr Campbells the third, Lt Scrivens the fourth and Lt Deas the fifth. I have conversed with all these gentlemen since the delivery of their parties, excepting Mr Campbell, and I believe they will concur with me fully in my views and opinions. With all these officers I held almost daily intercourse when upon the road, and I can bear testimony to the faithful discharge of the arduous duties that devolved upon them. They all complained of the difficulty in making the Indians keep up with the moving train.

The following is an extract of a letter from Lt Deas who was in the rear, addressed to me when I was waiting the arrival of my party from the rear.

"The Agent of the company with my party, requests me to write you upon the subject of your Indians that have remained behind your party. He says that he has ample means to bring up all that straggle from whatever party, and it is not my intention to allow any of the emigrating Indians to remain upon the route of emigration if I can possibly prevent it."

I believe every effort was made to keep them up, but nothing but the registor of military authority can ever effect it.

Many exagerated reports are in circulation respecting the miserable condition of these emigrating Indians. Let these be traced to the proper source and it will be found that the white-men with whom they have been associated for years past have been the principal cause. There is enough in support of this opinion. It is only necessary to advert to the allegations, in many instances well established, of the lands of the Indians having been purchased by some of these citizens at prices much below their real value, or of the purchase money having been in whole or in part, witheld; to the prosecutions for vaild or fictitious debts commenced at the moment of their departure for the west, and thereby extorting from them what little money they had.

Had they been permitted to retain the fair proceeds of their lands, they would have had the means of procuring any additional supplies required for their comfort.

The stipulations of the treaty were fairly executed; all that was to be furnished the Indians was provided, and if these were inadequate to their comfortable removal and subsistance, no blame can be attached to the Agents of the Alabama Emigrating Company or to the officers of Government.

I have the honour to be,
Very Respectfully
Your obt Servant
J. T. Sprague
Lt U.S.M. Corps
& Military Agent
5th Detachment Emigrating Creeks

To
C. A. Harris Esqur
Commissioner Indian Affairs
War Department
Washington City.

☾

Captain John Page reports to Alabama Emigrating Company partner Alfred Iverson on the circumstances that led Jim Island and his party of 135 as well as Ben Marshall and his party of seventy to relocate separately from detachment 5. Letter found at SIAC, Agent (Reynolds), Account (1687), Year (1838), NARA.

Mobile Point alab
8th July 1837

Sir

I have received your letter of the 19th of last month pointing out difficulties that have arose, that prevent the settlement of the alabama emigrating company for the removal of Creek Indians, that part which relates to 135 Indians under the charge of Jim Islands. I am not sufficiently acquainted with all the facts relative to the cause—when I paid out the annuity for the years 1836 and 1837 a large meeting of the chiefs of the Creek nation met at or near Tallassee in the Public square. the time was drawing near, the different parties had to commence their journey to their new countray, I urged the chiefs every day to hasten their business as a great many of them lived a long distance from home and they would scearcely arrive there before they would have to take up the line of march for their new countrey, the chiefs said it was impossible for them to get through with their business and comply with the order. I told them the order must be complyed with that I had Just been notified by the alabama Emigrating Company they were all ready; they went to Gen'l Jesup and stated to him they had so much business to attend to, that they could not comply with the order he then issued another order giving them five days longer, the chiefs still continued to council and with a great deal of argument I could break it, after the order giving them five days longer; the time nearley elapsed in the second order before the council broke. Jim Islands was not present himself, he was sick and unable to attend, he sent his brother[64] with several head men with full power to transact his business. Lieut Sprague was in Tallassee at the time and I requested him to proceede to his station about 50 miles and prepare his people to comply with the second order, he observed to me it was no use for him to leave until Islands and his people did, that they never would start unless he was present, and a great deal of business was to be done after Islands arrived and he did not think it was possible to comply with the second order. I told him it was necessary to comply with it as far as was in his power, and report the difficulties if any he had to contend with and the reason why the order was not carried into affect, and so soon as the council broke I would dispatch Islands and his people. Just before Islands left the council he stated to me he could only have time to get home before his people would have to start agreeable to the second order; he asked me if his people could have some few days longer. I told him no, and urged him to start off immediately: the next news I heard was, that Lieu't Sprague was on the road and Jim Islands party were left in the Rear. On my Return from Tallassee to Fort mitchell I made enquiry of some of the company who were present when this party started, they said Jim Islands was not ready and they could not wait for him if they complied with the last order, they stated to me, Lieu't Sprague was in Columbus Georgia when they started about 40 miles off and did not overtake them for several days after they had been on the Road with his party and that he over took Jim Islands in the rear bringing up his own people. the Emigrating company had no right to use forceable means to force these people off. If such measures were to be taken it was with Lieu't Sprague and he absent at the time (so say the company) and when he over took his party he was much offended at their leaving Islands' party in the rear, Do'ct Williams who had charge of this party told me he advanced a certain amount to Jim Islands for money he advanced to bring his people to memphis where they Joined. If this statement is correct you surely will be entitled to pay for the 135 Indians from Memphis to arkansaw in proportion to the distance. I have been exsplicit in detailing circumstances to show the Department difficulties will arise and they are unavoidable in doing business with a great number of people, and it is difficult for me to judge who is in the wrong when I am not present. I made it my business to start all the other parties and accompany them a day or two on the road, and endeavoured to have got to Lieu't Spragues party but could not reach it; If I could there would have been no difficulty, as to Ben Marshalls party of 70 Indians,[65] the Alabama Emigrating Company are intitled to pay at $28.50

per head at the time I started his Indians he could not go, the company prepared for him he had a law suit in court in which he was the defendant, Relative to a large Estate his deceast Brother left, he requested that I would permit him to remove his family with his Brothers, also his wifes Fathers family, negroes and all, consisted of 70 I told him I had no objection if such arraingments could be made so the company would secure to him the amount he could agree to move them for this he said he could arrainge himself, he done so and bound them to give him so much per head after he delivered them to the agent west and brought his certificate of their delivery. I signed the contract he entered into with the company, Ben Marshall is a man of wealth and a business man, his connections he took over were all wealthy and desired to go with Marshall in a squad by themselves, If I had appointed any person over Ben Marshall I doubt If I could ever started them. Cap't Bateman met them and offered assistance if required but they required none, had plenty. I hope this statement will be sufficient to enable you to close this part of your business.

Respectfully
your ob't Serv't
John Page capt &
Sup't Creeks

Honorable
A. Iverson
Washington City

Miscellaneous Letters of Creek Relocation

Page reports turning over 2,500 Creek prisoners to John W. A. Sanford and Company and reports that he has notified the Upper Creeks that they are required to be in camp for relocation by 10 August 1836. Letter found at SIAC, Agent (J. W. A. Sanford), Account (66), Year (1837), NARA.

Rec'd 2d Aug't
an'd 3 Aug't

Tuskeegee Alabama 20th July 1836

Sir

I have the honor to report that I turned over to the contractors to take to Arkansas 2500 hostile Indians I accompanied them to Montgomery alabama where they took water under the direction of Lieut Barry. I have just returned from a town among the upper creeks. I gave them a talk to assemble the 10th of next month to prepare for emigration at first they were much astonished (as they said) that they were to be rushed off so soon but when I explained their situation they yielded to my talk.

The ballance will be taken off on the old plan an officer will accompany each party, as things stand I cannot estimate what the expence per head will be, at all events I shall endeavour to get them off as soon as possible I am so much engaged I have not time to communicate to the department as I would wish. Lieu't Bateman is with me but is very sick consequently I have to attend to every thing.

I have received a Draft on the Branch Bank of Alabama at mobile for Twenty thousand Dollars. I will thank you to forward me blanks of various Kinds as a great many will be required, Blank bonds, contracts of agreement property returned. I have plenty on hand all others are required.

With respect
I have the honor to be
Your obt Servant
John Page Capt &
Sup't Creek Rem'l

Brig'r Gen'l George Gibson
Com Gen'l Sub'e
Washington City

☾

This letter—misdated as 6 August, instead of (probably) 6 September—reports on the movements of the various detachments of relocating Creek

Indians. Letter found at Records of the Adjutant General's Office, 1780s–1917, Entry 159-Q, Records of Major General Thomas S. Jesup, Container 19, Folder: "Letters Received Relating to Creek and Seminole Affairs, August 1836," NARA.

West Wetumpka, alabama
6th August 1836

Sir,

I have the honor to report that the Wetumpka Indians are all on their way to their New Homes: they camped four Miles from this place last night. The party is in charge of Lieut't R. B. Scrivens and consists of 3000 Indians.

Opoethle Yoholo's party in charge of Lieut Batman consists of 2,700 Indians and started Westward on the 1st instant. The Talladega Indians are also on their way for Arkansas as reported by Lieut't Deas who has charge of that District, and consists of about 3,800 or more.

The number of Hostile Indians shipped from Montgomery by water, on their way West, was 2,361.

From the foregoing report you will please find, that as near as can be ascertained at this time—the total number of Emigrating Indians—is 11,861.

With respect
I have the honor to be
General
Your Ob't Servant
John Page
Captain & Superintendant Creek Rem'l

Major Gen'l Tho's S. Jesup
Commanding army of the South
Montgomery, al'a

Another misdated letter from Captain John Page reports on the movements of various camps of Creek Indians. Letter found at CGS-IRW, Roll 6, 192.

Rec'd 16th Sept

Wetumpka, Alabama
6th August 1836

Sir,

I have the honor to report that on the 30th of last month, I turned over to the contractors a party of Indians headed by Opoethle Yoholo, and in charge of Lieut't Bateman; the Muster Roll calls for 2,700 Indians and they started on the 1st instant.

Another party headed by Wm McGilbray[66] turned over to the contractors on the 25th ult'o—have started this day in charge of Lieut't Scrivens and consists of ab't 3,000 Indians.

Lieut't Deas has charge of the Talladega District and from his last report about 3,800 were turned over to the contractors yesterday and are also, to be started this day.

I leave here tomorrow for the lower Creeks and will report on my arrival there—the situation &c. I have had so much to attend to, that it has been impossible for me to make reports as the regulations require:—but all vigilance on my part will be used to get the Indians off.

With respect
I have the honor to be, General
Your Ob't Servant
John Page
Captain & Superintendant Creeks

Brig'r Gen'l Geo Gibson
Comm'y Gen'l Sub'ce
Washington City

☾

Jesup reports on the movement of the detachments of relocating Creeks and the progress in raising a force to fight the Seminoles in Florida. Letter found at Records of the Adjutant General's Office, 1780s–1917, Entry 159-Q, Records of Major General Thomas S. Jesup, Container 20, Folder: "Documents Relating to the Creek War (1 of 3)," NARA.

Head Quarters Army of the South
Montgomery, ala: Sep't 5th 1836

Sir

I came hither to day to Examine into the state of the supplies on hand, and of selecting and forwarding such as may be spared from the service in this Country, for the use of the troops destined for Florida.

On my way to this place I passed Wetumpka, where there are about three thousand Indians who are to cross the Coosa to day, and take up their line of march westward. Hopoth-le-Yohola whose departure I reported a few days ago, is on his way to the west, with two thousand three hundred of his band—about four thousand, will move in a day or two from Talladega, if they have not moved already, and I hope to have the whole nation in motion by the 20th Except the families of some of the warriors who go to Florida whom I have consented to allow to remain until the warriors return.

Being able to dispense with the services of the Tennessee Volunteers I directed Brig'r Gen'l Armstrong[67] several days ago to proceed with them to Florida by Easy marches. I this day ordered the regular troops to concentrate at Fort Mitchell and Irwinton, they are dispersed, generally in single companies from Irwinton to Tallassee, a distance of a hundred & twenty miles, they will be pushed on to Florida about the 20th; and I hope to send under Captain Lane[68] from six hundred to a thousand Indian Warriors. This force, if the Seminoles can be found, should put an End to the war there in all October.

I have the honor to be Sir
Your Obt Servant
(signed) Thos. S. Jesup
Maj: Gen'l Com'g

Honb'le
Lewis Cass[69]
Secretary of War

☾

Edward Hanrick, one of the partners in the Alabama Emigrating Company, reports that all of the Upper Creeks will soon be in motion despite the presence of whites harassing the parties and stealing their horses. Letter found at Records of the Adjutant General's Office, 1780s–1917, Entry 159-Q, Records of Major General Thomas S. Jesup, Container 19, Folder: "Letters Received Relating to Creek and Seminole Affairs, September-December 1836," NARA.

Montgomery 9th September 1836

Maj'r Gen'l Thos S. Jesup

Dear Sir,

I arrived here last night from Twenty Two miles from Wetumpka where I left the Wetumpka Indians which party Consists of over three Thousand all going on well, with the exception of white men following and Stealing ponies and horses and harrassing the Indians for debt. Col Young[70] the Sheriff of Tallapoosa County that [had] the head Chief of the ufala Indians in Custety for debt has let him go finding that no person would do nothing further. We had to Send Waggons up after the balance of the Indians from Wetumpka, and I met yoholo micco[71] yesterday going on the way after the party. So that party will go on well, and all the Indians in the upper part of the nation is in motion, I understand that you will have to Send an order to Lieut. Bateman who has charge of the Tuckebatchee party of Indians respecting the payment of the anuity for 1837 and for other matters. I shall have to See them near Columbus Mississippi or in that State, and if you Should have any dispatches to Send on I will take them with pleasure.[72] I shall not leave untill I shall hear from you or untill you Shall Send on the order.

I have the pleasure to be
Your [obedient] and
Humble Servant
Edwd Hanrick

N.B. I send you a bundle of News papers by mail

E.H.

☾

William Armstrong reports on the meeting between Opothle Yoholo and Roly McIntosh and the strong feelings between the two parties. He also requests that some of the blankets designated for the Seminoles be given to the Creeks. Letter found at LR, CAE, Roll 238, 6–7.

Choctaw Agency
24 Dec 1836

C. A. Harris Esq'r
Comm'r of Ind affr's

Sir

I have just returned from Fort Gibson where I went for the purpose of seeing the Creek emigrants—there is now en camped around Fort Gibson about ten thousand of the Creeks—as I anticipated there is much feeling between the McIntosh party and those who have lately emigrated with their chief A poth le ho lo—the principal chiefs of each party met and appeared friendly—Apoth le ho lo and his followers will settle upon the Canadian and will be removed from Roly McIntosh and his people some distance, this side seperate them and for the

FIG. 10. Yoholo Micco of Upper Eufaula. From McKenney and Hall, *History of the Indian Tribes of North America* (1842). Courtesy of the Alabama Department of Archives and History, Montgomery.

present prevent any difficulty and ensure peace amongst them unless the life of Apoth le ho lo should be attempted—or some momentary excitement brought about to produce a difficulty. I am satisfied that their is no organized plan—or design to produce bloodshed between those parties Yet their is much excitement between the chiefs on both sides and the tribes immediately adjacent would be well pleased to see the breach widen. It is agreed between the parties that so soon as the emigrants now on their way arrive in their new country that a General council will be held at which I am to attend—they will probably be a month or two—I have directed the Sub agent to issue the blankets & to those arriving I fear those will not be a sufficiency to complete the issue—there are some five or six hundred Blankets designed for the Seminoles at Little Rock which Capt Brown will immediately send up—there is also some other goods such as Surveys & designed for the Seminoles—could any arrangement be made to give them to the Creeks—the Seminoles here have been supplied and the overplus is in consequence of the few who emigrated—

Capt Brown is now here preparing to pay the Choctaw annuity and from here proceed to Red river and furnish the nation—

Respectfully
Your Obt Serv't
Wm Armstrong
act Supt West'n Ter'y

☾

Captain James R. Stephenson reports on the issuance of rations and a correction to the muster roll of detachment 1. Letter found at LR, CAE, Roll 238, 705–6.

Fort Gibson
3rd January 1837

Sir

Your communication of the 2nd and 19th November have been received—The Rifles and Blankets directed to be turned over to Lieut Vanhorn[73] are ready whenever called for, there has never been any kettles in my possession. —On the opposite page you will find a statement showing the number of Creeks emigrated by the Alabama Emigrating Company and received by me.—The whole of the emigrants with the exception of 395 (Lieut Sprague and Co'l Gibsons party) was stopped at Fort Gibson by Order of Brig. Gen'l M Arbuckle, A contract for furnishing them with Subsistence during their encampment in this Vicinity was made by Cap't J Brown Prin'l disb'g ag't.—These Indians will all be on their own lands in the course of a day or two. So far Subsistence has been furnished them according to contract, in a few days the greater portion of them will move to the Canadian a distance of from 50 to 60 Miles from this place.—This location was not anticipated by the contractors, he has informed me that it is out of his power to furnish the corn part of the ration in consequence the difficulty of obtaining transportation in addition to the high price of corn—As the contractor has used every exertion in his power to comply with his contract and as he has an abundance of Beef and hogs on hand I have consented for him to continue to furnish the meat and Salt part of the ration and have taken it upon myself to furnish the corn on the best terms possible.—

When I Certified the Roll of the party of emigrant Creeks accompanied by Captain Batman and Dr Ingersoll I failed to deduct therefrom 37 Warriors who went to Florida in the Service of the U States—This Roll as it now stands calls for 2358 persons whereas the number should be 2321 as stated in the Opposite page.

I have written to Cap't John Page U.S. Army princ'l disb'g Ag't Creek emigration in relation to this alteration in the Roll.—

Very Respectfully
Your Ob't Sv't
Ja's R. Stephenson

Capt. U.S. Army
Disbg. Agt. (Creeks)

C A Harris Esq'r
Commissioner of Indian affairs
Washington DC

☾

William Armstrong reports that the situation of the Creeks is distressing as many are without clothing in the inclement weather. Letter found at LR, CAE, Roll 238, 26–27.

Choctaw Agency
January 27th 1837

C. A. Harris Esqr
Com'r Ind affrs

Sir

I enclose you the copy of a letter from Gen'l Arbuckle; and also two bills of the purchase of blankets made by Mr Audrain.[74] Upon recieving the letter of Gen'l Arbuckle, I wrote Mr audrain to purchase what blankets he could at Gibson, from the Suttlers; and in accordance therewith, he made the purchase of the enclosed bills. I had not then recieved your letter stating that an agent had been sent to New York, to purchase blankets. Upon recieving this information, I wrote to Mr audrain to cease to purchase. As yet no information, further, has been recieved, of the purchase made in New York.

The situation of the Emigrating Creeks is truly distressing—many of them are naked; and the weather most inclement. There is now, no alternative left, but to await the arrival of the blankets expected from New York, as there are no others in the country.[75] The Indians complain that they were promised these things when leaving their nation, and knowing their destitute and suffering condition, myself; and upon the letter of Gen'l Arbuckle I directed Mr Audrain to purchase what he could to supply a party then arriving under charge of Lieutenant Scrivner; and note the Department will sanction the purchase and direct it to be paid.

I have the honor to be
Your Ob't Servant
Wm Armstrong
act. Supt. West'n Ter'y

Captain John Page explains the reasons for the monetary losses incurred by John W.A. Sanford and Company. Of note is Opothle Yoholo's order directing the Creeks at the Wetumpka camp (detachment 2) not to move until he gives the word. Letter found at LR, CAE, Roll 238, 544–45.

Fort Mitchell Al'a
20 February 1837

Sir

I have the honour to acknowledge the receipt of your letter 6th February with an account claimed by J.W.A. Sandford & Co for removing a party of Hostile Indians, and extra expence occurred. This Company since the contract, have been busily engaged endeavouring to move the Creek Indians. They spared no pains or expense to fulfil the contract; at last succeeded in moving a small party of between five and six hundred.[76] The company stated to me they had lost considerable money on this party besides all their labour, but under the circumstances which they had taken the contract they would go through with it if possible. I encouraged them all I could to persevere. They had previous to the war's breaking out a considerable number encamped that they were feeding but Yo pothe la hola sent word to this camp of Indians not to move until he said the word. I heard of this and went to this chief for the purpose of prevailing on him to direct this Town of Indians to start, but he would not consent until I had made a proposition to the War Department to have the land claims settled. I made known his proposition to the War Department. The company still remained in the nation with a hope to effect something. This Chief was not opposed to being moved by the Company, but his only object was to hold out until he could effect his object in the land business. My ambition was to make a break with the upper Creeks (knowing at the same time) war was brewing with the lower Creeks, which facts I reported at the time. In a short time afterwards the War commenced and the Company gave up all hopes of doing any thing, and discharged their teams, Agents &c. After the War was supposed to have been brought to a close about nineteen hundred or two thousand Indians were in confinement at this place, and about the time I was to start, the Contract with this company expired. I requested General Jesup to issue the order to move them on a certain day, which I think, it was the day before the contract ceased, or the same day, so I could turn them over, as I discovered it was impossible for me to move them for a number of days. I immediately notified the Company, but they did not feel bound to move them knowing it would be ruinous to them unless they were compensated. I stated to them I would represent their situation and do all I could to aid them in a just settlement. If I had moved them on account of the U. States with all the economy I could have practised I could not have done better for the Government or moved them for a less sum, than the amount claimed by the Company.

With respect
I have the honour to be
Your Ob't Serv't
John Page Cap't &
Sup't Creek Removal

C A Harris Esq'r
Com'r of Indian Affairs
Washington City

15 Detachment 6

The sixth detachment was based at three camps in the former Creek Nation—Fort Mitchell, Echo Harjo's, and Polecat Springs—and consisted of the family members of the warriors fighting the Seminoles in Florida. Due to threats of arrest and violence by white militias, the camps were consolidated and moved to Mobile Point, Alabama, before relocation to Pass Christian, Mississippi. After their tour of duty was over the warriors joined detachment 6 on the Gulf. The most prominent headman of this party was Jim Boy, a Red Stick during the first Creek War (1813–14), who aided the United States against the Seminoles. The party was conducted to Indian territory by William A. Campbell and William J. Beattie on behalf of the Alabama Emigrating Company. Captain John Page of the 4th U.S. Infantry, Lieutenant John George Reynolds[1] of the U.S. Marine Corps, Lieutenant Thomas Theodore Sloan[2] of the U.S. Marine Corps, and Captain Mark W. Bateman of the 6th U.S. Infantry served as military oversight. Only Sloan accompanied the party up the Mississippi River as Bateman died on 31 July 1837; Page was ordered to Indian territory to pay out the rest of the Watson contract money in August 1837; and Reynolds became ill at Pass Christian, Mississippi and remained behind to recuperate in New Orleans.[3] Drs. John M. Woodfin, Gustavus Adolphus Nott,[4] and George W. Hulse were the attending physicians. When Nott became sick on the Gulf, he was replaced by Dr. Edmund Wiedemann.[5]

☾

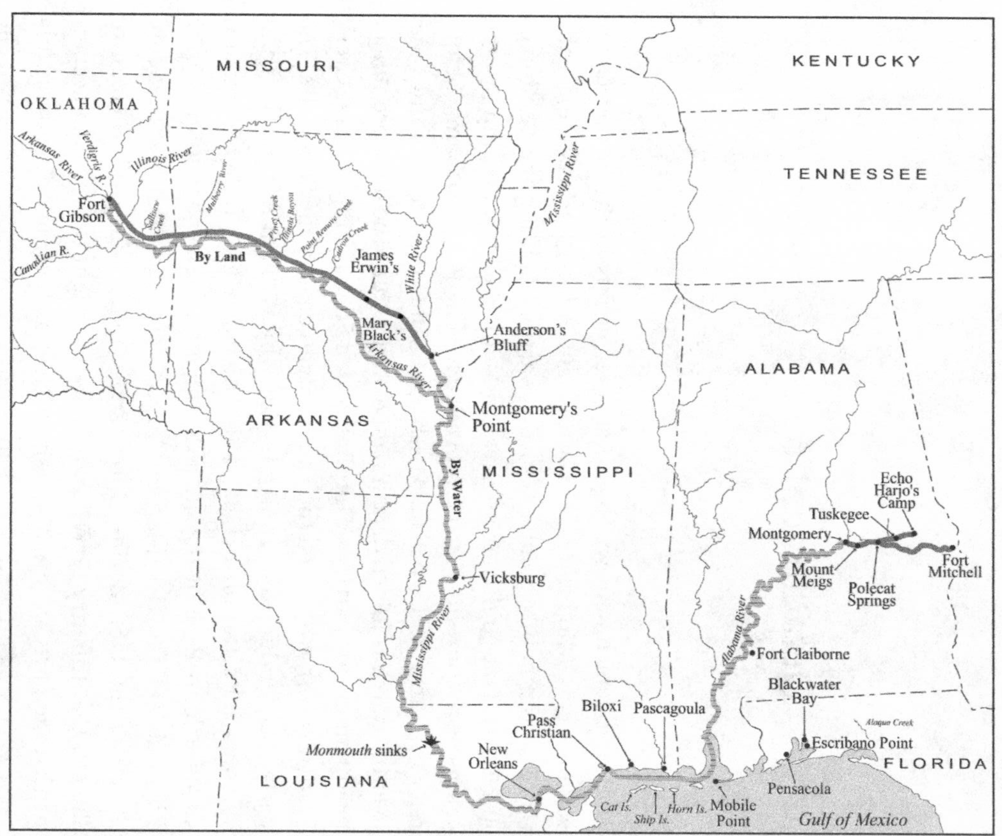

MAP 14. Route of detachment 6, March–December 1837 or January 1838. Place names correspond to stopping points or locations noted in the documentation. Route lines and locations are approximations. Route through the Mississippi Sound to Pass Christian may have required brief passage into the Gulf around Dauphin Island due to shallow water; see Lynn M. Alperin, *History of the Gulf Intracoastal Waterway*, 7–9. The location of Anderson's Bluff (approximately fifty miles south of the mouth of Cache) is from Frank M. Cayton, *Landings on All the Western and Southern Rivers* (1881), and A. E. Sholes, *Directory of the Taxing District of Memphis* (1883), 28. Cartography by Sarah Mattics and Kiersten Fish.

Lieutenant Thomas T. Sloan reports on the presence of "hostiles" (Creeks still participating in the Second Creek War) in and around Echo Harjo's camp and the desire of local white militias to remove the Creek men and boys to Tuskegee. This letter is one of the enclosures mentioned in Page's 21 February letter. Letter found at LR, CAE, Roll 238, 514–18.

(Copy)

Echo Harjos Camp
7th February 1837

Sir

I avail myself of the first leisure moments to acquaint you with the situation of this camp, and the scenes that have been enacted within the last few days. Immediately on learning the depredations that had been committed on the property of Dr Battle[6] I ordered the Indians at this camp to surrender their guns and remove within a smaller compass; that I could more conveniently observe their movements and prevent any intercourse with those that were still assuming a hostile attitude.

This order was promptly complied with by the old original camp of friendly Indians; and in less than twenty four hours sixty three guns were deposited in my quarters and the families (with but one <u>or</u> two exceptions, and those by my permission) were assembled within the space of less than one mile square. Those Hostiles who on the promise of protection had come into this camp, some time previous, refused to comply with my requisitions and during the night precipitantly left the camp. I presume to join their associates in arms.

These facts were forthwith communicated to you and such citizens as called on me for information.—A few days after the Hostiles had left this Camp I was informed by one of the friendly Indians that a small party was encamped about 20 miles North of this place on the Suchi Pocar Creek—I immediately assembled about 30 Warriors and went in pursuit of them the men fled and we took their women and children. I afterwards learned that two of their party was mortally wounded and have since died. This measure rendered the Indians, at this camp, as well as myself obnoxious to the Hostiles and I deemed it prudent, for our own safety, to return a part of the guns to the Warriors, this was not done until I received undoubted intelligence that they had been lying in wait for several nights, around my quarters and the houses of some of the principal men in this camp—Indeed my life and many of the friendly Indians had been threatened and one of them actually fired upon; their houses that had been recently abandoned broken open & pillaged, and their stock destroyed by the Hostiles, some of whom, who were still lurking in the neighbourhood had so enraged the friendly Indians at this camp that they proposed to go in pursuit of them—I consulted some of the Citizens of the neighborhood on the propriety of the measure, and it received their hearty Cooperation & I was making arrangements to fit out an expedition against them, when I received a note from Capt's Welborn[7] Jornigan[8] & Morris, asking an interview with me at the "Creek Stand". On meeting those gentlemen I learned with astonishment their intention of removing indiscriminately all the Indians at this camp to some point without the limits of their former territory—I expressed my decided disapprobation of the measure, and repeated to them the uniform and friendly disposition of those Indians towards the whites—That they were the first to take up arms against their own people and colour, in defence of the lives and protection of the property of the whites who had abandoned their homes—That they had sent 120 warriors to Florida, who were now side by side with the white troops encountering the fatigues of a Campaign and the dangers of the battle field to bring the Seminoles to subjection and restore peace to that distressed Country. That the faith of the Government had been solemnly pledged that their families should remain where they were and be fed and protected during their absence & that they had done nothing to forfeit that pledge. That the few remaining men left to mind their stock & assist their women and children, were willing at any time to join the whites and drive the hostiles from the swamps—That no intercourse had or would take place between them since they left this Camp—That the course suggested by them would be, in effect, reviving the same what exploded savage custom of wreaking vengeance on the innocent for the acts of the guilty—That the aggressors were now in the swamps and that it would be more humane & Soldierlike to pursue them, and chastise them than molest a few unarmed men & women & children—That any representations of the unfriendly character of this Camp, must have been obtained from persons remote and consequently unacquainted with its situation—That I lived in their midst, and appealed to every Citizen adjacent to the camps for the confirmation of what I said.

My ambition was then appealed to, and the need of glory, that awaited me was pointed out in glowing colours If I would give my consent, and join in this unhallowed crusade against our friends and allies—I informed them that I spurned distinction acquired by committing an outrage on the innocent & defenceless, and setting at defiance the plighted faith of my Government—That it was my duty as it was my pleasure, to render the settler every protection in my power and the most speedy and effectual means of doing this, was to hunt down and slaughter those hostiles that were laying waste the Country—It is due to Capt. Welborn that he acquiesced in my suggestions, and as a high minded gentleman & brave officer repaired where honour and duty called him, to scour the swamps and rid his country of their only enemies.

The interview being over I supposed the matter was at an end at least for the present—But on Sunday afternoon while superintending the issues of provisions I was astonished to find the men women and children driven up to my quarters at the point of the bayonet by a band of armed men led by Mr Jernigan. They seemed to have come without any settled purpose; at one time determined to pursue one course, then another. I used all the arguments with them that I had on a former occasion, and after keeping them guarded till ten oclock on Monday, without any thing to Eat and but few instances a blanket to cover them, they resolved to remove the men and boys to Tuskegee & encamp the women & children immediately around my quarters. I protested against the course they pursued as unnecessary unjust and uncalled for, by the occasion, but as they had the physical force they could do as they pleased. I have got the women pretty comfortably fixed and I do hope, as the action of the Government may be soon expected that I may not be again troubled by the unauthorised visit of irresponsible and self Constituted officers and soldiers.

I am with very great
respect Your Ob't Serv't
(Signed) T.T. Sloan
Lt & Mil Agent

Capt John Page
Commd'g in Creek nation

☾

Page reports on moving the families of the warriors fighting in Florida into three camps for their oversight and safety. But with the resumption of the Second Creek War in late 1836, Page is under increasing pressure to relocate these family members to the Gulf of Mexico. Letter found at LR, CAE, Roll 238, 508–10.

Fort Mitchell Al'a
9th February 1837

Sir

I have the honour to acknowledge the receipt of your letter dated 27th of last month requireing information relative to Creek Indians now remaining in the Creek Nation &c.

General Jessup issued an order requiring me to make arrangements to move all the Indians in the Creek Nation. I accordingly directed the contractors to make arrangements for that purpose, which they did. He was endeavouring at the same time to raise a Regiment of Creek Warriors, to go to Florida, several days elapsed before this object could be effected. At last, two or three towns of Indians, consented to go, on a certain condition (that is) if the families and connexions of the Warriors were permitted to remain in the Emigrating Camps they were then located and subsisted by the United States and protected until the Warriors returned, on these conditions the Indians consented. These were the arrangements made in council by Gen'r Jessup. Three camps were designated Viz, one at Polecat Springs, one at Echo Harjo's thirty miles East of Polecat Springs, and one at this place. L't Reynolds was directed to take charge of the Indians at Polecat Springs and L't Sloan at Echo Harjo's. I took charge of the Indians at this place, with a general Superintendence of the whole. General Jessup directed the Q'r Master's to furnish funds and provisions when required, since which time they have been ordered to Florida and I have furnished the means to subsist them. If General Jessup entered into any stipulations in writing with the warriors, I do not know it. I do know they were to remain here and subsisted by the U. States, until the warriors returned; I understood this was sanctioned by the President of the United States, but nothing to this effect was furnished me in writing. I supposed as a matter of course General Jessup had informed the Department on the subject. There is a great deal of excitement in the country in consequence of the late depredations that have been committed. What few warriors I have here, I have put them inside the Fort for <u>their</u> protection. The warriors at Echo Harjo's camp have also been put into the Pickets at Tuskegee. I have directed L't Reynolds to disarm all the warriors at Polecat Springs, and put a chain of sentinels around them, this is to let the Citizens know, there is no communication with the friendly Indians and the Hostiles that are now out. I thought at one time it would be out of my power to prevent the different companies that had collected, from killing the women and children. I am placed in a very awkward situation, committees calling on me, and Volunteer companies that I have mustered into service and expresses every day, to have me move these Indians to Mobile Point, and there to remain until the warriors return from Florida. My house is thronged from morning till night. I hope the government will take some steps to have them removed out of this nation to some place, I dislike to see the innocent punished for the guilty, and it must be the case so long as they remain here. I have no funds to subsist these people, and the Contractors are calling on me constantly. The Indians were left here pledged by General Jessup to be subsisted by the United States. The Emigrating Company are ready to receive them and move them to any point you may designate. I hope positive instructions will be given me and the means furnished to carry them into execution.

With respect
I have the honour to
be Your Ob't Serv't
John Page Capt
4th Infantry Comd'g &
Sup't Creek Removal

C A Harris Esq'r
Com'r of Indian Affairs
Washington City

☾

This letter, written by members of a company of Alabama Volunteers reports on the circumstances surrounding the apprehension of the Creek men at the encampments and the murder of and an elderly man by members of a white militia. This letter is one of the enclosures mentioned in Page's 21 February letter. Letter found at LR, CAE, Roll 238, 519–22.

(Copy)

Camp near Polecat Springs Al'a
19th February 1837

Sir,

It becomes necessary for us to communicate to you a painful circumstance happened last evening and one sir which is lamented by us and much disapprobated. In obedience to your request Capt Young's[9] Company repaired to this place for the aid of Lieut Reynolds—on its march formed a juncture with Capt Wilburn's, Harold's and Park's[10] companies who were on their way to the Indian camps near the Pole cat Springs, under the charge of Lt Reynolds—there to take into charge the warriors and place them into pickets; so that they might be conveniently guarded then the settlers of the country would no longer be excited, we proceeded to the Calebee when we despatched Lt Broadnax, to apprize the Lieut of our intentions and requested his Co-operation. He met us without delay, and readily acquiesced (but before we arrived at Calebee Capt Young received an express from the Lieut giving a list of such Indians as was permitted by him to remain on their improvements, this information was given to the different officers of companies all such as was not permitted to remain, he requested to be brought forthwith to him, and some he cared not how rough they were treated, for they had been very disobedient) requesting the officers to delay a small time to enable him to collect all the Indians together, that he had ordered all the warriors to assemble this day by 12 Oclock we proceeded at one Oclock to the camps and in a few minutes came in sight of the issuing house. When Capt Welburn & Young repaired to it, finding that the Lieutenant had discharged the duties confided in him in bringing the Indians, together. The Troops were ordered to surround the Indians which was done without the least resistance. The Indians appeared not at all alarmed, being of course anticipated by them. The Lieut treated us with every attention. He requested us to picket them in this vicinity this course was apposed by the company of Citizens from Russell with some of the other officers of which it was decided for the warriors to be confined at Tuskeegee.

About Eight Oclock at night we were alarmed with the fire of guns—orders immediately issued for the persons so offending to be gone in search of. Capt Young Parke & Lt Broadnax proceeded to near where the guns was supposed to have been fired, and to their surprise met with several men of Capt Parks company coming in. On meeting them, they stated Indians men had been seen near a swamp at fire and on their approach they broke and ran, they were then fired on, they then came into camp, nothing was more said believeing that nothing further of the kind would take place. A few moments afterwards we were again alarmed with a voley of guns in the same direction only further off. Lieutenant Reynolds exclaimed against such conduct stating he believed the Troops were murdering his innocent women and children for He was concious no men were out only a few sick and old which he had reported, in the day Gen'l Wilburn being much astonished at this, kind of conduct immediately summoned a few of his command, and went in person after the perpetrators. On reaching the place of firing He found several of the same company, about one mile from the camp and to his great mortification the band had killed a very old man of Jim boys Town by shooting and mashing his head. The General was not satisfied with his search for damage done, this morning went in company with Lt Reynolds Lt Stone and Gen'l Woodward,[11] and discovered, a small girl wounded, no further damages is yet ascertained, but from the number of guns fired we anticipate other mischief is done. Those circumstances caused us to come to the conclusion, to move the Camp West of Line Creek which was acceeded to by Lt Reynolds and shall take up the line of march day after to morrow   we were influenced to this course, from a belief that the settlers and Indians would not be safe otherwise. We hope that it will meet your approbation, and ample means will be furnished for their subsistence. The Indians are selling off everything they have and will be ready for moving in a few days.

With Great respect
Your Ob't Serv'ts
(Signed) Benj Young Cap't
Alabama Volunteers
(Signed) John H Broadnax Lt
Alabama Volunteers
(Signed) Cha's Stone 1st Lt
Alabama Volunteers

Cap't Jno Page
Emigrating Creek Agent
Fort Mitchell

☾

Lieutenant John G. Reynolds reports on the harassment of his camp by members of the Russell County militia who want to place the Creek men in pickets at Tuskegee. Reynolds has decided to move the camp to a safer location. This letter is one of the enclosures mentioned in Page's 21 February letter. Letter found at LR, CAE, Roll 238, 531–33.

Copy

Indian Issuing House
near Polecat Springs Al'a
19th February 1837

Sir

Since my last communication, my camp has been invaded by a force composed of three US companies of volunteers, and one composed of citizens of Russell County, on the approach of this force I met them at Durants and protested against any measures calculated to render the situation of the warriors uncomfortable, that I would convince them by occular demonstration that the Indians were perfectly peaceable and willing to submit to any terms I might suggest. I arranged a plan by which all the warriors were surrounded and made prisoners without difficulty, to shew you that they had perfect confidence in me and believed in my talk, instead of being frightened, as most persons would suppose, they jumped upon logs and appeared quite amused, at the unnecessary measures adopted to make prisoners of them—the Roll was called by me, and every Indian with the exception of some few old men who were absent with my permission in consequence of <u>old</u> age answered to their names—After which I gave up the camp to Gen'l Welborn a gentleman by the by that possesses the stern qualities of the soldier, and with whom I am much pleased, he stationed his troops in such a manner as to prevent any possible escape of the warriors, but I regret to inform you that in the course of the night a part of the <u>Russell County gentleman Company</u> attacked all the camps in the vicinity, stripped them of Provisions and <u>difiled</u> the helpless women moreover, Sir, shot an innoffensive old man of Jim Boys Town and wounded a young girl. My feelings could not passively brook such conduct and I called upon

General Welborn for protection, in as much as he had taken me and the warriors prisoners I demanded protection at his hands he freely extended it and advised with me the course necessary to pursue. I told him for his as well as my honour, it was of the utmost consequence that Company (Russell) should be disarmed, by so doing, it would reestablish me in the estimation of the Indians, for you cannot but allow that my talk proved eroneous, as every promise (in the event of submission) was made to wit that with my life protection should be afforded to them. I feel yet sour at the conduct of these men, I cannot say gentlemen.

It was the avowed determination of all to carry them to Tuskeegee and place them in the pickets to which I in a written communication protested, assigning for reason it was contrary to your wish for the Indians to be joined with those of Lt Sloan's, nothing but the breaking up of the Camp would satisfy them. I then made a proposition to remove them out of the nation provided the men were permitted to remain with their families they assented to this at the instance of General Welborn. I have therefore concluded to Remove the whole camp the day after to morrow to some convenient place beyond M't Meiggs which I hope will meet with your approbation indeed, Sir, I am now not in a situation to give in detail all the occurrences of my camp, but will make a full Report at a future period. The Indians I am happy to say do not murmer at any order I deem necessary to give I therefore feel bound to do all in my power to afford them comfort—Will the half breeds of every description Emigrate? Your answer to this will oblige.

Your Ob't Serv't
Signed, Jno G Reynolds
1st Lieut U.S.M.C.
& Military Agent

Capt John Page
Emigrating Creek Agent

☾

Captain John Page notifies the commissioner of Indian affairs that he has taken measures to try and protect the warriors' families from local militias. This letter includes three enclosures (Sloan to Page, 7 February 1837; Reynolds to Page, 9 February 1837; Young et al. to Page, 19 February 1837). Letter found at LR, CAE, Roll 238, 512–13.

Fort Mitchell Al'a
21st February 1837

Sir

I have the honour herewith to enclose letters from Lieut's Sloan and Reynolds Military agents and one from Capt: Young commanding a company of Alabama Mounted Volunteers. Lt Sloan's camp was the first that was surrounded. After all was quiet I took measures immediately to secure the Indians under the charge of Lt Reynolds, had all of them disarmed, and the Rifles boxed up and transported to montgomery. I then directed Capt: Young's company of Mounted Volunteers, to proceed to Pole cat springs and keep the Indians at that point, inside the chain of sentinels, and to assure the people all was correct. I also explained to this company or collection of Citizens, every measure was taken by me for the security of the Indians at Pole cat springs, and requested them to desist, lest they should do <u>acts</u>, that would bring disgrace upon themselves.

The enclosed letters will show their <u>acts</u> and the situation of the Indians, and in the mean time I think it will lessen the sympathies that have been manifested for the settlers in this section of country. The first camp that was visited by these people was the one I have charge of, I asked them the object of their visit I saw they were much excited I reasoned with them, and stated to them if massacre was their object, they could commence at once (pointing to five or six Indian children playing in the road and to an old woman that was sitting upon a log near my quarters.) I stated to them that what few warriors were here I had disarmed them, and had them under perfect controll. I then sent for them and directed them to go into the Pickets which order was promptly obeyed. I still have them there under the sentinels.

With respect
I have the honour to be

Your Ob't Serv't
John Page Capt &
Sup't Creek

C. A. Harris Esq'r
Com'r of Indian Affairs
Washington City

☾

Page reports that he has been ordered to move the families of the warriors fighting in Florida to Mobile Point, Alabama, and that the party will leave the following day. Page also reports that the Watson contract has been approved. Letter found at Records of the Adjutant General's Office, 1780s–1917, Entry 159-Q, Records of Major General Thomas S. Jesup, Container 14, Folder: "Letters Received from Officers, Captain John Page," NARA.

Fort Mitchell Ala'a
6th March 1837

Sir.

I have the honour to report, since my last communication no depredations have been committed. I have received orders to move all the Indians now in this nation to mobile point, there to await the arrival of the Warriors in Florida, who are ordered to meet their families at that point. I presume you have received the order before this. I acted under the orders I found at this post, for the government of the commanding Officer after you withdrew the Troops, and mustered into service seven companies of Volunteers. I start all the Indians tomorrow, what few are out I think will join us on the road. I shall direct all the Volunteers to search up whoever may be found lurking in the bush, and kill them if they find them. I think all will be quiet after I leave here. General Wellborn will be commanding officer of the Creek Nation after this date. I had an Election and he was elected Colonel. The contract you made with a company for the purchase of the fraudulent claims, is approved of by the President and I am directed to proceed there, and pay out the money to each individual, agreeable to the contract. I am also directed to proceed with the Indians. Lieu't R A Luther[12] is now in command of this post.

With respect
I have the honour to be
Your Ob't Serv't
John Page Capt
4th Infy Comd'g

Major Gen'l Tho's S Jesup
Commanding the Creek Campaign
Tampa Bay
East Florida

☾

Page assigns John Sims to go to Florida and bring a detachment of warriors to Mobile Point to meet their families. Letter found at SIAC, Agent (Page), Account (1701-B), Year (1838), NARA.

Fort Mitchell Alab
6th march 1837

Sir,

You are hereby appointed an Assistant agent in the Creek Removal to take affect from date. I must Request you to proceed immediately to Apalachicola and if any of the Creek warriors that went from this nation have arrived there, I wish you to take them to mobile Point where they will meet their families. Explain to them the cause of this movement and should they arrive their in large companies please show this to the officer in charge and make arraingements with the same conveyance that brings them there to proceede to mobile point if possible and I will see him paid for so doing—If this cannot bee arrainged, you are authorised to charter such boats or other transportation as circumstances Require.

John Page Capt 4th Inft'y
Sup't Creek Removal

John Sims Esqui
Asst Agent creek Emigration

N.B.
If you find any stragling Indians at the bay or any other point that belongs to this nation I wish you to arrest them and if necessary put them in Jail for safe Keeping and if you can take them to mobile Point I wish you to do so, three or four women have absconded from this camp and I am told they have been taken off in a Steam boat, please notice and find out if possible what boat took them off and the pearsons detaining them so I can commence a prosecution.

J Page

Should you not find the warriors at Apalachicola you will proceed to where you can find them.

John Page
capt Sup't creeks

☾

Page reports on the partial movement of the Creek volunteer families to Mobile Point and notes that he sent an agent to Florida to notify the warriors of this decision. Letter found at LR, CAE, Roll 238, 563.

Columbus Ga
18th March 1837

Sir

I have the honour to forward Duplicate muster Rolls of Creek Indians delivered to the agent west. There is no reason I can advance why the Emigrating company should not receive the amount called for by the Rolls. I have just returned from Montgomery where I turned over all the Indians to the Emigrating company they have transported or got them on the way to Mobille Point about 2,000; the balance will be started immediately. I have made arrangements for the company to feed them after they arrive until they are met by the warriors in Florida agreeable to your instructions. I have sent an ass't Agent to meet the warriors in Florida and accompany them to the Point where their families are and to Explain to them the cause of this movement &c. I shall proceed tomorrow again to accompany the Indians, some few hostiles are yet in the swamp. I have three companies of volunteers now in pursuit of them, they refused to join the Indians after I had sent them word what their fate would be if they did not come in.

With respect
I have the honour to be
your ob't serv't
John Page Capt &
Sup't Creeks

C. A. Harris Esq'r
Com of Indian affas
Washington Cty

☾

Reynolds reports on the events that led to his party being moved from Fort Mitchell to Mount Meigs, Alabama, including the violence committed on the Creeks and the loss of their property at the hands of roving bands of militias. Letter found at "Lieut. Jno G. Reynolds journal, of a party of Creek Indians, about to Emegrate to the west of the Mississippi, commencing 19th February and Ending 19th October 1837," Princeton University, Princeton, New Jersey (hereafter Reynolds Journal, Princeton University). Reynolds's journal is here transcribed in its entirety, but because it consists largely of a collection of letters he sent and received, they are interspersed chronologically among documents found elsewhere.

Fort Morgan
Mobile Point
31st. March 1837

Major;

In obedience to your calls for information respecting the causes which led to the removal of the families of the Indian warriors now in Florida, from the Creek nation, and the losses, sustained by them in consequence of such removal, I have to state in answer to the first. That I am entirely ignorant as to any just cause for such a measure—my indians were perfectly friendly and obedient were ever ready to carry into effect any measure or requirement I might deem necessary to make with the exception of a few residing near to the late chief Tuskeniahaw's residence, and they were not at all times othewise disposed, but at periods when Tuskenia put forth his influence under the guidance of some few designing white men, I have had trouble.[13] When the settlers became agitated by the depredation committed on the plantation of Doct Battle on Cowiga Creek, I deemed it prudent and proper to ally their fears by calling in their rifles. I appointed a day for that purpose and attended in person for the reception of those, of Jim Boy's and Elk Co Hadjo's[14] warriors, all were forthcoming the day subsequent was allotted for the handing in of Tuskenia's people. From the previous conduct of Tuskenia, I was apprehensive my requirements would not be complied with, in which event Mr Felton[15] my principal assistant was directed to repair to Tuskeegee and report the result. My anticipations being realized, I arrested Tuskenia that night, and brought him to Tuskeegee where he was detained three days during which period twenty one rifles were handed in, and he made perfectly sensible of his situation, he was permitted to return to his house, since when, I have experience not the slightest difficulty, he has done much towards bringing his people into camp. These facts were duly reported to Capt Page, the Emigrating Creek agent and commanding officer of the nation

On the evening of 9th February after the warriors of Lt Slones Camp had been placed in the pickets at Tuskeegee, a company under Capt Harrold returning by the Old Federal road[16] haulted at the house of Anne Cornells[17] a half breed Indian, secured and carried away two free negroes and an indian boy besides setting fire to and wholly destroying all her houses fodder stacks and moveable property generally including three hundred dollars in Bank Bills. This Sir, I have from the suffering woman herself and who is, now on the point[18] subject to interogations by yourself, the stolen indian I am happy to say subsequently made his escape and is also with me

On the 19th Ulto. I was informed a body of Troops under the command of Capt Wellborn usually styled General, were within two miles of my Camp, whither it was their intention to repair, for the purpose of scouring it, and make prisoners of all the warriors, Capt Brodnax was the bearer of Capt Wellborns intention and also a request for me to meet him at Durants stage stand on the edge of Calebee swamp, fearful some depredations might be committed upon the indians, I repaired without loss of time to the place appointed and much to my chagrin and mortification found some six or Eight of my warriors already prisoners.

I demanded of Capt Wellborn his authority for thus invading my camp. His reply was, "the people." I solemly protested [against] the measure, that it was unnecessary and impolitick, the faith of the Government was pledged to the warriors in Florida that those remaining behind should be wholy unmolested by the citizens, and placed under the protection of the Government, that I was the agent sent them by the Government and felt bound and was determined to protect the indians, I was then given to understand the object of their march would be accomplished, notwithstanding my protest. I then beged Capt. Wellborn to appoint a committee to wait on me at the issuing house at 3 o clock P.M., when I would pledge myself to present all the warriors of my camp, to this they also objected and were still determined to drive the camps. Finding such to be their purpose I deemed it prudent to cooperate with them, in order to prevent alarm and save the indians from being driven into the swamps than good will to my unwelcome visitors. Capt. W. was willing to adhere to any course that I would suggest; stratagem and deception were my only resort to carry into effect the object in view to wit, a continuance of good faith on my part to the indians. I therefore advised the immediate release of the warriors in custody and the counter march of the forces beyond the Calebee swamp, there to remain until the arrival of a messenger from me, I had an understanding with Capt Wellborn that we should take a formal parting and when he should again make his appearance I would possitively insist upon his retireing without molesting the indians that he might find assembled for the purpose of being mustered (an every other day practise.) This I considered the only course of preserving my standing. At 2. o'clock the temporary chiefs reported their people ready for roll call when I despatched a messenger to Capt Wellborn who in a short time with four companies three of which were mustered into the service viz. Capt Wellborn's, Capt. Harrold's and Capt. Young's and a Mr Park, with a company of citizens from Russel County surrounded my Issuing Houses much to the ammusement of the indians, for instead of being alarmed were delighted at what they deemed an unnecessary movement towards makeing them prisoners. I had stationed my interpreter near in order every thing that transpired might be communicated to the indians which being done they appeared perfectly satisfied with the course that I had pursued. I then assured them their being made prisoners was not the act of the Government, on the contrary General Jesup would not countenance such proceedings to remain perfectly quiet and every thing would end satisfactory. Their reply was they looked to me for protection that thus far it had been afforded and they knew the Government would not now desert them. I reassured them all that General Jesup had promised their chiefs would be rigedly adhered to. They appeared and I have every reason to believe were satisfied.

I stated to Capt Wellborn that in as much as the warriors were in bondage and taken away from their wives and children, protection should be afforded the latter that I as also the indians were apprehensive the soldiers would annoy them, he gave me positive assurance that they should not be molested. In order to satisfy Capt. Wellborn who appeared more anxious to gain the applause of his disorganised soldiery than the public good I called the roll, and found of Two hundred and fifty three warriors, fourteen absent, some of whom had been excused from attending muster in consequence of sickness, old age &c. He was satisfied with the order of the camp or rather so expressed himself to me. A little after dark I heard the report of a musket in the direction of Thlobthlocco town (Jim Boys) I stated to Capt. W. it was unusual to hear a musket or rifle fired in the camps at that hour, I was apprehensive some mischief was being done by his troops, and beged a party might be despatched to ascertain the cause. Few moments had elapsed after makeing this requisition, when a second report of muskets was heard in another direction, I then told Capt. W. he afforded me no protection; The warriors were restless, telling me my toungue was forked, and for the first time I was holding bad talk. Capt W headed a party in person and set out in the direction of the fireing, about 11 o'clock he returned and informed me an old man was Killed and a little girl wounded that the marrauders belonged to a Mr. Park's Company of citizens of Russel County Alaba. I demanded of Capt. W. the arrest of the whole of that Company as it was the only course to pursue in order to satisfy my warriors, that unless it was adopted a stigma would rest upon him and further it would be the means of reestablishing me in their confidence. He assented and said possitively my wishes should be carried forthwith into effect, but such was not the case. On the following morning Mr. Park together with his denominated officers attempted to make an apology for the offence of their company, I told them the matter now rested with the Government nothing could be done by me, but to pacify my agrieved indians, which was partially done by takeing Mr Park and his associates before the indians and pointing them out as the persons having authority over the men who committed the murder, I told the warriors, notice had already been taken of the offence and of their misfortunes, that an express had been sent to Fort Mitchell with all the facts connected with their sufferings that these men Mr Park and his associates, now regreted the occurences of the night and were willing to make any attonement for the losses sustained. The acting chief of Jim Boys town (Hillis Hadjo) replied it was out of their power to bring life back, he therefore would leave it to me to say, what was best to be done, I told them the old man was dead, died violently it was true, but life could not be restored, we therefore must submit, the reply was if I was satisfied they were, I told them no, far from it; but we were obliged to submit in this case, but justice should be rendered, General Jesup would not suffer them to be imposed upon. Previous to this in company with Capt Wellborn and Hillis Hadjo, I visited the house of the aged murdered man, who proved to be Loch chi yoholo about 90 years of age who had been excused, owing to the infirmities of age, deafness &c. from attending muster at the issuing house; found him lying in one corner shot in the breast and his head litterally stove in, with as I supposed butts of muskets, with some difficulty I obtained permission for the son of Loch chi yoholo to leave the chain of sentinels. I afterwards found the little girl who had been slightly wounded in the leg by a musket ball, she is the daughter of Cotch ar Fixico of the Ufalla town, about fifteen years old, she stated the men wished to ravish her, she refused and ran towards a thicket which was near by when she was fired at; I am happy however to say she has entirely recovered. There are two warriors by the name of Cotch ar Fixico belonging to the Ufalla town the father of the girl is with me, the other is in Florida upon prosecuting my inqueries further, I learned the same men had in several instances accomplished their diabolical views upon the frightened women and in many cases deprived them by force, of finger, Ear rings and blankets many of these women and whole families under a state of alarm ran to the swamp where the major part of them are still and no doubt viewed as hostile. I have used every possible means to draw them out without success. The most prominent measure [adopted] was causing staffs with white muslin attached to be carried through the camps as a token of friendship. The question (with the officers of the several companies) what was to be done with the warriors now presented itself; nine of twelve were in favor of removeing them to Tuskeegee. I formally protested against it and proffered to leave the nation with my whole party rather than consent to a separation of my people, it was some time before they assented to my proposition; as soon as informed of their assent, I repaired to montgomery County and consulted the citizens residing in the vicinity of Mount meiggs,[19] who readily acceeded to my wishes and aided in the selection of an eligable situation for Encamping. On my return I communicated with the indians gave them the choice, either of going to Tuskeegee as prisoners and separating from their families or leave the nation with them there was no hesitation they preferred the latter and in thirty Six hours afterwards with but four five horse teams, my party of upwards of nineteen hundred strong were on the march, on the 22nd inst I arrived at and Encamped near mount meiggs without any murmuring or discontent except regrets for loss of property and suffering for the acts of the guilty. The excitement of the settlers in the immediate vicinity of Polecat Springs, Capt Youngs company and a portion of Capt. Willborn's against the Russel County men was so great, that so soon as it was ascertained my camp would be removed; deemed it prudent, to leave at the earliest period, takeing with them some Eight or ten Ponies stolen from the indians, of this fact I was informed, by persons who met them on the road with the ponies in possession. Indeed the conduct of this party was of the most outrageous and disgraceful kind, even persons in the public employ and the stores, were wholly disregarded one of the former was most violently beaten and otherwise maltreated and stores for the subsistence of indians were taken by force.

As to the main inquiry, to wit. the probable loss sustained by the sudden and forced removal of my indians I answer it is impossible to form a correct estimate within the time required, but can do so in a few days as it will be necessary to call up the heads of families under the superentendance of their respective chiefs. I am convinced their losses were heavy in ponies, cattle, corn, furniture, and farming utensils &c.,

I am Sir.
Very Respectfully
Your Obt. Servt.
Jno G Reynolds
1st Lieut. U.S.M.C.
& Military agent

Major Henry Wilson[20]
4th Infantry
U.S. army
Mobile Point ala.

☾

Sloan reports on the events that led to his party being moved from Echo Harjo's camp to Tuskegee, and then to Montgomery, Alabama, and the loss of property suffered by the Creeks at the hands of roving bands of militias. Letter found at Records of the Adjutant General's Office, 1780s–1917, Entry 159-Q, Records of Major General Thomas S. Jesup, Container 19, Folder: "Letters Received Relating to Creek and Seminole Affairs, 1837," NARA.

Fort Morgan,
Mobile Point
March 31st 1837—

Major—

In answer to your enquiries in relation to the outrages that have been committed on the families of the Indian warriors serving in Florida, and the loss incident there to, I submit the following report—[21]

In consequence of a disturbance that occurred at the plantation of Dr. Battle, on the Cowiga creek, about the latter part of December last, thirty miles distant from the camp under my charge, (Echo Harjo's) I ordered the warriors forthwith to surrender their arms and remove within a smaller compass, so that they might be more immediately under my observation. This movement was made, not from a belief that the depredations were committed by my Indians (for I have no doubt it was the remnant of the old hostile party that have never surrendered) but to appease the citizens & prevent any intercourse with my camp, some of whom had previously been hostile—sixty three guns were deposited in my house.

This order was promptly obeyed, and all the old camp of Echo Harjo's Indians, & a few of those that had surrendered were encamped in less than half a mile square; the rest precipitately left the camp. They remained in this situation till the 5th of Febr'y when I found my camp suddenly surrounded by an armed populace headed by a Mr. Jernigan, and a party of citizens from Georgia, a Mr. Park at the head of the citizens from Russell county, Ala., and a Captain Morris of Franklin county, Geo., that had recently been mustered into the service of the United States. The Indians indiscriminately were driven up immediately around my quarters, and there guarded until twelve o'clock the next day, without provisions, & in most instances a blanket to shelter them from the inclemency of the weather.[22] I protested against their conduct as inhumane, uncalled for, and contrary to the solemn pledges of the Government; and that it would be more honorable and soldier-like to punish the aggressors than harrass a few unarmed men, women & children. After pillaging several of the Indian houses of property, & in one instance of money, they determined to remove the Indian men and boys to Tuskegee and place them within the stockade, under a strong guard, & permit the women & children to remain immediately around my quarters. The guns belonging to the Indians were also carried away by them & have not been returned. I have since learned they selected the best for their own private use. On the same evening my camp was again visited by two companies of citizens from Pike & Barbour counties, Ala., headed by a Mr. Curry and a Mr. Harrold, or Harrill;—the latter company was that day mustered into service. After some conversation I succeeded in satisfying them that no great danger was to be apprehended from a parcel of women and children; and after remaining until about midnight, & plundering the houses of the Indians that had been abandoned, they left to join their associates in arms, about five miles distant, where they, that night, had encamped with the Indian men & boys.

We had a respite from this time till the 20th of Feb. when Park and his mob returned, and after parading through the camp took six men that had been frightened off on his previous visit; and if the statement of some of his own men can be credited, stole two mules and a horse, & perhaps some ponies, & left the camp. On the 21st a Lt. ash, with a detatchment from Capt. Morris' company arrived at the camp and surrounded it, & after searching it thoroughly left for Tuskegee without making any discoveries of a very alarming character. On the next day I received a note from Capt. George (whose company was also in the U.S. service) & Lt. ash informing me that on the next morning they had determined to remove the women and children of my camp to Tuskegee. As I was that day making an issue of provisions for five days I begged them to defer it for four days, until they could consume their provisions, as no waggons was furnished for their transportation it would be impossible for them to carry it, and requested to hear from them that night by express. No intelligence was received, & I was convinced they adhered to their determination, & on the morning of the 23d ordered the Indians to prepare to remove to Tuskegee forthwith, & in half an hour the whole camp was on the march! In consequence of having no means of transportation, I directed them to deposit their effects in my quarters, &c., until waggons could be procured to remove them to Tuskegee; but in the mean time the house was broken open & plundered of most articles of any value. We had proceeded alone within four miles of Tuskegee before we met the companies that were to guard us. They escorted us to Tuskegee and encamped the women and children around the pickets under a guard, where they remained until the 7th of March, when they were marched off by the same companies to Montgomery, Ala.

The following is the discription & value of the property that has been lost as far as can be ascertained in so short a period—

145 Indian Ponies (average value, say $30.00)	4350.00
60 head of cattle, @ $12 pr. head.	720.00
200 head of hogs @ $3.00	600.00
100 bushels of corn @ $2.00 pr. bu.	200.00
Cooking & farming utensils, and crockery	200.00
63 guns (average value say $10.00)	630.00
sacrifice in hurried sales of property	1200.00
Money stolen by troops from Tallow-war-harjo	250.00
	$8150.00
100 bee hives @ $2.00	200.00
	$8350.00

I am, very respectfully
Your ob't. serv't.
T. T. Sloan
Lt. & Mil. Agent.

Maj. H. Wilson, U.S.A.
Mobile Point.

☾

Reynolds reports that the losses sustained by the wealthy Creek families in east Alabama were great and proposes giving each family an average of fifty dollars in compensation and allow the headmen to distribute the funds proportionally. Letter found at Reynolds Journal, Princeton University.

Mobile Point ala
12th April 1837

Major,

I have endevoured to ascertain the probable loss of property sustained by the indians under my charge in consequence of their sudden and unexpected removal from the nation, without being able to arrive at any just estimate of their losses—I called upon the head men for a return but find the amount so enormously great, that I have deemed it proper simply to return their statement—It is very certain many of them have been great sufferers in the lost of stocks running at large, where it was the intention of the families of the warriors to permit them to remain until the return of the young men from Florida—many of my indians were considered wealthy, nearly all of Jim Boy's immediate people were so, not being obliged to Encamp, reserved all their farming utensils &c. Tuskenia haw, and his connections were likewise large loosers.

I would respectfully suggest the propriety of covering all looses at an average of Fifty dollars to every family forced to move, in which event the chiefs would be enabled to proportion agreeably to the looses actually sustained, as I am convinced many families were worth nothing and consequently sustained no loss.

359 families
50

$17 950

I am Sir,
very Respectfully,
your obt. Servant
Jno. G. Reynolds
1st Lt. U.S.M.C.
& military agent

Major Henry Wilson
4th Infantry
US army
Mobile Point

☾

Major Henry J. Wilson reports on straggling Creeks (and Alabama governor C. C. Clay's demand that volunteers be raised to contain them), the need for the contractors to furnish fresh beef, the lack of firewood at Mobile Point, and John Oponee's lawyer sending his black slaves to the Gulf. Letter found at Records of the Adjutant General's Office, 1780s–1917, Entry 159-Q, Records of Major General Thomas S. Jesup, Container 17, Folder: "Letters Received from Officers, Major Henry Wilson," NARA.

Mobile Point Alabama
16th may 1837

General

I Received information the other day from pensacola of several Indian families loitering in the neighborhood of the perdido River, supposed to have straggled off from the point which I think is highly probable, from the fact, that several of Echo Harjos people were found missing about the time they were removed to new orleans—I have sent after them a command of five trusty, and confidential Indians, who I have no doubt—will succeed, in bringing them in.—I have enclosed to you a communication which was sent to me at the same time, Representing a number of fugitive Indians being on the Choctawhatchee, and pea River where they have been committing depredations—

I have to Report that within the last eight or ten days a Requisition was made on the contractors, for fresh Beef, for the Indian families at the point, which they Refused to furnish. I there upon directed a purchase to be made on account of Goverment, of two days Rations of fresh Beef, and at the same time authorised a contract to be made—to furnish the Indians whilst they Remained here, with one days Ration of fresh Beef—in each week.—the day to be designated: that it should not interfere with the issues of the company.—there can be no doubt in my opinion—of the necessity of there Requiring fresh provisions, at a place like this, where they are constantly Inhaling a salt atmosphere: Besides, the construction, I give the 4th article of agreement entered into—between Capt Page and the company; I think it obligatory on them to furnish fresh Beef, when it is Required by the officers—but it is true, they think differently, and contend, they have the Right to furnish fresh or salt provisions according to the contract, as they the contractors may think proper, and that the Goverment officers are bound to Receive it—the quality and quantity, not being objected to by them—I should like you would Refer to the contract; if Capt Page has a copy of it with him—and what his understanding was on the subject—I have submitted the matter to Mr Harris the commissioner of Indian affairs—the Indians at this place, are entirely destitute of wood—not a stick to be had at the point—I have therefore taken upon myself; the Responsibility of having it furnished, by contract, to be issued to them, in such quantities, as will enable them to cook there provisions—this I hope will meet your sanction—

I would General most Respectfully suggest, that the Instructions submitted to Capt Page, some time since for his decision by the department at Washington, be carried into effect that, of Removing to the west, the Indian families who are now here, unconnected with the warriors serving in Florida—there are at this place, of that description, Big and little, I understand, at least, one thousand souls—my opinion is their getting to there Homes in the west, would be both advantageous to them, and the Goverment—*

Governor Clay visited the point eight or ten days ago, on the following day, after he Returned to mobile, he met with Lieut't Reynolds, to whom he give a written order, directing him to muster into service for three months, unless sooner discharged—thirty volunteers with the priviledge of electing one 1st Lieutenant and one ensign.—and when organised to be placed subject to my order, as a Guard over the Indians at this place—to prevent their stragling off, and Restraining them, from committing any excesses—also for him Mr Reynolds to Repair in person, to collect, all straggling Indians, coming under the order of the Secretary of war, for emigration within the State.—on the order being handed me by the Lieutenant (although Irregularly Reaching me) I Readily assented to afford—, all the assistance I could towards carrying the Governors Instructions as to the volunteers into effect—the latter part that of withdrawing the Lieutenant the only commissioned officer, I had with me from the duties to which he had been assigned by you, with what I conceived an unlimited leave—to search for fugitive Indians through the State—I objected—not however without expressing my Readiness to afford at all times, every assistance with the means, within my controul, in obeying the Secretarys order in Relation to the Indians.—

Will you be pleased General, to say to John O; Pawney that his Negroes have been sent by his Lawyer, from the Nation, to this place.—

I am General
most Respectfully
your: ob't: Servent
HJ Wilson Maj'r U.S.A.
Temp'y Superintendant
Creek Emigration

* In a Conversation with Mr Reynolds previous to my writing the above, I understood from him there were the number of Indians as stated above, unconnected with the warriors in Florida, but I have

discovered since by a note received from him & herewith Enclosed, that I have been mistaken.

To
Maj'r General Thomas S. Jesup
Commanding Army of the South
Tampa Bay Florida

☾

Wilson reports that he will go to New Orleans and confer with Echo Harjo's people about coming back to Mobile Point. He also notes that fugitive Creeks are being shot down like "Black Birds." Punctuation has been silently emended for clarity. Letter found at Records of the Adjutant General's Office, 1780s–1917, Entry 159-Q, Records of Major General Thomas S. Jesup, Container 17, Folder: "Letters Received from Officers, Major Henry Wilson," NARA.

mobile point alabama
20th May 1837.

General,

I Received this morning by the Revenue Cutter, your letters of the 8th Inst: in relation to Echo Harjos' people, now at New orleans. I will leave here tomorrow for that place in order to Confer with them, as to their Removal back to the point, although I think general (pardon me for offering an opinion) from the length of time it has taken your letters to reach me, twenty days—that it would now probably be as well they should continue where they are, an account of the trouble, fatigue and inconvenience they would be obliged to undergo by a Removal and hardly become settled before they would be compelled to Return—I will name all these difficulties to them, and the prospect they have, of meeting their warriors in New orleans, in from twelve to fifteen days, after this, if they should desire to return to the point, your Instructions general, shall be strictly observed.

I directed Mr. Sloan previous to his leaving here that if they become sickly and it was thought necessary on account of their Health to Remove—to do so without the slightest hesitation.

I Received from pensacola on Sunday last thirty four, and this morning Ten, fugitive "Creeks", principally women & children. we have Accounts of their being a great many in the neighborhood of the Choctaw hatchee, and pea Rivers.—poor devils—we frequently hear of them being killed by the whites, who, (if reports are true) shoot them down, without regard to Age, or Sex! as they would Black Birds, without their making any Resistance—It would really be an act of humanity, general, that some plan could be devised to bring those poor creatures in—I would therefore suggest that an U.S. officer with four or five trusty, Confidential Creeks, and a good intelligent Interporetor, be stationed at pensacola, for the purpose of Receiving, and sending off to the point: such Indians as may be brought or should come to that place—with the priviledge of going in search of such as he may hear of, from time to time, within 50 or 100 Miles of pensacola.—I think a discreet officer with proper management could succeed in bringing in and save from the merciless hands of some who are worse than Savages, many of those poor Unfortunate wretches.

I am, Gen'l, very Respectfully
Yr. Ob. Servt.
H. J. Wilson Maj'r U.S.A.

To Maj'r Gen'l Thos S Jesup.
Comdg Army of the South
Tampa Bay Florida

☾

Reynolds reports on the progress of his expedition to find Creek Indians who had fled to Florida and were engaged in acts of violence against the white settlers. Letter found at Reynolds Journal, Princeton University.

La Grange Florida

4th June 1837

Major

I arrived at this place on 1st inst. made arrangements and departed immediately for a camp said to be about Eight or nine miles west of the Alaqua River, seven miles from here we came upon the ground where the indian massacre took place about twelve days since, a more shocking sight I never beheld; on the edge of a large swamp was a space of about fifteen or twenty feet in diameter, where the poor women with children upon their backs were inhumanly butchered the cries of the children were distinctly heard at a house distant a quarter of a mile, after their mothers were shot down the children's brains were deliberately knocked out—the women's Ears cut off, for the purpose of obtaining their Ear Rings and in several instances scalped—I am told this was done with the sanction of the Comd'g Colonel (Brown)[23]—we persued our course in the direction in which it was said the camps was situated; in our progress passed many old camp grounds, but not the least sign of indians being in the neighborhood of Alaqua for the previous ten or twenty days, it is the impression of the indians who are with me; that all the camps were broken up immediately after the murder—deeming it unnecessary to follow the trail further returned to this place where we arrived on the evening of the second day—

I inquired of the com'g officer if it was known by any person, where the indians were located it was represented, the head of chocktahatchee Bay, was full of them, that fires were constantly seen—I chartered a sail boat and made application to the officer then in command of this place for a guide, he could afford me no assistence although the indiviudals composing his company are residents of the place—under these unfavorable circumstances we set out to scour the point at which it was said indians had been seen, the person owning the boat accompanied me, but was wholly unacquainted with the waters above the inlet upon which La Grange is situated; we traversed the whole coast, the indians and myself at times going on shore with the hope of finding some traces of indians, but there was not the least sign wherewith to justify the report of the presence of indians—after two days absence—I returned, determined to give up all further search indeed it was not the design, that I should hunt them, I was under the impression that the people knew where the hostile camps were and could readily point them out, in that event I pledged myself to Enter and bring all in; the fact is, the people of this vicinity have committed so many barbarous outrages upon the poor devils, that they are now afraid to show themselves without their own camp and further it is my candid belief that the settlers care not whether the indians are brought in, for they all receive indiscriminately, Rations, from the Govt, on my return from my first scout west of this, I communicated to those who had moved into town for protection, that there was not the least danger to be apprehended, they appeared wholly indifferent and in my opinion choose to remain on the bounty of Govt—

Last night a plot was formed by a man named Lawrence in conjunction with a number of men who have been mustered into service to murder my party—this Lawrence is the one, who lost his wife by the supposed violence of the indians, this however is doubted many say, she fell by his own hand; I was in formed of his and his parties intention at a late hour, by an old worthy fellow named Bush, begging me to be on my guard, that an attempt would be made to destroy my party, I was located upon an old steam Boat lying beside the wharf, had my indians abaft the wheel house, Bush kept watch on the forecastle and I at the cabin door determined to resist with life any attempt of a hostile nature—Lawrence, by some means (I was informed this morning) was made acquainted with my watchfulness and Relinquished his design—I made an official call upon the commd'g officer for the arrest of all concerned with Lawrence—and requested civil action be had against the latter—The people are so outrageous & uncivilised. I have determined for the Safty of the indians to leave by the first opportunity for Escrevan's point, where I am all but positive many indians can be found, I shall remain at Black water—three days, after which Return to the point

Respectfully &c
Jno G Reynolds

Major H Wilson
US army
act'g Superentendent
Creek Removal

☾

Dr. John M. Woodfin reports that the soldiers at Fort Morgan have removed the plank boards upon which the sick Creeks were resting. Letter found at Reynolds Journal, Princeton University.

Mobile Point ala
10th June 1837

Sir

I deem it my duty to apprise You that in going my usual rounds to day visiting the sick, I find that planks upon which the beds of the sick Indians were made had been removed by the soldiers of the post

The sick consiquently have to lie on the hard bricks exposed to the dampness of the earth which must prove highly detrimental to their comfort and materially retard their recovery—

I am Sir Respectfully
Your obt. Servt
JM Woodfin
actg asst Surg

Lt John G Reynolds
Military agent
Creek removal

☾

Reynolds orders Captain Francis Smith Belton to accomodate the sick. Letter found at Reynolds Journal, Princeton University.

Mobile Point ala
10th June 1837

Sir

The asst Surgeon has reported to me that you have deprived his sick of plank, which was necessary for their comfort. I trust major Belton will render every convenience in his power to alleviate the sick. Any requisition for Stuff that may be necessary for the accommodation of the Indians will be cheerfully met by me.

I am Sir
Very Respectfully
Your Obt Servt
Jno G Reynolds
1st Lt. U S M C
& military agent

Major Belton
Com'g Fort morgan
Mobile Point

☾

Captain Belton reports on his decision to remove the planking. Letter found at Reynolds Journal, Princeton University.

Fort morgan 10th June 1837

Sir

Your note of this date I have just received—my course with respect to the plank, being that receipted for by me to the engineer Dept for the constructions here is this, it being much exposed to the Indians was put into store by my order for preservation for the purpose it was designed and partly worked up for, which I think I stated to you, as also that I was perfectly willing to let it go for any purpose in such quantities as would be proper—therefore I have shown every disposition to serve you and the sick I have had no requisitions from the asst Surgeon on the subject and have not deprived his sick of plank, and know nothing of his views on the subject. In the Army as you very well know there is a strict responsibility for property of all Kinds.

I remain
Very Respectfully
Your obt Servt
F S Belton
Capt 2nd art
com'g Post

To
Lt Reynolds
U S M Corps

☾

Reynolds requests permission to use the plank confiscated earlier. Letter found at Reynolds Journal, Princeton University.

Fort morgan mobile Point
12th June 1837

Sir

The Surgeon requires the sick within the Fort to be raised from the brick; for your information I enclose you a copy of his report to me—

I have to request, as there is Lumber belonging to the post, it be loaned to the asst surgeon for the convenience of his sick, as it will be the means of saving considerable Expense to the Govt—any deficiency in quantity at our final departure will be covered by a receipt.

I am Sir
Very Respectfully
Your obt Servt
Jno G Reynolds

1st Lt U.S.M.C.
& military agent

Major F S Belton
2nd Art U.S.A.
Comd'g Fort morgan
mobile Point

☾

Reynolds forwards Dr. John M. Woodfin's report on the condition of the Creeks at Mobile Point, Alabama. Letter found at Reynolds Journal, Princeton University.

Mobile Point ala
13th June 1837

Major

In consequence of a general complaint from the indians of my party in relation to the unhealthy situation of their present Encamping ground—I called upon act'g asst Surgeon Woodfin for a written Statement of the general health of the camp, which I herewith enclose for your consideration.

I am Sir
Very Respectfully
Your obt Servt
Jno G Reynolds
1st Lt U.S.M.C.
& military agent

Major Wilson
US army
act'g Superentendent
Creek Removal

☾

Woodfin reports that diarrhea is prevalent at the Mobile Point encampments which is caused by the drinking of stagnant water. Letter found at Reynolds Journal, Princeton University.

Mobile Point ala
13th June 1837

Sir

In compliance with your request in regard to the health of the Indians generally, the causes of sickness &c.

I report—That for some time past they have been exceedingly unhealthy and many of the children have died from Diarihae that being the complaint prevaling with all, nor do I see any prospect of a change in their condition as nearly all of those, who have died were under the severest Indian treatment,[24] which in connection with other causes must render their condition infinitily worse and prove fatal in almost every instance—

The principal cause of the diarihae prevaling at this time in my opinion is the water used by them, as you know every family has A Spring or properly speaking a hole dug Eighteen Inches or two feet in the sand which fills immediately on being dug with water, which has no chance of escape, nor can it be absorbed by the earth, consequently it remains in these holes without any chance of escape exposed to the heat of the Sun and in fact becoms stagnant and in this condition is drunk by the Indians, I have invariably proffered my services to all those under Indian treatment, and in every instance I have been refused, until all hope of recovery under their treatment was abandoned. Many, however, submit and are even anxious that I should attend them and in nearly every case I have had the happiness to witness a speedy and rapid recovery. Inflamation of the eyes prevails also with them, to a considerable extent owing to an almost entire exclusion of shade there being but few trees to protect them from the sun which for four or five hours of the day is very oppressive—

I am Sir
Respectfully
Your obt Servt
J m woodfin
act'g asst sur'g

Lt John G Reynolds
military agent
Creek removal

☾

The following are brief journal entries made by Reynolds listing the major events of detachment 6. The entries are scattered throughout Reynolds's journal but are consolidated here. Entries found at Reynolds Journal, Princeton University.

19th Feby. Issuing House surrounded by volunteers under the command of Gen'l Wilborn for the purpose of making the warriors prisoners.

21st Feby. Left the issuing house at 10 O Clock a.m. and Encamped 7 miles distant near to line creek—

22nd Feby. At 8 O clock a.m. marched for and arrived at the Encamping ground one and a half miles from mount meiggs, days march ten miles.

4th march At 9 o clock, a.m. left for montgomery arrived and Encamped on the ground of Gen'l Scott,[25] without any accident occuring to the people.

15th march Turned over to ala. Emigrating Company my party, consisting of _______ Strong for subsistence and were issued to by the company on 16th.

16 march Embarked on board the steamer John Nelson with first detachment of my party for mobile Point arrived and disembarked on 18th inst.

18th march Second and third detachments under charge of asst Conductor N Felton, Embarked on board the Steamers Chippawa and Bonnets O Blue, arrived and disembarked_______ Indians at mobile point on the 19th inst the first party subsisted by the company, as

Contractors commencing on ________ inst. that of the second on ________ inst.

3 April. Capt. Page Emigrating creek agent left mobile Point under orders to join the Comd'g General at Tampa Bay—during his temporary absence was relieved by Major Henry Wilson 4th Infantry.

22d April. Lieut Sloan left in the steamer "Far west" with a portion of the families of Echo Hadjo's warriors for New Orleans, whither he is to be joined by that chief and warriors, the remainder including the mother of Echo Hadjo (23 families 140 in number) refused to Embark; assigning for reason, that this was the point at which they were to be met by their friends in Florida—

On the same date I left with an interpreter for Pensacola under the orders of Major Wilson for the purpose of collecting fugitive creek then in the vicenity of that place, arrived at Pensacola and found one of them had been taken prisoner, after interogating him deem it proper to return to mobile Point with the indian prisoner that he might be Enabled to judge of the situation of the indians Encamped at this place.

April 24. Left for Pensacola with the indian prisoner, uchee and Creek interpreter for the purpose of Visiting the uchee Hostile Camp, and persuading them to come in—arrived at Pensacola at half pass 4 O.clock P.M. applied to: Commodore Dallas[26] for transportation to Escravans point, on Black water Bay; in consequence of the weather was obliged to return and accept of quarters on board the Frigate.[27]

25th April. At day light, left in the Frigate's 1st cutter[28] in company with act'g sailing master Boie,[29] arrived at the point at 3. o clock P.M.—left for the camp taking with me the two interpreters and uchee prisoner, at the distance of two miles the creek interpreter and a friendly indian, who I had taken with me from Mobile Point became alarmed and returned to Escrevants point, proceeded towards the uchee camp and Encamped about twelve miles distant.

26th April. At the solicitation of the uchee prisoner and the interpreter's alarm; returned to Escrevans-point for the purpose of remaining untill the coming in of the hostiles—

27th April. Two hostile men, a woman and child, at half pass 8 o clock reported themselves as also the fact of the whole camp moving for the purpose of giving up. Thirty seven friendly creek indians reported themselves, were Enrolled and received rations.

29th April. Joined from Tampa Bay nine creek volunteers with rations to 3rd May, inclusive.

30th April. At 3 o clock P.M. the hostile indians thirty three in number came in, were Enrolled and subsisted—at 4 o clock P.M. Embarked 70 indians on board the steamer "Watchman" for Pensacola, at 9 o clock P.M. came to under the Frigate "Consellation's" guns for protection—

1st May. at 7 o clock A.M. transfered the indians from on board the "Watchman" to the steamer "Champion" and left Pensacola for mobile Point at 8 o clock A.M.—at 1 o clock P.M. arrived at and disembarked at mobile point.

May 21st. Joined from Pensacola per Steam Boat champion thirty three Creek hostile Indians—also per same conveyance Ho bi o chee a creek volunteer warrior from Tampa Bay, who reported the death of his brother at Pensacola the latter was permitted to leave Tampa to join his family at this place.

May 23rd. The asst Surgeon reported the necessity of one of his patients having an arm amputated that for the want of instruments he was unable to do it himself and suggested the propriety of having the operation performed at the mobile Hospital—in consequence of which I took Echo Hadjo and two principal men of his Town to witness the amputation as also a boy to nurse and interpret while patient at the Hospital.

May 27th. Joined from Pensacola ten fugitive creek indians

May 30th. By order of the Tempo'y Superentendent, left with an interpreter and four indian creek runners, for La Grange situated at the head of the chocktehatchee Bay, for the purpose of collecting fugitive creek indians, said to be in that vicinity.

June 8th. Lieut Sloan returned with his party of indians from New Orleans.

June 14th. Joined two indians creek boys sent from near La Grange (W F) the parents of whom, reported as having been Killed—

June 16th. Capt Page with 133—Creek Indians including a portion of the Creek *volunteers who were permitted to visit their families on a leave of absence 30 days from 12th June—arrived at Mobile Point 16th June. * 112 volunteers

June 23. Left in the steamer "Farmer" under an order of the Superentendent, in search of a more healthy Situation for an encampment, returned on the Evening of 26th, the following are reports made in relation thereto.

Mobile Point, ala
27th June 1837

Sir,

In our late excursion to the different Islands ranging between this and the bay of St Louis the most important of which we visited and minutely examined Horn Island the first examined has not in my opinion any advantages over their present encampment for health, the Island is better timbered, but the water and character of the soil differes but little if any from their location on the point. we next examined Cat Island but owing to the obstinacy of an old Spaniard resident our examination was merely partial, however I am convinced that it does not differ from Horn Island materially, if any, in fact all the Islands differ but little in the nature and character of soil, water, timber, &c—being precisely that of their present encampment; Pass christian, and the bay of St. Louis, we also visited, the former places, presents more advantages decidedly for health and comfort, than any spot I have seen, its situation being high, dry, and airy, with three or four Springs of excellent water and beautifully shaded with large oaks hickory and other flourishing trees. my decided opinion is, that if the camp is moved to that place, it must be healthy and those already sick, will convaless rapidly—The fact of its being a retreat during the sickly season of summer, for the citizens of New orleans, is a convincing and strong proof of the healthiness of the situation, and the citizens, all testify to the facts, in the strongest terms.

Very Respectfully
Your Obt. Servt.
Signed J. M. woodfin
attend'g Physician.

Lt. John G. Reynolds
Disbursing agent,
Creek Emigration.

Mobile Point ala
27th June 1837

Capt John Page
Superentendent Creek Removal
mobile Point, ala.,

Sir,

In compliance with your instructions of 23rd Inst. I proceeded in the steam Boat Farmer, taking with me the asst. Surgeon of my party beside thirty eight principal indians to visit the several Islands in the vicinity or some place more suitable for Encamping the indians than our present location, all the Islands in succession; to wit, Horn, Ship and Cat, Islands were thouroughly examined, the two former I was informed, are the property of the United States, each affording a partial supply of both wood and water, but objected to by the indians, in consequence of the barrenness of the soil, the abundance of musquetoes and the low situation of the ground—Cat Island posseses more advantages than either of the former in Soil, wood and cattle; but the proprietor, who resides on the Island, objected in strong terms to the Indians occupying it on any terms—we then visited St Louis and Pass christian, the latter place is beautifully situated upon a high bluff and bears every appearance of being exceedingly healthy, the point below the village I was informed belonged to a citizen of new orleans who, I was given to understand, would have no objections to its being occupied by the Indians, provided they were restrained from committing depredations upon the property of settlers, to which I gave positive assurance that the Indians would in no way interfire with them—we all went over the ground, which is about a mile and a half from the landing and about the same distance from any habitation—the indians Expressed themselves delighted with the country and the Doctor was of the opinion, that the water, air &c. would do much towards restoring the sick and preserveing health.

The asst Surgeon's Report I herewith Enclose.

I am Sir
verry Respectfully
Your obt Servt
(Signed) Jno G Reynolds
1st Lt U S M C
& Disb'g agent Ind Dep't

July 7. Embarked at mobile Point with my party for Pass Christian on the Evening of the 7th July and arrived and disembarked safely on the afternoon of the 8th Inst about four o clock, also one interpreter detached under charge of Major Wilson on duty at Pensacola.

July 15. Yar tows Hadjo with Eleven warriors detached by order of Capt Page to visit their people in Florida, leaving the women and children behind.

July 22. Mustered and found several indians missing, some were reported as having Remained at mobile Point and others as having died and were buried without any return being made of the fact, consequently it was out of my power to keep the muster Roll accurate.

July 22. Joined from Montgomery under the charge of Lieut. Sloan's "asst. conductor," three indians.

Augst 19. Joined from "Tampa Bay" 208 Creek Volunters 157 of whom belongs to No 1 Party (Hopoth lo Yohola) thirty Eight to Lieut Sloans and 13 to Capt Page's.—

Augst 22. Capt Page left for arkansas under orders of the Deprt.

31st august. Joined from the choctihatchee Bay via Pensacola five creek Indians sent by major Wilson.

7th September. Joined from Gainestown nine fugitive indians under charge of asst Conductor Noah Felton, five of whom had Strayed from Lieut Sloan's party—

13th September. Joined from Tampa Bay Sixty Creek volunteers, including Echo Hadjo, chief of the Tallassee indians, all belonged and reported to Lieut Sloan.

15th September. Joined from Tampa Bay 78 Creek volunteers all of whom (78) belongs to no. 1 Party (Hopoth le Yoholo).

16th September. Joined from Tampa Bay 163 Creek volunteers of whom__________belongs to Lieut Sloans party 113 to Lieut J G Reynolds' party, also 17 fugitive Creek indians the latter collected and sent over from Pensacola by Major Wilson also an Interpreter and three friendly Indians (men) five of the fugitives, belonging to Lt. Jno. G. Reynolds' party and twelve belonging to Lt Sloans party.

29 Sept. Joined from Mobile two fugitive creek Indians.

19th Oct—Taken sick; transfered my party to Lieut Sloan, as also the public property in my possession—On 22nd Dec'r Received from the Indian Department a leave of absence for two months bearing date 6th Dec'r—to which Department I Reported for duty on 26th Jan'y 1838—

Jno. G. Reynolds
Lt U.S.M.C.
& Disb'g Agt. Ind. Dept.

☾

William A. Campbell asks Reynolds to confirm that the Alabama Emigrating Company has been in compliance with the contract regarding the issuance of rations. Letter found at Reynolds Journal, Princeton University.

Mobile Point June 16th 1837

Lieut J G Reynolds

Dr Sir

Will you have the kindness to state, if in the contract to furnish the creek Indians now at this place with rations, if they have not been the best of their kind and the quantity more than they have been enabled to consume. I make this request of you knowing you are in the habit, of visiting your encampment daily.

I am Sir your Obt Servt
Wm A Campbell
member & agent of the
Ala Emigrating Co

☾

Reynolds responds to William A. Campbell's 16 June 1837 letter. Letter found at Reynolds Journal, Princeton University.

Mobile Point ala

16th June 1837

Sir

I have received your communication of this date and hesitate not one moment in saying, that the kind of Rations furnished my party, has been good and the quantity ample; I have frequently discovered in making my daily Rounds through the several camps a great saving in both bacon and corn, which arrises from locality; the allowance per contract is more than can be consumed, and situated as at present, the Indians are deprived the opportunity of selling it as was frequently the case when in the nation.

I am Sir Respectfully
Your Obt Servt
Jno G Reynolds
1st Lt U.S.M.C. & military agent

Co'l W A Campbell
member & agent of the
Ala Em'g Company

☾

Captain Mark W. Bateman reports that the Creeks at Mobile Point are becoming discontented and that he and Captain Page will reconnoiter on Dauphin Island, Alabama, looking for a more suitable camp. Letter found at LR, CAE, Roll 238, 106–7.

Mobile Point Ala
18th June 1837

C. A. Harris Esq'r
Commissioner of Indian Affairs
Washington City

Sir

I have the honor to inform you that I arrived at this place yesterday. I found here on duty with the Indians, Major Wilson and Captain Page. Capt P. has recently returned from Florida, from whence I am sorry to say he brings but little good news. The Creek Indians at this place are becoming discontented, and should be removed immediately. The Citizens in the vicinity are becoming alarmed. Capt Page and myself will visit Dauphin Island tomorrow; with a view to select a new position for them.

I am gratifyed to learn direct from the western Creeks, that Opoth-lo-yo-ho-lo and his people are highly pleased with their new homes. Would to God that this part of the nation were with them.

I am Sir very
Respectfully
yr OSt
M. W. Bateman
Capt 6th U.S. Infantry
&c

P.S. I received on the 17th Inst at Mobile your communications dated 20th May and 1st June last.

M.W.B.

☾

Captain John Page reports on detachment 6's relocation to Pass Christian, Mississippi, due to the prevalence of sickness at Mobile Point, Alabama, and the difficulty he had getting the Creeks on board the steamboats while they were dying on the wharf. To make matters worse, bad weather delayed their movements. Despite this, the Creeks absolutely refused to return to their old encampment near Fort Morgan to wait out the storm. While the Creeks' sense of purity and balance precluded this, Page attributed it to the Indians' "superstitious notions." Letter found at Records of the Adjutant General's Office, 1780s–1917, Entry 159-Q, Records of Major General Thomas S. Jesup, Container 18, Folder: "Letters Received, July–December 1837," NARA.

Pass Christian Mississipipie
27th July 1837

Sir

I have the honor to Report my arrival at this place—with the Creek Emigrants.—Previous to the movement I employed a Steam Boat and sent a deputation in charge of Lieu't Reynolds and Doct Woodfin consisting of about fifty persons selected from the differrent towns by the Chiefs, to select a place for a summer residence; this course I found necessary as there had been so much sickness and so many deaths in camp at mobile Point that the Indians had got frightened and discouraged. If I had removed them to a place and it proved sickley the whole cause would have been attributed to me In a former communication I stated I exspected to move on Dauphin Island.—the Indians on examination thought there were no advantages in point of health than there was at mobile Point. after exploring all the Islands from Mobile Point to Cat Island they pitched on this place It being a noted place for health and maney other advantages they could realize—I have purchased cloth and made tents, the contractors furnish fresh Beef, Bacon, corn and Beans so the Indians have their choice of Rations. Maj'r

Wilson is at Pensacola with three Indians and an Interpreter to collect such fugitive Creeks as he can hear of, upwards of one hundred he has forwarded to this place and mobile Point. I also sent an agent back to the Creek nation and Brought seventy Creeks most of them had been taken prisoner by Gen'l Welborn, the last Detatchment from Mobile Point arrived here on the 18th Ins't. I had great difficulty getting them on board the Boat there were a great number sick maney of them died on the warf before they could get on board and some died immediately after they embarked and we had to bury them, this detained the Boats some time, on the return of the Boats for a second load I directed the Indians to break up their camps and be on the warf ready to embark the same night, all the sick were brought to the spot in litters a storm came up and the Boats could not lay a long side the warf, the storm lasted for two days this rendered the situation of the Indians very unpleasant, every thing was done to secure the sick from the storm that could be I endeavoured to get them to return to their old camps but they positively declined, saying it would spoil there Physic, they had so maney superstitious notions in cases of this Kind it is verry difficult to get along with them. I now think the camp is getting healthey, but few new cases have occured since our arrival and the Indians appear well satisfied. I enclose you reports of the officers having charge of the three Detatchments while at Mobile Point every officer and agent engaged in the Creek Emigration was sick and continued so until our arrival here this has prevented me from communicating to you more promptley, I was unable a considerable part of my time to set up.

With Respect
I have the honor to be
your ob't Serv't
John Page capt &
Sup't Creeks

Maj'r Gen'l T. S. Jesup
Commanding army of the South
St Augustine
East Florida

☾

Sloan reports on the number of deaths at his encampment during the month of July. Letter found at LR, CAE, Roll 238, 597.

Pass Christian, Miss
July 31–1837—

Sir—

In obedience to your instructions requiring the number of deaths that have taken place in the camp of Indians under my charge, during the present month, I submit the following report:

From the first to the seventeenth of July, inclusive, while stationed at Mobile Point, the deaths amounted to twenty—from the 18th to the 31st of July, since their removal to this place, there have been fifteen deaths—

These are all that have been reported to me, though it is probable others have occurred that were not communicated, notwithstanding the efforts to acquire correct information on the subject.

I am, sir, very respectfully
Your ob't Serv't.
T. T. Sloan
Lt. & Disb'g. Agent.

Capt. J. Page
Supr't. Creek removal

☾

Reynolds of the U.S. Marine Corps reports that 177 Creeks have died at his encampment since the party was moved to the Gulf of Mexico—93 at Mobile Point and 84 at Pass Christian, Mississippi. Letter found at LR, CAE, Roll 238, 593. A copy of this letter also appears in Reynolds Journal, Princeton University.

Pass Christian miss

31st July 1837

Capt,

In obedience to your call, I herewith furnish a Statement of the deaths that have occured in my party since our arrival at mobile Point, and at this place, the first death occured on the 20th march, from that to 31st July, 177 deaths have taken place, 93 of which number died at the point and 84 since disembarking at this place—On 20th July 13 persons died and on the following day 12 being the greatest number on any one day—

The attending Physicians Report, I here with Enclose.

I am Sir
very Respectfully
Your obt Servt
Jno. G. Reynolds
1st Lt. U.S.M.C.
& Disb'g. agt. Ind. Dept.

Capt John Page
Superentendent creek Emigrating
Pass Christian Miss

☾

Dr. Woodfin reports that the Creeks in his camp are convalescing rapidly. Letter found at LR, CAE, Roll 238, 595.

Pass Christian
July 31st 1837

Capt.,

Agreeable to Your request, I report that although many deaths have taken place since our landing here, owing to disease contracted while at Mobile Point, the camp is now in a better state of health than it has been for three months past, nor do I believe a single case of sickness has occurred since our landing here, the indians are decidedly in a better condition as regards health, and many of those who were sick when we landed convaless rapidly—

I am Sir Respectfly
Your Obt. Svt.
J. M. Woodfin
Attend'g Physician

Capt. John Page
Superintendant
Creek Emigration

☾

Alexander H. Sommerville reports on the number of deaths and births at his encampment. Letter found at Records of the Adjutant General's Office, 1780s–1917, Entry 159-Q, Records of Major General Thomas S. Jesup, Container 18, Folder: "Letters Received, July–December 1837," NARA.

(Copy)

Pass Christian mississippie
31st July 1837

Sir

Agreeable to your instructions requireing the number of Deaths and births that have taken place in the camp of Indians under my Charge, during the present month, I Submit the following Report.

From the 4th to the 17th July inclusive while stationed at Mobile point there were four deaths from the 18th July to the 31st July and since there Removal to this point there has been 11, deaths and one birth.

The above number of deaths are all that have ben Reported and agrees with the muster Roll and also the 1 birth.

I, am Sir very Respectfully,
your Ob't Serv't
Alex. H. Sommerville
asst agent Creek

Removal

To
Cap't John Page
Sup't and Disbursing agent
Creek Emigration

☾

Dr. Gustavus Adolphus Nott reports on the health of the party under his care. Letter found at LR, CAE, Roll 238, 591. A copy of this letter is found in Reynolds Journal, Princeton University.

Pass Christian
July 31st 1837

Capt. John Page,
Superintendant Creeks

Sir—

Being called on by you to report with regard to the health of the Encampment at present, the nature of diseases &c: I would say that the prevailing diseases are those of dearrhoea, & dysentery with a few cases of intermittent fever, contracted for the most part while at Mobile Point.

There have been but few new cases since our arrival here, wich I think are to be ascribed chiefly to the imprudence of the Indians in their diet &c.

G. A. Nott
Attend'ng Phys'n

☾

Lieutenant Jacob Edmund Blake[30] reports on the death of Bateman while serving on court of inquiry (court martial) at Mount Vernon Arsenal in Alabama.[31] He was thirty-seven years old. Letter found at LR, CAE, Roll 238, 118–19.

Mount Vernon Arsenal;
Alabama, July 31st 1837—

Sir;

I have the melancholy duty to perform of reporting the death of M. W. Batman late Capt. 6th— Regt. Inf—He died this morning at this Post most suddenly and unexpectedly. He rose at 7 o'clock in the morning, and after shaving himself, proceeded to the Bath-house—When discovered there, he was stretched upon the floor, having been seized with an apoplectic fit, and it is presumed had been in that situation from ½ to ¾ of an hour before he was discovered. The Surgeon of the Post (Dr Tunstall) was immediately sent for, and every means of restoring Capt Batman resorted to, without, unfortunately, success. He died at ½ past 10 o'clock this morning, about three hours after the commencement of the attack—In the death of Capt. Batman, the Army has lost a most efficient officer; and the Indian Department, a most zealous, indefatigable, and trust-worthy agent—

His death was immediately reported to Capt. Page at Pass Christian—

I am Sir;
with the greatest respect;
Your obdt Svt
J. Edm'd Blake
Lieut. 6th—Inf.

To,
C. A. Harris, Esq'r
Commissioner Indian Affairs,
Washington D.C.

☾

Page notifies the commissioner of Indian affairs on the appointments of Wooldridge and Carver to block the introduction of alcohol into the camps at Pass Christian. Page reports that while the Creeks are intoxicated they are a danger to the agents. Letter found at LR, CAE, Roll 238, 599.

Pass Christian Mississippie
4 august 1837

Sir

I have the honor to report Isaac N. Wooldridge and William Carver[32] as ass't agents in the Creek Removal during the period we Remain at that this place; one to be located in a little town one mile from the Indian Camp, the other at a point where small boats are in the habit of landing. I find these two appointments are absolutely necessary to suppress the sale of whiskey and other intoxicating liquors there is a certain class of people that will sell liquor to the Indians unless they are strictly watched: the Indians when drunk are perfectly uncontrolable and the lives of the agents are in dainger; the appointment of these two agents can suppress the sale of liquors to Indians. their appointments took affect on the 1st Ins't thus far our camps have been in perfect order, so large a body of Indians as we have got here without the aid of Troops are hard to controll, when the Indians have access to whiskey, when deprived of it all is quiet and good order.

With Respect
I have the honor to bee
your ob't serv't
John Page capt &
Sup't Creeks

To—
C. A. Harris Esq'r
Commissioner of Indian affairs
Washington City

☾

Page reports Dr. Edmund Wiedemann replaces Dr. Nott, who is sick, and that the newspapers have retracted their negative stories about the condition of the camp. Letter found at LR, CAE, Roll 238, 607.

Pass Christian Mississip
15th august 1837

Sir

I have the honor to report I have employed Doc't Edmund Weidemann, as physician to attend the sick—Doc't Nott is taken sick and the duties are too ardious for two physicians, the camp is about three miles in length and they are compel'd to be employed night and day to attend the calls of the Indians, (which I have Requested them to do)—Since my last report nothing of note has occured, the camp is getting healthy and thus far in most excellent order. I have stope'd the selling of intoxicating liquors to Indians, and shall hope to continue so during our stay here.—

There was a piece in one of the news papers that came out casting some reflections,[33] I sent Lieue't. Reynolds in advance with the first party, on his arrival the grog shops were thrown open to the Indians and of course most of them got drunk, this was unavoidable on the part of the agents; the man that wrote the piece happened to be here Just at that period, and although the camp with Jim Boy arm and arm both drunk and continued so during his stay: on my arrival here I took measures to suppress the liquor, and all who have visited our camp and see for themselves admit they never saw more regularity or Indians made more comfortable than those Indians. those papers that did come out with Reflecting pieces, have since retracted, having been an eye witness of the state of our camp.[34]

With Respect—I have
The honor to be your
obt Serv't
John Page Capt & Supt Creeks

C. A. Harris Esq'r

Commissioner of Indian affairs
Washington City

☾

Dr. Woodfin reports to Reynolds that the sick in his camp are improving in health. Letter found at LR, CAE, Roll 238, 652. A copy of this letter also appears in Reynolds Journal, Princeton University.

Pass Christian
26th Aug 1837

Sir

Since my last report, & since the removal of the indians to this place, a decided and happy change has taken place in the comfort and health of the camp. Many of those who were sick when I last reported are well, others convalescent; some it is true have died, but the deaths are comparitively few and a large portion of those who die are infants and infirm aged persons.

Yesterday in my division of the encampment there was not a death, to day I have to report the death of an aged man who had been for some time under indian treatment: The number of sick however has not increased and I do not think there is more sickness than could be expected from so large a number of men women & children. The prevailing diseases are Bilious fever, ague[35] & fever, dearrhae and some few cases of Dessentary.

very Respectly
Your Obt Svt
J M Woodfin
Attend'g Physician

Lieut J. G. Reynolds
Disbursing agent
Creek Emigra'tn

☾

Dr. Wiedemann reports that his camp is in good condition and that he only has thirteen who are sick. Letter found at Reynolds Journal, Princeton University.

Pass Christian

27th August 1837

Sir,

Having been called on by you for my report in relation to the health of the Camp.

I have the satisfaction to report, that the camp is in a good condition and the number of sick very few at present   I have only thirteen sick most of which are covalescent. The prevailing deseases are Diarrhoe, Dyssentary, ague and fever, and some few cases of Bilious fever of very mild type.

Very Respectfully
Your obt. Servt.
E Wiedeman
Att'g Phys

Lieut Jno G Reynolds
Disb'g agent
Creek Emigration

☾

Reynolds reports that a detachment of Creek volunteers arrived from Tampa Bay and large numbers of Creeks are at Fort Claiborne, Alabama. Letter found at LR, CAE, Roll 238, 650–51. A copy of this letter also appears in Reynolds Journal, Princeton University.

Pass Christian miss.
27 Augt 1837

Sir,

Since Capt. Page's departure, to wit. 22nd inst. no change has taken place, the indians are perfectly satisfied and the sick are convalescing very Rapidly; Enclosed you will Receive the Reports of the Physicians in Relation to the Deseases now prevailing in the Camp.

On 21st inst a detachment of upwards of 200 creek volunteers arrived from Tampay Bay, the act'g officer in charge wished to Retain the command of the Party, to which of course I could not consent, as they were to be Rationed upon Requisition from a seperate Dept, the reasons assigned, were, that they had not been mustered out of Service—I trust this step will meet with your approbation.

I have been informed there are a considerable number of creek indians (some of whom are fugitives) at Fort Claiborn about 200 miles above Mobile on the Ala. River, who are desirous to Emegrate, provided means were Extended, by which they could join the parties at this place—I have sent asst. Conductor Noah Felton, to afford the necessary transportation.

I am Sir,
very Respectfully
your Obt. Servant
Jno. G. Reynolds
1st Lieut. U.S.M.C.
& Disb'g Agt. Ind. Dept

C. A. Harris Esq'r
Comm'r of Indian Affairs
Washington City

☾

Reynolds reports on the events that led to his arrest for destroying the barrels of whiskey. Letter found at Reynolds Journal, Princeton University.

Creek Indian Encampment
Pass Christian mississippie
2d Sept 1837

Sir

I am pleased to have it in my power to represent upon the authority of the Physicians and personal observation,—the indians in a better condition as to health &c than they have been for some months, we have but few deaths reported since my last report Sixteen have died, as you will observe by the attending Physicians reports, which I have the honor herewith to enclose—

I have just returned from the Bay of St Louis distant six miles whither Lieut Sloan and my self were arrainged before a sivil court for a "riot" on the night of 26th July Inst. I say Riot, as the State attorney was pleased to term it as such I Know not whether Capt Page previous to his departure west informed the Department of the facts or not, but it was by his authority we went forth, the Court without hearing any mitigating circumstances, sentenced us to pay the sum of $100 Each for an assault upon three individuals, who were whiskey sellers, but no cencure as blame was attached for destroying the property, neither would theire have been a fine, could the law in any manner have been evaded by the Jury, the property was destroyed by Knocking in the heads of three whiskey Barrels, there is not one desenting voice as to the correctness of our course, as the subsequeant state of the Indians fully proves previous to the affair of that night, the indians were in a constant state of drunkenness, consequently dangerous, the sickness of the camp may in a great measure be attributed to the abundant use of whiskey—since that period, not only the inhabitants have become Reconsiled and Contented to remain at their homes, but it rarely occurs that an indian is seen drunk, previously, in consequence of their constant state of excitement they were wholly unmanageable—

The revised Regulations no. 4 forwarded for our goverment, had not been received, otherwise a verry differrent Course would have been persued, the Civil authority would have been appliyed too. Although six miles distant by water—the Lawyers fees (Mr Ives of New Orleans) are $100—fine $100 each and cost, those who were entitled to the latter, positively refused to accept—the Jury and the respectable citizens have Requested Gov'r Lynch[36] to Refund the fine. The Hon'r Harry Cage, volunteered his valuable Services, notwithstanding fifteen years absence from the bar his Eloquence made a great impression on all who heard him—the Reccord of the court together with exspences, so soon as obtained will be forwarded for your consideration.

The principal of the three Individuals above alluded to, has constantly annoyed us by bringing barrels of whiskey into the verry heart of the Encampment; he acknowledged before the Court of haveing sold a great many barrels of whiskey to the indians. A complaint was lodged against him, he was fined $20 for Every offence, being unable to pay, I am informed he has been committed to [jail].

I am Sir
Verry Respectfully
Your obt Servt—
Jno. G. Reynolds
1st Lieut U.S.M.C.
& Disbur'g Agt. Ind. Depart.

C. A. Harris Esq'r
Comm'sr Indian affairs
Washington City

☾

The following is the physician's report alluded to at the beginning of Reynolds's 2 September 1837 letter to C. A. Harris. Letter found at Reynolds Journal, Princeton University.

Pass Christian miss
2d September 1837

Sir

The weather being fine and no changes haveing taken place to alter the condition and health of the encampment I have to report the division to which I am attatched in the same good health and condition as when I last reported, seven death have taken place and no new cases since last Report.

Verry Respectfully
Your Ob't Servt—
J. M. Woodfin
attending Physician
Creek Emigration

Lieu't J. G. Reynolds
Disbursing Agent
Creek Emigration

☾

The following is the physician's report alluded to at the beginning of Reynolds's 2 September 1837 letter to C. A. Harris. Letter found at LR, CAE, Roll 238, 658; copy found at Reynolds Journal, Princeton University.

Pass Christian
2. Sept. 1837.

Sir,

Agreably to your orders, I herrwith furnish a statement of the Sick and deaths, in Your Camp for the last week.

Six Dyssentary
five Bilious fever[37]
two childern Rhachitis[38]

two old men Phtysis[39]
one child Tympanitis[40]

One only has died under my prescription five under Indian treatment.

Verry Respectfully
your Obt Servt
Dr E. Wiedemann
Attg Physician

To/
Lt. John G. Reynolds
Disb'g Agent
Ind. Depart.

☾

Reynolds, who became the acting superintendent of Creek relocation after the departure of Captain Page on 22 August, notifies the other officers that the Creeks are to stay within a five-mile radius of camp. Letter found at Reynolds Journal, Princeton University.

Circular

It haveing come to the Knowledge of the Acting Superintendant of Creek Removal that many of the Indians have Strayed to the distance of twenty to forty miles without the assent of the officers of the respective parties to which they belong, and contrary to a possitive assurance given by the Indians themselves previous to Disembarking at this place.—I have to entreat that the Citizens will extend no favours whatever to any Indians found beyond the distance of five miles from the encampment as passes for hunting, fishing, and other necessary amusements are in no instance given to extend beyound that distance.

The citizens will confer a great favour on the officers connected with the Emmigration, by demanding in every case the passes of the Indians found withought the limits of the encampment, and if found not to answer the date and distance will insist upon there immediate return to camp. Sternness and determination Seldom or ever fails to answer the purpose intended.

Jno G Reynolds
1st Lieut U.S.M.C.
& Disb'g agt Ind. Dept.
& act'g Sup't creek Removal

Indian Encampment
Pass Christian Mississippie
2d Sep't 1837

☾

Order no. 172 required the movement of the Creeks to Indian territory as soon as the volunteers were mustered out of service. Order found at Reynolds Journal, Princeton University.

H'd Qrs army of the South
Tampa Bay Sept 2nd 1837

order
no. 172

Par VII— The superentendant of creek Removal will require the contractors to commence the movement of the whole body of Indians westward so soon as the [regiments] be discharged and paid.

By order maj Gen'l Jesup
B Lennard[41]
a.D.C. & act'g adj Gen'l[42]

Superentendant creek Removal

☾

Reynolds reports on the deteriorated condition of the surplus baggage of detachments 1 and 6 left on the Gulf over the spring and summer of 1837. Letter found at Reynolds Journal, Princeton University.

Indian Encampment
Pass Christian mississ
5th Sept—1837

Sir,

The indians will not agree, that any contract be made whereby they will [be] seperated, from their baggage although they have a great deal more than the contract with the Alabamma Emigrating company obligees them to transport, the condition of the surplus baggage of party no. 1 now in store at mobile Point, has in a great degree determined the indians to resist any measure calculated to place them in a like situation. Indian Sagartee alias Yargee (brother to Tuskenia Haw, and son of the late celebrated chief Tustanuggee Locco or Big Wariors) the principal indian of the detatchment of the young Florida volunteers, drawn from party no. 1 (Hopothle Yohola's) has been informed of the total destruction of his clothes &c—by moths and says, it is useless to convey them west, as they will not be received by his people; I have seen the baggage alluded to, a considerable portion of which, is in a verry damaged state, the Iron of a wrought nature, such as Rifles barrels, plough—Shevres &c—are very much caroded and unfit for use—

As the proposals for conveying the surplus baggage of nos. 1 & 6 parties are advertised to be presented and opened on the 10th Ins't and Knowing the feelings of the Indians of the latter, I have considered it proper, to advise the Dept of the Difficulty that is likely to be encountered by embracing the surplus baggage of no. 6 with that of no. 1—I would Respectfully suggest the propriety of making seperate contracts for the transportation of the baggage of each party, unless the company will contract for the whole in which event, all the surplus baggage can be carried by the boats that carry the Indians as far as water conveyance will admit; land transportation should then be afforded for the surplus baggage of this party; as I fear they will not consent to haveing it stored—

Before acting upon any bid that may be given in Relation to the baggage, I shall wait for further instructions.—

I am Sir,
Verry Respectfully,
Your obt.—Servt.—
John G. Reynolds

1st Lieu't U.S.M.C.
& Disbur'g Agt. Ind Dept

C. A. Harris Esq'r
Commissioner of Indian affairs
Washington City

☾

Campbell and Beattie notify Lieutenant Reynolds's that they have purchased white beans and were directed by Captain Page to issue them. Letter found at Reynolds Journal, Princeton University.

Pass Christian
September 7th 1837

Sir

At the Special request of the Supt. Creek removal, the alabama Emigrating Company have purchased a large Quantity of white Beans and have been directed by the Sup't. to make issues of Beans every fourth day—The alabama Emigrating Company have to request that you receive the issue as directed by the Superentendant.

W/ respect
Your obt. Servts
Campbell & Beattie
members ala Em Co

Lt J G Reynolds
u s marine Corps
act Supt Creeks

☾

Reynolds notifies contractors William A. Campbell and William J. Beattie that they are not allowed to serve the Indians beans as a substitute for the rations specified in the contract. Letter found at Reynolds Journal, Princeton University.

Pass Christian
Indian Encampment
7th September 1837

Gentlemen,

As beans are not recognised in the contract Entered into by the United States and the alabama Emigrating Company, as contractors, and not knowing the views of the Superentendant in relation to the substitution of beans—I must decline forcing the Indians to receive any thing as a substitute, for any Expressed component part of the rations.

I am Gentlemen &c
very Respectfully
Your obt. Servt.
Jno G Reynolds
1st Lieut U.S.M.C.
& Disb'g. agt. Ind. Dept.

Messrs Campbell & Beattie
Contractors, and members of Alabama Emigrating Company

☾

Reynolds reports on the sickness in New Orleans, wandering Creek Indians, and settlers' fears that the Creeks are killing their livestock. Letter found at Reynolds Journal, Princeton University.

Indian Encampment
Pass Christian miss
9th September 1837

Sir,

The Encampment continues as to health, the same as when last reported—many persons arrive at this place from new orleans daily, to avoid the Epidemic, now so dreadfully prevailing in that city, my only fears are that the disease, may by accident get among the people, in which Event the mortality must be very great; Every measure of police to prevent the introduction of unseasonable and improper fruits has been adopted; whiskey and spirits of all kinds cannot now be reached by the indians—intoxication has entirely ceased.

On the 2nd inst. I was informed that many of the men had strayed to some distance in the interior, that the citizens were becoming alarmed, fearing depredations might be committed on their property, and requested measures be taken to get them in the Encampment—I knew of no other method to Effect it, than by issuing a circular, requesting the aid of the people, which you will find herewith Enclosed—

I was in hopes the circular would have the Effect designed, a gentleman direct from the country called at my tent and stated, the indians, in small parties of four to Six, had been hovering about his neighborhood for some time, that signs of killing stock, had in many instances been seen, in consequence of which, at the urgent solicitation of his neighbors, he was induced, before adopting any disided measures to confer with the officer—having charge—of the Emigration—I told him it was positivily against the superintendants wish and a recient order, which he would discover by reading the circular issued on 2nd inst. copies of which was furnished, he was perfectly satisfied and assured me the indians should be drove in. The large number of indians Encamped, with no physical means, renders it impossible for the officers to prevent, or know, when they absent themselves; the many fugitive creeks that have joined from time to time, doubtless are the ones complained of, as many are missing (without permission) from the camp.

In my report of 27th ult. I informed you of dispatching asst. conductor Noah Felton, to Fort Claiborn ala, he has returned with nine indians only, the others to the number of twenty or more refused to accompany him.

I am Sir
very Respectfully
Your obt. Servt.
Jno. G. Reynolds
1st Lt. U.S.M.C.
& Disb'g agt Ind Deprt

C A Harris Esqr
Commissioner Indian affairs,
Washington City.

☾

Jesup's instructions for the final relocation of the Creek warriors and their families from Pass Christian to Indian territory. These are the orders under which Lieutenant Reynolds was operating during his conflict with the Alabama Emigrating Company over the amount of transportation required. "Captain Boyd" refers to Capt. George Boyd. Letter found at Records of the Adjutant General's Office, 1780s–1917, Entry 159-Q, Records of Major General Thomas S. Jesup, Container 28, Folder: "Orders Sent by Gen. Jesup and Staff, September 1837 (1 of 2)," NARA.

Tampa Bay, Sept. 9th 1837.

Sir,

You will proceed with the last detachment of Creek Warriors on board the Tomochichi to Pass Christian where you will make arrangements to discharge the regiment.

Lieut. F. Searle[43] will muster and discharge them, and Major D. Fraser[44] will pay them—they are to be mustered and paid to the time of their discharge; for although they were mustered into service for twelve months, the contract with the chiefs was for an indifinite period, and they are entitled to pay for the time they will have been actually retained in service.

I desire you to see that every comfort and convenience which the contractors are bound to provide be secured to the Indians, and that they be put in motion to the west without unnecessary delay.

I desire you and Captain Boyd to assist them in the transacting of their business in New Orleans—They will desire to make many purchases for themselves and families; and they should be advised not to waste their money but to purchase such articles only as shall be really useful—they should be told of the necessity of providing against the cold weather which they will have to encounter before they arrive at their new homes; and I wish you and Captain Boyd to assist them in their purchases, so as to prevent imposition being practised upon them.

If on examining the contract for their removal you should find that the contractors are not bound to furnish sufficient transportation for the Sick, and infirm, nor for the articles necessary for their comfort on the route, you are authorized to direct Mr. Reynolds, or whosoever may be charged with Superintending the emigration, to make the necessary provision for these purposes.

You will cause a careful account of the Killed, and of all the Chiefs and Warriors who have died, to be taken; and furnish me a duplicate of it. You will send one copy direct to the War Department.

Advise them not to change their Bank notes at a discount: as the Govement Pay them in paper it is morally bound to *make good *any depreciation which may take place; the notes, in the mean time, will obtain for them any articles which they may have occasion to purchase; and should they sell them for specie at a loss the Government would not be bound for the loss. Advise them there to retain the same notes they receive, and to part with none but for such necessary articles as they may require.

It is desirable that the Second battalion be not detained by the slow progress of the other battalions; as the families of the chiefs and warriors are already west of the Mississippi, it is proper that they should be pushed on as rapidly as possible.

Should the 2nd battalion move seperately, & you think it adviseable, or the Indians desire it, Captain Boyd may be continued in service and accompany the second battalion to the west. In that event he will be instructed to proceed to Washington, on completing that service, for the settlement of his public accounts.

*Having accomplished the service with which you are now charged you will join me wheresoever I may be for special duty.

With great respect & regard

I am, Sir,
your ob't serv't
Th. S. Jesup
Major Gen'l Com'd

Major W. G. Freeman,[45]
Com'd Creek Volunteers,
Tampa Bay,—

*You will cause all accounts for express and other services performed by the Indians to be made out and properly certified; and they will be paid by Lt Searle who will have funds in his hands for that purpose.

Should any cases arise on which you have not specific instructions, you will consider yourself authorized to exercise a judicious discretion.

☾

Reynolds reports on the arrival of sixty volunteers and the forthcoming departure of detachment 6 for the West. He advises that a short detention in New Orleans will allow the Creeks to avoid sickness at New Orleans. Letter found at Reynolds Journal, Princeton University.

Pass Christian missi
13th Sept 1837

Sir

I have the honor to Report the arrival of sixty creek volunteers from Tampa Bay, the officer in charge informs me, the remainder are on their way hither; so soon as they arrive, mustered out of service and paid off, there will be nothing to detain us from moving—The sickness of new orleans can Easily be avoided with the aid of the civil authority, to prevent the indians from straying, we can pass through, with but a few hours detention.

The mustering out officer, and pay master will be here in a day or two—I hope your views as to an Early movement, will be given as soon as practicable—

I am Sir
Very Respectfully
Your obt. Servt
Jno G Reynolds
1st Lieut U.S.M.C.
& Disb'g agt Ind Deprt

C A Harris Esq'r
Comm'r Indian affairs
washington City

☾

Reynolds writes to New Orleans mayor Denis Prieur[46] requesting the use of a force to prevent the Creeks from deserting the party as they pass through the Crescent City. Letter found at Reynolds Journal, Princeton University.

Indian Encampment
Pass Christian miss.
14th Sept. 1837

Sir,

The Emegration of this party creek indians, will take place between the 5th and 10th of next month, in order to guard against the Epidemic so dreadfully prevailing in your city, and being necessarially obliged to pass through it; I have the honor to Request the aid of any disposable force within your authority, to prevent the indians from straying from the party, as they naturally will do, if not prevented—It is our intention to transport the party over the Rail Road, where Steam Boats will be in Readiness to Receive them, without any detention, other than the conveyance of the baggage from the cars to the Boats.

I have the honor
to be Sir,
Very Respectfully
Your Obt. Servt
Jno. G. Reynolds
Lt. & Emegrating agent

To his honor
mayor of the city
New orleans

☾

Reynolds notifies William A. Campbell that detachment 6 should be prepared to move between the 5th and 10th of October 1837. Letter found at Reynolds Journal, Princeton University.

Indian Encampment
Pass Christian miss.
14th Sept. 1837

Col. Wm A. Campbell
Agent & member
Ala. Emegt'g Company.

Sir,

It is the Department's wish, that the movement of this party west, should take place at the Earliest possible period, there being nothing that presents itself to me to debar that intention: I have to Request necessary measures be taken on behalf of the company, of which you are Agent and member, to carry into Effect the views of the Dept. on or before the 10th day of Oct. next, but not sooner than the 5 of that month.

I am Sir,
Very Respectfully
Your obt. Servt.
Jno. G Reynolds
1st Lieut. U.S.M.C.
& Disb'g Agt. Ind. Dept.
& Act'g Supt. creek Removal

☾

Campbell responds to Reynolds's 14 September letter and reports on the readiness of the Alabama Emigrating Company to move the Creeks to Indian territory. Letter found at Reynolds Journal, Princeton University.

Pass christian Missi
Sept 14th 1837

Lieut J G Reynolds
Disb'g agt &
act. Supt creek removal

Sir

Yours of this date has been rec'd, directing me on the part of the alabama Emigrating Company, to be in readiness with Suitable transportation for western Emigration from the 5th to the 10th Oct'r next.

I have the honor to inform you on the part of the company, that we have now in readiness all the transportation that is required of the company, agreable to their contract for the removal of the creek Indians west of the mississippi.

I am Sir
Your obt Servt
Wm A Campbell
agt & member of the Alabama Emigrating Company

☾

Reynolds apprises the commissioner of Indian affairs that the party is preparing to recommence its journey westward. Letter found at Reynolds Journal, Princeton University.

Indian Encampment
Pass christian missi
15th Sept. 1837

Sir,

Enclosed, you will receive copies of several letters in relation to Emigration; the object of giving so long a notice to the company to be in readiness, was in consequence of the sickness of new orleans, that the company might have ample time to make their arrangements with the rail road company for transportation, without being detained beyond the period necessary for the transfer of the baggage from the cars to the steam Boats—You will discover by Doct. weiderman's letter, that there is no danger to be apprehended from sickness in the short time that we would be detained, in the city, moreover, I have conversed with many gentlemen, Residents of New orleans, all of whom agree with Doctor Weiderman in opinion, but consider a nights exposure in the city would be fatal to many of us—The indians have had Everything Explained in relation to the disease, notwithstanding are willing to move: many particularly the warriors taken from no. 1 party are exceedingly anxious to Join their friends.

The company has informed me through their agent Col Campbell, they will deliver the Extra baggage of both parties at Fort Gibson without seperating it from the party, at Twenty dollars per hundred weight.

Be please to answer me by Express—it takes thirteen days by regular mail to recive a letter from Washington.

I am sir very Respectfully, Your obt. servt
Jno G Reynolds
1st Lieut U.S.M.C. & Disb'g agt Ind Deprt

C. A. Harris Eqr

Comm'r Indian affairs
washington city

☾

Dr. Wiedemann gives his professional opinion that the Creeks will not be exposed to the fever in New Orleans, if kept in the city for a short time. Letter found at Reynolds Journal, Princeton University.

Pass Christian miss
15th Sept. 1837

Sir,

I have Received your note of this date, to the principal inquiry, to wit, whether there will be danger in transporting the indians through the city of New Orleans, during the prevalence of the fever now Raging in that city? I will answer, having Reciently visited New orleans, for the purpose of purchasing medicines, for the Sick and witnessing the cause and Effects of the desease in one of the Hospital, do unhesitatingly give it as my opinion, that there is not the slightest danger of contracting the fever, for the Short period that the indians will Remain, before Embarking on board the boats.

I am Sir
your Obt. Servant
Edmund Wiedemann
Att'g Physician

Lieut. Jno. G. Reynolds
Act'g Supt. creek Removal

☾

Dr. Woodfin gives his professional opinion that the Creeks will not be exposed to the fever in New Orleans, if kept in the city for a short time. Letter found at Reynolds Journal, Princeton University.

Pass Christian
15th Sep't 1837

Sir

Your note of this morning requesting my opinion in regard to the danger and liability of transporting the Indians through New Orleans and the prevailing epidemic of that city has been received, I cannot conceive Sir that if the arrangement as expressed in your note are made the short period the Indians will be exposed to the atmosphere of orleans can materially effect their health nor do I believe that in their present good health they can possibly take the yellow fever from so slight an exposure, and I must give it as my decided opinion that it is neither dangerous nor injurious.

Very Respectfully
Your obt Servt
J. M. Woodfin
Attg Physician

Lieut Jno G Reynolds
Disb'g agent and
act'g Supt Creek Removal

☾

Reynolds seeks clarification on the type of transportation that will be used to transport the Creeks west. Letter found at Reynolds Journal, Princeton University.

Indian Encampment
Pass Christian miss—
15th Sept. 1837

Sir,

In your communication of yesterdays date, you informed me, that "all the transportation Required of the Ala. Emegrating Comp'y, agreeably to the contract, for the Removal of the creek indians west of the Mississippi was Ready"—Will you have the goodness to inform me, the kind of transportation it is the companies intention to afford this party; if by water, the number of Steam Boats, that will be Employed and the number of indians it is intended to be transported on Each boat, together with the tonage of Each and the conveniencies of transportation generally—

I make this Request, in consequence of the Season, the liabilities of sickness &c. &c. of which, you are as fully informed as myself.

I am Sir,
Very Respectfully
Your Obt. Servt.
Jno G Reynolds
1st Lt. U.S.M.C.
Disb'g Agt. Ind. Dept
& Act'g Supt. creek Removal

Col. Wm A. Campbell
Agent, & member
Ala. Emegt'g Comp'y

☾

Campbell responds to Reynolds's 15 September letter requesting information on the type of transportation to be used by the Alabama Emigrating Company. Letter found at Reynolds Journal, Princeton University.

Indian Encampment
Pass Christian miss—
15th Sept. 1837—

Lieut. Jno. G. Reynolds

Sir,

Yours of this date Requesting me to inform you the kind of transportation the ala E. Co. propose using in the removal of the creek Indians from this place west of the mississippi is before me. The Kind of transportation that we have is steam Boats the Tonage of which is from 150 to 280 Tons burthen we also design using with each st Boat, a Barge of 60 Tons, and on each boat with its barge we will transport from 800 to 1000 Indians, the barges of course cant be used untill we get in the mississippi river. This Kind of transporation will be used as far as the waters are navigable for St Boats, in the Land transportation you are aware the contract is explicit.

I am Sir
Your obt Servt
Wm A Campbell
agt & member
Ala. E. Co

Lieut J. G. Reynolds
Disbursing agt
& act Supt of
Creek Removal West

☾

Beattie and Campbell request a precise date of departure in order to anticipate when other transportation will be needed along the route. They also demand indemnities in case of detention. Letter found at Reynolds Journal, Princeton University.

Pass Christian
September 16th 1837

Sir

In your order of the 14th inst to the alabama Emigrating Company you have not specified any precise time you intend to turn over to the said Company the Creek Indians for emigration the Com'r of Ind affairs has notified the Emigrating Company, that a precise period should be fixed on to start & that the said Company should have ample notice of it. You will readily percieve the necessity of fixing a time precisely Look at the locality of this landing, and you will see that Boats are exposed in an open lake to all the gales and boistrous weather prevalent on this coast at this season of the year, there is also another Equally important consideration to the Co. you are aware that different Kinds of transportation have to be prepared on the route west, and to know the precise time of starting, will Enable the Company to have their different transportation all in readiness so that no delay may be Experience on the route, any delay on the part of the government after the day desinated for starting will cause the same delay with all the transportation intended to be used on the miss River and also all the teams intended for the route by land through arkansas, the Company will Expect to be fully indemified for all detention on the part of the Gov't from and after the time fixed for starting.

we are sir
mt Respectfully
Your obt Servts
Wm A Campbell and
Wm J Beattie
agts & member ala E company

J G Reynolds
1st Lt U.S.M.C.
Disb'g agt Ind Dept
& act'g supt creek removal

☾

Reynolds reports that detachment 6 will be ready to move on 5 October 1837. Letter found at Reynolds Journal, Princeton University.

Indian Encampment
Pass Christian miss
16th Sept 1837

Gentlemen,

I have received your communication of this date, and must acknowledge that I am not a little surprised at the position you have assumed, on behalf of the company of which you are members, in regard to the period of departure—A latitude of five days was given in my notice of the 14th inst Entirely to suit the convienance of the Company; this proving disagreeable, in consequence of the precise day not being fixed—I now state that on the 5th day of next month the whole party of creeks Encamped at this place will be ready to Embark.

I am
very Respectfully
Your obt. Servt—
Jno G Reynolds
act'g Supt creek removal

Messrs Wm A Campbell
& Wm J Beattie
members ala Emigt'g Comp'y.

☾

Reynolds orders the Alabama Emigrating Company to procure a steamboat for every five hundred Creeks and to double land transportation (double the number of wagons specified in the contract). Letter found at Reynolds Journal, Princeton University.

Indian Encampment
Pass Christian miss
18th Sept 1837

Gentlemen,

The contract Entered into by the united States with your company, not Embracing water conveyance for the Emigration of the creeks, and it being the positive directions of Major Gen'l Jesup, Comd'g army of the south, that this party be transported with Every Ease and convenience as well as comfort—I have to request, in obedience to the wish of the Commd'g General, that the company will provide by the date specified in my communication of the 16th inst, steam Boats for their transportation, Each boat to accommodate and carry, not to exceede five hundred indians. The land transportation, as defined in the contract, is such as will render the sick and infirm Exceedingly uncomfortable, you are therefore directed that instead of one wagon for the number of persons and weight of baggage as Expressed in the contract, to furnish two, the best of their kind.

As it is the wish of the Major Gen'l Commd'g that Every necessary article for the comfort of the party on the Route be furnished—I have to request you to inform me, the kind of provisions it is the intention of the company to issue, agreeably to the contract.

I am Gentlemen
very Respectfully
Your obt. Servt
Jno. G Reynolds
1st Lieut U.S.M.C.
Disb'g agt. &c

Messrs Wm a Campbell
& Wm J Beattie
agents and members
of the ala Emgt'g Company

☾

Campbell and Beattie demand to see the written orders that require them to procure a steamboat for every five hundred Creeks and to double land transportation. Letter found at Reynolds Journal, Princeton University.

Pass Christian
Septr 18th 1837

Sir

We have the honor to acknowledge the receipt of yours of this inst, ordering the ala. Em. Co. to furnish Extra transportation &c. for the Emigrating Indians, which you say is in complyance of the Special orders of Major Gen'l Jesup Commanding the army of the south will you be pleased Sir, to furnish us extracts, of such of your instructions as require you to cause Extra transportation to be prepared for the Emigrating creek Indians—

In Complyance Sir You will
much oblige
your most obt Servts
Wm A Campbell
Wm J Beattie

J G Reynolds
1st Lt U.S.M.C.
Disb'g agt Ind Dept
& act Supt creek removal

☾

Major William G. Freeman reiterates that no more than five hundred Creeks should be placed on any one steamboat and that the number of wagons provided under the contract with the Alabama Emigrating Company is woefully inadequate. Letter found at Reynolds Journal, Princeton University.

Pass christian miss
Sept 18th 1837

Sir

By direction of major Genl Jesup comdg the army of the south I have examined the contract entered into between the u. states and the alabama Emigrating company, for the removal of the creek Indians west of the mississippi—By the terms of this contract, it appears that land transportation—only was contemplated by the contracting parties as I learn that it is the intention of the Emigrating company to make use of steam navigation for a great portion of the journey, you are here by directed in that Event, to order a board of survey to assemble and report what number of Indians should be transported in Each Boat with a due regard to their health and comfort—In my own opinion, not more than five hundred should be put on Each—the transportation of a greater number, taking into consideration the extent of sickness prevalent among them, and the heat of the season, would be attended with fatal consequencies, as regards land transportation, the quantity provided by contract is greatly less than that authorised by the revised Regulations, concerning the Emigration of Indians; and totally insufficient for the proper conveyance of the sick and infirm togeather with the baggage, you are therefore authorised by direction of maj. Gen'l Jesup, to make the necessary provision for those purposes—

The above remarks are in conformity with my instructions from the commanding General, and intended principally to apply to the Regiment of creek volunteers: but I may state in general terms, that he is exceedingly anxious that every attention be paid to the wants of the Indians, so that all may reach their new homes with no other feeling than those of friendship towards the whites.

I am sir most Respectfully
Your obt Servt
W G Freeman
maj. cK vols
comd'g Rgt

For
Lieut John G Reynolds
1st Lieut U.S.M.C.
Disbursing agent Ind Dept
& act'g supt creek removal
Pass christian miss

☾

Reynolds asks the attending physicians, Woodfin, Wiedemann, and Hulse, to research the number of people who can safely travel on board a steamboat during the low stage of the Mississippi River. Letter found at Reynolds Journal, Princeton University.

Indian Encampment
Pass Christian miss
19th Sept 1837

Gent

It is desirable that comfortable transportation be Extended to the indians more particularly at this season of the year; the Ala. Emegt'g Comp'y not being obliged by their contract to transport or move with less than one thousand to Each party and Steam Boat conveyance not being Expressed in the contract I have to Request that you will in your official capacity consult together, and Report the number of indians you consider it would be safe to Embark on board of Each boat—If you are uninformed as to the danger of steam Boat navigation on the Mississippi at the low Stage of its waters, you will be pleased to obtain information from such gentlemen, natives of New orleans, as are temporareally Residents of this place and Report the Effect of your inquiries.

Respectfully
your Obt Servt
Jno G Reynolds
1st Lt U.S.M.C.
Disb'g Agt. Ind Dept
& Act'g Supt. creek Rem.

Docts Woodfin
Widermann
Hultz

☾

Dr. Woodfin forwards the opinions of Drs. Wiedemann and Hulse, and encloses a letter from steamboat owners and captains, regarding the proper number of people that can safely ride a steamboat during low water. Letter found at Reynolds Journal, Princeton University.

Pass Christian miss
22nd Sept. 1837

Sir,

I have availed myself of the first opportunity to obtain the necessary information in Regard to the num— of indians to be transported on Each St Boat up the Mississippi River, in its present low stage of its waters—I herewith Enclose you a communication from several owners and Capts of St Boats; which I believe contains the most correct informa— in my power to obtain, it is founded on several years Experience in the navigation of the Mississi—I have also consulted Drs Hultz and Widerman on the subject, the former of these Dr H has had Some Experience in the transportation of indians and says he has never known more than four to five hundred indians transported on Steam Boats or seven superficial square feet to Every indian, Embracing men, woman and children—In Regard to my own opinion on the subject, I can say but little, however I cannot differ with those gentlemen whoes communication I have Enclosed, nor with Dr Hultz they having had much Experience in the transportation of indians and St. Boat navigation generally—It is absolutely necessary to promote the health of the indians, that they should not be crowded on Boats, Each one should have ample space and by all means the different departments should be kept clean and [also] ventulated.

Respectfully &c &c
J. M. Woodfin

Lieut Reynolds

☾

The following is the enclosed letter from steamboat owners and captains mentioned in Woodfin's 22 September letter. Letter found at Reynolds Journal, Princeton University.

Pass christian, Sept. 21. 1837

To/
Dr J. M. Woodfin
Directing Physian
Creek Emigration

Sir,

In compliance with your request to state our opinion in regard to the number of Indians that it would be safe to transport up the mississipi River, at this season of the Year, on board of steam Boats of 150 tons burden & upwards, and the liability to sickness to submit it the following as our opinion founded in several years expirience and intimate connection with steam Boats navigation in the Western Waters. The scale below we believe to exhibit the greatest number of Indians, including children that can be carried with safety on Board of Boats of the Burden there described—viz:

Boat of 150 tons to carry 375

200	425
250	500
300	625
400	750
500	875

In the foregoing scale we suppose the Boats to be built as they are generaly for the navigation of the mississippi.

As to the danger of sickness that they may be exposed to, we consider the greatest that of being crowded, and a want of room to exercise and the consequent uncleanliness, therefore we consider the most important to the preservation of health, that they Indians should be allowed each day from one to two hours for the purpose of exercise on shore, and to give time for a through cleansing of the Decks of the Boat.

We are very respectfully
Your ob't Servts
(Signed) Calvin T. maynard
(Signed) P. M. Turner
(Signed) N. Beckwith
(Signed) Francis Turner

☾

The Alabama Emigrating Company gives the reasons why they cannot and will not comply with the order to provide double the land transportation and to limit the number of Creeks per steamboat to five hundred people. Letter found at Reynolds Journal, Princeton University.

Pass Christian
September 23d 1837

Sir

You have this moment favored us with the perusal of the orders of major Genl Jesup to WG Freeman major commanding creek volunteers also maj Freemans orders to you of the 18th inst together with your correspondence with the direct'g physician &c—your order of the 18th inst to the alabama Emigrating company directing a Steam Boat to each five hundred persons to be furnished and Land transportation double the amount required by our contract cannot be complied with for these reasons—.

1st The superintendant has not the right to order the company to furnish double the transportation required by contract.

2nd maj Genl Jesup's order to maj Freeman as also maj Freeman's instructions to you are confined to the creek volunteers, and does not in our opinions extend to the Creek Emigration.

3d The contract specifies that no party shall move of less number than one thousand persons see art (3d)

4th You have not given the company any assurance of receiving pay for the Extra transportation you have been pleased to order.

The company Sir are ready with all the transportation required for their travel by land and with more Tonnage of water transportation than has been the custom of the Govt or the company to Employ in all former removals of Indians which the company considers amply sufficient for the present—

If in compliance of the wish of maj Genl Jesup you require Extra transportation we would be happy to make any special contract to furnish it for you on individual account—

with Respect
we have the honor to be &c.
Signed Wm J Beattie
Wm a Campbell

To
Jno G Reynolds
1st Lt U.S.M.C.
Disb'g agt & act'g,
Suptdt creek removal

☾

Reynolds notifies Campbell and Beattie that he has suspended the relocation of the detachment from Pass Christian indefinitely. Letter found at Reynolds Journal, Princeton University.

Indian Encampment
Pass Christian miss
24th Sept 1837

Gentlemen,

Circumstances are such, that I deem it a duty to suspend the movement of the party until further orders are received, from the Com'r of Indian affairs, of which due notice will be given to

Enable you to prepare for such further requesitions as the Dept may authorise.

I am Gent
Your obt. Servt.
Jno G Reynolds
1st Lt U.S.M.C.
Disb'g agt Ind Dept &
act'g Supt creek Removal

Messrs William A Campbell
William J Beattie

☾

Reynolds reports that he has suspended the departure of detachment 6 from Pass Christian, Mississippi, until the conflict over transportation can be resolved. Letter found at Reynolds Journal, Princeton University.

Indian Encampment
Pass christian miss
24th Sept'r 1837

Sir,

I enclose herewith the Order of maj. Gen'l Jesup to maj'r Freeman and maj'r Freeman's Order to me in relation to the emegration of the Warriors and their families, upon the receipt of which, and the authority reposed in your letter of 1st inst. I notified the Ala Emegrating Company that additional transportation was required, in consequence of the season &c. the correspondence, I also enclosed for the information of the Dept.

It was not my intention, of course, that the Ala. Emegrating Company should furnish the surplus transportation without additional compensation but I did not consider myself authorised to enter into a new contract to carry into effect the Orders of Gen'l Jesup, this in conjunction with the information contained in a letter received yesterday from Capt. Page (a copy of which is enclosed) I have deemed it proper to suspend the movement until your orders are received.

You will observe by the Directing Physian's Reports, a considerable increase of sick.

Mr George Boyd, a recient Capt. of Creek Vol's has been appointed "conductor" of that portion of the Warriors drawn from Hopothe Yohola's party. I have not considered it prudent to dispatch them ahead, as there would be no means of transportation, by land. I have also to report the joining of Doct. Hultz by Order of Gen'l Jesup. Be pleased to inform me, whether Mr Boyd's appointment will be confirmed.

Be pleased to favour me with an immediate answer instructing me fully how to proceed, as I have this morning notified the agents of the company, of putting off the day of departure.

I have the honor
to be Sir
Very respectfully
Your ob't serv't
(Signed) Jno. G. Reynolds
1st Lieut u.s.m.

C. A. Harris Esq'r.
Comm'r of Indian Affairs
Washington City

P.S.—The agents of the company inform me that in the event of extra transportation beeing required, they are without funds for carrying the Order into effect. I have about $3500.

(Signed) Jno G Reynolds

☾

Dr. Woodfin reports on the condition of the sick in the various encampments at Pass Christian, Mississippi. Punctuation has been lightly edited for clarity. Letter found at LR, CAE, Roll 238, 687.

Pass Christian

24th Sept 1837

Sir

I have this morning received the attending Physicians report; the following is a correct statement. No. of sick in Dr. Weidemanns camp 28. of that number three have died & 14 convalescent. in Dr. Hults division 52 are reported. of that No. 5. well 1 dead 26 convalescent. It may be well to remark here that the most of Dr Hults division are soldiers who lately returned from Florida sick, & that since their arrival many are convalescing but the late sudden change of weather, which has been for the last week very cold & unreasonable with frequent showers of rain, has materially retarded their recovery and added some few cases of Cataulaul fever to the sick report; amongst those who were exposed to the inclemency of the weather. The division of the encampment to which I attend has not Suffered much from the late change of weather, there has been during the past week four new cases, but they are convalescing & out of danger.

Very Respectfully
Your Obt. Svt.
J M Woodfin
Direct'g Phys

Lt. J G Reynolds
Disb'g Agent
& Act'g. Supt. Creek Emigtn

☾

Reynolds reports on the sickness of the party and the lack of ponies and wagons to transport the infirm. Letter found at Reynolds Journal, Princeton University.

Indian Encampment
Pass Christian miss

25 Sept 1837

Sir,

I forwarded by yesterdays mail copies of several letters in Relation to our western movement, I called upon the contractors for double land transportation, in accordance with the wish of Major Gen'l Jesup and desired to move on the 5th Oct. they denighed the Right of the Gen'l to Require additional transportation, in consequence of which, I was obliged to defer the movement, until your instructions are Received.

I Enclose an Estimate for the quarter Ending 31st Dec'r—the several amounts are as near as can be Reached on supposition; the amount pr head ($24) was fixed by the agents of the company.

The party labours under greater disadvantages; owing to the absence of ponies, indian wagons &c. than any other creek indians, Excepting hostiles, that have Emegrated; the many sick that we have had and who are now convalecent but too weak to travel on foot will necessarially be obliged to Ride.

The sickness of New Orleans, by the daily Reports Received here has been abating for the last week, but it is said, it Prevails to a considerable Extent on the shores of the Mississippi River.

Jno. G. Reynolds

C. A. Harris Esq'r

☾

Reynolds reports on a number of Creeks who have gone to Biloxi, Mississippi, in search of alcohol. Here he orders Isaac N. Wooldridge to be on constant alert at the encampment at Pass Christian. Letter found at SIAC, Agent (Page), Account (1701-B), Year (1838), NARA.

29th Sept. 1837

Sir,

I have just been informed that there were many indians at Buloxie after whiskey, and that they would be in this Evening, I wish you would discover who they are, the only way by which it can be done is by your personal and constant appearance upon the Pass—

Jno G Reynolds
Lt &c—

☾

Reynolds orders the prosecution of whites who sold alcohol to the Creeks on the Gulf and the return of money stolen by unscrupulous white traders. Letter found at SIAC, Agent (Page), Account (1701-B), Year (1838), NARA.

Indian Encampment
Pass Christian Miss—
30th Sept. 1837

Sir,

You will proceede to Bolexie and take such measures for the prosecution of all persons who are in the habit of selling whiskey to fugitive indians from this Encampment as in your judgment may seem proper.

Respectfully
Your Obt. Servt.
Jno G Reynolds
Lt & Superintendant Creek
Emegration

Mr. I. Wooldridge
Agent
Creek Emegration—

P.S. I understand many of the indians who have been at Bolexie, when intoxicated have lost their pocket books or walletts containing considerable amount of money—You will be pleased to call upon such persons having in their possession such monies lost. Represent your office and abtain all monies of that description and deliver it to me on your Return to your station.

Jno. G. Reynolds
Lt & Supt. Creek Removal

☾

The physician's report shows two deaths in the preceding week. Letter found at LR, CAE, Roll 238, 693.

Pass christian
Octo 1. 1837

Sir

From the reports of attending physician Dr. Hults & Weirdemann handed me this day, it appears that during the past Week a more favourable change has taken place in the health of the camp, many reported sick are convalescing since last weekly report and their health & condition has much improved; In my division only two deaths reported during the past week and a decided change in the health of those who were sick has taken place. There is no malignant or contagious disease in the camp the prevaling diseases are the common Bilious & Intermittent fever of the climate.

very Respectfly
Your obt Svt
J. M. Woodfin
Direct'g Phys

Lt. J. G. Reynolds
Disb'g agent
Creek Emigration

☾

Sloan reports that Chisse Harjo was cheated out of $50 worth of silver and orders Wooldridge to retrieve it. Letter found at SIAC, Agent (Page), Account (1701-B), Year (1838), NARA.

Pass christian Oct 3d 1837

Sir

The bearer of this Chisse Hajo[47] states he left $50 in the hands of a Merchant in Beloxi to be exchanged for silver & that he closed his store & Kept it shut while he remained there & that he had to leave it—He will show you the house—you will take measures to have it restored.

Respectfully
T. T. Sloan
Lt. & Disb'g. Agent.

I wooldridge
Regulating officer

☾

Reynolds reports to Campbell and Beattie that he is waiting for a response from the commissioner of Indian affairs. Letter found at Reynolds Journal, Princeton University.

Indian Encampment
Pass Christian miss
5th Oct 1837

Sir

Your letter of this date informing me that the ala Emigrating Company are in readiness to carry into Effect my orders of 14th and 16th ultimo has been received. In reply I beg leave to refer you to my communication dated 24th Sept. wherein the alabama Emigrating Company, through their agents Messrs Campbell and Beattie were informed that circumstances arrising from communications with those gentlemen, made it necessary to postpone Emigration, until further instructions be received from the comm'r of Indians affairs—when due notice would be given the company for preparation on their part, which however was Entirely unnecessary on the part of the United States, if the letter of Col Campbell date 14th Sept in answer to my requisition of the same date be taken into consideration—you will discover in answer to that requisition, that all of the transportation required of the company agreeably to the contract, was then, in a state of readiness and until the receipt of your letter of this morning I rested under the belief—consequently the notice of twenty two days or indeed any number of days was unnecessary—nevertheless, so soon as I hear from the Dept you will receive immediate notice, that no unnecessary delay be had in the movement.

I am Respectfully
Your obt Servt
Jno G Reynolds
1st Lt U.S.M.C.
Disb'g agt Ind Dept
& act'g Supt creek removal

Wm J Beattie
agt & member
ala Emigrating Company

☾

Beattie protests Reynolds's decision to move between 220 and 300 Creeks of detachment 1 to Indian territory early because it would mean a loss to the company. Letter found at Reynolds Journal, Princeton University.

Pass Christian
October 6th 1837

Sir

My attention has been Called to your public notice of this date, solicititing proposals to transport, & subsist to Fort Gibson, from 220 to 300 of the Emigrating creek Indians, now at this place—in your order of the 16th ultimo, you have made it the duty of the alabama Emigrating Company, to be in readiness on the day therein named, to receive the whole party of creek Emigrants, now at this place.

The Company Sir, have made positive contracts in obedience to that order for transportation & Subsistence, both by water and the travel by land, on the Entire route west—for and on behalf of the alabama Emigrating Company, I protest against your sending off any number of the Creek Emigrants now at this place; unless in conformity with the articles of agreement between the united States of america and the said Company; the company are prepared with transportation and Subsistence, for the entire party and consequently any number of Emigrants taken from them, must inevitably be a loss to the Company, and the united States will be chargable with the same.

with Respect
I am Sir
yr most obt. Servt
W J Beattie
agt & member
ala Em Co

Jno G Reynolds
U.S.M.C.
Disb'g agt
& act'g Supt.
Creek Removal

☾

Reynolds reports that if the Alabama Emigrating Company is willing to relocate the Creek volunteers immediately, he will withdraw his advertisement for moving and subsisting the warriors. Letter found at Reynolds Journal, Princeton University.

Indian Encampment

Pass Christian
7 Oct 1837

Sir

I have received your letter of yesterday's date, protesting on the part of the company against the removal of any portion of the creek Emigrants now at this place—The number of warriors designated to be sent off, say from two to three hundred, are those drawn from a party that Emigrated some twelve months since, their long absence from their families and Gen'l Jesup's order has induce me to make arrangements for their removal forthwith, not however, without consulting the agents of the company upon the propriety of such removal, their acquiesance apart from the contract with the company and the Indians great anxiety to join their families are in my opinion sufficient reasons for anticipating the final removal of the whole with regard to the immediate removal of the warriors above mentioned if however the company are prepared to Emigrate the warriors of No. 1 party, immediately, that portion of my notice for contract with regard to their removal and subsistence will be withdrawn and they transferred to the ala Emigrating Company, for Emigration without delay.

I am Sir
very Respectfully
your obt Servt
Jno G Reynolds
1st Lt U.S.M.C.
Disb'g agt Indian Dept
& act'g Supt Creek Removal

W J Beattie Esqr
agt. & member
ala Em Co

☾

Beattie responds to Reynolds's 7 October letter by declaring that the Alabama Emigrating Company is not willing to remove such a small number of Creeks. Letter found at Reynolds Journal, Princeton University.

Pass christian
October 7th 1837

Sir

I have this moment received yours of this morning, in answer to that portion enquiring if the alabama Emigrating Company will immediately receive transport and Subsist the warriors of party no. 1 creek removal numbering from two to three Hundred persons, I have to state that the alabama Emigrating Company are not willing to send agents and furnish transportation for so small a number.

I readily confess as an individual connected with the removal, I would be happy to part with those warriors and many others Encamped here as there is no military force to keep them under subjection.

with Respect
I am Sir
Your most obt Servt
W J Beattie
agt & member
ala Em Co

Lt Jno G Reynolds
U.S.M.C.
Disb'g agt & act'g
Supt creek Removal

☾

Alabama Emigrating Company partner Edward Hanrick demands that his bid to transport the extra baggage of detachments 1 and 6 be accepted. Letter found at Reynolds Journal, Princeton University.

Pass Christian
Oct 8th 1837

Sir

I am ready with ample security to comply with my bid made to you yesterday agreeable to your advertisement for proposals for the transportation of the Extra baggage of party no. 6 now at this place and in as much as Jesse Hart has withdrawn his bid for the Extra baggage of Party no 1 at mobile Point and also the warriors of party no 1 at this place my bid being the next lowest, I am also Ready with my security to comply with your requisition, I am Ready and insist upon my Right of having the contract closed according to your advertisement.

I am Sir
with Respect
your obt & Humble servt
E Hanrick

Lt Jno G Reynolds

☾

Reynolds responds to Hanrick by noting that he has pulled the advertisement due to the high cost of the bids. Letter found at Reynolds Journal, Princeton University.

Indian Encampment
Pass Christian miss
8th Oct 1837

Sir,

I have received your note of this morning insisting upon your bid for the Extra baggage of parties no. 1 & 6 be taken or closed—you also refer to the withdrawal of Mr Jesse Hart who was a lower bidder than yourself for the transportation of Indians and baggage of party

no. 1 I have to say, that in consequence of a communication_____ [48]
received from the Indian Dept subsequently received to the one authorising the proposals for the transportation above alluded to—it became necessary to withdraw on my part as I was convinced any contract bordering on anything like the amount which you had proposed would not be authorised—the same notice was given to Mr Jesse Hart who immediately withdrew any claim that he might have on the United States in consequence of being the lowest bidder—

I shall Refer all the papers, including your letter to the Dept.

Respectfully
Your obt Servt
Jno G Reynolds
Lt & Disb'g agt Ind Dept

E Hanrick Esq'r
Pass Christian

☾

Reynolds updates the commissioner of Indian affairs on the status of the Creeks' extra baggage. Letter found at Reynolds Journal, Princeton University.

Indian Encampment
Pass Christian
8th October 1837

Sir

In complyance with the instructions contained in yours of 21st Ultimo, which was received by me at this place on the morning of 6th inst I immediately advertised for proposals and was about closing with the lowest bidder, when yours, by Express dated 30th Sept arrived and of course put a stop to further action on my part the instructions however if attempted to be carried into Effect with the aid of force, will, rest assured create great Excitement with the warriors; since my letter of 5th ultimo advising the Dep't of the difficulty likely to be Encountered, if the baggage Should be seperated from them on the route, has been measurably realised, by the conduct of some of the principal men when the subject of your letter was communicated to them yesterday morning—my whole object and study has been to render justice both to the united States and the people who I have been placed in charge, if all that has been from time to time promised the Indians by the agents—are not fully carried out, and one is that their baggage should not be seperated from them, it will be difficult to say what the result will be when an attempt is made to Enforce your instructions—The Indians very readily have told me that their losses have been Exceedingly great already, by their families being forced to remove from their homes while they were fighting for the country, which was contrary to the positive assurance given them by Gen'l Jesup, and they are not now disposed to be put to a similar inconvenience by the loss of such of their articles as may have been collected since their removal; there is hardly day that passes but I am applied for the payment of property lost in consequence of leaving the nation, the reasons assigned for not seperating from the baggage they have now is the fear of its being damaged or kept from them as that of No. 1 party has been—

It is impossible to obtain a responsible bid for the delivery of the baggage as directed by your, indeed those putting in consider notwithstanding your subsequent instructions that I am in duty bound to take, up their bid, but duty to myself prevents me from doing any thing, whereby the discountenance of the Dept is at all likely to be the result.

I have forwarded the two notices as also the several bids and other papers that you may observe how far I had progressed. If it is possible to persuade the Indians to leave the movement will commence without delay with such transportation as the Company by their contract are bound to furnish, unless instructions of a different nature are received in the interem as regards the purchase and additional transportation considerable discontent is therefore anticipated. Mr Beattie agt of the company has consented to receive all the Extra baggage and transport it until the permanant superentendant joines us, when a contract for a fair compensation will be made by him, this is the only resort I have.

The warriors alluded too, in one of the notices are those of no. 1 party, whom Genl Jesup was desirous should leave at the Earliest possible period under the conduct of Mr G Boyd of whoese appointment as conductor I asked for, in mine of 24th ultimo.

I am Sir
very Respectfully
Your obt Servt
Jno G Reynolds
1st Lt U.S.M.C.
Disb'g agent Ind Dept &c

C A Harris Esqr
Commr of Indian affairs Signed
washington City

☾

This is the last letter in Reynolds's journal; his 19 October entry declaring that he had become too sick to accompany the party any further (he turned it over to Lieutenant Thomas T. Sloan), is the last notation of any kind in his journal. At the top of this letter Reynolds wrote: "This letter alludes to bids for Extra baggage of parties no. 1 & 6 at mobile Point and Pass Christian." Letter found at Reynolds Journal, Princeton University.

Indian Encampment
Pass Christian miss
10th Oct 1837

Sir

Enclosed you will receive the papers alluded to in mine of yesterday by which, you will discover the pecular Situation in which I am placed—I was in hopes Capt Page would have rejoined us, long Ere this, that a relief might have been afforded to my perplexity.

I shall do that, which I conceive to be my duty, (in the absence of positive instructions) regardless of consequencies.

I am Sir
very Respectfully
your Obt Servt
Jno G Reynolds
Lt & Disb'g agt Ind Dept

C A Harris Esqr
Comm'r Ind affairs
Washington City

☾

Sloan reports that two thousand Creeks of detachment 6 under his charge have been relocated to New Orleans and he is awaiting the arrival of more. Noah Felton would conduct Lieutenant Reynolds's party as Reynolds had become sick with fever and would not accompany the party. Letter found at LR, CAE, Roll 238, 860–61.

Pass Christian, Miss
23d Oct. 1837—

Sir—

I have the honor to inform you that agreeably to the arrangements made by Lt. Reynolds, I have this day embarked two thousand emigrating Creek Indians from this place to New Orleans, where ample transportation is in readiness to receive them. Such arrangements have been made by the contractors that the party will remain but a few hours in New Orleans, whence they will proceed with all reasonable expedition to their place of destination. I shall accompany the first party to New Orleans to attend their final embarkment, where I shall remain until I am joined by the last party which will be on the 25th inst—Every arrangement having been previously made for the comfortable and speedy removal from this place of the party under my charge I deem it most advisable to remain in New Orleans and see Lt. R's party on the way and make arrangements for the reception of my own.

I have appointed Noah Felton, who was formerly assistant conductor under Lt. Reynolds, conductor of the principal part of his party and I hope it will meet your approbation. Mr. Felton has had considerable experience, and I conceive every way qualified for the appointment.

I am very respectfully
Your obt. Servt.
T. T. Sloan
Lt. & Disb'g. Agent

C. A. Harris
Comm'r Indian affairs
Washington City.

☾

Sloan, writing from the steamboat *Black Hawk*, reports that although the party was briefly detained at Pass Christian, the Creeks of detachment 6 are ascending the Mississippi River. Letter found at LR, CAE, Roll 238, 863–64.

Steam boat "Black Hawk"
near Vicksburgh Miss
Nov. 3d 1837—

Sir—

In my communication to you of the 23d Oct. I apprised you that two thousand emigrating Creek Indians had left Pass Christian for Arkansas.

I have the honor to inform you that the whole party are now on the move to their new homes in the west—In consequence of the inclemency of the weather, the last party was detained several days at Pass Christian, the first party in the mean time moving twelve or fifteen miles above New Orleans so as to be beyond the influence of the yellow fever which was then raging in that city. They remained at that place until they were joined by the other party, which was on the 29th Oct. when the whole party in fine health and spirits proceeded up the river—

Agents have been placed on each boat to attend to the wants of the Indians, and a physician accompanies each party to provide for the comfort of the sick—

I directed Dr. Halse to remain at Pass Christian with Lt. Reynolds until he could be relieved—He will join us soon as Lt. R. had sent to Mobile for a physician—

Very respectfully
Your Ob't. Serv't.
T. T. Sloan
Lt. & Disb'g. Agent

C. A. Harris, Esq
Comm'r Indian Affairs
Washington City—

☾

The Alabama Emigrating Company responds to the orders to halt at the mouth of the White River and forwards the daily costs of the detention. Letter found at SIAC, Agent (Reynolds), Account (1687), Year (1838), NARA.

(Copy)

St Bt Black Hawk
Vicksburg 4th Nov 1837

Sir

In Compliance with your order of this date the Steam Boats Farmer, Far West, & Black Hawk with the party of Indians will remain at the mouth of White River until otherwise directed the following are the daily expenses incident to their detention.

Respectfully

N F Collins[49]
Ag't. Ala Emg Co

Lt T. T. Sloan

Disb Agt Ind Dept

Charter of St Bt Farmer $300 p day	300.00
Subsistence of Indians	41.00
Agent p day—	5.00
	$346.00
Charter of St Bt Far West p day	300.00
Subsistence of Indians—	46.00
Agent p day—	5.00
	$351.00
Charter of St Bt Blk Hawk p day	300.00
Subsistence of Indians p day	43.00
Agent p day	5.00
	348.00

P.S. You will state from your Knowledge of the Circumstances as to the Correctness of the above Expenses.

☾

Page reports that the main body of detachment 6 has arrived at Fort Gibson. Repeating a common refrain among the military agents, Page asserts that the journey (the sinking of the *Monmouth* notwithstanding) was very "pleasant and agreeable" for the Creeks. Letter found at LR, CAE, Roll 238, 621.

Fort Gibson
28th—December 1837

Sir

I have the honor to Report this day the arrival of all the Creek Indians in the new Countrey allotted them, the movement with the exception of the disaster on board the Monmouth has been a verry pleasant and agreeable Emigration on the part of the Indians; Each party was conducted through the countrey with a great deal of caution—no complaints on the part of the Indians or the Inhabitants of arkansas for depredations committed; as I passed through the countrey I promised the citizens every depredation committed this year by the Creek Indians, I would ensure them pay for it provided they would inform me who conducted them; on my return I made all enquiry, no complaint, but all pleased in the manner the Creeks were conducted through the countrey, the extra baggage was also landed at Fort Gibson agreeable to contract and Divided by Ho. poth. le. yoholo and the other chiefs. I should have been more prompt in communicating to you but my health has been so bad, that I was unable to do so. I am at this time in so low a state of health that I am compeled to Keep my bed two thirds of my time, I shall however in two or three days make a start for Columbus Georgia, with a hope, travelling may improve my health, I will render my accounts so soon as I arrive at Columbus.

With Respect
I have the honour to
be your ob't Serv't
John Page Capt &
Sup't Creeks

To—
C, A, Harris Esqu'r
Commissioner of Indian
affairs Washington C'ty

☾

E. W. B. Nowland, the postmaster at Fort Gibson, notifies William J. Beattie's father, James, that his son died of fever at the mouth of the White River. Letter found at Beattie Family Papers, 1814–1884, MS 158, Folder 6, Vermont Historical Society, Barre, Vermont.

Fort Gibson
March 29— 1838

Mr James Beatty[50]

D Sir

Yours of the 21 Feby came to hand making Enquire respecting Mr Wm J. Beaty. I am sorry to say that he died at the mouth of the arkansas River the last of November or 1st December on his way to this place with a party of Emigrating Indians, he died of Fever. Coln Campbell of Montgomery ala can give you all infirmation desired, he was Engaged in the same business.

Yours &c
EWB Nowland[51]
P Master Ft Gibson

☾

Page reports that the Alabama Emigrating Company was not liable for the expense of moving detachment 6 from Mobile Point, Alabama, to Pass Christian, Mississippi. Letter found at SIAC, Agent (Alabama Emigrating Company), Account (1722), Year (1838), NARA.

Augusta Georgia
31st May 1838

Col Wm A Campbell

Sir

Your letter dated Washington City 26th Inst has just been received and in reply I must state that about the middle of March 1837 party no. 6 of the Creek Indians for Emigration west were turned over to the Alabama Emigrating Company by me at Fort Mitchell and Montgomery Ala and were removed by said company to Mobile Point where they were taken charge of by me and detained there by order of the commissioner of Indian affairs and Gen'l Jesup. These Indians were to remain at this Point until the warriors returned from Florida and subsisted at the Expense of the U States as will be seen by a contract now in the possession of the 2d comptroller.[52] About the middle of July the Emigrants became very sickly, sometimes thirty or forty deaths per day. I was directed by the commissioner of Indian affairs and Genl Jesup to remove them to some healthy place. I selected Pass christian and so soon as I could procure steamboats I removed the Emigrants to that place.

I did not consult the Alabama Emigrating Company as I considered they had nothing to do with the Emigrants until they were remustered and turned over to them for Emigration.

After the warriors returned from Florida all were remustered at Pass christian and on the 23d of October 1837 the Emigrants were turned over to the Alabama Emigrating Company to be transported to their new country west. The Emigrating company had nothing to do with the movement of the Emigrants from Mobile Point to Pass christian. It was done at the Expense of the Government. I am aware the Emigrating company sustained a considerable injury by this sudden movement, as they had deposited large quantities of Provisions at the Point, suffering the families would remain there until the warriors returned from Florida, but in consequence of the sickness I was compell'd to make this movement. The Expense Embarking these Emigrants from Pass christian was much greater than it could have been if they had taken them from Mobile Point.=

I certify on honor the above statement is correct and true.

John Page Capt &
Supt Creek Rem'l

☾

Campbell gives some insight into the crash of the steamboat *Monmouth*, including that there were 462 survivors. Letter found at LR, CAE, Roll 239, 168–69.

Washington June 7th 1838

C. A. Harris

Sir

In presenting the within account the undersigned does it with a hope that the Gov't will reimburse him for monies Expended for the use of the surviving Creek Indians that were on board the steamer Monmouth, at the time she was wrecked on the evening of the 31st Oct'r 1837. It was an act of humanity on my part, & the money expended, out of my private funds & unconnected with the alabama emigrating Company. The accompanying documents, together with a letter of Lieut Sloan to the department dated the early part of Nov'r 1837 will shew the destitute condition those people were in for the want of Cloathing at the time, the purchases were made by me.

I have the Honor to
be Sir Your Obt Svt
Wm A. Campbell

P.S. Mr. Noah Feton[53] whose affadavit is annexed to the account rendered was at the time an acting agent for the U. States in the Creek removal, there were 462 survivors; seventeen Dollars & 50/100 is near the amt expended for each Indian & from the acts rendered it will be seen that articles of comfort alone was purchased for them, the Indians had just retired to their beds, at the time of the wreck is perhaps one of the causes, of their saving so small a portion of their property, & from the fact of the whole of their valuable property was placed in lower part of the boat.

Wm A. Campbell

☾

Michael M. Cravens, a subagent for detachment 6, reports on the circumstances surrounding the decision to take Tuskenehaw, along with his friends and relatives, by water to Fort Gibson. Affidavit found at SIAC, Agent (Alabama Emigrating Company), Account (2755), Year (1839), NARA.

Washington City

Personally appeared before me Clement T Coote[54]—a Justice of the Peace for the County of Washington D.C.—M.M. Cravens, who being sworn, saith that he was employed by the Alabama Emigrating Company as an assistant Agent in the removal of creek Indians from Pass christian to Fort Gibson in the fall of 1837—That he had charge of a party of Indians in the Steam Boat Cavalier from New orleans up the Mississippi to the mouth of White river—That when the whole Party left New orleans it was supposed that the Boats could ascend White River as far as Rock Roe, where waggons had been prepared to meet them But that upon experiment it was found that they could not go up higher than Andersons Bluff. That when they got to Andersons Bluff finding that they could not go farther by water, the Indians & baggage were landed & waggons were sent for to convey them by land to Fort Gibson and all the Boats discharged Except the John Nelson which was the property of the company. After the discharge of these Boats and before the waggons had all assembled, this affiant concluded to make an effort to ascend the arkansas with a party of the Indians on the John Nelson. This was agreed to for the accommodation of the warriors & the chief Tuskenah, who was a very large helpless man & at that time so unwell, that he could not go by land & insisted on attempting a conveyance by Water—That he was permitted to select a party of his friends, relatives &c who were placed on board the John Nelson & under the charge of this Deponent as the agent of the Company & Capt. Boyd as the office of the Government, proceeded thro' the Cut off into the Arkansas & after much difficulty succeded in reaching Fort Gibson—The water was very low, but the Boat met an occasional rise in the river and after some delay finally reached her destination—(The ballance of the Party took the land route from Andersons Bluff and did not reach Fort Gibson for upwards of three weeks after the affiant arrived with his party). This Affiant states that none of the Extra baggage of the Indians was put on board the John Nelson Except a few trunks of cloathing &c belonging to one of the chiefs, as it was considered very doubtful whether the Boat could get up with the Indians and their regular baggage—The number of Indians which were thus conveyed on the John Nelson, as receipted for by the Government office at Fort Gibson, as near as this deponent can remember was four hundred & fifty.

M. M. Cravens
Sworn to & Subscribed before on this 2d August 1838—
Clement T. Coote J. Peace

I do hereby certify that I am well acquainted with Mr Michael M Cravens whose name appears to the foregoing affidavit—Mr Cravens resides very near me in the State of Alabama, and I take pleasure in stating that he is a man of integrity & that his statements are entitled to the fullest credit.

August 2nd 1838.

Joseph Bryan[55]

☾

In this letter to Reynolds, Finley B. Hiern[56] reports on the number of Creek Indians who deserted detachment 6 and remain at Pass Christian and New Orleans. Letter found at LR, CAE, Roll 239, 515.

Pass Christian 30th Janry 1839

My Dear Sir

Yours of the 29th inst came safe to hand, and I hasten to give you all the information that I possess or can obtain in relation to the creek Indians that remained here after the main body were removed from this place.—From what I can learn from the old Indian Bearfoot there were about twenty in number men women

& children who remained behind eleven of whom left this during the winter of 1839 for N. Orleans where they have remained ever since all the rest are at this place and vicinity with the exception of one man who has left some time since for alabama.

Tom Pigeon[57] and family are at Wolf River[58]—consisting of himself and four others, there are also five others who are liveing at this place.

I remain sir respectfully yours
Finley B. Hiern

Part 4

The Refugee Removals, 1837

16 Removal of the Refugee Creeks in the Cherokee and Chickasaw Countries

Creeks in Cherokee Country

Soon after conducting detachment 3 to their destination at Fort Gibson, Edward Deas was commissioned to travel into the Cherokee country and apprehend any Creeks found hiding there. Deas noted in his muster roll that these were Creeks who had fled the Creek Nation soon after the signing of the 1832 Treaty of Washington. In reality many Creeks had fled to the Cherokee nation in the years after the first Creek War as well as after the signing of the treaties of Indian Springs and (1826) Washington. In fact, many of these Creeks had actually returned to Alabama after the signing of the 1832 Treaty of Washington, hoping to receive a half-section of land. Still, by 1837 there were several hundred Creeks living among the Cherokees, many intermarried and raising families.

In May 1837 over five hundred Creeks left Gunter's Landing for the Indian territory. Most of the refugees were found around Coosawattee (eighteen miles from New Echota) and near Red Clay on the Tennessee-Georgia line. There were also untold numbers of Creeks "scattered" in the North Carolina mountains or on the banks of Valley River. In addition, there were 150 Creeks already under guard at Gunter's Landing when Deas first arrived. Deas chose to move these Creeks solely by water—a smart choice considering their proclivity to try and escape. Indeed, dozens of Creeks did desert the party over a two-night period when, due to high winds on the Tennessee River, the boats were forced to come to shore.

Only one small party of refugees from the Cherokee country made the journey to the West. The remainder—imbedded among the Cherokee people through marriage or hard to collect due to the remoteness of their camps—were allowed by Cherokee headmen to remain. Federal agents, not willing to risk a confrontation, allowed to these Creeks to share the fate of the Cherokees.[1]

The detachment of Creek refugees captured in the Cherokee country was conducted west by Hugh G. Barclay[2] of the Alabama Emigrating Company and Lieutenant Edward Deas, who served as military oversight. Doctor James G. Morrow served as attending surgeon.

Journal of Refugee Creek (Cherokee) Removal

Found at LR, CAE, Roll 238, 251–81.

Journal of Occurrences

On the Route of a Party of Emigrating Creek Indians, kept by Lieutenant Edw. Deas U.S. Army Disbursing Agent in the Creek Emigration; in charge of the Party.

16th May 1837.

To day the Party of Creek Indians, the collection of which for Emigration, I have been charged with, was turned over by me to an Agent of the "Alaba'a. Emigrating Company," at a point about four miles south of Gunter's Landing N. Alabama.

The Party numbers 543, as shewn by the muster Rolls. After due consideration of all the circumstances, I find that the Route by water to the new Indian Country, west of the Mississippi River, at the present time, is preferable to that by land. I have therefore indicated this mode of Transportation, for the present Party.

These Indians are a part of those Creeks, that fled from their own country in Alabama, after the Treaty with that Tribe of 1832; hoping probably by taking refuge among the Cherokees to be placed upon the same footing, with the latter people, in reference to the necessity of Emigrating to the West.

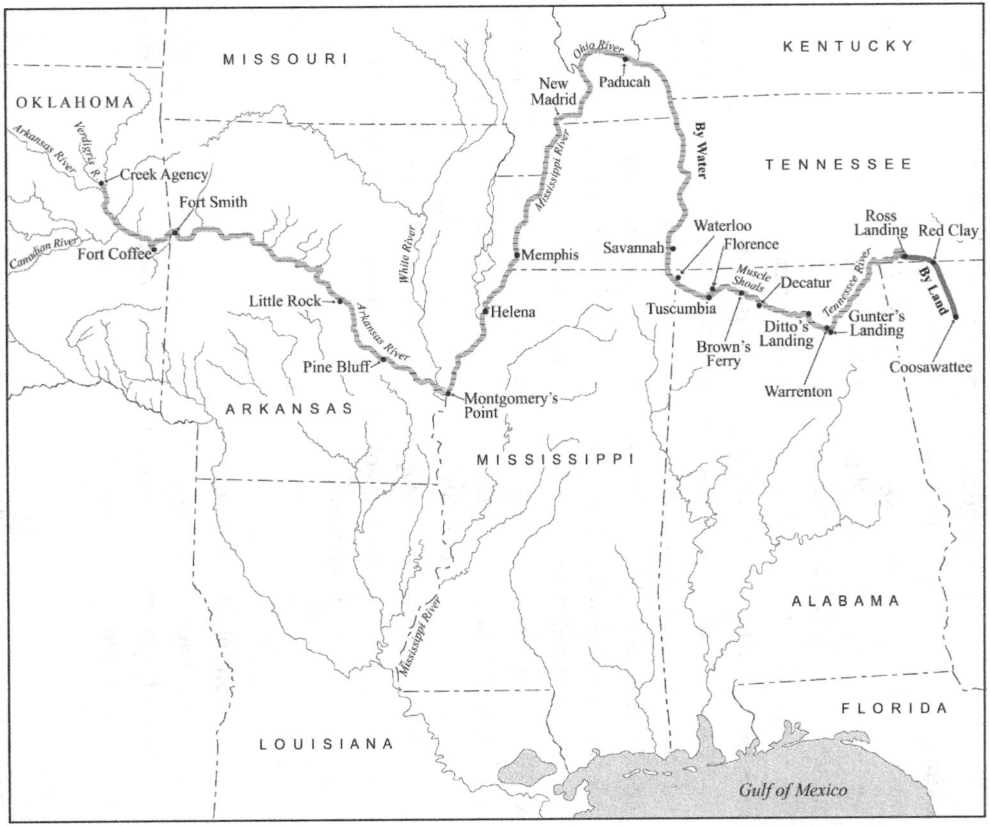

MAP 15. Route of Creek refugees in Cherokee country, May–June 1837. Place names correspond to stopping points or locations noted in the documentation. Route lines and locations are approximations. Cartography by Sarah Mattics and Kiersten Fish.

They have been apprehended at various points in the Cherokee Nation, scattered over an extensive tract of thinly settled, or barren country. For this reason, and owing to the inaccessible retreats in which they were found by the Troops, and the difficulty of procuring Subsistence and Transportation in such places; and also the necessity of employing Agents of intelligence to take charge of the Indians when apprehended; it has required a good deal of Expense to prepare the present Party for Emigration. Nine Flat-Boats have been purchased by the Contractor, to be used until steam conveyance can be procured below the Muscle Shoal Falls, in the Tennessee River.[3] Four of these Flats, are of the largest class, about 80 feet long, the others 50 & 40 feet in length. This allowance is sufficient to ensure health and comfort to the people. I turned the Party over this morning at the Encampment of Tennessee Volunteers about 4 miles south of Gunter's Landing, where the Indians have been guarded for the last week. They were mooved to the water's edge by noon, and about sun-set the whole embarked on the Flat-Boats & are at this time (10 o'clock P.M.) progressing slowly by the force of the current.

There are but very few cases of sickness at present, and the weather is very favourable in this respect.

17th May.

The Boats continued to float all last night, and until to-day at noon, when they reached Ditto's Landing 30 miles from the point of starting.[4] They were then obliged to stop until 5. P.M., on account of wind, when they again set out, and are still floating (10 o'clock P.M.)

18th May.

About 2 o'clock[5] this morning a heavy wind suddenly arose, by which the Boats were compelled to land, in the dark, and we were so unfortunate as to loose Fifteen of the Indians, who took this opportunity of making their escape. Owing to the continuation of the wind the Boats could not re-embark until near sun-set, and are still floating (10 o'clock P.M.).

19th May.

The Flat Boats with the Party on board continued to float all last night, and to-day until 3 o'clock P.M., when they were landed on account of wind, a few miles above Decatur; which place is 60 miles from Gunter's Landing. The Party re-embarked about sun-set, and is still progressing slowly (10 o'clock P.M.).

20th May.

Early this morning the weather became stormy and the Boats were obliged to land before day light, and in consequence we have lost more of the Indians by Desertion. The Boats were seperated when they were landed, and immediately after some of the smaller ones touched the shore, the people on board of them, took advantage of the Darkness, and Rain, to make their escape.

As soon as the other boats landed, every exertion was made to overtake & bring them back. By offering a Reward of one dollar for each that should be returned, I recovered 15. The remainder 56 in number, could not be overtaken in time, and succeeded in making their escape to the mountains, 5 miles distant.

The weather has continued rainy thro' the day. No progress has been made, but we shall probably start to night. We are at Present at Brown's Ferry, 12 miles below Decatur.

21st May

About midnight the Boats set-out & came thro' the Elk River Shoals to Lamb's Ferry, 16 miles. We there stopped long enough to procure Pilots & hands to pass the Muscle Shoals, which are some-what difficult of navigation. The Boats entered the Rapids at 10 o'clock A.M. and reached the foot of the Shoals at 4. P.M. without any accident.

The length of the shoals is 15 miles and at some places the river is 2 or 3 miles wide, and is filled with small Islands. Many of the passes are very rapid, and experienced Pilots are necessary, to carry a Boat thro' in safety, though in case of accident, there is no other danger than the loss of the Boat & cargo.

The Party is at present landed on the north bank of the River, about 6 miles above Florence.

22nd May

The Boats started this morning at 4. o'clock floated 14 miles, and again landed the Party 6 miles below Tuscumbia. An arrangement was made at that place to-day, for a S-Boat at Waterloo, 30 miles below, at the foot of the Rapid waters. Nothing of consequence has occurred; the Indians continue healthy, generally, and apparently well satisfied. No further desertions have taken place.

For the last week it has been uncommonly cool for this country, at this season. Yesterday and to-day the weather has been very fine.

I should have mentioned, that on the 20th near Decatur I engaged a Dr. Morrow to accompany the Party at $85—per month, & expenses; in place of the physician who started from Gunters Landing, at which place one could no [illegible] be hired, for less than $5 per day.

23rd May

Early this morning the Party again started, and reached Waterloo at 10 o'clock A.M. The Steam Boat Black Hawk was then got in readiness for the reception of the Indians. One large Keil[6] and two of the large Flats were taken in Tow, and at 4 o'clock P.M. the whole Party re-embarked, and we have since come 40 miles & landed for the night, at the foot of an Island in order to prevent desertions, should any of the Indians yet be so disposed. The Black Hawk is of about the middle size of steam-Boats, & her guards have been covered, and every thing done to accommodate the Indians to the best advantage on board of her.[7]

24th May.

The Boats got under way this morning early, and reached Savannah Tenn'e an hour afterwards. One of the Flats was left at that place, as it impeded very much our progress, and was not at all necessary, to the comfort of the People. The other Boats have been rendered as convenient for them as possible by constructing temporary sheds & Cooking-Hearths, in the Flat Boats, & on the Deck of the Keil. all appear well pleased with the rapid progress we are making, about 8 miles an hour. a child that has been sick for some time back, died to-day & was buried in the afternoon at a wood-landing.[8]

Nothing else of importance has occurred thro' the day.

25th May.

The Boats continued to run thro' last night, passed Paducah to-day at one o'clock, and stopped for the night about sun-set, near the mouth of the Ohio, on the Illinois shore.

Another child Died to-day, owing probably to the folly of its mother, in putting it in cold water.[9] Since leaving Gunter's Landing, the weather has been uncommonly cool, for the season. Since yesterday after-noon, there has been an almost constant drizzling rain. Up to the present time the Rations have been issued without any failure. I had 17 Bushells (all that could be had) of dried Peas, issued at Tuscumbia in place of part of the meat-Ration, which is too great for the present inactive situation of the people.

26th May.

This morning about day-light the Boats started, the weather fine and still cool. In the forenoon we reached New-Madrid, where a short stop was made, to procure corn. Since that time no interruption has occurred, & the boats will continue to run thro' the night.

27th May.

The Boats passed Memphis this morning early, but we made no stop, as intimation had been given, that some of the Indians wished to visit the Chicasaw country, & would attempt to leave the Party for that purpose.

28th May

The Boats continued to run thro' last night, & reached Montgomerie's-point, this morning about day light. We entered the mouth of white River at 8 o'clock having stopped a short time at the Point, and passed thro' the cut-off into Arkansas R., about ½ past nine. We have since come about 50 miles, up the latter stream, and stopped for the night at 8 o'clock P.M.

The Arkansas is at a very good stage at present, for small Boats, and is on the rise, which will probably continue for some time.

The Spring-Fresh has just begun.[10] Had we arrived 2 or 3 days sooner, we should have been delayed, as several boats were fast on the Bars above, until yesterday. The rise of this River at this season, is said to be owing to the melting of Snows in the Rocky Mountains, and consequently depends upon its time of occurrence, which of course varies with the season.[11] as last winter was a severe one, & the warm weather having set in late this spring, it is reasonable to expect a heavy rise this summer.

No thing of importance has taken place to-day, the weather continues fine tho' warm.

The Boats stopped for the night at dark, having come about 50 miles.

29th May.

An Indian man & a very old woman both of whom have been sick since starting, Died to-day. as it is necessary at present to stop at night, on account of navigation, and as the people can therefore go on shore to sleep & cook, if they choose, we left the Flat Boat this morning; the Steam Boat & Keil being sufficient to transport the Party, under such circumstances.

The Boats got under way early this morning, and stopped at sunset having come about 75 miles.

30th May.

The people came on board & the Boats started at 6 o'clock A.M. and passed Pine Bluffs in the forenoon. As we shall be able to reach Lt. Rock early to-morrow by running to-night, and the Indians wishing to do so, I have consented to its being done. The River has risen so suddenly within the last few days, that the Pilots thinking there is no longer danger from snags, or other obstruction at night.

31st May.

We reached Little Rock this morning at 7 o'clock, stopped there about an hour, and then continued to run until 7. P.M. having come about 50 miles.

When the Boats landed a very few of the people went on shore, and as they appeared generally desirous of continuing to run thro' the night, we accordingly started again at 11. P.M. It rained last night but cleared up this morning before reaching Lt. Rock, and the weather is at present fine tho' warm in the day time. a female child died this afternoon, but nothing else of importance has occurred thro' the day.

The River is now said to be 12 or 14 feet above low water mark.

1st June 1837.

We continued to run thro' last night, and to-day; the weather very fine tho' warm. An old woman who has been ill with the consumption more than a year died this afternoon.[12] We are still running (10 o'clock P.M.) and are about 200 miles above Little Rock by water.

2nd June

We continued to travel through last night & to-day and reached Fort Smith this evening at dark, and are still progressing at the rate of between 3 & 4 miles an hour (10 o'clock P.M.). It should have been mentioned that every day a considerable stop has been made in day time, at Wood landings, giving the Indians an opportunity of leaving the Boats, and Bathing, and also of taking Exercise, the want of which to people of their habits is the greatest objection to Transporting them by water. I do not think that the present Party has suffered on this account.

3rd June.

We reached Fort Coffee[13] this morning about 2 o'clock, stopped there a half an hour, and then continued to run until 11. A.M. when the Boats were obliged to stop 2 or 3 hours to procure wood, which was gathered and cut, by the Hands and Indians, who were hired to do so. So little navigation takes place on this part of the River, that wood landings are very few in number.

After laying in a sufficient supply, the Boats again started and will continue to run thro' the night.

We passed the mouth of Canadian River about Sun-set and are now between 50 & 60 miles above Fort Coffee and about 30 from Fort Gibson (10 o'clock P.M.)

Another Death occurred this morning at Fort Coffee (an infant). For 5 or 6 days after we entered the Arkansas, we travelled at an average of some thing over 4 miles per hour, but since then, the current has become so much more rapid, that we have been gradually running slower, and at present the speed of the Boats does not exceed 3 miles.

4th June 1837.

We continued to travel through last night, and this forenoon at 7 o'clock passed the mouth of Grand River. The Indians had said to me, that they wished to be landed on the west bank of the Verdigris, near the Creek Agency. When we reached the mouth of Grand River, I sent an Indian Runner to inform the Disbur'g. agent of the Creeks (west), that the Party was in the vicinity, in order that arrangements might be made for its immediate reception, at the point of Debarkation. The Boats reached the Creek Agency at 8 o'clock, and the Indians were immediately mustered, with as much accuracy, as it was possible for that operation to be performed with. The Party was received immediately after its arrival, and the number after deducting Desertions and Deaths upon the Route, amounted to Four hundred and sixty-three.

Fort Gibson Arkansas Territory
June 5th 1837.

To day the muster Roll of the Party of Indians that was yesterday delivered over by me, at the Creek Agency on the Verdigris R. was certified by the Disbursing Agent of the Creeks (West.) I have no fault to find with the "Emigrating Company" in regard to the Removal of this Party. I believe the Indians have received every allowance they were entitled to, and with one trifling Exception, were treated in conformity with the requirements of the letter and Spirit of the Emigrating Contract. This exception was the failure to have constructed some necessary fixtures which were essential to Cleanliness in the Boats and which I was promised should be put up, before starting. Their construction was delayed several days and never were finished as I wished them to be. Had not their necessity been superseeded on a few days, by the freequent stopping of the Boats, I should have employed carpenters to make them & have charged the expense to the Contractors.

When the miserable and empoverished condition of many of these people, some months previous to starting, is considered, and the injurious effects that such circumstances, was calculated to produce upon the health & constitutions of many of them; and when it is also remembered that they were necessarily closely confined under Guard, for several weeks previous to setting out; and when the unhealthy season of the year is also taken into account; I do not think that the amount of sickness & number of Deaths upon the Route, has been by any means great.

The foregoing Remarks embrace every occurrence of any importance that has taken place to my Knowledge, from the time the Party started from Gunter's Landing, until its arrival and delivery, in the new country west of the Mississippi River.

Edw— Deas
1st Lt. U.S. Army &
Disburs'g. agent in the
Creek Emigration.

Supplemental Letters of Edward Deas and Assistants

Lieutenant Edward Deas reports on the probable locations of the refugee Creeks living in the Cherokee country and offers the opinion that it would be best to remove a small party by water as soon as possible in order to take advantage of the current state of the rivers than to wait until all the Creeks were brought in and would be forced to go by land. Letter found at LR, CAE, Roll 238, 199–202.

New Echota Geo'a
30th March 1837

To,
C. A. Harris esquire
Commissioner of Indian Affairs

Sir,

I have the honour to inform you of my arrival at this place, which I reached yesterday, & reported to General Wool,[14] and have received his instructions, upon the subject of Collecting the Refugee Creeks in the Cherokee country.

I left Gunter's Landing on the 26th instant, after settling with the Contractor for subsisting the Creek Indians Encamped at that point. I found the number there to amount to 150, and Gen'l Andrew Moore Assis't Agent has charge of the camp.

It appears from information received that the other principal bodies of the Refugee Creeks, are in the neighbourhood of Coosawattie, 18 miles to the eastward of this point, and in the neighbourhood of Red Clay, a point 30 or 40 miles to the east of Ross's Landing.

There are also a number scattered in the mountains of N— Carolina, and near the banks of valley River, and the whole number of those in the Cherokee Country is thought to be over 1000, but of course there is much uncertainty upon this point.

General Wool has issued orders to the commanders of stations, to furnish detachments for their collection, upon my requisition & I shall immediately take measures to have them assembled for Emigration. It appears most expedient to collect those that may be found to the eastward of Ross's Landing, at that point, & then remove them to Gunter's Landing by water, to join those that now are or may hereafter be there assembled, and then enroll them & turn the whole over to the Emigrating Company.

There are many of these people in a miserably destitute condition, having scarcely clothing enough to cover their nakedness. General Wool has directed me to supply decent clothing to those of this description. I shall be glad however to receive further instructions from the Department as soon as possible, upon this point.

There are at present the following Assistant Agents employed in this Emigration under my direction (viz)—General Andrew Moore at Gunter's Landing,—Mr. A. R. Barclay[15] who will proceed immediately to the vicinity of Red Clay,—Mr. W. H. Griffith who is stationed near Coosawattie and Mr. Stidham a Conductor & Interpreter.

I shall also have to employ an Agent to attend to subsisting those that may be brought in near Valley River N.C. After the Indians are collected & turned over for Emigration the services of all of these Agents will of course no longer be necessary & I shall be glad to receive direct authority to discharge those that may no longer be required.

I am of opinion that if only 5 or 6 hundred of the Creeks can be collected for Emigration, without the whole number being brought in, in time to start soon enough in the season, to enable the Party to reach Fort Gibson by water; it would be better to turn those over that were ready to go, & let the remainder, if any, depend upon going in a separate Party when they should be collected. I believe it is known that the Arkansas River is highest in may & June generally, & after that time, there is no certainty of Steam Boats reaching Fort Gibson. I shall also be glad to know if this view is approved, but mention it only as a measure of precaution, as I trust that we shall be able to collect the whole in time, so as to render only one Party necessary.

I shall also be glad to receive the acknowledgement of the receipt of my accounts for Disbursements in the Creek Removal, for the 2nd 3rd & 4th Quarters of 1836, which I have not yet done. Ross's Landing[16] Hamilton Co'y Tennessee will be the best point to which to direct to me, any communication.

I have the honour to be Sir
very Respect'y your Obe't Servant.
Edw— Deas
Lt. U S Army &
Disburs'g Agent Creek Emigration

☾

Deas reports that there are approximately 250 refugee Creeks encamped at various locations throughout the Cherokee country. Letter found at LR, CAE, Roll 238, 207–8.

Fort Cass Cherokee Agency
E—Tennessee
6th April 1837.

To,
C. A. Harris Esquire
Commissioner of Indian Affairs

Sir,

I have the honour herewith to forward my accounts for Disbursements in the Removal & Subsistence of Indians for the 1st Quarter of 1836.

I have Endeavoured to make the accounts & vouchers, as plain and explicit as possible, but owing to the manner in which some of the accounts for Subsisting the Refugee Creeks, were incurred, it was impossible to preserve entire uniformity in making them out.

Nothing of particular importance has occurred in reference to the collection of these Indians for Emigration, since I last had the honour to address you upon this subject. All exertions have been made to apprehend them & upwards of 250 are reported, as now encamped & guarded at different stations. I shall proceed immediately to the mountains of N. Carolina, to urge on the collection of those in that section of country, and will report without delay, all information of interest in reference to this business.

I have the honour to be, Sir,

very Respecfully
your Ob't Servant
Edw— Deas
Lieut. U S Army &
Disburs'g Agent in the
Creek Emigration

☾

Deas reports that he has collected about 545 Creeks (actual number 543), who were captured at various points in the Cherokee country. Encamped near Gunter's Landing, the agent notes that some of these Creeks have contracted dysentery, requiring the attendance of an additional physician and a delay in the commencement of the journey, which did not subsequently begin until 16 May. Letter found at LR, CAE, Roll 238, 214–17.

Gunter's Landing N. alaba'a
10th May 1837.

To,
C. A. Harris Esq'e
Commissioner of Indian affairs

Sir,

Since I last had the honour to address you, there have been collected for Emigration, about 545, of the Refugee Creek Indians, and these are now encamped, and guarded, within four miles of this place.

Near a hundred of them, were apprehended in the mountains of N. Carolina, and were conducted by myself to Ross' Landing. Two other Detachments, one from Red Clay, & the other from Coosawattie, were brought to the same point, and on the 2nd ins't about 350, were there assembled.

I then had them removed by water, to the neighbourhood of this place, which they reached in safety on the morning of the 7th instant.

There had already been collected near this point, about 195, of which number, about 40, have been brought in by the Troops within the last ten days.

On the 5th instant I received your communi'n of the 24th March, but have as yet, received no answers to my letters addressed to yourself, since my arrival in the Cherokee Country. Therefore under the instructions which I have at present, I had determined, to turn over for Emigration on tomorrow (the 11th), to the Agent of the "alabama Emigrating Company", now present, all the above named Indians. For the following reason however, I have determined, in order to ensure the health & safety of these people, to defer doing so, for a few days at least. Within the last two or three days, a disorder has made its appearance in the Camp, of the nature of a Dysentery, and has affected a large number of the Children. I immediately employed a Physician to attend them, and after due consideration find, it would be extremely hazardous to Embark the Indians on their journey until this disorder is checked. The Physician is of opinion that this may be done effectually, in the course of a Week, at the expiration of which time, at furthest, I hope the Party will be enabled to set out.

I am unable by any means to discover the number of Creek Refugees, still remaining at large in the Cherokee Country. All those that could be heard of, and found, have been apprehended by the Troops, but I have doubt that there are still many of them scattered & secreted amongst the Cherokee People. I think however, that those still remaining, are so well provided for, that they will not become a nuisance to the Citizens of the Country, as many of those now in Camp have been. Numbers of them were found in the most wretched condition, and in some cases, naked, & starving.

I hoped to receive before leaving Ross' Landing on the 3rd instant, a communication from yourself, in answer to two of mine, the former dated New Echota 30th March, & the latter from the same place, enclosing an Estimate of Funds, on the 2nd April.[17] I may still have an opportunity of hearing from Ross' Landing by Express, before leaving this place. That is the point to which I requested you, in my letter of the 29th March, to direct to me.

Provisions have been, and still are, extremely high in this country. Bacon from 12 to 15 cents per pound. Corn from 75 cents to a dollar per Bushell, and Fresh Beef not to be had in any quantity.

I still hope that I shall receive a communication in regard to Funds, as I have not enough on hand at present, to discharge the expenses which I have necessarily incurred in subsisting, & collecting this Party for Emigration.

I think at present that it will be most expedient for it to perform the whole route by water, going as far as the foot of the Muscle shoals in Flat Boats, & thence to Fort Gibson, by Steam, with large Keils in tow.

I shall continue to report all circumstances of Interest connected with this business, as they may occur.

I have the honour to be,
Sir, Very Respectfully
your Obed't Servant.
Edw— Deas
1st Lieut. U.S. Army &
Disb'g Agent in the
Creek Emigration

☾

Brevet Brigadier General John E. Wool reports to Roger Jones,[18] the adjutant general of the U.S. Army of the transfer of approximately 420 Creeks captured in the Cherokee country to Gunter's Landing, Alabama. Letter found at LR, CAE, Roll 238, 920.

Head Quarters
Army of the C N
New Echota Geo.
May 11th 1837

To/.
Brig: Genl R Jones Adjt. Genl

Sir,

Herewith I transmit for the information of the General in Chief letters from one to nine to officers and others relating to my command.

The detachments, sent in pursuit of the Creek Indians, apprehended about four hundred and twenty. These have been sent to Gunters Landing, Ala. for emigration to the West. The Agents sent to receive the Creeks having left this Country, my detachments have been called in from further pursuit.

I am Sir,
Verry respectfully
your obdt. Servt.
John E. Wool
Brig Genl
Comdg

☾

Written almost a week after reporting the presence of dysentery in the camp, Deas's 16 May letter updates the commissioner of Indian affairs, Carey A. Harris, on the status of the party, including that the refugees have been brought to the Tennessee River's edge and are about to embark on boats for the West. Letter found at LR, CAE, Roll 238, 219–20.

Encampment of Indians
(near) Gunter's Landing
North alabama
16th May 1837.

To,
C. A. Harris Esquire
Commissioner of Indian affairs

Sir,

I have the honour herewith to forward to you the muster-Roll of the Party of Creek Indians, to-day turned over by me, to the Agent of the "alabama Emigrating Company".

The Indians are now at the water's Edge a mile below Gunter's Landing, on the point of Embarking in Flat Boats.

I had the honour to inform you on the 10th instant, that some delay had occurred, in consequence of sickness, but at present, the Party is as healthy as can be expected in this country, at this season.

I have found it impossible to provide a Physician to attend the Party, west, on lower terms than Five dollars a day, and have therefore made a Contract with one to this effect, to continue only until I can procure medical attendence on lower terms.

I have as yet received no communications whatever from your office, other than mentioned in my letter of the 10th instant.

There are some other points of interest which I have to mention on the subject of the Emigration, that there is not time left, to go into, at present, so as to send this by the next mail from this place. I shall take the first opportunity of addressing you again upon these points, & in reference to the progress of the Party, which I shall of course accompany on the Route of Emigration, having received no instructions to the contrary.

I am Sir, Very Respectfully
your Obed't Servant
Edw— Deas
Lieut. U S Army &
Disb'g Agent in the
Creek Emigration

☾

Three days after leaving the neighborhood of Gunter's Landing, Deas again updates the commissioner of Indian affairs on the progress of the party. Writing from Decatur, Deas laments the loss of sixteen Creeks (his journal entry from 18 May says fifteen) who deserted the party when their flatboat was forced to come to shore due to high wind. Letter found at LR, CAE, Roll 238, 233–36.

Decatur N. alabama
19th May 1837.

To,
C. A. Harris esq'e
Commissioner of Indian affairs.

Sir,

I have the honor to inform you that the Party of Creek Indians under my charge, reached this place a few moments ago, (7 o'clock P.M.) and will proceed immediately.

I regret to say that on the evening of the 17th when the Boats were compelled to land, on account of wind 16 of the Indians made their escape, and have not since been heard of.

With this exception every thing thus far, relative to the removal of the Party has gone on well. Nine Flat Boats are employed, four of them of the largest class. This mode of travelling is however, very slow, and it is intended to employ steam conveyance as soon as possible, after passing the Muscle Shoals.

The Indians remain healthy, and I hope that we shall meet with no impediments from any cause. I have engaged a Physician, at this place to attend the Party, at $85—per month, as was done last year.

In my letter from Gunter's Landing of the 16th inst't, I stated that there were several points upon which I then, had not time to write, which I therefore take the present opportunity of doing.

It appears that General Andrew Moore of Claysville, from letters in his possession, was appointed by Gen'l Jesup last summer, to take charge of the business connected with the Emigration of the Creeks in the Cherokee Country, and until my arrival at Gunter's Landing, in march last, continued to have charge of a Camp of Creek Indians near that place, which had been formed a short time after the Emigration from that neighbourhood, last September.

Gen'l Moore has incurred a number of accounts consisting of the hire of agents, Wagons, &c, to the payment of which I first wished to have your approval. I therefore wrote to Gen'l Moore upon the subject, and a copy of the letter is herewith enclosed, which also informed him that his services were no longer required.

I shall be glad to hear if this is approved & whither the accounts are to be paid.

When I reached the Cherokee country, I made two Contracts for subsisting the Indians, at different points, duplicates of which are herewith enclosed. Under the former with Mr. Childress[19] at Gunter's Landing, about 3500 Rations have been furnished amounting to something over $1200—, which I had not the necessary Funds to settle before leaving that place.

Under the latter with Mr. H. G. Barclay about 5250, Rations still remain to be paid for at 16 cents amounting to near $850—.

All other accounts that I know of, other than those mentioned or referred to above and connected with the Creek Emigration in the Cherokee Country, are at this time settled.

I left directions for any communications that might arrive for me, to be forwarded to Memphis.

After delivering the present Party at Fort Gibson, I take it for granted, that the unsettled business at Gunters Landing, will render it necessary for me to return to that place.

I will thank you Sir, to give me instructions upon this point, and to direct this Communication to Little Rock Arkansas, if it is written soon after the receipt of this.

It will require about $2100—to discharge all the accounts at Gunters Landing, besides what I shall have on hand probably, at the end of the present Quarter.

I am Sir.
Very Respectfully
your Obed't Servant
Edw— Deas
Lieut U.S.A. & Dis'g agent
C— Emig'n

☾

Two days after fifteen (or sixteen) Creeks escaped the flats on 18 May, seventy-one more Creeks fled the party as the boats came to shore after passing Decatur, Alabama. Here Deas notifies the commissioner of Indian affairs of the new desertions, while also reporting the successful passage of the Muscle Shoals. Letter found at LR, CAE, Roll 238, 240–42.

Steam-Boat "Black Hawk"
(near) Helena, Arkansas:
27th May 1837.

To,
C. A. Harris Esq'e
Commissioner of Indian affairs.

Sir,

I have the honour to report to you, that the Party of Emigrating Creek Indians under my charge, passed Memphis this morning, at 4 o'clock A.M. It was thought advisable to make no stop, at that place, least some of the Indians should succeed in escaping from the Boats, for the purpose of visiting the Chicasaw country, of which intention, on the part of some of them, several intimations have been given.

On the 19th inst. the Party passed Decatur Alabama, as I then reported. Early the next morning the weather became stormy, and the Flat Boats were compelled to land, before daylight, in consequence of which, we were so unfortunate as to loose a number of the Indians, by Desertion. The Boats were seperated at the time of landing, and immediately after some of the smaller ones touched the shore, the Indians on board took advantage of the darkness of the night, and the Rain, to make their escape.

As soon as the other Boats landed every exertion was made to overtake and bring them back. By offering a reward of one dollar, for each one that should be returned, I succeeded in recovering 15. The others 56 in number, could not be overtaken in time, and succeeded in making their escape to the mountains 5 miles distant.

On the 21st we passed thro' the Muscle Shoals without accident, on the 23rd the Party reached Waterloo Alaba'a at noon, and re-embarked at 4 o'clock on Board the S— Boat Black Hawk with a Keil & two Flats in tow. We have continued to run since that time, in day light, and stopped the greater part of Each night except last night.

We shall probably enter the Arkansas River, tomorrow, and will ascend that Stream, with two Keils in tow. I have had every thing done, to secure the health and comfort of the People under my care, and they now appear well satisfied in all respects. Two deaths have occurred amongst the Children, since starting, one of them caused by imprudence; but at present the Indians are generally healthy.[20] The weather has been extremely favourable, and the Removal of the Party, thus far, on the part of the Emigrating Company; has been well conducted in all respects.

Nothing else of importance has occurred upon the Route, since I last had the honour to address you upon this subject.

I have left directions for all my communications to be forwarded. I therefore, expect to receive at Little Rock all those that have not yet reached me.

I am Sir, Very Respectfully
your Obedient Servant.
Edw— Deas
Lieut. U.S. Army &
Disburs'g Agent in the
Creek Emigration

☾

Superintendent of Cherokee removal Nathaniel Smith[21] reports on the destitute condition of the Creeks living in the Cherokee country. Letter found at LR, CAE, Roll 238, 792–94.

Cherokee Agency East
29th May 1837.

Hon'l
C. A. Harris
Com. Ind. affairs,

Sir,

Doct. J. S. Young,[22] conducting Agent, shewed me a letter, in which you direct, that he, shall make out an account, of the expenses of transporting the 5 creeks, to the cherokee country West.

Shortly after I entered on the duties of Sup. C. Removal, I was informed that some 80 or 100 creeks, were encamped in the mountains, about Eighteen miles, from this place, and that they were not only destitute of subsistance but almost naked. I immediately sent out an agent, to invite them to come in and inform them, I would furnish them with rations and clothing. The agent with his Interpreter reached their Camps, in the evening, where he found about 60 destitute of clothing and without any thing to eat. He told them his business and they agreed to come in with him. He went about 5 miles, to stay all night and when he returned the next morning, they had all fled. He was told that nine had encamped, between where he was and the agency & he came by and found them. 5 of them had some little clothing, the other 4, a Woman and 3 children, were so nearly in a state of nudity, that I had to send blankets out, for them to cover their nakedness, before they would come in, and without a shoe to their feet.

This woman is the daughter of chinnubby[23] who was a friendly chief, during the late war.

I had to send her half Brother, who is half cherokee, (and who was amongst the emigrants, that went west, in the last detachment) before I could induce her, and the others to come in. The only piece of covering she had for herself and children was part of an old blanket, not a yard square. When they reached camp, the blood was runing out of her and her childrens legs; they had parched them so by the fire, to keep warm that where the twigs, touched them, as they came in the blood ran freely.

I gave them all clothing and rations and they became well satisfied, untill the first night after I left this, with the detachment; The woman, then took her 3 children, and left us, and I have not heard of them since. The other five went on very well satisfied.

I have thought it best to enclose you the whole account, that you may have it paid to the Cherokee fund. the 9 Blankets, given them, was out of a parcel left on hand in this office, by the late Superintendent.

There has lately been taken out of the cherokee nation East 4 or 500 creeks and from reports I beleive there are still 3 or 400 more lurking in the mountains; generally subsisting on what they can beg from the cherokees and nearly naked.

The prices charged for the rations and transportation I cannot precisely ascertain, but the am't charged I am sure will cover all expenses.

I have the honour to remain

very respectfully
Nat Smith
Sup't C. Removal

☾

Writing from Helena, Arkansas, Deas reports on the status of the party, including the deaths of two people. According to his 29 May journal entry, one was a Creek man and the other "a very old woman." Letter found at LR, CAE, Roll 238, 244.

Steam Boat Black Hawk
(at) Little Rock Ark's
31st May 1837.

To,
C. A. Harris esq'e
Commiss'r of Indian affairs

Sir

On the 27th ins't I had the honour to report to you from Helena Arkan's every thing of interest up to that time, relative to the Removal of the Party of Creek Indians under my charge.

We have just reached this place (7 o'clock A.M.) and will proceed immediately towards Fort Gibson, which place I hope we shall be able to reach by water as the Arkansas is at present at a good stage, and on the rise.

Two deaths occurred on the 29th, but the Party at present is healthy and nothing else of particular importance has occurred since I last had the honour to address you upon this subject.

I am Sir
Very Respect'y your Obed't Servant

Edw— Deas
Lieut. U.S. army and
Disb'g agent Creek Emigra'n

☾

Deas reports on the party's arrival on 4 June and forwards his journal to the department. Letter found at LR, CAE, Roll 238, 249.

Fort Gibson Ark's Ty.
5th June 1837.

To,
C. A. Harris Esq'r
Commission'r of Indian affairs

Sir,

I have the honour to forward to you herewith, my Journal of occurrences upon the Route of the Party of Creek Emigrants, which yesterday reached its place of Destination, under my charge.

The Journal itself contains every thing of interest, that I have at present to communicate, upon the subject of the Indians.

I shall return Eastward immediately, and will probably receive at Little Rock, some intelligence from your office, to govern me in my future movements.

I have the honour to be, Sir,
Very Respect'y your Obe't Servant
Edw— Deas
Lieut. U.S. Army &
Disbursing agent
In the Creek Emigration.

☾

Lieutenant Deas reports that there are still several hundred Creek Indians living among the Cherokees. Letter found at LR, CAE, Roll 238, 246–47.

Steam Boat Black Hawk
near Little Rock Arkan's
7th June 1837.

To,
C. A. Harris esq'r
Commissioner of Indian affairs

Sir,

On the 5th instant, I had the honour to address you from Fort Gibson, and to forward my Journal of Occurrences upon the Route of the Party of Indians which I delivered near that place, the day before.

I supposed that on my return to Little Rock I should probably receive some communication from your office, to govern me in any further duties that I may have to perform in the Indian Department. I was disappointed in this respect, & shall therefore return to Gunter's Landing, having left directions for any letters to be forwarded to that place, that may arrive for me, at Little Rock.

I have already mentioned that there are several hundreds of the Creeks, still remaining in the Cherokee Country, (East), which I suppose it is the intention of the Department to have removed west, as soon as it may be practicable, and Expedient to do so.

Any further instructions for myself, either upon this or any other Subject I will be glad to have forwarded to Gunter's Landing, N. Alabama.

I have the honor to be, Sir,
Very Respectfully
Your Obed't Servant
Edw— Deas
Lieut. U.S. Army &
Disburs'g Agent in the
Creek Emigration

☾

Captain James R. Stephenson reports on the arrival of the 463 Creeks captured in the Cherokee country and that many of them fled upon the steamboat's landing, which delayed his certifying the rolls. Letter found at LR, CAE, Roll 238, 815.

Fort Gibson
June 13th 1837

Sir

On the 4th Inst. I received in their new Country Four hundred and sixty three Emigrant Creeks, conducted by H. G. Barclay Agent for the Alabama Emigrating Company, and accompanied by Lieut Edw'd Deas U.S. Army.—These Emigrants arrived on board of a Steam Boat, and immediately on their landing a large number of them dispersed through the Country with their friends, although every precaution was taken by Lieut Deas to detain them until a re-muster could be effected; in consequence of this fact, and the impossibility of collecting them for several days I felt bound to certify the Rolls as I have done heretofore, determined however to have a re-muster as soon as it could possibly be done, this I have effected and find the Roll to be correct.

The Contractors for furnishing the Emigrant Creeks with Provisions, have at this time within this vicinity an ample supply of Beef, Corn and Salt for all present purposes, and from their present movements no apprehension of a failure to fully comply with their Contract may be anticipated.

Very Respectfully
Your Obedt. Servt.
Ja's. R. Stephenson
Capt. U.S. Army
Disbg. agt. (Creeks)

C. A. Harris Esqr.
Com. of Ind. Affairs
Washington
D.C.

☾

Deas explains his decision to close down the subsistence camps in the Cherokee country, noting that all the refugees who could be captured had been captured. The remainder were embedded with Cherokee families. Letter found at LR, CAE, Roll 238, 285–87.

(Copy)

Gunter's Landing, alaba'a
23rd June 1837.

To,

Brig'r General John E. Wool
U.S. Army

Sir,

I have just reached this neighbourhood, on my return from Arkansas, and a few minutes ago, had some conversation with Mr. Childress, who was the contractor for furnishing the Creeks encamped near here, previous to the late Emigration. He states that he has heard of a number of these Indians still in the Cherokee country, & that he thought from what he heard you say, to, or in the presence of General Moore of Claysville, that you were of the opinion that a Camp for Subsistence aught to have been left open, for their reception; or something to that effect.

If Mr. Childress is correct, the following are the reasons why I closed up the business of the Emigration upon my departure for Arkansas.

If the Creeks were in want of Food, they had had ample opportunity of coming in and receiving their regular subsistence. It is therefore manifest that all those that would come in of their own accord, did come in, before the last Party started west, which was the opinion of Every disinterested Agent that I knew. Hence it was only for such Indians as the Troops might apprehend that a Camp for Subsistence could be required. The Troops had searched the country at every point and the different commanders had said that they had apprehended all the Refugees that could be apprehended, at that time.

I had no doubt that this was the case, for I had very good reasons to believe, that the Creek Indians still remaining in the Cherokee Country, were not living in Towns, or Camps; but were connected with Cherokee Families, and were living with, and concealed by those people.

I therefore conceived that all those that were left when I started for Arkansas, were provided for, for the present, and would not become a nuisance to the country, by their destitute condition, and consequent depredations, as had been the Case with those that composed the last party, for the most part.

I was well aware that after that Party started, no other could go before the latter part of the Summer or Fall, as the annual June Rise in the Arkansas River would be over, which would prevent water Transportation, and provisions could not be had upon the land Route, west of the Mississippi River, before the next crop of Corn in September.

For the above reasons I did not think the Expense of an Agent, or Agents, would be required until my return, at least, and on other accounts I wished to close up the business, and put a stop to further Expenses, until a responsible Agent of the Government could be present to superintend them.

I have the honour to be, Sir,
Very Respectfully
your Ob't Servant
Edw— Deas
Lieut. U.S. Army
Superinten'g the Creek
Emigration in the Cherokee Country.

Creeks in the Chickasaw Country

While federal agents were combing the Cherokee country looking for refugee Creeks, agents were also sent to Mississippi to apprehend those who had fled to live among the Chickasaws. Officials estimated that there were approximately five hundred Creek Indians hiding among the Chickasaws in Mississippi. Some of these Creeks had likely absconded from the 1834 voluntary emigrating party led by John Page, while others may simply have fled the Creek country as the problems in the former Creek Nation became worse in the 1830s. In 1833 sixty-six families consisting of over 230 Creeks petitioned Washington for permission to emigrate to the Chickasaw Nation. Claiming that they were "all our family connections," the Creeks proposed living among the Chickasaws until that nation emigrated to the west. In fact, early Cusseta migration legends describe the close relationship between the Creeks of Alabama, Abihka, and Cusseta towns and the Chickasaws.[24]

Reuben E. Clements,[25] a native of Lafayette, Tennessee, and a former surveyor in the Creek country, conducted the party west in the fall of 1837. Lieutenant Gouverneur Morris[26] served as military oversight, and Dr. Jesse Mays accompanied the party as the attending surgeon. The journey appears to have been relatively uneventful, although a physician named "Dr. McCoole"[27] died on 11 December 1837 near the St. Francis River when a tree limb fell on his head while he was dressing the wound of "an old Indian" man who was burned by the accidental explosion of his powder horn.[28]

Letters of the Detachment of Refugee Creeks in the Chickasaw Country

Chickasaw agent Arthur M. M. Upshaw[29] reports on the appointment of Kemp S. Holland[30] as agent to remove the refugee Creeks (he declined the appointment). Upshaw believes the Creeks should not travel in company with the Chickasaws to Indian territory. Letter found at LR, CAE, Roll 238, 883.

Pulaski July 21st 1837
Hon'l. C. A. Harris

Sir,

I had the honor to receive your communications of the 23d June, last evening, informing me of the appointment of Kemp S. Holland, Esqr as agent to remove the refugee Creek Indians: who are now Settled in the Chickasaw country. I would observe that besides those that are in Itawamba County, there are, I am informed, about one hundred on

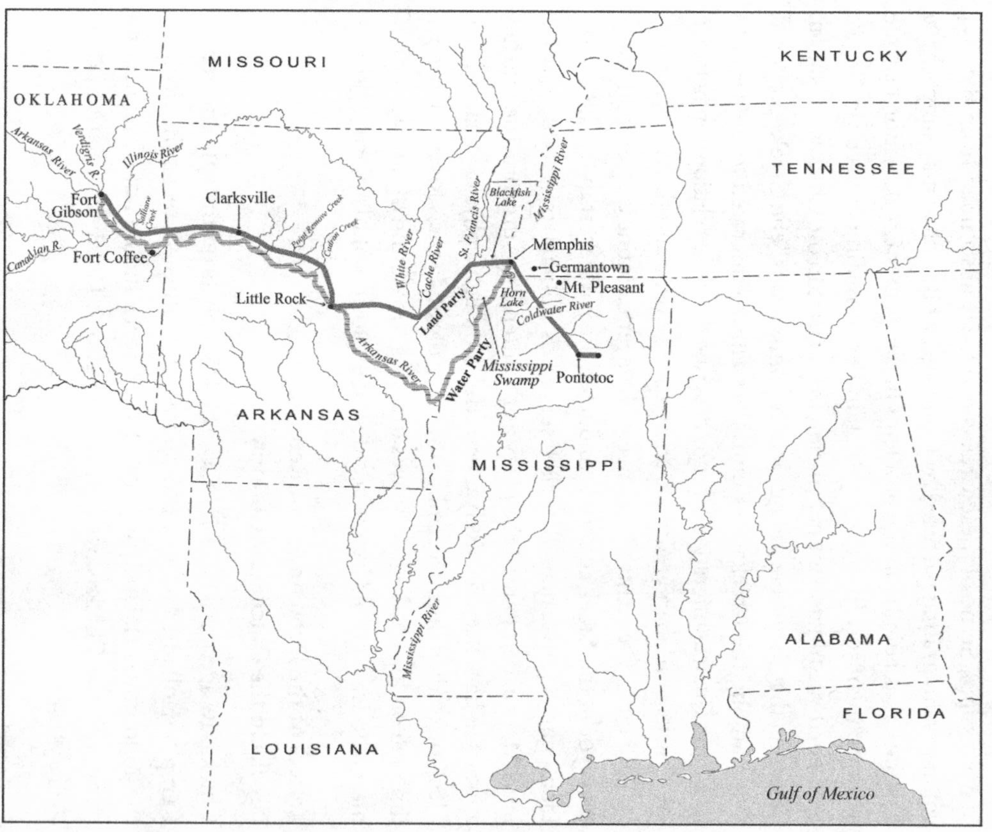

MAP 16. Route of Creek refugees in Chickasaw country, October–December 1837. Place names correspond to stopping points or locations noted in the documentation. Route lines and locations are approximations. Cartography by Sarah Mattics and Kiersten Fish.

Horn Lake or near there, a greater part of those Creeks I understand, ran off from the emigrating parties last fall; In the same package I received a coppy of your instructions to Capt Philips,[31] instructions to Holland, and also a coppy of Mr. W.M.M. Owen's[32] letter to the Hon'l Secretary of War.

I have not heard from Mr Holland whether he accepts the appointment or not, but So far as I can without interfering with my own duties, render Mr. Holland every assistance; But I must be permited to object to their going in company with the Chicksaws for two reasons, the 1st is, the Chicksaws are a well disposed people, the Creeks are mean and Contrary, and I should dislike for the Chicksaws to be corrupted by them, the 2nd is, Some thing might happen to create unkind feeling between the Conductors of the parties.

With high, regard, I have the honor, to be
Yr Mo ob't St &c
A.M.M. Upshaw
Supt. Reml. Chicksaws

☾

Reuben E. Clements, who was appointed superintendent after Holland declined, reports on the appointment of agents, the establishment of camps, and the disposition of the refugee Creeks to move west. Letter found at LR, CAE, Roll 238, 163–64.

Pontotoc Sept 20th 1837

Hon C. A. Harris

Sir

I have the honor to Inform you that I have Appointed Robert B Crockett Assistant supertendant of the Emigration of the Creek Indians who have setled in the Chickasaw Nation his compensation will be four Dollars per day and nessary expences paid commencing upon the 15th Inst. I also have the honor to inform you that I have

Appointed Thomas B Carroll & Wm M. M. Owen Enrolling agents there Day to commence the 17th Ins't at four Dollars per day and nessary travling Expences paid.

I have the Honor to inform you that I held a counsel with those in Itawamba county about 30 miles East of this they are Disposed to Emegrate soon I am to have a counsel with those that are about 30 miles south of Memphis and I have no doubt but what I shall be able to get them all off in about 20 days or Perhaps Less. I have appointed two places of Enrolling one about 20 miles East of this and the other about 30 miles from Memphis. I shall endeavour to Join them a few miles from Memphis—You will please write If you sanction the appointments of Messrs Crockett Carroll and Owen. Crockett & Carroll are from Tennessee and Owen from this state. They are men that I can plase the utmost confidence In.

with Resp't
Yo ob't ser't
R. E. Clements
Supt Creek Removal

☾

Clements notifies the commissioner of Indian affairs that there are probably more Creeks (five hundred) in the Chickasaw country than originally anticipated, and he wants funds arranged for the impending removal. Letter found at LR, CAE, Roll 238, 161.

Pontotoc Sept 23rd 1837

Hon C. A. Harris

Sir

I have the honor to Inform you that there is more Creek Indians than you Expected. I think there are about 500 Hundred and the amount of money you Instructed Capt Philips to hand over to me or to who he appointed my Disbursing officer will not more than Defray the Expence farther than Memphis. I have conversed with

Capt Philips about the Probable amount he thinks will take about Seven Thousand Dollars more about half of which I would like to have at Memphis and the Balance at Little Rock, that at Memphis might be drawn upon the Resivor of Public moneys at this plase. Capt Philips Informed me that Leut Morris would Disburse for me he has not arrived at this plase yet But Is Looked for Daily.

with Respt
Yo ob't Serv't
R. E. Clements
Supt Creek Removal

☾

Clements reports on the appointment of a surgeon and interpreter. Because the refugee Creeks in Mississippi were so opposed to removal and to federal agents in particular, finding a Muskogean speaker willing to aid the government proved difficult. Luther Smuttie (or "Smut Eye") was willing to do it, for a price. He drove a hard bargain and was paid nearly a dollar more than other interpreters were paid. Letter found at LR, CAE, Roll 238, 172.

Pontotoc Oct 8th 1837

Hon. C. A. Harris

Sir

I have the honor to inform you that I have appointed Doct Jesse Mays as surgeon of the Creek Emegration he is a man of high standing in his profession his compensation will be five dollars per day and nessary travling Expences paid.

I also have the honor to Inform you that I have appointed Luther Smuttie Interperter. I had much trouble to get an Interperter and have to give this one Two Dollars and fifty cents per day and pay his Expences while travling from one Rendezvous to the other you will please write me If you sanction those appointments Doct Mays Is from Tennessee and my Interperter is the most sober Indian I ever saw.

Respectfully
Yo mo obt sert
R. E. Clements
Supt. Creek Removal

☾

Clements reports on the progress of enrolling the refugee Creeks and on the arrival of Captain Gouverneur Morris, who served as disbursing agent. Letter found at LR, CAE, Roll 238, 174.

Pontotoc Oct'r 11th 1837

Hon C. A. Harris

Sir

I have the honor to inform the Department that since the 1st Inst I have made as good progress in Enrolling the Indians as could be expected considering there dispursed situation.

Capt Morris Dis. Agent arrived and reported for duty on the 6th Inst we shall leave here on the 12th and visit the portion in Pontotoc Itawambie and Desoto counties and attend to the colection of the Creeks in those Districts.

I also deem it my duty to inform the Department that Capt Morris has made a contract with Maj'r N. A. Bryan of Tallahatchie Marshall county to furnish these Indians at the Rendezvos and on the route as far as Memphis with rations at sixteen cents per ration the same that Col upshaw pays for the Chickasaws. It is the lowest rate that a contract could be made in this section of country.

I have the honor to be
very respectfully
yo mo obt sert
R. E. Clements
Sup't Creek Removal

☾

Clements reports that he was only able to enroll approximately three hundred Creek refugees. The party moved from Pontotoc toward Memphis behind one thousand Chickasaws. Letter found at LR, CAE, Roll 238, 176–77.

Pontotoc Nov'r 1st 1837

Hon C. A. Harris

Sir

I have the honor to report my progress since I wrote you last   I have Enroled about 3 hundred Indians and have been on the march some 3 days.

I have had great difficulty to get those Indians in camp and will not be able to get off more than Three hundred.

Owing to the situation of the Country I was compeled to have my Rendezvous in one mile of the Chickasaw camp and after I got ready to move I made an effort to start and my Indians bid defiance and said they would not start untill the Chickasaw started   Those Creeks are very hostile and I have had great difficulty to get along with them without Assistant   upon one occasion there came a Chickasaw into my Camp very Drunk and was trying to ride over my camp   I led his horse out and he returned with his Knife in his hand and I had to have him taken off and the Creeks was Drinking very much and they rose with their Knifes and It was with much difficulty that I could get them satisfied. I then tryd to move them and they said they would not move untill the Chickasaws started and I have been compeled to wait untill the Chickasaws started and travel after them and with much difficulty that I can move them. I am now upon the march Just in the rear of Mr Millard[33] who is conducting about one thousand Chickasaws   I think we will cross the River in about 8 or 10 day.

I Remain very respecfully
your mo obt Sert
R. E. Clements
Supt Creek Removal

(

Clements reports on funds, the appointment of subagents, and the violence among the Creeks in camp. He also notes that the party will leave Memphis the following day in the steamboat *Itasca*. Letter found at LR, CAE, Roll 238, 179–81.

Memphis Tenn
November 18th 1837

C. A. Harris Esqr
Comm'r Indian affairs

Sir

I have the honor to acknowledge the receipt of your letters of the 23rd and 26th ultimo relative to the Appointments of assistant agents and advising me of funds transmitted to the Disbursing Officer for the creek emegration.[34]

When I recived the appointment of Supertendent for the collection and removal of these Indians I was informed by several Gentleman of respectability, who have resided a number of years among the Chickasaws that there were scatterd over the sission[35] more than five hundred creeks acting under this impresion and considering the carictor of the Indians and their dispursed situation I entertained the fullest confidence that the Department would sanction the appointment I made. I consulted col upshaw on the subject who concurd with me in the nicisity and propriety of the measure the greater part of these Indians are outlaws have fled from own tribe for murders and crimes they have committed on there people and taken refuge among the chickasaws. They are affraid to return to their nation Knowing Indian law life for life will be enforsed. Since I have had them collected several savage and inhuman acts have been committed on cold water[36] one of them attacked another for Killing his brother several years ago, cut his scull in several places and opened his lungs and would have finished him had he not been prevented by some friends of his victim and the other day within three miles of this plase another was stabed to death in the camp by the brother of an Indian whom he had Killed and the same night they had another Indian to put to death who had been given up by his relation to receve his sentence he was released by the Agents and a wagoner by the name of Miller[37] the next day two of the Indians came painted to Miller and told him he had released the Indian who had Killed there brother and prevented them from Killing him that if he did not return him to them they would take his life in fire they are the most hostile and savage Indians I have ever Known. I have been compeled to gard and take the most desive measure with them at this time I have two in double irons and am fearful that I shall be unable to compell some of them to quit the Chickasaws as they have refused to come Into camp.

I shall embark tomorrow with about 300 on board steam boat Itasca[38] commanded by Capt Buckner[39] and shall send the Ponies with some ten or twelve through by land in charge of one or two Assistants the melancoly misfortune which occurd a few days since has had its effect upon this emegration. I have in compliance with your letter dispenced with the service of Mr. Owen.

In relation to the funds I did not make the proper and usal estimate supposing the Disbursing Officer would make the proper Disbursments should the sum transmitted exceed the amout required the balance will be accounted for in the usal way.

In the accomplish of the emegration the Department may rest assured that every thing will be conducted to its satisfaction.

I have the honor to be
Sir yo mo obt sert
R. E. Clements
Supt Creek Removal

☾

Clements reports that all of the Creek refugees captured in the Chickasaw country have arrived at Fort Gibson. The water party arrived on 30 November, the land party on 28 December. Letter found at LR, CAE, Roll 239, 161.

Fort Gibson
December 31st 1837

Sir

I have the honor to inform the Department that all of the creek Indians who were scatterd over the Chickasaw cession in Mississippi have been removed west, the rolls and Indians were severally transferd to the Gov't Agent Capt J. R. Stephenson as they arrived at the Post on the 30th November and 28th December 1837.

I have completed the emegration of this party as soon and have been as economical as Possible in the expenditures considering there Sick and helpliss condition and dispursed situation and I trust my acts will meet the approbation of the Department.

I have the honor sir
to be your mo obt sert
R. E. Clements
Supt creek Removal

Hon'r.
C. A. Harris
Commissioner Indian affairs
washington

Part 5

The Voluntary Self-Emigrations and Reunification Emigrations, 1831–77

17 The Reunification Emigrations

Although the major operations of the Creek Indian removal era ended in late December 1837 as the last of the *Monmouth* survivors made their way to Fort Gibson, there were still Creek Indians in Alabama. Some were ancestors of the Poarch Band of Creek Indians, who throughout the nineteenth and twentieth centuries petitioned for legal rights to their land. They were granted federal recognition in 1984 and remain in Alabama to this day. A small number of Creeks went through the tedious legal process of obtaining clear title to the reserves granted to them under the 1832 Treaty of Washington. In 1837 a number of Creeks of African descent in Macon County, Alabama, along with a number of Indian countrymen, all of whom were enrolled on the census as heads-of-families, requested patents for their land in the former Creek Nation. Others, like Powis Harjo and Neharlocco Harjo, both from Pucantallahassee, sold their reserves but continued living on their land, apparently with the permission of the white owners, into the 1840s.[1] Still others were somehow tied to a piece of land. Their status is unclear, but many may have been day laborers, sharecroppers, or even slaves on a white man's plot of land. Some may have held a life estate that guaranteed the Creek reservee rights to an allotment under the 1832 Treaty of Washington, until death. Many probably were tricked into working for whites; Luther Blake reported that a number of Alabamians and Georgians "told them such tales—as would but induce them to remain" (through promise of pay), only to find themselves living among the whites' black slaves without money. Just how many Creeks were living in this manner was a matter of conjecture, but a rough draft of a contract drawn up to remove these Creeks noted that there were approximately

160 still in Alabama. Luther Blake, who had helped conduct the 1829 voluntary emigrating party, reported that there were 51 men, 54 women, and 54 children. Of this total, 44 were slaves. Blake took an interest in these Creeks, hoping to conduct them west for $100 per person, although the government felt the cost too extravagant. Many of the Creeks were anxious to rejoin their townspeople in the west, while others pilfered from local farms without much apparent desire to leave.[2]

Whatever their reasons for staying, a longing to be reunited with friends and family ultimately brought them back together. Throughout the 1840s and beyond, dozens of Creeks, in family-sized parties voluntarily emigrated from Alabama to Indian territory. Unlike the voluntary parties of the 1820s and early 1830s, which cleaved the Creek Nation in half, these reunification emigrations were attempts to make it whole.[3]

The 1841 Reunification Emigration

In 1841 John H. Brodnax, a planter and trader who held great influence over the Creeks, conducted a party of eighteen people (seventeen Creeks and one slave) to Indian territory. Brodnax had previously served as a legal advisor to the Creek National Council in Alabama, and he accompanied to Washington the delegation of headmen who signed the Treaty of Washington in March 1832. Brodnax, in fact, was one of the lead negotiators of that document. He also speculated in Creek reserves after 1832.[4]

1841 Reunification Emigration Muster Roll

Found at LR, CAE, Roll 240, 522.

William Low 4 members consisting of 1 male under ten, 1 male of twenty-five and under fifty, 1 female of ten and under twenty-five, and one male slave.

Nancy Low 7 members consisting of 1 male under ten, 3 males of twenty-five and under fifty, 1 female of twenty-five and under fifty, and 2 females over fifty.

Leah McIntosh 4 members consisting of 1 male over fifty, 2 females under ten, and 1 female of ten and under twenty-five. On a copy of this muster roll the name is listed as "Leah McIntosh Brodnax."[5]

Claiborne Low 1 member consisting of 1 male of ten and under twenty-five.

Tony 1 member consisting of 1 male of twenty-five and under fifty.

Richard Harrod 1 member consisting of 1 male of twenty-five and under fifty.

The 1846 Reunification Emigration

In 1845 Moses K. Wheat,[6] a resident of the Alabama town of Cusseta, in Chambers County, secured the contract to transport a group of Creek Indians at $47.25 per person. Wheat was no stranger to the Creeks (or profiting off them) as he had provided rations to a number of towns during the Second Creek War in 1836 as part of an outfit he called "Moses Wheat & Son."[7] On 10 January 1846, sixty-four Creeks and thirty-nine of their slaves rendezvoused at Montgomery and waited for boats to take them westward. The wait was a bit longer than expected as the party's commencement was delayed by the low stages of the Alabama River. Wheat also had difficulty collecting the Creeks and keeping them in camp as local whites tried to persuade the emigrants to come back and work for them as laborers. Moreover, a "considerable number" of Creeks, primarily women, were still in Barbour, Henry, Dale, Covington, and Pike counties, being held against their will, allegedly as slaves. At one point Wheat collected fifty-seven Creeks in Coosa and Talladega counties and ordered them into camp. Before they reached the encampment, whites convinced the Creeks to flee by falsely claiming that the emigrants would be placed in chains and sold as slaves in the Indian territory. While Wheat remained behind collecting more emigrants, the party left under the charge of Arnold Seale (a notorious land speculator in Creek reserves in the mid-1830s) and Leroy Driver.[8]

The Creeks left Montgomery by steamboat and traveled to Mobile and New Orleans. One infant was born while on the steamboat on Lake Pontchartrain seven miles below New Orleans. The Creeks proceeded up the Mississippi River and overtook a self-emigrating Creek Indian at the mouth of the White River, who then joined the party. The Creeks continued by water and arrived at the Creek agency on 15 February 1846. On 1 March, two weeks after the party arrived in the west, the adult male who had joined the party at the White River, died of exposure.[9]

1846 Reunification Emigration Muster Roll

Found at LR, CAE, Roll 240, 391, 393, 401.

1. **Abraham Foster** 39 members consisting of 1 male of ten and under twenty-five, 1 male of twenty-five and under fifty, 14 male slaves, and 23 female slaves. In margin under "Remarks" is written "One Infant, (boy) Born on the way."
2. **William Moore** 8 members consisting of 4 males of ten and under twenty-five, 1 male over fifty, 1 female of ten and under twenty-five, and 2 male slaves.
3. **Roger Barnett** 7 members consisting of 2 males under ten, 1 male of ten and under twenty-five, 1 male of twenty-five and under fifty, 1 female under ten, 1 female of ten and under twenty-five, and 1 female of twenty-five and under fifty.
4. **Big Jack** 9 members consisting of 2 males under ten, 2 males of ten and under twenty-five, 2 females under ten, 2 females of ten and under twenty-five, and 1 female of twenty-five and under fifty.
5. **James Johnson** 6 members consisting of 1 male under ten, 3 males of ten and under twenty-five, and 2 females of ten and under twenty-five.
6. **John Barnett** 7 members consisting of 1 male under ten, 1 male of ten and under twenty-five, 2 males of twenty-five and under fifty, 2 females under ten, and 1 female of ten and under twenty-five.
7. **Betsey Watley** 8 members consisting of 3 males under ten, 2 males of ten and under twenty-five, 1 female of ten and under twenty-five, and 2 females of twenty-five and under fifty.
8. **Sam Brown** 2 members consisting of 1 male of twenty-five and under fifty and 1 female of twenty-five and under fifty.
9. **Joe** 5 members consisting of 2 males of ten and under twenty-five, 2 females under ten, and 1 female of ten and under twenty-five.
10. **Tom & Tallapoosa** 2 members consisting of 2 males of ten and under twenty-five.
11. **Sally Randall** 9 members consisting of 4 males under ten, 2 males

of ten and under twenty-five, 2 females of ten and under twenty-five, and 1 female of twenty-five and under fifty.

12. **Daniel** 2 members consisting of 1 male of ten and under twenty-five and 1 female of ten and under twenty-five.

Supplemental Letters on 1846 Emigration

Robert M. Cherry[10] reports that 102 Creek emigrants have assembled at Montgomery en route to the Indian territory via Mobile and New Orleans. Letter found at LR, CAE, Roll 240, 380–82.

Montgomery Alabama
January 11th 1846

Sir,

In a communication received from T. Hartley Crawford Esq'r,[11] late commissioner of Indian Affairs, of 9th September last I was instructed to advise him "of the time when the Indians shall assemble preparatory to starting, their number &c."

I have now to inform your department, that a party, of the emigrating Creek Indians amounting in all to one hundred & two (102), are now assembled at this place (having reached here on yesterday) on their way to their Western homes via Mobile & New Orleans—The contractor informs me that the party will leave this, to-day or to morrow as they are only waiting the arrival of a Boat, which is under contract, and now up the River some 15 miles & which is expected in the evening—. Of the above party, thirty-eight are slaves—the property of, or said to be the property of Indians & as such named in the muster Rolls of the contractor.

I went to their encampment and found the number to be as above stated & have taken a copy of the muster Roll, of the contractor & compared it by examination of the Indians & slaves, shewing their ages, sex, name &c, as near as may be, which if desired I will forward to the department.

I have not been enabled to give this information, as desired in the letter of 9th Septr last, at an earlier date, as the contractor did not furnish me with any definite information as to the number being assembled, for emigration hertofore, which he says, he could not furnish, from the fact that he could not Keep any fixed numbers in camp, as parties of the Indians were frequently collected & would again disperse from various causes; many of them being persuaded off by whites from interested motives touching their labour & services for the whites.

From the information of Mr Wheat & others—I presume there must be yet remaining in Georgia & Alabama, (principally in the latter state), Two hundred Indians or more of the Creeks, who have not joined the emigrating party, a number of these I learn from Gen Luther Blake of Russell County, Ala, are children in the possession of white persons who in many instances hold them for the benefit of their present & future services.

Agreeable to request contained in letter of the 27th Septr last I have advised Col James Logan,[12] Creek agent West of the time of departure of the emigrating party &c &c.

I remain respectfully
your obedient servant
R. M. Cherry
late S.A. &c

To Wm Medill Esqr[13]
com'r Indian Affairs
Department of War
Washington City
D.C.

☾

Moses K. Wheat notes that many Creeks want to move to Indian territory but are being held against their will as slaves by whites. Letter found at LR, CAE, Roll 240, 412–13.

Cusseta ala January 20th 1846

Dear Sir

On the 10th Inst I Started a party [of] Indians—from Mongomery—which presume you have been advised of. I have been doing all in my power to get the party off ever Since I got the contract—I did not at the time expect to have any difficulties in geting them off but have with great opposition from white persons—I have had from five to ten men engaged in trying to collect and emegrate the Indians and have been informed by them that there is Still Some remaining that wish to go to their new homes—but are prevented by white persons—who are making Slaves of them—for refference of the fact I refer you to Col'l John Crowel Gen'l Luther Blake, Capt Arnold Seale who I presume you are acquainted with from character if not in person The party now on the way are in charge of Capt A Seale & Mr Leroy Driver two Responsable—and good men. In one Instance which I attend to in person in Coosa and Talladega Counties I collect Some 57 in number and put them in charge of the wagoner to carry them to camp—and when on the Journey wer—persuaded to Abscond—By persons telling them that they wer to be chained and carried off and sold as slaves—; Gen'l Blake—writes me that in a scout in Barbour Henry Dale Covington & Pike Counties he found A considerable number but mostly females—and those who hold them as Slaves and they consider them as souch he also found others that are willing and anxious to emegrate but cannot arrange their matters to do so before Spring—when they will be ready to emegration.

I [am respectfully] yours &c
Moses K. Wheat
Contracter

☾

Wheat reports that a number of Creeks were "deceived" by white men and "carried off" from the emigration camps last winter. Letter found at LR, CAE, Roll 240, 418–19.

Cusseta Chambers co ala
July 13th 1846

D'r Sir

I recd a Letter from Coosa and one from Talledega counties informing me that the Indians in that Region had now become anxious to emegrate, and Say they wer deceived and carried off from camp on Last winter by designing men, they Say they will prefer going by Land which they urged as an objection Last fall to emegration   The citizens through that region are very anxious that the Indians Should Leave and have written to me on the Subject Several times   I think there is about 18 or 20 [members] of the Carr family that was verry anxious to Emegrate Last fall if they could have got ready (disposes of their property &c) I Should have made an effort to have got them off but the ageant R. M. Cherry Seem to think I had better here from the Department on the Subject as I did not Get them off as Soon as he thought agreeable to contract—

I am able to Satisfy the department that I did all in my power to carry out the contract in every portion. If you think proper I would Like to here from you on the Subject and Know whether I can bee allowed to carry them off and whether or not by Land if they prefer it as I presum the waters will not admit.

Your Obt Servent
Moses K. Wheat

To Wm Medill Esqr
Commission of Indian
affair Washington city
D.C.

☾

Creek agent James Logan reports on the child who was born on Lake Pontchartrain and the man who passed away soon after the party arrived. Letter found at LR, CAE, Roll 240, 405–6.

Creek Agency July 29th 1846,

Sir,

Your letter of the May 5th has been duly Rec'd on the subject of the acct. of Moses K. Wheat for Emigrating the Creek Indians. The Infant or Child refered too was born at Lake Ponchetrain below New Orleans some seven miles, some Ten or Twelve hundred miles from this place. The man refered too was taken up at the Mouth of this River (Ark) some Five Hundred miles from this place so here he was recived.[14] The above is all that I know in regard to the matter, and this much I learned from Mr Abram Foster an Intelligent Creek that was emigrated at the same time. And I have reason to belive the above is correct. I should have sent this at the time I sent the Roll but not being in possession of the facts I failed to do so.

Very resp'y
y'r obed't Serv't
James Logan
Creek agent

William Medill Esq

Over

P.S. From the best calculations I can make the two persons within named was emigrated something like one half of the way, and should be so considered in the settlement.

Yours &c.
J.L.

Paddy Carr's Emigration (1847)

Paddy Carr, the Cusseta land speculator, returned to Russell County, Alabama, in November 1837 after serving his tour of duty in Florida. Discovering "no indians Left in The old Creek Nation," Carr vowed to stay in Alabama no "longer than I Can Settle up mi Bizzanness." Whether Carr traveled to Indian territory soon after making that declaration is unclear;

however, in 1847 Carr petitioned the federal government for permission to move himself and some family members west.[15]

Muster Roll

Found at LR, CAE, Roll 240, 428.

1. **Paddy Carr** 1 member consisting of 1 male of twenty-five and under fifty.
2. **Milly Carr** 1 member consisting of 1 female of twenty-five and under fifty.
3. **Ariadne Carr** 1 member consisting of 1 female of ten and under twenty-five.
4. **Arianne Carr** 1 member consisting of 1 female of ten and under twenty-five.
5. **Syche** 1 member consisting of 1 male of twenty-five and under fifty.
6. **Thomas C. Carr** 1 member consisting of 1 male of twenty-five and under fifty
7. **Marianne Rogers** 1 member consisting of 1 female of twenty-five and under fifty.
8. **Betsey Rogers** 1 member consisting of 1 female of twenty-five and under fifty.
9. **Georgian Rogers** 1 member consisting of 1 female of ten and under twenty-five.
10. **Georgianna** 1 member consisting of 1 female of ten and under twenty-five.
11. **Thomas L. Rogers** 1 member consisting of 1 male of twenty-five and under fifty.
12. **Tom** 1 member consisting of 1 male slave.
13. **Joe** 1 member consisting of 1 male slave.
14. **Scepio** 1 member consisting of 1 male slave.
15. **Louisiana** 1 member consisting of 1 female slave.
16. **Polly** 1 member consisting of 1 female slave.
17. **Pierson** 1 member consisting of 1 male slave.
18. **Judy** 1 member consisting of 1 female slave.
19. **Philip** 1 member consisting of 1 male slave.

☾

Paddy Carr and Fanny Lovett report that there are a number of Creeks who wish to emigrate to Indian territory and asks that either Moses K. Wheat moves them west or they go on their own. Punctuation emended in places for clarity. Letter found at LR, CAE, Roll 240, 424.

Fort Mitchell 15th Dec 1846

Sir

Gov. let a contract to take of what Creeks were remaining here, to Mr Wheat—he took to Arkansas all that could then go, leaveing a part of us here, to dispose of our property such as we had, with the promise to take us last spring—thinking it would make no diferense with the government—and was much obligeing us—But now the government does not outherise Mr Wheat to carry out his engagements. Moust of our family are in Arkansas, the balance here, and in readiness to go to their Brothern west. We wish the Dept. to order Mr Wheat, who is ready at any moment to take us off—or will it pay us, if we go at our own   your attention in our behalf will be acknowledged.

Your Humble Servants
Fanny Lovett
Paddy Carr.

Hon D Lewis U.S.S.[16]

The 1848 Reunification Emigration

In the spring of 1848 Ward Cochamy (also Coachman)[17] traveled back to Alabama from the Indian territory to remove a number of his family members who still resided on the Coosa River. Throughout April and May Cochamy collected a number of emigrants, including forty in Autauga, Bibb, Coosa, and Talladega counties. These Creeks were sent to Wetumpka, while over twenty members of Cochamy's family rendezvoused at Montgomery. On 30 May the party of sixty-five Creeks, traveling by boat, left for the Indian territory and reached New Orleans by the first week of June and Fort Smith, Arkansas, on June 24, before taking wagons due to the low stage of the Arkansas River. There was only one death reported on this journey—Echo Fixico, a Chehaw man "considerably over 100 years old," who died as the steamboat was being cleaned at Lewisburg, Arkansas.[18]

Cochamy became the principal chief of the Muscogee (Creek) Nation in 1876 when Principal Chief Lochar Harjo was removed from office. Serving as second chief at the time, Cochamy served out the remainder of Lochar Harjo's term. Born at Wetumpka in Alabama, Cochamy lived with his uncle Lachlan Durant in Macon County, Alabama, until the 1840s, when he moved to Indian territory. After arriving in the west, Cochamy became an interpreter, trader, and farmer before becoming the clerk of the district court of Deep Fork District in 1868 and then a member and speaker of the House of Warriors in 1875. That year Cochamy became second chief, and he served in this capacity until the impeachment of Lochar Harjo in 1876. Cochamy was defeated for reelection in 1879 by Samuel Checote (who had emigrated with his family to Indian territory in 1829).[19]

The original muster roll is missing the first page, so the transcribed list shows only thirty-seven of the sixty-five people who left Montgomery in May 1848 (although I have numbered them here from 1 to 37). The first page contains column headings that denote age ranges, which are consequently unavailable. The original document does not group names by family, so every individual member of the party is listed separately (that is, on this roll bold type does not necessarily denote head-of-family).[20]

1848 Reunification Emigration Muster Roll (Partial)

Found at LR, CAE, Roll 240, 485.

1. **Hien** 1 member consisting of one female slave.
2. **Sarah** 1 member consisting of 1 female slave.
3. **Isaac** 1 member consisting of one male slave.
4. **William Durant** 1 member consisting of 1 male of ten and under twenty-five.

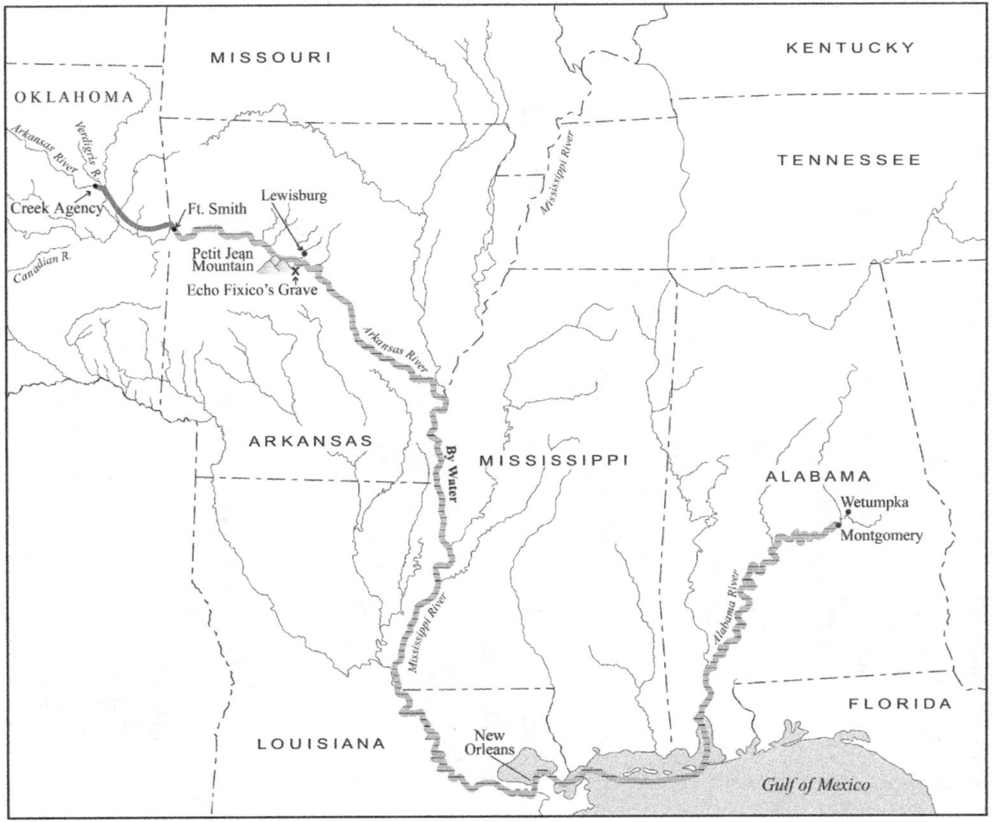

MAP 17. Route of the 1848 reunification emigration. Place names correspond to stopping points or locations noted in the documentation. Route lines and locations are approximations. Cartography by Sarah Mattics and Kiersten Fish.

5. **Eusekiah Harjo** 1 member consisting of 1 male over fifty.
6. **Gehogee** 1 member consisting of 1 female of twenty-five and under fifty.
7. **Jack** 1 member consisting of 1 male of ten and under twenty-five.
8. **Hay ar nubbe** 1 member consisting of 1 male of ten and under twenty-five.
9. **Billy** 1 member consisting of 1 male under ten.
10. **Chusk ur hoie** 1 member consisting of 1 male under ten.
11. **Te wil gu bee** 1 member consisting of 1 male over fifty.
12. **Nao boache Yoholo** 1 member consisting of 1 male over fifty.
13. **Le uth li ga** 1 member consisting of 1 male of twenty-five and under fifty.
14. **Lum a nut che** 1 member consisting of 1 male of ten and under twenty-five.
15. **Lin o git che** 1 member consisting of 1 male under ten.
16. **Oshut talie** 1 member consisting of 1 male over fifty.
17. **Lunsy** 1 member consisting of 1 male over fifty.
18. **Joe** 1 member consisting of 1 male under ten.
19. **O sit che Emathla** 1 member consisting of 1 male over fifty.
20. **Te har ga** 1 member consisting of 1 female over fifty.
21. **Kitta to che** 1 member consisting of 1 male of ten and under twenty-five.
22. **I ar ux tarhe** 1 member consisting of 1 male of twenty-five and under fifty.
23. **Te gur le** 1 member consisting of 1 male of twenty-five and under fifty.
24. **O sit che Micco** 1 member consisting of 1 male of twenty-five and under fifty.
25. **Che wit che** 1 member consisting of 1 female over fifty.
26. **Leehe** 1 member consisting of 1 male of ten and under twenty-five.
27. **Toma che** 1 member consisting of 1 male of ten and under twenty-five.
28. **Lin cho ki lotta** 1 member consisting of 1 male of ten and under twenty-five.
29. **Sally Stouse** 1 member consisting of 1 female of twenty-five and under fifty.
30. **Wag la tie harkie** 1 member consisting of 1 female of ten and under twenty-five.

31. **James N. Wilkenson** 1 member consisting of 1 male of twenty-five and under fifty.
32. **Rachail L. Wilkenson** 1 member consisting of 1 female of ten and under twenty-five.
33. **Me at hi ie** 1 member consisting of 1 female of ten and under twenty-five.
34. **David** 1 member consisting of 1 male under ten.
35. **Nar boache e Fixico** 1 member consisting of 1 female of ten and under twenty-five.
36. **Fi ye pe Stouse** 1 member consisting of 1 female under ten.
37. **Echo Fixico** 1 member over fifty. In margin is written "died at Lewisburgh, Arks, June 18th 1848."

Letters of the 1848 Reunification Emigration

Ward Cochamy seeks authorization to act as an emigration agent in order to move approximately fifty to sixty Creeks who remain in Alabama. Letter found at LR, CAE, Roll 240, 446–48.

Wetumpka, Alabama April 7th 1848—

Sir

I arrived at this place a few days since. The object of my Coming to alabama is to remove to the West some of my relations still remaining here—I Came last fall with the same object in view, but their Connections with the Whites were such that I Could not do it without sacrificing what little property they had in this Country—I then told them prepare by Spring, and I would Return for them—I have now Come to Carry them to their own Country—There are some others here not my relations that say they want to go to the West—but I am not able to pay their expenses to Arkansaw I think I Could pick some 50 or 60 individuals—I thought that the General Government had an agent yet in Alabama and was told that Robert M. Cherry Esq. was impowered to Contract for the removing of the residue of the Creeks to the west—but I got a friend to see him about it and he says that he has nothing to do with it & refers me to

Government—Mr. Cherry further stated to my friend that unless a Contract was made the General Government would not pay anything for Carrying them out to Arkansaw.

I want the Government to give me a Contract to Carry all that I can persuade to go with me to Arkansaw and pay me for it when I get them there, and pay me as much a head as they paid for the last emigration—I have sett to leave here for Arkansaw in four weeks from this time if the Government will give me a Contract   I want to Know it soon—I shall Carry as many as I shall have money to pay the passage any how.

And having been raised and Educated in this Town, I have friends that will lend me as much money as will pay the passage of all the Creeks that will go with me provided I Could assure them that the money would be paid back to them, as soon as I Could get to Arkansaw—I have only resided in the Creek Nation west three years my father is the Tustenuggee Emarthlar of the Alabama Town of Creeks—I have traveled the route frequently and as to my integrity, capacity, and ability to do what I undertake to do I refer you to the Creek Chiefs now at Washington, Benj—Marshal and Tuckabatchee Micco,[21] more—particularly the latter Chief—If the Government will give me a Contract I think that I will get off the last of my people now remaining on the Coosa River before the 1st day of June, I think I can have them in Arkansaw by 15th June—If the Government Concludes to give me the Contract the arrangement Can be made with the Chiefs now in Washington—I will offer no appology for troubling you with these propositions I hope to get an answer within two weeks from this time   I also inclose with this a letter to the Chiefs which I hope you will deliver to them as soon as it comes to hand—direct an answer to me at this place.

Respectfully Yours &c
Ward Co-cha-my

To Col Medil
Commissioner of
Indian affairs
Washington City
D.C.

☾

This letter reports on the arrival of Cochamy's party at New Orleans and the desire of the author to engage in a government contract to subsist these Creeks for a year after their arrival in Indian territory. Letter found at LR, CAE, Roll 240, 454.

New Orleans June 6, 1848,

Sir,

There is a small party of some 70 Creeks here, en route for Arkansas, and presuming they will be subsisted 12 months after their arrival to the Creek Nation, and not knowing that any proposals have been issued I have been induced to propose to the Department, to subsist them for 12 months Furnishing rations, at such times and places as may be designated by the agent, or other officer of the Department, at four cents for each ration (understood to be the commonly furnished ration as issued in subsistence of Indians)—

For The faithful performance of which I will enter into bond, with surety, approved by the Agent, or other officer* of the Department.

*Refering to Jos Bryan Esq.[22]

I am Respectfully
Wm C Dickson[23]

Hon W. Medill
Commissioner Ind. affrs.
Washington City

☾

Cochamy reports that he left Montgomery, Alabama, on 30 May 1848 with sixty-five people. There was some sickness in the party (diarrhea) and one death—that of Echo Fixico, who was "Considerably over 100 years old." Letter found at LR, CAE, Roll 240, 450–51.

Tuckabatchee July 16th 1848

Sir

Your favor of the 17th April last was received by due course of Mail, and I was glad to get it as it enabled me to remove home a part of my people—Previous to its reception I had prepared to remove my relations—as soon as your letter came I visited all the Creeks I could, & found all I talked to anxious to remove West—I gathered in the Counties of Autauga, Bibb, Coosa & Talladega about forty souls—these I assembled at Wetumpka-Ala my relations I assembled at Montgomery.

I left for Arkansaw on the 30th May with sixty five souls and arrived at Fort Smith on the 24th June, (this being as far as there was water for Boats) from this point I had the emigrants moved in wagons—the health of the party was good, generally. Diarhea & slight fever are natural to the Red man when he first drinks the brackish waters of the Arkansaw river—I have however to report the death of one of the party—Echo Fixico of the Che he haw Town—the oldest man I ever saw (by his own account Considerably over 100 years old) sickened—and on the night of the 18th June while the Boat was lying up at Lewisburg—expired—I had him buried at the foot of the Petit John Mountain[24]—I had to wait for C'ol Logan, to return from below (thither he had gone to have his Bond approved) 10 days. I had understood your letter to mean that each emigrant would receive 20$ Cash in lieu of subsistence immediately on their arrival, and had told them so—you may judge my astonishment as well as the emigrants' when informed by Col Logan that he had no orders from or money from Government for that purpose.

I talked to Jim Boy and Tomathla Micco[25] and showed them your letter after which they requested Col Logan to advance each emigrant 10$ out of the lost property fund[26] (as there would be time to replace it before it would be needed) which the Agent Kindly did, this relieved me of a great responsibility and relieved the immediate wants of the emigrants—I had to borrow some money in Ala. to pay for subsistence & transportation of emigrants

& I had supposed that my account could be divided & a draft sent direct from Washington to Ala so that the money would have been replaced in less than 60 days from the date of borrowing, but Col. Rutherford[27] says that so small an account cannot well be divided, so I have put the whole matter in his hands with a view to the early refunding the amount thus borrowed at best it will take a long time for the Muster Roll to get to Washington & a Draft returned to C'ol Rutherford and the money forwarded to Ala—I Crave your prompt attention to my account; to facilitate the early settlement of which, I have omitted to charge any thing for the dead one[28]—yet I hope you will allow me full pay, as I had paid his passage to Fort Smith and his Coffin & burial expenses were considerable—I think there yet remains in Alabama not less than 100 Creeks—and most of them in a deporable condition—A man by the name of Dickerson in Coosa County has one family—a woman & her children 7 in number A Mr Floyd[29] and a Rev. Mr Hays[30] both of Autauga County have each a number of Creeks I tried to get these but was prevented from doing so by threats of their would be masters—I shall yet get them—but not this season—when the waters are in good Boating order next season you will hear from me again. My thanks are due Cols Rutherford & Logan for their Kind attention to me.

Yours Respecfuly
Ward Co-cha-my

C'ol Medill

The 1849 Reunification Emigration

William H. Durant, a relative of Cochamy who emigrated with his party in 1848 (no. 4, 1848 reunification emigration roll), returned to Alabama in early 1849 to conclude some unsettled business. After arriving, Durant was approached by a number of Creeks who were anxious to emigrate to Indian territory. Newspapers reported the arrival of a small detachment of Creeks, perhaps from this very party, reaching Fort Gibson in June 1849.[31]

Letters of the 1849 Reunification Emigration

Durant requests permission and money to emigrate a small number of Creeks from Alabama to Indian territory. Letter found at LR, CAE, Roll 240, 500–01.

Wetumpka, March 7th 1849

Sir

I have In my possession a letter from the office of Indian affairs dated 17th April 1848 directed to Ward Co cha my a Creek Indian authorising him to remove a portion of the remnant of the Creeks remaining in Alabama also extending the same privilege to any other individual Indian or the head of any Creek family. I emigrated with the party that Co cha my carried out last spring and have now returned to close up my business that I left unfinished, and I find a number of Creeks ankious to go to their own Country and I have Concluded to take them with me but there is one difficulty In Carrying emagrants they need Subsistence as soon as they arrive In Arkansas It would be a grate advantage to the emagrant If your department would order the Agent to pay them the $20 In lieu of Subsistence as soon as they arrive at the agency as they will be In greate need of money when arrive there. I expect to start to arkansas some time in next month and Shall carry a few emagrants with me and Should like to be Informed from your department at whot time the emergrants will certainly receive the money to be paid them in lieu of the one years Subsistence.

Your early attention Is desired to this matter address me at this place.

very Respectfully your &c
William H. Durant

To the Commissioner
of Indian affairs
Washington City
D.C.

Durant reports that he has almost three dozen Creeks encamped and ready to begin their journey to Indian territory. Letter found at LR, CAE, Roll 240, 503.

Wetumpka May 2d 1849

Dear Sir

Your answer of the 21st march was Received by due corse of mail. I had concluded until a very recent date not to attempt to carry any of my people with me to Arkansaw this Spring on account of the prevalence of Cholera In New Orleans and on the Mississippi river but being now well assured that the Cholera has greatly abated and disapeard as an epidemic and some of my people very anxious to go west I have determined to carry them. I have at this place 28 Indians and half breeds near Fort Claiborn there are 35 more all now ready to start and I believe there are some 10 or 15 more that will go from Fort Claiborne I think the party will number from sixty five to seventy five. I shall start on Satturday next the fifth Inst and expect to get to the Creek agency by 25th of the present month.

I should be glad to receive a letter from you when I get to Fort Gipson informeing me whot instrucktions are giveing to Col Rutherford.

Very Respectfully your &c
Wm H Durant

To Col. Medill
Comm. Indian aff.
Washington City

The Voluntary Self-Emigrations

The following are muster rolls of Creeks or Indian countrymen who emigrated to Indian territory without the immediate aid of the federal government (and separate from any of the aforementioned federally sponsored voluntary emigrating parties) from 1831 to the 1880s. Their reasons for doing so are myriad. Some, due to their wealth, could travel in a more leisurely and comfortable manner than those who were hurried along in the larger government emigrations. Others may have been willing to move with the voluntary emigrating parties if the timing had been right but could not sell their large amounts of property in time. Some moved out of immediate necessity. Arpekoche Emathla (Ar pek ko che marthla, no. 140 on Stidham's roll, later in this chapter) hastily moved his Fish Pond family of ten westward in the winter of 1834–35 because "one of the Young men of the family was charged with being too intimate with the wife of another man," and he wanted to escape clan justice. All of the Creeks who voluntarily self-emigrated were due to receive federal compensation for their travels. The following is not an exhaustive list.

1831 Self-Emigrations

Muster roll found at LR, CAE, Roll 237, 575.

1. **Susannah McIntosh** 13 members consisting of 5 members over eight years old and 8 slaves. Arrived in Indian territory in November 1831. At bottom of muster roll western Creek Agent John Campbell notes that "all the above emigrants are entitled to one years' provisions under the Treaty of 1826, that Susannah McIntosh and Jane Hawkins have been paid the allowance for emigrating their families to this country." Susannah McIntosh (née Coe) was the widow of William McIntosh.
2. **Jane Hawkins** 1 member consisting of 1 person over eight years old. Arrived in Indian territory in November 1831. At bottom of muster roll western Creek Agent John Campbell notes that "all the above emigrants are entitled to one years' provisions under the Treaty of 1826, that Susannah McIntosh and Jane Hawkins have been paid the allowance for emigrating their families to this country—Jane Hawkins is entitled to the allowance for emigrating Pascopha & Jackson as she paid their expenses and brought them to this country." Jane Hawkins was the daughter of William McIntosh and daughter-in-law of Stephen Hawkins (no. 66 on the first McIntosh party roll, chap. 1) and

brother-in-law of Benjamin Hawkins (no. 65 on the first McIntosh party roll, chap. 1). Jane Hawkins later married Paddy Carr.

3. **Pascopha** 1 member consisting of 1 person over eight years old. Arrived in Indian territory in November 1831. Travel paid for by Jane Hawkins. Not listed as a slave.
4. **Jackson** 1 member consisting of 1 person over eight years old. Arrived in Indian territory in November 1831. Travel paid for by Jane Hawkins. Not listed as a slave.
5. **Samuel Brown** 1 member consisting of 1 person over eight years old. Arrived in Indian territory in August 1831. At bottom of muster roll western Creek Agent John Campbell notes "Samuel Brown and John Winslett to the allowance for Emigrating themselves at their own expence."
6. **John Winslett** 1 member consisting of 1 person over eight years old. Arrived in Indian territory in August 1831. At bottom of muster roll western Creek Agent John Campbell notes "Samuel Brown and John Winslett to the allowance for Emigrating themselves at their own expence."

1833 Self-Emigrations

Muster roll found at LR, CAE, Roll 237, 420.

1. **Timothy Fisher** 1 member consisting of 1 male over sixteen years old. Arrived in Indian territory on 27 June 1833.
2. **William Fisher** 1 member consisting of 1 male over sixteen years old. Arrived in Indian territory on 27 June 1833.

1836 Self-Emigrations

Muster roll found at LR, CAE, Roll 237, 647.

1. **Ho-hon-ho-ye** 2 members consisting of 1 male under ten and 1 female of ten and under twenty-five. Arrived in Indian territory on 1 April 1836.
2. **Opothle Yoholo's negroes** 12 members consisting of 6 male slaves and 6 female slaves. Arrived in Indian territory on 19 May 1836.

3. **Tuckabatchee Micco's negroes** 7 members consisting of 3 male slaves and 4 female slaves. Arrived in Indian territory on 19 May 1836.
4. **Tol-lo-wa Harjo** 1 member consisting of 1 male of twenty-five and under fifty. Arrived in Indian territory on 19 May 1836.

1835–36 Self-Emigrations

Muster roll found at LR, CAE, Roll 237, 657.

1. **John P. Moore** 4 members consisting of 2 males under ten, 1 male of ten and under twenty-five, and 1 female of ten and under twenty-five. The son of Indian countryman James Moore (no. 84 on second McIntosh party roll, chap. 2). Arrived in Indian territory on 10 February 1836.
2. **Michael Kennard**, 1 member consisting of 1 male of ten and under twenty-five. Arrived in Indian territory on 20 January 1836.
3. **Jackson Doyle** 1 member consisting of 1 male of ten and under twenty-five. Arrived in Indian territory on 1 January 1836.
4. **Islemolika** 1 member consisting of 1 female of twenty-five and under fifty. Arrived in Indian territory on 15 December 1835.
5. **Lizzy Kennard** 1 member consisting of 1 female of ten and under twenty-five. Arrived in Indian territory on 16 February 1836. Originally enrolled with fifth voluntary emigrating party (no. 13 on fifth voluntary party muster roll, chap. 6), Kennard left the group on 19 December 1835 and joined some of her friends who were traveling separately from the government-sponsored emigration.
6. **John W. Thomas** 2 members consisting of 1 male of twenty-five and under fifty and 1 female of ten and under twenty-five. Arrived in Indian territory on 4 February 1836.

1836–37 Self-Emigrations

Muster roll found at LR, CAE, Roll 238, 834.

1. **David Barnett** 15 members consisting of 2 males of twenty-five and under fifty, 9 male slaves, and 4 female slaves. Arrived 4 April 1837.
2. **Thlan e hum gee Emathla** 5 members consisting of 2 males of ten

and under twenty-five, 1 male of twenty-five and under fifty, and 2 females of ten and under twenty five. Arrived 31 May 1837.

3. **Simme ho ke or Widow Prince** 8 members consisting of 1 female under ten, 1 female of ten and under twenty-five, 1 female of twenty-five and under fifty, 3 male slaves, and 2 female slaves. Arrived 31 May 1837.

G. W. Stidham's Rolls of Self-Emigrant Creek Indians, 1885–86

The following is a composite list of self-emigrating Creek Indians created from two rolls (one prepared in 1870–71 and the other in 1885–86). The 1870–71 roster was ultimately rejected by the Department of the Interior in 1872 for, among other things, insufficient proof and because it included the names of over four hundred Creeks who had emigrated to Texas in 1811 (well before the start of the Creek removal era) and were therefore considered ineligible for compensation as guaranteed under the 1826 and 1832 Treaties of Washington. In 1885 another roll was commissioned with the aid of Hitchiti headman G. W. Stidham to replace the rejected roll.[32] The 1885–86 roll (called the "corrected" roll) serves as the standard for this composite list.

Names that are italicized are those that only appear on the original 1870–71 roll but for some reason were rejected for the 1885–86 roll (the Creeks who emigrated to Texas in 1811 are one example). Italicized names that are sprinkled among non-italicized names indicate cases where a head-of-family appears on both rolls but there are discrepancies in the number of family members (for example, Kun nup pe—no. 2—is listed on the 1885–86 roll as traveling by himself to Indian territory, while the 1870–71 roll shows he traveled with six other people). Finally, this composite list also includes a few names that do not appear on either roll, but proof of their emigration was confirmed by depositions of Creek Indians taken in the 1880s.

Of note: the ages given are not necessarily accurate. As Tul mo chus Micco noted in a deposition in 1886: "the ages are not correctly stated—The Indians did not Keep family Records, and the ages can only be estimated; and some instances their age is stated when the Roll was prepared, when it should represent the date they came into the Territory."

Rolls found at Special Files of the Office of Indian Affairs, 1807–1904, Special File 285: Creek Self-emigration claims, 1886–1904, Microcopy 574, Roll 77, 2–170.

Okfuskee Town

1. **Tusekiah Charte** (male, age 50) 6 members consisting of Fi yar ti ke (female, age 31), Ar ar to Harjo (male, age 22), Mo har ye (female, age 8), Polly (female, age 17), and Martha (female, age 21). Remarks: Emigrated from Alabama to Texas in the year 1839 and from Texas to the Creek Nation, Indian territory in the year 1842. *Heirs: Tar co sar, Te sar ke, and Rebecca*. Tul mo chus Micco (b. 1813 or 1814, and town king of Okfuskee), an acquaintance of these people in Alabama, stated in testimony that this family moved from Texas to Indian territory because they were "sent for by their relatives in the Territory."
2. **Kun nup pe** (male, age 40) *7 members consisting of Is ny kee (female, age 31), Lar se (male, age 15), Imfitta Harjo (male, age 29), Ho ye (female, age 16), Is e no le (male, age 19), Sar kiu na (female, age 14)*. Remarks: Emigrated from Alabama to the Chickasaw Nation, Indian territory in 1838 and to the Creek Nation, Indian territory in 1840. *Heirs: Sar kiu na and Jackson.*
3. **Konip Harjo** (male, age 31) 8 members consisting of So me kar (female, age 17), To loaf Harjo (male, age 31), *War ne (female, age 25), Mil le ke (male, age 19), I e ne (female, age 21), Mar to char (female, age 34)*, Joseph (male, age 28). Remarks: Emigrated from Alabama to the Chickasaw Nation, Indian territory in 1838 and to the Creek Nation, Indian territory in 1840. *Heirs: Tal loaf Harjo, War ne, Mil le ke, I e ne, Mar to char, and Joseph.*
4. **Hotulke Harjo** (male, age 27) 10 members consisting of In to war (female, age 31), Sal e far ne (female, age 30), Yo thle ke (female, age 39), Char ke (male, age 48), Jimmy (male, age 25), Yo pose kar (female, age 14), Wycey (female, age 15), E mo chee (female, age 29), *Pi see (female, age 24)*. Remarks: Emigrated from Alabama to the Chickasaw Nation, Indian territory in 1838 and to the Creek Nation, Indian territory in 1840.

5. **Qua kus see** (male, age 40) 6 members consisting of Is tar holth kar se ke (female, age 35), Charney (male, age 28), Po to ke (female, age 34), *Lin ti che (male, age 31)*, Tar we (male, age 28). Remarks: Emigrated from Alabama to the Chickasaw Nation, Indian territory in 1838 and to the Creek Nation, Indian territory in 1840. *Heirs: Micco chupco (male) and Sar no ke cher (male).*
6. **Kun charte Fixico** (male, age 42) 7 members consisting of So kar ke (female, age 60), Mar pe yar (female, age 8), Lucy (female, age 5), Lit ho kee (male, age 3), Ho mar har thle (female, age 4), and Wattie (female, age 40). Remarks: Emigrated from Alabama to the Chickasaw Nation, Indian territory in 1838 and to the Creek Nation, Indian territory in 1840. *Heirs: Mar pe yar, Lucy, and Lit ho ke.*
7. **Sar che ne che** (male, age 39) 4 members consisting of *He tar (female, age 2)*, In to te (female, age 45), and *O fo lote ker (female, age 5)*. Remarks: Emigrated from Alabama to the Chickasaw Nation, Indian territory in 1838 and to the Creek Nation, Indian territory in 1840. *Heir: He tar.*
8. **Ok char ye ne har thlocco** (male, age 38) 7 members consisting of Se me toh ka (female, age 60), Se wy ke (female, age 39), Me te woh lee (male, age 20), *Tar cey (male, age 24)*, Sar ya mi ka (male, age 35), *Cul low we (female, age 22)*. Remarks: Emigrated from Alabama to the Chickasaw Nation, Indian territory in 1838 and to the Creek Nation, Indian territory in 1840. *Heirs: Tar cey, Cul low we, and Patcher.*
9. **Tal war Micco** (male, age 45) 4 members consisting of *So har te (female, age 60), Mone tul ker (male, age 35), Mosey (male, age 15)*. Remarks: Emigrated from Alabama to the Chickasaw Nation, Indian territory in 1838 and to the Creek Nation, Indian territory in 1840. *Heirs: Loneza (female) and Le mar (male).*
10. **Tar chok cus se ho ke** (female, age 60) 5 members consisting of War suk te (male, age 32), Nar he cher (male, age 35), Kin nar ye (female, age 28), Par chies ser (female, age 18). Remarks: Emigrated from Alabama to the Chickasaw Nation, Indian territory in 1838 and to the Creek Nation, Indian territory in 1840. *Heirs: Cully and Cho ne ker.*
11. **Har lit ho ke** (female, age 42), 6 members consisting of Phlar se me ke (female, age 28), Le nar (female, age 18), Is mar ley (male, age 19),

Se mar (male, age 15), Oh pe ne (male, age 10). Remarks: Emigrated from Alabama to the Chickasaw Nation, Indian territory in 1838 and to the Creek Nation, Indian territory in 1840. *Heirs: Chin nar (female), Lasley (male), and Baby che.*

12. **John Danley** (male, age 35) 4 members consisting of Te ye che Danley (female, age 33), Te cum the Danley (male, age 12), Jackson Danley (male, age 10). Remarks: "Emigrated from ala in the year of 1836." *Heir: Milly.* Probably John Danely (Tulse Fixico), a Horse Path Town[33] man, who was a proponent of voluntary emigration and in 1829 was driven from his town by the Okfuskee chief Menawa. Menawa told his men at a ball play that "Dannily must be killd that he talked of going to arkansas, and was trying to persuade his friends to go with him, that he should be killd, and his property taken, and his children should be raised up as other Indians were, and then they would comply with the customs of the nation and that this should be the fate of all his men who spoke of going to arkansas." This followed the death of Danely's brother Jim, who was shot and killed for practicing "witchcraft." In late 1827 Jim Danely had been charged by the Creeks with "rapidly accumulating wealth . . . that appeared to them so strange and unaccountable." Fearing the same fate, John fled to the Creek Agency and sought the protection of the authorities.[34]
13. **Suk ho ye che** (female, age 62) 6 members consisting of Sin te ker (female, age 43), We lar ke (female, age 28), Hul ke (female, age 30), We sar (female, age 34), Chu wil le (male, age 48). Remarks: "Emigrated from ala to the Chickesaw Country in 1838, and to the Creek nation in 1840." *Heirs: Tomone Yoholo (male) and So me (female).*
14. **Captain Tarcey** (male, age 55) 12 members consisting of Micco Harjo (male, age 36), Lucy (female, age 40), Brok luf ke (male, age 42), Lou wi ne (female, age 34), Hannah (female, age 20), Ha ney (male, age 2), Suckey (female, age 28), Me char ley (male, age 23), Se le ann (female *servant*, age 18), To ney (male servant, age 15), Nelly (female *servant*, age 13). Remarks: *"Emigrated from ala.—in the fall of 1836."*
15. **Ne har Yoholo** (male, age 60) 8 members consisting of So thla (female, age 56), Se he we (male, age 25), Pi ka (male, age 20), Sim me ye (male, age 18), Ars he che (female, age 61), Is fi yut ho ke (female, age 50), Se

moke ho ke (female, age 40). Remarks: "Emigrated from ala to the Chickesaw Country in 1838, and to the Creek nation in 1840." *Heir: Arpeka Yoholo.*

16. **Ar pe kar Harjo** (male, age 70) 8 members consisting of Is ya pok la te ke (female, age 65), Ets mon day (female, age 3), Is mut ti ye (male, age 2), In su me ke (male, age 1), Artus ho po eth le (male, age 38), Tun tis che (female, age 80), Se moke tars ke (male, age 4). Remarks: "Emigrated from ala to the Chickesaw Country in 1838, and to the Creek nation in 1840."
17. **Tholk mal i ke** (female, age 72) 9 members consisting of Lot tee (female, age 40), Fah tar (female, age 38), Ful lup per (male, age 30), Sor te ke (male, age 40), Char ki ye che (male, age 5), Jo kah (male, age 3), Jackson (male, age 34), Youth ker (female, age 2). Remarks: "Emigrated from ala to the Chickesaw Country in 1838, and to the Creek nation in 1840." *Heir: Arpekar Harjo.*
18. **Mickie Emathla** (male, age 43) 9 members consisting of Suckey (female, age 37), Le yok har me ke (female, age 19), Kar nar ye (female, age 17), Ki te he (male, age 15), Thlar kar ke (female, age 13), *Sour (female, age 11), To tal li ke (female, age 8), Mok nar ke (male, age 10).* Remarks: "Emigrated from ala to the Chickesaw Country in 1838, and to the Creek nation in 1840." *Heirs: Sour, To tal li ke, and Mok nar ke.*
19. **Eliza** (female, age 25) 2 members consisting of Yar per (male, age 23). Remarks: "Emigrated from ala to the Chickesaw Country in 1838, and to the Creek nation in 1840." *Heir: In see.*
20. **Ok tar har sars Harjo** (male, age 62) 7 members consisting of *Conchart Harjo (male, age 53), Hatti che (female, age 40), Co chubbee (male, age 35),* E yar see (male, age 38), *Se ho ke (female, age 19), Ful lut ho ke (female, age 4).* Remarks: *"Emigrated from the Creek nation in ala. the winter of 1836–7, reached the Creek nation west, Indian Territory the Fall of 1837—"*
21. **Tus ke he ne har** (male, age 70) 6 members consisting of Kar war pi ke (female, age 65), Cocksey (male, age 40), Jacob (male, age 37), Sammy (male, age 16), Basey (male, age 14). Remarks: "Emigrated from ala to the Creek nation in 1836." *Heir: Cocksey.*
22. **Hugh Henry** (male, age 22) 8 members consisting of M. A. Henry

(female, age 20), James Henry (male, age 4), Patrick Henry (male, age 19), Ezekial Henry (male, age 25), Paralcie Henry (female, age 28), Caroline Henry (female, age 31), James C. Henry (male, age 33). Remarks: "Emigrated from Ala to Texas in the year 1838, And from Texas to the Creek nation I. Ty in 1866." Born in Nacogdoches County, Texas, Hugh Henry (b. 1848) was the son of Woodson. D. Henry (a white man from Georgia, see no. 40 this roll) and Levicey (Levisa) Hutton (d. 1852), a Creek woman of mixed ancestry. After his mother's death, Henry was raised by his grandmother in East Texas and later became a cowboy and frontiersman and served with the Confederate Creeks during the Civil War. Henry married Anne Dickerson (d. 1883) of Texas and had three children: James (b. ca. 1874), Levisa (b. ca. 1875), and Luella (b. ca. 1883). He had three additional children by his second wife Mittie Exon (a white woman from Missouri): Patrick (b. ca. 1887), Mack (b. ca. 1889), and Annie May (b. ca. 1891). Henry was described as being "about six feet in height, of robust build, and weighs 172 pounds—showing little of the aborigine in his appearance."[35]

23. **Nancy Hutton** (female, age 57) 1 member. Remarks: "Emigrated from Ala to Texas in the year 1838, And from Texas to the Creek nation I. Ty in 1866." Nancy Moore Hutton was the daughter of James Moore (no. 84, second McIntosh party roll, chap. 2), and brother of James P. Moore (no. 1, 1835–36 muster roll, this chapter). By the 1850s Hutton was widowed and living in Garden Valley, Van Zandt County, Texas.[36]
24. **Cusseta Harjo** (male, age 25) 2 members consisting of Po ko te kee (female, age 20). Remarks: "went to chickasaw N & then to Creek N in 1838 or 1839."
25. **Peggy Kennard** (female, age 46) 12 members consisting of Lyman Moore (male, age 2), James Moore (male, age 5), Buck Moore (male, age 6), Moses Moore (male, age 16), Elizabeth Moore (female, age 14), Wash Moore (male, age 1), *Jackson Moore (male, age 41), Daniel (male servant, age 73), Adam (male servant, age 63), Lucinda (female servant, age 58), Ebenezer (male servant, age 35)*. Remarks: "Emigrated from ala to Texas in 1838, and from Texas to the Creek nation in 1849."
26. **Coppetcher Harjo** (male, age 50) 5 members consisting of Toc was ho ke (female, age 40), Hok to chee (female, age 20), Fickley (female,

age 15), Wa thloc co Harjo (male, age 30). Remarks: "Emigrated from ala to chickasaw N. I.T. in 1838, and from there to the Creek nation in 1840."

27. **Mar tol la** (female, age 30) 4 members consisting of Te he a cha (male, age 30), To wi sey (female, age 10), I sey (female, age 8). Remarks: "Emigrated from ala to chickasaw N. I.T. in 1838, and from there to the Creek nation in 1840."
28. **Thlar se kee** (male, age 30) 2 members consisting of Au fu lo tee kee (female, age 25) Remarks: "Emigrated from ala to chickasaw N. I.T. in 1838, and from there to the Creek nation in 1840."
29. **Au wo tol le ko** (male, age 50) 6 members consisting of Thle se me (female, age 40), In hol li kee (female, age 30), Ni ca (female, age 20), Sa cha la kee (male, age 25), Ki chee (male, age 16). Remarks: "Emigrated from ala to chickasaw N. I.T. in 1838, and from there to the Creek nation in 1840."
30. **Itch ars** Yoholo (male, age 50) 2 members consisting of Sike ley (female, age 38). Remarks: "Emigrated from ala to chickasaw N. I.T. in 1838, and from there to the Creek nation in 1840."
31. **Locher we na** (male, age 58) 2 members consisting of Washington (male, age 50). Remarks: "Emigrated from ala to chickasaw N. I.T. in 1838, and from there to the Creek nation in 1840."
32. **Oso che** Harjo (male, age 45) 4 members consisting of Nan ney (female, age 14), So na (female, age 12), I chin ne (female, age 10). Remarks: "Emigrated from ala to chickesaw nation in 1838, and from the chickesaw nation to the creek nation in 1841."
33. **Le cher** (male, age 29) 2 members consisting of Me yeh pe (male, age 25). Remarks: "Emigrated from ala to chickesaw nation in 1838, and from the chickesaw nation to the creek nation in 1841."
34. **Kotchar** Harjo (male, age 36) 3 members consisting of Eufaula Fixico (male, age 15), Nar tol li kee (female, age 34). Remarks: "Emigrated from ala to chickesaw nation in 1838, and from the chickesaw nation to the creek nation in 1841."
35. **Okfuskee Micco** (male, age 63) 5 members consisting of Se me se hoh kee (female, age 30), To na ye (female, age 33), Pin Harjo chee (male, age 30), He ya ya kee (male, age 10).

36. **Is far ne marthle** (male, age 40) 2 members consisting of Tin ha lah tee (female, age 60). Remarks: "Emigrated from Ala to the Creek nation direct."
37. ***Ho ye chi che*** *(female, age 20), 13 members consisting of Is fok ose ke (female, age 40), To ma li ke (female, age 36), Ho ne chi ke (female, age 18), Jim see (male, age 24), Son no ke che (male, age 20), Nar he le (male, age 18), Che co sar (male, age 39), Te ho yar ne (female, age 54), Char we che (male, age 34), Is kar yun cher (male, age 60), Kar sum kar (male, age 53), Sal le ti ke (male, age 42). Remarks: Emigrated from Alabama to the Chickasaw Nation, Indian territory in 1838 and to the Creek Nation, Indian territory in 1840. Heirs: Euganla Fixico and Char ne.*
38. ***Oc ti ar che Yoholo*** *(male, age 41) 7 members consisting of Tim au i che (female, age 51), Mo mar (female, age 22), Mo sey (male, age 35), Se har ye (female, age 18), Tee nar (female, age 16), Lele kar (female, age 21). Remarks: Emigrated from Alabama to the Chickasaw Nation, Indian territory in 1838 and to the Creek Nation, Indian territory in 1840. Heirs: Te con ni he (female), Te mar se (male), and Susey (female).*
39. ***Sar pok pot te*** *(female, age 30) 3 members consisting of Wal ly (female, age 11) and Sen ne ke ye (male, age 9). Remarks: "Emigrated from ala.—in the fall of 1836." Heir: Tuckabatchee (son of Wal ly).*
40. ***Woodson. D. Henry*** *(male, age 55) 12 members consisting of Levicey Henry (female, age 51), James C. Henry (male, age 33), Caroline Henry (female, age 31), Paralcie Henry (female, age 28), Ezekiel Henry (male, age 25), Hugh Henry (male, age 22), M. A. Henry (female, age 20), Patrick Henry (male, age 19), James Henry (male, age 4), Susan Grayson (female, age 38), George Heard (male, no age given). Remarks: "Emigrated from Ala. to Texas in the year 1838—& from Texas to the Creek Nation, I.T. in the year 1849—" W. D. Henry was a white man from Georgia who married Levicey (Levisa) Hutton (d. 1852), a Creek woman of mixed ancestry. According to Harry F. O'Beirne and Edward S. O'Beirne, Henry and Levicey emigrated to Texas in 1832. See no. 22, this roll.*[37]
41. ***Charles Simmons*** *(male, age 60) 8 members consisting of Chu ko locco (female, age 63), Pas sey (female, age 32), Jackson (male, age 40), Martin (male, age 35), Wilson (male, age 42), Eliza (female, age 33), David*

(male, age 26). Remarks: "Emigrated from ala. to the Creek nation, I.T. in the year 1838—" Heir: Ho pey.

Coweta Town

42. **Conip Emathla** (male, age 56) 8 members consisting of Molly (female, age 30), Se ho ker (female, age 31), To kol la kul lar (male, age 18), Sor tas che (male, age 9), Mish chie (male, age 7), Par nee (male, age 5), Sickney Greenwood (male, age 3). Remarks: "Emigrated from ala to the creek nation in the winter of 1836 & 7." *Heir: Sickney Greenwood.* In an 1849 letter Chilly McIntosh noted that James Island led a party of four families which included Conip Emathla's family.[38]
43. **Mar ye** (female, age 70) 2 members consisting of Rhoda (female, age 25). Remarks: "Emigrated from ala to the creek nation in the winter of 1836 & 7." *Heirs: Jimmy (male), Mike (male), Lo see (female).*
44. **Hotulke Harjo** (male, age 47) 6 members consisting of Cho ne kar (male, age 12), Kizzie (female, age 18), Hep sey (female, age 18), Eliza (female, age 20), Oak char te (male, age 12). Remarks: "Emigrated from ala to the creek nation in the winter of 1836 & 7."
45. **Nannie Miller** (female, age 41) 5 members consisting of Maria (female, age 25), Susey (female, age 10), Loueza (female, age 6), John Tiger (male, age 8). Remarks: "Emigrated from ala to the creek nation in the winter of 1836 & 7." In an 1849 letter Chilly McIntosh noted that James Island led a party of four families, which included Nannie Miller's family.[39]
46. **Yar kin har Micco** (male, age 30) 2 members consisting of Hiley (female, age 26). Remarks: "Emigrated from ala to the creek nation in the winter of 1836 & 7." May also have been known as Yar kin har Fixico.
47. **Se war ke kee** (male, age 49) 2 members consisting of Kizzie (female, age 45). Remarks: "Emigrated from ala to the creek nation in the winter of 1836 & 7."[40]
48. **Charle Harjo** (male, age 60) 6 members consisting of Le pix ie (female, age 53), *Palo Carr (male, age 78)*, Para Carr (male, age 18),[41] *Mahala (female, age 30)*, Lucy (female, age 21), Wat tie (female, age 18).

"Emigrated from ala to the creek nation in the winter of 1836 & 7." *Heirs: Limbo "& other heirs."*

49. **Is fi e cher** (male, age 47) 6 members consisting of Soh he lin ter (female, age 40), Po lo co che (female, age 20), Fo lot ho ke (female, age 18), Cho na lar (male, age 16), Parmar (male, age 14). Remarks: "Emigrated from ala to the creek nation in the winter of 1836 & 7." *Heir: Parmar.*
50. **Ninne chupper Harjo** (male, age 43) 9 members consisting of Chas ne he ye (female, age 40), Nar kof te che (female, age 36), Me si ne (female, age 12), Sar chick larf kar (male, age 14), Soh tar lar ke (male, age 12), Thlo chup ho ke (female, age 20), Nit tar he che (female, age 15), Jane o chee (female, age 8). Remarks: "Emigrated from ala to the creek nation in the winter of 1836 & 7." *Heir: Jane o chee.* Jane o chee (b. ca. 1828), the daughter of Ninne chupper Harjo, was about sixty years old in 1886 when she testified that she and her family left Alabama in the fall of 1836 and arrived in Indian territory toward the spring of 1837. It appears that multiple families emigrated together with this family, including those led by Nannie Miller (no. 45), Is fi e cher (no. 49), Arparlar Harjo (no. 64), Tal loaf Harjo (no. 51), Hart kar (no. 52), Soh lot ti ke (no. 53), Lucy locco (no. 54), Par hose Harjo (no. 55), So me che (no. 57), Wox e ho lar ter (no. 59), Tuc ko Harjo (no. 62), and Chullo (no. 229).[42]
51. **Tal loaf Harjo** (male, age 63) 9 members consisting of Polly (female, age 54), Muk lar che (male, age 14), Sar nar (female, age 18), Cheis quar che (female, age 12), Car cho fe (female, age 10), Lose char te (female, age 10), *Chepon hat kee (male, no age given), Lucy che (female, age 9)*. Remarks: "Emigrated from ala to the creek nation in the winter of 1836 & 7." *Heirs: Chepon hat kee and Lucy che.*
52. **Hart kar** (female, age 40) 3 members consisting of Tar ley (male, age 18), Lose ki ar le (female, age 30). Remarks: "Emigrated from ala to the creek nation in the winter of 1836 & 7."
53. **Soh lot ti ke** (female, age 30) 4 members consisting of Ar har lot Harjo (male, age 28), Che lo ke (male, age 26), Se leat kar (male, age 20). Remarks: "Emigrated from ala to the creek nation in the winter of 1836 & 7." *Heir: Che lo ke.*

54. **Lucy locco** (female, age 33) 5 members consisting of Polly (female, age 13), Na ra (male, age 11), Elijah (male, age 9), Amy (female, age 7). Remarks: "Emigrated from ala to the creek nation in the winter of 1836 & 7." *Heirs: Polly and Na ra.*

55. **Par hose Harjo** (male, age 49) 9 members consisting of To kar (female, age 40), Ar chu le (male, age 44), Si ley (female, age 20), Chu ille (male, age 18), Che par ney (male, age 16), O so che Emathla (male, age 30), Soo na le (male, age 14), Ca to (male, age 12). Remarks: "Emigrated from ala to the creek nation in the winter of 1836 & 7." *Heirs: Soo war le and Ca to.*

56. **Mar lis sa** (female, age 35) 1 member. Remarks: "Emigrated from ala to the creek nation in the winter of 1836 & 7." *Heir: Warrior.*

57. **So me che** (female, age 60) 1 member. Remarks: "Emigrated from ala to the creek nation in the winter of 1836 & 7." *Heir: Fit to thle.*

58. **Locher Harjo** (male, age 62) 4 members consisting of Sar che (female, age 46), Char ye Yoholo (male, age 36), Sar me (male, age 16). *Heir: Sar me.*

59. **Wox e ho lar ter** (male, age 46) 4 members consisting of Che yo ke (female, age 42), Sam se (male, age 22), Bet sey (female, age 16). Remarks: "Emigrated from ala to the creek nation in the winter of 1836 & 7." *Heir: Co sis te Harjo.*

60. **Elijah Beaver** *(male, age 20)* 1 member. Remarks: "Emigrated from Ala to Kentuckey to R M Johnson's school[43] in 1836 & from Kentuckey to the Creek nation I T in 1840." *Heir: Tommy Yoholo.*

61. **Daniel** (male, age 23) 1 member. Remarks: "Emigrated from ala to the Creek nation in the summer of 1841." *Heir: Tommy Yoholo.*

62. **Tuc ko Harjo** (male, age 45) 8 members consisting of Che lar (female, age 41), Thlars che yar (female, age 37), Tar tar ho ye (female, age 27), Sar war ne (female, age 22), Funnie (female, age 21), David (male, age 18), Chu lar (male, age 16). Remarks: "Emigrated from Ala to the Creek nation in the winter of 1836 & 7." *Heir: Honey (daughter of Tuc ko Harjo).*

63. **Ho lah ta** (male, age 59) 6 members consisting of Loneza (female, age 39), Sam me (male, age 7), Wicey (female, age 5), Co ney (male, age 4), Billy (male, age 2). Remarks: "Emigrated from ala to the creek

nation in the Spring 1837 in Company with Ja's Island." His age is likely wrong, by his own testimony he was born ca. 1816 in Alabama. He also testified that he emigrated in 1839.[44]

64. ***Arparlar Harjo*** *(male, age 52) 8 members consisting of Che wo ner (female, no age given), Peter Gibson, (male, no age given), John Gibson (male, no age given), Halkar (no sex or age given), Jimmy (male, no age given), Lucinda (female, no age given), Hoke to che (female, no age given). Remarks: "Emigrated from ala to the creek nation in the winter of 1836 & 7." Heirs: Lucy che and Chepon hat kee.*
65. ***Ar nar he che*** *(male, age 48) 5 members consisting of Hart kar (female, age 40), Billy (male, no age given), Tar ley (male, age 18), Lose ki ar le (female, age 30). Remarks: "Emigrated from ala to the creek nation in the winter of 1836 & 7." Heir: Lose ki ar le.* See no. 52.
66. ***Tallassee Fixico*** *(male, age 50) 9 members consisting of Oh ke (no sex or age given), Polly (female, no age given), Susey (female, no age given), Humlie (male, no age given), Kizzie (female, no age given), Ars wo li ke (no sex or age given), Lose charte (female, no age given), Che par ne (male, no age given). Remarks: "Emigrated from ala to the creek nation in the winter of 1836 & 7." Heir: Ti to.*
67. **Holo Barnett** *(female, age 20) 1 member. Remarks: "Emigrated from ala. to the Creek Nation, I.T. in 1830—at her own charges and expense." Heir: Cheparne Gibson.*
68. ***Sipper*** *(female, no age given) 1 member. Remarks: "Emigrated from ala to the Creek Nation I.T. the winter of 1836–7—at her own charges and expense." Heir: Lose ki ar le (female).*

Broken Arrow Town

69. **Hillabee Harjo** (male, age 50) 5 members consisting of Pe thlar me (female, age 46), Nar ke (female, age 26), Locey (female, age 21), Mary (female, age 18). Remarks: "Emigrated from ala to the creek nation in the Spring 1837 in Company with Ja's Island."
70. **Eliza** (female, age 48) 7 members consisting of Yar har Fixico (male, age 37), Betsey (female, age 20), Lucy (female, age 13), Tommy (male, age 10), Jimmy (male, age 22), Chil la chopco (male, age 11). Remarks:

"Emigrated from ala to the creek nation in the Spring 1837 in Company with Ja's Island."

71. **Ho yar ne cher** (male, age 24) 4 members consisting of Me lis sa (female, age 22), Litch ar (male, age 3), Par ley (female, age 1). Remarks: "Emigrated from ala in 1839." *Heirs: Danille and Me har ke.*
72. **Sam Sells** (male, age 50) 23 members consisting of Patsey Sells (female, age 45), John Sells (male, age 14), Daniel Sells (male, age 23), Cherokee Sells (female, age 12), King (male, age 40), Nancy (female, age 6), Bob (male servant, age 33), Abraham (male servant, age 28), Andrew (male servant, age 14), Sharp (male servant, age 10), Ellick (male servant, age 18), Peggy (female servant, age 14), Mary (female, age 9), Charlotte (female *servant*, age 19), Isaac (male *servant*, age 18), Peter Randall (male, age 60), Suckey (female, age 65), Joseph (male, age 16), Ben (male, age 23), Polly (female, age 21), Lucretia (female, age 14), Adaline (female, age 6). Remarks: "Emigrated from Ala to the Creek nation in the year 1830." *Heir: Patsey Sells.* Sells emigrated with the second McIntosh party in 1828 (see no. 3, second McIntosh party muster roll, chap. 2) but returned to Alabama to emigrate the rest of his family and property. Sells's party traveled to Indian territory in 1830 accompanied by a group led by Benjamin Hawkins. Sarah Davis, a black slave owned by Jane Hawkins (daughter of William McIntosh; sister of Chilly McIntosh, no. 1 on first McIntosh roll, chap. 1; sister-in-law of Benjamin Hawkins, no. 65 on first McIntosh party roll, chap. 1; daughter-in-law of Stephen Hawkins, no. 66 on first McIntosh party roll, chap. 1; and widow of Samuel Hawkins—who was executed over his support of the 1825 Treaty of Indian Springs; and ex-wife of Paddy Carr, no. 16 on fifth voluntary party roll, chap. 6), who traveled with Hawkins's group, testified in December 1885 that Sells "had two large wagons and one carriage, Besides these he had plenty of horses and I saw a good many of the Sells party riding on horseback all of the way along until we reached the Verdigris river in the Creek Nation Indian Territory. I Know that both Ben Hawkins and Sam Sells bought provisions for their respective parties all along the way as I among

other slaves was required to help pack bacon and other things into the camps. I did not Know of any one else buying provisions for the two aforesaid parties but Hawkins and Sells as herein before stated. The two parties continued near together all the way from the starting point [near Columbus, Georgia] to the Creek Nation." Benjamin Hawkins was in Alabama in 1830 on the invitation of federal officials who hoped he (and Roly McIntosh, whom he accompanied) would serve as ambassadors and help soothe the hostilities between the McIntosh faction and those Creeks who opposed William McIntosh and emigration. Neither McIntosh nor Hawkins was successful in recruiting Creeks to move west, and in fact Secretary of War John H. Eaton asserted that Benjamin Hawkins's presence in the eastern Creek Nation did "'much injury to the cause of emigration.'" On Hawkins's return to Indian territory, he accompanied Sells's party while also conducting family members west, including his nephew Pinkney (no. 76, this roll).[45]

73. **Lewina Wadsworth** (female, age 40) 5 members consisting of Joshua Wadsworth (male, age 14), Mary Wadsworth (female, age 12), Caddo Wadsworth (male, age 10), Josephine Wadsworth (female, age 8). Remarks: *"Emigrated from ala. to Texas in the year 1833 and from Texas to the Creek Nation, I.T. the Spring of 1842."* Lewina Kennard married James Wadsworth and had five children (Mitchell Wadsworth is not listed). Daughter Mary Wadsworth married Thomas Watts, a Cherokee Indian, while daughter Josephine married Richard Berryhill (b. 1852), the grandson of Alexander Berryhill (no. 2 on the first McIntosh party roll, chap. 1).

74. **Muskogee Sutbury** (female, age 53) 7 members consisting of *father (no name or age given), mother (no name or age given)*, Archie Doyle (male, age 16), Susan (female servant, age 33), Seaborn Hardage (male, age 9), *Mary Hardage (female, age 26)*. Remarks: *"Emigrated from Ala. to Texas in 1838. Her father & mother died in Texas—She Emigrated from Texas to the Creek Nation, I.T. in the year 1848, bringing Archie Doyle, Susan the servant and her two children born in Texas—Seaborn and Mary Hardage."*

Hillabee Town

75. **Thomas Grayson** (male, age 45) 6 members consisting of Levy Grayson (male, age 15), Samson Grayson (male, age 13), Millie Grayson (female, age 11), Lizzie Grayson (female, age 9), David Grayson (male, age 7). Remarks: "Emigrated from ala to the creek nation in 1830." See Thomas Grayson, no. 102, second McIntosh party roll, chap. 2.
76. **Pinkney Hawkins** (male, age 17) 1 member. Remarks: "Emigrated from ala to the creek nation in 1830." The son of Samuel Hawkins (who was executed for his support of the 1825 Treaty of Indian Springs), Pinkney (or Pink) was born in 1816 on the Tallapoosa River in Alabama. After first settling in Indian territory, Hawkins moved to Texas (near Nacogdoches) and married Annie Pigeon, with whom he had one daughter. There he had a large plantation worked by over twenty slaves. During the Mexican-American War Hawkins's slaves escaped, and he returned to Indian territory penniless. He resettled near Eufaula on the Canadian River and remarried twice: once to an orphan girl named Aggy, then to Liddie Benson after Aggy's death. With Benson, Hawkins had five children: John, Billy, Louisa, Michael, and Rose. Hawkins served with the Confederate Creeks under Chilly McIntosh and later served fourteen years in the House of Warriors and as Second Chief for four years. He was described (ca. 1890) as "straight, broad-chested and in excellent health, in appearance not over sixty." In October 1886 seventy-year-old Pinkney Hawkins gave a sworn statement declaring that he emigrated in 1831 and was "in company with an uncle of mine by the name of Benjamin Hawkins." Pinkney Hawkins probably emigrated with the same group that his uncle and Sam Sells conducted west in 1830 (see no. 72, this roll).[46]
77. ***Sampson Grayson** (male, age 30) 5 members consisting of Lucinda Grayson (female, age 26), Simpson Grayson (male, age 4), Melvina Grayson (female, age 2), Lydia A. Grayson (female, age 6 months). Remarks: "Emigrated from ala. to the Creek Nation, I.T. the Spring of 1837—" Heir: Simpson Grayson. Unclear if this is the same Sampson Grayson who accompanied the 1834 voluntary party then returned to Alabama and accused the emigrating agents of not having enough*

provisions and threatening to enslave the Creeks on Mississippi sugar plantations (see no. 1, fourth voluntary party muster roll, chap. 5). In the margin below Grayson's name is written "One of this name with 1—M & 3 F [emigrated] in 1836 by U.S."

78. ***Ar fut che che*** *(female, age 41) 2 members consisting of Sun thlar pe (female, age 33). Remarks: "Emigrated from ala. to the Creek Nation I.T. Spring of 1839." Heir: Lin i de.*
79. ***Field Grayson*** *(male, age 37) 4 members consisting of Sul a ti ge (female, age 23), Jim (male, age 13), Joseph Grayson (male, age 4). Remarks: "Emigrated same as above the Spring of 1837." Heir: Thle war le.*
80. ***Te mar se ne che*** *(female, age 50) 8 members consisting of Polly (female, age 5), Maria (female, age 8) Fi ho ke (female, age 12), Rachel (female, age 14), Abby (female, age 3), Choctaw (male, age 1), Te me ho sar (female, age 65). Remarks: "Emigrated same as above the Spring of 1837." Heir: Ar wi ke.*
81. ***Har far boaf Harjo*** *(male, age 42) 7 members consisting of Tim min no che (female, age 30), Ki heo gee (female, age 21), Nannie (female, age 10), Winey (female, age 14), Hamley (male, age 13), Simon (male, age 8). Remarks: "Emigrated same as above the Spring of 1839." Heir: E dy.*
82. ***Se mar he*** *(male, age 38) 5 members consisting of Tha at ly (male, age 36), Anna (female, age 34), Par ne (male, age 12), Sally (female, age 10). Remarks: "Emigrated same as above the Spring of 1839."*
83. ***Tim e te wi ke*** *(male, age 60) 4 members consisting of Nic kic ker (female, age 50), Ser en ker (female, age 18), Al ac (male, age 12). Remarks: "Emigrated same as above the Spring of 1839."*
84. ***Tim fi e che*** *(male, age 33) 8 members consisting of Hetty (female, no age given), Tic ar sum me (female, no age given), Ser ther mar ke (female, no age given), Er mar ne (female, no age given), Andy (male, no age given), Ne har thloc co (male, no age given), O har ho ye (no sex or age given). Remarks: "Emigrated same as above the Spring of 1839."*
85. ***Is po oak Harjo*** *(male, age 38) 10 members consisting of In ter hi ar (female, age 30), Yo puk a la li ke (female, age 17), Is per ti ke (female, age 14), Ya ea che (male, age 12), Is ter chok ot ho ye (male, age 10), Ar*

se put che (male, age 20), Suk har lo che (male, age 30), Mar se ho ke (female, age 25), Is ke li ke (male, age 16). Remarks: "Emigrated same as above the Spring of 1839."

86. ***Ar ho tul Harjo*** *(male, age 35) 7 members consisting of Thlatho ke hoker (female, age 30), Sar ho Yohola (male, age 28), Is te hi ar (female, age 60), Mun tar whe cher (male, age 16), Sut ler hi a ye (male, age 20), Cher ki ye (female, age 18). Remarks: "Emigrated from Creek Nation in ala. in 1837."*

87. ***Elijah Carr*** *(male, age 40) 23 members consisting of Lydia Carr (female, age 30), Thomas Carr (male, age 8), Vicey Carr (female, age 5), Washington Carr (male, age 1), George (male servant, age 30), Judy (female servant, age 25), Sarah (female servant, age 15), Seaman (male servant, age 15), Hill (male servant, age 25), Pow ho ser (male, age 10), Is ter fe kub he (male, age 18), Pe for whe che (male, age 25), Emarthlo che (male, age 30), Mubby ho ma ye (female, age 26), Taylor (male, age 38), Yo po her (female, age 24), I chin ne (female, age 7), In ke la ker (female, age 8), Coody (male, age 2), So look hat ker (female, age 42), Dave (male, age 40), Molly (female, age 37). Lydia Carr, her husband Elijah, and her three children "did not start with the 'last big drove' (of Creeks) but overtook the party at Memphis and arrived at Fort Gibson with Opothleyaholo." Ethan Allen Hitchock reported that Lydia Carr came in a party of thirty-one people—"Jackey, wife and eight children, Elijah Carr, wife and three children, her own aunt and four children, an old man and his wife (Davy) and four negroes, in all 31." Carr complained that her family did not receive any provisions during the journey west and only "a small issue" after arriving at Fort Gibson. This party suffered from sickness and malnutrition during the first year of their resettlement and as a result, Carr noted that "'This man (the man who came with her) lost four children, one of mine is gone. I just got two." Hitchock subsequently recorded in his journal: "Twelve deaths from 31!'"*[47]

Thlobthlocco Town

88. **Millie Reed** (female, age 45) 10 members consisting of Elizabeth Sells (female, age 23), Juda Reed (female, age 20), Sallie Reed (female, age

16), Rosanna Reed (female, age 14), William Reed (male, age 10), Susan Reed (female, age 8), James Reed (male, age 18), Hepsey (female, age 16), David (male, age 6). Remarks: "Emigrated from Ala to the Creek nation I T in 1830." John S. Porter (no. 233) of Broken Arrow testified in October 1886 that "the Reed family came here in 1829—that is in the winter of 1829. In January 30, I passed the family at Fort Smith, Ark." Polly Island, a woman of African descent, testified in November 1886 that she traveled in the company of Reed's and Austin's parties (no. 89) from Alabama to Indian territory, "moving a little ahead of them, but camping together at night" and that she "came along West as they did in or about 1830, and whilst we moved in day time in separate squads we camped together at night." John Berryhill's group (no. 90) and Sam Sells's party (no. 72) may also have accompanied the Reed and Austin parties.[48]

89. **Pleasant Austin** (male, age 40) 6 members consisting of Polly Austin (female, age 30), Daniel Austin (male, age 8), Nathaniel Austin (male, age 6), Jefferson (male servant, age 40), Sookey (female servant, age 12). Remarks: "Emigrated from Ala to the Creek nation I T in 1830." Scipio Sancho (b. ca. 1816), the brother of Sookey, declared in a November 1886 statement that "I do not understand that Jefferson, a servant, came with the Austin family to the Nation. He was purchased by them after their arrival." Sancho also testified that he had heard members of the party recall that "they located 1 season at (10) Islands near Mobile, ala, and then came on West, landing finally in the Creek Nation, I.T."[49]
90. **John Berryhill** (male, age 30) 3 members consisting of Te na Berryhill (female, age 22), Rainey Berryhill (female, age 1).

Tallassee Town

91. **Tus ton nop chup co** (male, age 60) 8 members consisting of Eu pock lotte kee (female, age 54), Nar komey (male, age 30), Tar co sar Harjo (male, age 28), Tina (female, age 24), Che par ney (male, age 16), Tos sin ne chee (male, age 14), Phillip (male, age 18). Remarks: "Emigrated from ala to the Creek nation in 1838." In October 1886 Parhose Harjo (also known as Phillip) testified that his family, led

by his father Tus ton nop chup co, "came after the 'big emigration', because sickness in the family detained us in Alabama."[50]

92. **George Washington** (male, age 44). 1 member. Remarks: *"Emigrated from ala. to the Creek Nation, I.T. the Spring of 1845."*

Tuckabatchee Town

93. **O so che ho thle bo yer** (male, age 50) 6 members consisting of Mar wo be (female, age 40), Ar to te (male, age 15), Ar ho yei che (female, age 8), Tommy Harjo (male, age 15), Cap pe tan ne (male, age 20). Remarks: "Emigrated from Ala to the creek nation in 1835."
94. **Micco yar holles** (male, age 65) 4 members consisting of Cussup hoh ye (female, age 50), Potty (female, age 35), Toka (female, age 40). Remarks: "Emigrated from ala to Texas in 1838 and from Texas to the Creek nation in 1840."
95. **Is tar ke na he** (male, age 40) 2 members consisting of Echo Emathla (male, age 30). Remarks: "Emigrated from Ala to the Creek nation I T in 1840."

Tolowarthlocco Town

96. **Tommy Harjo** (male, age 58) 2 members consisting of Eliza (female, age 4). Remarks: "Emigrated from Ala to the Creek nation in 1839."

Fish Pond Town

97. **Hillis Harjo** (male, age 21) 1 member. Remarks: "Emigrated from ala to the Creek nation in 1840." This name replaces Kar war pi ke (no. 100) on the corrected roll. According to an 1886 statement, Hillis Harjo "was arrested under a false charge, tried and acquitted in Alabama, and afterwards worked his way West, and reached his tribe in the Territory," and "Had he not been wrongfully detained, he would have come with the main body of emigrants who removed some time before."[51]
98. **Ar pek ko che marthla** (male, age 60) 10 members consisting of Sa wa he che (male, age 22), Tol lot hoh ke (male, age 22), Chon e hoh ye (male, age 20), Pin ka lee (male, age 10), Ars ho ye (male, age 16), Te wa lee (female, age 20), Ar pa kee (female, age 20), E meh kee (female,

age 16), Sim ma hah kee (female, age 50). Remarks: "Emigrated from Ala to the creek nation in 1834 & 5." Ar pek ko che marthla hastily emigrated to the west in the winter of 1834–35—according to Ho tul ke Emathla (b. ca. 1818), a chief of Fish Pond—because "one of the Young men of the family was charged with being too intimate with the wife of another man, and in order to escape punishment, which was severe under the Creek law or custom, the family came to the Territory."[52]

99. ***Milly** (female, age 50) 9 members consisting of Te cum the (male, age 20), Che kar ne (male, age 18), Jennie (female, age 13), Susan (female, age 12), Won tee (male, age 22), Jane o chee (female, age 9), Sar ho ni ye (female, age 60), Jim co (male, age 19). Remarks: "Emigrated from ala. to the Creek Nation, I.T. the Fall and Spring of 1839–40."*
100. ***Kar war pi ke*** [corrected roll states that this name is incorrect, it should be Hillis Harjo; see no. 97, this roll] *(male, age 21) 3 members consisting of Cho nits cher (male, age 18), Mar fo pe cher (male, age 10). Remarks: "Emigrated from ala. to the Creek Nation, I.T. the Fall and Spring of 1839–40."*
101. ***Sin nok ho ke** (female, age 32) 5 members consisting of Tim pfi e che (male, age 58), Mun nuch ho ye (female, age 16), Har pith ho ke (female, age 14), Sim now ho ye (female, age 8). Remarks: "Emigrated from ala. to the Creek Nation, I.T. the Fall and Spring of 1839–40."*
102. ***Is ke nar ye** (male, age 21) 4 members consisting of Sin pil ho ye (female, age 30), Thars wol ker (male, age 8), Inter hop ke (female, age 53). Remarks: "Emigrated from ala. to the Creek Nation, I.T. the Fall and Spring of 1839–40."*

Abeika Town

103. **To thlar tar ke** (female, age 51) 2 members consisting of Sim ho mar har ke (female, age 19). Remarks: "*Emigrated from ala. to the Cherokee nation, I.T. in 1840, and from Cherokee to the Creek nation I.T. in 1848.*"
104. **Thlom ne hum ke Emathla** (male, age 45) 5 members consisting of Lucy (female, age 40), Sop pe hoh ye (female, age 30), Tol mo chus Harjo (male, age 30), John Lasley (male, age 15). Remarks: "Emigrated from Ala to the creek nation in 1839." John Lasley (b. ca. 1824) lived

on the North Fork River, twelve miles northwest of Eufaula, and was the only surviving member of his family when he gave his statement in 1886.[53]

Ottissee Town

105. **Saf o he kee** (male, age 20) 1 member. Remarks: "Emigrated from Ala to the creek nation in 1841." According to testimony from Ho pe chee (also known as Eliza, b. ca. 1827), Saf o he kee was left "back in Alabama, and he emigrated to the Indian Territory in 1841, at his own expense. He was an orphan boy & remained over in Alabama for a few years in Alabaman before he rejoined his people."[54]
106. **Fok lote ka** (male, age 20) 4 members consisting of Mo thle che (female, age 18), Betsey (female, age 15), Charkey (male, age 13). Remarks: "Emigrated from Ala to the Creek nation in 1840."
107. **Ar tah thle** (female, age 30) 2 members consisting of To kee (female, age 27). Remarks: "Emigrated from ala to the Creek nation in 1854."
108. **Hol th ka see** (female, age 40) 3 members consisting of Sal o wee (female, age 13), Sa cha kee (female, age 11). Remarks: "Emigrated from Ala to the Creek nation in 1843."
109. ***Cotchar Tustunnuggee*** *(male, age 55) 12 members consisting of Marley (female, age 45), Suckey (female, age 38), Mar ho ye (female, age 13), I e char (female, age 9), Te ho see (female, age 6), Chu ty (female, age 4), Pink saul (male, age 25), M e pe (male, age 1), Charley (male, "infant"), Lucy (female, age 2), Betsey (female, age 2). Remarks: "Emigrated from ala. to the Creek Nation, Ind. Ter. in 1837.—" Heir: Micco nupper.*

Lower Eufaula Town

110. **Henry Burgess** (male, age 23) 1 member. Remarks: "Emigrated from Ala to the Creek nation in 1838." *Heir: William Burgess.*
111. **Okfuskee Micco** (male, age 45) 5 members consisting of Yolth ka (female, age 40), Te mo chee (male, age 30), Lucy (female, age 26), Che pon chloco (male, age 10). Remarks: "Emigrated from ala to the Creek nation in 1846." Probably emigrated with Yar te ka (no. 112) and Walker (no. 113).
112. **Yar te ka** (male, age 30) 5 members consisting of Oak lo cey (female,

age 28), In ka kee (female, age 23), Iney (female, age 10), John (male, age 8). Remarks: "Emigrated from ala to the Creek nation in 1846." Iney was the daughter of Yar te ka, and noted that she emigrated with her family in 1846 "but was several years on the road." Probably emigrated with Okfuskee Micco (no. 111) and Walker (no. 113).[55]

113. **Walker** (male, no age given) 2 members consisting of Miser (female, no age given). Walker and Miser were husband and wife and do not appear on either muster roll. Iney (no. 145) testified in 1886 that these two "came along slowly and finally reached the Creek Nation, Ind. Ter." Probably emigrated with Okfuskee Micco (no. 111) and Yar te ka (no. 112).[56]

Hitchiti

114. **Thomas Morris** (male, age 18) 1 member. Remarks: "Emigrated from ala. to the Creek nation I.T. the winter 1852–3 at his own charges & expense."
115. **Mary Ann Jones** (female, 40) 2 members consisting of Thomas T. Rogers (male, age 2). Remarks: "Emigrated from ala. to the Creek Nation I.T. in the year" 1847. Heir: Eliza J. Checote.
116. **John Shepherd** (male, age 30) 1 member. Remarks: "Emigrated from Ala to the Creek nation in 1852." *Heir: Mon ar chik che.* G. W. Stidham (b. ca. 1817), testifying in October 1886, claimed that Shepherd "was left a small boy in Alabama, & came west and found his own mother by whom he was identified."[57]
117. **Toh far lich che** (female, age 20) 1 member. Remarks: "Emigrated from ala to the Creek nation in 1847." *Heirs: David and Polly.*
118. **Cup pit cher Fixico** (male, age 65) 4 members consisting of Ho le (female, age 60), *Kar ho ker (female, age 32),* Yar wil ho ye (female, age 33). Remarks: "Emigrated from Ala to the Creek nation in 1840."
119. **Fol lin ho ye** (female, age 50) 8 members consisting of *Sar hal le (male, age 40),* Billy (male, age 32), Jackson Lewis (male, age 6), Sut che mi ke (female, age 39), Lucy (female, age 3), *Johnson (male, age 1),* Ful lich ho ye (female, age 30). Remarks: "Emigrated from Ala to the creek nation in 1847." *Heir: Jackson Lewis.* Next to Sar hal le's name on original roll is written: "Died on the way here." Next to Johnson's

name is written: "Died on the way here—" In October 1886 Jackson Lewis (b. ca. 1831) testified that his family left Alabama then "stopped for several years in the Choctaw Nation near Doaksville."[58]

120. **So fop ha kee** (male, age 40) 3 members consisting of Ton ner cha (male, age 42), Sa wa chick ey (male, age 39). Remarks: "Emigrated from Ala to the Creek nation in 1841."
121. ***Ar wi ke** (male, age 38) 1 member. Remarks: "Emigrated as above in the year 1855." Heir: Pars co far.*
122. **Ar che wi che** (male, age 30) 1 member. Remarks:"Emigrated from Ala to the Creek nation 1833." *Heir: Ti ke.* Listed under Oke te yark ney town; however, on 1870–71 roll it notes that Oke te yark ney was an "obsolete" name and that the emigrant should be listed under Hitchiti.

Hickory Ground Town

123. **Emathla Harjo** (male, age 50) 8 members consisting of Hon ni che (male, age 18), Tim par he che (male, age 22), Ho wi che (male, age 10), Mon tal le (male, age 15), Hoke te (female, age 23), Tow we lar ke (female, age 40), Pol ey (female, age 14). Remarks: "Emigrated from Ala to the Creek nation in the spring of 1837." See no. 128. Chowee Colbert (b. ca. 1822) testified in 1886 that Emathla Harjo "was a man who had crazy spells, and did not like to mix in crowds, and, therefore, would not come in the 'big Emigration.'"[59]
124. **Samuel Fisher** (male, age 53) 13 members consisting of Vicey Fisher (female, age 45), Ninity Fisher (female, age 29), William Fisher (male, age 17), Jane Fisher (female, age 18), Ann Fisher (female, age 21), George Fisher (male, age 19), Rebecca Fisher (female, age 15), Richard Fisher (male, age 13), Lucy Fisher (female, age 55), Washington (male, age 28), Darcus (female, age 27), *John (male, age 17)*. Remarks: "Emigrated from Ala to the Creek nation in 1847." *Heir and administrator: George Fisher*. George Fisher (b. ca. 1828), the son of Samuel Fisher, testified that his family emigrated in 1847. William Fisher was another son of Samuel Fisher, who, according to Harry F. O'Beirne and Edward S. O'Beirne, was "two-thirds white, and a farmer and stock-raiser by occupation." He was described as being "five feet eleven inches in height, of excellent intelligence and superior business capacity. . . .

Although part Indian, yet he shows a large preponderance of white blood." After arriving in the West, William Fisher was sent to the Shawnee Mission in Kansas for two years. He married Sarah P. Lampkins, a white woman from Tennessee, in 1850 and with her had nine children. He joined the Confederate Army under Chilly McIntosh and served on the National Council after the war."[60]

125. **Angeline McCombs** (female, age 50) 2 members consisting of Cornelia McCombs (female, age 45). Remarks: "Emigrated from Ala to the Creek nation 1877."

126. **Eliza Ancil** (female, age 27) 5 members consisting of Stephen Ancil (male, age 33), William Ancil (male, age 7), Malissa Ancil (female, age 5), Sarah Ancil (female, age 3). Remarks: *"Emigrated from the Creek Nation, ala. to Mississippi in 1843, from Miss to arkansas in 1845, from ark. to the Choctaw Nation in 1847, and from that to the Creek Nation, I.T. in 1849."*

127. **Benjamin Knox** (male, age 10) 4 members consisting of William Harvison (male, age 8), Thomas C. Harvison (male, age 6), Silla (female servant, age 14). Remarks: "Emigrated from ala to the Creek nation in 1846. The parents of these children died while on the Journey through." Thomas C. Harvison (b. ca. 1838) was the half-brother of Benjamin Knox and testified in 1886 that his "Parents died on the way to the Indian Territory at Memphis, Tenn. The family at the outset consisted of (7) persons but the two old ones & a child died. When the family reached the Territory it embraced Benj. Knox, William Harvison, Silla, a servant, & myself."[61]

128. ***Polly Chisholm** (female, age 56) 8 members consisting of Emathla Harjo (male, age 50), Hon ni che (male, age 18), Tim par he che (male, age 22), Ho wi che (male, age 10), Mon tal le (male, age 15), Hoke te (female, age 23), Tow we lar ke (female, age 40). Remarks: "Emigrated from ala. to the Creek Nation I.T. the Spring of 1837." See no. 123, this roll.*

129. ***John Ward** (male, age 36) 20 members consisting of Mahala Ward (female, age 61), Suckey Ward (female, age 34), Betsey Ward (female, age 24), Hetty Ward (female, age 12), Suckey Ward (female, age 4), Malinda Ward (female, age 2), Finner (female servant, age 81), Bittey (female servant, age 42), Larry (male servant, age 26), Lemuel*

(male servant, age 26), Jack (male servant, age 16), Nancy (female servant, age 14), Judy (female servant, age 12), Polly (female servant, age 8), Dick (male servant, age 12), Jeffrey (male servant, age 6), Willis (male servant, age 26), Bucher (male servant, age 20), Te ner (female servant, age 8). Remarks: "Emigrated same as above in 1834." Heir and "administratrix": Suckey Ward (age 4). A Creek man of mixed ancestry, John Ward was the son of Mahiga Ward (his mother) and son-in-law of Hickory Ground mile chief William McGillivray. Sometime in 1833 Ward petitioned President Andrew Jackson for a new reserve under the 1832 Treaty of Washington, claiming that locating agents did not assign him the piece of land that he had lived on and had been cultivating since 1820. Ward stated that his original land was not remarkably fertile but was in the midst of "his relations and friends." It is unclear whether Ward was assigned his old land but his voluntary emigration the next year may not have been coincidence.[62]

130. ***Josiah Fisher*** *(male, no age given) 10 members consisting of Pilista Fisher (female, age 39), Maria Fisher (female, age 13), Eliza Fisher (female, age 10), Susan Fisher (female, age 8), Rosanna Fisher (female, age 23), Matilda Fisher (female, age 21), Martha Fisher (female, age 19), James Fisher (male, age 17), Joshua Fisher (male, age 15). Remarks: "Emigrated same as above in 1839." Heir and administrator: George Fisher.*

131. ***James Gentry*** *(male, age 42) 7 members consisting of Caroline Gentry (female, age 43), William E. Gentry (male, age 13), L. L. Gentry (male, age 11), A. J. Gentry (male, age 9), N. R. Gentry (female, age 7), S. P. Gentry (female, age 3). Remarks: "Emigrated from the Creek Nation in ala. to Miss. in 1840, & from Miss. to Creek Nation I.T. in 1855." William E. Gentry (born 11 March 1842) was the second son of James Gentry and Caroline Bush, an American citizen. He was the grandson of Elijah Gentry, who married a Catawba woman. William attended school in Mississippi before moving to Indian territory in 1855, where he attended the Asbury Mission in Eufaula. He joined the Confederate Army (Second Creek Regiment) under Chilly McIntosh. He was elected to the House of Warriors in*

1887. William Gentry, who married three times, had eight children: Albert James (b. 1873), William (b. 1879), Caroline (b. 1881), Mary E. (b. 1883), Sallie P. (b. 1885), Bobby Lee (b. 1887), Bluford (b. 1889), and Rachel Jane (b. 1891).[63]

Co was sar da Town

132. **Chook McNac** (female, age 50) 4 members consisting of John McNac (male, age 16), Polly McNac (female, age 18), Jane McNac (female, age 14). Remarks: "Emigrated to the Creek nation I T in 1847."

Kialiche Town

133. **Tim mon mar fiche** (female, age 34) *7 members consisting of Sup pow we (male, age 60), It chars war che (male, age 30), Se yar par ho ye (female, age 33), Tar ho si che (male, age 20), Tommy (male, age 18), Bobby (male, age 28).* Remarks: "Emigrated to the creek nation in 1843."
134. **Jon ny** (male, age 40) 6 members consisting of Par tee (female, age 30), Wat tie (male, age 10), *Lum ber (male, age 7),* You par te (female, age 22), Ar to thli ke (female, age 30). Remarks: "Started with Emigration in 1836 were left on Mississippi river, stayed There 2 years arrived in the creek nation in 1838."
135. **Cosiste Harjo** (male, age 60), 6 members consisting of *Fun par ke (female, age 30),* Sampson (male, age 18), *Loneza (female, age 14), Eliza (female, age 10).* Remarks: *"Emigrated from ala. to the Creek nation, I.T. the Fall of 1837—"* Cosiste Harjo's wife, Suf fol la kee, was incorrectly omitted from both rolls. According to the testimony of Thla thlo Yoholo, also known as Siah Fish (b. ca. 1810), who was an acquaintance, Cosiste Harjo and family first went "to Texas, and he & family were brought to the Territory. that is, they were sent for by their people."[64]
136. ***Jim** (male, age 50) 12 members consisting of We lar ke (female, age 42), Fart sar (male, age 12), Ah he che (female, age 15), Chok i kee (male, age 30), Mar ho ye (female, age 20), Cow war pi ke (male, age 40), Yo thli ke (female, age 10), Sea ley (female, age 13), Ar ko si le (male, age 13), Hagey (male, age 25), Johnson (male, age 56). Remarks: "Emigrated*

from the Creek nation ala. to Texas about the year 1811, & from Texas to the Creek nation I.T. in the year A.D. 1843."

137. ***Ar par le che*** *(male, age 52) 8 members consisting of Is chil lar ye (male, age 31), Par le cher (male, age 22), Has ho ker (female, age 55), Te mo har ye (male, age 63), O ye cher (female, age 60), Har lut har ye (female, age 22), Mar tar ho ye (female, age 15). Remarks: "Emigrated from the Creek nation ala. to Texas about the year 1811, & from Texas to the Creek nation I.T. in the year A.D. 1843."*

Hatcheechubba Town

138. **Chular Fixico** (male, age 51) 4 members consisting of Se yar fan nar ke (female, age 45), Sal lar ho ke (female, age 42), Poh he (female, age 35). Remarks: "Emigrated from Ala to the Creek nation in 1839."

Tars ke kee Town

139. **Dick McNac** (male, age 45) 10 members consisting of Adam (male, age 40), *Ketch (male, age 55)*, Jeffrey (male, age 18), Hardey (male, age 16), Creacy (female, age 14), *Phillis (female, no age given)*, George (male, age 12), Toney Spaniard (male, age 30). Remarks: "Emigrated from ala to the Creek nation in 1838." Dick McNac's nephew, Silas Jefferson (b. ca. 1831), testified in 1886 that his uncle "made efforts in his life time to get his pay, or to get his money back" for emigrating but never received compensation.[65]

Chehaw Town

140. **Powhattan Sims** (male, age 20) 1 member: Remarks: "Emigrated from Ala to Creek nation in 1855."

Cusseta Town

141. ***Pin Harjo*** *(male, age 30) 1 member. Remarks: "Emigrated from ala. in 1835, worked his way through Mississippi & Arkansas to the Creek nation, I.T. paying for Transportation & Subsistence." Heir: Thlar fe che (female).*
142. ***Tus ke ne har thlocco*** *(male, age 60) 2 members consisting of Loneza (female, age 34). Remarks: "Emigrated from Ala. in 1837."*

Quassartie Town of Arkansas

143. ***Efar Yoholo*** *(male, age 65) 5 members consisting of Linda (female, age 23), Pe thlar ne (female, age 15), Se me ho ke (female, age 45), Che parne (male, age 8). Remarks: "Emigrated from ala. to the Creek Nation, I.T. in 1835."*

144. ***Par toc Harjo*** *(male, age 30) 7 members consisting of Sar pok le (male, age 35), Ho thle po yar (male, age 20), Se mar lum he (female, age 15), Tic ke ye (male, age 15), Lar ne (female, age 10), Ha lubbe (male, age 20). Remarks: "Emigrated from ala. to the Creek Nation, I.T. in 1835."*

145. ***Tom mar the*** *(male, age 30), 6 members consisting of Tim par le che (female, age 35), So fut che (female, age 20), So tar we (female, age 15), Kar par ke (female, age 13), Tar lo pe (male, age 40). Remarks: "Emigrated from ala. to the Creek Nation, I.T. in 1835."*

146. ***Tom me Yoholo*** *(male, age 40) 6 members consisting of Yar ke tar ne (female, age 50), Sar nar ho ke (female, age 25), So the (female, age 15), Thle sar we (male, age 8), Yar tub bee (male, age 5). Remarks: "Emigrated from ala. to the Creek Nation, I.T. in 1835."*

147. ***Tusekiah Harjo*** *(male, age 38) 5 members consisting of Char ke (male, age 30), Se mar te (female, age 15), So che ye (female, age 8), Ko nar he (female, age 6). Remarks: "Emigrated from ala. to the Creek Nation, I.T. in 1835."*

148. ***Par hose Yoholo*** *(male, age 33) 9 members consisting of Sar ko nar he (male, age 42), Cho thlo te (female, age 25), Tar pe che (female, age 15), Nun ny (female, age 30), Mis sar (female, age 35), Mosey (male, age 10), Susey (female, age 5), Sun thlar te Yoholo (male, age 25). Remarks: "Emigrated from ala. to the Creek Nation, I.T. in 1835."*

149. ***Hil lis war*** *(male, age 36) 7 members consisting of No sar pe (male, age 30), Tos ker (female, age 25), Fo ti pe (male, age 22), Po ni ye (female, age 14), Sar tar le che (male, age 10), Hun ke (female, age 2). Remarks: "Emigrated from ala. to the Creek Nation, I.T. in 1835."*

150. ***Tom mus se yer*** *(male, age 25) 5 members consisting of Che par nar ke (male, age 15), Ho te see (female, age 30), Wa to (female, age 10), La der (female, age 8). Remarks: "Emigrated from ala. to the Creek Nation, I.T. in 1835."*

151. ***Ho mar ho te*** *(female, age 25) 4 members consisting of Sar fis sar (female, age 21), So yo thli ke (female, age 15), Chow ho ye (female, age 8). Remarks: "Emigrated from ala. to the Creek Nation, I.T. in 1835."*

152. ***Micco*** *(male, age 44) 10 members consisting of Hun thler (female, age 40), To po ye (male, age 36), Ho tul ke Harjo (male, age 23), Mock le (male, age 24), Johnny (male, age 15), Se le (female, age 10), Se le che (female, age 7), Ul see (male, age 8), Tul war Micco (male, age 25). Remarks: "Emigrated from ala. to the Creek Nation, I.T. in 1835."*

153. ***Kot char*** *(male, age 50), 3 members consisting of Sar pe fot ker (female, age 32), Pos tar lar (male, age 15). Remarks: "Emigrated from ala. to the Creek Nation, I.T. in 1835."*

154. ***He thle*** *(female, age 35) 5 members consisting of Ko nar he (female, age 46), Te mar thle (female, age 25), He che (male, age 22), Ho lar ter Harjo (male, age 25). Remarks: "Emigrated from ala. to the Creek Nation, I.T. in 1835."*

155. ***Ko le cher*** *(male, age 36) 3 members consisting of Se mar lar ho ke (female, age 32), Un ter ler (male, age 25). Remarks: "Emigrated from ala. to the Creek Nation, I.T. in 1835."*

156. ***Kus ker sus ke*** *(male, age 53) 3 members consisting of Char we (female, age 36), Sar par we (male, age 22). Remarks: "Emigrated from ala. to the Creek Nation, I.T. in 1835."*

157. ***In kar par*** *(male, age 54) 7 members consisting of Pin Harjo (male, age 39), Johnny (male, age 8), Fo lo te (female, age 15), Se ke ye (female, age 24), Sur che mi ke (female, age 5), Lucy (female, age 3). Remarks: "Emigrated from ala. to the Creek Nation, I.T. in 1835."*

158. ***Yar too che*** *(male, age 35) 2 members consisting of Sar nic thle (female, age 29). Remarks: "Emigrated from ala. to the Creek Nation, I.T. in 1835."*

159. ***Fe no ke*** *(female, age 50) 5 members consisting of Nancy (female, age 37), Se no che (female, age 15), Sar late ker (male, age 2), Mary (female, age 5). Remarks: "Emigrated from ala. to the Creek Nation, I.T. in 1835."*

160. ***Chisse Harjo*** *(male, age 36) 5 members consisting of Chisse ho lar ter (male, age 35), Te mar tul ke (female, age 27), Ar pi e che (female, age 8), Okfuske (male, age 5). Remarks: "Emigrated from ala. to the Creek Nation, I.T. in 1835."*

161. ***Se tar thle*** *(male, age 30) 7 members consisting of Jimmy (male, age 15), Par se mar (female, age 15), Suk lut ke (male, age 20), So ko ye (female, age 5), Lucy (female, age 10), Johnny (male, age 7). Remarks: "Emigrated from ala. to the Creek Nation, I.T. in 1835."*

162. ***Sar po ke*** *(female, age 35) 7 members consisting of Tar nar (female, age 30), To ho ther (male, age 21), Pe fot ho ke (female, age 15), War ke (female, age 15), Eliza (female, age 8), O fo li ke (female, age 5). Remarks: "Emigrated from ala. to the Creek Nation, I.T. in 1835."*

163. ***Nip pe Emathla*** *(male, age 42) 2 members consisting of Sar pok le (female, age 33). Remarks: "Emigrated from ala. to the Creek Nation, I.T. in 1835."*

164. ***Ar see*** *(male, age 39) 3 members consisting of Tar par ye (female, age 25), Lucy charte (female, age 5). Remarks: "Emigrated from ala. to the Creek Nation, I.T. in 1835."*

165. ***Oc ti ar che*** *(male, age 55) 4 members consisting of Susey (female, age 38), Te le cher (male, age 15), Har lar te (male, age 8). Remarks: "Emigrated from ala. to the Creek Nation, I.T. in 1835."*

166. ***So har ho ye*** *(female, age 38) 3 members consisting of Ful ley (female, age 25), Sar pe ye (female, age 10). Remarks: "Emigrated from ala. to the Creek Nation, I.T. in 1835."*

Alabama and Quasartee of Canadian

167. ***Sim mi ye*** *(female, age 50) 8 members consisting of Che lo ka (male, age 80), Ho ya (female, age 40), Si ha ya che (male, age 82), Park li ya (male, age 75), To har te (female, age 70), Ti ar che (female, age 40), Cotcher Yoholo (male, age 70). Remarks: "Emigrated from the Creek Nation, alabama, to Texas, in or about 1811, and from Texas to the Creek Nation, I.T. in 1843." Heir: Cotcher Yoholo.*

168. ***Cow wop ka*** *(male, age 70) 14 members consisting of Sit tok ki ye (female, age 75), Ho lar te (male, age 81), Sok gur che (male, age 78), You po lut ke (male, age 30), Stof fok ches ti e (male, age 20), Nok til list che (male, age 22), To mo pul li ke (female, age 60), To hi ye (female, age 30), Much a catch ha (female, age 35), Kei par ke (female, age 25), To ni ye che (male, age 30), Sim o kar pe (female, age 28), Sim i pi ye ke (female, age 50). Remarks: "Emigrated from the Creek Nation, alabama,*

to Texas, in or about 1811, and from Texas to the Creek Nation, I.T. in 1843." Heir: Sim i pi ye ke.

169. ***Tim ma ho ye*** *(male, age 80) 13 members consisting of Sim me che (female, age 40), Te wak ke (male, age 35), Yeat che (male, age 40), Wa he che (male, age 35), Thler kar ke (female, age 78), Char he che (male, age 40), Sirn mat ho ye (female, age 28), Betsey (female, age 76), Ti e che (female, age 79), O so no (female, age 30), Ma ho ye (female, age 22), Meis ter (female, age 60). Remarks: "Emigrated from the Creek Nation, alabama, to Texas, in or about 1811, and from Texas to the Creek Nation, I.T. in 1843." Heir: Meis ter.*
170. ***Pla lut te*** *(male, age 50) 8 members consisting of In char re (female, age 20), Son e tar (male, age 35), Ar lit ke (male, age 22), Tomme Harjo (male, age 40), Sox sue me (female, age 60), Mil le cher (female, age 64), Sar yonth ke (male, age 40). Remarks: "Emigrated from the Creek Nation, alabama, to Texas, in or about 1811, and from Texas to the Creek Nation, I.T. in 1843." Heir: Sar yonth ke.*
171. ***My he che*** *(female, 45) 10 members consisting of My ho he (female, age 40), Char tu che (female, age 35), Chit te (male, age 45), Sim ma ho ye (female, age 60), Sar u bus ke (male, age 72), Sim a wil lar ke (male, age 22), To war ke che (male, age 70), Chis so qua (male, age 45), Micco nupper (male, age 50). Remarks: "Emigrated from the Creek Nation, alabama, to Texas, in or about 1811, and from Texas to the Creek Nation, I.T. in 1843." Heir: Micco nupper.*
172. ***Tar che pe*** *(female, age 70) 8 members consisting of Yar hi ke (male, age 28), Char ke (male, age 35), Fix o me che (male, age 26), Is fun ke (male, age 20), Sim ma ho ye che (female, age 30), Eu war ne (female, age 36), Cotchar Micco (male, age 70). Remarks: "Emigrated from the Creek Nation, alabama, to Texas, in or about 1811, and from Texas to the Creek Nation, I.T. in 1843."*
173. ***Sim mar pil ke*** *(female, age 20) 17 members consisting of Is ha pul le (female, age 40), Im me to ker par ke (female, age 50), Te wer nar ke (female, age 40), Thle se (female, age 50), Pal lar pe (male, age 42), George (male, age 30), Co al lup pe (male, age 27), Sox sue me che (male, age 30), To was si ye (male, age 20), Mun te le che (male, age 21), Sim mo nar ye (male, age 38), Ti a ke (female, age 60), Is wi ke (male, age*

40), Sar yo ye (male, age 54), Te mars ho ye (female, age 32), Teacher (female, age 55). Remarks: "Emigrated from the Creek Nation, alabama, to Texas, in or about 1811, and from Texas to the Creek Nation, I.T. in 1843." Heir: Teacher.

174. ***Okfuskee Tustunnuggee*** *(male, age 60) 6 members consisting of Sar pi e ye che (female, age 45), Tok how war ke (female, age 24), Ti ke (male, age 29), Tar hin ne (male, age 27), Sar hul ho te (female, age 54). Remarks: "Emigrated from the Creek Nation, alabama, to Texas, in or about 1811, and from Texas to the Creek Nation, I.T. in 1843." Heir: Sar hul ho te.*
175. ***Ho te se*** *(male, age 60) 5 members consisting of Kar che he (female, age 22), Willis (male, age 27), Kin chart ke (male, age 28), Martha (female, age 45). Remarks: "Emigrated from the Creek Nation, alabama, to Texas, in or about 1811, and from Texas to the Creek Nation, I.T. in 1843." Heir: Martha.*
176. ***Se lit ke*** *(male, age 72) 13 members consisting of Char ker (male, age 36), Sar te che (female, age 60), Sar wa le (male, age 75), Is wun ke (female, age 30), Is ter chu be (male, age 28), Cor sar (female, age 40), Ar ko ye (male, age 50), E po se (female, age 75), Chok kar you be (male, age 45), Par ye ar (male, age 28), War sar se (male, age 32), Cotchar Fixico (male, age 35). Remarks: "Emigrated from the Creek Nation, alabama, to Texas, in or about 1811, and from Texas to the Creek Nation, I.T. in 1843." Heir: Cotchar Fixico.*
177. ***Ful li ke*** *(female, age 68) 7 members consisting of Te war he char (female, age 45), Ne kar che (female, age 25), Sin me lar we (male, age 40), Much che kil le (male, age 37), Sa yo har (female, age 28), Min ni cher (female, age 48). Remarks: "Emigrated from the Creek Nation, alabama, to Texas, in or about 1811, and from Texas to the Creek Nation, I.T. in 1843." Heir: Min ni cher.*
178. ***War le*** *(male, age 59) 9 members consisting of Sea le (female, age 60), Tim me mar (female, age 18), Ho yar ni te (male, age 49), Sook sin (male, age 14), Wes ta lor (male, age 35), To ta ye (male, age 10), Chis ti lar (female, age 40), Jennie (female, age 40). Remarks: "Emigrated from the Creek Nation, alabama, to Texas, in or about 1811, and from Texas to the Creek Nation, I.T. in 1843." Heir: Jennie.*

179. ***Cow e tar*** *(male, age 50) 9 members consisting of Ka te tee (male, age 54), La ser (male, age 15), Lon war sar (female, age 43), Lar te (female, age 48), Me e lar (female, age 16), To nar ye (male, age 14), Sam se (male, age 13), Abel (male, age 42). Remarks: "Emigrated from the Creek Nation, alabama, to Texas, in or about 1811, and from Texas to the Creek Nation, I.T. in 1843." Heir: Sel in ne.*

180. ***In ho war tub bee*** *(male, age 40) 1 member. Remarks: "Emigrated from the Creek Nation, alabama, to Texas, in or about 1811, and from Texas to the Creek Nation, I.T. in 1843." Heir: Gibson.*

181. ***Billy*** *(male, age 45) 5 members consisting of Ful li che (male, age 40), Te mar le che (male, age 38), Kar wop ke (female, age 48), Quar sart Yoholo (male, age 52). Remarks: "Emigrated from the Creek Nation, alabama, to Texas, in or about 1811, and from Texas to the Creek Nation, I.T. in 1843." Heir: Chil le le.*

182. ***Billy*** *(male, age 40) 7 members consisting of Sar war li che (male, age 70), Par he char (male, age 60), Jackson (male, age 12), Char le le char (male, age 58), Os ho ke (female, age 53), Tom me Emarthlo che (male, age 30). Remarks: "Emigrated from the Creek Nation, alabama, to Texas, in or about 1811, and from Texas to the Creek Nation, I.T. in 1843." Heir: Tom me Emarthlo che.*

183. ***Lucy*** *(female, age 60) 6 members consisting of Sallie (female, age 53), Lydia (female, age 18), Yon par yar ke (male, age 22), Tar chie (male, age 35), Louina (female, age 55). Remarks: "Emigrated from the Creek Nation, alabama, to Texas, in or about 1811, and from Texas to the Creek Nation, I.T. in 1843." Heir: Louina.*

184. ***Sim se*** *(male, age 42) 7 members consisting of Ar wul ke (male, age 56), Sar nar ke (female, age 50), Tim mo ho ke (male, age 21), Sar par le (female, age 37), O no che (male, age 70), Fix o me che (male, age 50). Remarks: "Emigrated from the Creek Nation, alabama, to Texas, in or about 1811, and from Texas to the Creek Nation, I.T. in 1843." Heir: Fix o me che.*

185. ***Yon pok lot te*** *(female, age 50) 7 members consisting of Jennie (female, age 10), Chok ke pe (male, age 25), Tim me poe che (female, age 45), Fil le more tub bee (male, age 20), Fil le se (male, age 25), Si e me (female, age 35). Remarks: "Emigrated from the Creek Nation, alabama, to*

Texas, in or about 1811, and from Texas to the Creek Nation, I.T. in 1843." Heir: Si e me.

186. ***Ar fo be** (male, age 60) 5 members consisting of Loniza (female, age 24), Boney (male, age 27), Car li na (female, age 17), Rosey (female, age 60). Remarks: "Emigrated from the Creek Nation, alabama, to Texas, in or about 1811, and from Texas to the Creek Nation, I.T. in 1843." Heir: Rosey.*
187. ***Sim mar wi ke** (female, age 50) 3 members consisting of **Sar thlun ar ke** (female, age 48), Ho mo (male, age 23). Remarks: "Emigrated from the Creek Nation, alabama, to Texas, in or about 1811, and from Texas to the Creek Nation, I.T. in 1843." Heir: Thlar e che che.*
188. ***Eufaula** (male, age 50) 5 members consisting of Tumme Harjo (male, age 42), Sarful le (female, age 57), Nancy (female, age 47), Tal Yoholo (male, age 42). Remarks: "Emigrated from the Creek Nation, alabama, to Texas, in or about 1811, and from Texas to the Creek Nation, I.T. in 1843." Heir: Rosinda.*
189. ***Is te mar cho che** (male, age 45) 5 members consisting of Se te he che (female, age 42), Lin te (female, age 33), Billy (male, age 48), Te yar kar (male, age 29). Remarks: "Emigrated from the Creek Nation, alabama, to Texas, in or about 1811, and from Texas to the Creek Nation, I.T. in 1843." Heir: Te yar kar.*
190. ***Neak thler** (male, age 51) 5 members consisting of Te co lar (male, age 39), Te he che che (male, age 22), Is ho yar ne (male, age 41), To sa (male, age 40). Remarks: "Emigrated from the Creek Nation, alabama, to Texas, in or about 1811, and from Texas to the Creek Nation, I.T. in 1843." Heir: To sa.*
191. ***Sar yar kar pe** (male, age 68) 5 members consisting of Ho yau ne cher (female, 38), Sim mo thlol ke (female, age 28), Se ho mi che (male, 30), Is par ne Harjo (male, age 50). Remarks: "Emigrated from the Creek Nation, alabama, to Texas, in or about 1811, and from Texas to the Creek Nation, I.T. in 1843." Heir: Tar che pe.*
192. ***Cho lar ke** (female, age 70) 13 members consisting of Co sar (male, age 19), Sim mi li ke (male, age 16), Susie (female, age 14), Sil le che (female, age 12), Sim mar po che (female, age 50), Sar cum se (female, age 18), Sar ko le cher (male, age 65), Karpit cher (male, age 20), Co we Harjo*

(male, age 22), Co war ko che (male, age 25), War ner (male, age 36), Co war sart Emathla (male, age 45). Remarks: "Emigrated from the Creek Nation, alabama, to Texas, in or about 1811, and from Texas to the Creek Nation, I.T. in 1843." Heir: Co war sart Emathla.

193. ***Mulcey*** *(female, age 50) 6 members consisting of John (male, age 35), Fisher (male, age 45), Joshua (male, age 24), Yar kee (female, age 22), Nancy (female, age 45). Remarks: "Emigrated from the Creek Nation, alabama, to Texas, in or about 1811, and from Texas to the Creek Nation, I.T. in 1843." Heir: So lin ne.*

194. ***Dickey*** *(male, age 50) 8 members consisting of Char ke (female, age 45), Mi cey (female, age 34), Tar ke (male, age 24), Co sar (male, age 45), Sem me (male, age 23), O way (male, age 48), Jackson (male, age 30). Remarks: "Emigrated from the Creek Nation, alabama, to Texas, in or about 1811, and from Texas to the Creek Nation, I.T. in 1843." Heir: Jackson.*

195. ***Tomme Yoholo*** *(male, age 50) 7 members consisting of Quarsard Emathla (male, age 75), Is par ne (male, age 40), Is par ne Harjo (male, age 45), Judy (female, age 18), Par ne (male, age 12), Eu pus ke (male, age 60). Remarks: "Emigrated from the Creek Nation, alabama, to Texas, in or about 1811, and from Texas to the Creek Nation, I.T. in 1843."*

196. ***Se he che*** *(male, age 40) 8 members consisting of Jennie (female, age 70), Peggy (female, age 21), Pi e cher (male, age 20), Kal lar ne (male, age 18), Fannie (female, age 16), Eu pho nie (male, age 50), Nocose ille Harjo (male, age 60). Remarks: "Emigrated from the Creek Nation, alabama, to Texas, in or about 1811, and from Texas to the Creek Nation, I.T. in 1843." Heir: Nocose ille Harjo.*

197. ***To war ke che*** *(male, age 50) 4 members consisting of In le ti ke (male, age 40), Charle (male, age 35), Is tar che ye (male, age 70). Remarks: "Emigrated from the Creek Nation, alabama, to Texas, in or about 1811, and from Texas to the Creek Nation, I.T. in 1843." Heir: Chi se.*

198. ***Ar to way ke*** *(male, age 66) 4 members consisting of Lum hi che (male, age 58), Tal mar se (male, age 23), Sal e cher (female, age 18). Remarks: "Emigrated from the Creek Nation, alabama, to Texas, in or about 1811, and from Texas to the Creek Nation, I.T. in 1843." Heir: David.*

199. ***Is tin char ke*** *(male, age 23) 5 members consisting of Siah (no sex or*

age given), Peter (no sex or age given), Louiza (no sex or age given), Se me ho ker (no sex or age given). Remarks: "Emigrated from the Creek Nation, alabama, to Texas, in or about 1811, and from Texas to the Creek Nation, I.T. in 1843." Heir: Se me ho ker.

200. ***To say ye che*** *(male, age 32) 1 member. Remarks: "Emigrated from the Creek Nation, alabama, to Texas, in or about 1811, and from Texas to the Creek Nation, I.T. in 1843." Heir: Georgia.*
201. ***Tomme Harjo*** *(male, age 60) 5 members consisting of Char we pe (male, age 58), Par chis ke (male, age 62), Cho lar ke (male, age 40), Tar thlar (male, age 36). Remarks: "Emigrated from the Creek Nation, alabama, to Texas, in or about 1811, and from Texas to the Creek Nation, I.T. in 1843." Heir: Susanna.*
202. ***Sim se*** *(male, age 26) 8 members consisting of Oak char ye Micco (male, age 58), God de (male, age 40), Fus Harjo (male, age 60), Echo Emathla (male, age 72), Arthlun Harjo (male, age 38), Amey (female, age 32), Artus Fixico (male, age 46). Remarks: "Emigrated from the Creek Nation, alabama, to Texas, in or about 1811, and from Texas to the Creek Nation, I.T. in 1843." Heir: Artus Fixico.*
203. ***Mas sar nay*** *(female, age 40) 8 members consisting of Fut char li ke (male, age 42), Lucy (female, age 36), Flar ma (female, age 28), To lun cher (male, age 23), O los kar (female, age 40), Sar way ka (female, age 38), Char ka (male, age 20). Remarks: "Emigrated from the Creek Nation, alabama, to Texas, in or about 1811, and from Texas to the Creek Nation, I.T. in 1843." Heir: Char ka.*
204. ***Kar par ke*** *(female, age 40) 5 members consisting of Lo cho che (female, age 38), Ko to le (female, age 28), Kar pit cher (male, age 25), Sal o che (female, age 50). Remarks: "Emigrated from the Creek Nation, alabama, to Texas, in or about 1811, and from Texas to the Creek Nation, I.T. in 1843." Heir: Co war sar te Emathla.*
205. ***Adam*** *(male, age 35) 5 members consisting of Martin (male, no age given), Bar tiese (male, no age given), Bur fe tar tub be (male, no age given), No war tar tub bee (male, no age given). Remarks: "Emigrated from the Creek Nation, alabama, to Texas, in or about 1811, and from Texas to the Creek Nation, I.T. in 1843." Heir: No war tar tub bee.*
206. ***Willis*** *(male, age 50) 7 members consisting of Jimmy (male, age 20),*

Yones star (female, age 20), Yon te (female, age 12), Sall (male, age 21), Is me (male, age 10), Par sa Fixico (male, age 70). Remarks: "Emigrated from the Creek Nation, alabama, to Texas, in or about 1811, and from Texas to the Creek Nation, I.T. in 1843." Heir: Par sa Fixico.

207. ***Char tee*** *(male, age 68), 5 members consisting of Lar tee (male, age 27), No cos ho lar te (male, age 32), No cos Harjo che (male, age 22), Sar me che (female, age 25). Remarks: "Emigrated from the Creek Nation, alabama, to Texas, in or about 1811, and from Texas to the Creek Nation, I.T. in 1843." Heir: Ho lar te.*

208. ***Har key*** *(female, age 70) 6 members consisting of Ar pal ho ke (female, age 50), Ne he che (male, age 60), Katey (female, age 18), Bar te sar (male, age 40), Lo char (female, age 40). Remarks: "Emigrated from the Creek Nation, alabama, to Texas, in or about 1811, and from Texas to the Creek Nation, I.T. in 1843." Heir: Lo cher.*

209. ***Thlar war ye che*** *(female, age 60) 5 members consisting of War ke che (male, age 42), Se te to cars ke (male, age 52), Sar ho yar (female, age 63), Nicey (female, age 35). Remarks: "Emigrated from the Creek Nation, alabama, to Texas, in or about 1811, and from Texas to the Creek Nation, I.T. in 1843." Heir: Nicey.*

210. ***Suu nar*** *(male, age 70) 6 members consisting of Ar kar ke (female, age 60), Kar wap ho ke (female, age 35), Ah se che (male, age 22), So har pe ye (female, age 18), Sun e ke (male, age 49). Remarks: "Emigrated from the Creek Nation, alabama, to Texas, in or about 1811, and from Texas to the Creek Nation, I.T. in 1843." Heir: Sun e ke.*

211. ***Sart ho ye che*** *(female, age 50) 4 members consisting of In no che (female, age 23), Sim mis se (female, age 35), Hul ho ke (female, age 70). Remarks: "Emigrated from the Creek Nation, alabama, to Texas, in or about 1811, and from Texas to the Creek Nation, I.T. in 1843." Heir: Susie.*

212. ***Mar tol lar*** *(male, age 50) 9 members consisting of Milly (female, age 78), Annie (female, age 67), Wal ta (male, age 71), Jimmy (male, age 45), Sin se (male, age 40), Jo (male, age 18), Willis (male, age 16), Tal loaf Harjo (male, age 40). Remarks: "Emigrated from the Creek Nation, alabama, to Texas, in or about 1811, and from Texas to the Creek Nation, I.T. in 1843."*

213. ***Billy*** *(male, age 48) 8 members consisting of Caesar (male, age 50), Ma*

lee (female, age 43), To yer ker pe (male, age 60), Yon thle ke (female, age 41), Eufaula Harjo (male, age 39), Sam sey (male, age 27), Sar ne (male, age 40). Remarks: "Emigrated from the Creek Nation, alabama, to Texas, in or about 1811, and from Texas to the Creek Nation, I.T. in 1843." Heir: Sar ne.

214. ***Ar lin ger*** *(male, age 40) 2 members consisting of Yoak po ka (female, age 45). Remarks: "Emigrated from the Creek Nation, alabama, to Texas, in or about 1811, and from Texas to the Creek Nation, I.T. in 1843." Heir: Charles Jones.*

215. ***Char lar ke*** *(male, age 50) 3 members consisting of Bo loo (male, age 36), Hotulke Yoholo (male, age 28). Remarks: "Emigrated from the Creek Nation, alabama, to Texas, in or about 1811, and from Texas to the Creek Nation, I.T. in 1843." Heir: War near ye.*

216. ***Sall ley*** *(male, age 40) 4 members consisting of Billy (male, age 35), Ma lin (female, age 50), Ar par le Harjo (male, age 40). Remarks: "Emigrated from the Creek Nation, alabama, to Texas, in or about 1811, and from Texas to the Creek Nation, I.T. in 1843." Heir: Ar par le Harjo.*

217. ***Se you ke*** *(female, age 60) 7 members consisting of Sar to se che (male, age 70), Ar cher (male, age 40), Mikey (male, age 41), Ar way (female, age 45), Ar sar wa (female, age 21), Te war ho ye (female, age 35). Remarks: "Emigrated from the Creek Nation, alabama, to Texas, in or about 1811, and from Texas to the Creek Nation, I.T. in 1843." Heir: Te war ho ye.*

218. ***Ar thlun Harjo*** *(male, age 50) 10 members consisting of Narke (male, age 20), Lo char Yoholo (male, age 35), Qus ke (female, age 18), Tar ke (female, age 28), Sar thlar he che (female, age 33), Se he che (male, age 22), No ke che (male, age 25), Se le sar (female, age 10), Mar le (male, age 70). Remarks: "Emigrated from the Creek Nation, alabama, to Texas, in or about 1811, and from Texas to the Creek Nation, I.T. in 1843." Heir: Mar le.*

219. ***So te che*** *(female, age 45) 6 members consisting of Billy (male, age 35), Tomme (male, age 18), Tar lar we lub bee (male, age 40), Ben ne (male, age 70), Pars coaf Harjo (male, age 72). Remarks: "Emigrated from the Creek Nation, alabama, to Texas, in or about 1811, and from Texas to the Creek Nation, I.T. in 1843." Heir: Tie che.*

220. ***Par he che*** *(male, age 60) 5 members consisting of Jackson (male, age 21), Char le che (male, age 40), Os ho ke (female, age 55), Tom Emarthlo che (male, age 40). Remarks: "Emigrated from the Creek Nation, alabama, to Texas, in or about 1811, and from Texas to the Creek Nation, I.T. in 1843."*

221. ***War lin te*** *(male, age 35) 6 members consisting of Hoke te larne (female, age 18), Loniza (female, age 50), Tom me (male, age 27), Do ce na (male, age 25), Hotulke Yoholo (male, age 37). Remarks: "Emigrated from the Creek Nation, alabama, to Texas, in or about 1811, and from Texas to the Creek Nation, I.T. in 1843." Heir: Hotulke Yoholo.*

222. ***So we na*** *(male, age 25) 8 members consisting of Polly (female, age 70), Sallie (female, age 50), Me la yo che (female, age 22), Wash lear (male, age 60), Tor tues (male, age 40), Flarn soc kis (female, age 35), Tus ke he ne har (male, age 35). Remarks: "Emigrated from the Creek Nation, alabama, to Texas, in or about 1811, and from Texas to the Creek Nation, I.T. in 1843." Heir: Tus ke he ne har.*

223. ***Se har ye*** *(female, age 35) 7 members consisting of Sar fut charge (female, age 30), Im me yar che (female, age 22), Lucy (female, age 27), Ohe e kar (female, age 25), Micco (male, age 18), Hotulke Fixico (male, age 40). Remarks: "Emigrated from the Creek Nation, alabama, to Texas, in or about 1811, and from Texas to the Creek Nation, I.T. in 1843." Heir: Hotulke Fixico.*

224. ***Se me har ke*** *(female, age 40) 10 members consisting of Is se mo (male, age 30), Ful che ye (female, age 32), Ko nar ye (female, age 18), Tom me (male, age 12), Che thlic nar (male, age 70), Kan tar ye (female, age 22), War sar se (female, age 70), E to we lar ke (female, age 60), Ho mar te Harjo (male, age 32). Remarks: "Emigrated from the Creek Nation, alabama, to Texas, in or about 1811, and from Texas to the Creek Nation, I.T. in 1843." Heir: Ho mar te Harjo.*

225. ***Ar se he*** *(female, age 35) 1 member. Remarks: "Emigrated from the Creek Nation, alabama, to Texas, in or about 1811, and from Texas to the Creek Nation, I.T. in 1843." Heir: Daniel.*

226. ***Ke nar te*** *(male, age 75) 6 members consisting of Se he che pe (male, age 38), Is wi ke (female, age 40), Tar hui na (male, age 26), Kotchar Harjo (male, age 35), Sar cui ho ke (female, age 40). Remarks: "Emigrated*

from the Creek Nation, alabama, to Texas, in or about 1811, and from Texas to the Creek Nation, I.T. in 1843." Heir: Sar cui ho ke.

227. *[Illegible]* ***car Harjo*** *(male, age 28) 1 member. Remarks: "Emigrated from the Creek Nation, alabama, to Texas, in or about 1811, and from Texas to the Creek Nation, I.T. in 1843." Heir: No cose Yoholo of Tuckabatchee.*

Creeks Accidentally Omitted from Both Rolls

228. **William B. Crabtree** (male, no age given) 2 members consisting of Pricilla Crabtree (female, age 59). William (1817–1882) and Pricilla Crabtree (née McGirth, b. ca. 1815) do not appear on either list, but proof of their emigration is shown in sworn statements accompanying the Stidham roll. In November 1886 Pricilla Crabtree testified that she and her husband, William, emigrated from Alabama and arrived in Indian territory (residents of Eufaula) in 1874 or 1875 after "having stopped on the way several years." The son of an Irishman, William Crabtree moved from Alabama to McKinney Bayou, Miller County, Arkansas, in 1837. He served in the Mexican-American War before emigrating to the Creek Nation and becoming an extensive slave trader (purchasing slaves in Indian territory then carrying them to the South for sale). William had nine children, including: Susan (b. 1841), William Frentin (1846–1900), and James II (b. 1849). Crabtree was described as "a fine-looking man, six feet high and weighed 220 pounds." He died of kidney disease in the fall of 1882 at Eureka Springs, Arkansas.[66]

229. **Chullo** (female, age 30) 3 members consisting of Ok lar ne (female, age 8) and Top pot te tar kee (male, age 6). Jane o chee testified that Chullo and her family left with her family from Alabama in the fall of 1836 and arrived in Indian territory toward the spring of 1837.[67]

230. **Sar pa we** (male, no age given) 5 members consisting of It chas war che (male, no age given), Se yar par ho ye (female, no age given), and Tar ho si che (male, no age given). See no. 133. According to testimony, this family moved first to Texas before settling in the Indian territory.[68]

231. **A. J. Doyle** (male, no age given) 1 member. It is unclear if this is

Archie Doyle (see no. 74, this roll). G. W. Stidham testified in 1886 that Doyle "emigrated himself in 1836."[69]

232. **Kibto** (male, age over 13) 1 member. Emigrated in company with Hillabee Harjo (no. 69) and Ho yar ne cher (no. 71) and their families, with James Island. Kibto (b. after 1826) claims he emigrated in 1839.[70]

233. **John S. Porter** (male, age 21) 1 member. Born ca. 1808, Porter emigrated to Indian territory in 1829.[71]

234. **Samuel C. Brown** (male, no age given) 1 member. "Emigrated from Alabama to Kentucky for education, & thence to the Indian Territory reaching there in 1834." According to John McIntosh (b. ca. 1819), Samuel C. Brown and Goliah Harrod (no. 235), were students at the Choctaw Academy.[72]

235. **Goliah Harrod** (male, no age given) 1 member. "Emigrated from Alabama to Kentucky for education, & thence to the Indian Territory reaching there in 1834."[73]

NOTES

ABBREVIATIONS

ASP-MA	*American State Papers: Documents, Legislative and Executive of the Congress of the United States*, vols. 6–7: *Military Affairs*
Blount-ADAH	Richard Blount Journal, Alabama Department of Archives and History
CGS-IRW	Files of the Office of the Commissary General of Subsistence, Indian Removal to the West, 1832–1840, University Publications of America, Bethesda MD
CRR-Misc.	Miscellaneous Creek Removal Records, ca. 1827–59, Record Group 75, Entry 300, NARA
HR 98	U.S. Congress, House Report 98, *Report of the Select Committee*
LR CA	Letters Received by the Office of Indian Affairs, Creek Agency, Record Group 75, Rolls 219–227, NARA
LR, CAE	Letters Received by the Office of Indian Affairs, Creek Agency Emigration, Record Group 75, Rolls 237–240, NARA
NARA	National Archives and Records Administration
NYPL	New York Public Library
RG 94, 159-Q	Records of the Adjutant General's Office, 1780s–1917, Record Group 94, Entry 159-Q, Records of Major General Thomas S. Jesup, NARA
SFOIA	Special Files of the Office of Indian Affairs, 1807–1904, Record Group 75, Microfilm M574, NARA
SIAC	Settled Indian Accounts and Claims, Record Group 217, Entry 525, NARA

INTRODUCTION

1. John Stuart (d. 1838). Born in Kentucky, Stuart served as private, 39th Infantry in 1814. His military history includes: promoted sergeant, 39th Infantry (1815); appointed second lieutenant, 7th Infantry (1819); promoted first lieutenant, 7th Infantry (1822); promoted captain, 7th Infantry (1828); Fort Gibson, Indian

territory (ca. 1824–33); at Fort Smith, Arkansas Territory (1833–34); at Fort Coffee, Indian territory (1834–38); engaged in establishing Camp Illinois, Indian territory (1838); died 8 December 1838 at Camp Illinois, Indian territory. Foreman, "Captain John Stuart's Sketch of the Indians," 667–72.

2. Stuart to Jones, 15 January 1837, Letters Received by the Office of Indian Affairs, Creek Agency Emigration (hereafter cited as LR, CAE), Roll 238, 19–22, Record Group 75, NARA.
3. Haveman, *Rivers of Sand*, 200–33.
4. Anderson, *Conquest of Texas*; Carson, "'The Obituary of Nations'"; Anderson, *Ethnic Cleansing and the Indian*; Madley, "Reexamining the American Genocide."
5. Kakel, *The American West and the Nazi East*.
6. See Prucha, "Andrew Jackson's Indian Policy"; Remini, *Legacy of Andrew Jackson*; Remini, *Andrew Jackson and His Indian Wars*.
7. Haveman, *Rivers of Sand*, xv. See also Bowes, *Land Too Good for Indians*, 3–18.

1. THE FIRST MCINTOSH PARTY

1. William McIntosh (1778–1825). Born in the Creek town of Coweta, McIntosh was the son of Captain William McIntosh, a loyalist British officer during the American Revolution and a Coweta woman from the Wind clan. McIntosh, commanding Creek warriors as a major and then as brigadier general, fought on the side of Andrew Jackson during the first Creek War and First Seminole War. McIntosh later became speaker of the Lower Towns, and the fifth ranking member of the Creek National Council. McIntosh was also closely involved in Creek land cessions in Georgia in 1805, 1814, 1818, and 1821. Despite a law passed prohibiting the cession of land without National Council approval, McIntosh agreed to ceded large amounts of Creek land in Georgia and Alabama in the 1825 Treaty of Indian Springs. This decision ultimately cost him his life, and McIntosh was executed on 30 April 1825. Green, *Politics of Indian Removal*, 54–56; Frank, "The Rise and Fall of William McIntosh," 18–48.
2. Green, *Politics of Indian Removal*, 69–97.
3. Haveman, *Rivers of Sand*, 42–57. Slavery had long been a feature of Creek Indian society. By the late eighteenth century almost all slaves were black. Wealthy Creeks like William McIntosh lived on southern-style plantations and had dozens of slaves to do their bidding. Snyder, "Conquered Enemies"; Snyder, *Slavery in Indian Country*; Braund, "Creek Indians, Blacks, and Slavery"; Littlefield, *Africans and Creeks*, 100–2.
4. Cantonment Gibson was constructed in 1824 as a replacement for Fort Smith (in present-day Arkansas). The garrison was located on the Grand River in present-day Oklahoma and served to protect the frontier as the United States commenced moving eastern Indians to Indian territory. Cantonment Gibson became an official fort in 1832. Agnew, *Fort Gibson*.

5. For more on the first McIntosh party emigration, see Haveman, *Rivers of Sand*, 42–57; Haveman, "'With Great Difficulty and Labour.'"
6. David Brearley (1780–1837). Born in New Jersey, Brearley was appointed captain, Light Dragoons, in 1808. His civil and military history includes: resigned U.S. Army (1811); rejoined U.S. Army and appointed lieutenant colonel, 15th Infantry (1812); colonel, 15th Infantry (1813); in War of 1812, being engaged in the defense of New York harbor and the Narrows, New York (1814); disbanded and honorably discharged (1815); reinstated as lieutenant colonel and brevet colonel, 7th Infantry (1816); colonel, 7th Infantry (1817); in Florida, being engaged in First Seminole War (1817–18); at Fort Scott, Florida, having been tried and acquitted in a general court martial (1818); resigned (1820); appointed U.S. Indian agent to the western Cherokees and Quapaws; opened the first store at Dardanelle (along with his brothers Charles and Pearson) that catered to the Indian market (1820); U.S. agent for McIntosh party (1826–29); engaged in conducting first McIntosh party west (1827–28); engaged in conducting second McIntosh party west (1828); fired as U.S. agent to the western Creeks (1829); died at Dardanelle, Arkansas, December 1837. Hamersly, *Complete Regular Army Register*, 317; Gardner, *A Dictionary of All Officers*, 82; Heidler and Heidler, *Old Hickory's War*, 91, 123–25, 132, 192; *Biographical and Historical Memoirs of Western Arkansas*, 125; *New York City and Vicinity*, 1:108, 2:138; Moser et al., eds., *Papers of Andrew Jackson*, vol. 5: *1821–1824*, 218n5; Cooley et al., *Genealogy of Early Settlers in Trenton and Ewing*, 13–16; James, *The Raven*, 111–12.
7. Dr. William Lewis Wharton (d. 1846). Born in Washington DC, Wharton was appointed assistant surgeon, U.S. Army Medical Department in 1828. His military history includes: at Fort Mitchell, Alabama (ca. 1828–34); at Fort Moultrie, South Carolina (1835); at Fort Johnston, North Carolina (1835–36); major and surgeon, U.S. Army Medical Department (1837); at Fort Leavenworth, Kansas (ca. 1842–44); at Fort Jesup, Louisiana (ca. 1844–45); died at Port Lavaca, Texas, 4 October 1846. Heitman, *Historical Register*, 1:1022; Gardner, *A Dictionary of All Officers*, 479; Hamersly, *Complete Regular Army Register*, 851; *ASP-MA*, 5:278, 6:35, 6:211; *Register of the Army*, 1844–46; *Army and Navy Chronicle*, 22 January 1835; 20 August 1835.
8. Dr. John Walker Baylor, Sr. (1782–1835). Born in Virginia, Baylor was appointed assistant surgeon, U.S. Medical Department in 1824. His military history includes: dismissed (1825); reinstated (1825); at Fort Gibson, Indian territory (1826–33); Jefferson Barracks, Missouri (1833); dropped (1833); died near Natchez, Mississippi, 1835. Heitman, *Historical Register*, 1:201; Hamersly, *Complete Regular Army Register*, 288; *ASP-MA*, 4:209, 4:261; Feller et al., *The Papers of Andrew Jackson*, 7:349n2; Gardner, "The Lost Captain," 217–49.
9. Meserve, "The MacIntoshes"; Bonner, *Georgia's Last Frontier*, 8–9, 49; O'Beirne and O'Beirne, *Indian Territory*, 194–95; McCoy, *Annual Register of Indian Affairs*,

20; Declaration of western Creeks, Settled Indian Accounts and Claims (hereafter cited as SIAC), Agent (Kendall Lewis), Account (18,271), Year (1834), Record Group 217, Entry 525, NARA; Current-Garcia and Hatfield, eds., *Shem, Ham, and Japheth*, 44; Levasseur, *Lafayette in America*, 76; List of signers to the treaty at Indian Springs, HR 98, 255. Chilly is shortened from "Chillicothe." See Smithers and Newman, *Native Diasporas*, 440n39.

10. Thelma Nolan Cornfeld, unpublished manuscript, Muscogee (Creek) Nation Library, Okmulgee OK.
11. "Law menders" was the name for the Creek police force. It was created with the encouragement of Creek agent Benjamin Hawkins (1754–1816; agent 1796–1816) and was designed to take law and order out of the hands of the clans and give it to the Creek National Council. Green, *Politics of Indian Removal*, 37.
12. Kappler, *Indian Affairs*, 2:214–17; List of signers to the treaty at Indian Springs, U.S. Congress, House Report 98, *Report of the Select Committee of the House of Representatives, to Which Were Referred the Messages of the President U.S. of the 5th and 8th February, and 2d March, 1827*, Serial 161, 255 (hereafter cited as HR 98); Enclosure No. 1, HR 98, 565.
13. Kappler, *Indian Affairs*, 2:214–17; Receipt of Brearley, 19 April 1827, SIAC, Agent (Brearley), Account (14,487), Year (1830), NARA; Haveman, "'With Great Difficulty and Labour'"; List of signers to the treaty at Indian Springs, HR 98, 255.
14. Journal kept by Richard Blount while serving on the Georgia-Alabama Boundary Survey Commission, July 17 to 26, 1826, Richard A. Blount Papers, Alabama Department of Archives and History, Montgomery AL (hereafter cited as Blount-ADAH).
15. Enclosure No. 1, HR 98, 565.
16. Receipt of Brearley, 19 April 1827, SIAC, Agent (Brearley), Account (14,487), Year (1830), NARA. Affidavit of Nichols, 30 June 1825, HR 98, 426–27.
17. Receipt of Brearley, 19 April 1827, SIAC, Agent (Brearley), Account (14,487), Year (1830), NARA.
18. Enclosure No. 1, HR 98, 565; Kappler, *Indian Affairs*, 2:214–17; List of signers to the treaty at Indian Springs, HR 98, 255.
19. Affidavit of Hambly, 4 July 1825, HR 98, 393–99; United States to Daniel Perryman, SIAC, Agent (Crowell), Account (15,814), Year (1831), NARA.
20. Green, *Politics of Indian Removal*, 96–99; HR 98, 338; Enclosure No. 3, HR 98, 259–63; Pickett, "The Death of McIntosh, 1825"; Valuation of Improvements, Special Files of the Office of Indian Affairs, 1807–1904 (hereafter cited as SFOIA), SF 207, Roll 61, 570–83, Record Group 75, Microfilm M574, NARA; Peggy and Susannah McIntosh to Campbell and Meriwether, 3 May 1825, Letters Received by the Office of Indian Affairs, Creek Agency (hereafter cited as LR CA), Roll 219, 636–38, Record Group 75, NARA. Haveman, *Rivers of Sand*, 57, 130–31, 270–71, 287.

21. Explanatory memorandum HR 98, 573; Saunt, *Black, White, and Indian*, 15, 34; Swanton, *History*, 259n10; SFOIA, SF 136, Roll 27, 1043.
22. Journal, June 26 to July 6, 1826, Blount-ADAH; Enclosure no. 2, HR 98, 566; Current-Garcia and Hatfield, eds., *Shem, Ham, and Japheth*, 99.
23. Journal, June 26 to July 6, 1826, Blount-ADAH; Enclosure No. 2, HR 98, 566. Lewis McIntosh, William McIntosh's son with his wife Peggy, was also known as "Interfleckey" or "Interlifkey" McIntosh, although James C. Bonner notes that Lewis McIntosh died at Lockchau Talofau at age fifteen. The name "Interlifkey McIntosh" appears with other McIntosh party members in an 1825 letter. Bonner, *Georgia's Last Frontier*, 8; Creeks to Gaines, 18 June 1825, HR 98, 596–98.
24. Woodward, *Woodward's Reminiscences*, 61–62; Rogers to the Secretary of War, 27 February 1829, SIAC, Agent (Rogers), Account (14,999), Year (1831), NARA; Declaration of western Creeks, SIAC, Agent (Kendall Lewis), Account (18,271), Year (1834), NARA; Kappler, *Indian Affairs*, 2:214–17; List of signers to the treaty at Indian Springs, HR 98, 255.
25. Meserve, "The Perrymans." George Catlin wrote that Benjamin and Samuel Perryman were brothers. Catlin, *Catlin's Notes of Eight Years' Travels*, 1:276.
26. Pickett, *History of Alabama*, 2:315; Woodward, *Woodward's Reminiscences*, 83; Claiborne, *Life and Times of Gen. Sam. Dale.*
27. Meserve, "The Perrymans," 166–84; Debo, *Road to Disappearance*, 117; Grant Foreman, *Advancing the Frontier*, 141–42; Barclay, *Early American Methodism*, 2:197. There was a James Perryman educated at Union Mission in Indian territory who served as interpreter to Presbyterian missionary John Fleming before becoming a Baptist pastor in Indian territory. Perryman aided in the translation of Ephesians, Titus, James, and part of the Book of Acts into the Muskogean language as well as the first Christian primer, *I stutsi in Naktsokv*—The Child's Book. Missionaries described Perryman as "'an excellent interpreter, a good preacher, deeply pious, and withal much beloved, and very popular in the nation.'"
28. Meserve, "The Perrymans," 166–84; Tomer and Brodhead, eds., *A Naturalist in Indian Territory*, 136–37; Saunt, *Black, White, and Indian*, 169–70.
29. Meserve, "The Perrymans," 166–84; Richard A. Blount, who served on the Georgia-Alabama Boundary Survey Commission, encountered a Henry Perryman in 1826, although it is unclear if it is the same one listed on the roll. The Perryman Blount saw was a student at Asbury Mission School near Fort Mitchell in Alabama. During his encounter, Blount recorded the following: "Henry Parryman who in his prayer months ago, said J Christ died for all—Iste Hautkee or Iste Hadkee—Iste chartee & Iste Lustee—the white man, the red man—and the blackman—It is said he is a composition of the whole—and his hair rather exhibits the latter." Blount also noted that Perryman "sings well—His voice is strong and yet sonorous, and he appears pious." Journal, August 9 to 14, 1826, Blount-ADAH.
30. Enclosure no. 1, HR 98, 565; SFOIA SF 207, Roll 61, 306.

31. Enclosure no. 1, HR 98 565; List of signers to the treaty at Indian Springs, HR 98, 255.
32. McCoy, *Annual Register of Indian Affairs*, 20; Declaration of western Creeks, SIAC, Agent (Kendall Lewis), Account (18,271), Year (1834), NARA.
33. Enclosure no. 4, HR 98, 567; Declaration of western Creeks, SIAC, Agent (Kendall Lewis), Account (18,271), Year (1834), Record Group 217, Entry 525, NARA.
34. Enclosure no. 4, HR 98, 567.
35. Enclosure no. 4, HR 98, 567.
36. Enclosure no. 2, HR 98, 566.
37. Zellar, *African Creeks*, 43.
38. John Ridge, "The Cherokee War Path, 1836–1840," HM 1730, Huntington Library, San Marino CA; Carolyn Thomas Foreman, "The Cherokee War Path"; Grant Foreman, *Indians and Pioneers*, 234.
39. James Barbour (1775–1842). Born near Gordonsville, Orange County, Virginia, Barbour received no formal education although he studied under Presbyterian minister James Waddel at Gordonsville. His civil and political history includes: deputy sheriff of Orange County; admitted to Virginia bar (1794); served in Virginia House of Delegates (1798–1804, 1808–12); speaker of Virginia House of Delegates (1809–12); governor of Virginia (1812–14); U.S. Senate (1815–25) and engaged as chairman of Senate Committees on Military Affairs and Foreign Relations and on Committee of District of Columbia; secretary of war in John Quincy Adams administration (1825–28); minister to Great Britain (1828–29); Virginia House of Delegates (1830–31); president of the Virginia Agricultural Society; helped establish the Orange County Humane Society, for education of the poor; died at Barboursville, Virginia, 7 June 1842, at age 66. Lowery, *James Barbour*; Dodge and Koed, eds., *Biographical Directory of the United States Congress*, 607; Bell, *Secretaries of War*, 40.
40. Refers to the boundary line separating Arkansas Territory from Indian territory.
41. Agent, Indian Affairs.
42. The party took the following steamboats: *Fort Adams* from Montgomery to Mobile; *Columbia* from Mobile to New Orleans; *Catawba* from New Orleans to Dardanelle Rock. Receipts, SIAC, Agent (Brearley), Account (14,487), Year (1830), NARA.
43. New Orleans.
44. Dardanelle, Arkansas Territory.
45. Matthew Arbuckle (1778–1851). Born in Greenbrier County, Virginia, Arbuckle was appointed ensign, 3rd Infantry in 1799. His military history includes: first lieutenant, 3rd Infantry (1799); transferred to 2nd Infantry (1802); captain, 2nd Infantry (1806); major, 3rd Infantry (1812); lieutenant colonel, 3rd Infantry (1814); in Georgia, being engaged at the Battle of Fowltown (1817), and in Florida during the First Seminole War (1817); colonel, 7th Infantry (1820); at Fort Smith, Arkansas

(1822); at Fort Gibson, Indian territory (1824–34, 1835–41); brevet brigadier general, for ten years faithful service in one grade (1830); at Baton Rouge, Louisiana (1840s); commander, Seventh Military District, Fort Smith, Arkansas (1848); died at Fort Smith, Arkansas, 11 June 1851. Hamersly, *Complete Regular Army Register*, 263; Gardner, *A Dictionary of All Officers*, 43; Bearss and Gibson, *Fort Smith*; Ryan, "Matthew Arbuckle Comes to Fort Smith"; Frazer, *Forts of the West*, 116–18.

46. Steamboat *Courtland*. Receipt, SIAC, Agent (Brearley), Account (14,487), Year (1830), NARA.
47. The McIntosh party was settling on former Osage land. The cession referred to is found in the 1825 Treaty of St. Louis. Kappler, *Indian Affairs*, 2:217–21.
48. Brearley, not the Creek deputation, selected this location. The Creeks preferred the land between the Arkansas and Canadian rivers, but Brearley refused to provide provisions from that distance. Haveman, *Rivers of Sand*, 46.
49. Clermont II (also spelled Claremore II) was (probably) the son of a prominent Osage headman of the same name. By the end of the eighteenth century bands of Osages living on the Pomme de Terre, Niangua, Sac, and White rivers in Missouri and Arkansas coalesced around Clermont II ("Town Maker") and established villages on the Grand and Verdigris Rivers. These were the "Clermont bands" (also known as the "Arkansas bands" or "People of the Oaks") to whom Brearley refers. Socially, the Osages organized themselves into two divisions (moieties), each led by a *Ga-hi-ge* (chief). Clermont II was *Tsi-zhu Ga-hi-ge*—the chief of the sky moiety. Burns, *A History of the Osage People*, 30; Rollings, *The Osage*, 22–24, 199.
50. Tally (Deer with Branching Horns, or possibly *Ta-ha-ka-ha*—Antlered Deer) was *Hon-ga Ga-hi-ge* (chief of the earth moiety) and vice president of the Osage National Council, which was created by Major Matthew Arbuckle (the commander of Cantonment Gibson) and David Barber (the subagent for the Arkansas Osages) in 1824 as a mode of controlling the Osages in anticipation of moving eastern Indians onto their ceded land. Because the *Tsi-zhu Ga-hi-ge* was considered the dominant chief in Osage tradition, Clermont II served as the president of the Osage National Council. Tally had also served as the chief counselor to Black Dog (another Osage leader) and as the temporary head chief of the two Black Dog bands during a period when Black Dog was absent. Rollings, *The Osage*, 244–45n65, 253–56; Burns, *A History of the Osage People*, 17, 51–52, 63–64.
51. The Osages are a Dhegiha-Siouan speaking people who once lived along the lower Ohio River. Pushed west by powerful eastern nations in the early seventeenth century, the Dhegians splintered into autonomous groups—Quapaw, Kansa, Omaha, Ponca, and Osage—as they resettled west of the Mississippi. Oral tradition states that Osage social and political organization was created by the merging of five villages or subdivisions. By the end of the 1700s they consisted of three core groups: (1) the Little Osages (the northernmost group) occupied

the land between present-day Malta Bend and Glasgow, Missouri; (2) villages on the Osage River in Missouri; and a third group consisting of random bands that eventually coalesced around the headman Clermont II and lived on the lower Grand and Verdigris rivers in present-day Oklahoma. The McIntosh party encountered this third core group of Osages when they arrived at Chouteau's trading house in 1828. Burns, *A History of the Osage People*, 3–30; Rollings, *The Osage*, 1–7, 45–46; Mathews, *The Osages*.

52. These expressions of friendship did not last long. Thinning buffalo herds, harsh winters, land cessions, and encroaching Indian nations (including those immigrating from the east), put pressure on the Osages. To ameliorate their suffering, Clermont's band repeatedly raided the western Creeks' property. On 10 May 1831 a council was organized by agents and military personnel at Cantonment Gibson in which a punishment of up to thirty-nine lashings for stealing was implemented. This did little to stop the Osages, however, and by 1835 the Creeks estimated that they had lost $10,000 in property at the hands of the Osages. Haveman, *Rivers of Sand*, 163–64.

53. Brearley planned on moving the first party entirely by land, if possible. In a 3 August 1827 letter to Secretary of War James Barbour, Brearley writes: "The Calculations [for the cost] are founded upon the Supposition that the distance by land [from the Creek Nation to Cantonment Gibson] is 800 miles and that takeing into View all the Casualties incident to Such a movement they Will not average more than ten miles a day . . . although it is expected they Will perform the journey on foot, or by the aid of Such means as they Can Command, nevertheless it is Certain that a great portion of them have no means whatever, and that frequent Cases Will Occur when persons must be Carried or left On the road or the whole party detained." Brearley to Barbour, 3 August 1827, LR, CAE, Roll 237, 50–51.

54. Brearley was likely concerned about punctuality for the second party because the first McIntosh party was several weeks delayed in commencing their journey west. The appointed day for each camp to consolidate was initially 15 September, with departure scheduled for 1 October. The party, however, ran late in part because Chilly McIntosh, who had stopped at Kymulga and merged with the camp there, arrived at Harpersville sometime after the main party. Haveman, *Rivers of Sand*, 48.

55. John Crowell (1780–1846). Born in Halifax County, North Carolina, Crowell moved to Alabama in 1815 and served in the U.S. House of Representatives from Alabama Territory (1818–19) and Alabama (1819–21). Crowell was appointed Creek agent in 1821. During his time amongst the Creeks, Crowell redirected the flow of goods away from Coweta headman William McIntosh and toward his brother, Thomas Crowell's store, in the Creek Nation. Crowell was dismissed as agent by President Andrew Jackson in 1835, and died at Fort Mitchell, Alabama,

25 June 1846, at age 65. Dodge and Koed, eds., *Biographical Directory of the United States Congress, 1774–2005*, 899.

56. The 1826 Treaty of Washington lays out policies for emigration and emigrants, including:

Article 7: "The emigrating party shall remove within twenty four months and the expense of their removal shall be defrayed by the United States. And such subsistence shall also be furnished them, for a term not exceeding twelve months after their arrival at their new residence, as, in the opinion of the President, their numbers and circumstances may require";

Article 8: "An agent, or sub-agent and Interpreter, shall be appointed to accompany and reside with them. And a blacksmith and wheelwright shall be furnished by the United States. Such assistance shall also be rendered to them in their agricultural operations, as the President may think proper";

Article 9: "In consideration of the exertions used by the friends and followers of General McIntosh to procure a cession at the Indian Springs, and of their past difficulties and contemplated removal, the United States agree to present to the Chiefs of the party, to be divided among the Chiefs and Warriors, the sum of one hundred thousand dollars, if such party shall amount to three thousand persons, and in that proportion for any smaller number. Fifteen thousand dollars of this sum to be paid immediately after the ratification of this treaty, and the residue upon their arrival in the country west of the Mississippi"; and

Article 10: "It is agreed by the Creek Nation, that an agent shall be appointed by the President, to ascertain the damages sustained by the friends and followers of the late General McIntosh, in consequence of the difficulties growing out of the Treaty of the Indian Springs, as set forth in an agreement entered into with General [Edmund Pendleton] Gains, at the Broken Arrow, and which have been done contrary to the laws of the Creek Nation; and such damages shall be repaired by the said Nation, or the amount paid out of the annuity due to them." Kappler, *Indian Affairs*, 2:264–68.

57. Men of age who enrolled with the first McIntosh emigration were to receive a rifle, powder, blanket, knife, flints, lead, a beaver trap, and brass kettle. Estimate of Cost, LR, CAE, Roll 237, 52.
58. The second McIntosh party did not leave the Creek Nation until October 1828.
59. Horse-drawn wagons.
60. The steamboat *Facility* was captained by Virginia-born Phillip Pennywit (1793–1868). Eno, *History of Crawford County*, 101–3.
61. A trading house established at the Three Forks and operated by Auguste P. Chouteau. Foley and Rice, *First Chouteaus*; Hoig, *The Chouteaus*, 83, 103, 136.
62. The *Arkansas Gazette*, 13 February 1828, reported that Clermont also offered two of his daughters to Brearley.
63. Nathaniel Hale Pryor (1772–1831). Born in Amherst County, Virginia, Pryor

moved with his family to Jefferson County, Kentucky. Pryor was appointed volunteer sergeant on the Lewis and Clark expedition in 1803. His civil and military history includes: on Lewis and Clark expedition (1804–6); commissioned ensign, 1st Infantry (1807); second lieutenant, 1st Infantry (1808); resigned U.S. Army (1810); Indian trader and operator of lead-smelting furnace, Galena River, Illinois (1810–11); appointed second lieutenant, 24th Infantry, declined (1812); appointed first lieutenant 44th Infantry (1813); captain, 44th Infantry (1814); in War of 1812, being engaged at the Battle of New Orleans (1815); disbanded and honorably discharged (1815); licensed trader among Osage Indians (1819–31); appointed subagent for the Osage Indians (1830); died at Osage subagency, Arkansas Territory, 9 June 1831, at age 59. Heitman, *Historical Register*, 1:808; Gardner, *A Dictionary of All Officers*, 369; Morris, *The Fate of the Corps*, 197–98; Holmberg, *Dear Brother*, 137–38n17; Foreman, *Pioneer Days in the Early Southwest*, 38, 76–77, 196; Foreman, "Nathaniel Pryor," 152–63.

64. Auguste Pierre Chouteau (1786–1838). Born in St. Louis, Chouteau graduated from the United States Military Academy, West Point, New York, in 1806 (4th of 15) and was promoted to ensign, 2nd Infantry (1806). His military history includes: on the Southwest Frontier and threatened by Spanish forces in Texas (1806–7); aide-de-camp to Brigadier General James Wilkinson; resigned U.S. Army (1807); licensed trader in Indian territory (1808–38); U.S. commissioner to treat with Comanche Indians (1837–38); died at "La Saline," 25 December 1838. Although of limited military experience, Chouteau's nickname was "colonel." Cullum, *Biographical Register* (1868), 1:98. See also Foley and Rice, *First Chouteaus*; Christian, *Before Lewis and Clark*; Hoig, *The Chouteaus*.
65. Probably referring to his desire to commence the second McIntosh party in early March 1828.
66. It is unclear if Brearley meant actual presents or if he intended to say "presence."
67. Affobo Harjo, no. 71 on the first McIntosh party roll.
68. Hos pi tack Harjo, no. 49 on the first McIntosh party roll.
69. Alexander Lashley, no. 98 on the first McIntosh party roll.
70. Thomas Anthony, a subagent under Brearley.

2. THE SECOND MCINTOSH PARTY

1. Haveman, *Rivers of Sand*, 61–66.
2. *Cherokee Phoenix*, 5 November 1828; *Alabama Journal*, 31 October 1828.
3. Frank, *Creeks and Southerners*, 43, 92; Woodward, *Woodward's Reminiscences*, 54–55; United States Indian Department to Kendall Lewis, Record Group 75, Entry 300, Box 5, Receipt number 3; Collins, "A Swiss Traveler in the Creek Nation," 269; Abstract of Licenses Granted, LR CA, Roll 219, 92; Deposition of Kendall Lewis, SFOIA SF 136, Roll 27, 777; Hodgson, *Letters from North America*, 1:127–29,

134; Valuation of Improvements, SFOIA SF 207, Roll 61, 570–83; Declaration of western Creeks, SIAC, Agent (Kendall Lewis), Account (18,271), Year (1834), NARA; Creeks to Brearley, 3 June 1828, LR, CAE, Roll 237, 154–56.

4. Creek self-emigration claims, SFOIA SF 285, Roll 77, 6–7, 27, 30–31, 100–1, 103, 109–10; Affidavit of Samuel Sells, 28 June 1825, HR 98, 428–29; Major Andrews' Report to the Secretary of War, HR 98, 305–47.
5. Creeks to Brearley, 3 June 1828, LR, CAE, Roll 237, 154–56.
6. Kappler, *Indian Affairs*, 2:214–17; List of signers to the treaty at Indian Springs, HR 98, 255.
7. Thelma Nolan Cornfeld, unpublished manuscript, Muscogee (Creek) Nation Library, Okmulgee OK (hereafter cited as Cornfeld manuscript).
8. Cornfeld manuscript.
9. Abstract of Licenses Granted, LR CA, Roll 219, 92; SFOIA, SF 136, Roll 27, 784.
10. Meserve, "The Perrymans," 166–84.
11. Woodward, *Woodward's Reminiscences*, 46; Hiern to Reynolds, 30 January 1839, LR, CAE, Roll 239, 515.
12. Testimony of Reed, 18 May 1828, LR CA, Roll 221, 750; Shorter to Scott et al., 1 March 1835, LR, CAR, Roll 243, 929–30.
13. Cornfeld manuscript; Receipts SIAC, Agent (Brearley), Account (14,487), Year (1830), NARA.
14. Cornfeld manuscript; Testimony of Berryhill, 18 May 1828, LR CA, Roll 221, 752.
15. Cornfeld manuscript; Anthony to Brearley, 23 March 1829, LR, CAE, Roll 237, 303–4.
16. Cornfeld manuscript. See also Affidavits of John and Andrew Berryhill, HR 98, 427–28.
17. Anthony to Brearley, 23 March 1829, LR, CAE, Roll 237, 303–4.
18. Haveman, "'With Great Difficulty and Labour,'" 468; SFOIA SF 207, Roll 61, 398.
19. Cornfeld manuscript.
20. Cornfeld manuscript.
21. Cornfeld manuscript.
22. Cornfeld manuscript; Receipts SIAC, Agent (Brearley), Account (14,487), Year (1830), NARA.
23. Cornfeld manuscript; Memorial No. 81, Miscellaneous Creek Removal Records, ca. 1827–1859, Record Group 75, Entry 300, NARA; Testimony of John Reed, 18 May 1828, LR, CAE, Roll 221, 750.
24. Meserve, "The Perrymans," 166–84; Testimony of John Winslett, 21 December 1833, in *American State Papers*, vol. 6: *Military Affairs* (hereafter cited as *ASP-MA*), 6:453; Herring to Phagan, 4 June 1832, *ASP-MA*, 6:459–60.
25. Cornfeld manuscript; Receipts SIAC, Agent (Brearley), Account (14,487), Year (1830), NARA.
26. SFOIA SF 207, Roll 61, 424.

27. Affidavit of William Lott, 28 June 1825, HR 98, 432; Deposition of Haynes Crabtree, 4 July 1825, HR 98, 692–93; Haveman, *Rivers of Sand*, 18–19.
28. SIAC, Agent (Kendal Lewis), Account (18,271), Year (1834), NARA.
29. Grant Foreman, *Indian Removal*, 125; Milton to Cass, 18 June 1833, LR, CAE, Roll 237, 397–99.
30. The letter appears to have been altered later to read that all members of the McIntosh party, not just Chilly McIntosh, were invited back to the nation. Affidavit of John Owens, 2 July 1825, HR 98, 433–34; Affidavit of Samuel Sells, 2 July 1825, HR 98, 435.
31. Receipts SIAC, Agent (Brearley), Account (14,487), Year (1830), NARA; SFOIA SF 285, Roll 77.
32. Walker to McKenney, 3 March 1828, LR, CAE, Roll 237, 181–84; Receipts SIAC, Agent (Brearley), Account (14,487), Year (1830), NARA; SFOIA SF 285, Roll 77.Walker to McKenney, 8 March 1828, LR, CAE, Roll 237, 174–75; Hoole, ed., "Echoes from the 'Trail of Tears,' 1837" and "Echoes from the 'Trail of Tears,' 1837," part 2; Wright, *Creeks and Seminoles*, 313.
33. Ingersoll, *To Intermix With Our White Brothers*, 113–14.
34. Baird, ed., *Creek Warrior*, 19; Saunt, *Black, White, and Indian*, 15; SFOIA, SF 136, Roll 27, 782.
35. Saunt, *Black, White, and Indian*, 15, 44.
36. Saunt, *Black, White, and Indian*, 5.
37. Green, *Politics of Indian Removal*, 89; Meserve, "The MacIntoshes," 310–25; Meserve, "Chief Samuel Checote"; Grant Foreman, ed., *A Traveler in Indian Territory*, 121–22; List of signers to the treaty at Indian Springs, HR 98, 255.
38. Crowell to Barbour, 10 September 1827, LR CA, Roll 221, 248–49; Remarks, SIAC, Record Group 217, Entry 525, Agent (Crowell), Account (15,814-G), Year (1831), NARA; Frank, *Creeks and Southerners*, 118–19; Haveman, "The Indomitable Women of the Creek Removal Era, " 10–39.
39. Thomas Loraine McKenney (1785–1859). Born in Maryland, McKenney worked in the family business on the Eastern Shore until his father's death forced the sale of the business. Moving to Georgetown at twenty-three, McKenney worked in dry goods until the outbreak of the War of 1812, when he joined the army and subsequently served in a number of militias. In April 1816 McKenney was appointed superintendent of Indian trade. Although the War of 1812 had largely disrupted the Factory System, McKenney transitioned the department away from solely an economic concern to one that focused on all aspects of Indian life (he supported the 1819 Indian Civilization Fund Act, for example). Soon after the abolition of the Indian trade office in 1822, McKenney (through the connections with Secretary of War John C. Calhoun) became head of a new Indian affairs office in 1824 and served until he was dismissed by President Andrew Jackson in 1830. McKenney died in Brooklyn, New York, 20 February 1859, at age 73. Viola, "Thomas L. McKenney 1824–30"; McKenney, *Memoirs, Official and Personal.*

40. Tuskenehaw of Tuckabatchee. When Big Warrior died in 1825, Tuskenehaw became the principal headman of the Upper Creeks, a move that was unusual in that he was not chosen in the usual manner (through the matrilineal line) but was put in power by a few powerful men. Tuskenehaw was subsequently "broken" or removed from office, (after having been reinstated) on three occasions (1827, 1830, 1835). He opposed emigration and threatened to kill his brother-in-law William Walker (among others) for working as an emigration subagent. Tuskenehaw tried to stymie voluntary emigration in 1835 when he participated in a plot to trade valuable Creek reserves (assigned under the 1832 Treaty of Washington) for a plot of land owned by Walker just south of the Federal Road near Fort Hull, Alabama. Federal agents subsequently rejected this agreement. He also participated, albeit half-heartedly, in the Second Creek War. Green, *Politics of Indian Removal*, 108, 131–32; Ellisor, *Second Creek War*, 26–27; Haveman, *Rivers of Sand*, 131.
41. John Davis (1800–1840). Davis was a Creek man of African ancestry, probably from Weogufka, who was a converted Christian. He was a pupil of the Baptist missionary Lee Compere and educated at Withington Station. Davis was a proponent of voluntary emigration and had been threatened "'with death'" for trying to induce others to move west. Haveman, *Rivers of Sand*, 60–61; Frank, *Creeks and Southerners*, 91. According to John D. Benedict, *Muskogee and Northeastern Oklahoma*, 1:177, Davis was born in Tennessee and "captured by an American soldier in the War of 1812."
42. James Moore. See no. 84, second McIntosh party muster roll.
43. Thomas Triplett served as a subagent for Brearley.
44. See no. 15 on first McIntosh party roll and no. 32 on second McIntosh party roll.
45. Probably referring to Thomas Pidgeon and his son, Joseph Pidgeon, who deserted the camp. See no. 42, second McIntosh party roll.
46. Zachariah McGirth (b. 1770). Born in South Carolina, McGirth moved to the Creek Nation (living at various times at Tuckabatchee and the Tensaw). He married Vicey Cornells, Alexander McGillivray's widow, in 1794. McGirth escaped Fort Mims just moments before it was attacked on 30 August 1813. Waselkov, *A Conquering Spirit*, 56–59.
47. See no. 67, second McIntosh party roll.
48. Tuskenehaw.
49. This letter was transcribed in typeface on the microfilm roll.
50. Matthew Arbuckle and Chilly McIntosh helped construct the western Creek agency building, which was built on the eastern bank of the Verdigris River about three or four miles from the river's mouth, near a high sandstone bluff. This was near the highest point at which steamboats or keelboats could ascend the river, as there was a five- or six-foot fall in the river about seven hundred yards above. U.S Congress, House Report 87, Serial 190, 35–48. The original agency complex

consisted of two log cabins in the dogtrot style with a passage in between the two buildings, all under one roof. Sometime later the agency was expanded to include five rooms (one of which was an office), a kitchen, an outhouse, and crib surrounded by eighty acres of cleared land. Dawson to Crawford, 5 January 1843, LR CA, Roll 227, 46.

51. Luther Blake accompanied four Creek Indians—Coe Emathla, Tuskenehaw, and Choeste—to Indian territory via St. Louis in 1828. A fourth member, interpreter Harper Lovett, went as far as St. Louis before dying of measles. The party initially planned on leaving St. Louis sometime around August with delegates of Ottawas, Potawatomis, Chickasaws, and Choctaws, but the Chickasaws postponed the commencement until October. Once in Indian territory the Creek delegates did not do much exploring, choosing instead to remain at the western Creek agency visiting with the McIntosh emigrants (the exploratory party members were not associated with the McIntosh party) while the Chickasaws and Choctaws explored the region on their own. It was while they were visiting with the McIntosh party at the Creek agency that Brearley's land party arrived. McCoy to Porter, 29 January 1829, U.S, Congress, House Report 87, 6–24; Creeks to Adams, 22 January 1829, U.S. Congress, House Report 87, 5.

52. The 1828 Treaty of Washington, signed by the western Cherokees, in which they agreed to cede their domain in the Arkansas Territory for land farther west in present-day northeast Oklahoma. Unbeknownst to anyone at the time, the western Cherokees acquired land that had already been granted to the McIntosh party. Neither the Creeks nor the Cherokees were willing to concede the land, however, and the problem was exacerbated by the fact that Cherokee settlers had already moved into the Creek territory and established farmsteads. Although treaties signed at Fort Gibson with the western Creeks and western Cherokees in 1833 appeared to settle the controversy by adjusting the boundary lines, western Creek headman Roly McIntosh later complained that the redrawn boundaries were inaccurate. In 1842 he and other Creek headmen wrote to Washington and complained that they had "lost much country and suffer great wrong" at the hands of the surveyors. The Creeks received monetary compensation under a treaty signed in 1845. Kappler, *Indian Affairs*, 2:288–92, 385–91, 550–52; Creeks to Secretary of War, 15 January 1842, LR CA, Roll 226, 604–8; Hitchcock to Spencer, 9 April 1842, LR CA, Roll 226, 464–65.

53. Peter Buell Porter (1773–1844). Born in Salisbury, Connecticut, Porter graduated from Yale College (1791) and studied at the Litchfield Law School. His civil, political, and military history includes: law practice in Canandaigua, New York (beginning 1793); clerk of Ontario County, New York (1797–1804); New York state assembly (1802); lawyer in Black Rock, New York; U.S. House of Representatives (1809–13), having served on the New York State Canal Commission (1810–16); in War of 1812, being engaged as quartermaster general of New York Volunteers (1812–15), and in bloodless duel with General Alexander Smyth (1812), as major

general being engaged in the raid on Black Rock, New York (1813), commanded brigade of New York militia and Six Nations Indians in the Battle of Chippewa, Upper Canada (1814), the Battle of Lundy's Lane, Niagara Falls, Upper Canada (1814), and the Siege of Fort Erie, Upper Canada (1814), and the recipient of a gold medal under joint resolution of Congress "'with suitable emblems and devices' presented 'in testimony of the high sense entertained by Congress of his gallantry and good conduct in the several conflicts of Chippewa, Niagara and Erie'" (1814); U.S. House of Representatives (1815–16); secretary of state of New York (1815–16); U.S. commissioner appointed to survey U.S.-Canadian boundary under articles of the Treaty of Ghent; regent of the University of the State of New York (1824–30); New York state assembly (1828); U.S. secretary of war, and advocate of the removal of eastern Indians west of the Mississippi River (1828–29); presidential elector on Whig ticket (1840); died at Niagara Falls, New York, 20 March 1844, at age 70. Dodge and Koed, eds., *Biographical Directory of the United States Congress*, 1753; Bell, *Secretaries of War*, 42; Gardner, *A Dictionary of All Officers*, 364; Stagg, "Between Black Rock and a Hard Place."

3. THE THIRD VOLUNTARY PARTY

1. Emigrating Creeks to John H. Eaton, 12 April 1829, LR, CAE, Roll 237, 263–64; Creeks to Andrew Jackson, 14 August 1829, LR, CAE, Roll 237, 267–68.
2. O'Beirne and O'Beirne, *Indian Territory*, 397–98; Meserve, "The MacIntoshes"; Current-Garcia and Hatfield, eds., *Shem, Ham, and Japheth*, 110.
3. Samuel Checote (1819–84) Meserve, "Chief Samuel Checote," 401–9.
4. Testimony of Crowell, 14 November 1827, LR CA, Roll 221, 362; Frank, *Creeks and Southerners*, 38; Receipt of Abram M. Mordecai and Robert Grierson, SIAC, Agent (Crowell), Account (15,814), Year (1831), NARA.
5. Houston quoted in Grant Foreman, *Indians and Pioneers*, 260. John W. Flowers furnished goods to the second McIntosh party in 1828. Abstract of Disbursements by David Brearley, SIAC, Agent (Brearley), Account (14,487), Year (1830), NARA.
6. Thomas Crowell (d. 1835). Born in Halifax County, North Carolina, Crowell was a trader and ran a store at Fort Mitchell in the Creek Nation.
7. Luther Blake Blake was a licensed trader in the Creek Nation living on the Flint River reserve in Georgia prior to the Treaty of Indian Springs and had been among the Creeks since 1823. Affidavit of Blake, 19 July 1825, HR 98, 407–9; HR 98, 342.
8. Robison was from Columbus, Georgia, and served as physician to the western Creeks from August 1829 to December 1830. Robison married Elizabeth Reed, a Creek woman of mixed parentage from Thlobthlocco. Their first child, William, was born in Indian territory in 1833. O'Beirne and O'Beirne, *Indian Territory*, 255–58; U.S. Congress, House Report 30, *Alexander J. Robison*, 1.
9. Nathaniel F. Collins.
10. John Henry Eaton (1790–1856). Born near Scotland Neck, Halifax County,

North Carolina, Eaton attended the University of North Carolina at Chapel Hill (1802–4) before studying law and moving to Williamson County, Tennessee sometime around 1808. His civil, political, and military history includes: law practice in Franklin, Tennessee; served as a private with the western Tennessee militia in the War of 1812; served in Tennessee House of Representatives (1815–16); co-author of *The Life of Andrew Jackson, Major General in the Service of the United States* (1817); appointed to the U.S. Senate to fill the term of George W. Campbell after his resignation (1818–21); elected to U.S. Senate (1821–29); U.S. secretary of war (1829–31); resigned as secretary of war over controversy regarding his second wife Margaret O'Neale (June 1831); governor of Florida Territory (1834–36); minister to Spain (1836–40); died at Washington DC, 17 November 1856, at age 66. Dodge and Koed, eds., *Biographical Directory of the United States Congress*, 999; Bell, *Secretaries of War*, 44; Copeland, "Eaton, John Henry," 130; Ratner, *Andrew Jackson and His Tennessee Lieutenants*, 84; Marszalek, *Petticoat Affair*; Reid and Eaton, *The Life of Andrew Jackson*. See also Latner, "The Eaton Affair Reconsidered"; Lowe, "John H. Eaton, Jackson's Campaign Manager."

11. Neah Emathla was a Mile Chief (one of the ninety preeminent headmen who were assigned a mile-square reserve of land under the 1832 Treaty of Washington) from the Lower Creek town of Hitchiti. At some point in his youth he moved to Florida and served as a prominent headman among the Mikasuki band of Seminoles. Neah Emathla supported the British in the War of 1812, helped start the First Seminole War, and participated in the Second Creek War before he was captured on 14 June 1836. He was also the lead negotiator for the Florida Indians in the Treaty of Moultrie Creek in 1823. Florida Territory governor William DuVal declared that Neah Emathla was "'Uncommonly capable, bold, violent, restless, unable to submit to a superior or to endure an equal,'" while John B. Hogan reported that the headman had "a high reputation as an assassin." Neah Emathla was also a staunch opponent of voluntary emigration and in 1829 led an assault on a group of emigrants as they waited in camp at Fort Bainbridge in Alabama. Mahon, *History of the Second Seminole War*, 24, 29–50, 52–53; McReynolds, *The Seminoles*; Missall and Missall, *The Seminole Wars*; Haveman, *Rivers of Sand*, 75; Ellisor, *Second Creek War*, 32, 247; Hogan to Cass, 8 March 1836, *ASP-MA*, 6:751–53. See also Irving, "The Conspiracy of Neamathla."
12. First Seminole War (1817–18).
13. William Walker accompanied the water party as far as Little Rock before he was relieved by Luther Blake (who to that point had conducted the land party). Walker subsequently returned to Alabama to enroll more Creeks. Haveman, *Rivers of Sand*, 79.
14. Steamboat *Virginia*.

4. MCINTOSH'S AND HAWKINS'S PARTIES

1. Haveman, *Rivers of Sand*, 82–110; Haveman, "'Last Evening I Saw the Sun Set'"; Green, *Politics of Indian Removal*, 173; Ellisor, *Second Creek War*, 47–96; Young, *Redskins, Ruffleshirts, and Rednecks*, 73–113; Crowell to Cass, 25 January 1832, LR, CA, Roll 223, 113; Crowell to Cass, 29 February 1832, LR, CA, Roll 223, 117.
2. Haveman, *Rivers of Sand*, 114–15; Ellisor, *Second Creek War*, 81–82.
3. Haveman, *Rivers of Sand*, 116–18; Parsons to Herring, 7 June 1833, LR, CA, Roll 223, 1025–27.
4. John James Abert (1788–1863). Born in Frederick, Maryland, Abert graduated from the U.S. Military Academy, West Point, New York, in 1811 (19th of 19). Abert declined his appointment, resigned upon graduation, and entered civilian life as a counselor at law in Washington DC and in Ohio (1813–14). He served in the District of Columbia militia during the War of 1812, being engaged at the Battle of Bladensburg, Maryland (1814). He was reappointed in the U.S. Army with a rank of brevet major (staff) in the Topographical Engineers (1814). His military history includes: honorably discharged (1815); reinstated (1816); assistant in the geodetic survey of the Atlantic coast (1816–18); reconnaissance of East River, New York (1818); as superintending topographical engineer of the following surveys—Chesapeake Bay (1818), Dutch Island and the western entrance of Narragansett Bay, Rhode Island (1819), East River, New York (1819), Fall River, Massachusetts (1819), Louisville canal, Kentucky (1819), Mount Hope Bay, Newport Neck, Narragansett road, Rhode Island (1819), Cox's Head, Maine (1821), Patuxent River, Maryland (1824), Chesapeake and Ohio Canal (1824–25), in Maine (1826–27); brevet lieutenant colonel for faithful service, ten years in one grade (1824); head of topographical bureau, Washington DC (1829–61); U.S. commissioner in Indian removal (1832–34); in Creek country implementing 1832 Treaty of Washington (1832–33); with the Wyandot Indians, Ohio (1833–34); in command of Corps of Topographical Engineers (1838–61); colonel, Corps of Topographical Engineers (1838); member of the Board of Visitors to the U.S. Military Academy, West Point, New York (1842); retired from active service from disability resulting from long and faithful service (1861); member of the Société de Géographie of Paris, France; died 27 January 1863, Washington DC, at age 74. Cullum, *Biographical Register* (1891), 1:101–2; Heitman, *Historical Register*, 1:150.
5. Enoch Parsons (d. 1841). He was a lawyer, originally from Tennessee. McAdory, *History of Alabama*, 4:1323.
6. Jefferson Van Horne (ca. 1802–57). Born in Pennsylvania, Van Horne graduated from the U.S. Military Academy, West Point, New York, in 1827 (30th of 38) and was appointed brevet second lieutenant of Infantry (1827) and second lieutenant, 3rd Infantry (1827). His military history includes: frontier duty at Jefferson Barracks, Missouri (1827–29); at Fort Leavenworth, Kansas (1829); at Jefferson Barracks, Missouri (1829–30); on Red River, near Natchitoches, Louisiana (1830–31); at Fort Towson, Indian territory (1831–32); on commissary duty, subsisting

Indians removed to Indian territory (1832–39); first lieutenant, 3rd Infantry (1836); in Second Seminole War (1840–41, 1841–42); captain, 3rd Infantry (1840); at Fort Stansbury, Florida (1842–43); at Jefferson Barracks, Missouri (1843); sick leave (1843–44); frontier duty, Fort Jesup (Camp Wilkins), Louisiana (1844–45); in military occupation of Texas (1845–46); recruiting service (1846–47); in Mexican-American War, being engaged in the Battle of Tolome (1847), Battle of Paso de Ovejas, Mexico (1847), Skirmish of Ocalaca (1847), Battle of Contreras, Mexico (1847), Battle of Churubusco, Mexico (1847), Storming of Chapultepec, Mexico (1847), capture of Mexico City (1847)—promoted brevet major for gallant and meritorious conduct during Battles of Contreras and Churubusco (1847); at East Pascagoula, Mississippi (1848); frontier duty at San Antonio, Texas (1848–49); march to El Paso, Texas (1849); at Fort Bliss, Texas (1849–51); San Elizario, Texas (1851); Fort Fillmore, New Mexico (1851–52); recruiting service (1852–54); frontier duty at Fort Stanton, New Mexico (1855–56); at Albuquerque, New Mexico (1856–57); died at Albuquerque, New Mexico, 28 September 1857, at age 55. Cullum, *Biographical Register* (1868), 1:320–21; Heitman, *Historical Register*, 1:983.

7. Hallis Fixico, no. 13 on McIntosh's 1833 muster roll. Hugh Love was a Georgian who became a licensed trader in the western Creek Nation. He operated a store near the falls of the Verdigris, across the river from Auguste P. Chouteau's store. Mulroy, *Seminole Freedmen*, 107; Gregory and Strickland, *Sam Houston with the Cherokees*, 113–14; Grant Foreman, *Pioneer Days*, 77, 84n113, 107–8, 119–20, 193; Jesup to Bell, 9 June 1841, Records of the Adjutant General's Office, 1780s–1917, Record Group 94, Entry 159-Q, Records of Major General Thomas S. Jesup (hereafter cited as RG 94, 159-Q), Container 2, Folder: "Letters Received 1836–1841, Quartermaster," NARA.
8. Cholar Fixico, no. 9 on McIntosh's 1833 muster roll.
9. Billy Williams, no. 10 on McIntosh's 1833 muster roll.
10. Sin thee key, no. 12 on McIntosh's 1833 muster roll.
11. Isaac Pennington. Grant Foreman, *Pioneer Days*, 158.

5. THE FOURTH VOLUNTARY PARTY

1. Jackson was frustrated by the small emigrating parties and, in an attempt to put pressure on the headmen to move west, halted all federally funded emigrations in 1830. Jackson no doubt believed that starvation, white encroachment, and living under Alabama jurisdiction (which had been extended over the Creek Nation between 1827 and 1832) would create enough problems that it would force the chiefs' hand and compel them to agree to a mass voluntary emigration to Indian territory. Haveman, *Rivers of Sand*, 89–90, 116–17.
2. Cass to Hogan, 11 July 1834, Files of the Office of the Commissary General of Subsistence, Indian Removal to the West, 1832–1840, University Publications of America, Bethesda MD (hereafter cited as CGS-IRW), Roll 5, 45.

3. John Page (ca. 1797–1846). Born in Fryeburg, Maine, Page joined the army and was appointed second lieutenant, 8th Infantry in 1818. His military history includes: promoted first lieutenant, 8th Infantry (1819); transferred to 4th Infantry (1821); assistant commissary of subsistence (1823); brevet captain, for ten years' faithful service in one grade (1829); captain, 4th Infantry (1830); emigrating and disbursing agent in removal of the Choctaws (1833); conducted fourth voluntary emigrating party of Creek Indians to Indian territory (1834–35); as superintendent in the removal of the Creek Indians (1835–37); in Mexican-American War, being engaged in the Battle of Palo Alto, Texas (1846); died 12 July 1846 near Cairo, Illinois, from wounds sustained at the Battle of Palo Alto. An account of Page's wound was recorded by Second Lieutenant Ulysses S. Grant, who was standing a few feet away as artillery fire severed the head of an enlisted man and took off Page's lower jaw. In his *Personal Memoirs* Grant noted: "One cannon-ball passed through our ranks, not far from me. It took off the head of an enlisted man, and the under jaw of Captain Page of my regiment, while the splinters from the musket of the killed soldier, and his brains and bones, knocked down two or three others, including one officer, Lieutenant Wallen [Georgia-born, Henry D. Wallen],—hurting them more or less. Our casualties for the day were nine killed and forty-seven wounded." Severely injured, Page lived for over two months. He was taken to Point Isabel, Texas, then sent to New Orleans, where he met his wife (on 6 July) who had rushed from Baltimore to see him (she first went to Point Isabel before discovering Page had been sent to New Orleans). The two commenced ascending the Mississippi River on the steamboat *Missouri.* Page died on 12 July 1846 near Cairo, Illinois. Page County, Iowa, is named in his honor, and in 1904 Page had a battery named after him at Fort Dade, Florida. Hamersly, *Complete Regular Army Register*, 675; Gardner, *A Dictionary of All Officers*, 347; Grant, *Personal Memoirs*, 1:96; Haecker and Mauck, *On the Prairie of Palo Alto*, 44–45, 49–50; *Niles' National Register*, 8 August 1846; General Orders, No. 194, in *General Orders and Circulars, War Department, 1904*, 6–7; Leyden, *Historical Sketch of the Fourth Infantry*, 13.
4. Hogan to Cass, 24 July 1834, CGS-IRW, Roll 5, 47.
5. William John Beattie (1809–1837). Born in Ryegate, Vermont, Beattie moved to Alabama in the 1830s looking for business opportunities. He became a speculator in Creek Indian reserves after the signing of the 1832 Treaty of Washington and worked as an agent during the fourth voluntary emigrating party. Beattie later became a silent partner in J.W.A. Sanford & Company, a contracting firm hired by the federal government in 1835 to move Creek Indians at $20 per person. Beattie also accompanied the fifth detachment of Creeks west in 1835–36. When J.W.A. Sanford & Company reorganized under the new name Alabama Emigrating Company, Beattie again worked removing the Creeks during the coerced relocations of 1836–37. Beattie died at the mouth of the Arkansas River,

9 November 1837, at age 28, while helping conduct detachment 6 to Indian territory. Miller and Wells, *History of Ryegate, Vermont*, 284; Whalen, "A Vermonter on the Trail of Tears."

6. Page to Gibson, 13 May 1835, CGS-IRW, Roll 5, 654–55.
7. Estell to Hogan, 3 July 1835, *ASP-MA* 6:734; Conner to Hogan, n.d., *ASP-MA*, 6:734; Creek Self-Emigration Claims, SFOIA, SF 285, reel 77, 35, 96, 112, 119, 156, 162; Saunt, *Black, White, and Indian*, 44; SFOIA, SF 136, Roll 27, 1000.
8. *Niles' Weekly Register*, 24 January 1835.
9. Baird, ed., *Creek Warrior*, 19; Saunt, *Black, White, and Indian*, 15, 44.
10. Green, *Politics of Indian Removal*, 87, 124; Ellisor, *Second Creek War*, 72, 213; Haveman, "'Last Evening I Saw the Sun Set,'" 94.
11. Ellisor, *Second Creek War*, 72, 213–14, 327; Haveman, *Rivers of Sand*, 264.
12. Crowell to Marshall, 6 November 1829, SIAC, Agent (Crowell), Account (15,814), Year (1831), NARA; HR 98, 565; Haveman, *Rivers of Sand*, 21, 95.
13. Saunt, *Black, White, and Indian*, 5, 44.
14. George Gibson (1775–1861). Born in Spring Township, Pennsylvania, Gibson was appointed captain, 5th Infantry in 1808. His military history includes: promoted major, 7th Infantry (1811); in the War of 1812, being captured at the Battle of Queenston Heights, Upper Canada (1812); exchanged (January 1813); lieutenant colonel, 5th Infantry (1813); honorably discharged after regiment disbanded on first reduction of the army after the treaty of peace (1815); appointed colonel and quartermaster general, U.S. Army (1816); assigned to the Southern Division under Major General Andrew Jackson (1816); engaged in the First Seminole War, including at Fort Gadsden, Florida in defense of that garrison (1817–18); commissary general of subsistence with rank of colonel, U.S. Army (1818–61); brevet brigadier general for ten years faithful service in one grade (1826); brevet major general for meritorious conduct during War with Mexico (1848); died at Washington DC, 29 September 1861, at age 87. Heitman, *Historical Register*, 1:453; Henry, *Military Record of Civilian Appointments*, 1:22; Eicher and Eicher, *Civil War High Commands*, 253; Newell and Shrader, *Of Duty Well and Faithfully Done*, 109, 337n4; Roberts, *Memoirs of John Bannister Gibson*, 228–31; H. H. Hain, *History of Perry County, Pennsylvania*, 700; *Niles' Weekly Register*, 27 March 1819.
15. Tuckabatchee Harjo was a mile chief of Cusseta and a staunch opponent of emigration and removal. He was ultimately relocated west with detachment 5 in 1836 (see chap. 14).
16. Return Jonathan Meigs (1801–1891). Born in Winchester, Kentucky, Meigs was a lawyer practicing in Athens, Tennessee, when President Andrew Jackson tapped him to travel to the former Creek Nation to investigate the implementation of the 1832 Treaty of Washington. Meigs's presence in the Creek country was seen by many Creeks as a sign that he was there to restore reserves that were sold

(illegally or otherwise) to the original Creek owners. This was not the case, but it stalled emigration because many would-be emigrants waited, hoping Meigs would give them their land back. Wright, "Return Jonathan Meigs, 1801–1891," 28:125–28; Haveman, *Rivers of Sand*; Ellisor, *Second Creek War*, 99–100.

17. William Armstrong (1800–1847). Born in Tennessee, Armstrong was appointed superintendent of Indian affairs in the Western Territory and served as agent in the removal of the Choctaws. He died near Fort Towson, Indian territory, 12 June 1847. Foreman, "The Armstrongs of Indian Territory," 292–308.
18. Alexander H. Sommerville of Montgomery, Alabama, was an assistant agent during the fourth voluntary emigration. Sommerville served previously as an assistant agent in the removal of the Choctaws prior to 1834. In 1834 Sommerville was ordered to remove all white squatters who were illegally occupying Creek reserves and were considered "obnoxious to the Indians." Hill to Gibson, 12 September 1834, CGS-IRW, Roll 5, 166–68; Crawford to Cass, 2 March 1834, U.S. Congress, House Document 276, *Letter from the Secretary of War, Transmitting Documents in Relation to Hostilities of Creek Indians*, 115; Hook to Sommerville, 1 July 1833, U.S. Congress, Senate Document 512, *Correspondence on the Subject of the Emigration of Indians*, vol. 1, 280.
19. Mississippi Swamp about twenty-five miles west of Memphis.
20. Linens, cloth.
21. Disbursing agent.
22. Jacob Brown (1789–1846). Born in Charlton, Berkshire County, Massachusetts, Brown joined the U.S. Army as a private, 11th Infantry, in 1812. His military history includes: sergeant, 11th Infantry (1814); in War of 1812, being engaged in the Battle of Crysler's Farm, Upper Canada (1814); commissioned ensign, 11th Infantry (1814); third lieutenant, 11th Infantry (1814); in War of 1812 being engaged in the Battles of Chippewa, Upper Canada (1814), and Lundy's Lane, Niagara Falls, Upper Canada (1814); second lieutenant, 11th Infantry (1814); transferred to 6th Infantry (1815); appointed regimental quartermaster (1816–21); at Council Bluffs (1818–25); engaged in Yellowstone expedition (1819); first lieutenant, 6th Infantry (1819); captain, 6th Infantry (1825); on detached service at Little Rock, Arkansas Territory, being engaged at different times as principal disbursing agent, in speculating in commercial and agricultural land in Arkansas Territory, and as president of the Arkansas State Bank (1831–40); rejoined 6th Infantry (1840); major, 7th Infantry (1843); assigned as acting commander of 7th Infantry (1845); in Mexican-American War being assigned to Brigadier General Zachary Taylor's Army of Occupation (1846); at Fort Texas, Texas (1846); died 9 May 1846, at age 56, from infection caused by the amputation of his leg after explosion of Mexican shell during the defense of Fort Texas, 6 May 1846. Brownsville, Texas, is named after Jacob Brown. Heitman, *Historical Register*, 1:252; Cutrer, "Brown, Jacob," in *Encyclopedia of the Mexican-American War*,

1:91; Gardner, *A Dictionary of All Officers*, 88; Chance, ed., *My Life in the Old Army*, 310–311n32, 311n34.

23. Dr. John T. Fulton. Fulton was the brother of Arkansas Territory governor and U.S. Senator William Savin Fulton. He had a medical practice and ran a drug store in Little Rock and served at different times as a postmaster. In the 1830s Fulton became a removal agent for the Choctaws. Brown to Gibson, 19 October 1835, CGS-IRW, Roll 5, 288; Satz, *American Indian Policy in the Jacksonian Era*, 76.
24. John B. Hogan (d. 1845). Born in Virginia, Hogan was appointed ensign, 20th Infantry in 1812. His military history includes: at Flint Hill, Buffalo, New York (ca. 1812–13); promoted second lieutenant, 20th Infantry (1813); in War of 1812, being engaged in the capture of Fort George, Upper Canada (1813), and in the Siege of Fort Erie (1814); assigned assistant deputy quartermaster general with rank of captain (1813); major, deputy quartermaster general (1814); regiment disbanded and honorably discharged (1815); retained as paymaster, 7th Infantry (1817); transferred to 4th Infantry (1818); served in Florida under Andrew Jackson (1818); regiment disbanded and honorably discharged (1821); Alabama senator (1829–35); superintendent of Creek Indian removal (1835–36); engaged in investigating land frauds associated with 1832 Treaty of Washington (1835–36); adjutant and inspector general, Alabama Volunteers, being engaged in Second Creek War (1836); brigadier general, Alabama Volunteers (1836); customs collector, Mobile, Alabama (1836–41); died 17 May 1845. Gardner, *A Dictionary of All Officers*, 232; Heitman, *Historical Register*, 1:535; Hogan to Marcy, 7 April 1845, LR, CAR, Roll 248, 622–27. Hogan was born in Pennsylvania, according to *Register of All Officers and Agents, Civil, Military, and Naval, in the Service of the United States, on the Thirtieth September, 1835*, 85; Cutler and Hall, eds., *Correspondence of James K. Polk*, 9:126n2.
25. Page is likely referring to his experience as conductor of a party of Choctaws to Indian territory in 1833. Page to Gibson, 20 January 1834, CGS-IRW, Roll 5, 93–94.
26. Chilblains are skin ulcers caused by extreme cold.
27. The average cost per person of the first two McIntosh party emigrations was $43.58, while the third voluntary party averaged $21.22 per person. Here Page is noting that it cost upward of $60 just to get one Creek Indian as far as Little Rock. Herring to Cass, 4 March 1834, Letters Sent by the Office of Indian Affairs, Roll 12, 161–62.
28. Article 13 of the 1832 Treaty of Washington states: "There shall also be given to each emigrating warrior a rifle, moulds, wiper and ammunition and to each family one blanket." Kappler, *Indian Affairs*, 2:341–43.
29. This footnote appears in the documentation and refers to Page's 25 April letter, in which he reported that he was "well Convinced if we had attempted to have

Laid by in Consequence of the severity of the weather that one half would have died of that Complaint it proved so fatal with the inhabitants when I Called at a house and found almost Every member of the family down with this disease."

6. THE FIFTH VOLUNTARY PARTY

1. Haveman, *Rivers of Sand*, 127.
2. Hogan to Cass, 24 July 1834, CGS-IRW, Roll 5, 47 ("stupidly ignorant"); Hogan to Gibson, 18 October 1834, CGS-IRW, Roll 5, 52; Haveman, *Rivers of Sand*, 128.
3. Haveman, *Rivers of Sand*, 80; Contract of J.W.A. Sanford & Co., 17 September 1835, *ASP-MA*, 6:782–83; "A brief of the transactions connected with the formation of the Contract with the Alabama Emigrating Company for the removal and subsistence of Creek Indians, and other Contracts for subsistence and transportation subsequent thereto," SIAC, Agent (Reynolds), Account (1687), Year (1838), NARA; Iverson to Forsyth, 7 November 1834, LR, CAE, Roll 237, 430–34; Sanford & Co. to Gibson, 30 September 1835, *ASP-MA*, 6:753–54.
4. Letter to Hogan, 21 September 1835, *ASP-MA*, 6:777–78; Hogan to Gibson, 24 August 1835, *ASP-MA*, 6:738; Hogan to Gibson, 4 November 1835, *ASP-MA*, 6:744–45; Blue to Hogan, 13 July 1835, CGS-IRW, Roll 5, 562–63; Hunter to Hogan, 12 August 1835, *ASP-MA*, 6:739–40 ; Creeks to Jackson, 14 January 1836, LR CA, Roll 225, 38–41.
5. Haveman, *Rivers of Sand*, 140.
6. Edward Deas (ca. 1812–49). Born in South Carolina, Deas graduated from the U.S. Military Academy, West Point, New York, in 1832 (15th of 45) and was promoted brevet second lieutenant, 4th Artillery (1832). His military service includes: Black Hawk War, but "not at the seat of war" (1832); at Fort Gratiot, Michigan (1832–33); at Fort Hamilton, New York (1833–34); second lieutenant, 4th Artillery (1833); assigned to fifth voluntary party of Creek Indians (1835–36); first lieutenant, 4th Artillery (1836); assigned to detachments 3 and 4 of relocating Creek Indians (1836–37); appointed to remove party of Creek refugees from the Cherokee country (1837), and in removing Indians (1837–39); at Fort Columbus, New York (1839); at Camp of Instruction, near Trenton, New Jersey (1839); on the northern frontier during the Canada independence movement, Cleveland, Ohio (1839–40); recruiting service (1840); on special duty (1840–41); at Detroit, Michigan (1841); at Sackett's Harbor, New York (1841–42); at Fort Monroe, Virginia (1842–43); Carlisle Barracks, Pennsylvania (1843–44); Fort Monroe, Virginia (1844–45); engaged in the military occupation of Texas (1845–46); in Mexican-American War, being engaged in the Battle of Monterrey, Mexico (1846); quartermaster duty (1846–47); captain, 4th Artillery (1847); at Buena Vista, Mexico (1847–48); dismissed (April 1848) but reinstated at former rank (June 1848); drowned in the Rio Grande River, near Fort Ringgold, Texas, 16 May 1849, at age 37. Cullum, *Biographical Register* (1868), 1:404; Gardner, *A Dictionary of All Officers*, 144.

7. Dr. Burton Randall (1805–1886). Born in Maryland, Randall was appointed assistant surgeon, U.S. Army, in 1832. His military service includes: at Fort Jackson, Louisiana (1832–33); at Cantonment Cass, Indian territory (1833); at Fort Jackson and in Louisiana (to 1836); Fort Wood and New Orleans, Louisiana (to April 1836); hospital duty at Bay St. Louis, Mississippi (to October 1835); attending physician for fifth voluntary emigrating party of Creek Indians (to August 1836); at Washington DC (to October 1838); surgeon, U.S. Army (1838); at Philadelphia, Pennsylvania (to April 1839); in Florida, being engaged in the Second Seminole War (to March 1842); at Forts Stansbury and Pickens, Florida (to June 1842); at Jackson Barracks, New Orleans, Louisiana (to April 1843); at Fort Gibson, Indian territory (to January 1847); with the U.S. Army of Invasion and Occupation of Mexico (to July 1848); at Fort Barrancas, Florida (to September 1849); at Jackson Barracks, New Orleans, Louisiana (1850–53); at Fort Gibson, Indian territory (to August 1857); at Carlisle Barracks, Pennsylvania (to October 1861); hospital duty, Annapolis, Maryland (to July 1862); at Fort Hamilton, New York Harbor (to April 1866); brevet lieutenant colonel, U.S. Army, for faithful and meritorious service during the Civil War (March 1865); at Fort Trumbull, Connecticut (beginning September 1867); on sick leave (to September 1868); admitted to Government Hospital for the Insane, Washington DC (1878–86); died at Washington DC 8 February 1886, at age 81. Randall's son, John K. Randall, a lawyer and librarian at Baltimore's Mercantile Library committed suicide (at age 32, by shooting himself in the heart), 8 February 1886, upon hearing of his father's death. Dual funerals were held at St. Anne's Church, Annapolis, Maryland, 10 February 1886. Henry, *Military Record of Civilian Appointments*, 1:107; Randall to Hook, 11 October 1835, CGS-IRW, Roll 5, 695; U.S. Congress, House Report 2561, *Virginia Taylor Randall*, 49th Cong., 1st Sess., 1886, 1–2; *Army and Navy Journal: Gazette of the Regular and Volunteer Forces*, 13 February 1886; *Library Journal*, February 1886; *Maryland Medical and Surgical Journal*, 2:314; Memorandum of Expenses (Randall), SIAC, Agent (Page), Account (220), Year (1837), NARA.
8. Randall to Gibson, 8 November 1835, CGS-IRW, Roll 5, 689.
9. John William Augustine Sanford, Sr. (1798–1870). Born in Baldwin County, Georgia, Sanford attended Yale College before returning south and becoming engaged in agriculture. In 1834–35 he headed the John W.A. Sanford and Company, a private contracting firm hired to emigrate the Creek Indians to Indian territory. Sanford stepped down from the company to run for Congress and was elected a U.S. representative from Georgia (served 4 March 1835–25 July 1835), but stepped down before Congress convened. After the 1832 Treaty of Washington signing, Sanford became a certifying agent in Russell and Barbour counties in Alabama. Sanford served as major general during the Second Creek War and was later appointed Creek agent in Indian territory in 1837. He was

elected to the Georgia Senate (1837) but never took his seat, and later became the secretary of state of Georgia in 1841–43. Sanford died 12 September 1870 at Milledgeville, Georgia, at age 72. Dodge and Koed, eds., *Biographical Directory of the United States Congress, 1774–2005*, 1862; Ellisor, *Second Creek War*, 97, 110; Owen, *History of Alabama*, 4:1500–1; Boyd, "Creek Indian Agents, 1834–1874."

10. Alfred Iverson Sr. (1798–1873). Born in Liberty County, Georgia, Iverson was the son-in-law of former Georgia governor John Forsyth and was a lawyer and the editor of the *Columbus Sentinel* newspaper. He graduated from the College of New Jersey (Princeton University) in 1820, was admitted to the bar in 1822, and started his law practice in Clinton, Georgia. He was a member of the Georgia House of Representatives (1827–30) before moving to Columbus, Georgia, in 1830, and becoming a judge on the state superior court (1835–37) and a Georgia state senator (1843–44). He speculated in Creek lands under the 1832 Treaty of Washington and was a member of the notorious M. W. Perry & Company land company based in Columbus. He was a partner in John W.A. Sanford and Company as well as the Alabama Emigrating Company. On the eve of their relocation west in August 1836, Creek headmen signed a contract with the James C. Watson & Company in which they sold 656 half-sections of land that had been stolen by speculators. When a number of land buyers protested, arguing that they had purchased the reserves legally, Alfred Iverson provided legal representation for the Watson company against the claimants. Iverson served in the U.S. House of Representatives as a Democrat (1847–49), and as a judge on the state superior court (1850–54), before serving as a U.S. senator (1855–61). He was a pro-slavery, pro-states' rights secessionist (he resigned from the Senate when Georgia seceded from the Union). Iverson died in Macon, Georgia, 4 March 1873. Northen, *Men of Mark in Georgia*, 2:339–40; Duckett, *John Forsyth*, 6; Ellisor, *Second Creek War*, 118; List of Land Companies, CRR-Misc, Box 11, NARA; Young, *Redskins, Ruffleshirts, and Rednecks*, 88; Mellichamp, *Senators from Georgia*, 141–43; Dodge and Koed, eds., *Biographical Directory of the United States Congress, 1774–2005*, 1247.
11. John David Howell (b. 1810). Born in St. Luke's Parish, Beaufort District, South Carolina, Howell was a land speculator and ran a store in the former Creek Nation. He was described by Alfred Iverson as, "a young man living [at Columbus] not much known abroad, but highly respectable and an active business man." List of Land Companies, CRR-Misc, Box 11, NARA; Hogan to Cass, 8 March 1835, *ASP-MA*, 6:751–53; Owen, *History of Alabama*, 4:1591; Iverson to Forsyth, 7 November 1834, LR, CAE, Roll 237, 430–34.
12. Marshall replaced Samuel C. Benton, a founder of the company and one-time clerk to former Creek agent John Crowell, who stepped down due to illness. Despite his signature, Hogan argued that Marshall had a bond with members of the company "that they will keep him free from all expense and harm." Sanford

& Company, however, noted with regard to pecuniary liability that Marshall was "fully as responsible as Mr. Benton." Hogan to Gibson, 6 November 1835, *ASP-MA*, 6:746; Sanford & Co. to Gibson, 30 September 1835, *ASP-MA*, 6:753–54; Letter from Sanford & Co., 23 October 1835, *ASP-MA*, 6:754–55.

13. Luther Blake was a justice of the Inferior Court of Muscogee County, Georgia. He helped conduct the third voluntary party in 1829 and presided over a delegation of Creeks who visited the Indian territory in 1828. Blake and Howell owned a store together, and Blake was an important member of the company because of his alleged influence over the powerful Cusseta headman Neah Micco. Statement of Crowell, 14 November 1827, LR CA, Roll 221, 362; *Arkansas Gazette*, 1 July 1829, 15 July 1829, 22 July 1829; Hogan to Cass, 8 March 1835, *ASP-MA*, 6:751–53.
14. Stephen Miles Ingersoll (1792–1872). Ingersoll was physician and a land speculator (member of Michael W. Perry & Company). List of Land Companies, CRR-Misc, Box 11, NARA.
15. Also called the Florida Cracker Horse, Indian ponies were smallish in stature (with some breeds larger than others) and are believed to have descended from the Spanish horses brought to the Americas during the colonial period. Francis de Laporte, Comte de Castelnau (1812–1880), a London-born French naturalist, visited Florida in 1837–38 and noted that "the Floridian horse, such as it is today, and which is called generally Indian pony is small, long haired and bright eyed, lively, stubborn, and as wild as the Indians themselves; it has wonderful endurance of fatigue and hardship; it has a singular instinct in finding its way in the dense woods. Its food consists only of the high grass that covers the prairies and it does not require any care." See Comte de Castelnau, "Essay on Middle Florida"; Hendricks, *International Encyclopedia of Horse Breeds*, 16–17, 188.
16. The disbursing agent at Fort Gibson was Captain James R. Stephenson.
17. William C. Easton was a Maryland-born agent charged with correspondence and examination of all accounts and returns of agents involved in Choctaw removal in the early 1830s. By the time the John W.A. Sanford contract was negotiated, Easton served as the principal clerk in "the Emigration of Indians, under the direction of the Commissary General of Subsistence." Gibson to Cass, 25 August 1831, SD 512, 1:42; *Register of All Officers and Agents*, 84.
18. Massachusetts-born William Browne was one of four clerks who served directly under William C. Easton in Washington. *Register of All Officers and Agents*, 84.
19. "Osenubba Indians" is written directly above Kotchar Tustunnuggee's name, a reference to Cusseta (on Osenubba Hatchee or Tuckabatchee Harjo's Town), a town listed on the 1832 Creek census. Kotchar Tustunnuggee was from Coweta, and there is no Kotchar Tustunnuggee who appears on the Cusseta-Osenubba census. Osenubba Hatchee means "Moss Creek" in the Muskogean language. Journal, July 9 to 26, 1826, Blount-ADAH.
20. Haveman, *Rivers of Sand*, 34–35.

21. Journal (Deas), CGS-IRW, Roll 6, 33–55.

22. Hogan to Cass, 8 March 1836, *ASP-MA*, 6:751–53; McKenney and Hall, *History of the Indian Tribes of North America*, 2:23–24; List of Land Companies, CRR-Misc., Box 11, NARA; Fanning to Jones, 9 February 1837, RG 94, 159-Q, Container 21, Folder: "Letters, Reports from General Jesup to War Department Offices," NARA; O'Beirne and O'Beirne, *Indian Territory*, 33; Motte, *Journey into Wilderness*, 8.

23. Journal (Deas), CGS-IRW, Roll 6, 33–55.

24. Hogan to Gibson, 6 November 1835, *ASP-MA*, 6:746; Hogan to Gibson, 12 October 1835, *ASP-MA*, 6:741–42; Sanford & Co. to Gibson, 30 September 1835, *ASP-MA*, 6:753–54; Letter from Sanford & Co., 23 October 1835, *ASP-MA*, 6:754–55.

25. Uriah Blue (1775–1836). Born in Virginia, Blue was appointed second lieutenant, 8th Infantry in 1799. His military history includes: honorably discharged (1800); appointed second lieutenant, 2nd Infantry (1801); disbanded and honorably discharged (1802); appointed first lieutenant, 7th Infantry (1808); captain, 7th Infantry (1809); engaged in Creek War (1813–14); major, 39th Infantry (1814); in Florida, being engaged in commanding Choctaw warriors in the Battle of Pensacola (1814), and in scouring the swamps and bays of West Florida for fugitive Creek Indians with a force of mounted men (1814–15); disbanded and honorably discharged (1815); reinstated as captain, 8th Infantry to rank from 9 May 1809 and with brevet of major from 13 March 1814 (1815); resigned U.S. Army (1816); engaged as assistant to John B. Hogan in emigrating Creek Indians (1835); died at Mobile, Alabama, May 1836. Pickett, *History of Alabama*, 2:368; Thrapp, *Encyclopedia of Frontier Biography*, 1:129; Waselkov, *A Conquering Spirit*, 144, 149–52, 156, 192, 195; Rucker, "In the Shadow of Jackson", 325–38; Heitman, *Historical Register*, 1:226; Gardner, *A Dictionary of All Officers*, 73; Hamersly, *Complete Regular Army Register*, 97, 305; Quarterly Return, 30 June 1835, CGS-IRW, Roll 5, 539–40; Hogan to Page, 3 November 1835, CGS-IRW, Roll 5, 556–57; Coues, *The Expeditions of Zebulon Montgomery Pike*, xxviii.

26. No. 63 on Deas's muster roll.

27. Under Creek clan justice.

28. The Mulberry Fork is one of three forks (along with the Sipsey and Locust) that form the Black Warrior River.

29. See no. 13 and no. 79 on Deas's muster roll.

30. May also be misspelled "impassible."

31. Courtland was composed of "many large and elegant brick buildings." Anne Royall visited the town in June 1821 and noted that it was "now a considerable town, consisting of fine brick houses, was a cornfield 18 months ago, and the corn furrows are still visible in many parts of the town." LR CA, Roll 219, 226–34; Royall, *Letters from Alabama on Various Subjects*, 137.

32. The steamer *Alpha* was a 51-ton sternwheeler built at Rising Sun, Indiana in 1834–35. The vessel transported goods to and from Cincinnati, Ohio. By 1836

the *Alpha* was transporting goods from Portsmouth, Ohio (items that had come through the Erie Canal from New York City) to Cincinnati. The *Alpha* was later wrecked "somewhere in the Red River country." *History of Dearborn and Ohio Counties, Indiana*, 374–75; Autobiography of John H. Jones IU; Neville, *Directory of Tennessee River Steamboats*, 13; Banta, *The Ohio*.

33. Owens Island in the Tennessee River.
34. Many small and large businesses emerged along navigable rivers, all catering to passing steamboat traffic. Steamboats burned a considerable amount of wood, and landings appeared every four or five miles on the Mississippi River by the 1860s. Business owners also sold fresh water, fruits and vegetables, beef, and other rations to passing steamboats; see Gudmestad, *Steamboats and the Rise of the Cotton Kingdom*, 154.
35. The *Arkansas Gazette* reported that the boat was anchored in the river near Little Rock for about an hour. *Arkansas Gazette*, 12 January 1836.
36. Snags were trees that had fallen into the river and were commonplace along the Mississippi and Arkansas rivers. In fact, hundreds of snags were pulled out of the Arkansas River by snag boats each year. The trees often lay submerged only a few feet under the water and could do considerable damage to a boat and its cargo.
37. At this point pages are missing from CGS-IRW, Roll 6, 33–55. Entries from 16 January, 17 January, and part of 18 January are transcribed from Gaston Litton, "The Journal of a Party of Emigrating Creek Indians," 238.
38. The transcription from Litton, "Journal of a Party of Emigrating Creek Indians," ends here. Original journal found at CGS-IRW, Roll 6, 33–55 resumes.
39. Coweta mile chief Kotchar Tustunnuggee.
40. Fort Smith was established in 1817 on the Arkansas River at Belle Point near the mouth of the Poteau. The garrison was created in order to prevent Indian hostilities in the area. Bearss and Gibson, *Fort Smith*, 8–165; Haskett, "The Final Chapter." From "A no. 3," *ASP-MA* 7:977: "Fort Smith is situated on the south side of the Arkansas river, and is immediately below the mouth of the Poteau. The river at this point runs north ten degrees east for several miles. The ground which is the best calculated for a military site is about fifty or sixty feet above low-water mark. There is from this point a handsome view of the river, and the site, in a military point of view, is naturally good. The highland around Fort Smith, as well as the river bottom, contains pools of standing water. The best timber, for miles around the place, has been cut. Stone can be procured in the river banks by blasting."
41. James R. Stephenson (1801–1841). Born in Virginia, Stephenson graduated from the U.S. Military Academy, West Point, New York, in 1822 (29th of 40) and was promoted second lieutenant, 7th Infantry (1822). His military history includes: frontier duty at Fort Jesup, Louisiana (1823–24); Fort Towson, Indian territory (1824–26); first lieutenant, 7th Infantry (1825); Fort Gibson, Indian territory

(1826–27); commissary duty at Fort Towson, Indian territory (1827–29); frontier duty at Fort Jesup, Louisiana (1829–30); frontier duty at Calcasieu, Louisiana (1830); frontier duty at Fort Gibson, Indian territory (1830); commissary duty subsisting Indians, Fort Gibson, Indian territory (1830–39); captain, 7th Infantry (1834); in Second Seminole War (1840); on sick leave (1840–41); died at Palatka, Florida, 26 November 1841. Cullum, *Biographical Register* (1868), 1:235.

42. John Scott was an Indian countryman married to a Creek woman. Far from having "a deep interest" in the welfare of the Creeks, as these headmen asserted, Scott was a notoriously corrupt land speculator who cheated the Creeks out of countless reserves. Ellisor, *Second Creek War*, 34, 73, 82, 224. Winn, *Triumph of the Ecunnau-Nuxulgee*, 345–46.
43. "Senr" many also be "Jun." Walter Grayson Jr., number 10 on 1832 Chattoksofke town census.
44. Possibly refers to the Upper Creek town of Oselarneby.
45. Young's Ferry was near present-day Dadeville, Alabama. Irons, "River Ferries in Alabama."
46. John Hewitt Jones (1814–82). Born in Milford, Clermont County, Ohio, Jones was raised in Rising Sun, Indiana. He worked in various businesses, including a number of dry goods operations. John Hewitt Jones, "Autobiography," Lilly Library, Indiana University, Bloomington.
47. Lewisburg, Arkansas.
48. Big Sandy River, a tributary of the Tennessee River south of the Tennessee-Kentucky border.
49. Question mark appears in the documentation.
50. A wave crashing over a shoal.
51. Diamond Island is ten miles west of Henderson, Kentucky.
52. The owners of the *Alpha* were S. Hathaway, Samuel Best Sr., Jacob La Rue, Moses Turner, William Cullen, J. C. Wagoner, John H. Jones, and Robert Thompson.

7. FIRST DETACHMENT OF CREEK PRISONERS

1. Ellisor, *Second Creek War*, 279–283; Haveman, *Rivers of Sand*, 186–87; Barry to Gibson, 12 July 1836, SIAC, Agent (Barry), Account (507), Year (1837), NARA; Grant Foreman, *Indian Removal*, 155n; Milton to Jesup, Records of the Adjutant General's Office, 1780s–1917, Record Group 94, Entry 159, Thomas S. Jesup, Box 12, Folder "Letters Received from Officers of the Army '36–'37: Names Beginning with 'M,'" NARA.
2. John Waller Barry (1810–37). Born in Kentucky, Barry graduated from the U.S. Military Academy, West Point, New York, in 1830 (8th of 42) and was promoted brevet second lieutenant, 1st Artillery, and second lieutenant, 1st Artillery (1830). His military service includes: Fort Washington, Maryland (1831–32); on leave of absence (1832–34); at Fort Washington, Maryland (1834–35); at Washington DC

Arsenal (1835); on quartermaster duty at Washington DC (1835); first lieutenant, 1st Artillery (1835); assistant quartermaster (1835–36); at Newport, Kentucky (1836); assigned to conduct first detachment of Creek prisoners to Fort Gibson (1836); resigned from army (1836); assistant engineer on Charleston and Cincinnati Railroad; died of tuberculosis near Lexington, Kentucky, 2 June 1837, at age 27. Cullum, *Biographical Register* (1868), 1:363; *Army and Navy Chronicle* 16 November 1837. See also Conover, ed., "'To Please Papa'"; Conover, ed., "Kentuckian in 'King Andrew's' Court."

3. Dr. Eugene Hilarian Abadie (1809–1874). Born in France, Abadie came with his father to Philadelphia when he was six, graduated from the University of Pennsylvania, and was appointed assistant surgeon, U.S. Army from Pennsylvania in 1836. His military service includes: engaged in the Second Creek War, Alabama (1836); accompanying detachment 1 of Creek prisoners to Indian territory (1836); in Second Seminole War (1837–39); at New York harbor (1839–40); at Fort Smith, Arkansas (1840–44); Fort Mifflin, Pennsylvania (1844–46); in Florida (1846–47); in Mexico-American War (1847–48); at Point Isabel, Texas (1848–49); at St. Louis, Missouri (1849–52); at Santa Fe, New Mexico (1852–56); surgeon, U.S. Army, (1853); at Jefferson Barracks, Missouri (1856–58); at New Orleans, Louisiana (1858–60); at San Antonio, Texas (1860–61); paroled prisoner of war, New York City, New York (1860–61); at Washington DC (1861–62); chief medical officer at U.S. Military Academy, West Point, New York (1862–64); on temporary leave at U.S. Military Academy, West Point, New York, to serve on medical board, Philadelphia, Pennsylvania (1862–63), and in New York City (1863); chief medical officer of the Military Division of West Mississippi (1864–65); brevet lieutenant colonel and brevet colonel, for faithful and meritorious service during Civil War (1865); medical director of the Department of the Missouri (1865–66); assistant medical purveyor, not confirmed by Senate (1866); acting assistant medical purveyor, St. Louis, Missouri (1866–67); died at St. Louis, Missouri, 12 December 1874. Cullum, *Biographical Register* (1868), 1:66; Henry, *Military Record of Civilian Appointments*, 51; Pittman, ed., *Americans of Gentle Birth*, 1:xiii–xiv; Motte, *Journey into Wilderness*, 2.
4. Dr. William Stout Chipley (1810–1880). Born in Lexington, Kentucky, Chipley graduated with a medical degree from Transylvania University in 1832. He moved to Columbus, Georgia, where he started a medical practice that extended into the Creek country in Alabama. Due to the large numbers of sick Creeks, Chipley was hired to accompany the first detachment of Creek prisoners to Indian territory. Returning to Lexington in 1844, Chipley served on the faculty of Transylvania University before becoming superintendent of the Eastern Lunatic Asylum in 1855. He resigned the superintendency in 1870 and opened a private hospital in Lexington that year. In 1875 he became superintendent of the Cincinnati

Sanitarium, a position he held until his death from "structural disease" in 1880. Chipley took an early interest in eating disorders and in 1859 defined the term "sitomania"—the "intense dread of food"—an early diagnosis of what is now known as *anorexia nervosa*. Memorandum of expenses (W. S. Chipley), SIAC, Agent (Page), Account (1490), Year (1838), NARA; "Proceedings of the Association of Medical Superintendents," 177–79; Peter, *History of the Medical Department*, 147–53; Chipley, "Sitomania," 1–42; Brumberg, *Fasting Girls*, 104–11; Jones, *Taming the Troublesome Child*, 19; Silver, *Victorian Literature and the Anorexic Body*, 1.

5. John Archer Elmore, Jr. (1809–1878). Born in South Carolina and educated at South Carolina College (University of South Carolina), Elmore was the son of John Archer Elmore (namesake of Elmore County, Alabama). He opened a law practice in Hayneville, Lowndes County, Alabama, shortly after being admitted to the bar in 1832. He was captain of the 1st Battalion, Alabama Infantry, during the Second Creek War and later was elected a state senator from Lowndes County. After moving to Montgomery County, Alabama, Elmore worked in the law firm of fire-eater William L. Yancey. Index to Compiled Service Records of Volunteer Soldiers who Served During the Creek War in Organizations from the State of Alabama, A-J, Microcopy 244, Roll 1, National Archives and Records Administration, Washington dc; Brewer, *Alabama*, 457–58; Doliante, *Maryland and Virginia Colonials*, 297.
6. Drury A. Gaffney (1805–1851). Born in Fairfield District, South Carolina, Gaffney was a Lowndes County planter. Information from Smyrna Cemetery, Lowndes County, AL.
7. John Milton (1807–1865). Born near Louisville, Jefferson County, Georgia, Milton attended Louisville Academy and the University of Georgia. He practiced law in Louisville before moving to Columbus, Georgia (where he ran unsuccessfully for Congress), and then to Mobile, Alabama, where he had a large legal practice. Milton was a land buyer and purchased a number of the claims from the emigrants of Chilly McIntosh's emigrating party in 1833 as well as the five full sections of land granted to the western Creeks. Milton served as the captain of a volunteer company during the Second Creek War and Seminole War (1835–37) before returning to law in stops at Marion, Alabama; New Orleans, Louisiana; and (part-time) in Jackson County, Florida. Soon after arriving in Florida in 1846, Milton became a leader of the Democratic Party and was elected to the state senate in 1849, then served as Florida governor (1861–65). In January 1861 he ordered the seizure of the U.S. arsenal at Apalachicola, Fort Marion, and the navy yard at Pensacola. He supported slavery and Florida's secession movement, but the stresses of office and Confederate losses took their toll. Milton committed suicide at Marianna, Florida, 1 April 1865. *National Cyclopædia of American Biography*, 11:378–79; Eicher and Eicher, *Civil War High Commands*, 391; Parker, "John Milton, Governor of Florida"; *New York Times*, 1 May 1865.

8. Alabama Artillery No. 1, also known as the State Artillery Company No. 1. The company was organized around 18 May 1836 just after news of the Second Creek War's commencement reached Mobile. The soldiers left Mobile on 27 May on the steamboat *Meridian* and reached Stockton, Alabama, that afternoon. The party continued to Fort Claiborne (31 May); Greenville, Alabama (ca. 5 June); Irwinton, Alabama (ca. 7 June); Hitchiti—High Log town (ca. 16 June); and Montgomery (July), where they accompanied the *Lewis Cass* and *Meridian* with 2,300 Creeks on board. Terry, ed., "Record of the Alabama State Artillery."
9. Thomas Sidney Jesup (1788–1860). Born in Berkeley County, Virginia and raised in Mason County, Kentucky, Jesup was commissioned second lieutenant, 7th Infantry in 1808. His military service includes: brigade quartermaster at Newport, Kentucky (1808); first lieutenant, 7th Infantry (1809); at Baton Rouge, Louisiana, (1811); recruiting service (1812); in the War of 1812, being engaged as major and acting adjutant general under General William Hull (1812), as prisoner of war after the British capture of Detroit (1812), captain, 7th Infantry (1813), as deputy quartermaster general in charge of supervising the construction of "Schenectady boats" at Cleveland, Ohio (1813), major, 19th Infantry (1813), at Fort Stephenson, Ohio (1813), as witness during General William Hull's court martial, Albany, New York (1814), transferred to 25th Infantry (1814), engaged at the capture of Fort Erie, Upper Canada (1814), and at the Battle of Chippewa, Upper Canada (1814); brevet lieutenant colonel for distinguished and meritorious service in the Battle of Chippewa (1814); engaged and wounded in the shoulder, neck, right hand, and chest at the Battle of Lundy's Lane, Niagara Falls, Upper Canada (1814); recuperating at Buffalo, New York (1814); brevet colonel for "'gallant conduct and distinguished skill'" at the Battle of Lundy's Lane (1814); at Fort Erie during the Siege of Fort Erie, Upper Canada (1814); in Hartford, Connecticut during the Hartford Convention (1814–15); transferred to 1st Infantry (1815); appointed commander, 8th Military Department (1815); at New Orleans and Baton Rouge, Louisiana (1816–17); lieutenant colonel, 3rd Infantry (1817); appointed adjutant general of the Northern Division, Brownville, New York (1818); colonel, 3rd Infantry (1818); quartermaster general of the U.S. Army with rank of brigadier general, Washington DC (1818–60); supervising transportation for the Mississippi and Missouri expeditions (1819); at Washington DC (1819–21); on inspection tour of Southern states (1821–22); at Washington, DC (1822–28); brevet major general for ten years faithful service in one grade (1828); on sick leave at Kentucky (1828); at Washington DC (1828–32); on sick leave (1832); at Washington DC (1832–36); in Alabama, being engaged in commanding forces during the Second Creek War (1836), and overseeing the removal and relocation of the Creek Indians (1836–37); in Florida, being engaged in command of the Army of the South during the Second Seminole War (1836–38); at Washington DC (1838–45); on inspection duty of western frontier (1845); at Washington DC (1845–46); at New

Orleans directing supply operations during Mexican-American War (1846); on inspection and support duty during the Veracruz amphibious landing, Mexico (1847); engaged in forwarding transportation and supplies for General Winfield Scott's inland march to Mexico City (1847); at Washington DC (1847–51); leave of absence (1851); at Washington DC (1851–60); died as the result of a stroke at Washington DC, 10 June 1860, at age 72. Kieffer, *Maligned General*; Fredriksen, *American Military Leaders*, 1:372–73; Ellisor, *Second Creek War*, 229; Heitman, *Historical Register*, 1:573.

10. Captain John Page, who superintended Creek removal, reported that this detention "operated very severe on the contractors, as they had fifteen hundred [Creeks] in charge that I turned over to them and they were paying Eight and ten dollars per day for each five horse team" when the typical price for a team per day prior to the Second Creek War was $3.50. Page to Gibson, 8 August 1836, SIAC, Agent (Sanford), Account (66), Year (1837), NARA.
11. The Creek captives used myriad strategies to avoid being forced to Indian territory in chains. Suicide, desertion, and violence against their captors were the most common. Jacob Rhett Motte, an army surgeon who served in the Second Creek and Second Seminole Wars, recorded a number of instances of suicide in his journal, including: "There were several who committed suicide rather than endure the sorrow of leaving the spot where rested the bones of their ancestors. One old fellow was found hanging by the neck the night before he was to leave Fort Mitchell for the far West; preferring the glorious uncertainty of another world, to the inglorious misery of being forced to a country of which he knew nothing, but dreaded every thing bad"; and "One of this very party of emigrating Indians on his arrival at Montgomery [Alabama] attempted his escape; but when caught and secured in a waggon, by some accident got possession of a very dull knife; with this he made several ineffectual efforts to cut his throat, but it not proving sharp enough, he with both hands forced it into his chest over the breast-bone, and by successive violent thrusts succeeded in dividing the main artery, when he bled to death." Motte, *Journey into Wilderness*, 19, 20.
12. The steamboats were *Meridian* and *Lewis Cass*.
13. The source of the strife is unclear, although the Creeks and Yuchis (who belonged to the Creek Nation but did not speak the Muskogean language) had a complex relationship dotted with periods of friendship and hostility. Hahn, "'They Look upon the Yuchis as Their Vassals.'"
14. Captain Walter Smith, commander of the Alabama Artillery Number 1. When the company formed in May 1836 John Milton was elected first lieutenant and served under the command of Captain Smith. In June of that year Smith was elected colonel and Milton was promoted to captain. It does not appear that Smith accompanied the Creeks to Mobile. Terry, ed., "Record of the Alabama State Artillery," 148–49.

15. Sylvester Churchill (1783–1862). Born in Woodstock, Vermont, Churchill was commissioned first lieutenant, 3rd Artillery in 1812. His military service includes: in War of 1812, being engaged in building parapets on Lake Champlain, Burlington, Vermont, in defense of Commodore Thomas McDonough's fleet (1813); captain, 3rd Artillery (1813); ordnance officer during the Battle of Chateauguay, Lower Canada (1813); appointed major and assistant inspector general (1813–15); engaged at the Battle of Lacolle Mills, Lower Canada (1814); on the staff of General George Izard while on the march from Lake Champlain to Niagara River (1814); transferred to Corps of Artillery (1814); on the staff of General Alexander Macomb at the Battle of Plattsburgh, New York (1814); retained as captain, Corps of Artillery (1815); at Plattsburgh, New York (1815–16); at Governor's Island and Bedloe's Island, New York Harbor, and at The Narrows, Brooklyn, New York; transferred to 1st U.S. Light Artillery (1821); brevet major, U.S. Army, for ten years faithful service in one grade (1823); ordnance duty, Allegheny Arsenal, Pittsburgh, Pennsylvania (1824–28); leave of absence (1828); at Fort Johnston, North Carolina (1828–35); major, 3rd Artillery (1835); at Fort Sullivan, Maine (1835–36); at Fort Mitchell, Alabama, being engaged in the Second Creek War (1836); in Florida, being engaged in the Second Seminole War (1836–37); in Vermont during Canada independence movement (1838); in Florida, being engaged in Second Seminole War (1838–39, 1839–41); colonel and inspector general of U.S. Army (1841); in Mexican-American War, being engaged in the Battle of Buena Vista, Mexico (1847); brevet brigadier general, U.S. Army, for meritorious conduct at the Battle of Buena Vista, Mexico (1848); discharging volunteers at New Orleans, Louisiana (1847, 1848); engaged in various inspection duties (1848–59); senior Inspector General, U.S. Army (1849–61); retired from U.S. Army "for incapacity, resulting from long and faithful service, from wounds or injury received, from disease contracted, or from exposure in the line of duty;" (1861); died at Washington DC, 7 December 1862, at age 79. Eicher and Eicher, *Civil War High Commands*, 172; Henry, *Military Record of Army and Civilian Appointments*, 2:62; Churchill, *Sketch of the Life of Bvt. Brig. Gen. Sylvester Churchill*, 7–27, 33–36.
16. John Archer Elmore Jr.
17. John Breckinridge Grayson (1806–1861). Born in Fayette County, Kentucky, Grayson graduated from the U.S. Military Academy, West Point, New York, in 1826 (22nd of 41) and was promoted brevet second lieutenant, 3rd Artillery (1826), and second lieutenant, 2nd Artillery (1826). His military history includes: at Artillery School for Practice, Fort Monroe, Virginia (1825–28); topographical duty (1828–32); at Augusta Arsenal, Georgia (1833); Fort Mitchell, Alabama (1833–34); Fort Wood, Louisiana (1834); first lieutenant, 2nd Artillery (1834); at Bay St. Louis, Mississippi (1834); Fort Wood, Louisiana (1834–35); in the Second Seminole War (1835–36), being engaged at Battle of Camp Izard (1836) and Battle of Oloklikaha (1836); assistant commissary of subsistence at Montgomery, Alabama, during the

Second Creek War, having replaced Major Joshua B. Brant (1836); commissary duty at New Orleans (1836–47); captain (staff), commissary of subsistence (1838); captain, 2nd Artillery (1838–46); in Mexican-American War (1847–48), being engaged as chief of commissariat of the army under Major General Winfield Scott; engaged in the Siege of Veracruz, Mexico (1847), Battle of Cerro Gordo, Mexico (1847), Battle of Churubusco, Mexico (1847); brevet major for gallant and meritorious conduct in the Battles of Contreras and Churubusco (1847); engaged in the Battles of Molino del Rey, Mexico (1847), Battle of Chapultepec, Mexico (1847), and capture of Mexico City (1847); brevet lieutenant colonel for gallant and meritorious conduct in the Battle of Chapultepec (1847); commissary duty, Detroit, Michigan (1848–55); chief of commissariat of the Department of New Mexico (1855–61); major (staff), commissary of subsistence (1852); resigned U.S. Army (1861); brigadier general, North Carolina Militia (1861); brigadier general, Confederate Army in command of the Department of Middle and East Florida, Fernandina, Florida (1861); died of tuberculosis and pneumonia at Tallahassee, Florida, 21 October 1861, at age 55. Grayson was the step-son of Secretary of War Peter B. Porter (1828–29) and cousin of Congressman John C. Breckinridge. Cullum, *Biographical Register* (1868), 1:298; Wilson and Fiske, eds., *Appletons' Cyclopædia of American Biography*, 2:732; Warner, *Generals in Gray*, 115–16; Porter to Clay, 12 February 1823, in Hopkins and Hargreaves, eds., *Papers of Henry Clay*, 3:378–79n3; Eicher and Eicher, *Civil War High Commands*, 264–65, 872; Johnson, *A History of Kentucky and Kentuckians*, 1:589; Grayson to Gibson, 15 July 1836, CGS-IRW, Roll 5, 953; Chambers to Grayson, 10 August 1836, CGS-IRW, Roll 6, 70; Memorandum of an agreement, SIAC, Agent (Bateman), Account (3797), Year (1839), NARA.

18. Possibly E. B. Robinson, captain of the Washington City (DC) Volunteers. Orders No. 39, RG 94, 159-Q, Container 26, Folder: "Orders, July 1836," NARA; Index to Compiled Service Records of Volunteer Soldiers who Served During the Creek War in Organizations from the State of Alabama, A-J, Microcopy 244, Roll 2, National Archives and Records Administration, Washington DC; *Army and Navy Chronicle*, 23 June 1836; Elmore to Jesup, 14 July 1836, RG 94, 159-Q, Container 8, Folder: "Letters Received from Officers, Captain John Elmore," NARA.
19. This contradicts Barry's letter of 16 July 1836, which states that the party left on 14 July.
20. The *Meridian* was a 195-ton sidewheeler built in New Albany, Indiana, in 1836; the *Lewis Cass* was a 111-ton sidewheeler built in Cincinnati in 1835. Neville, *Directory of River*, 22, 23.
21. This is a slightly different version of the same event noted in Barry's 12 July 1836 letter to George Gibson.
22. Isaac Heylin Erwin (1807–1843). Erwin was an ensign when the Alabama Artillery Number 1 formed in May 1836. Just before leaving Mobile the volunteers passed

down Royal Street to the house of W. J. Ledyard, whose wife presented the "neat, tasteful flag" she had made for the company (which was received by Erwin). He died of yellow fever in 1843. By June 1836 Erwin was serving as lieutenant. Terry, ed., "Record of the Alabama State Artillery," 146–47; Index to Compiled Service Records of Volunteer Soldiers who Served During the Creek War in Organizations from the State of Alabama, A-J, Microcopy 244, Roll 1, National Archives and Records Administration, Washington DC; Patton, *Biography of James Patton*, 32.

23. The hurricane deck was the third deck of the steamboat (also called upward deck or roof) that was located above the main and boiler decks. The name "hurricane" name comes from the fact that the breeze was typically the strongest on this uppermost deck. The hurricane deck served as a promenade for passengers who wanted a better view of the river or to enjoy the breeze off the water. Above the hurricane deck was the pilothouse. For post-1840s boats, the "Texas" (a suite of rooms for the officers and crew) was built on the hurricane deck and the pilothouse above the Texas. Kane, *The Western River Steamboat*, 67, 90–91; Chittenden, *History of Early Steamboat Navigation*, 112–14; Kotar and Gessler, *The Steamboat Era*, 67, 274.
24. Neah Emathla.
25. The Alabama Artillery Number 1 did not accompany the Creek prisoners farther than Mobile.
26. Mobile.
27. Construction on the New Canal or New Basin Canal began in 1832; it was filled with water on 24 December 1835 and opened to traffic in 1838. During the early years of the canal, only small boats that drafted less than six feet of water could navigate its six-mile length. When this party used the canal in July 1836, it was so shallow that only a flatboat towed by the Creeks could make it up the passage; von Gerstner, *Early American Railroads*, 745–54.
28. The basin was near the foot of Julia Street in New Orleans.
29. Mo git har was a Creek man from Wetumpka and was part of Neah Micco's party during the Second Creek War. He reportedly was "Well known" to many of the headman, suggesting that he was an active participant during the uprising. Thompson to Van Ness, 3 July 1836, RG 94, 159-Q, Container 19, Folder: "Letters Received Relating to Creek and Seminole Affairs, July 1836 (1 of 3)," NARA.
30. John F. Lane (ca. 1809–1836). Born in Kentucky, Lane graduated from the U.S. Military Academy, West Point, New York in 1828 (10th of 33) and was promoted brevet second lieutenant of Artillery and second lieutenant, 4th Artillery (1828). His military history includes: assistant professor of mathematics, U.S. Military Academy, West Point, New York (1828–29); assistant professor of natural and experimental philosophy, U.S. Military Academy, West Point, New York (1829); at Fort McHenry, Maryland (1829–31, 1831–32); served under direction

of commissary general of subsistence during the Choctaw removals (1832–34); quartermaster duty in the quartermaster general's office, Washington DC (1834); constructing Delaware breakwater (1834–35); assistant quartermaster (1834); at Fort Monroe, Virginia (1835); on quartermaster duty (1835); captain, 2nd Dragoons (1836); engaged in Second Creek War as aide-de-camp to Major General Thomas S. Jesup (1836); colonel, Regular Mounted Creek Volunteers (September–October 1836); in Second Seminole War being engaged in skirmish at Tampa Bay (September 1836); died at Fort Drane, Florida, 19 October 1836, at age 26. Details surrounding Lane's death are somewhat cryptic. One account notes that Lane had suffered from "oppressive pain in the forehead, and it was thought that he exhibited some symptoms of insanity." Once arriving at Fort Drane, however, the report claims Lane "appeared to be in good spirits, and conversed freely with the officers; while in Captain Galt's [Patrick Henry Galt of the 4th Artillery] tent, he again complained of the severe pain in his forehead. He soon after retired to his own tent, and when some persons entered they found him reclining on his knee, with his sword pierced through his right eye, so as to penetrate the brain; he lingered about half an hour." Previous to this, Lane invented a portable and adjustable pontoon bridge that was first tested during the Second Creek War. In 1834 Thomas S. Jesup, who as quartermaster general had been interested in the development of modern and efficient field equipage, suggested the development of a new type of easily transportable pontoon bridge. Lane took up this challenge, and after receiving permission from the secretary of war, began work in 1835. The bridge Lane created consisted of pontoons made of India rubber "with a frame work of timber placed over them; and upon this laid a flooring of pine boards; and all so united and arranged as to present a strong and handsome bridge." This replaced the older bridges, which had "cumbrous and bulky" pontoons made of wood, sheet iron, and copper. Lane's bridge was first presented for testing to the Army Board of Examination (which included Colonel Archibald Henderson) on 24 August 1836 at Tallassee, where it was stretched across the Tallapoosa River. A column of U.S. Marines (acting as infantry), a detachment of cavalry, and a wagon "easily and safely" crossed the 350-foot-long bridge that consisted of "fourteen feet width of roadway," and was supported by sixteen pontoons. The pontoons and cordage could be transported in "a single wagon." Concerned about the distance between the pontoons and the amount of pressure the gaps could sustain, officials conducted a second test on 16 September 1836 at Woolfolk's Ferry on the Chattahoochee River. The second bridge was 294 feet long, 13 feet wide, and held 31 pontoons. The tests included: "A column of more than two hundred men of the regular army, with mounted officers, all armed and equipped for war, were marched upon it in the cadenced step to the sound of martial music. After being there halted, closed and made to stand by their arms for the space of ten or fifteen minutes, the divisions were all countermarched at the same moment, and subsequently moved to shore. The next and final experiment was made by drawing over a six pounder [a gun that shoots a 57 mm, approximately 6-pound ball] attended by the proper complement of matrosses [a gunner's mate who helped load ammunition], and its caisson [a chest] filled with ammunition." Cullum, *Biographical Register* (1868), 1:328; U.S. Congress, House Document 60, *Letter from the Secretary of War, A statement of the names* (1834), 2; *Army and Navy Chronicle*, 27 October 1836. If the report of the Board of Examination is to be believed, Lane's design was revolutionary for pontoon bridge design. While the pontoons and cordage for Lane's Tallapoosa bridge (350 feet long) could be transported in only one wagon, the most advanced British model of the time (stretching an equal 350 feet) would have required the use of 17 four-horse wagon teams. One wagon could only transport a 21-foot section of a British pontoon bridge. *Reports on India Rubber Air Pontoons*, 3–23.

31. A warehouse where rope was made and woven together.
32. The *Revenue* was a 122-ton sidewheeler constructed in Louisville, Kentucky, in 1835; Neville, *Directory of Tennessee River Steamboats*, 23. The *Lamplighter* was a 200-ton steamboat rated to carry 1,200 bales of cotton; Gudmestad, *Steamboats and the Rise of the Cotton Kingdom*, 143. Sometime after transporting the Creeks the *Majestic* blew a boiler, causing a "dreadful destruction of life." Eighteen months later, in November 1837, the *Majestic* had its boiler flue collapse ten miles from Memphis, killing two and "badly scalding" eight people; *Memphis Enquirer*, 2 December 1837. The *Arkansas State Gazette* reported three people dead (two firemen and a deckhand) in the November 1837 accident; *Arkansas State Gazette*, 19 December 1837.
33. Cussetas.
34. William F. Pope, an early settler in Arkansas, visited Montgomery's Point in 1832 and noted that the settlement still contained some of the original 1766 log buildings erected by French fur trader Francois D'Armand, which were located "about three hundred yards back from the river." Pope also reported: "Two large log ware-houses, built upon piling, stood near the water's edge and were used by the firm of Montgomery, Miller & Co., for storing freight destined for points along the Arkansas and White rivers. The extensive business of this firm was under the management of Mr. Moses Greenwood, who afterwards became a prominent and wealthy commission merchant of New Orleans, and who was well known and highly respected throughout the South for his many excellent traits of character.

    The hotel at the Point was owned by Gen. [William] Montgomery and was situated about two hundred and fifty yards from the river. The hotel building was elevated some distance above the ground on high brick pillars and had wide verandas on all sides." Pope, *Early Days in Arkansas*, 62.

35. Neah Micco (d. 1836). Neah Micco was a mile chief from the town of Cusseta. He became the principal headman of the Lower Towns after the death of Little Prince in April 1828.
36. Now called Campylobacter: diarrhea common to children who eat contaminated food in the hot summer months.
37. Refers to John W.A. Sanford & Company. Although Sanford & Company was transporting the prisoners to Indian territory, their original contract with the government, signed in 1835, had expired.
38. This contract with the Alabama Emigrating Company would be signed on 13 August 1836.
39. Rock Roe, seven miles below the mouth of the Cache River near present-day Clarendon, Arkansas.
40. Ball games were played on fields that could exceed one hundred yards and could include over one hundred players. The goal was to strike a pole with a stuffed deerskin ball. Hudson, *Southeastern Indians*, 408–20.
41. James Erwin frequently provided provisions to emigrating Indians as they passed by his homestead. Deposition of H. Reynolds, 25 December 1844, SFOIA SF 62, Roll 7, 378.
42. Probably refers to LaGrue Bayou (the Crane River), a watershed that stretches from Big LaGrue Bayou (near present-day Carlisle, Arkansas) in the north to Little LaGrue Bayou (in the vicinity of Stuttgart, Arkansas) in the south. They merge near present-day DeWitt, Arkansas, before emptying into the White River. U.S. Congress, House Document 48, *Letter from the Secretary of War, Transmitting . . . Cost of Improvement of La Grue River, Ark.* (1921), 4.
43. For more on the Busk, see Payne, "Green-Corn Dance"; Foster, ed., *Collected Works of Benjamin Hawkins*, 75s–78s; Hudson, *Southeastern Indians*, 365–75.
44. Dysentery is an infection of the intestines that causes bloody diarrhea.
45. Dr. William Stout Chipley.
46. John Waller Barry.
47. Armstrong probably means the "former"; that is, Chilly McIntosh.

8. SECOND DETACHMENT OF CREEK PRISONERS

1. Biography of F. S. Belton, New York Public Library (hereafter cited as NYPL).
2. Francis Smith Belton (1791–1861). Born in Baltimore, Maryland, Belton was commissioned second lieutenant, 1st U.S. Light Dragoons, in 1812. His military history includes: first lieutenant, 1st U.S. Light Dragoons (1813); regimental paymaster (1813); in War of 1812, being engaged in the skirmish at Hoople's Creek, Upper Canada (1813), and as aide-de-camp to General Edmund Pendleton Gaines (1814), and engaged in raising a detachment of Oneida Indians to fight at the Battle of Big Sandy Creek, New York (1814), and being engaged in the Siege of Fort Erie, Upper Canada (1814), as aide-de-camp to

General Winfield Scott (1814–15); appointed assistant adjutant general with the rank of major (1814); chief of staff to General Alexander Macomb (1815); retained as first lieutenant, 4th Infantry (1815) reinstated as major and assistant inspector general to rank from 18 October 1814 (1816); on inspection tour of Great Lakes forts (1817); reinstated to the lineal rank of captain, 4th Infantry to rank from 31 July 1817—served as major, assistant inspector general to 1 June 1821 (1820); transferred to the 2nd Artillery with the rank of captain (1821); Artillery School for Practice, Fort Monroe, Virginia (1827–28); at Fort Johnson, South Carolina (1828–29); at South Carolina State Arsenal, Charleston, South Carolina (1829–31); in command of Fort Moultrie, South Carolina (1831); in Cherokee Nation, being engaged in removing intruders (1832, 1833); at Fort Mitchell, Alabama (1834); at Fort Morgan, Alabama (1834–35); in Florida, being engaged in Second Seminole War as commander of Fort Brooke, Florida (1835–36), and in Battle of Camp Izard (1836); at Tuscaloosa, Alabama (1836); engaged in discharging the Alabama volunteers, Montgomery, Alabama (1836); assigned to conduct second detachment of Creek prisoners to Indian territory (1836); leave of absence, New Orleans, Louisiana (1836); in Florida, being engaged in Second Seminole War (1837); at Fort Morgan, Alabama (1837); at Tuscaloosa, Alabama (1837); at Fort Foster, Florida (1837–38); major, 1st Artillery (1838); transferred to 4th Artillery (1838); at Camp of Instruction, near Trenton, New Jersey (1838–39); at Detroit, Michigan during the Canada independence movement (1839–40); in command of Fort Gratiot, Michigan (1840–41); in command of Sackets Harbor, New York (1841–42); at Fort Monroe, Virginia (1842–45); at Fort McHenry, Maryland (1845–46); lieutenant colonel, 3rd Artillery (1845); in Mexican-American War, being engaged in occupying the city of Tampico, Mexico (1846–47), and the landing at Veracruz, Mexico (1847), and as commander of Castle of San Juan de Ulúa, Veracruz, Mexico (1847), and at the Battle of Cerro Gordo, Mexico (1847), and in occupying San Carlos Fortress, Perote, Mexico (1847), appointed civil and military governor of Puebla, Mexico (1847), and engaged at the Battles of Churubusco, Mexico (1847), and Molina del Rey, Mexico (1847), and the Battle of Chapultepec, Mexico (1847), as lieutenant governor of Mexico City, Mexico (1847); brevet colonel for gallant meritorious conduct at the battles of Contreras and Churubusco, Mexico (1847); at Fort Trumbull, Connecticut (1849–53); colonel, 4th Artillery (1857); retired from active service (1861); died at Brooklyn, New York, 10 September 1861. Heitman, *Historical Register*, 1:209; Henry, *Military Record of Civilian Appointments*, 1:508; Belton, Biography of F. S. Belton, NYPL; Journal of Amos B. Eaton, University of Miami Special Collections, Miami FL; Letter from Belton, 2 January 1838, RG 94, 159-Q, Container 4, Folder: "Letters Received from Officers, Captain F. S. Belton," NARA. Letter of Belton, 21 September 1854, Colonel Francis S.

Belton, Mexican War Letters, 1846–1854, GA51, Special Collections, University of Texas at Arlington Library, Arlington, Texas.

3. Hiram William Cooke (1817–88). Born in Mount Sterling, Montgomery County, Kentucky, Cooke was an eighteen-year-old clerk at a mercantile store when he enlisted as a private, 1st Regiment of Tennessee Mounted Volunteers, on 13 June 1836 (he was mustered into service on 1 July 1836 at Fayetteville, Tennessee). On 1 August 1836 Cooke was appointed "Issuing Commissary to Emigrating Indians at Montgomery, Ala." Mary A. Cooke, in a deposition while seeking her late husband's military pension, noted that "I have often heard my husband speak of helping to remove the Creek Indians to the Indian Territory," and "my husband often spoke of Col. Belton removing the Creek Indians to the Indian Territory and my husband was detailed to go with the colonel." While fighting in the Second Seminole War in Florida, Cooke served in Captain Alexander D. Bradford's (and later Jesse H. McMahon's) company of the 1st Regiment of Tennessee Mounted Volunteers (honorably discharged at New Orleans, 17 January 1837). Later, he was captain of a company in the 3rd Battalion, Tennessee Infantry (commanded by Col. Henderson King Yoakum) stationed at Fort Cass, Tennessee (May–June 1838), during the Cherokee removals (Cooke was discharged at Fort Poinsett, Florida, 28 June 1838). After moving to Texas, Cooke served as captain in the Mounted Ranging Company (Coryell County, Texas) in Lieutenant Colonel Thomas C. Frost's company (Henry E. McCulloch's 1st Texas Cavalry) in the Confederate Army during the Civil War. According to his widow, Cooke was later conscripted into the Confederate Army and served as first lieutenant and adjutant in Colonel James M. Norris's Frontier Regiment, 46th Texas Cavalry. He died at Dripping Springs, Texas, 26 January 1888. Cooke's widow described his appearance as a young man as: "fully 6 feet tall" and with graying hair when they met, but which was "originally very black and was curly and silkey. He had large dark eyes, a Roman nose, and his skin was rather dark." Hiram W. Cooke file (number 10,652), Pension and Bounty Land Records (Indian Wars service case files), Record Group 15, Records of the Department of Veterans Affairs 1773–1985, National Archives and Records Administration, Washington DC; Crockett to Lewis, 26 January 1839, LR, CAE, Roll 239, 389; Bixler, ed., *Decisions of the Department of the Interior*, 14:409; *Austin Daily Statesman*, 28 January 1888; Hale and Merritt, *A History of Tennessee and Tennesseans*, 3:806; Rives, ed., *The Congressional Globe*, 30:531; Ivey, *The Texas Rangers*, 105, 114–18; Henderson, *Texas in the Confederacy*, 144; *The Iron Age*, 16 May 1895.

4. Dr. James Jones (1807–73). It is unclear if this is the same James Jones who served as the chair of obstetrics and later as "Chair of Practice of Medicine" at the Medical College of Louisiana in New Orleans (now Tulane University School of Medicine). He served on the faculty for thirty-seven years beginning in 1836. Dr. James Jones receipt, 15 January 1868, Medical Documents Collection, 1759–1952,

Louisiana Research Collection, Tulane University, New Orleans LA; Fenner, ed., *Southern Medical Reports*, 1:461–62; "Miscellaneous," 684; "The Medical Department of Tulane University of Louisiana"; Chaillé, *Historical Sketch of the Medical Department*, 6–7.

5. Joshua Bosworth Brant (1790–1861). Born in Hampshire, Hampton County, Massachusetts, Brant worked at a drug store in Troy, New York and then became a partner in a distilling business in Dutchess County, New York until the outbreak of the War of 1812, when he joined as private, a detachment of troops at Rhinebeck, New York, commanded by Captain Azariah W. Odell (1813). His military history includes: Engaged in Battles of Fort George, Upper Canada (1813), and Forty-Mile Creek, Upper Canada (1813); major, 23rd Infantry (1814); commissioned ensign, 23rd Infantry (1814); engaged in Battle of Lundy's Lane, Upper Canada (1814), and the Siege of Fort Erie (1814); second lieutenant, 23rd Infantry (1814); brevet first lieutenant, 23rd Infantry, for gallant conduct in Siege of Fort Erie (1814); retained and transferred to 2nd Infantry (1815); regimental quartermaster, 2nd Infantry (1815–19); at Sackets Harbor, New York (1818); assistant deputy quartermaster general with rank of captain (1819); at St. Louis, Missouri (1823–39); captain, 2nd Infantry (1832); quartermaster with rank of major (1832); ordered to Alabama for duty in the field, being engaged in Second Creek War (1836); leave of absence to St. Louis, Missouri and replaced by John Breckinridge Grayson (1836); in Florida, being engaged in Second Seminole War (1838); deputy quartermaster general with rank of lieutenant colonel (1838); resigned U.S. Army after being court-martialed for fraud, violation of official trust and neglect of duty, and of conduct unbecoming an officer and a gentleman (1839). After leaving the army in 1839, Brant went into the construction business and was responsible for building many of the tallest buildings in St. Louis. His second wife was the niece of Missouri senator Thomas Hart Benton, who stayed with the couple often when he was in St. Louis. Edwards and Hopewell, *Edwards's Great West*, 197–98; *Proceedings of a Court Martial Convened for the Trial of Lt. Col. Joshua B. Brant*. Herr and Spence, *Letters of Jessie Benton Frémont*, 127n3, 238n1; Gardner, *A Dictionary of All Officers*, 82; Heitman, *Historical Register*, 1:241; Stevens, *St. Louis*, 2;543, 697; Memorandum, *ASP-MA*, 6:793; Wilson, *Jim Beckwourth*, 86; Hamersly, *Complete Regular Army Register*, 316, says Brant was born in Connecticut.
6. Quartermaster, United States Army.
7. This is the first of many times when Belton appears to talk in the third person.
8. Jesse H. McMahon's company, 1st Regiment Tennessee Mounted Volunteers. Hiram W. Cooke file (number 10,652), Pension and Bounty Land Records (Indian Wars service case files), Record Group 15, Records of the Department of Veterans Affairs 1773–1985, National Archives and Records Administration, Washington DC.

9. Possibly "indefinite."
10. The word is somewhat illegible but Cooke was appointed "Issuing Commissary to Emigrating Indians at Montgomery. Ala. 1st August 1836," and Belton's son and biographer noted that Cooke helped the agent issue provisions to the Creeks during the journey west. Hiram W. Cooke file (number 10,652), Pension and Bounty Land Records (Indian Wars service case files), Record Group 15, Records of the Department of Veterans Affairs 1773–1985, National Archives and Records Administration, Washington DC; J. F. Belton, Biography of F. S. Belton, Belton-Kirby-Dawson-Todd Families Papers, Manuscripts and Archives Division, NYPL.
11. Possibly W. W. Fry of Mobile. In 1838 Fry and other entrepreneurs sought to import iron-hulled steamboats into Alabama. *Niles' National Register*, 14 July 1838. Brant to Belton, 1 August 1836, SIAC, Agent (Belton), Account (528), Year (1837), NARA.
12. A lighter is a flat-bottomed barge.
13. In 1835 the pilot of the steamer *Mazeppa*, angry with the owner for taking a barge in tow, deliberately ran into a snag, killing three slaves (a woman and two children) along with twenty-three horses riding on the flatboat. Kotar and Gessler, *The Steamboat Era*, 157.
14. William C. Sutton was the captain of the *Mazeppa*. U.S. Customs Service, Slave Manifests, Mobile, Alabama Inward, Record Group 36, Box 2, 5, National Archives and Records Administration at Atlanta, Morrow, Georgia.
15. The "keys" refers to the barrier islands off the coast of Alabama and Mississippi, which include (east to west) Dauphin Island, Petit Bois Island, Horn Island, Ship Island, and Cat Island. At certain times it was too shallow to pass inside the keys. During low tides Dog Key Island, between Horn and Ship Islands, can appear. Due to shallow water near Dauphin Island, many steamboats were forced into the Gulf, which subjected the vessels to rough water. In describing the routine 190-mile voyage between Mobile and New Orleans on board the 130-ton, forty-five-horsepower, low pressure engine steamer *Mount Vernon*, British traveler James Stuart noted that "the passage is almost entirely within a range of islands, which breaks the force of the sea, so that it is generally made in still water. We had rather rough weather on the evening on which we left Mobile,—and, finding that we touched the bank within Dauphin Island, we were obliged to go without it into the Gulf of Mexico." Stuart, *Three Years in North America*, 2:225–26; Alperin, *History of the Gulf Intracoastal Waterway*, 7–9; for more on the shallows near Dauphin Island and in Mobile Bay, see Prichard et al., "Southern Louisiana and Southern Alabama in 1819."
16. Belton's son and biographer later wrote that the party stayed at the Old Ursuline Convent, Belton, Biography of F. S. Belton, NYPL; Wilson, "An Architectural History of the Royal Hospital."

17. Isaac Clark Jr. (1787–1842). Born in Castleton, Rutland County, Vermont, Clark was commissioned ensign, 11th Infantry, in 1812. His military history includes: third lieutenant, 11th Infantry (1813); second lieutenant, 11th Infantry (1813); first lieutenant, 11th Infantry (1814); severely wounded at the Siege of Fort Erie, Upper Canada (1814); at Sackets Harbor, New York (1814–15); honorably discharged (1815); reinstated, 5th Infantry (1815); transferred to 6th Infantry (1816); at Plattsburgh, New York (1816); at Rouses Point, New York (1818); assistant commissary of subsistence (1819); at St. Louis, preparing provisions for Yellowstone Expedition (1819); captain, 6th Infantry (1822); engaged in survey of Florida coast (1824–25); brevet major for ten years' faithful service in one grade (1832); paymaster (1836); quartermaster with the rank of major, 6th Infantry (1838); at New Orleans, Louisiana (1835–41); drowned himself in the Ohio River, 22 July 1842. Heitman, *Historical Register*, 1:304; Gardner, *A Dictionary of All Officers*, 116; Hamersly, *Complete Regular Army Register*, 359; *Army and Navy Chronicle*, 16 December 1841; Hammond, "The Spanish Fisheries of Charlotte Harbor," 355–80; Clark to Clark 10 January 1815, Colonel Isaac Clark Papers, University of Vermont Special Collections, Burlington (hereafter Clark-VT); Clark to Clark, 31 August 1816, Clark-VT); Clark to Clark, 6 August 1818, Clark-VT); Littlefield, *Africans and Seminoles*, 40. Belton's biography reports that Clark furnished water transportation only as far as Montgomery's Point. Belton, Biography of F. S. Belton, NYPL.
18. Grant Foreman, *Indian Removal*, 158, notes that the steamboat was the *Mobile*, but Belton calls it *Moine* in his journal and *Moyne* in another letter. Belton to Gibson, August 1836, CGS-IRW, Roll 5, 870–71. There was a steamboat named *Mobile* that ran between New Orleans and Madisonville and Mandeville across Lake Pontchartrain in Louisiana. There was also a mail boat named *Mobile*; *New-Orleans Bee*, 10 August 1836.
19. Dr. James Jones was paid $150 a month for his services attending to the sick of the party to Fort Gibson and ten cents a mile for his return to New Orleans, see Contract with Jones, SIAC, Agent (Belton), Account (528), Year (1837), NARA.
20. The first steamboat to reach Little Rock was the 113-ton *Eagle* in 1822. It is unclear if this is the same boat. Moffatt, "Transportation in Arkansas, 1819–1840."
21. Belton entered into an agreement with William Mahon of Arkansas County, Arkansas, to conduct a portion of the party from the mouth of the White River to the old Arkansas Post in a keel boat "to be furnished with suitable bunks or birth places, and a Cabin partition and proper flooring to keep the Indians dry and wholesome and also a fire place on deck for cooking"; see Articles of Agreement, SIAC, Agent (Belton), Account (2195), Year (1838), NARA.
22. Julian Menard (b. ca. 1812). According to Belton's biographer, Menard provided provisions and fruit for the party. Receipts, SIAC, Agent (Belton), Account (528), Year (1837), NARA; Belton, Biography of F. S. Belton, NYPL. Population Schedules

of the Seventh Census of the United States, Arkansas, Vol. 1, Microcopy 432, Roll 21, NARA.

23. Luther Chase (b. 1810). Born in Massachusetts, Chase was a resident of Pulaski County, Arkansas. He was employed by Jacob Brown as a disbursing agent for Creek emigration as far back as 1834. He later served as a U.S. marshal. Deposition of Luther Chase, 13 January 1845, SFOIA SF 62, Roll 7, 379; Population Schedules of the Seventh Census of the United States, Arkansas, Vol. 2, Microcopy 432, Roll 24, NARA.
24. Captain Jacob Brown, a principal disbursing agent based in Little Rock.
25. Refers to lieutenant colonel Absalom Fowler's command of a battalion of five companies of Arkansas Volunteers that left for the Red River in 1836 out of fear that Mexicans in Texas were attempting to start an Indian war. Brown, *A Life of Albert Pike*, 155–56.
26. Fort Towson was established in 1824 on the Red River near the mouth of the Kiamichi. Morrison, "Fort Towson."
27. Angelico Island was one of many timber islands in the Grand Prairie (the prairie stretched for about forty miles in length and was up to fifteen miles wide). Angelico Island was about eleven miles south of Stuttgart, Arkansas, near the northern part of the prairie. *Biographical and Historical Memoirs of Eastern Arkansas*, 633.
28. Probably Harold Stillwell (1783–1850). The Stillwells were one of the earliest families in the Grand Prairie. Born in New Jersey, Harold Stillwell, represented Arkansas County in the territorial legislature. *Biographical and Historical Memoirs of Pulaski, Jefferson, Lonoke*, 577; *Biographical and Historical Memoirs of Eastern Arkansas*, 635, 640–41, 668.
29. Mary Black's settlement was on the Grand Prairie and was a popular stopover among travelers passing between Little Rock and Memphis. George Archibald McCall (1802–68), who stayed at Mary Black's in 1835, described her as "a widow of goodly proportions: I have seen fatter women, but not many." The public house was described as "a log building, a point of fine timber land stretching out from the south to within half a mile of the house, which was one of those structures called in the West '*two pens and a passage*,' which means two rooms from ten to twenty feet apart, the whole under one roof. One of these was the dining-room, the other the sleeping-room [which contained four single beds]; the kitchen and other apartments occupied by the family, built likewise of logs, were in the rear." McCall, *Letters from the Frontiers*, 280–81.
30. Belton rented two wagons from Thomas Baker near Mary Black's settlement; see United States to Thomas Baker, SIAC, Agent (Belton), Account (528), Year (1837), NARA.
31. James Erwin.
32. Under the contract for the keelboat, Captain Jacob Brown was to furnish payment

to William Mahon (or Joseph Smith, who Mahon appears to have contracted with) at Little Rock. As the party moved toward Mary Black's, either Mahon or Smith followed and threatened a lawsuit for nonpayment. This delayed the party and "After much argument" Belton turned over a draft for the amount. The following day Luther Chase met Belton with $2,000; Chase turned over all but the $250 dollars that went to pay off the charge of the keelboat. Belton to Lewis, 19 September 1838, SIAC, Agent (Belton), Account (2195), Year (1838), NARA; Articles of Agreement, SIAC, Agent (Belton), Account (2195), Year (1838), NARA.

33. Daniel Greathouse (1802–1836). Born in Kentucky, Greathouse moved to Arkansas at age 13 and settled in Pulaski County, Arkansas. In 1835 Greathouse secured a contract with the federal government to subsist large voluntary emigrating parties of Seminoles. Greathouse, along with James Erwin, contracted to supply corn, beef, fodder, wagons, and teams to help transport the Indians from Rock Roe across the state. The Indians never came, however, and Greathouse and Erwin lost considerable money. Deposition of H. Reynolds, 25 December 1844, SFOIA SF 62, Roll 7, 378; United States to Daniel Greathouse, 28 July 1829, SIAC, Agent (Crowell), Account (15,814), Year (1831), NARA; Daniel Greathouse Materials, 1934–1973, Box 1, Folder 7, Hardin-Stark Family Materials, University of Arkansas Libraries, Special Collections, Fayetteville.

34. The homestead of Samuel Newell, a Pulaski County magistrate, or James C. Newell, a judge; Marcy to Sevier, 3 March 1847, SFOIA SF 62, Roll 7; Carter, ed., *Territorial Papers of the United States*, 19:810; United States to James C. Newell, 29 July 1829, SIAC, Agent (Crowell), Account (15,814), Year (1831), NARA; Ross, "Cadron."

35. Receipts show that the payment was made to Mary E. Mathers on the Cadron River. Mary was married to Colonel Thomas Mathers (d. 1839), a native Pennsylvanian who served in the War of 1812 before settling in Pulaski County in 1820. He served in the territorial legislature (1823–25), and became clerk of the county (1832–36), and postmaster of the town of Cadron. Together, they regularly provided provisions to emigrant Indians. Receipts, SIAC, Agent (Belton), Account (528), Year (1837), NARA; United States to Thomas Mathers, SIAC, Agent (Page), Account (20,726), Year (1836), NARA; Shinn, *Pioneers and Makers of Arkansas*, 220–21; Ross, "Cadron."

36. Frederick Fletcher ran a toll and ferry. He charged Belton one dollar per wagon, twelve and a half cents a horse, and six and a quarter cents per person; see Receipts, SIAC, Agent (Belton), Account (528), Year (1837), NARA; Herndon, ed., *Centennial History of Arkansas*, 1:746.

37. Reuben J. Blount (1795–1841). Born in Georgia, Blount came to Arkansas in 1811 and settled in Conway County. SIAC, Agent (Crowell), Account (15,814), Year (1831); Shinn, *Pioneers and Makers of Arkansas*, 221, 260; Ross, "Squatters Rights," 51–66.

38. Kirkbride Potts (1803–79). A native of Pennsylvania, Potts moved to Arkansas via Missouri in 1828. He served in the Arkansas legislature, was a government Indian agent, and operated an inn near Dardanelle in Pope County, Arkansas. His settlement was approximately 220 miles west of Memphis. Morris, "Potts, Kitkbride," 227–28; Worley, "Arkansas and the 'Hostile' Indians"; Deposition of Dempsey Odom, SIAC, Agent (Alabama Emigrating Company), Account (2282), Year (1838).
39. Ben was a Creek Indian and a member of this party. His name appears on the muster roll. He was between twenty-five and fifty years old and traveled alone. Muster Roll (Belton), Entry 299, Box 1, NARA.
40. Belton is referring to himself.
41. William Lewis Lovely (1750–1817). Born in Dublin, Ireland, Lovely moved to Virginia and served in the American Revolution. Moving to Tennessee, Lovely became subagent to the Cherokees. When bands of Cherokees began emigrating to Arkansas Territory Lovely relocated his subagency in 1813 to the Illinois Bayou, a mile north of the Arkansas River. Carter, ed., *Territorial Papers of the United States*, 21:133–35; Nuttall, *Journal of Travels into the Arkansa Territory*, 191; Bergherm, "Lovely, William Lewis," 173–5. Lovely died in 1817 but his widow, Persis, continued to live on the plantation. Duval to Eaton, 10 December 1829, SIAC, Agent (Persis Lovely), Account (15,832), Year (1831), NARA; Agnew, "The Cherokee Struggle for Lovely's Purchase.".
42. Dwight Mission School was a school for Cherokee children that operated between 1820 and 1829 and was named for Timothy Dwight IV (1752–1817), president of Yale College (1795–1817). Carter, ed., *Territorial Papers Papers of the United States*, 21:136–41.
43. Jesse May moved from Dixon County, Tennessee, to Arkansas in 1833 and established a homestead on a tract of land that stretched from near the mouth of Piney Creek to the Pope County line. Starling May and Thomas May also lived in the area. Langford, *Johnson County, Arkansas*, 169.
44. Probably Wesley Garrett (b. ca. 1785). Born in Virginia, Garrett moved to Arkansas in 1828 and was coroner in Pope County, Arkansas, and later a territorial legislator. He lived on Spadra Creek. When Johnson County was created Garrett was the driving force in naming it after his friend Benjamin Johnson, an Arkansas Territory judge. Langford, *Johnson County, Arkansas*, 22, 60, 155.
45. According to Belton's son and biographer, the owner of the Lassiter homestead had been shot and killed only ten days before Belton and the Creeks arrived at the property on 25 September. The matriarch had been sick for many years with scrofula, an infection of the lymph nodes caused by tuberculosis (now called mycobacterial cervical lymphadenitis). The only person on the property able to aid the party was a sixteen-year-old boy. Here Belton turned the detachment over to the physician Dr. Jones and, according to his son and biographer,

remained in one of the Lassiters' outhouses "in a state of unconsciousness from continued fever, and without medicines for five days." Belton, Biography of F. S. Belton, NYPL, 60.

46. Belton went to Florida and served in the Second Seminole War before returning to Alabama as commander of Fort Morgan. Journal of Amos B. Eaton, University of Miami Special Collections, Miami FL.

9. DETACHMENTS 1–6

1. Opothle Yoholo (1790s–1863) was a mile chief of Tuckabatchee and arguably the most powerful Creek leader during the removal era. Prior to the Treaty of Indian Springs signing, Opothle Yoholo served as speaker to Tuckabatchee headman Big Warrior, and as a result of that position, served as the speaker for the Upper Towns. Opothle Yoholo, in fact, had confronted William McIntosh on behalf of the National Council at Indian Springs in 1825, warning the Coweta headman that by selling their country, he was putting his life in danger. When Big Warrior died while in Washington protesting the Indian Springs agreement, Opothle Yoholo filled the political vacuum becoming "'prime minister or Chief Councillor of the Nation'" (and commencing a political rivalry with Big Warrior's son, Tuskenehaw). Opothle Yoholo opposed voluntary emigration and removal, but lost this battle and led detachments 1 and 2 to Indian territory in 1836. Members of William McIntosh's family never forgave Opothle Yoholo for his role in the Coweta headman's death and, during the American Civil War, Opothle Yoholo and his followers (who opposed the McIntosh confederates) were driven by regiments of Confederate Creeks to Kansas. Opothle Yoholo died there in 1863. Green, *Politics of Indian Removal*, 108, 110, 132. See also Taylor to Hanrick, 12 September 1850, Hanrick Family Papers, 1803–1948, New York Historical Society, New York NY.
2. Haveman, *Rivers of Sand*, 200–9; *Arkansas State Gazette*, 25 April 1837; for more on the plates see Adair, *History of the American Indians*, 208–9.
3. Haveman, *Rivers of Sand*, 234–40; Ellisor, *Second Creek War*, 2, 409; Mahon, *History of the Second Seminole War*; Laumer, *Massacre!*; Laumer, *Dade's Last Command*; Bemrose, *Reminiscences of the Second Seminole War*; Sprague, *Origin, Progress, and Conclusion*, 162; Missall and Missall, *The Seminole Wars*.
4. Haveman, *Rivers of Sand*, 234–69.
5. James C. Watson (d. 1843). Born in Cumberland County, North Carolina, Watson was the president of the Insurance Bank of Columbus and served as intendant (mayor) of the city of Columbus in 1835. He was the brother-in-law of Thomas S. Woodward. *New Charter of the City of Columbus*, 111; Ellisor, *Second Creek War*, 324.
6. Edward Hanrick (ca. 1797–1865). Born in Ireland, Hanrick came to Wilmington, North Carolina in 1817, before moving to Montgomery, Alabama in 1819 and

engaging in various mercantile businesses. Hanrick was also a prolific land speculator who, as a member of a land company headed by Indian countryman William Walker, purchased a large number of Creek reserves under the 1832 Treaty of Washington. Hanrick also invested heavily in Texas lands in the 1830s, was a supporter of the Texas revolution, and even raised money to send a battalion to Texas in 1836. In the 1840s he was instrumental in moving the state's capital from Tuscaloosa to Montgomery. Hanrick was known as "Horse-shoe Ned" for always carrying a silver horseshoe in his pocket for luck. Hanrick died at Montgomery, Alabama, 3 December 1865, at age 68. *Montgomery Advertiser*, 22 August 1871; Young, *Redskins, Ruffleshirts, and Rednecks*, 106; List of Land Companies, CRR-Misc, Box 11, NARA; Scarborough, "The Georgia Battalion in the Texas Revolution"; Hudson, "Jane McManus Storm Cazneau"; *Cases Argued and Decided in the Supreme Court of the State of Texas*, 54:103; Edward Hanrick Papers, 1831–1869, Dolph Briscoe Center for American History, University of Texas, Austin.

7. James Abercrombie (1795–1861). Born in Hancock County, Georgia, Abercrombie settled in what is now Dallas County, Alabama, around 1812. He was a corporal in Major Frederick Freeman's Squadron of Georgia Cavalry during the War of 1812. He moved to Montgomery County in 1819 (and later Russell County) and served a number of times in both the Alabama House of Representatives and Senate between the 1820s and 1850s before being elected as a Whig to the U.S. House of Representatives in 1850 and 1852. He moved to Florida in 1856 and died at Pensacola, 2 July 1861. Dodge and Koed, eds., *Biographical Directory of the United States Congress, 1774–2005*, 538; Dorman, *Party Politics in Alabama*, 56–60, 77, 87–88.
8. William A. Campbell lived in Montgomery, Alabama.
9. T. W. Gilman.
10. Other side of the page.
11. Anderson Abercrombie (1785–1867). Born in Hancock County, Georgia, Abercrombie was the older brother of James Abercrombie and Charles Abercrombie. Abercrombie served under General Floyd at the Battles of Ottissee and Calebee during the first Creek War (1813–14). He served in the Georgia legislature (1826–27) before moving to Russell County, Alabama, in 1832. Anderson was one of three men (the others were Thomas M. Martin and Hardeman Owens—a notorious squatter on Creek Indian lands who was famously shot and killed while being evicted by marshals in 1833) charged with finding a location for the first Russell County courthouse. Both Anderson and Charles were members of M. W. Perry & Company, a notorious land company based in Columbus, Georgia, that speculated in Creek reserves under the 1832 Treaty of Washington. Brewer, *Alabama*, 510–11; Ellsworth, "Raiford and Abercrombie," 247–60; List of Land Companies, CRR-Misc, Box 11, NARA; Page to Howell, 10 July 1837, Anderson

Abercrombie Papers, 1836–1867, University of North Carolina Libraries, Chapel Hill; Cherry, "The History of Opelika," 243–49, esp. 245–46.

12. George Whitman was one of the first merchants in Montgomery, Alabama and a prolific land buyer. Whitman served as a lieutenant in the town's first volunteer company, the Montgomery Light Infantry, which was incorporated in 1824. By 1835 he was on the board of directors of the Montgomery and Chattahoochee Railroad Company, and when the Second Creek War started, Whitman served as captain of the "Montgomery Guards," one of two companies organized on 10 May 1836. His speculation in land was notorious to the point that an acquaintance noted that Whitman "owned real estate sufficient to make him a millionaire, which he would undoubtedly be at this moment—*if he had held on to it*." His land business brought him into partnership with Edward C. Hanrick; both were members of an Alabama land company, which sought to colonize large swaths of Texas land in 1835. Beale, Phelan, and Blue, *City Directory and History of Montgomery, Alabama*, 9–11, 19, 27–28, 47, 79; Barker, "Land Speculation as a Cause of the Texas Revolution," 76–95; Smith, *Theatrical Journey-Work*, 45.
13. Attorney.
14. Captain John Page.
15. Lieutenant John George Reynolds.
16. Archibald Henderson (1783–1859). Born in Dumfries, Virginia, Henderson was appointed second lieutenant, U. S. Marine Corps in 1806. His military history includes: first lieutenant, U.S. Marine Corps (1807); captain, U. S. Marine Corps (1811); at Charleston Navy Yard, Boston, Massachusetts (to 1812); in War of 1812, on board the frigate *Constitution*, and participating in the capture of the HMS *Java* (1812); brevet major, U. S. Marine Corps (1814); and HMS *Cyane* and HMS *Levant* (1815); at Boston, Massachusetts (1815); at Portsmouth, New Hampshire (1816); at Washington DC (1819); commandant, U.S. Marine Corps (1820–59), with rank of lieutenant colonel (1820); brevet colonel for ten years faithful service (1830); colonel, U. S. Marine Corps (1834); in Alabama, being engaged in patrolling the Alabama-Georgia border while guarding supply convoys and stagecoach waystations during the Second Creek War (1836); in Florida, being engaged in commanding a battalion of marines in at Battle of Hatcheelustee during the Second Seminole War (1837); brevet brigadier general, U. S. Marine Corps for gallant and meritorious service in Second Creek War and Second Seminole War (1837); stationed at Washington DC (1837–46); died at Washington DC 6 January 1859, at age 75. Fredriksen, *American Military Leaders from Colonial Times to the Present*, 1:333–34; Gardner, *A Dictionary of All Officers*, 224; Henderson to Jesup, 30 August 1836, *ASP-MA*, 7:358; Millett, *Semper Fidelis*, 42, 70–72; *Evening Star*, 10 January 1859; Lewis, *Famous American Marines*, 75–88; Dawson, "With Fidelity and Effectiveness," 727–53; Diary of Thomas Sidney Jesup, 1836, Ethan Allen Hitchcock Collection

on Indian Removal, Box 2, Folder 6, Beinecke Rare Book and Manuscript Library, Yale University, New Haven CT.

17. Barent Dubois (1798–1849). A native of Albany, New York, Dubois married a Tuckabatchee woman named Milly and served as witness to many of Opothle Yoholo's letters. John B. Hogan believed that Opothle Yoholo was under the influence of a number of white men including Dubois. His appointment as assistant agent to M. W. Bateman was almost certainly to appease Opothle Yoholo; see Hogan to Cass, 8 March 1836, *ASP-MA*, 6:751–53.

18. Dr. John B. Bussy. Born in Georgia, Bussy graduated from the University of Pennsylvania in 1835 with a medical degree specializing in "Influence of Cold." *American Journal of the Medical Sciences*, 16:262.

19. Richard Bedon Screven (1808–51). Born in South Carolina, Screven graduated from the U.S. Military Academy, West Point, New York, in 1829 (46th of 46) and was promoted brevet second lieutenant, 2nd Infantry (1829), and second lieutenant, 2nd Infantry (1829). His military service includes: Hancock Barracks, Maine (1829–31); transferred to 4th Infantry (1831); Baton Rouge, Louisiana (1831–32); Fort Jesup, Louisiana (1832); Baton Rouge, Louisiana (1832–35); Bay St. Louis, Mississippi (1835); Fort Wood, Louisiana (1835–36); first lieutenant, 4th Infantry (1836); in Second Seminole War, being engaged in battle at Camp Izard and in Battle of Oloklikaha (1836); conducting detachment 2 of Creek Indians to Indian territory (1836–37); in Second Seminole War, being engaged at the Battle of Okeechobee (1837); captain, 8th Infantry (1838); at Ogdensburg, New York, during Canada independence movement (1839–40); recruiting service (1840); Jefferson Barracks, Missouri (1840); in Second Seminole War (1840–42); Fort Brooke, Florida (1842–44); Key West, Florida (1844); Fort Brooke, Florida (1844–45); in military occupation of Texas (1845–46); in Mexican-American War, being engaged at Battle of Monterrey, Mexico (September 1846); brevet major for gallant and meritorious conduct during the Battle of Monterrey (1846); at siege of Veracruz, Mexico (1847), Battle of Cerro Gordo, Mexico (1847), capture of San Antonio, Mexico (1847), Battle of Churubusco, Mexico (1847), Battle of Molino del Rey, Mexico (1847); brevet lieutenant colonel for gallant and meritorious conduct in Battle of Molino del Rey (1847); recruiting service at Albany, New York (1848–50); on sick leave (1850–51); died at New Orleans, Louisiana, 15 May 1851, at age 43. Cullum, *Biographical Register* (1868), 1:359–60; Heyward, ed., *Genealogy of the Pendarvis-Bedon Families*, 122–23; Brown, *Touching America's History*, 54–63.

20. James Hervey Simpson (1813–83). Born in New Brunswick, New Jersey, Simpson graduated from the United States Military Academy, West Point, New York, in 1832 (18th of 45) and was promoted brevet second lieutenant, 3rd Artillery (1832). His military history includes: at Fort Preble, Maine (1832–33); second lieutenant, 3rd Artillery (1833); on recruiting service (1833–34); at Fort Monroe,

Virginia (1834); at Fort King, Florida (1835); on commissary duty, Wetumpka, Alabama (1836); on commissary duty, Charleston, South Carolina (1836–37); first lieutenant, 3rd Artillery (1837); in Florida, being engaged in Second Seminole War, on commissary duty (1837), as aide-de-camp to Brevet Brigadier General Abraham Eustis (1837–38), at the Battle of Loxahatchee (1838); first lieutenant, Corps of Topographical Engineers (1838); assistant topographical engineer on Lake Erie harbor improvements (1838–39); constructing roads in Florida (1839–40); improvements on Erie Harbor, Pennsylvania (1840–41); surveying northwest lakes (1841–45); Lake Erie harbor improvement (1845–48); construction of lighthouse at Monroe, Michigan (1847–49); A.M. degree, College of New Jersey (Princeton University) (1848); exploring a route from Fort Smith, Arkansas, to Santa Fé, New Mexico (1849); appointed chief topographical engineer in the Department of New Mexico (1850); oversaw construction of roads in Minnesota (1851–56); captain, Topographical Engineers (1853); on survey of coasts (1856–58); appointed chief topographical engineer with the U.S. Army in Utah (1858); exploring new wagon route from Salt Lake City to the Pacific Ocean, portions of which are now part of U.S. Route 50, and dubbed the "Loneliest Road in America" by *Life* magazine in 1986 (1859); writing and preparing his report on his reconnaissance (1860–61); in the Civil War, being engaged in mustering Ohio volunteers (1861), as chief topographical engineer in the Department of the Shenandoah (1861); major, Topographical Engineers (1861); joined 4th New Jersey Volunteers with the rank of colonel (1861); engaged in defense of Washington DC (1861–62); in the Peninsula Campaign, being engaged in the Battle of Eltham's Landing, Virginia (1862), and captured at Gaines's Mill, Virginia (1862); prisoner of war at Richmond, Virginia (28 June to 12 August 1862); exchanged (1862); with his regiment on march from Harrison's Landing, Virginia to Alexandria, Virginia (1862); resigned voluntary commission (1862); chief topographical engineer (1862–63), and chief engineer (1863) of the Department of the Ohio; promoted lieutenant colonel, Corps of Engineers (1863); engaged in constructing and repairing railroads, erecting temporary defenses, and in general charge of the fortifications in Kentucky (1863–65); engineer agent at Cincinnati, Ohio (1864–65); chief engineer of the District of Kentucky (1865); brevet colonel and brevet brigadier general, U.S. Army for meritorious service during Civil War (1865); chief engineer of the Department of the Interior, Washington DC, overseeing inspection of the Union Pacific railroad and federal wagon roads (1865–67); colonel, Corps of Engineers (1867); superintending engineer of defenses at Key West and Tortugas, Florida (1867–68), at Fort Madison, Maryland (1868–69), at Baltimore, Maryland (1868–69); navigation improvement of Patapsco and Susquehanna rivers (1868–70); improvements of Fifth and Sixth Lighthouse Districts (1868–70); improvements at mouth of Cape Fear and Nags Head, North Carolina (1870); improvements at Cambridge and Queenstown harbors, Maryland (1870);

improvement of defenses at Mobile, Alabama; Pensacola, Florida; Ship Island, Mississippi; improvements of Mobile Bay, Alabama; river surveys of Coosa River, Tombigbee River, and Apalachicola River; improvements at Eighth Lighthouse District, east of Pearl River, Mississippi (1870–72); surveys of Choctawhatchee River, Chattahoochee River, and St. Marks River, and surveys of Tampa Bay and Apalachicola Bay (1871–72); improvement of Tombigbee River, dredging Cedar Key bar, Florida (1872); obstruction removal on Mississippi River, Missouri River, Arkansas River, White River, and St. Francis River, and survey of Forked Deer River, Tennessee (1873); improvement of Ouachita River and Yazoo River (1873); improvement of Little Missouri River and Current River (1873–75); improvement of Osage River (1873–77); improvement of Mississippi River, between the mouths of the Illinois River and Ohio River (1873–80); survey of the "Mississippi Route" between Alton, Illinois, and mouth of Ohio River (1874–75); member of the board on improvement of Appomattox River (1870), and Mobile Harbor, Alabama (1872–73); preservation of Vicksburg, Mississippi, waterfront (1877–78); preservation of bridges at east Boston, Massachusetts (1868), Montgomery, Alabama (1872), Nebraska City, Nebraska (1873), Little Rock, Arkansas (1873), Louisiana, Missouri (1873), St. Louis, Missouri (1873), Carondelet, Missouri (1874), Cincinnati, Ohio (1874), Clinton, Iowa (1874), over Mississippi River (1876–77), Beaver, Pennsylvania (1877); retired from active service (1880); died at St. Paul, Minnesota, 2 March 1883, at age 70. Cullum, *Biographical Register* (1879), 3:91; Cullum, *Biographical Register* (1891), 1:515–6; Wilson and Fiske, eds., *Appletons' Cyclopædia of American Biography*, 5:538; "James Hervey Simpson," *Northwest Review*; Eicher and Eicher, *Civil War High Commands*, 490; *An Account of the Receipts and Expenditures of the United States, for the Year 1836*, 128; Simpson, *Journal of a Military Reconnaissance, from Santa Fé, New Mexico*; Simpson, *Report of Explorations across the Great Basin.*

21. James H. Simpson was angry that he had not been appointed military oversight of one of the detachments after Orders nos. 63 and 67 were issued. In a tersely worded 25 August 1836 letter to Captain John Page, Simpson writes: "'Orders No: 67' I have just read. In those Orders, I perceive that all the principle military agents, have been appointed, & I left out—I know not why I have been left out; but that my claims to one of those appointments were prior & Superior, to say the least, to Either of the Marine officers, [Lts. Reynolds and Sloan] I positively affirm & can maintain—Independent of my being an officer of the Army, my having already been assigned to Indian Service, not to say any thing about Rank, Should have given me the preference—My having been uselessly superseded by Lt: Scriven, I should have thought would have satisfied your disposition to do me injustice, without your adding injury to injustice, by fixing me to a second place, when right, propriety, & opportunity, pointed out to you for me a first place,—one of the principle agencies—As to Lt: Scriven as also yourself, I am

disposed & willing at all times to accord a favor; but it must not be at the Expense of justice to myself—I have never Complained of my having been thrust down in to a subordinate station under Lt: Scriven; because I knew his anxiety to get off soon, as also yours to satisfy that anxiety; and because, in doing Lt: Scriven a kindness, I still had the prospect of being appointed principle military agent of another Detachment—That prospect however is now gone, & I do now most positively assert, that you have treated me with injustice; that I ought not only to have been kept principle agent over the 2nd Detachment,—for Lt: Scriven could have been assigned to another, & then one of the Marine officers dispensed with,—but that in the appointment of Lt: Scriven as principle military agent of the 2nd Detachment, I ought at least to have been transferred to the principle agency of another Detachment. As it is, I have not only been deprived of my just situation as principle Agent of 2nd Detachment, & have been thrust & kept in a Subordinate station, when the opportunity was offerred you to retrieve your previous act of injustice to me, by transferring me to the principle agency of the 3d, 4th, or 5th Detachment; but, further, that you have left it to a mere Contingency or Contingencies, to determine whether I am to be Continued on Indian Emigration service,—whether I am to accompany one of the Emigrating parties west. I say you have left it to Contingencies &c: for the Certainty of a division of the 2nd Detachment in to two parties is a Contingency, & the Certainty of my being the officer ordered to accompany one of those parties is another Contingency.

"Another Cause of dissatisfaction & Complaint with me, is,—that the very same act upon your part, which should have been done in respect to myself, on the ground of justice,—you have done in the Care of Lt: Reynolds, where Consideration of justice could scarcely have influenced you. I hold, that if any officer were transferred from a subordinate agency to a principle one, I should have been that officer.

"I have felt aggrieved, Sir, by your treatment to me in this matter of the assignment of officers to their Subordinate Station in the Emigration service, & therefore have made this frank avowal to you, as the Chief Superintendent, of my feelings & opinions with Regard to that treatment." Simpson to Page, 25 August 1836, RG 94, 159-Q, Container 14, Folder: "Letters Received from Officers, Lieutenant J. H. Simpson," NARA.

22. It is unclear what Lieutenant James H. Simpson meant by "a favor" and "anxiety to get off soon" when referencing Lieutenant Richard B. Screven (in his 25 August 1836 letter to Captain John Page), but Screven's 25 July 1836 application letter to serve as military agent for one of the detachments gives some insight. In his communication to Thomas S. Jesup, Screven writes: "I respectfully request to be considered an Applicant for service in the Emigration of Indians.

"I do not presume to present to you considerations having reference to the situation of my family or my own health—however urgent they may be.—but I do request you to take into consideration the fact that I have been seven years a Lieutenant, and have not during the whole period, been on any Kind of duty whatever detatched from my Regiment.

"Should you think that my detail for the duty, would be consistent with the good of the service, I shall be greatly obliged, if you will cause it to be made." Screven to Jesup, 25 July 1836, RG 94, 159-Q, Container 14, Folder: "Letters Received from Officers, Lieutenant R. B. Screven," NARA.

23. Henry Stanton (1796–1856). Born in Vermont, Stanton was appointed third lieutenant, Light Artillery in 1813. His military history includes: captain (staff), assistant deputy quartermaster general (1813–14); in War of 1812, being engaged in quartermaster duty (1813–14), as aide-de-camp to Major General George Izard on the northern frontier (1814); second lieutenant, Light Artillery (1814); leave of absence (1815–17); resigned from U.S. Army (1817); reappointed in the U.S. Army with rank of captain (staff), assistant deputy quartermaster general with the rank of captain (1818); quartermaster at U.S. Military Academy, West Point, New York (1818); quartermaster duty at Atlantic posts (1818–22); major (staff), deputy quartermaster general (1820); quartermaster duty at New Orleans, Louisiana (1822–23), at Detroit, Michigan Territory (1823–26), at New York (1826–36); brevet lieutenant colonel, for faithful service, ten years in one grade (1830); as senior quartermaster of the army (to 1836); in Alabama, being engaged in Second Creek War, as acting adjutant general under major general Thomas S. Jesup (1836); in Florida, being engaged in Second Seminole War, as acting adjutant general under major general Thomas S. Jesup (1836–37); chief quartermaster at New York, New York (1837–46); colonel (staff), assistant quartermaster general (1838); in charge of quartermaster general's office, Washington DC (1846–47); brevet brigadier general, U.S. Army for meritorious conduct during Mexican-American War (1847); chief quartermaster at Philadelphia, Pennsylvania (1847–51); at St. Louis, Missouri (1851–56); on leave of absence and awaiting orders (1856); died at Fort Hamilton, New York, 1 August 1856. Cullum, *Biographical Register* (1868), 1:59–60; Wilson and Fiske, eds., *Appletons' Cyclopædia of American Biography*, 5:649.

24. Jim Boy (ca. 1793–1851). Also known as Tustunnuggee Emathla, Jim Boy was a prominent headman associated with the Clewalla or Thlobthlocco towns (he is often listed as headman of both). He was present during the attack on Fort Mims in August 1813 and later became one of the ninety "mile chiefs" selected by the Creeks in Council to receive a full section of land under the 1832 Treaty of Washington. In 1836 Jim Boy joined the Americans in arresting the rebels of the Second Creek War, and he participated in the Florida campaign against the Seminoles. While en route to Indian territory in the fall of 1837, four of Jim Boy's children died on the *Monmouth* steamboat disaster. Thomas L. McKenney and

James Hall noted that Jim Boy was "a fine-looking man, six feet and one inch in height, and well proportioned, of manly and martial appearance and great physical strength." Painter John Mix Stanley noted while painting him in 1843 that he was "vigorous and active, and is still able to undergo much fatigue and hardship." McKenney notes he was born around 1793, while Stanley estimated Jim Boy to be 52 years old in 1843 (born in 1791). McKenney and Hall, *History of the Indian Tribes of North America*, 2:95–96; Woodward, *Woodward's Reminiscences*, 88–89; Stanley, *Portraits*, 10–11; Thrapp, *Encyclopedia of Frontier Biography*, 2:727.

25. Dr. George B. McKnight (d. 1857). Born in New York, McKnight served in a volunteer company during the War of 1812, before graduating from the College of Physicians and Surgeons, New York City (Columbia University School of Medicine) in 1816. His civil and military history includes: surgeon's mate, 1st Infantry (1817); resigned, U.S. Army (1818); post surgeon (1820); resigned, U.S. Army (1824); resided in Chambersburg, Pennsylvania (ca. 1824–29); appointed assistant surgeon, U.S. Navy in 1829; assistant surgeon on the sloop *Natchez*, West Indies Station, patrolling Atlantic Coast (1829–30); briefly on sloop *Grampus*, tending to Simón Bolívar as he was dying (1830); at Washington DC (1830); at naval hospital, Philadelphia, Pennsylvania (1832); leave of absence (1832); on sloop *Natchez*, being engaged in cruising the Atlantic coast (1832–33); leave of absence (1833); on schooner *Experiment*, West Indies Station (1833–34); on sloop of war *Vandalia* (1834); leave of absence (1834); passed assistant surgeon, U.S. Navy (1835); at marine barracks, Washington DC (1836); in Alabama, being engaged in Colonel Archibald Henderson's regiment patrolling the Alabama-Georgia border while guarding supply convoys and stagecoach waystations during the Second Creek War (1836); in Florida, engaged in Second Seminole War (1836–37); surgeon, U.S. Navy (1838); on leave at Washington DC (1838); on leave at Washington DC (1842–43); on sloop *Vincennes* (1846–47); died at Washington DC 13 May 1857. Gardner, *A Dictionary of All Officers*, 300; Collum, *History of the United States Marine Corps*, 69; *Catalogue of the Alumni, Officers and Fellows of the College of Physicians and Surgeons*, 28; Richard, "History of Franklin County," 280; *Military and Naval Magazine of the United States* 4, no. 1 (September 1834): 80; *ASP-MA*, 4:61, 4:245, 4:457, 4:482, 4:891, 4:948; Register kept by Assistant Surgeon George B. McKnight, 1833–34, Columbia University Health Sciences Library, New York NY; Force, *Register of the Army and Navy*, 140; *Naval Magazine*, January 1836; *Register of the Commissioned and Warrant Officers of the Navy*, 99; Slatta and De Grummond, *Simón Bolívar's Quest for Glory*, 291.

26. Mann Page Lomax (1787–1842). Born in Portobago, Caroline County, Virginia, Lomax graduated from the College of William and Mary, and studied law before being appointed second lieutenant, Artillery in 1807. His military history includes: promoted first lieutenant, Artillery (1811); transferred to 1st Artillery (1812); in

War of 1812, being engaged as assistant adjutant general with the rank of major, under General James Wilkerson at the St. Lawrence River (1814–15); transferred to Corps of Artillery (1814); captain, Corps of Artillery (1814); retained (1815); transferred to 3rd Artillery (1821); brevet major, ten years faithful service in one grade (1824); at Fort Wolcott, Newport, Rhode Island (ca. 1828–36); in Alabama, being engaged in Second Creek War (1836); in Florida, being engaged in the Second Seminole War (1836–38); major, Ordnance Corps (1838); at Watertown Arsenal, Massachusetts (1838–42); died of tuberculosis at Watertown Arsenal, Massachusetts, 27 March 1842, at age 65. Lomax reportedly returned from Florida in 1838 "with a shattered constitution and health so impaired, he was unable to walk without assistance." U.S. Congress, Senate Committee Report 142, *In Senate of the United States*, 1–3; Lomax, *Genealogy of the Virginia Family of Lomax*, 19, 39–42; Heitman, *Historical Register*, 1:639; Hamersly, *Complete Regular Army Register*, 585; Gardner, *A Dictionary of All Officers*, 283; White, Jr., "The Journals of Lieutenant John Pickell, 1836–1837," 142–71.

27. Thomas Theodore Sloan. For biography see note 2 to chapter 15.

10. DETACHMENT 1

1. Mark W. Bateman (ca. 1799–1837). Born in Pennsylvania, Bateman graduated from the U.S. Military Academy, West Point, New York, in 1823 (16th of 35) and was promoted to second lieutenant, 6th Infantry in 1823. His military service includes: frontier duty at Fort Atkinson, Council Bluffs (1823–25); engaged in Missouri expedition (1825); at Fort Atkinson, Council Bluffs (1825–26); first lieutenant, 6th Infantry (1826); on recruiting service (1826–28); at Jefferson Barracks, Missouri (1828–31); on recruiting service (1831–33); at Jefferson Barracks, Missouri (1833–34); Indian service (1834–36); disbursing agent for Cherokees, Calhoun, Tennessee (1835); on quartermaster duty and conducting detachment 1 of Creek Indians west (1836–37); captain, 6th Infantry (1836); frontier duty, Camp Sabine, Louisiana (1837); assigned to detachment 6 of relocating Creek Indians (1837); died at Mount Vernon Arsenal, Alabama, 31 July 1837, at age 38. Cullum, *Biographical Register* (1868), 1:247; *Register of Commissioned Officers of the Sixth Regiment of Infantry*, 11, 17, 27; Gibson to Bateman, 21 November 1835, SIAC, Agent (Bateman), Account (3797), Year (1839), NARA.
2. United States to John B. Bussy, M.D., SIAC, Agent (Bateman), Account (3817), Year (1839), NARA.
3. Detachment 1 was originally ordered to begin their march on 20 August 1836. On 19 August Opothle Yoholo declared to Jesup that his people would not be ready to proceed by that time, so an order was issued, which pushed back the commencement five days. On 25 August the chiefs declared that they would not be able to raise an army to fight the Seminoles in Florida unless given some more time, so Jesup pushed the departure day back another five

days. Page to Gibson, 9 November 1836, SIAC, Agent (Barry), Account (507), Year (1837), NARA.

4. John F. Lane (see note 30 to chapter 7).
5. Probably "Spanny Fixico," number 316 on the 1832 Tuckabatchee town census.
6. Cahaba River.
7. The *Farmer* was a 250- to 300-ton steamboat that could carry up to two thousand bales of cotton or up to three thousand barrels of goods. The typical complement of officers and men for a vessel of this size was eleven people, "besides 8 firemen & 4 deck hands." The vessel commanded between $200 and $300 per day on the Alabama and Mississippi rivers. Polk to Lewis, SIAC, Agent (Alabama Emigrating Company), Account (2282), Year (1838), NARA.
8. Bateman misdates Friday, 14 October, and continues this succession unaware.
9. Bateman remained in camp for two weeks. Monday, 31 October 1836 is the correct date.
10. James Erwin.
11. Bateman left the party for Fort Gibson to deliver two letters to William Armstrong (see Bateman to Armstrong, 9 November 1836, and Jesup to Bateman, 3 October 1836, as well as Armstrong's letter to Harris, 24 November 1836).
12. John T. Sprague was the military commander of detachment 5. Although detachment 1 was designated the advance party, Sprague decided to take his party by water from Memphis to Little Rock in order to avoid the congestion at Rock Roe. As a result, detachment 5 was ahead of the other four detachments at this point in the journey.
13. Post oak (*Quercus stellata*) is a tree common to the American Southeast. The bad road Bateman describes may be the result of the fact that post oaks grow best on dry, sandy soils, or on gravelly clays with poor surface drainage. Gilman and Watson, "*Quercus stellate*: Post Oak," 1–2; Nelson et al., *Trees of Eastern North America*, 312.
14. Old Dwight Mission.
15. For a description of this area see "Site at the mouth of Lee's creek, B No. 1," *ASP-MA*, 7:981–82, which was provided by Lieutenant Colonel William Whistler and Captain John Stuart, both of the 7th Infantry: "The point of highland at the mouth of Lee's creek is on the north side of the Arkansas river, about five miles below Fort Smith, and about one and a half mile above Van Buren. It is the south end of a considerable mountain, which terminates abruptly at the river and on Lee's creek, ranging parallel and close to the river for the distance of one and a half mile, and about one mile on the creek. This ridge or mountain runs back on a northeast course for many miles, becoming higher as it leaves the river. Immediately at the point, and a little below the mouth of the creek, the summit of the hill is tolerably level, and the surface smooth, to an extent sufficiently great to give ample room for the erection of an extensive military

establishment. A square of four or five hundred feet can be got by levelling about six feet—or, in other words, by taking off about that depth of clay from the highest point within that space.

"The height of the bluff from the river edge at the mouth of the creek to the site is four hundred feet and six inches, according to a measurement which we had by means of a well-constructed plumb-level [a carpenter's line with a plumb line at a right angle]. The face of this rise on the side of the river, as well as on the creek, is extremely precipitous. The rocks in some places at the summit of the precipice are perpendicular, at other places there are brakes and winding ways among the crags and piles of stone, through which persons on foot can with great care, and by holding on to the rocks and shrubs, ascend and descend from the bottom to the top. We were told that horses had at some particular point ascended it; but from the appearance of the bluff, one would suppose it to be impossible for a horse to ascend it in its present condition. A cannon placed on the brink of this precipice cannot be so depressed as to rake the face of the hill. A man standing twenty yards back from the brink can barely see the edge of the water on the opposite side of the river, and cannot see the creek when he is even twenty feet back from the brink. At the site the river can only be seen at a great distance above and below—that part of the river, being immediately abreast of the site, being obscured from view at that point for near a mile both above and below.

"The scenery from the extreme point of this precipice is seldom surpassed, either in extent or beauty of appearance. A birdseye view of the country from north, round by south, to northeast, can be had to the distance of twenty miles at one glance, and without changing the position more than to turn the head.

"The land on this hill is poor, and the timber on it consists entirely of black jack, black oak, and post oak, which stand thickly on the surface, and is of a very short and stunted growth, and is calculated for little else than fence rails and for fuel. The timber above the mouth of Lee's creek consists of the cup oak, red oak, ash, and other timber common to the Arkansas bottom, which would have to be hauled near a mile, and that, too, across the creek, either by means of a boat or bridge, which would have to be constructed for the purpose, and would then have to be hauled up a steep and rocky road. There is no timber below the mouth of the creek of that kind within several miles of the site; and that description of timber is absolutely necessary for making shingles, &c.

"There is an abundant supply of red sandstone to be found in almost every direction; but there is no limestone near the site that we could hear of.

"There is one spring, about a half mile from the site, which is said to run during the whole of the summer. Another spring was pointed out to us, within a fourth of a mile of the site, which runs during the winter and spring months only. There are no creeks or large branch on the hill for the distance of some miles from the site.

"No wells have been dug on the hill, and it is therefore impossible to say whether water can be procured by digging or not. The spring that was shown to us nearest to the site rises in a flat place near the top of the mountain. It is supported by rains that fall on the surface and sink.

"About a fourth of a mile up the creek from the site the hill slopes off towards the creek in such a manner that a road could be made, though with much labor, that would be passable for horses, and even for teams; which road would make a communication between the site and the creek, within about the distance of a half mile, or near it. In making this road much digging would be required, and extensive masses of stone would have to be removed; and the road would even then be steep. A little further on the same direction a road might be got to the creek, on a much more gradual slope, which would strike it about a mile and a half distant from the site.

"The road marked on the enclosed sketch, crossing the mountain from Van Buren to the present crossing of Lee's creek, passes within a half mile of the site. This road, on leaving Van Buren, ascends the side of the mountain, over rocks and steep points, for the distance of about six or seven hundred yards, when it reaches the summit of the mountain, and then passes over a level space for near a mile, when it begins to descend, by a long and much more gradual slope, to the creek, which it crosses about a mile and a half from the site. A road might be, with much labor and expense, cut in the side of the hill from the site to the river; and might, by taking it along the side of the hill to the distance of five or six hundred yards, be rendered passable, and suitable for all military purposes on that side of the site. It could not, however, be commanded or covered by guns from the site; and it is doubtful whether it could be covered from any other point on the hill.

"There is a narrow pass of a few yards in width along the river, and at the base of the hill, extending from Van Buren round to a point on Lee's creek, north of the site, and where the point of the mountain comes directly to the creek, which can now be passed over by horses all of that distance. There is a good point on the river for a ferry, about a half mile below the site. Directly opposite the site is an extensive sand-bar, extending from above the mouth of Lee's creek some distance down the river.

"Lee's creek, near the mouth, appears to be about thirty yards wide, and it is of precisely the same character and description of the Poteau. Its banks are soft and miry, as is also the bottom. It is backed up by the Arkansas, at every rise of that river, to the distance of some miles, when it has the appearance and character of a mill-pond, and when that takes place in the summer, it is said that its water is stagnant, and that it is usually covered with a scum, and when in that state it must be unhealthy; but whether its deleterious effects would reach the top of the hill or not, is beyond our ability to determine. Various accounts have been given respecting the settling of the fogs on this hill; some say that they do settle there, and are often seen there, when they cannot be discovered below. The country in the vicinity of the site, from the north round by south to northeast, is low and flat, and contains some pools of stagnant water, as is the case on all parts of the Arkansas bottom.

"There is no apparent cause on the hill to produce sickness; but whether the site would be healthy or not is out of our power to determine.

"There are but very few persons living on the mountain near the site, and none have been there long enough to prove the health of the place. Van Buren, situated on the river about a mile and a half below the site, and directly at the foot of the mountain is considered to be one of the most sickly places in the country.

"The few families settled above the mouth of Lee's creek (it is said) have been sickly this last season."

16. Principal military agent.
17. Pearly S. Gerald, Henry W. Russell of Tallassee, Alabama, and Spire M. Hagerty (ca. 1810–49). The United States entered into a contract with Russell and Gerald to supply rations to the Creeks of detachment 1 at Tallassee over the summer of 1836. Hagerty also sold rations to the Creeks. Hagerty married Rebecca McIntosh (1815–86, daughter of William McIntosh), in Texas in 1838. Provision returns, SIAC, Agent (Page), Account (1490), Year (1838), NARA; Batman to Jesup, 16 July 1836, RG 94, 159-Q, Container 15, Folder "Letters Received During the Creek War, 1836–38, From Camps & Forts," NARA; Carroll, *Homesteads Ungovernable*, 37.
18. James A. Chambers (1800–1838). Born in Maryland, Chambers graduated from the U.S. Military Academy, West Point, New York, in 1820 (8th of 30) and was promoted to second lieutenant, Light Artillery (1820). His military history includes: transferred to Corps of Artillery (1820); Fort Columbus, New York (1820–21); Fort Mackinac, Michigan Territory (1821–23); transferred to 2nd Artillery in reorganization of the army (1821); New York harbor (1823–24); Artillery School for Practice, Fort Monroe, Virginia (1824–26); Fort Columbus, New York (1826); on commissary and quartermaster duty, Baltimore, Maryland (1826); on ordnance duty (1826–28); Savannah, Georgia (1828–29); Augusta Arsenal, Georgia (1829); Savannah, Georgia (1829–30); Augusta Arsenal, Georgia (1830); in Cherokee Nation (1830); brevet first lieutenant, for faithful service, ten years in one grade (1830); Savannah, Georgia (1830–31, 1831–32); first lieutenant, 2nd Artillery (1832); Fort Pike, Louisiana (1833–35); in Florida, being engaged in ordnance duty during Second Seminole War (1835–36); assistant quartermaster (1836–38); in Alabama, being engaged as chief quartermaster and commissary during Second Creek War (1836); in Florida, being engaged in Second Seminole War, as aide-de-camp to Major General Thomas S. Jesup (1836–38), as acting assistant adjutant general

of the Army of the South (1837, 1837–38), and being engaged in the Battle of Hatcheelustee Creek (1837), and the Battle of Loxahatchee (1838); captain (staff), assistant quartermaster and captain, 2nd Artillery (1838); quartermaster duty at Baltimore, Maryland (1838); died at Baltimore, Maryland, 10 December 1838, at age 38 of disease from service in Florida. Cullum, *Biographical Register* (1868), 1:199; Gardner, *A Dictionary of All Officers*, 109.

19. Thomas J. Abbott. A Tuscaloosa, Alabama lawyer, Abbott was appointed to take a Creek population census in accordance with the 1832 Treaty of Washington (Abbott conducted the Lower towns census, Benjamin S. Parsons conducted the Upper towns). Abbott later served as a certifying agent (appointed to approve Creek land sales) and as lawyer for James C. Watson & Company. Ellisor, Second Creek War, 50, 56, 193.
20. Mad Blue, one of the mile chiefs of Tuckabatchee; Little Doctor (Nahetluc Hopie), one of the mile chiefs of Tuckabatchee, and a signer of the 1826 Treaty of Washington; James Island, one of the mile chiefs of Coweta; Tuscoona Harjo, the mile chief of Fish Pond; Menawa, one of the mile chiefs of Okfuskee; Kotchar Emathla, one of the mile chiefs of Okfuskee; Hatcheechubba Tom, the mile chief of Upper Hatcheechubba; Yoholo Micco, one of the mile chiefs of Upper Eufaula; Hobie Fixico, one of the mile chiefs of Emarhe; Tustunnuggee Chopco, one of the mile chiefs of Tallassee; Ko-nip-pe Emathla, one of the mile chiefs of Thlakatchka. For Little Doctor, see Rhees, *An Account of The Smithsonian Institution*, 56.
21. Spoak-oak Micco, a Mile Chief of Kialiga. This headman may have been the same one who, according to Albert James Pickett, led the procession of chiefs who carried the sacred Tuckabatchee brass plates to Indian territory. Pickett writes: "When the inhabitants of this town, in the autumn of 1836, took up the line of march for their present home in the Arkansas Territory, these plates were transported thence by six Indians, remarkable for their sobriety and moral character, at the head of whom was the Chief, Spoke-oak, Micco. Medicine, made expressly for their safe transportation, was carried along by these warriors. Each one had a plate strapped behind his back, enveloped nicely in buckskin. They carried nothing else, but marched on, one before the other, the whole distance to Arkansas, neither communicating nor conversing with a soul but themselves, although several thousands were emigrating in company; and walking, with a solemn religious air, one mile in advance of the others." Pickett, *History of Alabama*, 1:86–87.
22. One of the most prominent types of fraud was "personation," whereby another Indian was bribed by a white land speculator to impersonate the true owner of a reserve. The impersonator was versed in the pertinent facts certifying agents would ask (the name of the victim, his town, the location of the town's square ground, etc.) and would then "sell" the half-section to the speculator for a discounted price. Once the certifying agent left, the impersonator gave all but five

or ten dollars (the bribe) back to the speculator. Haveman, "'Last Evening I Saw the Sun Set.'"

23. Under the provisions of the 1832 Treaty of Washington, those Creeks who chose to remain in Alabama after five years from the date of ratification (4 April 1837) would receive a fee-simple patent to their reserve and, theoretically, become citizens of the state of Alabama.
24. Dr. Robert W. McHenry was the certifying agent for Chambers and Macon counties, Alabama, where some of the heaviest frauds occurred. Ellisor, *Second Creek War*, 97–136.
25. Alfred Balch and Thomas Hartley Crawford (the future commissioner of Indian affairs) were appointed as special commissioners to investigate the frauds and the causes of the Second Creek War.
26. John Floyd (1769–1839). Born in Beaufort, South Carolina, Floyd moved to Camden County, Georgia in 1791. He worked as a shipwright and became brigadier general of the First Brigade of Georgia Militia (1813–14, 1814–15) after the Red Stick attack on Fort Mims in 1813. He was injured at the Battle of Ottissee and engaged the Red Sticks at the Battle of Calebee Creek. Floyd later commanded a brigade at Savannah, Georgia, charged with protecting the coast against a British attack. He served in the Georgia House of Representatives (1820–27), and as U.S. representative from Georgia (1827–29). He died near Jefferson, Georgia, 24 June 1839, at age 69. Dodge and Koed, eds., *Biographical Directory of the United States Congress*, 1065.
27. Under Article 2 of the 1832 Treaty of Washington, twenty reserves were set aside for the benefit of Creek orphans. This land was subsequently rented out to white farmers for a few years after the allotments were located. In 1835 the headmen notified President Jackson that they wanted to sell the orphan reserves because they needed money and because the renters, according to the chiefs, were depreciating the value of the land because they were not careful "of the timber or the mode of cultivation." The twenty reserves were subsequently divided into quarter sections and sold at auction in Mardisville, Alabama on 25 and 26 April 1836. The unsold reserves were auctioned at Tuskegee on 8 February 1837. The proceeds were then invested. Due to federal negligence, the Creeks did not receive the orphan funds until 1882. Haveman, "Last Evening I Saw the Sun Set for the Last Time."
28. James L. Alexander was an Indian countryman who was a member of detachment 1. According to Harry F. O'Beirne and Edward S. O'Beirne, Alexander married the niece of Tuckabatchee Micco and served as "forage master for the Indians on their trip to this country. At the time of his death he was clerk of the council and correspondent for his people." O'Beirne and O'Beirne, *Indian Territory*, 245–47.
29. Mile chief of Tuckabatchee. John Mix Stanley painted Tuckabatchee Micco in June

1843 and wrote that he was "the great Medicine or Mystery Man of the Creeks" or "Physic-maker" and that his countrymen "suppose him to be indued with supernatural powers, and capable of making it rain copiously at will." These supernatural powers were used, according to Stanley, to plan the Tuckabatchee town rotunda that was built in Indian territory. Stanley notes that Tuckabatchee Micco "cut sticks in miniature of every log required in the construction of the building, and distributed them proportionately among the residents of the town, whose duty it was to cut logs corresponding with their sticks, and deliver them upon the ground appropriated for the building, at a given time. At the raising of the house, not a log was cut or changed from its original destination; all came together in their appropriate places, as intended by the designer. During the planning of this building, which occupied him six days, he did not partake of the least particle of food. Stanley, *Portraits of North American Indians*, 12–13.

30. Your Obedient Servant.
31. The person referenced here was Captain John F. Lane; see Bateman's journal entry for Friday, 2 September 1836.
32. Mississippi Swamp.
33. In Bateman's journal entry for Sunday, 17 October, he notes that the boats originally landed at the mouth of Cache River, but due to the high water the party dropped down several miles to Rock Roe. The high water at Rock Roe also made crossing difficult.
34. James Sevier Conway (1796–1855). Born in Greene County, Tennessee, Conway was the first governor of Arkansas after statehood was granted in 1836. Before reaching the governor's office, Conway served as an Arkansas Territory public land surveyor (an appointment secured by his uncle Elias Rector). President Andrew Jackson appointed Conway as a commissioner of Arkansas, whereby his duties included surveying the boundary between Arkansas Territory and Louisiana. He also helped survey the Arkansas Territory boundary with the Choctaws in 1825, during which Conway deviated from his instructions, resulting in the loss of 130,000 acres of Choctaw land. He ran as a Jacksonian Democrat in the 1836 gubernatorial election. His governorship was marred by controversy over the failed Arkansas State Bank and a territorial dispute with Texas. Ill health, a deteriorating economy, and a challenge from popular congressman Archibald Yell led Conway not to seek a second term. Williams, "James Sevier Conway 1836–1840," in Donovan and Gatewood, Jr., eds., *The Governors of Arkansas*, 1–5.
35. James Erwin's.
36. Edmund Pendleton Gaines (1777–1849). Born in Culpeper County, Virginia, and lived in North Carolina, Gaines was appointed ensign, 6th Infantry, in 1799. His military history includes: promoted second lieutenant, 6th Infantry (1799); honorably discharged (1800); appointed second lieutenant, 4th Infantry (1801); engaged in constructing military road along portions of old Natchez

Trace (1801–2); transferred to 2nd Infantry (1802); first lieutenant, 2nd Infantry (1802); Fort Stoddert, Mississippi Territory (1804–11), and instrumental in the arrest of Aaron Burr, Mississippi Territory (1807); captain, 2nd Infantry (1807); leave of absence (1811); judge of the parish of Pascagoula, Mississippi Territory (1811); commissioned major, 8th Infantry (1812); lieutenant colonel, 24th Infantry (1812); colonel, 25th Infantry (1813); adjutant general with the rank of colonel (1813); in War of 1812, being engaged at the Battle of the Thames, Upper Canada (1813), and the Battle of Crysler's Farm, Upper Canada (1813); brigadier general (1814); commander at Sackets Harbor, New York (1814), engaged and severely wounded in the Siege of Fort Erie, Upper Canada (1814); brevet major general for gallantry and good conduct in defending Fort Erie, Upper Canada (1814); in surveying Creek Nation boundary line in accordance with the Treaty of Fort Jackson (1815–16); engaged in the destruction of Negro Fort, Florida (1816); engaged in the capture of Amelia Island, Florida (1817); in Florida, being engaged in the First Seminole War at the Battle of Miccosukee (1818); on southeastern frontier (1818–21); commander of the Western Department of the U.S. Army (1821–36, alternating terms); commander of the Eastern Department of the U.S. Army (1821–36, alternating terms); in Creek Nation investigating the Treaty of Indian Springs (1825); leave of absence (1830–31); in Illinois, being engaged in negotiations to remove Black Hawk and his followers (1831); in Florida, being engaged in the Second Seminole War at the skirmish on the Withlacoochee River (1836), and having been shot in the jaw at the Battle of Camp Izard (1836); in Louisiana and Texas, being engaged in protecting American border during Texas revolution (1836); Jefferson Barracks, Missouri (1836–37); New Orleans, Louisiana (1845–46); New York City (1846–48); New Orleans, Louisiana (1848–49); died of cholera at New Orleans, Louisiana, 6 June 1849, at age 72. Silver, *Edmund Pendleton Gaines*; Wilson and Fiske, eds., *Appletons' Cyclopædia of American Biography*, 2:571–73; Heitman, *Historical Register*, 1:442; Thian, *Notes Illustrating the Military Geography*, 63.

37. The women and children of the warriors attached to Opothle Yoholo accompanied detachment 1 west in 1836. The warriors of the Lower Towns requested that their women and children remain in Alabama until their tour of duty in Florida was over. Haveman, *Rivers of Sand*, 241.

38. Francis Wells Armstrong (ca. 1783–1835). Born in Virginia, Armstrong was appointed captain, 24th Infantry in 1812. His military history includes: promoted major, 24th Infantry (1813); honorably discharged (1815); reinstated as captain, 7th Infantry with brevet of major from 26 June 1813 (1815); resigned U.S. Army (1817); served in Alabama legislature (1820–21, 1823–25); U.S. marshal for Alabama (1823–27); engaged in taking a census of the Choctaw Indians (1831); as agent for Choctaws, Indian territory (1831–35); died at Choctaw Agency, 6 August 1835. Armstrong was the brother of William Armstrong

and Robert L. Armstrong. Foreman, "The Armstrongs of Indian Territory," 292–308; Heitman, *Historical Register*, 1:169; Gardner, *A Dictionary of All Officers*, 44; DeRosier, *Removal of the Choctaw Indians*, 150n; Pate, ed., *Reminiscences of George Strother Gaines*, 202n18.

39. Stephen Watts Kearny (1794–1848). Born in Newark, New Jersey, Kearny attended King's College (Columbia University) before being commissioned ensign, 5th Regiment, First Brigade of Militia of the City and County of New York, in 1810. His military history includes: lieutenant, Militia of the City and County of New York (1811); assigned to 13th Infantry with rank of first lieutenant (1812); in War of 1812, being captured at the Battle of Queenston Heights, Upper Canada (1812); prisoner of war (1812–13); acting adjutant, 13th Infantry (1812); captain, 13th Infantry (1813); Sackets Harbor and Plattsburgh, New York (1813–15); retained and transferred to 2nd Infantry, (1815); on recruiting service and at Sackets Harbor, New York (1815–19); Camp Missouri, Nebraska, and engaged in finding a route between Camp Missouri and Camp Coldwater, Minnesota (1819–20); transferred to 3rd Infantry, Detroit, Michigan (1821); transferred to 1st Infantry (1821); Baton Rouge and New Orleans, Louisiana (1821–23); on sick leave due to malaria (1821); brevet major for ten years faithful service in one grade (1823); commander of companies attached to second Yellowstone Expedition (1824–25); engaged in the construction of Jefferson Barracks, Missouri (1826, 1827); engaged in military action against Winnebago Indians, Wisconsin (1826–27); leave of absence (1827–28); in command of Fort Crawford, Wisconsin (1828–29); Jefferson Barracks, Missouri (1829); major, 3rd Infantry (1829); Fort Leavenworth, Kansas (1830–31); Fort Towson, Indian territory (1831); recruiting service, New York City (1832–33); lieutenant colonel, 1st Dragoons (1833); Jefferson Barracks, Missouri (1833); on Dodge-Leavenworth Expedition (1834); in command of Fort Des Moines, Iowa (1834–36); colonel, 1st Dragoons (1836); Fort Leavenworth, Kansas (1836–42); in command of Third Military Department, U.S. Army (1842); Jefferson Barracks and St. Louis, Missouri (1842–45); and on circuit through Great Plains, being engaged in expedition from Fort Leavenworth along Oregon Trail to front range of Rocky Mountains and along Santa Fe Trail back to Fort Leavenworth (1845); brigadier general, 1st Dragoons (1846); in Mexican-American War, as commander of the Army of the West, and being engaged in the invasion and capture of New Mexico (1846), in California Campaign, being engaged in the Battle of San Pasqual, California (1846); engaged in the Battle of Rio San Gabriel, California (1847), and the Battle of La Mesa, California (1847); military governor of California (1847); commander, 10th Military District (1847); commander and military governor of Veracruz (1848); military governor of Mexico City (1848); brevet major general for gallant and meritorious conduct in New Mexico and California, to date from Battle of San Pasqual in which he was twice wounded (1848); Jefferson Barracks, Missouri (1848); died at St. Louis,

Missouri, 31 October 1848, at age 54, from the effects of yellow fever contracted at Veracruz. Heitman, *Historical Register*, 1:586; Gardner, *A Dictionary of All Officers*, 259; Clarke, *Stephen Watts Kearny*; Ball, "Stephen W. Kearny." See also Lucas, "Kearny, Stephen Watts."

40. Jacob Brown served as the first president of the Arkansas State Bank, largely because of the backing of Chester Ashley (1791–1848), one of the founders of the city of Little Rock and arguably the wealthiest man in Arkansas (he also served in the U.S. Senate, 1844–48). Ashley successfully blocked from the bank's presidency Terence Farrelly (a wealthy Irish-born Arkansas Post merchant and planter who served in the territorial legislature and was adjutant general of the Arkansas militia), and instead placed his friend, Brown, at its head. Brown did not resign from the U.S. Army when he took the bank job, but serving in simultaneous positions caused controversy, and he stepped down as president in 1837. Hempstead, *Historical Review of Arkansas*, 142–43, 170; Brown, *A Life of Albert Pike*, 37–38, 59–60, 114–15, 126–27.
41. The Arkansas State Bank (1836–43) was one of two banks (along with the Real Estate Bank of Arkansas) created by the Arkansas legislature in 1836. In addition to serving as a depository for state funds, the purpose of the Arkansas State Bank was to fund commercial projects, facilitate land sales, and serve the general public (while the Real Estate Bank of Arkansas facilitated agricultural development). The Arkansas State Bank suffered a number of problems over its short history—it officially opened around the time of the Panic of 1837 and operated during the recession that lasted into the 1840s; sufficient local demand for the bank never arose; and inflationary lending practices caused many borrowers to default on their loans—before it ceased operations in 1842–43 with almost two million dollars in liabilities. Hempstead, *Historical Review of Arkansas*, 142–43, 170; Worley, "The Arkansas State Bank: Ante-Bellum Period," 65–73; Worley, "The Batesville Branch of the State Bank"; Worley, "Arkansas and the Money Crisis."
42. Principal Disbursing.
43. James C. Watson.
44. Carey Allen Harris (1806–42). Born in Williamson County, Tennessee, Harris was a partner in the *Nashville Republican* newspaper before quitting to practice law in 1827. Moving to Washington DC, Harris became a clerk under Secretary of War Lewis Cass and leveraged his talents and relationship with President Andrew Jackson to become commissioner of Indian affairs in 1836. Harris supported Indian removal and advocated for more federal control over the Indians who had been relocated west. He promoted the establishment of schools and missions in Indian territory for the benefit of "civilization." Although he was retained as commissioner of Indian affairs by the Van Buren administration, he resigned in 1838 after it was disclosed that he schemed to speculate in Indian allotments

in the South. He later became president of the Real Estate Bank of Arkansas in Little Rock before moving back to Franklin, Tennessee. He died in Franklin of tuberculosis, 17 June 1842, at age 35. Satz, "Carey Allen Harris," 17–22; Rockwell, *Indian Affairs and the Administrative State*, 168–69, 201.

45. Detachment 3 reached Fort Gibson on 23 January 1837.
46. Member, Alabama Emigrating Company.
47. Disbursing Agent, Creek Removal.

11. DETACHMENT 2

1. Dr. Madison Mills (1810–73). Born in New York City, Mills was commissioned assistant surgeon, U.S. Army in 1834. His military history includes: Fort Armistead, Florida (to July 1835); Fort Mitchell, Alabama (to August 1836); surgeon with detachment 2 of relocating Creek Indians (to April 1837); with U.S. Dragoons at Fort Gibson, Indian territory (to April 1839); in Florida, being engaged in Second Seminole War, including at Fort Brooke (to September 1840); Fort Brady, Michigan (to October 1841); Fort Niagara, New York (to August 1845); in Texas (to May 1846); major and surgeon, U.S. Army Medical Corps (1847); in Mexican-American War, being engaged with the Army of Occupation of Mexico (to July 1848); with the 3rd Infantry in Texas (to January 1850); Fort Leavenworth, Kansas (to May 1855); Fort Columbus, New York (to May 1857); appointed medical director in the Department of Utah, but unable to assume the duties due to sickness; Fort Leavenworth, Kansas (temporary duty, to May 1859); Fort Riley, Kansas (1860–61); hospital duty, St. Louis, Missouri (to May 1862); medical director of the Department of the Missouri (1862–63); medical director, Army of the Tennessee (1863); brevet lieutenant colonel and brevet colonel for meritorious service at siege of Vicksburg, Mississippi (1864); colonel, U.S. Army Medical Corps inspector general (1863–65); brevet brigadier general, U.S. Army for faithful and meritorious service during Civil War (1865); discharged (1865); died at Fort Columbus, New York, 28 April 1873, at age 62. Henry, *Military Record of Civilian Appointments*, 1:98–99; Eicher and Eicher, *Civil War High Commands*, 391; Hamersly, *Complete Regular Army Register*, 639; Mills to Green, 20 July 1839, William Davenport Papers, Special and Area Studies Collections, George A. Smathers Libraries, University of Florida, Gainesville; Omer, "An Army Hospital"; Gillett, *The Army Medical Department*, 217–19; Madison Mills Diary, 1846–1847, Filson Historical Society, Louisville KY; Wilcox, *History of the Mexican War*, 612.
2. Screven to Jesup, 27 August 1836, RG 94, 159-Q, Container 15, Folder "Letters Received during the Creek War 1836 Montgomery, Ala," NARA.
3. Florence, Alabama, was located on the Tennessee River at the foot of the Muscle Shoals. The town sits on "an eminence," which commands "an extensive view of the surrounding country, and Tennessee river, from which it is three quarters

of a mile distant." Anne Newport Royall (1769–1854) visited in 1821 and noted: "Many large and elegant brick buildings are already built here, (although it was sold out, but two years since,) and frame houses are putting up daily. It is not uncommon to see a framed building begun in the morning and finished by night." Royall estimated that the site had "one hundred dwelling houses and stores, a court house, and several ware houses" as well as two taverns and "several *Doggeries*" (taverns that did not sell food). Ferriage across the Tennessee River was done "in a large boat worked by four horses, and crosses in a few minutes." Royall, *Letters from Alabama*, 143–51; Bowes Reed McIlvaine (1795–1866), the son of a senator from New Jersey, visited north Alabama at the time the Chickasaws were being forced west. He described the region between Florence and Decatur, Alabama, as a place of "horrid ugly sickly women, & the swearing, tobacco spitting, whiskey drinking men." Parsons, ed., "Letters on the Chickasaw Removal of 1837."

4. Alexander H. Sommerville of Montgomery, Alabama.
5. The *John Nelson* was a 200-ton steamboat that could carry one thousand bales of cotton or two thousand barrels of goods. The typical complement of officers and men for a vessel of this size was eleven people, "besides 8 firemen & 4 deck hands." Polk to Lewis, SIAC, Agent (Alabama Emigrating Company), Account (2282), Year (1838), NARA.
6. The vantage point the Creeks would have seen as they approached Little Rock around this time was described by William F. Pope, who noted that from the north bank of the Arkansas looking toward the town: "But little of the capital could be seen from the north side of the river when I first saw the town in 1832, on account of the high and irregular bluffs on the south bank, which time and the march of improvement have greatly lowered and depressed. . . . On the east side of First, or Commerce street, and near the river, stood two large log warehouses, owned and used by Enezy Wilson & Son for storing freight brought by steamboats to this port.

   "On the north side of Elm street, near First street, there was a group of small log houses occupied as dwellings and owned by Richard C. Byrd. Scattered about in this vicinity were a number of small log houses and shanties extending along the river bank to Cumberland street.

   "Still viewing Little Rock from the north side of the river, no other buildings came in sight until a point opposite Spring street was reached. Here a steam saw mill came in view, and on the bluff immediately west two or three neat cottages which were owned and occupied by Dr. John H. Cocke and Dr. Bushead W. Lee. At the foot of and on the east side of Arch street was the residence of Samuel Hall, Esq., a prominent lawyer of the town.

   "The buildings here mentioned were the only ones in Little Rock that could be seen from the North Side." Pope, *Early Days in Arkansas*, 99–101.

7. This likely refers to a cluster of fallen trees and debris that littered the road as a result of high winds or a tornado.
8. Dr. Samuel Grandin Johnston DeCamp (1788–1871). Born in Upper Longwood, New Jersey, DeCamp graduated from the College of Physicians and Surgeons (now Columbia University School of Medicine) in 1808 and began his practice in Petersburg, New Jersey in 1809. He served as a surgeon's mate during the War of 1812 before returning to Petersburg. He reenlisted in the U.S. Army and was appointed assistant surgeon in 1823. His military history includes: at Fort Jackson, Louisiana (1823–24); with the 4th Infantry (1824–28); at U.S. Military Academy, West Point, New York (1828); at Sackets Harbor, New York (1828–32); at Fort Dearborn, Illinois during the Black Hawk War (1832); at Fort Trumbull, Connecticut (1833); promoted surgeon, U.S. Army (1833); at Jefferson Barracks, Missouri (1833–34); at Fort Gibson, Indian territory (1834–37); at Jefferson Barracks, Missouri (1837–38); in Florida, being engaged in the Second Seminole War (1838–39); at Jefferson Barracks, Missouri (1839–44); at Fort Leavenworth, Kansas (1844–46); in Mexican-American War, being engaged in expedition to California (1846–47); at Fort McHenry, Maryland (1847–48); at Carlisle Barracks, Pennsylvania (1848–49); at Fort Columbus, New York (1849–54); at St. Louis, Missouri (1854–61); at Allegheny Arsenal, Pennsylvania (1861–62); at Watervliet Arsenal, New York (1862–63); retired "for incapacity resulting from long and faithful service, from disease contracted, or from exposure in the line of duty, in conformity with section 16 of the Act of Congress, of August, 1861." (1862); died at Saratoga Springs, New York, 8 September 1871, at age 83. Cullum, *Biographical Register* (1868), 1:67; Henry, *Military Record of Civilian Appointments*, 1:69–70; *History of Medicine and Surgery*, 19–21; Moses and Kirkland, eds., *History of Chicago*, 2:226; Wilcox, *History of the Mexican War*, 612.
9. Screven misspells "C.A." Harris.
10. Lieutenant James Hervey Simpson.
11. Order No. 69, issued 25 August 1836.
12. Robert Armstrong (1792–1854). Born in Abingdon, Virginia, and lived in Tennessee, Armstrong enlisted with the Tennessee volunteers as a sergeant of artillery at the outbreak of the War of 1812. His military and personal history includes: promoted lieutenant, Tennessee volunteers (1813); in Mississippi Territory, being engaged in Creek War (1813–14) having been severely wounded at the Battle of Enitachopco Creek (1814), and as aide-de-camp to General Andrew Jackson at the Battle of New Orleans (1814–15); postmaster of Nashville, Tennessee (1829–45); in Florida, being engaged in Second Seminole War, as brigadier general, Tennessee mounted volunteers (1836–37), and having seen action at the Battle of Wahoo Swamp (1836); appointed U.S. Consul to Liverpool, England (1845–49); publisher of *Washington Union*, Washington DC (1851); official publisher

of U.S. House of Representatives; died, in Washington DC, 23 February 1854, at age 61. Armstrong was the brother of Francis Wells Armstrong and William Armstrong. Ewing, "Portrait of General Robert Armstrong"; Pierpaoli, "Armstrong, Robert," 21; Gardner, *A Dictionary of All Officers*, 45; Weaver and Cutler, eds., *Correspondence of James K. Polk*, 4:15n16.

13. Commissary General of Subsistence.

12. DETACHMENT 3

1. United States to James W. Townsend, 25 January 1837, SIAC, Agent (Deas), Account (1180), Year (1837), NARA.
2. Dr. James G. Morrow (1808–1888). Born in Greenville County, South Carolina, Morrow moved to Alabama in 1818. He died of heart disease at Somerville, Alabama, 25 April 1888, at age 80. *Alabama Enquirer*, 28 June 1888. Morrow traveled with the second Talladega party for some distance before joining the first Talladega party when Dr. Milo Smith (who was the surgeon assigned to the first party) was only able to go as far as Memphis. United States to Dr. James G. Morrow, SIAC, Agent (Deas), Account (506), Year (1837), NARA.
3. Horseshoe Bend (Tohopeka) was the site of the last major battle in the first Creek War (1813–14). The battlefield is located four miles west of the Okfuskee town square on the Tallapoosa River. See Braund, ed., *Tohopeka*.
4. Gideon Riddle and Sylvanus Walker. Riddle & Walker's store was later known as Curry Station in Talladega County, Alabama. Jemison, *Historic Tales of Talladega*, 58, 196.
5. Refers to detachment 4, which was also under the charge of Edward Deas.
6. Owned by Eli M. Driver. Driver's Ferry was on the Benton–St. Clair county line near the town of Alexandria. Irons, "River Ferries in Alabama Before 1861"; Vandiver, "Pioneer Talladega," 25.
7. The homestead of Edward Cox (b. 1786), near Raccoon Mountain in north Alabama; United States to Edward Cox, SIAC, Agent (Deas), Account (1180), Year (1837), NARA.
8. General Andrew Moore of Claysville, Alabama, was appointed by Secretary of War Lewis Cass as an assistant agent in the Creek relocations in May 1836. Gibson to Page, 11 May 1836, RG 94, 159-Q, Container 20, Folder: "Documents relating to Creek War," NARA.
9. R. W. Williams, a partner in the Alabama Emigrating Company. Opinion on M. K. Hammond's claim, LR, CAE, Roll 239, 414–16.
10. Deposit Ferry was located on the north side of the Tennessee River and connected to Deposit Landing (also called Fort Deposit) on the south side. The ferry is sometimes referred to as Fort Deposit Ferry. In 1813 Andrew Jackson established a depot of supplies at Deposit Ferry during the first Creek War. DeLand and Smith, *Northern Alabama*, 248; Foscue, *Place Names in Alabama*, 47.

11. Tuscoona Harjo was a "mile chief" (one of the ninety preeminent headmen in the Creek Nation) from the town of Fish Pond.

12. Okfuskee headman Menawa. Menawa fought Andrew Jackson at Horseshoe Bend in 1814, carried out the execution of William McIntosh in 1825, accompanied the delegations that signed the 1826 and 1832 Treaties of Washington, and aided the Americans against the Creek rebels during the Second Creek War. Menawa also sent his oldest son to fight with the Americans against the Seminoles during the Second Seminole War. He was also staunchly opposed to emigration to Indian territory, even if it meant living under Alabama law (as would be the case under the 1832 treaty). In fact, according to Thomas L. McKenney and James Hall, Menawa visited the Catawbas in North Carolina to determine how they were faring under state law and came to the realization "that there was no insurmountable objection to such a mode of life." This was not to be, however. The night before his party left Talladega, Menawa returned to his *talwa* and spent his final night in Alabama at his Okfuskee home. Commencing the march the next day, Menawa declared that "Last evening I saw the sun set for the last time, and its light shine upon the tree tops, and the land, and the water, that I am never to look upon again." Menawa also gave a portrait of himself to a white man just prior to his departure and noted that "I am going away. I have brought you this picture—I wish you to take it and hang it up in your house, that when your children look at it you can tell them what I have been. I have always found you true to me, but great as my regard for you is I never wish to see you in that new country to which I am going—for when I cross the great river my desire is that I may never again see the face of a white man!" According to McKenney and Hall, in his younger days Menawa (which means "The Great Warrior") was known as Hothlepoya, or "The crazy war hunter" as a result of his "daring feats as a marauder upon the frontiers of Tennessee." Accordingly, he "was widely known and feared by the new settlers along the border, as a bold and successful adept in this species of warfare, which he practised with the least possible breach of the public peace—seldom shedding blood if unresisted, but fighting with desperation when opposed." He later received a mile reservation under the 1832 Treaty of Washington. McKenney and Hall, *History of the Indian Tribes of North America*, 2:97–106.

13. Chattoksofke was a village of Okfuskee.

14. Running gear consisted of an assembly of the frame, axles, wheels, and tongue (or shafts).

15. The flywheel is a large, heavy circular wheel that stores rotational energy, and moderates the speed of the engine by its weight and inertia. Kane, *The Western River Steamboat*, 115–16.

16. A bushel was a measurement of dry weight and varied based on the commodity. One bushel of corn ca. 1850s was fifty-six pounds.

17. William Strong's stand was located at the St. Francis Post Office, two miles

west of the St. Francis River crossing. Strong was appointed postmaster at St. Francis on 1 November 1826; Deas to Gibson, 22 November 1836, LR, CAE, Roll 237, 553–56; Carter, ed., *Territorial Papers of the United States*, 20:750. Strong regularly provided rations to emigrating Indians and provided provisions for the first two McIntosh Parties in 1827 and 1828; Abstract of Disbursments by David Brearley, SIAC, Agent (Brearley), Account (14,487), Year (1830), NARA; Gerstacker, 133, 191, 196.

18. There are no entries for December 14–18.
19. There are no entries for December 20–24.
20. Samuel Plummer (1801–76). This station is near the current site of Plumerville, Arkansas. Abstract of Disbursements, Letters Received by the Office of Indian Affairs, 1824–81, Chickasaw Agency Emigration, 1837–50, Microcopy 234, Roll 143, 433, 465.
21. This is the first of a number of times Deas appears to miswrite P.M. for A.M.
22. Tuckabatchee Harjo, who traveled with detachment 5, had fallen behind his party. He was a mile chief of Cusseta, not Coweta as the journal notes.
23. Thomas, Philip, and James Madden were wealthy planters who lived on the north side of the Arkansas River in Johnson County. The crossing point over Piney Creek was called Madden Ford. The homestead and its environs included a schoolhouse and several slave cabins. Langford, *Johnson County, Arkansas*, 165.
24. Spadra Creek near Clarksville, Arkansas.
25. John Ward (b. 1773). Born in Virginia, Ward first settled on Horsehead Creek in 1834 before moving to Clarksville. Langford, *Johnson County, Arkansas*, 22, 159; Population Schedules of the Seventh Census of the United States, 1850, Microcopy 432, Roll 22. There were many Wards in this area during this time.
26. Alfred E. Pace, an Arkansas magistrate and the son of Twitty Pace, the postmaster of Scotia, Arkansas, in Pope County. In December 1838 the Cherokees were provisioned by Alfred Pace on Horsehead Creek. Hempstead, *A Pictorial History of Arkansas*, 946.
27. Joseph Russell on White Oak Creek. Hull to Sevier, 6 December 1833, Carter, ed., *Territorial Papers of the United States*, 21:858–59.
28. The Dwight Mission was moved to Sallisaw Creek after 1828 when the western Cherokees ceded their Arkansas Territory land for land in present-day Oklahoma. Grant Foreman notes that by 1830 the new complex looked like "a little village" consisting of: "'a double log house with two rooms, each twenty feet square, with two stone chimneys, shingle roof, with a passage ten feet wide through the middle, which was occupied by Miss [Ellen] Stetson and the girls' school. The dining room and kitchen, built of hewn logs, was twenty-four by fifty-four feet in size and two stories high. One stone chimney provided two fireplaces and there was a cellar twenty-four by thirty-four feet, walled and pointed.

    Mrs. [Susanna Washburn] Finney and Miss [Cynthia] Thrall were each provided a log cabin sixteen by twenty-one feet in size, a story and a half high, made of hewn logs, chinked with stone, pointed with lime mortar and whitewashed. The boys' school shared with Mr. A. Hitchcock a two-story log house with two rooms below, eighteen by twenty-two feet, and similar rooms above. One large stone chimney in the center furnished two fireplaces on each floor. There was a similar two-story house for Mr. [Cephas] Washburn and Mr. Gray. Mr. Jacob Hitchcock and Mr. [James] Orr were provided with story and a half houses, each with two fireplaces. A gallery eight feet wide ran across the front of each of these log houses. Two cabins were built for the laborers and another for an office.

The missionaries tilled the fertile soil near the mission and in 1830, on their little fifty-acre well fenced farm, they raised 1,800 bushels of corn, 250 bushels of potatoes and owned '200 head of horned cattle.' Besides these they inventoried kitchen and household furniture, beds, bedding, library, books, and stationery to the value of $1,600 or an aggregate of mission property valued at $8,520.'" Foreman, *Advancing the Frontier*, 311–12; *Report of the American Board of Commissioners for Foreign Missions*, 91. Carolyn Thomas Foreman, "The Cherokee Gospel Tidings of Dwight Mission."

29. John Thompson Drew (1795–1865). Born in Georgia, Drew was a Cherokee interpreter, merchant, and trader. His home was on Bayou Menard, about six miles east of Fort Gibson. Allardice, *Confederate Colonels*, 133; Grant Foreman, *Advancing the Frontier*, 26.
30. Major General John H. Patterson of the First Division of Alabama militia. Ellisor, *Second Creek War*, 208.
31. William Winslett was part of a partnership called "Cravens, Winslett, & Cravens" (Michael M. Cravens, William Winslett, and Nehemiah A. Cravens) to provide rations to the encamped Creeks. Provision receipts, SIAC, Agent (Page), Account (1650), Year (1838), NARA. See also William Winslett deed conveyed to Edward Hanrick, November 1853, Hoole Special Collections, University of Alabama, Tuscaloosa.
32. Jacob D. Shelly (1795–1860). Born in Guilford County, North Carolina, Shelly was captain of a company of Talladega Rangers during the Second Creek War. He died in DeSoto Parish, Louisiana, in 1860. Population Schedules of the Seventh Census of the United States, 1850, Vol. 2, Alabama, Microcopy 432, Roll 51, NARA.
33. Joseph D. McCann (b. 1811). McCann was born in Tennessee. Population Schedules of the Seventh Census of the United States, 1850, Vol. 2, Alabama, Microcopy 432, Roll 51, NARA.
34. Dr. Milo Smith (1807–69). Born at Smith's Cross Roads, Tennessee (present-day Dayton), Smith attended medical school in Philadelphia, Pennsylvania. Smith was mayor of Chattanooga, Tennessee, for a number of one-year terms (1842,

1852, 1862, and 1863). Armstrong, *The History of Hamilton County*, 1:10, 300–1; McGuffey, *Standard History*, 51–52.

35. Dr. James W. Townsend. United States to James W. Townsend, 25 January 1837, SIAC, Agent (Deas), Account (1180), Year (1837), NARA.
36. Alabama Emigrating Company.
37. David S. Walker served as a subagent under Edward Deas. Testimony of Walker, 13 March 1838, SIAC, Agent (Alabama Emigrating Company), Account (2282), Year (1838), NARA.
38. William A. Campbell was the agent of the Alabama Emigrating Company accompanying detachment 4. Provision receipts, SIAC, Agent (Page), Account (1650), Year (1838), NARA.
39. Refers to detachment 4, which was under the principal control of Deas but accompanied west by Joseph D. McCann and William A. Campbell.
40. Refers to detachments 1 and 2, which were the first to cross the Mississippi River.
41. Detachment 5.
42. The three enclosed letters are: Conway to Deas, 6 December 1836; Deas to Conway, 8 December 1836; and Deas to Conway, 11 December 1836, all presented immediately before Deas's letter of 19 December.
43. The 17 January 1837 edition of the *Arkansas State Gazette* reports: "It will be recollected by some of our readers, that a few weeks since information was received here that a party of Creek Indians, under their chief, Tuck.i.batch.i.had.jo, had made a stand a few miles west of Potts'—and after remaining there a longer time than was necessary for them to recruit, were ordered away, on their march, by Mr. Potts, which they peremptorily refused—saying they were west of the Mississippi, and it was not in the power of any one to compel them to go on. They said the threats of the whites might alarm little boys—but *they* were men! Intelligence being conveyed to Col. [William G. H.] Teevault, commandant of the Pope county militia, of the audacious language held by this chief, he, by authority of two proclamations issued by the Governor of this State, on the 22d of Oct. and 6th Dec.—made a requisition, dated Dec. 26, on the companies of his regiment, for an armed force—and in two or three days, upwards of 100 mounted men appeared under arms, for a forcible expulsion. But they were not needed—the Indians getting wind of the movement, decamped in the night about the first of January, and made a precipitate flight."

13. DETACHMENT 4

1. Chambers to Shelly, 1 September 1836, letter found at RG 94, 159-Q, Container 22, Folder: "Orders and Letters Sent by General Jesup and Staff, September 1836 (2 of 2)," NARA; Vandiver, "Pioneer Talladega," 16, 19, 25; United States to Jacob D. Shelly, SIAC, Agent (Deas), Account (506), Year (1837), NARA

2. United States to Doctor Milo Smith, SIAC, Agent (Deas), Account (506), Year (1837), NARA.

14. DETACHMENT 5

1. Charles Abercrombie (b. 1790). Born in Hancock County, Georgia, Charles Abercrombie was the brother of Anderson and James Abercrombie. Ellsworth, "Raiford and Abercrombie," 247–60; Causey, ed., *Some Descendants of Charles Abercrombie*; Cherry, "The History of Opelika," 249.
2. John Titcomb Sprague (1810–78). Born in Newburyport, Massachusetts, Sprague was commissioned second lieutenant, U.S. Marine Corps in 1834. His military history includes: in Alabama, being engaged as aide-de-camp, acting commissary of subsistence, and assistant quartermaster to Major General Thomas S. Jesup during Second Creek War (1836); assigned to conduct detachment 5 of relocating Creek Indians to Indian territory (1836–37); resigned U.S. Marine Corps (1837); appointed second lieutenant, 5th Infantry (1837); disbursing agent in the removal of the Pottawatomis (1837–38); on frontier during Canada independence movement (1838); transferred to 8th Infantry (1838); first lieutenant, 8th Infantry (1839); in Florida, being engaged as aide de camp to brevet major general Alexander Macomb (1839), and as disbursing agent with Seminoles during treaty negotiations (1839), and as regimental adjutant, 8th Infantry (1839–42), and being engaged at the Battle of Pilaklikaha, Florida (1842); brevet captain, for meritorious and successful conduct in Second Seminole War (1842); regimental adjutant, 8th U.S Infantry (1843–45); aide de camp to Colonel William Jenkins Worth (1844); captain, 8th Infantry (1846); commander, 9th Military Department of Florida (to 1848); brevet major, 8th Infantry (1848); in Texas (1849–52); commander at Fort Inge, Texas (1850); in command of government wagon train to El Paso, Texas (1850); Fort McKavett, Texas (1852); commanding post of Governor's Island, New York Harbor (1852–54); in New Mexico (1855–59); leave of absence (to 1861); major, 1st U.S Infantry (1861); chief of staff to General John Pope (1861); captured at San Antonio, Texas (1861); paroled (1861); nominated for promotion to brigadier general, but nomination tabled (1862); mustering and disbursing officer, Albany, New York (1861–65); lieutenant colonel, 11th Infantry (1863); adjutant general of New York Militia (1863–64); lieutenant colonel, 11th Infantry (1863); chief of staff and assistant adjutant general to General John Pope (1865); promoted brevet brigadier general, U.S. Army (1865); colonel, 7th Infantry (1865); assistant commissioner, Bureau of Refugees, Freedmen, and Abandoned Lands, for Florida (1866–68); unassigned (1869); retired (1870); died at New York City, 6 September 1878, at age 68. Heitman, *Historical Register*, 1:912; Eicher and Eicher, *Civil War High Commands*, 503; Henry, *Military Record of Civilian Appointments*, 1:459; Hamersly, *Complete Regular Army Register*, 776–77; Thrapp, *Encyclopedia of Frontier Biography*, 3:1350; Carson, *Against the Grain*, 73; Sprague,

The Origin, Progress, and Conclusion of the Florida War; Harris to Sprague, 3 April 1837, SIAC, Agent (Sprague), Account (3218), Year (1839), NARA; Sprague to Harris, 13 March 1838, SIAC, Agent (Sprague), Account (3218), Year (1839); United States in Account Current, SIAC, Agent (Sprague), Account (4736), Year (1840), NARA.

3. Dr. Green Washington Hill (1812–1844). The son-in-law of John Claiborne Webb, Hill was appointed a commissioner of the town of West Point, Georgia, in 1835. Abstract of Expenses, SIAC, Agent (Sprague), Account (547), Year (1837), NARA; *Acts of the General Assembly of the State of Georgia*, 68–69.
4. James Island was a McIntosh party member from Coweta. After the Treaty of Indian Springs forced him into exile in Georgia, he returned to the Creek Nation and was even awarded a full mile reserve under the 1832 Treaty of Washington. When the Second Creek War broke out in 1836, Island aided the Americans in bringing the rebels to capture. When the majority of the Creek population was relocated in August and September 1836, Island and 135 of his followers camped opposite West Point, Georgia, in preparation for their journey. Sickness delayed their commencement, however, and their party did not join detachment 5 until reaching Memphis. Haveman, *Rivers of Sand*, 21, 95, 202, 210; Ellisor, *Second Creek War*, 213–14.
5. Arnold Seale (1795–1871), who ran a store at Cusseta and was also a speculator in Creek Indian reserves. Ellisor, *Second Creek War*, 106–7; Gamble, *Alabama Catalog*, 199.
6. Horatio Nelson Crabb (1800–1857). Born in Middletown, Dauphin County, Pennsylvania, Crabb was commissioned second lieutenant, U.S. Marine Corps in 1822. His military service includes: at naval headquarters, Washington DC (1823); at Philadelphia (1824); in command of marine guard on corvette *John Adams*, West India Station, and being engaged in Foxardo incident, Puerto Rico (1825); navy yard, Washington DC (1826); Philadelphia, Pennsylvania (1827–30); first lieutenant, U.S. Marine Corps (1830); in command of marine guard on sloop *Concord*, to Maó-Mahón, Minorca (1830); in command of marine guard on frigate *Constellation* on its return to the United States (1830–31); on sloop *Concord* (1831); Philadelphia, Pennsylvania (1832); Gosport, Virginia (1833); on sloop *Ontario* (1834); marine officer on board sloop *Natchez*, along coast of Brazil (1835); in Alabama, being engaged as assistant quartermaster under Colonel Archibald Henderson during Second Creek War (1836); leave of absence (1837); resigned U.S. Marine Corps due to disability—double inguinal hernia (December 1837); naval storekeeper (civilian appointment) at Honolulu, Hawaii (1847–50); dismissed (1850); died at Honolulu, Hawaii, 4 November 1857, at age 57. *Saturday Press*, 17 February 1883; *Army and Navy Chronicle*, 9 June 1836; U.A. Congress, House Report 47, *Horatio N. Crabb and John G. Reynolds*, 1–2; *Register of the Commissioned and Warrant Officers of the Navy* (1825); *Register of the Commissioned and Warrant Officers of the Navy* (1835),

91; *Journal of the House of Representatives of the United States* (1843), 112; 242; *Naval Magazine* 2, no. 3 (May 1837): 84; U.S. Congress, Senate Report of Committee 307, *In the Senate of the United States* (1852); Bockstruck, *Naval Pensioners of the United States*, 47; *A Register of Officers and Agents* (1830), 144; *American State Papers*, vol. 2: *Naval Affairs*, 2:457, 2:806; *American State Papers*, vol. 4: *Naval Affairs*, 4:264, 4:477.

7. Dr. Green Washington Hill of West Point, Georgia. Abstract of Expenses, SIAC, Agent (Sprague), Account (547), Year (1837), NARA.
8. Cusseta.
9. Columbus, Georgia, was platted soon after the Creeks were forced from Georgia under the 24 January 1826 Treaty of Washington. When Anne Royall visited Columbus in 1830 she marveled at its rapid growth and sophistication. She observed in her memoirs that the town had "2 Churches; 1 Bank; 18 Stores; 11 Doctors; 12 Lawyers; 1200 inhabitants, and only TWO years old!!!" James Stuart (1775–1849) also visited Columbus in 1830 and noted that in March of that year the town had "a population of 1500 people, three churches, a post-office, several brick buildings, and above 130 frame buildings of wood, most of them painted without, and the whole erected on a regular plan." When British traveler James Silk Buckingham (1786–1855) visited in 1839 he noted that the boomtown had approximately eight thousand inhabitants "in nearly equal proportions of black and white." Buckingham described the town's buildings as "substantial, commodious, and ornamental." By the end of the 1830s Columbus had "a more than usual number of the places called 'Confectionaries,' where sweetmeats and fruits are sold;" however, the town's staple supplies were "peach-brandy, whiskey, rum, and other ardent spirits, of which the consumption here, by all classes and in various forms, is said to be considerable." Before removal and relocation, the town of Columbus, Georgia, and its environs became a magnet for Lower Creeks looking for work, to trade, or seek handouts from the local populace. There were "generally hundreds" of Creeks in Columbus by day but all Creeks were required to return to their homes on the west side of the Chattahoochee River at night. Local residents noted that the Creeks "were generally friendly and harmless while on this side of the river, but sometimes annoying, as they would go to private houses to the alarm of some of the ladies, but their object was to get something to eat or steal." Columbus was also home to a large number of land speculators. As a Georgia frontier town, Columbus invited its share of hardscrabble, violent settlers. Buckingham noted that the town allowed "the open sale of dirks, bowie-knives, and a long kind of stiletto, called the 'Arkansas toothpick.' These are sold by druggists, in whose shops or stores these deadly weapons are hung up for public inspection, and sold by them as part of the legitimate wares of their calling; thus plainly indicating, that weapons to kill, as well as medicine to cure, could be had at the same shop; and placing, beside

the deadly poisons of arsenic, laudanum [an opiate], hemlock, and hellebore [*Veratrum viride* Ait, a medicinal plant], the deadly weapons of no less fatal power." Royall, *Mrs. Royall's Southern Tour*, 2:138–41; Stuart, *Three Years in North America*, 2:130–31; Buckingham, *The Slave States of America*, 1:246–47; Martin, ed., *Columbus Geo from Its Selection as a "Trading Town,"* 10.

10. Henry Marshall is number one on the 1832 Coweta (Toosilkstookee Hatchee) town census.
11. Likely a typo. Almost certainly P.M.
12. Felix G. Gibson (d. 1841), a contractor with the Alabama Emigrating Company. Gibson died on 13 April 1841 in Florence, Stewart County, Georgia. *Macon Georgia Telegraph*, 25 May 1841.
13. Jesse Carr, a member of a prominent Creek family. Abstract of Expenses, SIAC, Agent (Sprague), Account (547), Year (1837), NARA.
14. Cussetas
15. Matthew McCrary (1798–1855). McCrary is buried in Hillsboro, Alabama, about ten miles east of Courtland. Alabama Land Grants and Land Patents Collection, 1810–1854, Box 6, Folder 4, Alabama Department of Archives and History, Montgomery; Gentry, *Life and Legend of Lawrence County, Alabama*, 96; Corum, *From Whence We Came.*
16. Dempsey Odom, an employee of the Alabama Emigrating Company. Odom was a subagent on the third voluntary emigrating party in 1829. SIAC, Agent (Alabama Emigrating Company), Account (2282), Year (1838), NARA; United States to Ellis, SIAC, Agent (Crowell), Account (15,814), Year (1831), NARA.
17. Probably referring to 10th Article.
18. Sprague's 24 September 1836 order demanded that the party halt on 25 September. The order appears later in chapter 14.
19. James Webb (b. ca. 1788). Born in North Carolina, Webb lived with his wife, Manima Crisp Webb (b. ca. 1800), and three children in Bolivar, Tennessee. *Hardeman County*, 227; Population Schedules of the Seventh Census of the United States, 1850, Microcopy 432, Roll 881, 125B, NARA.
20. Thomas Jones Hardeman (1788–1854). Born near Nashville, Tennessee, Hardeman served as lieutenant in Thomas Hart Benton's 39th Infantry and then under Brigadier General John Coffee in the First Regiment of Volunteer Gunmen. He was taken prisoner at the Battle of New Orleans and injured in the head by a British officer's saber while in custody. In 1818 Hardeman moved to southwest Tennessee and Hardeman County was created in 1823. That same year Hardeman built a mill on Pleasant Run Creek, a few miles west of Bolivar, Tennessee, and served as clerk of the county court in Bolivar (1823–33). He moved with his family to Matagorda County, Texas, in the 1830s, and served in the Congress of the Republic of Texas (1837–39), was elected associate justice and chief justice of Bastrop County and Travis County, Texas (1840s), and served in the U.S. House

of Representatives from Texas (1847–51). In the 1850s he was president of the Colorado Navigation Company. Hardeman died in Bastrop County, Texas, 15 January 1854, at age 74. Hardeman, *Wilderness Calling*, 65–69, 121–22, 133–34.

21. William Claiborne Dunlap (1798–1872). Born in Knoxville, Tennessee, Dunlap studied at Ebenezer Academy and Maryville College (1813–17). He served in the First Seminole War (1818–19) before returning to Knoxville and practicing law. He moved to Bolivar, Tennessee, in 1828 and was elected to the U.S. House of Representatives in 1832 and 1834 as a Jacksonian Democrat. He lost in his attempt at a third term. He later served as judge of the Eleventh Circuit Court of Tennessee (1840–49) before serving in the both the Tennessee State Senate and House of Representatives in the 1850s. He died near Memphis, Tennessee, 16 November 1872. Dodge and Koed, eds., *Biographical Directory of the United States Congress*, 989.
22. William A. Campbell, a contractor with the Alabama Emigrating Company. Provision receipts, SIAC, Agent (Page), Account (1650), Year (1838), NARA.
23. Detachment 4.
24. Probably Lieutenant Joseph D. McCann. According to the Alabama Emigrating Company, McCann was the agent of record for detachment 4. The U.S. in account current with the Alabama Emigrating Company, SIAC, Agent (Reynolds), Account (1687), Year (1838), NARA.
25. Stephen Miles Ingersoll, a contractor with the Alabama Emigrating Company and formerly of J.W.A Sanford & Company. He accompanied the 1835 Creek emigration.
26. Robert Lawrence.
27. Farmers and Merchants Bank, the first bank organized in Memphis (1834). Robert Lawrence was president of the bank. Schweikart, "Antebellum Southern Bankers"; *Goodspeed's History*, 890.
28. In Bateman's 12 October journal entry he notes: "Some delay occasioned, owing to a misunderstanding with the Chiefs." This probably refers to Opothle Yoholo's initial refusal to go by water. Another account, in which Opothle Yoholo "'actually refused to move and willfully detained the party for two days longer, without excuse or reason'" just as detachment 1 was preparing to cross the Mississippi River may also have been his protest against river travel. Haveman, *Rivers of Sand*, 223.
29. Steamboat *Farmer*.
30. William J. Freeman, assistant military agent. Quarterly statements, LR, CAE, Roll 238, 732; Abstract of Expenses, SIAC, Agent (Sprague), Account (547), Year (1837), NARA.
31. Jim Island's party consisted of 135 members. Island was sick in August 1836 and needed extra time before commencing the journey west. Unwilling to wait, the contractors gave Island some traveling money and started moving without him.

Island and his people did not rejoin detachment 5 until reaching Memphis. Page to Iverson, 8 July 1837, SIAC, Agent (Reynolds), Account (1687), Year (1838), NARA.

32. Edward Hanrick.
33. The same William J. Beattie who helped conduct the fourth and fifth voluntary emigrating parties in 1835–36.
34. Detachment 4.
35. Emzy Wilson (1791–1863). Wilson who owned a bridge over Palarm Creek, SIAC, Agent (Page), Account (20,726), Year (1836), NARA.
36. Reuben J. Blount in Conway County, Arkansas. SIAC, Agent (Crowell), Account (15,814), Year (1831); Shinn, *Pioneers and Makers of Arkansas*, 221, 260.
37. John H. Love. Receipt no. 15, SIAC, Agent (Reynolds), Account (1687), Year (1838), NARA.
38. The Alabama Emigrating Company wanted compensation for detachment 5's delay at Kirkbride Potts's settlement, claiming that "every proper means was used by the Co. throughout the entire route to induce the Indians to keep up and that the Indians *would* linger behind in spite of all the exertions of the Co. & its agents." Comments upon the Statement of "facts & principles," SIAC, Agent (Reynolds), Account (1687), Year (1838), NARA.
39. Jesse May, who moved from Dixon County, Tennessee, to Arkansas in 1833 and established a homestead on a tract of land that stretched from near the mouth of Piney Creek to the county line of Pope County, Arkansas. Langford, *Johnson County, Arkansas*, 169.
40. Among the Wards who were living in Clarksville or Spadra Township during this period were John Ward (b. ca. 1773 in Virginia), Augustus M. Ward (b. ca. 1815 in Virginia), and David Ward (b. ca. 1816 in Missouri). Population Schedules of the Seventh Census of the United States, 1850, Microcopy 432, Roll 22.
41. Alfred E. Pace, an Arkansas magistrate and the son of Twitty Pace, the postmaster of Scotia, Arkansas, in Pope County. In December 1838 the Cherokees were provisioned by Alfred Pace on Horsehead Creek. Hempstead, *A Pictorial History of Arkansas*, 946; Langford, *Johnson County, Arkansas*, 139.
42. The first sentence of Article 13 of the 1832 Treaty of Washington states: "There shall also be given to each emigrating warrior a rifle, moulds, wiper and ammunition and to each family one blanket." Kappler, *Indian Affairs*, 2:341–43.
43. In the margins of the journal Sprague adds 2,087 and 156, for a total of 2,237.
44. Opothle Yoholo.
45. John Claiborne "Bridger" Webb (1790–1840). Born in Elbert County, Georgia, Webb fought in the War of 1812 and served as major in an Alabama volunteer company during the Second Creek War. He was the father-in-law of Dr. Green W. Hill, who accompanied detachment 5 to Indian territory. Ellisor, *Second Creek War*, 282; Trent, ed., *Narrative of James Williams*, 102n21; Lindsey, *Reason for the Tears*, 185.
46. Samuel Miller (1775–1855). Born in Massachusetts, Miller was commissioned

second lieutenant, U.S. Marine Corps, in 1808, at the age of 33. His military history includes: first lieutenant, U.S. Marine Corps (1809); captain, U.S. Marine Corps (1814); in the War of 1812, being engaged at the Battle of St. Leonard Creek, Maryland (1814), and severely wounded while commanding a battalion of Marines at the Battle of Bladensburg, Maryland (1814); brevet major, U.S. Marine Corps for distinguished service at the Battle of Bladensburg (1814); West India Station (1823); commanding at Philadelphia, Pennsylvania (1825–36); brevet lieutenant colonel, U.S. Marine Corps (1827); major, U.S. Marine Corps (1834); in Alabama, being engaged in the Second Creek War (1836); in Florida, being engaged in the Second Seminole War (1837); lieutenant colonel, U.S. Marine Corps (1841); commanding Marine guard (1842–43); died at Philadelphia, Pennsylvania, 9 December 1855, at age 80. Gardner, *A Dictionary of All Officers*, 319–20; Simpson, *The Lives of Eminent Philadelphians*, 697–98; *ASP-MA*, 1:864; Names of officers, RG 94, 159-Q, Container 30, Folder: "Morning Reports, July 1836 (2 of 5)," NARA; Samuel Miller Papers, Archives Branch of the Marine Corps History Division, Quantico VA.

47. Captain John D. Still, commander of a company of LaFayette volunteers.
48. Levi Twiggs (1793–1847). Born in Richmond County, Georgia, Twiggs was commissioned second lieutenant, U.S. Marine Corps in 1813. His military history includes: in the War of 1812, on Patuxent River in defense of that river against British attack (1814), and in commanding marines on board U.S. frigate *President* against its engagement with the HMS *Endymion* (1815); imprisoned in Bermuda (1815); first lieutenant, U.S. Marine Corps (1814); New York station (1815–23); Philadelphia, Pennsylvania (1823–24); brevet captain, U.S. Marine Corps (1825); on frigate *Constellation* (1825–27); furloughed (1828); Philadelphia, Pennsylvania (1829–30); captain, U.S. Marine Corps (1830); at headquarters, Washington DC (1831); Navy yard, Washington DC (1832–35); commanding officer at Navy Yard at Gosport, Virginia (1835–36); in Alabama, being engaged in the Second Creek War, under the command of Colonel Archibald Henderson (1836); in Florida, being engaged in Second Seminole War, (1836–37), at the Battle of Hatcheelustee Creek (1837); major, U.S. Marine Corps (1840); under orders at Washington DC (1842); commanding marine guard, New York (1842); commanding marine barracks, Philadelphia PA (1842–46); in Mexican-American War, being engaged in the storming party on right flank, under Major General John A. Quitman, at the Battle of Chapultepec, Mexico (1847); killed at the Battle of Chapultepec, 13 September 1847. Gardner, *A Dictionary of All Officers*, 457; U.S. Congress, Senate Report 641, *Priscilla Decatur Twiggs*, 1–3; Aldrich, *History of the United States Marine Corps*, 58, 72; *Military and Naval Magazine of the United States* 6, no. 3 (November 1835): 236; *The Mexican War and Its Heroes*, 212–16.
49. Paddy Carr or one of his relatives.
50. This was not laziness but a resistance strategy. Many Creeks deliberately stalled their movements and traveled at their own pace to delay reaching Fort Gibson.

51. The interpreter was Jesse Carr. See Sprague's 21 September 1836 journal entry.
52. William A. Campbell, a partner in the Alabama Emigrating Company, who accompanied detachment 4.
53. Billy Spiller. Receipt no. 15, SIAC, Agent (Reynolds), Account (1687), Year (1838), NARA.
54. Sprague's 1 April 1837 letter states that the Creeks joined on the ninth night.
55. Detachments 1 and 2.
56. The muster roll was important for the Alabama Emigrating Company because it showed how many Creeks the company transported to the west. Without the roll, the contractors would not receive compensation based on the number of Creeks they relocated.
57. The steamer was the *John Nelson*.
58. Sprague's 10 December 1836 entry in his journal reports that the 395 Creeks on board the *John Nelson* arrived at (or near) Fort Gibson on 20 November. Sprague's 1 April 1837 letter to C. A. Harris reports that the party arrived at or near Fort Gibson on 22 November.
59. Referring to the detachments of Creek prisoners that left in July and August 1836.
60. Sprague's 16 October 1836 letter states that the Creeks joined on the third night.
61. See note 58, this chapter.
62. Those "settled in the country" were most likely McIntosh party members.
63. The Alabama Emigrating Company officially claimed twenty-five deaths.
64. His brother was Absalom Island.
65. Marshall's muster roll shows seven heads of families with seventy-three people total. The heads of families were: Benjamin Marshall, Lucy Thlocco, Lucy Watley, Anne Barnard, Cussena Barnard, Little Sims, and Patsey. Seventy people arrived at Fort Gibson after one "old Negro" remained behind because he was "not able to travel by old age"; one woman deserted camp before the party commenced their journey west; and one child died at Pontotoc, Mississippi. Muster Roll (Marshall), SIAC, Agent (Reynolds), Account (1687), Year (1838), NARA.
66. William McGillivray was a mile chief from Hickory Ground. Cashin, *Lachlan McGillivray, Indian Trader.*
67. Brigadier General Robert Armstrong of the Tennessee Volunteers.
68. Captain John F. Lane.
69. Lewis Cass (1782–1866). Born in Exeter, New Hampshire, Cass studied at Philips Exeter Academy before practicing law and being elected prosecuting attorney of Muskingum County, Ohio, in 1804. His military and political history includes: Ohio House of Representatives (1806–7); federal marshal of Ohio (1807–12); colonel, third regiment of Ohio volunteers (1812); in War of 1812, being engaged in the invasion of Canada (1812), and the Battle of River Canard (1812), and captured at the Siege of Detroit (1812); elected major general, Ohio militia (1812); appointed colonel, 27th Infantry (1813); brigadier general, U.S. Army (1813); in War of 1812,

being engaged in the Battle of the Thames (1813); governor of Michigan Territory (1813–31); U.S. secretary of war in Andrew Jackson administration (1831–36); minister to France (1836–42); U.S. Senate (1845–48); Democratic candidate for President of the United States (1848); U.S. Senate (1849–57); U.S. secretary of state in James Buchanan administration (1857–60); died at Detroit, Michigan, 17 June 1866, at age 83. Klunder, *Lewis Cass and the Politics of Moderation*; Gardner, *A Dictionary of All Officers*, 108.

70. Harrison Young (d. 1838), the first sheriff of Tallapoosa County. *Tallapoosa County: A History*, 62.

71. Yoholo Micco (ca. 1786–1836) was a mile chief from Upper Eufaula. He was an ally of William McIntosh during the first Creek War, served as speaker to the Upper Towns, and signed the 1826 Treaty of Washington that nullified the controversial 1825 Treaty of Indian Springs. Yoholo Micco was also granted a mile reserve under the 1832 Treaty of Washington. According to Thomas L. McKenney and James Hall, Yoholo Micco was an eloquent orator (as speakers were), and during one council spoke "in a manner so clear and pointed as not to be easily forgotten by those who heard him." McKenney and Hall also noted that the headman "fell a victim to the fatigues of attending the emigration, in his fiftieth year, while on his way to the land of promise," suggesting that he died en route. Probably traveling with Yoholo Micco was his son Mistippee, also known as "Mr. Ben" or "Benny" after agent Benjamin Hawkins. Among the Creeks, "Mr. Ben" morphed into "Mistiben" and later "Mistippee." Mistippee accompanied his father to Washington when that delegation signed the 1826 Treaty of Washington. In their *History of the Indian Tribes of North America*, McKenney and Hall write that "Of Mistippee there is little to tell. When at Washington, in 1826, he was a remarkably handsome boy, and in all respects prepossessing. His father gave him unusual advantages in regard to education, which he is supposed to have improved. When at maturity he wedded a comely woman of the Hillabee towns, and soon after emigrated to the new home provided for his people, west of the Mississippi." Kappler, *Indian Affairs*, 2:264–68; McKenney and Hall, *History of the Indian Tribes of North America*, 2:17–18, 19–22.

72. Detachment 1 was originally assigned to pass through this part of Mississippi, but due to the headmen of detachment 2 demanding to follow in the footsteps of Opothle Yoholo, Bateman altered his route through Russellville, Alabama.

73. Jefferson Van Horne.

74. Francis Audrain. Audrain became an agent to the Creeks in Indian territory. *Army and Navy Chronicle*, 1 December 1836.

75. Three thousand five hundred blankets arrived at Fort Gibson on 6 March 1837. Boyd to Harris, LR, CAE, Roll 238, 98–99.

76. Page is referring to the fifth voluntary emigrating party that left Alabama in late 1835.

15. DETACHMENT 6

1. John George Reynolds (1801–65). Born in New Jersey, Reynolds was appointed second lieutenant, U.S. Marine Corps in 1824. His military history includes: at Portsmouth, New Hampshire (1825); Charlestown navy yard, Massachusetts (1826); on sloop *Lexington* (1827); at New York (1828); assistant quartermaster, U.S. Marine Corps (1828–31); on sloop *Fairfield* (1829); on frigate *Java* (1830); on frigate *Constellation* (1831); at Philadelphia, Pennsylvania (1833–34); first lieutenant, U.S. Marine Corps (1833); at New York (1835–36); in Alabama, being engaged in Second Creek War as acting adjutant (1836); in Florida, being engaged in Second Seminole War (1836–37); assigned to detachment 6 of relocating Creek Indians (1837); on leave of absence (1839); on frigate *Constellation*, East India Squadron (1842–44); marine barracks, Brooklyn, New York (1845); captain, U.S. Marine Corps (1847); in Mexican-American War (1846–48), being engaged in leading advance party that stormed the Castle of Chapultepec, Mexico (1847); brevet major, U.S. Marine Corps (1847); on recruiting duty, New York (1849); with Pacific Squadron (1850); on recruiting duty, New York (1852–55); at marine barracks, Warrington, Florida (1856); on frigate *St. Lawrence* to Montevideo, Uruguay, to protect the American consulate (1857–59); on Paraguay Expedition (1858); at marine barracks, Portsmouth, New Hampshire (1860); led a battalion at the first Battle of Bull Run (1861); brevet major, U.S. Marine Corps (1861); lieutenant colonel, U.S. Marine Corps (1861); with West Gulf Blockade Squadron (1862); commanding officer Boston Marine Barracks (1862–63). *American State Papers*, vol. 4: *Naval Affairs*, 4:273; *The Marine Corps in Mexico*, 15–16; Yates and Yates, *The Boston Marine Barrack*, 196; Broadwater, *Civil War Special Forces*, 134–35; Aldrich, *History of the United States Marine Corps*, 73, 122–23, 133–36, 143, 242; Daugherty, *The Marine Corps and the State Department*, 32; *A Naval Encyclopædia*, 468, 550, 559; Melton, *The Best Station of Them All*, 71.
2. Thomas Theodore Sloan (d. 1850). Born in Kentucky, Sloan was appointed second lieutenant, U.S. Marine Corps in 1834. His military service includes: junior officer of the guard of frigate *Constitution* (1835); at New York (1835–36); in Alabama, being in charge of the camp at Echo Harjo's and conducting detachment 6 of Creek Indians to Indian territory (1836–37); on U.S. steamer *Poinsett*, being engaged in Second Seminole War, in shore duty at Tea Table Key, Florida (1839–40); at Marine Barracks, Washington DC (1840); first lieutenant, U.S. Marine Corps (1840); commander of U.S. Navy "Mosquito Fleet" in Florida (1840–42); on leave, Frankfort, Kentucky (1842); at Washington DC (1843); court martialed and suspended until 1 March 1844 (1843); sentence commuted by President John Tyler (1843); on leave (1844); on board frigate *United States*, African Squadron (1847–49); died at Naval Hospital, Brooklyn, New York, 10 February 1850. *Military and Naval Magazine of the United States* 5, no. 1 (March 1835): 80; Collum, *History of the United States Marine Corps*, 72; *American Railroad Journal, and*

Advocate of Internal Improvements, 25 October 1834; *Register of All Officers and Agents* (1843), 245; *Army and Navy Chronicle*, 29 October 1835, 20 June 1839, 16 July 1840; *Stryker's American Register and Magazine* 4 (July 1850): 449. Aldrich, *History of the United States Marine Corps*, 79–80; *Register of the Commissioned and Warrant Officers of the Navy* (1847), 122; Shappee, "Fort Dallas," 13–40.

3. Ruff to Harris, 15 November 1837, LR, CAE, Roll 238, 697.
4. Gustavus Adolphus Nott (1810–75). Born in Columbia, South Carolina, Nott moved to Louisiana in the 1830s where he became professor of anatomy at the University of Louisiana (now Tulane University Medical School) in 1839. Later he was professor of materia medica and therapeutics, before becoming dean of the faculty in 1849. He served as a surgeon in the Confederate Army. He died at Montgomery, Alabama, on 6 June 1875. Nott was the younger brother of physician and racial theorist Josiah Clark Nott (1804–73). Barnard and Guyot, eds., *Johnson's New Universal Cyclopædia*, vol. 3, part 1, 888; *Supplement to Encyclopædia Brittanica, Ninth Edition*, 4:551. See also Cashin, *A Family Venture*, 135–36.
5. Dr. Edmund Wiedemann (ca. 1805–44). Although it is unclear if this is the same person, in the 1840s an Estonian-born Wiedemann went to San Antonio, Texas, and served as the town's physician. An odd fellow, he claimed that he had been sent by the "Emperor of Russia" to collect all the information he could find on the flora and fauna of Texas. During the 19 March 1840 Council House Fight (where thirty-five Comanches, including five women and children, were killed) he attended to the injured Texas Rangers, for which he was later appointed assistant surgeon for the Texas army. After the battle at the council house, Wiedemann reportedly took his cart and collected the corpses of the dead Comanches for scientific research. On two others, he simply severed and stole the heads. In her memoirs Mary A. Maverick noted that while she was at a friend's house Wiedemann came up to the "grated front window, and placed a severed Indian head upon the sill. The good doctor bowed courteously and saying, 'With your permission, Madam,' disappeared. Soon after he returned with another bloody head, when he explained to us that he had viewed all the dead Indians, and selected these two heads, male and female, for the skulls, and also had selected two entire bodies, male and female, to preserve as specimen skeletons." Wiedemann subsequently boiled the two heads and two bodies in a large soap boiler before dumping the waste water into a ditch that provided drinking water for the town, and that led to the San Antonio River, which, along with San Pedro Creek, was used by the townspeople for washing and bathing. When the locals discovered this, "'There arose a great hue and cry and all the people crowded to the mayor's office—the men talked in loud and excited tones, the women shrieked and cried—they rolled up their eyes in horror, they vomited, and many thought they were poisoned and must die. Dr. Wiedemann was arrested and brought to trial, he was overwhelmed with abuse, he was called

'diabolo,' 'demonio.' 'sin verguenza,' etc., etc. He took it quite calmly, told the poor creatures they would not be hurt—that the Indian poison had all run off with the water long before day—paid his fine and went off laughing." Wiedemann died ca. 1844 at Gonzales, Texas, after drowning in Peach Creek. Maverick and Maverick, *Memoirs of Mary A. Maverick*, 38–41; Moore, *Savage Frontier*, 3:21–34; Cox, "Frontier Medicine"; Geiser, "Some Frontier Naturalists."

6. Dr. Cullen Battle (1785–1879). Born in Edgecombe County, North Carolina, Battle was a doctor for a number of years before turning his attention to his growing planting interests. He moved to Hancock, Georgia in 1818 (settling in Powelton), before arriving in Alabama in 1836. He was living at the north fork of Cowikee Creek when his house was raided on 29 December 1836 by a dozen Creeks during the Second Creek War. Battle escaped but his plantation was burned to the ground. Battle moved to Tuskegee, Alabama, in 1853 before returning to Eufaula, Alabama, in 1870. Boykin, *History of the Baptist Denomination in Georgia*, 2:28–30; Ellisor, *Second Creek War*, 342; *Greenville Advocate*, 26 June 1879.
7. William Wellborn (1792–1867). Born in Georgia, Wellborn was one of the early founders of Irwinton (Eufaula), Alabama, in Barbour County. Wellborn was also a speculator in Creek lands and served in the Alabama senate before moving to Texas. He died in Houston, Texas, in 1867 at age 75. Brewer, *Alabama*, 125; Ellisor, *Second Creek War*, 127, 345, 348.
8. Henry W. Jernigan (1805–49). Born in Jones County, Georgia, Jernigan was a founding member of the town of Florence, Georgia in 1837. Clark, "State Industrial Interests," 2:284; Lupold and French Jr., *Bridging Deep South Rivers*, 98.
9. Captain Benjamin Young. Page to Harris, 15 January 1837, LR, CAE, Roll 238, 497–98.
10. Dr. E. E. Parks of Russell County, Alabama; Ellisor, *Second Creek War*, 351.
11. Thomas Simpson Woodward (1794–1859). Born in Elbert County, Georgia, Woodward was an ally of William McIntosh and served with him in the Creek War, the First Seminole War, and the Second Creek War. He was an Indian countryman, land speculator, and states' rights nullifier. He lived in Macon County, Alabama, before leaving the state in 1841 and living for a time in Arkansas and later Louisiana. Woodward was the brother-in-law of Alabama Emigrating Company partner James C. Watson. He died in Winn Parish, Louisiana. *Macon Daily Telegraph*, 21 February 1860; Ellisor, *Second Creek War*, 159, 235, 245, 316; Woodward, *Woodward's Reminiscences*, 138–41; Brewer, *Alabama*, 339.
12. Roland Augustus Luther (1815–53). Born in New Holland, Pennsylvania, Luther graduated from the U.S. Military Academy, West Point, New York in 1836 (17th of 49) and was promoted second lieutenant, 2nd Artillery (1836). His military history includes: at Fort Mitchell, Alabama (1836–37); in Florida, being engaged in Second Seminole War (1837–38); first lieutenant, 2nd Artillery (1838); in Cherokee Nation,

being engaged in removing Cherokee Indians (1838); on northern frontier during Canada independence movement, Detroit, Michigan (1838–39); Buffalo, New York (1839–41); Lewiston, New York (1841); Buffalo, New York (1841); Fort Monroe, Virginia (1841); recruiting service (1841–42); Fort Monroe, Virginia (1842); Fort Hamilton, New York (1842); Fort Adams, Rhode Island (1842–43); Fort Columbus, New York (1843–44); Frankford Arsenal, Pennsylvania (1844–45); Fort Columbus, New York (1845); in military occupation of Texas (1845–46); in Mexican-American War, being engaged and wounded in the Battle of Palo Alto, Mexico (1846); recruiting service (1847); Fort Hamilton, New York (1847); captain, 2nd Artillery (1847); Fort Moultrie, South Carolina (1848–50, 1850–51); in Florida (1852); died at New Holland, Pennsylvania, 9 July 1853, at age 38. Cullum, *Biographical Register* (1868), 1:502; Heitman, *Historical Register*, 1:647; Diffenderffer, "Historical Sketch," 51–52.

13. Tuskenehaw, son of the late Big Warrior.
14. Echo Harjo also aided the Americans against the Seminoles in the Second Seminole War. Ellisor, *Second Creek War*, 218, 244–45, 339.
15. Noah Felton (1808–89). Born in Gates County, North Carolina, Felton died in Lee County, Alabama, 21 May 1889, at age 81. Information from Pine Hill Cemetery, Auburn, Alabama.
16. Opened in 1811, this road was a widened postal horse path linking Fort Stoddert, (present-day) Alabama, with Fort Wilkinson, Georgia. Southerland and Brown, *The Federal Road*.
17. Anne Cornells was a Tuckabatchee woman (number 184 on 1832 census). Thomas S. Woodward claimed that she was the daughter of Big Woman and Tom Low. Alexander B. Meek, however, believed that her father was Joseph Cornells, the interpreter. Meek also noted that she married one of Big Warrior's sons. Meek, *Romantic Passage*, 274; Woodward, *Woodward's Reminiscences*, 112.
18. Mobile Point, Alabama.
19. Mount Meigs, Alabama, about thirteen miles east of Montgomery, Alabama.
20. Henry J. Wilson (ca. 1792–1872). Born in Philadelphia, Pennsylvania, Wilson was commissioned ensign, 32nd Infantry in 1813. His military history includes: second lieutenant, 32nd Infantry (1814); honorably discharged (1815); reinstated in 4th Infantry (1815); first lieutenant, 4th Infantry (1816); in Florida, being engaged in First Seminole War, at the Battle of Pensacola (1818); regimental adjutant, 4th Infantry (1816–19); captain, 4th Infantry (1819); brevet major for ten years faithful service in one grade (1829); commander of Cantonment Clinch, Pensacola, Florida (1830); in Florida, engaged in Second Seminole War; as army agent in settling dispute between U.S. military personnel and Alabama Emigrating Company over failure of the contractors to issue beef rations, Mobile Point, Alabama (1837); major, 3rd Infantry (1838); lieutenant colonel, 1st Infantry (1842); brevet colonel for gallant and meritorious conduct at Monterrey, Mexico (1846); military governor of Veracruz, Mexico (1847); colonel, 7th Infantry (1851); commander

of Fort Smith, Arkansas (1852, 1853–55); commander of Fort Gibson, Indian territory (1855–57); resigned U.S. Army (1861); died at New Orleans, Louisiana, 21 February 1872. James, "Wilson, Henry," 848; Henry Wilson Papers, Western Americana Collection, Beinecke Rare Book and Manuscript Library, Yale University; Heitman, *Historical Register*, 1:1046; Henry J. Wilson Papers, Mss. 559, Series I, Papers, 1779–1885, Box 1, Folder 3, Louisiana and Lower Mississippi Valley Collections, Louisiana State University Special Collections, Baton Rouge; Coker and Watson, *Indian Traders of the Southeastern Spanish Borderlands*.

21. The original letter says, "and the loss incident thereto." The copy found at LR, CAE, Roll 238, 403–7 says, "and the loss of property incident thereto."
22. Letter has "most" written over "many," or vice versa. The copy found at LR, CAE, Roll 238, 403–7 says "most."
23. Colonel Leavin Brown. Ellisor, *Second Creek War*, 382, 384; Rucker, "West Florida's Creek Indian Crisis of 1837," 315–34.
24. It is unclear what treatment Woodfin is referring to but a common form of "Indian treatment" was boiling roots and medicinal plants, then having an Indian doctor blow into the elixir through a long reed. Augustus Loomis visited the Indian territory in the 1850s and recorded the following: "This Indian's wife was taken sick, but he would not call the white physician, nor send to the Mission for medicines. He calls a 'blower,' that is, a native doctor; or perhaps a conjuror. A large kettle of roots and herbs is selected according to prescription, and boiled together; but it has no efficacy till the breath of the blower has been infused into it.

   "Perhaps he is called to the house, or perhaps the liquid is prepared and taken away to the blower, and it may be ten or fifteen miles distant. He takes a reed two or three feet long, and blows through it into the medicine, and perhaps performs some other conjuration over it. Then the vessel is covered over tightly, lest the virtue should escape on the way home. This is given to the patient in large doses; she dies nevertheless." In another instance, Loomis noted, "Roots and herbs are gathered and boiled down to make a 'black drink;' but it has no efficacy till the doctor has given it a healing power by his own breath blown into it through a long tube, together with certain mummeries performed over it." Loomis, *Scenes in the Indian Country*, 194, 235.
25. Winfield Scott (1786–1866). Born near Petersburg, Virginia, Scott attended the College of William and Mary and practiced law before being commissioned captain, U.S. Army Light Artillery in 1808. His military history includes: recruiting service (1808–9); at New Orleans and Terre aux Boeufs, Louisiana, and Natchez (1809–10); suspended from the U.S. Army for un-officer-like conduct (1810–11); at Baton Rouge and New Orleans, Louisiana (1811–12); major, 2nd Artillery (1812); lieutenant colonel, 2nd Artillery (1812); Fort Mifflin, Pennsylvania (1812); in War of 1812, being captured at the Battle of Queenston Heights, Upper Canada (1812);

prisoner of war (1812); colonel, U.S. Army (1813); colonel and adjutant general, U.S. Army (1813); engaged and wounded in the shoulder by splinters from an exploding magazine during the capture of Fort George, Upper Canada (1813); brigadier general, U.S. Army (1814); Buffalo, New York (1814); engaged in the Battle of Chippewa, Upper Canada (1814), and being severely wounded in the left shoulder by low velocity cannonball at the Battle of Lundy's Lane, Upper Canada (1814); brevet major general for conduct at the Battle of Chippewa and Niagara, Upper Canada (1814); in resolution passed by Congress "that the President of the United States be requested to cause a gold medal to be struck, with suitable emblems and devices, and presented to Major General Scott, in testimony of the high sense entertained by Congress of his distinguished services in the successive conflicts of Chippewa and Niagara, and of his uniform gallantry and good conduct in sustaining the reputation of the arms of the United States" (1814); on tour of Europe (1815–16); in command of Military District no. 3, New York (1816); on furlough (1817–19), and being engaged in writing *General Regulations for the Army* (1818–21); at New York; commander of the Western Department of the U.S. Army (1821–36, alternating terms); commander of the Eastern Department of the U.S. Army (1821–37, alternating terms); in Illinois, being engaged in negotiating the Treaty of Fort Armstrong to end the Black Hawk War (1832); in South Carolina monitoring nullification crisis (1832–33); in Florida, being engaged in the Second Seminole War (1836); in Alabama, being engaged in the Second Creek War (1836); in Washington DC to stand in court of inquiry over his conduct in Second Seminole War and Second Creek War (1836–37); on northern frontier during the Canada independence movement (1838); in Tennessee, engaged in the removal of the Cherokee Indians (1838); on northern frontier during Canada independence movement (1838); in Maine during Aroostook War (1839); in Buffalo, New York, keeping the peace after the arrest of Alexander McLeod (1840–41); major general, U.S. Army (1841); general-in-chief, U.S. Army (1841–61); in Mexican-American War, being engaged in commanding forces during the amphibious assault and capture of Veracruz, Mexico (1847), and in campaign to capture Mexico City, Mexico (1847); recipient of the Thanks of Congress presented to "Winfield Scott, Major-General commanding in chief of the army in Mexico, and through him to the officers and men of the regular and volunteer corps under him, for their uniform gallantry and good conduct conspicuously displayed at the siege and capture of the city of Veracruz and Castle San Juan de Ulloa, March twenty-ninth, eighteen hundred and forty-seven; and in the successive battles of Cerro Gordo, April eighteenth; Contreras, San Antonio, and Churubusco, August nineteenth and twentieth; and for the victories achieved in front of the city of Mexico, September eighth, eleventh, twelfth, and thirteenth, and the capture of the metropolis, September fourteenth, eighteen hundred and forty-seven in which the Mexican troops, greatly superior in numbers, and in every advantage of position, were in every conflict signally defeated by the American arms, and that the President of the United States be, and he is hereby, requested to cause to be struck a gold medal with devices emblematical of the series of brilliant victories achieved by the army, and presented to Major-General Winfield Scott as a testimony of the high sense entertained by Congress of his valor, skill, and judicious conduct in the memorable campaign of eighteen hundred and forty-seven" (1848); interim U.S. secretary of war (1850); as Whig candidate for President of the United States (1852); in Pacific Northwest, being engaged in negotiating the joint occupation of San Juan Island (1859); retired from U.S. Army (1861); died at West Point, New York, 29 May 1866, at age 79. Johnson, *Winfield Scott*; Eisenhower, *Agent of Destiny*; Peskin, *Winfield Scott and the Profession of Arms*; Eicher and Eicher, *Civil War High Commands*, 475–76.

26. Alexander James Dallas, Jr. (1791–1844). Born in Philadelphia, Pennsylvania, Dallas was appointed midshipman, U.S. Navy in 1805. His military history includes: acting lieutenant, U.S. Navy (1810); in War of 1812, on board U.S. frigate *President*, being engaged in military action against HMS *Belvidera* (1812), and being engaged in military action against the British man-of-war *Little Belt* (1811); lieutenant, U.S. Navy with rank from June 1810 (1811); in command of *Spitfire* of the Mediterranean Squadron, being engaged in military operations against Algiers (1815); master commandant (1817); Philadelphia, Pennsylvania (1820–23); on corvette *John Adams*, West India Station, being engaged against pirates in Caribbean (1824–25); Philadelphia, Pennsylvania (1826–29); captain, U.S. Navy (1828); naval board of examination (1830); commandant, navy yard, Pensacola, Florida (1831–34); commander, West India Squadron (1835–39), while in command of U.S. frigate *Constellation* (1835–36), in command of U.S. sloop *Concord* (1836–37), and in command of U.S. frigate *Constellation*, being engaged in the Second Seminole War (1837); Pensacola Naval Yard (1839); New York (1842); commander of Pacific Squadron (1843–44); died on the sloop *Vandalia*, while in the harbor at Callao, Peru, 3 June 1844, at age 53. Was the son of Secretary of the Treasury (James Madison) Alexander James Dallas Sr. and brother of Vice President of the United States (James K. Polk) George M. Dallas. *Ships' Data*, 372; *Congressional Record: Containing the Proceedings and Debates of the Forty-Sixth Congress*, 10:2578; *National Cyclopædia of American Biography*, 8:307–8; U.S. Congress, House Report 250, *U.S. Frigate "Constellation,"* 1–8; Castleman, *Knickerbocker Commodore*, 166.

27. United States frigate *Constellation* (launched 1797; scrapped 1853). Built at the Sterrett Shipyard in Baltimore, Maryland, the *Constellation* first sailed in 1798. Its military history includes: convoying merchant ships to sea (1798); naval war with France (1798); West India Squadron, being engaged in the capture of the *L'Insurgente* at Nevis (1799), and in the capture of the French privateers *Diligent*

and *Union* (1799); engaged with the frigate *Vengeance* (1800); repair and refitting (1801–2); Mediterranean Squadron, being engaged in the blockade of Tripoli (1802); patrolling Mediterranean (1804); engaged in evacuating Marines and diplomats from Tripoli (1805); engaged against Tunis (1805); in ordinary at Washington Navy Yard (1805–12); refitting to add 14 inches to beam (1812–13); engaged with British fleet (1813); Mediterranean Squadron, being engaged in the capture of the Algerian frigate *Mashuda* (1815); in Brazilian Station, engaged in protecting American commerce (1819–20); in Pacific Ocean, engaged in patrolling coast of Peru (1820–22); West India Squadron (1827); repair (1828–29); carrying American ministers to France and England and patrolling Mediterranean (1829–31); repair (1831–32); patrolling Mediterranean (1832–34); repair (1834–35); in Gulf of Mexico, being engaged in the Second Seminole War (1835–37); West India Squadron (to 1838); repair (1838–39); East India Squadron (1841–43); in ordinary at Norfolk, Virginia (1845–53); scrapped (1853); replaced as a 22-gun sloop of war (1854–55). During the Second Seminole War the *Constellation* was commanded by Commodore Alexander James Dallas. Mooney, *Dictionary of American Naval Fighting Ships*, 2:171–73; Footner, *USS Constellation*; Toll, *Six Frigates*; Gilliland, ed., *USS Constellation.*

28. United States Revenue Cutter *Jefferson* (launched 1833; wrecked 1847). Built at the Webb and Allen shipyard in New York for the United States Revenue Cutter Service, the *Jefferson* first sailed in January 1833. The *Jefferson* was stationed at Norfolk, Virginia (1833–34), before being transferred to Savannah, Georgia, in 1834. In 1836 the *Jefferson* was assigned to the U.S. Navy and deployed to Florida against the Seminole Indians. It subsequently patrolled the coasts of Florida, Alabama, Mississippi, Texas, and Mexico and had a number of deployments to the islands of the Caribbean. The vessel's name was changed to *Crawford* in 1839 and was lost at Gardiner's Point, Long Island, New York, 15 December 1847. *Army and Navy Chronicle*, 23 June 1836; Mooney, *Dictionary of American Naval Fighting Ships*, 3:513; Canney, *U.S. Coast Guard and Revenue Cutters*, 15.

29. James K. Bowie (d. 1843). Born in Maryland, Bowie was appointed midshipman, U.S. Navy, in 1828. His military history includes: on board frigate *Constellation*, West India Squadron (1830); on board frigate *Java* (1831); on board schooner *Shark* (1833); at naval school, Norfolk, Virginia (1834–35); passed midshipman (1834); on board frigate *Constellation* (1836–37), being engaged on board revenue cutter *Jefferson* (1836); on board sloop *Concord* (1838–39); lieutenant, U.S. Navy (1840); on board sloop *Levant*, West India Squadron (1842); on board sloop *Ontario* (1842); on board receiving vessel, New Orleans, Louisiana (1843); inspector of provisions and clothing, Pensacola, Florida (1843); died at Pensacola, Florida, 25 December 1843. *Army and Navy Chronicle*, 23 June 1836; 15 March 1838; 22 January 1842; 11 January 1844.

30. Jacob Edmund Blake (1812–1846). Born in Pennsylvania, Blake graduated from

the U.S. Military Academy, West Point, New York, in 1833 (25th of 43) and was promoted to brevet second lieutenant, 6th Infantry (1833). His military history includes: at Jefferson Barracks, Missouri (1833–34); as quartermaster at the U.S. Military Academy, West Point, New York (1835–36); Subsistence Department, Washington DC (1836–37); second lieutenant, 6th Infantry (1836); in adjutant general's office, Washington DC (1837–38); first lieutenant, 6th Infantry (1837); transferred to Topographical Engineers (1838); assistant topographical engineer during Second Seminole War (1838–39); in constructing the harbors at east end of Lake Erie (1839–41); surveying boundary between United States and Texas (1841); reconnaissance of defensive approaches to New Orleans (1841–42); on the staff of General William J. Worth in Florida (1842–44); in charge of surveys and improvements in Florida Territory (1844–45); in occupation of Texas (1845–46); in War with Mexico, being engaged in surveying terrain from Padre Island to mouth of Rio Grande River (1846); the Battle of Palo Alto, in which he performed a daring reconnaissance of the enemy's position (1846); killed 9 May 1846, after accidental discharge of his pistol while taking off his holster. Cullum, *Biographical Register* (1868), 1:435; Lewis, *Trailing Clouds of Glory*, 40–41; Haecker and Mauck, *On the Prairie of Palo Alto*, 32, 52.

31. Congress approved the establishment of Mount Vernon Arsenal, located in present-day Mobile County, Alabama, in 1828 at the site of Mount Vernon Cantonment (which was built in 1811 as a replacement for Fort Stoddert). The arsenal was in the possession of the Confederacy during the Civil War and was designated Mount Vernon Barracks in 1873. In 1887 Apache chief Geronimo and 450 of his followers were incarcerated at the site after their capture before being transferred to Oklahoma. Sledge, *The Mobile River*, 76, 250; Utley, *Geronimo*.
32. Carver subsequently turned down the appointment and Page hired Thomas Batson in his place. Page to Harris, 6 August 1837, LR, CAE, Roll 238, 601–2.
33. Page is likely referring to the 10 August 1837 edition of the *New-Orleans Bee*, which ran a long opinion piece that declared: "The condition of the Indian at Pass Christian is any thing but creditable to the agents of the government under whose charge they have been placed. Sick, without any of the comforts of life, exposed to the inclemency of the weather, without cloathing and with apparently little provisions they are objects calculated to excite the liveliest sympathy in the bosom of all who have seen them; and to call forth such denunciations as may serve to arouse those under whom they are placed to a sense of their duty, and to those sentiments of humanity that they seem entirely to have forgotten. It certainly is grievious enough to remove the red-man from the home of his fathers, his hunting grounds and the thousand associations that endear that peculiar spot where he became first conscious of existence, but motives of policy, the stern law of necessity dictates this to us, and as much as we may deplore the seeming injustice, it is reconciled by the danger incurred by our own citizens,

and by the ultimate benefit to the race whose modes of life and habit, unfit them from being in the midst of our population. But, with the necessity, there is an imperitive obligation on our part to make the removal in the most tender and humane manner. They should be conveyed with expedition, and not suffered to pine, sicken and die, the victims of oppression and cruelty. The government is accused by some persons very unjustly, with its want of liberallity, in not having made ample provision for this purpose. Those who make this charge are unacquainted with the sollicitude that Congress, the several Presidents and the Indian department have shown; but their bounty has to pass through the hands of persons who are careless or disinterested, and who in place of rendering the Indian comfortable abandon him without the least remorse to a fate compared with which death if inflicted would be mercy.

"Not a person who saw the exposed situation of a party of Indians at _______ wharf at Pass Christian last Sunday, but felt indignant at the treatment they received, and such expressions were made use of on that occasion, as certainly testified popular resentment to be in no limited degree. These Indians were lying on the wharf, several of them sick and enfeebled under the rays of a meridian sun, without covering, and apparently half famished, as, they were eagerly devouring some water melons that the liberality of some benevolent persons had enabled them to purchase. They had been previously conveyed to this city, back again to Mobile point, and finally to Pass Christian, and what will be the disposition made of the remnant, after disease shall have thinned their ranks it is impossible to surmise; for the design of the government appears to have been totally forgotten. We did not visit the camp, and cannot tell what are the accomodations there, but surely, the spectacle we saw was quite sufficient to justify the conclusion, that inhumanity was the prevailing feature in the arrangements made. At any rate, the policy that dictates their removal to the west, dictates at the same time, that it should be carried into immediate effect, and that if deprived of one home, they should be supplied with another, when they may resume their former habits."

34. The 15 August 1837 edition of the *New-Orleans Bee* retracted their earlier op-ed and printed the following: "A late visit to the camps of the Indians at Pass Christian have convinced us that we were wrong in concluding that their treatment did not conform to the humane dispositions of the government. We went through the establishments examining particularly the provision that had been made for them, and found that nothing was wanting to conduce to their comfort and make their change of residence as favorable as possible. The agents are sensitively alive to all their wants, and while they supply them liberally they take care that they shall not indulge in ardent spirits, by which they might commit many excesses and become entirely ungovernable. We feel sorry that we should have done the agents the injustice we did in our preceding article, for had we had a knowledge of the facts we now have, we would have panegerised rather than

censured them. One of the gentlemen, Lieut. Reynolds is deservedly popular among the whole tribe; and governs more by mildness and limited indulgence than by the authority he is invested with or by the fear of punishment. He is very polite and obliging to strangers, and readily communicates all the knowledge about the Indians of which he may be possessed.

"The camps stretch along the whole border of the Pass, each camp being generally allotted to one family. The presence of these Indians afford an opportunity to those who wish to possess an accurate knowledge of their manners and habits, their religion and their polity, that may never again be offered, as the native children of the forest are destined in the course of a very few years to be all transported beyond convenient travelling distance.

"Their favorite game of racket we are told, on Sunday, was exceedingly animated, and was quite a feast to those who witnessed it. The party under Jim Boy carried the victory, after which a dance took place, that was equally a novelty.

"Among the head-men and people the influence of this Jim Boy is immense. He is one of the finest specimens of the human species we ever saw; his form is symmetry itself, and his contenance quick and expressive. At a single glance you are convinced that his mental superiority is not inferior to his physical; and half an hour conversation is sufficient to shew you, that he has not been inattentive to the instruction he has received from the white men. Cunning and discreet he might hold his own against the most accomplished double-dealing politician, or the most ingenuous sophist you can find. He is particularly guarded in what he says, and appears fully aware of the value of that sage remark of a Greek philosopher that men have but one tongue and two ears, for the purpose of hearing more than they say.

"He is expected to be in the city in a few days, and will put up at the St. Charles Hotel."

35. Ague, an archaic term (from the French, *fièvre aigue*—"acute fever") often associated with malaria. By the early nineteenth century physicians believed they had identified three primary types of ague (1) *quotidian*—a fever that returns every day, (2) *tertian*—returns every other day, and (3) *quartan*—occurring on the first and fourth day. There were disagreements about what caused ague but "marsh miasma" and "exposure to dews, loaded with unwholesome air" were typically agreed upon. Some argued that drunkenness also caused ague. Medical books in the early to mid-nineteenth century recommended anything from Peruvian Bark, mercurial ointments, calomel, opium, arsenic, to bloodletting as possible treatments. Graham, *Modern Domestic Medicine*, 193–97; Brewer, *The Military and Naval Medical Reference Book*, 224–26; Fagge and Pye-Smith, *Text-Book of the Principles and Practice of Medicine*, 1:322–38; Wesley, *Primitive Phyfick*, 29–33; Pettigrew, *On Superstitions Connected with the History and Practice of Medicine and Surgery*, 92–98.

36. Charles Lynch (1783–1853), governor of Mississippi (1833, 1836–38).
37. Bilious fever was a generic term for any fever that caused the expulsion of bile ("bilious") in the form of vomiting or diarrhea. Tissot, *An Essay on Bilious Fevers*; Buchan, *Domestic Medicine*, 186–87.
38. Rickets, the weakening of bones in children and caused by a vitamin D deficiency. The word *rickets* comes from the Old English *wrickken*—"to twist." The archaic term *rachitis* comes from *rachis*, the Greek word for spine. Mayow, *'Ρ'αχιτιδολογια: or, A Tract of the Difeafe Rhachitis Commonly called the Rickets*; Hochberg, ed., *Vitamin D and Rickets*, 1.
39. Phthisis, an archaic term for tuberculosis. Originally, phthisis characterized a range of diseases in which the body wasted away or was "consumed." Marten, *A New Theory of Confumptions*; Bynum, *Spitting Blood*, 10–22; Frith, "History of Tuberculosis."
40. Tympanites, also called meteorism, is the painful distension of the abdomen due to excessive gas. Ogle, *On the Relief of Excessive and Dangerous Tympanites.*
41. Thomas B. Linnard (1810–1851). Born in Pennsylvania, Linnard graduated from the United States Military Academy, West Point, New York, in 1830 (9th of 42) and was promoted brevet second lieutenant and second lieutenant, 2nd Artillery (1830). His military history includes: ordnance duty (1830–33); Fort Wood, Louisiana (1834); Fort Clinch, Florida (1834); Fort Pickens, Florida (1834); Fort Brooke, Florida (1834–35); topographical duty (1835–36); first lieutenant, 2nd Artillery (1835); in Florida, being engaged in Second Seminole War (1836–38), at the Battle of Camp Izard (1836), at the Battle of Oloklikaha (1836), skirmish near Tampa Bay (1836); brevet captain for gallant conduct in Second Seminole War (1836); engaged in the Battle of Loxahatchee (1838), and as aide-de-camp to Brevet Major General Thomas S. Jesup (1836–38), and as acting assistant adjutant general (1837, 1838); first lieutenant, Corps of Topographical Engineers (1838); assistant topographical engineer in the improvement of harbors on the Delaware River and bay (1838); superintending topographical engineer of Whitehall, New York, and engaged in harbor improvements and the construction of Delaware breakwater (1839–40), and improvement of Mobile harbor, Alabama (1841–43); inspector of Red River improvement, Louisiana (1841–45); captain, Corps of Topographical Engineers (1842); engaged in examination of Lafourche and Lake Pontchartrain harbors, Louisiana (1845); overseeing Red River improvement (1845–46); engaged in the military occupation of Texas (1846); in Mexican-American War, being engaged in the march through Chihuahua, Mexico (1846–47), and the Battle of Buena Vista, Mexico (1847); brevet major for gallant and meritorious conduct in the Battle of Buena Vista (1847); in charge of the construction of iron lighthouses on Carysfort Reef and Sand Key, Florida (1849–51); died at his brother's residence, Philadelphia, Pennsylvania, 24 April 1851, at age 40.

Cullum, *Biographical Register* (1891), 1:452–53; *United Service Journal: Devoted to the Army, Navy and Militia of the United States*, 3 May 1851.

42. Aide-de-camp & acting adjutant general.
43. Frederic Searle (ca.1803–53). Born in England and appointed from Massachusetts, Searle graduated from the U.S. Military Academy, West Point, New York, in 1823 (10th of 35) and was promoted brevet second lieutenant, 1st Artillery and second lieutenant, 4th Artillery (1823). His military history includes: topographical duty (1823–24, 1824–25); Artillery School for Practice, Fort Monroe, Virginia (1828); Fort Columbus, New York (1828–30); topographical duty (1830–32); first lieutenant, 4th Artillery (1831); in Black Hawk War but "not at the seat of war" (1832); Fort Columbus, New York (1832–33); Fort Gratiot, Michigan Territory (1833–34); Fort Columbus, New York (1834, 1835–36); in Second Creek War, being engaged as captain, Regiment of Mounted Creek Volunteers (1836); in Second Seminole War (1836–39); as chief of commissariat (1836–38), and being engaged in the Battle of Wahoo Swamp (1836), Battle of Hatcheelustee Creek (1837), Battle of Loxahatchee (1838); captain (staff), assistant quartermaster (1838); severely wounded from an ambush while on the road between St. Augustine and Picolata, Florida (1839); brevet major, for gallant and good conduct during Second Seminole War (1838); on sick leave of absence being disabled by his wound (1839–53); died at Sulphur Springs, Virginia, 19 July 1853, at age 50. Cullum, *Biographical Register* (1868), 1:244–45.
44. Donald Fraser, Jr. (1791–1860). Born in New York, Fraser was commissioned ensign, 15th Infantry in 1812. His military history includes: second lieutenant, 15th Infantry (1813); in War of 1812, as aide-de-camp to Brigadier General Zebulon Pike, and being wounded by exploding magazine at the Battle of York, Upper Canada (1813), assistant deputy paymaster general (1813–14), as aide-de-camp to Brigadier General George McClure (1813), first lieutenant, 15th Infantry (1813), as aide-de-camp to Major General Peter Buell Porter (1814), engaged in Battle of Lundy's Lane, Upper Canada (1814), engaged and severely wounded in the Siege of Fort Erie (1814); transferred to 8th Infantry (1815); brevet captain for gallant conduct in the Battle of Niagara Falls (1815); brevet major for gallant conduct at Siege of Fort Erie, Upper Canada (1815); retained in 8th Infantry (1815); aide-de-camp to Major General Jacob Brown (1815–16); resigned, U.S. Army (1816); U.S. commissioner appointed to survey U.S.-Canadian boundary under articles of the Treaty of Ghent; resigned (1816); owner of ferry at Black Rock, New York (1826); sutler at Fort Niagara (1828); superintendent of the Buffalo and Black Rock Jubilee Water Works Company (1832); appointed paymaster with rank of major (1836); in Florida, being engaged as paymaster, U.S. Army during Second Seminole War (1836–40); resigned, U.S. Army (1841); officer at New York Custom House (to 1860); died at Brooklyn, New York, 5 March 1860, at age 69. Gardner, *A Dictionary of All Officers*, 179; Heitman, *Historical Register*, 1:434;

Vincent, *Vincent's Semi-Annual United States Register*, 169; *New York Times*, 7 March 1860; Smith, ed., *History of the City of Buffalo*, 2:55, 523; Norton, "The Old Black Rock Ferry," 91–109.

45. William Grigsby Freeman (1815–66). Born in Virginia, Freeman graduated from the U.S. Military Academy, West Point, New York, in 1834 (15th of 36) and was promoted brevet second lieutenant, 4th Artillery (1834). His military history includes: at Fort Monroe, Virginia (1834–35); Fort Hamilton, New York (1835–36); in Alabama, being engaged in Second Creek War (1836); second lieutenant, 4th Artillery (1836); in Florida, in command of regiment of mounted Creek volunteers and being engaged at the Battle of Wahoo Swamp (1836); brevet first lieutenant, regiment of mounted Creek volunteers for gallantry and good conduct in Second Seminole War (1836); captain, regiment of mounted Creek volunteers (1836–37); major, regiment of mounted Creek volunteers (1837); as aide-de-camp to Brevet Major General Thomas S. Jesup (1837–38); engaged in the Battle of Loxahatchee (1838); first lieutenant, 4th Artillery (1838); Fort Columbus, New York (1838); in Florida, being engaged in Second Seminole War (1838–39); Fort Columbus, New York (1839); recruiting service (1839–40); at U.S. Military Academy, West Point, New York, as assistant instructor of Infantry and Artillery Tactics (1840–41); on northern frontier at Buffalo, New York, during Canada independence movement (1841); brevet captain (staff) and assistant adjutant general (1841); assistant in Adjutant General's Office, Washington DC (1841–49); member of the Board of Visitors to the U.S. Military Academy, West Point, New York (1843); brevet major (staff) and assistant adjutant general (1847); captain, 4th Artillery (1847); brevet lieutenant colonel for meritorious conduct in Mexican-American War (1848); chief of staff to Lieutenant General Winfield Scott at New York (1849–50); assistant adjutant general at Washington DC (1850–53); on tour of inspection of the Department of Texas (1853); assistant in Adjutant General's Office, Washington DC (1853–56); resigned from U.S. Army (1856); died at Cornwall, Pennsylvania, 12 November 1866, at age 51. Cullum, *Biographical Register* (1868), 1:450–51; Heitman, *Historical Register*, 1:436

46. Denis Prieur (1791–1857), was the Jacksonian mayor of New Orleans between 1828 and 1838. Castellanos, *New Orleans as It Was*, 134–66.

47. Chissee Harjo was possibly the same man who had served in Florida against the Seminoles and was in Courchus Micco's Company E, Creek volunteers. Reynolds to Jesup, 24 September 1836, RG 94, 159-Q, Container 17, Folder: "Letters Received from Officers, Various USMC Officers, 1836," NARA; Creeks enrolled for Florida, letter found at RG 94, 159-Q, Container 17, Folder: "Letters Received from Officers, Various USMC Officers, 1836," NARA.

48. C. A. Harris letter, 30 September 1837.

49. Nathaniel F. Collins. Collins was the brother-in-law of Alabama Emigrating

Company partner James C. Watson, and served as his lawyer. Giddings, *The Exiles of Florida*, 201.

50. James Beattie (1776–1866). Born near Antrim, Ireland, Beattie came to the United States in 1801 and lived in Armenia, New York, before settling in Ryegate, Vermont. James and his wife Margaret (née Gillespie, 1789–1861) had twelve children. William John Beattie was their oldest. Miller and Wells, *History of Ryegate, Vermont*, 284; Beattie Family Papers, 1814–1884, MS 158, Vermont Historical Society, Barre, Vermont.
51. Edward William Benjamin Nowland (1806–41). Born in Harford County, Maryland, Nowland lived in Tennessee before becoming sutler at Fort Gibson in 1832, and later postmaster. He was the brother-in-law of Arkansas Territory governor and U.S. Senator William Savin Fulton. Nowland was shot and killed over a disputed horse race in Crawford County, Arkansas, 15 November 1841, at age 35. *Arkansas Gazette*, 8 December 1841; Stouffer, "The E.W.B. Nowland Family," 38–44.
52. Albion Keith Parris (1788–1857). Born in Hebron, Maine (Massachusetts), Parris graduated from Dartmouth College in 1806. He practiced law before serving in the Massachusetts house of representatives and senate (1813–15), and U.S. Congress (1815–18). Parris later became governor of Maine (1822–27), U.S. Senator from Maine (1827–28), and a judge on the Maine supreme court (1828–36). Between 1836 and 1850 Parris served as Second Comptroller of the United States Treasury. Parris died 11 February 1857 in Portland, Maine. Dodge and Koed, eds., *Biographical Directory of the United States Congress*, 1701.
53. Noah Felton.
54. Clement Tubbs Coote (1784–1849). Born in Cambridgeshire, England, Coote came to the United States in 1817 and was naturalized in 1822. He became a Washington DC alderman (1827–36), a justice of the peace, and owned the Washington Brewery. He was a freemason and helped lay the cornerstone of the Washington Monument in 1848. He died in Baltimore, Maryland, 12 May 1849. Tyler, ed., *Encyclopedia of Virginia Biography*, 5:1079–80; Harper, *History of the Grand Lodge*, 342–43; *Evening Star* (DC), 11 October 1892; Bundy, "A History of the Office of Justice of the Peace."
55. Joseph Bryan (1801–63). Born in Mount Zion, Georgia, Bryan was a locating agent and speculator who served as attorney for the land speculators opposed to the James C. Watson contract. Haveman, "'Last Evening I Saw the Sun Set.'"
56. Finley Bodam Hiern (1805–90). Hiern served as postmaster at Pass Christian. Population Schedules of the Seventh Census of the United States, 1850, Mississippi, Microcopy 432, Roll 372, NARA.
57. The same Thomas Pidgeon as no. 42 on the second McIntosh party roll. His son, Joseph, was executed in Mobile sometime around this time.
58. Wolf River flows into Bay St. Louis between Bay St. Louis and Pass Christian, Mississippi.

16. REMOVAL OF THE REFUGEE CREEKS

1. Haveman, *Rivers of Sand*, 242–50; Ellisor, "Like So Many Wolves."
2. Hugh Gaylord Barclay (1805–62), the clerk of the county court of Talladega County (elected March 1833), who also served as its first postmaster (ca. 1833–40). Vandiver, "Pioneer Talladega," 16; Jemison, *Historic Tales of Talladega*, 80, 102–3.
3. The Muscle Shoals were considered at the time "'the greatest single barrier to navigation of the Tennessee [River].'" The shoals consisted of a mix of hard, non-eroding rock overlying the softer rock of the riverbed. This mix helped create an extensive series of rapids that saw the Tennessee drop more than three and a half feet for every mile beginning at Elk River and continuing forty miles to Florence. Moreover, the shoals dropped 163 feet between the eastern shoals and Florence, twenty miles to the west. The Tennessee River also contained many natural obstacles such as islands, reefs, and sand and rock bars that made navigating this stretch of the river very difficult, especially at night. Davidson, *The Tennessee*, 1:12–13; *Tuscumbia Telegraph*, 19 July 1828. For a detailed description of a journey through the shoals see U.S. Congress, House Report 284, *Letter from the Secretary of War, Transmitting . . . an Examination of the Muscle Shoals* (1828), Serial 175, 5–20.
4. James Ditto established a ferry on the Tennessee River at this site in 1807.
5. Handwriting suggests it could also be 4 o'clock.
6. Keelboat.
7. Guards are the part of the deck of a steamboat that extends beyond the hull. Guards provided additional deck space for more cargo. See Gudmestad, *Steamboats and the Rise of the Cotton Kingdom*.
8. The Creeks were generally opposed to using steam or keel boat transportation. Sickness, caused by the close quarters, was one concern; however, the "greater dread was being thrown overboard when dead" and denied a proper Creek burial. The burial of the Creek child at a wood landing suggests this did not occur. *Arkansas State Gazette*, 15 November 1836; Haveman, *Rivers of Sand*, 223.
9. Deas probably misread this episode. The mother was not guided by foolishness but by the Creeks' firmly held views on purity and strength. She was either trying to cleanse the child or make the child strong by exposing her progeny to the elements. Deas notes in his muster roll that this girl was an adolescent—"between 10 & 25"—so the family was likely "going to water" in order to cleanse as the Creeks did daily. Many southeastern Indians preferred cold water, and infants were even submerged in order to give them strength. In fact, Lieutenant Henry Timberlake believed that the Cherokee practice of bathing babies daily in cold water gave them strength and prevented deformities. The Creeks also valued the practice of "going to water" and would ritually bathe in nearby streams. Dutch botanist and writer Bernard Romans noted that Creek children were submerged

in cold water immediately after birth. Once in the Indian territory, Creek women rolled their offspring in the snow "to make them hardy." Muster roll (Deas), SIAC, Agent (Reynolds), Account (1687), Year (1838), NARA; Perdue, *Cherokee Women*, 33; Grant Foreman, ed., *A Traveler in Indian Territory*, 130; Romans, *A Concise Natural History of East and West Florida*, 148. Another possibility, albeit less likely, was that the mother committed infanticide in order to spare the infant from the horrors of removal. This was not unusual during times of extreme desperation. In fact, during the Second Creek War, American soldiers reported that Creek women had killed six of their children "who were unable to keep up with them in their flight." McIntosh to Jesup, 13 August 1836, RG 94, 159-Q, Box 12, Folder "Letters Received from Officers of the Army," NARA. Some children were poisoned by Creek women while others were suffocated with their mouths stuffed with dry grass and moss to prevent American soldiers from hearing them. Ellisor, *Second Creek War*, 293–94. See also, Haveman, "The Indomitable Women of the Creek Removal Era," 10–39.

10. More commonly, *freshet*, a thawing of snow during the spring months.
11. The Arkansas River originates in the Rocky Mountains near Leadville, Colorado.
12. Consumption was the archaic name for tuberculosis. See Rothman, *Living in the Shadow of Death*; Dormandy, *The White Death.*
13. Fort Coffee was established in 1834.
14. John Ellis Wool (1784–1869). Born in Newburgh, New York, Wool served as color bearer for the Troy Invincibles (1808–9). His military history includes: ensign and quartermaster of cavalry, Rensselaer, New York militia (1809–12); captain, 13th Infantry (1812); in the War of 1812, being severely wounded in both thighs at the Battle of Queenston Heights, Upper Canada (1812), and being engaged in the Battle of Frenchman's Creek, Upper Canada (1812); major, 29th Infantry (1813); and in the Battle of Plattsburgh, New York (1814); brevet lieutenant colonel, U.S. Army, for meritorious conduct at the Battle of Plattsburgh (1815); transferred to 6th Infantry (1815); colonel and inspector general of Northern Division, U.S. Army (1816); on inspection duty of northern commands (1816); lieutenant colonel, 6th Infantry to rank from 1818 (1820); vacated lineal grade as lieutenant colonel (1821); inspector general, U.S. Army (1821); on inspection duty of western posts (1822); on inspection duty of Atlantic coast and Great Lakes arsenals and forts (1824); brevet brigadier general, U.S. Army for ten years faithful service in one grade (1826); on tour of Europe (1832); in Cherokee country engaged in preserving the peace in wake of the Treaty of New Echota, subsisting Cherokees, and overseeing the round up of fugitive Creek Indians (1836–37); in Vermont and New York during the Canada independence movement (1838); in Maine planning defenses during lead-up to Aroostook War (1838); commander, Department of the East, New York City (1838–46); brigadier general, U.S. Army (1841); in Utica, New York standing guard during trial of Alexander McLeod

(1841); in Mexican-American War, being engaged at the Battle of Buena Vista, Mexico (1847), and in military occupation of Coahuila, Mexico (1847); brevet major general, U.S. Army, for gallant and meritorious conduct at the Battle of Buena Vista (1847); commander, Army of Occupation, Mexico (1847–48); commander, Department of the East (1848–54); commander, Department of the Pacific (1854–57); commander, Department of the East (1857–61); commander, Department of Virginia, Fort Monroe, Virginia (1861–62); commander, Middle Department, Baltimore, Maryland (1862–63); commander, Department of the East (1863); major general, U.S. Army (1862); retired (1863); died at Troy, New York, 10 November 1869, at age 85. Eicher and Eicher, *Civil War High Commands*, 581; Henry, *Military Record of Civilian Appointments*, 1:47–48; Hinton, "The Military Career of John Ellis Wool"; Prosch, "The United States Army in Washington Territory"; Warner, *Generals in Blue*, 573–74; Cherokee Subsistence Receipts, January–June 1837, Box 26, Folder 1, John Ellis Wool Papers, 1810–1869, SC 15361, New York State Library, Albany.

15. Archibald Rhea Barclay (1802–69) was the brother of Hugh Gaylord Barclay and one of the largest slave owners in Talladega County. Barclay's bid to help conduct the Creeks west was endorsed by Alabama Governor C. C. Clay in 1836. Population Schedules of the Seventh Census of the United States, Alabama Slave Schedules, Microcopy 432, Roll 24, NARA. DeLand and Smith, *Northern Alabama*, 46; see also Sevier and Madden, *Sevier Family History*; Kennamer, *History of Jackson County*, 31.
16. Ross's Landing is modern-day Chattanooga, Tennessee.
17. In addition to notifying the commissioner of Indian affairs that he was forwarding his estimate of funds for the emigration, Deas's 2 April 1837 letter, written from New Echota, specifies what type of funds would be most acceptable along the route west. Deas writes that "it is well to observe that Alabama money, or that of Nashville or West Tennessee is the most current in the section of country thro' which the Emigration is generally conducted; but I think it would be better, to have part of the amount Estimated for, in a Bank of North Alabama with authority to Draw upon the War Department, in case more should be required." Deas to Harris, 2 April 1837, LR, CAE, Roll 238, 204–5.
18. Roger Jones (1789–1852). Born in Westmoreland County, Virginia, Jones was commissioned second lieutenant, U.S. Marine Corps, in 1809. His military history includes: first lieutenant, U.S. Marine Corps (1809); resigned, U.S. Marine Corps (1812); appointed captain, 3rd Artillery (1812); brigade major, 3rd Artillery (1813); assistant adjutant general with the rank of major (1813); transferred to Corps of Artillery (1814); in War of 1812, being engaged in the Battle of Chippewa, Upper Canada (1814), and the Battle of Lundy's Lane, Upper Canada (1814), and in the Siege of Fort Erie, Upper Canada (1814); brevet major for distinguished service in the Battle of Chippewa, Upper Canada (1815); brevet lieutenant colonel for gallantry

and good conduct during sortie from Fort Erie (1815); retained in artillery (1815); aide-de-camp to Major General Jacob Brown (1815); adjutant general with the rank of colonel (1818–21); retained and transferred to 3rd Artillery (1821); brevet colonel for ten years faithful service in one grade (1824); adjutant general of the army (1825–52); major, 2nd Artillery (1827); brevet brigadier general (1832); lieutenant colonel, 4th Artillery (1834); relinquished his rank in line (1835); brevet major general for meritorious conduct in performance of duties prosecuting Mexican-American War (1849); died at Washington DC, 15 July 1852. Gardner, *A Dictionary of All Officers*, 255–56; Heitman, *Historical Register*, 1:582; Jones, *Captain Roger Jones*, 71–73.

19. James Childress. Estimate of Funds, LR, CAE, Roll 238, 296.
20. Imprudence refers to the child who was placed in cold water by its mother and died, as reported in Deas's 25 May journal entry.
21. Nathaniel W. Smith (1791–1841). Born in McMinn County, Tennessee, Smith served as a ensign in the Tennessee volunteers (1812–13). His military history includes: lieutenant, Tennessee volunteers (1813–14); appointed first lieutenant 39th Infantry (1813); in Mississippi Territory, being engaged and wounded at the Battle of Horseshoe Bend (1814); honorably discharged (1815); reinstated, in 1st Infantry (1815); resigned U.S. Army (1816); colonel, East Tennessee volunteers (1836); resigned, East Tennessee volunteers (1837); superintendent of Cherokee Removal (1837–39); died at Fort Houston, Texas, 17 September 1841. Heitman, *Historical Register*, 1:902; *Daughters of the Republic of Texas: Patriot Ancestor Album*. Paducah KY: Turner Publishing Company, 1995.
22. Dr. John S. Young (1804–57), Tennessee secretary of state (1839–47). Graf and Haskins, eds., *Papers of Andrew Johnson*, 1:27n1.
23. Chinnabee. An ally of Andrew Jackson during the first Creek War (1813–14), Chinnabee's son was the mile chief Selocta (a Natchez Creek Indian who also aided Andrew Jackson during the First Creek War). Selocta also went by (or was misidentified as) "General Chinubbee." McKenney and Hall, *History of the Indian Tribes of North America*, 2:193–96; Ellisor, *Second Creek War*, 55.
24. Petition of Creek Indians, LR, CAE, Roll 237, 411–13; Hahn, "The Cussita Migration Legend."
25. Reuben E. Clements (1812–68). Born in Fayetteville, Tennessee, Clements was a former surveyor in the Creek Nation. He moved to Texas in 1848 and became postmaster of Brownsville, Texas, in 1849. He later worked for the city of San Antonio as an engineer before serving in the Texas state legislature. Johnson, *A History of Texas and Texans*, 3:1206–7; Upshaw to Harris, 13 September 1837, LR, CAE, Roll 238, 885.
26. Gouverneur Morris (d. 1868). Born in New York, Morris attended the U.S. Military Academy, West Point, New York (1818–23), but never graduated. He was appointed second lieutenant, 4th Infantry, in 1824. His military history includes: first lieutenant, 4th Infantry (1831); captain, 4th Infantry (1837); engaged as

military oversight of a detachment of refugee Creeks from Chickasaw territory (1837); in Mexican-American War, being engaged at the Battle of Palo Alto, Texas (1846), and the Battle of Resaca de la Palma, Texas (1846); brevet major for gallant and meritorious conduct in the Battles of Palo Alto and Resaca de la Palma (1846); major, 3rd Infantry (1850); in command of Fort Union, New Mexico (1852–53); lieutenant colonel, 1st Infantry (1857); in command of Fort Duncan, Texas (to 1859); retired from U.S. Army (1861); died 18 October 1868. Heitman, *Historical Register*, 1:727; Hamersly, *Complete Regular Army Register*, 649; Kiser, *Dragoons in Apacheland*; Thompson, *Civil War to the Bloody End*, 81; Thompson, *Fifty Miles and a Fight*, 66n8.

27. Dr. Nic McCoull. Voucher No. 11, SIAC, Agent (Morris), Account (1837), Year (1838), NARA.
28. *Arkansas State Gazette*, 19 December 1837.
29. Arthur Martin Montgomery Upshaw (1803–77). Born in Essex County, Virginia, Upshaw moved to Pulaski, Tennessee, as a young man. He served with the Tennessee Volunteers in the Second Creek War and Second Seminole War. He was later appointed by President Martin Van Buren as agent for the Chickasaws and participated in their removal to Indian territory. He remained as agent to the Chickasaws in the West until 1850, when he was fired by President Zachary Taylor. Upshaw and his family eventually settled in Washington County, Texas, where he became a two-term state legislator. *A Memorial and Biographical History of Johnson and Hill Counties*, 473; Gibson, *The Chickasaws*, 182; Satz, *Tennessee's Indian Peoples*, 56; Paige et al., *Chickasaw Removal*, 81.
30. Kemp S. Holland (ca. 1803–46). Born in Virginia, Holland served in the Mississippi legislature and was assistant commissary with the rank of captain during the Mexican-American War. He died in Mexico in 1846. Gardner, *A Dictionary of All Officers*, 233; McIntosh, ed., *Papers of Jefferson Davis*, 2:678–79.
31. Joseph Augustus Phillips (1805–46). Born in New Jersey, Phillips graduated from the U.S. Military Academy, West Point, New York, in 1823 (26th of 35) and was promoted second lieutenant, 7th Infantry (1823). His military history includes: on frontier duty at Fort Gibson, Indian territory (1824–25); adjutant, 7th Infantry, at regimental headquarters (1825–30); first lieutenant, 7th Infantry (1828); on frontier duty at Fort Gibson, Indian territory (1830); on recruiting service (1830–32); commissary duty subsisting Indians (1832–34); assistant instructor of Infantry Tactics and quartermaster, U.S. Military Academy, West Point, New York (1834–35); captain, 7th Infantry (1835); on frontier duty at Fort Gibson, Indian territory (1835–36); Camp Desire, Indian territory (1836); transferring Indians and as disbursing agent (1836–38); transferred to 8th Infantry (1838); Watertown, New York, during Canada independence movement (1838–39); Sackets Harbor, New York (1839); on recruiting service (1839); Jefferson Barracks, Missouri (1840); resigned U.S. Army (1840); died at Quincy, Illinois, 4 January 1846, at age 41.

Cullum, *Biographical Register* (1868), 1:252; Heitman, *Historical Register*, 1:789; Receipt of Morris, SIAC, Agent (Morris), Account (1837), Year (1838), NARA.

32. William M. M. Owen. Owen served as an enrolling agent from 17 September to 18 November 1837 and was discharged at Memphis. Census records show Owen was from Itawamba County, Mississippi. Population Schedules of the Sixth Census of the United States, Mississippi, Vol. 2, Microcopy 704, Roll 215, NARA; SIAC, Agent (Gouverneur Morris), Account (1837), Year (1838), NARA. See also Rowland, *Official and Statistical Register*, 106; Lowry and McCardle, *A History of Mississippi*, 495.
33. John Michael Millard (1803–83). Millard conducted detachments during Chickasaw removal. Millard died at Baltimore, Maryland, 21 June 1883. *Saint Mary's Beacon*, 28 June 1883.
34. The disbursing agent was Gouverneur Morris.
35. Probably "cession."
36. Coldwater River in northwest Mississippi.
37. Daniel Miller. Abstract of disbursements, SIAC, Agent (Morris), Account (1837), Year (1838), NARA.
38. Several Creeks were also transported on the steamboat *DeKalb* from Memphis to Fort Coffee in late 1837. Receipt of Buckner, SIAC, Agent (Morris), Account (1837), Year (1838), NARA. Approximately eight hundred Chickasaws traveled on the *Itasca* as well. Paige et al., *Chickasaw Removal*.
39. Simeon Buckner (1797–1843). Cantrell, *The Annals of Christ Church Parish*, 30; Crozier, ed., *The Buckners of Virginia*, 79.

17. THE REUNIFICATION EMIGRATIONS

1. Paredes, "Back from Disappearance"; Ellsworth and Dysart, "West Florida's Forgotten People"; Waselkov, "Formation of the Tensaw Community;" Haveman, "Last Evening I Saw the Sun Set for the Last Time," 85.
2. Blake to Abert, 8 May 1841, LR, CAE, Roll 240, 129; Blake to Crawford, 8 June 1844, LR, CAE, Roll 240, 298; Blake to Crawford, 25 June 1841, LR, CAE, Roll 240, 142–43; War Dept. to Blake, 7 July 1841, LR, CAE, Roll 240, 150; Blake to Crawford, 21 August 1841, LR, CAE, Roll 240, 145; Crawford to Porter, 17 November 1843, LR, CAE, Roll 240, 284–87; Lewis to Lewis, 12 December 1843, LR, CAE, Roll 240, 308.
3. Haveman, *Rivers of Sand*, 295.
4. Ellisor, *Second Creek War*, 47, 94–95; Haveman, *Rivers of Sand*, 92–95, 265.
5. Muster roll (Brodnax), LR, CAE, Roll 240, 524.
6. Moses K. Wheat (1781–1849).
7. Francis Asbury Wheat (ca. 1812–38). *Columbus Enquirer*, 9 April 1838; Wheat & Son to Page, 27 June 1836, CGS-IRW, Roll 6, 247–49.
8. Leroy Driver (b. ca. 1813). Born in Georgia, Driver served as jailer of Chambers

County, Alabama, for a time. Cherry to Crawford, 28 August 1845, LR, CAE, Roll 240, 344–47; Muster roll (Wheat), LR, CAE, Roll 240, 393; Cherry to Crawford, 3 October 1845, LR, CAE, Roll 240, 356–57; Wheat to Commissioner of Indian Affairs, 20 January 1846, LR, CAE, Roll 240, 412–13.

9. Logan to Medill, 29 July 1846, LR, CAE, Roll 240, 405; Logan to Medill, 5 March 1846, LR, CAE, Roll 240, 387; Muster roll (Wheat), LR, CAE, Roll 240, 393; Abstract of Provisions, LR, CAE, Roll 240, 389.

10. Robert M. Cherry (b. ca. 1810). Born in South Carolina, Cherry was a Wetumpka, Alabama, lawyer. Lewis to Crawford, 30 April 1845, LR, CAE, Roll 240, 372. Population Schedules of the Seventh Census of the United States, 1850, Vol. 4, Alabama, Microcopy 432, Roll 51, NARA.

11. Thomas Hartley Crawford (1786–1863). Born in Chambersburg, Pennsylvania, Crawford graduated from the College of New Jersey (Princeton University) in 1804. He was admitted to the bar in 1807 and practiced law before serving as U.S. representative from Pennsylvania (1829–33) and in the Pennsylvania state legislature (1833–34). In 1836 he was appointed (along with Alfred Balch) a special commissioner charged with investigating the causes of the Second Creek War as well as the frauds committed against the Creeks in the sale of their reserves under the 1832 Treaty of Washington. In 1838 President Martin Van Buren appointed Crawford to replace Carey A. Harris as commissioner of Indian affairs (1838–45). Crawford supported Indian removal and "civilization" efforts (in the form of manual labor schools) designed to coerce and compel Indians to live like whites. In 1845 President James K. Polk appointed Crawford as a judge in the criminal court of the District of Columbia (1845–61). He died in Washington DC, 27 January 1863, at age 76. Satz, "Thomas Hartley Crawford," 23–27; Dodge and Koed, eds., *Biographical Directory of the United States Congress*, 891–92.

12. James Logan (1792–1859). Born near Danville, Kentucky, Logan moved to Arkansas Territory and served in the territorial legislature. He served as Creek agent in the 1830s and 1840s. Hempstead, *A Pictorial History of Arkansas*, 1138.

13. William Medill (1802–65). Born in New Castle County, Delaware, Medill graduated from Newark Academy in 1825 and commenced a law practice in Lancaster, Ohio in 1830. He served in the Ohio state legislature (1835–38), the U.S. House of Representatives from Ohio (1839–43), and became lieutenant governor of Ohio (1852–53), and governor of Ohio (1853–56). He was part of the Van Buren wing of the Democratic Party, and this faction pressured President James K. Polk into placing Medill in positions within his administration, including assistant postmaster general (1845), and commissioner of Indian affairs (1845–49), despite the fact that Medill had no prior experience dealing with native peoples. Medill believed in "civilizing" Indians and assimilating them into American society through manual labor schools. Medill also supported cracking down on the illegal whiskey trade in Indian territory and supported reforming the

way annuities were distributed. After being removed as commissioner of Indian affairs, Medill served as first comptroller of the U. S. treasury (1857–61). Medill died in Lancaster, Ohio, 2 September 1865. Trennert, "William Medill," 29–39; Dodge and Koed, eds., *Biographical Directory of the United States Congress*, 1568; Wilson and Fiske, eds., *Appleton's Cyclopædia of American Biography*, 4:285.

14. In the margin of the muster roll under "Remarks" is noted: "One overtaken, & emigrated from the [mouth] Of White River—the same died on the 1st March, 1846." Muster Roll (Wheat), LR, CAE, Roll 240, 393.
15. Haveman, *Rivers of Sand*, 265.
16. Dixon Hall Lewis (1802–1848). Born in Dinwiddie County, Virginia, raised in Hancock County, Georgia, and educated at South Carolina College (University of South Carolina), Lewis moved to Autauga County, Alabama in 1820. He was admitted to the bar in 1823 and began a law practice in Montgomery, Alabama, before becoming a member of the state's house of representatives (1826–28), a member of the U.S. House of Representatives (1829–44), and the U.S. Senate (1844–48). He was a States' Rights Democrat, opposing the bank and internal improvements, and supported nullification. During his time in Congress, Lewis chaired the Committee on Indian Affairs and supported Jackson's Indian removal program. Lewis died in New York City, 25 October 1848, from complications due to obesity. Dodge and Koed, eds., *Biographical Directory of the United States Congress*, 1444; Williams, "Dixon H. Lewis"; Owen, *History of Alabama*, 4:1043; Doss, "Lewis, Dixon Hall," in *American National Biography*, 13:566–68.
17. Ward Cochamy (1823–1900). Born in the Creek town of Wetumpka, Cochamy was descended from the Scotsman Lachlan McGillivray and the celebrated headman Alexander McGillivray. Orphaned at a young age, Cochamy was raised by his uncle Lachlan Durant and remained with him in Macon County, Alabama, through the removal era. Cochamy moved to Indian territory in 1845 and became a trader, interpreter, farmer, and clerk in the West. He joined the Confederacy during the American Civil War and served under Chilly McIntosh's regiment. After the war Cochamy served in the House of Warriors and House of Kings and as Second Chief before becoming Principal Chief in 1876 after the impeachment and removal of Locher Harjo. Cochamy was described in his later years as being "a very large heavily built man 6 ft high & weighs about 200 lbs—dark hazel eyes, black hair, thin whiskers & has a very pleasant address" and "his whiskers are dark, tinged with grey & very thin & scattering." Cochamy married Lizzie Carr (d. 1864) and had three children: Peter (b. 1852), Visey (b. 1854), and Charles (b. 1856). He had another child with his second wife. Cochamy died near Wetumka, Indian territory, 13 March 1900. Current-Garcia and Hatfield, eds., *Shem, Ham & Japheth*, 91, 158; Meserve, "Chief Samuel Checote," 406–7; O'Beirne and O'Beirne, *Indian Territory*, 341–43.
18. Cochamy to Medill, 7 April 1848, LR, CAE, Roll 240, 446–48; Dickson to Medill,

6 June 1848, LR, CAE, Roll 240, 454; Cochamy to Medill, 16 July 1848, LR, CAE, Roll 240, 450–51.

19. Meserve, "Chief Samuel Checote."
20. The muster roll has eleven columns so I have used the following assumptions for the age ranges: (1) males under ten, (2) males of ten and under twenty-five, (3) males of twenty-five and under fifty, (4) males over fifty, (5) females under ten, (6) females of ten and under twenty-five, (7) females of twenty-five and under fifty, (8) females over fifty, (9) male slaves, (10) female slaves, (11) aggregate. Muster roll (Cochamy), LR, CAE, Roll 240, 485.
21. Benjamin Marshall and Tuckabatchee Micco were in Washington in 1848 on authority of the Creek Nation to pursue, among other things, a claim for two thousand dollars for the one hundred slaves caught by the Creek warriors who were serving in Florida against the Seminoles. General Thomas S. Jesup promised the Creeks twenty dollars "for each slave captured by them belonging to the whites," and the warriors apprehended approximately one hundred. Creeks to Medill, 5 June 1848, LR, CAE, Roll 240, 462–63.
22. Joseph Bryan, the same as in chapter 15.
23. William C. Dickson was a merchant in Indian territory. Gideon, *Indian Territory*, 161, 349.
24. Petit Jean Mountain in Arkansas.
25. A mile chief from Tuckabatchee.
26. Possibly a reference to the 1838 Treaty of Fort Gibson, which compensated Creeks who lost property during the 1836–37 relocations. Kappler, *Indian Affairs*, 2:524–25.
27. Samuel Morton Rutherford (1797–1867). Born in Goochland County, Virginia, Rutherford moved with his family to Gallatin, Tennessee at the age of 12. During the War of 1812 he enlisted in the Tennessee volunteers and served under Andrew Jackson at the Battle of New Orleans. After the war he established a trading post at the mouth of the Verdigris River. He later served as sheriff of Clark and Pulaski Counties, Arkansas Territory (1826–27); was elected to the Arkansas territorial legislature (1831); appointed special agent for the removal and subsistence of the Choctaws (1832); appointed treasurer of the Arkansas Territory (1833); appointed register of the United States land office in Arkansas (1835). He was the acting superintendent of Indian affairs for the Western Territory until May 1849. In the 1850s he served as Seminole agent and returned to Florida to help move Seminoles to Indian territory. Rutherford died at Fort Smith, Arkansas at age 70. Hempstead, *Historical Review of Arkansas*, 3:1105–8; Rand "Samuel Morton Rutherford"; Grant Foreman, "Nathaniel Pryor"; Foreman, *The Five Civilized Tribes*, 74n22, 272, 274.
28. Echo Fixico.
29. According to an 1850 census there was only one Floyd family in Autauga County,

headed by Joel Floyd (b. 1782), a sixty-eight-year-old farmer born in Virginia. Population Schedules of the Seventh Census of the United States, 1850, Vol. 2, Alabama, Microcopy 432, Roll 1, NARA.

30. Possibly Rev. Enoch Hayes (d. 1853), pastor of the Mulberry Baptist Church (1828–40) and later of a church in Kingston, Alabama, which was the county seat of Autauga County at the time. Abrams, *History of Mulberry Baptist Church*, 22–23.
31. Haveman, *Rivers of Sand*, 268.
32. George Washington Stidham (1817–91). Born in the Creek Nation, Alabama, Stidham was the son of the "white explorer" (Hopaychutke), a man of Scotch-Irish heritage and a Hitchiti mother. He was a businessman, a judge, and served in the House of Warriors in Indian territory. O'Beirne and O'Beirne, *Indian Territory*, 185–87.
33. This town was named Cho lock co Ninne, after the horse path that passed near it (the path was also known as the Okfuskee Trail). The route was described as "plain and 12 or 15 Inches wide and probably has been used 100 years." Journal, July 17 to 26, 1826, Blount-ADAH.
34. Coffee to Eaton, 16 November 1829, LR, CAE, Roll 237, 248–50; *Macon Telegraph*, 7 January 1828.
35. O'Beirne and O'Beirne, *Indian Territory*, 298–99.
36. Hoole, "Echoes from the 'Trail of Tears,' 1837" and "Echoes from the 'Trail of Tears,' 1837," part 2.
37. O'Beirne and O'Beirne, *Indian Territory*, 298–99.
38. McIntosh to Medill, 29 January 1849, LR, CAE, Roll 240, 513.
39. Se war ki ke (no. 47) may have been a part of this family. See Exhibit B, SFOIA SF 285, Roll 77, 93; McIntosh to Medill, 29 January 1849, LR, CAE, Roll 240, 513.
40. Se war ki ke may have been a part of Nannie Miller's family. See Exhibit B , SFOIA SF 285, Roll 77, 93.
41. May be the same as Palo Carr.
42. Exhibit B, SFOIA SF 285, Roll 77, 93–94.
43. Also known as the Choctaw Academy (1825–48). The school was founded as a partnership between the Choctaws and Richard Mentor Johnson (1780–1850), who served as a representative and senator from Kentucky and as Martin Van Buren's vice president. The school was established in 1825 at Johnson's farm five miles west of Georgetown, Kentucky. The institution educated a diverse student body of Indians from across the continent in spelling, grammar, mathematics, surveying, history, and later in trades. Snyder, *Great Crossings*; Carolyn Thomas Foreman, "The Choctaw Academy."
44. "Ja's Island" refers to James Island. For Ho lah ta see Exhibit C, SFOIA SF 285, Roll 77, 96.
45. Exhibit E, SFOIA SF 285, Roll 77, 100–1; Meserve, "The MacIntoshes"; Haveman, *Rivers of Sand*, 88–89.
46. Exhibit F, SFOIA SF 285, 103; O'Beirne and O'Beirne, *Indian Territory*, 171–72.

47. Ethan Allen Hitchcock Notebooks, Creeks, Box 4, Folder 17, Beinecke Rare Book and Manuscript Library, Yale University, New Haven CT.
48. Exhibit G, SFOIA SF 285, Roll 77, 107, 109–10.
49. Exhibit G, SFOIA SF 285, Roll 77, 105–6, 107, 109–10.
50. Exhibit H, SFOIA SF 285, Roll 77, 112.
51. Exhibit I, SFOIA SF 285, Roll 77, 114–15.
52. Exhibit I, SFOIA SF 285, Roll 77, 114.
53. Exhibit J, SFOIA SF 285, Roll 77, 117.
54. Exhibit K, SFOIA SF 285, Roll 77, 119.
55. Exhibit L, SFOIA SF 285, Roll 77, 152.
56. Exhibit L, SFOIA SF 285, Roll 77, 152.
57. Exhibit AA, SFOIA SF 285, Roll 77, 6.
58. Exhibit M, SFOIA SF 285, Roll 77, 154.
59. Exhibit N, SFOIA SF 285, Roll 77, 156.
60. Exhibit O, SFOIA SF 285, Roll 77, 158; O'Beirne and O'Beirne, *Indian Territory*, 214–16.
61. Exhibit Q, SFOIA SF 285, Roll 77, 162.
62. Ward to Jackson, n.d., Letters Received by the Office of Indian Affairs, 1824–81, Creek Agency Reserves, 1832–50, Microcopy 234, Roll 241, 755–59.
63. O'Beirne and O'Beirne, *Indian Territory*, 152–54.
64. Exhibit R, SFOIA SF 285, Roll 77, 164.
65. Exhibit S, SFOIA SF 285, Roll 77, 166.
66. Exhibit X, SFOIA SF 285, Roll 77, 168; O'Beirne and O'Beirne, *Indian Territory*, 258–59; Benedict, *Muskogee and Northeastern Oklahoma*, 3:323–25.
67. Exhibit B, SFOIA SF 285, Roll 77, 93–94.
68. List of omitted names, SFOIA SF 285, Roll 77, 86–87; Exhibit R, SFOIA SF 285, Roll 77, 164.
69. Exhibit AA, SFOIA SF 285, Roll 77, 6–7.
70. Exhibit D, SFOIA SF 285, Roll 77, 98–99.
71. Exhibit G, SFOIA SF 285, Roll 77, 107, 109–10.
72. Exhibit Z, SFOIA SF 285, Roll 77, 175.
73. Names omitted from corrected roll, SFOIA SF 285, Roll 77, 173–74.

BIBLIOGRAPHY

ARCHIVAL SOURCES

Alabama Department of Archives and History, Montgomery AL
  Alabama Land Grants and Land Patents Collection.
  Richard A. Blount Papers.
Archives Branch of the Marine Corps History Division, Quantico VA
  Samuel Miller Papers.
Columbia University Health Sciences Library, New York NY
  Register kept by Assistant Surgeon George B. McKnight, 1833–34.
Filson Historical Society, Louisville KY
  Madison Mills Diary, 1846–1847.
Huntington Library, San Marino CA
  John Ridge, "The Cherokee War Path, 1836–1840."
Indiana University, Lilly Library, Bloomington IN
  Autobiography of John H. Jones, 1814–82.
Louisiana State University, Special Collections, Baton Rouge LA
  Henry J. Wilson Papers, 1779–1885.
Muscogee (Creek) Nation Library, Okmulgee OK
  Thelma Nolan Cornfeld. Copy of unpublished manuscript.
National Archives and Records Administration, Atlanta GA
  Record Group 36, Records of the U.S. Customs Service, 1745–1997.
    Coastwise Slave Manifests, 1820–1860.
    Mobile, Alabama Inward.
National Archives and Records Administration, Fort Worth TX
  Record Group 36, Records of the U.S. Customs Service.
National Archives and Records Administration, Washington DC
  Record Group 15, Records of the Department of Veterans Affairs, 1773–1985.
  Record Group 29, Records of the Bureau of the Census, 1790–1996.
  Record Group 75, Records of the Bureau of Indian Affairs, 1793–1989.
    Documents—Entry 299, Emigration Lists, 1836–38.

Documents—Entry 300, Miscellaneous Creek Removal Records, ca. 1827–59.
Microcopy 21—Records of the Office of Indian Affairs, Letters Sent, Roll 12.
Microcopy 234—Letters Received by the Office of Indian Affairs, 1824– 81.
Chickasaw Agency Emigration, 1837–50, Microcopy 234, Roll 143.
Creek Agency, 1824–76, Rolls 219–27.
Creek Agency Emigration, 1826–49, Rolls 237–40.
Creek Agency Reserves, 1832–50, Rolls 241–48.
Creek Agency West, 1826–36, Roll 236.
Microcopy 275—1832 Census of Creek Indians Taken by Parsons and Abbott, Roll 1.
Microcopy 574—Special Files of the Office of Indian Affairs, 1807–1904.
Special File 62, Roll 7—James Erwin and Erwin & Greathouse, claims for losses under contracts made in 1834–35 for transporting and providing subsistence for Creek and Seminole Indians, 1847–55.
Special File 136, Roll 27—McIntosh party, claims for property destroyed by hostile Creek Indians in 1825, 1825–26.
Special File 207, Roll 61—Creek claims for property left in the East and lost during removal, 1838.
Special File 285, Roll 77—Creek self-emigration claims, 1886–1904.
Record Group 94, Records of the Adjutant General's Office, 1780s–1917.
Record Group 217, Records of the Accounting Officers of the Department of the Treasury.
National Library of Medicine, Bethesda MD
Army Medical Department Album, vol. 1.
New York Historical Society, New York NY
Hanrick Family Papers, 1803–1948.
New York Public Library, New York NY
Biography of F. S. Belton. Belton-Kirby-Dawson-Todd Families Papers, ca. 1763–1892. Astor, Lenox, and Tilden Foundations, Manuscripts and Archives Division.
New York State Library, Albany NY
John Ellis Wool Papers, 1810–1869.
Princeton University, Department of Rare Books and Special Collections, Princeton NJ
John G. Reynolds Journal.
Tennessee State Library and Archives, Nashville TN
Fergusson Family Papers, 1784–1927.
Tulane University, New Orleans LA
Louisiana Research Collection, Medical Documents Collection, 1759–1952.
University of Alabama, Hoole Special Collections, Tuscaloosa AL
William Winslett deed conveyed to Edward Hanrick, November 1853.
University of Arkansas Libraries, Special Collections, Fayetteville AR

Hardin-Stark Family Materials.
University of Florida, George A. Smathers Libraries, Gainesville FL
Special and Area Studies Collections, William Davenport Papers.
University of Miami Libraries, Miami FL
Journal of Amos B. Eaton.
University of North Carolina, Chapel Hill NC
Anderson Abercrombie Papers, 1836–67.
University of Texas at Arlington Library, Arlington TX
Colonel Francis S. Belton, Mexican War Letters, 1847–1854.
University of Texas, Dolph Briscoe Center for American History, Austin TX
Edward Hanrick Papers, 1831–1869.
University of Vermont Libraries, Special Collections
Colonel Isaac Clark Papers.
University of Virginia, Albert and Shirley Small Special Collections Library, Charlottesville VA
Burton Randall Papers, 1827–1865.
University Publications of America, Bethesda MD
Indian Removal to the West, 1832–1840. Files of the Office of the Commissary General of Subsistence, Rolls 1, 4–6, 7, 10.
Vermont Historical Society, Barre VT
Beattie Family Papers.
Wisconsin Historical Society, Madison WI
Draper Manuscripts, Frontier Wars Papers.
Yale University, Beinecke Rare Book and Manuscript Library, New Haven CT
Ethan Allen Hitchcock Collection on Indian Removal.
Henry Wilson papers 1829–1858.

PUBLISHED SOURCES

Abrams, Ulysses H. *A History of Mulberry Baptist Church, 1818–1968: Written for Its Sesquicentennial Celebration*. Chilton County AL: N.p., 1968.

Acts of the General Assembly of the State of Georgia, Passed in Milledgeville at an Annual Session in November and December, 1835. Milledgeville GA: John A. Cuthbert, 1836.

Adair, James. *The History of the American Indians*. Ed. Kathryn E. Holland Braund. Tuscaloosa: University of Alabama Press, 2005.

Agnew, Brad. "The Cherokee Struggle for Lovely's Purchase." *American Indian Quarterly* 2, no. 4 (Winter 1975–76): 347–61.

———. *Fort Gibson: Terminal on the Trail of Tears*. Norman: University of Oklahoma Press, 1980.

Akers, Donna L. *Living in the Land of Death: The Choctaw Nation, 1830–1860*. East Lansing: Michigan State University Press, 2004.

Alcaraz, Ramón, et al. *The Other Side: or, Notes for the History of the War between Mexico and the United States.* Translated and edited by Albert C. Ramsey. New York: John Wiley, 1850.

Aldrich, M. Almy. *History of the United States Marine Corps.* Boston: Henry L. Shepard, 1875.

Allardice, Bruce S. *Confederate Colonels: A Biographical Register.* Columbia: University of Missouri Press, 2008.

Allsopp, Fred W. *History of the Arkansas Press for a Hundred Years and More.* Little Rock: Parke-Harper, 1922.

Alperin, Lynn M. *History of the Gulf Intracoastal Waterway.* Washington DC: U.S. Army Engineer Water Resources Support Center, 1983.

The American Journal of the Medical Sciences. Vol. 16. Philadelphia: Carey, Lea & Blanchard, 1835.

American State Papers: Documents, Legislative and Executive, of the Congress of the United States, From the First Session of the First to the Second Session of the Eighteenth Congress, Inclusive: Commencing March 3, 1789, and Ending March 5, 1825, vol. 1: *Naval Affairs.* Ed. Walter Lowrie and Walter S. Franklin. Washington DC: Gales and Seaton, 1834.

American State Papers: Documents, Legislative and Executive, of the Congress of the United States, From the First Session of the Eighteenth to the Second Session of the Nineteenth Congress, Inclusive: Commencing May 13, 1824, and Ending January 5, 1827, vol. 2: *Naval Affairs.* Ed. Asbury Dickins and John W. Forney. Washington DC: Gales and Seaton, 1860.

American State Papers: Documents, Legislative and Executive, of the Congress of the United States, From the Second Session of the Twenty-First to the First Session of the Twenty-Fourth Congress, Commencing March 1, 1831, and Ending June 15, 1836, vol. 4: *Naval Affairs.* Ed. Asbury Dickins and John W. Forney. Washington DC: Gales and Seaton, 1861.

American State Papers: Documents, Legislative and Executive, of the Congress of the United States, vols. 6–7: *Military Affairs.* Ed. Asbury Dickins and John W. Forney. Washington DC: Gales and Seaton, 1861.

An Account of the Receipts and Expenditures of the United States, for the Year 1836. Washington DC: Blair and Rives, 1837.

Anderson, Gary Clayton. *The Conquest of Texas: Ethnic Cleansing in the Promised Land, 1820–1875.* Norman: University of Oklahoma Press, 2005.

———. *Ethnic Cleansing and the Indian: The Crime That Should Haunt America.* Norman: University of Oklahoma Press, 2014.

Armstrong, Zella. *The History of Hamilton County and Chattanooga Tennessee*, vol. 1. Chattanooga: Lookout Publishing, 1931.

Baird, W. David, ed. *A Creek Warrior for the Confederacy: The Autobiography of Chief G. W. Grayson.* Norman: University of Oklahoma Press, 1988.

Baldwin, Leland D. *The Keelboat Age on Western Waters*. Pittsburgh: University of Pittsburgh Press, 1941.

Ball, Durwood. "Stephen W. Kearny." In *Soldiers West: Biographies from the Military Frontier*, ed. Paul Andrew Hutton and Durwood Ball, 43–71. Norman: University of Oklahoma Press, 2009.

Banks, Wayne. *History of Yell County, Arkansas*. Arkansas Historical Series no. 9. Van Buren AR: Press-Argus, 1959.

Banta, R. E. *The Ohio*. New York: Rinehart, 1949.

Barclay, Wade Crawford. *Early American Methodism 1769–1844*, vol. 2. New York: Board of Missions and Church Extension of the Methodist Church, 1950.

Barker, Eugene C. "Land Speculation as a Cause of the Texas Revolution." *Quarterly of the Texas State Historical Association* 10, no. 1 (July 1906): 76–95.

Barnard, Frederick A. P., and Arnold Guyot, eds. *Johnson's New Universal Cyclopædia: A Scientific and Popular Treasury of Useful Knowledge. Illustrated with Maps, Plans, and Engravings*, vol. 3, part 1. New York: A. J. Johnson and Company, 1883.

Beale, Phelan, and M. P. Blue. *City Directory and History of Montgomery, Alabama, With a Summary of Events in that History, Calendarically Arranged, Besides Other Valuable and Useful Information*. Montgomery AL: T. C. Bingham and Company, 1878.

Bearss, Edwin C., and Arrell M. Gibson. *Fort Smith: Little Gibraltar on the Arkansas*. 1969; reprint, Norman: University of Oklahoma Press, 1988.

Bell, William Gardner. *Secretaries of War and Secretaries of the Army: Portraits and Biographical Sketches*. Washington DC: Center of Military History, United States Army, 2003.

Bemrose, John. *Reminiscences of the Second Seminole War*. Ed. John K. Mahon. Gainesville: University of Florida Press, 1966.

Benedict, John D. *Muskogee and Northeastern Oklahoma: Including the Counties of Muskogee, McIntosh, Wagoner, Cherokee, Sequoyah, Adair, Delaware, Mayes, Rogers, Washington, Nowata, Craig and Ottawa*. Vols. 1–3. Chicago: S. J. Clarke, 1922.

Bergherm, Brent G. "Lovely, William Lewis." In *Arkansas Biography: A Collection of Notable Lives*, ed. Nancy A. Williams and Jeannie M. Whayne, 173–75. Fayetteville: University of Arkansas Press, 2000.

Biographical and Historical Memoirs of Eastern Arkansas: Comprising a Condensed History of the State, a Number of Biographies of Distinguished Citizens of the same, a Brief Descriptive History of each of the Counties named herein, and numerous Biographical Sketches of the Prominent Citizens of such Counties. Chicago: Goodspeed, 1890.

Biographical and Historical Memoirs of Pulaski, Jefferson, Lonoke, Faulkner, Grant, Saline, Perry, Garland and Hot Spring Counties, Arkansas, Comprising a Condensed History of the State, a Number of Biographies of Distinguished Citizens of the same, a Brief Descriptive History of each of the Counties above named, and numerous Biographical Sketches of their Prominent Citizens. Chicago: Goodspeed, 1889.

Biographical and Historical Memoirs of Western Arkansas: Comprising a Condensed History of the State, a number of Biographies of Distinguished Citizens of the same, a brief Descriptive History of each of the Counties mentioned, and numerous Biographical Sketches of the Citizens of such Counties. Chicago: Southern Publishing Company, 1891.

Bixler, John W., ed. *Decisions of the Department of the Interior in Appealed Pension and Bounty-Land Claims; Also a Table of Cases Reported, Cited, Overruled, and Modified, and of Statutes Cited and Construed*, vol. 14. Washington DC: Government Printing Office, 1904.

Bockstruck, Lloyd de Witt. *Naval Pensioners of the United States, 1800–1851*. Baltimore: Genealogical Publishing Company, 2002.

Bolton, S. Charles. *Territorial Ambition: Land and Society in Arkansas 1800–1840*. Fayetteville: University of Arkansas Press, 1993.

Bonner, James C. *Georgia's Last Frontier: The Development of Carroll County*. 1971; reprint, Athens: University of Georgia Press, 2010.

Bowes, John P. *Land Too Good for Indians: Northern Indian Removal*. Norman: University of Oklahoma Press, 2016.

Boyd, Joel D. "Creek Indian Agents, 1834–1874." *Chronicles of Oklahoma* 51, no. 1 (1973): 37–58.

Boykin, Samuel. *History of the Baptist Denomination in Georgia, With Biographical Compendium and Portrait Gallery of Baptist Ministers and Other Georgia Baptists*, vol. 2. Atlanta: Jas. P. Harrison & Company 1881.

Braund, Kathryn E. Holland. "The Creek Indians, Blacks, and Slavery," *Journal of Southern History* 57, no. 4 (November 1991): 601–36.

Braund, Kathryn E. Holland, ed. *Tohopeka: Rethinking the Creek War and the War of 1812*. Tuscaloosa: University of Alabama Press, 2012.

Brewer, Willis. *Alabama: Her History, Resources, War Record, and Public Men. From 1540 to 1872*. Montgomery AL: Barrett and Brown, 1872.

Brewer, W. *The Military and Naval Medical Reference Book; Containing Directions to Young Medical Men, and the Responsible Heads of Military Detachments and Ships' Crews, How to Discriminate and Treat Diseases Incident to Europeans in Different Countries, and How to Preserve and Restore the Sick and Wounded.* London: H. Silverlock, 1841.

Broadwater, Robert P. *Civil War Special Forces: The Elite and Distinct Fighting Units of the Union and Confederate Armies*. Santa Barbara: Praeger, 2014.

Brown, Meredith Mason. *Touching America's History: From the Pequot War through World War II*. Bloomington: Indiana University Press, 2013.

Brown, Walter Lee. *A Life of Albert Pike*. Fayetteville: University of Arkansas Press, 1997.

Brumberg, Joan Jacobs. *Fasting Girls: The History of Anorexia Nervosa.* 1988; reprint, New York: Vintage, 2000.

Buchan, William. *Domestic Medicine; or, The Family Physician: Being an Attempt To render the Medical Art more generally ufeful, by fhewing people what is in their own power both with refpect to the Prevention and Cure of Diseases. Chiefly Calculated to recommend a proper attention to Regimen and Simple Medicines.* Second American Edition. Philadelphia: Joseph Crukshank, 1774.

Buckingham, J. S. *The Slave States of America*, vol. 1. London: Fisher, Son, and Company, 1842.

Bundy, Charles S. "A History of the Office of Justice of the Peace in the District of Columbia." *Records of the Columbia Historical Society* 5 (1902): 259–93.

Burns, Louis F. *A History of the Osage People.* Tuscaloosa: University of Alabama Press, 2004.

Bynum, Helen. *Spitting Blood: The History of Tuberculosis.* Oxford: Oxford University Press, 2012.

Canfield, Frederick A. *A History of Thomas Canfield and of Matthew Camfield With a Genealogy of their Descendants in New Jersey.* New Haven CT: Tuttle, Morehouse and Taylor Press, 1897.

Canney, Donald L. *U.S. Coast Guard and Revenue Cutters, 1790–1935.* Annapolis: Naval Institute Press, 1995.

Cantrell, Ellen Harrell, comp. *The Annals of Christ Church Parish of Little Rock, Arkansas from A.D. 1839 to A.D. 1899.* Little Rock: Press of Arkansas Democrat Company, 1900.

Carroll, Mark M. *Homesteads Ungovernable: Families, Sex, Race and the Law in Frontier Texas, 1823–1860.* Austin: University of Texas Press, 2001.

Carson, James. *Against the Grain: Colonel Henry M. Lazelle and the U.S. Army.* Denton: University of North Texas Press, 2015.

Carson, James Taylor. "'The Obituary of Nations': Ethnic Cleansing, Memory, and the Origins of the Old South." *Southern Cultures* 14, no. 4 (Winter 2008): 6–31.

Carter, Clarence Edwin, ed. *The Territorial Papers of the United States*, vol. 19: *The Territory of Arkansas, 1819–1825.* Washington DC: Government Printing Office, 1953.

———. *The Territorial Papers of the United States*, vol. 20: *The Territory of Arkansas, 1825–1825–1829.* Washington DC: Government Printing Office, 1954.

———. *The Territorial Papers of the United States*, vol. 21: *The Territory of Arkansas, 1829–1836.* Washington DC: Government Printing Office, 1954.

Cases Argued and Decided in the Supreme Court of the State of Texas, During Part of the Tyler Term, 1880, the Galveston Term, 1881, and a Part of the Austin Term, 1881, vol. 54. Reported by A. W. Terrell. St. Louis: Gilbert Book Company, 1883.

Cashin, Edward J. *Lachlan McGillivray, Indian Trader: The Shaping of the Southern Colonial Frontier.* Athens: University of Georgia Press, 1992.

Cashin, Joan E. *A Family Venture: Men and Women on the Southern Frontier*. New York: Oxford University Press, 1991.

Castellanos, Henry C. *New Orleans as It Was: Episodes of Louisiana Life*. 1895; reprint, Baton Rouge: Louisiana State University Press, 2006.

Castleman, Bruce A. *Knickerbocker Commodore: The Life and Times of John Drake Sloat 1781–1867*. Albany: State University of New York Press, 2016.

Catalogue of the Alumni, Officers and Fellows of the College of Physicians and Surgeons in the City of New York, From A.D. 1807, to A.D. 1859. New York: Baker & Godwin, 1859.

Catlin, George. *Catlin's Notes of Eight Years' Travels and Residence in Europe, With His North American Indian Collection: With Anecdotes and Incidents of the Travels and Adventures of Three Different Parties of American Indians Whom He Introduced to the Courts of England, France and Belgium*, vol. 1. New York: Burgess, Stringer & Company, 1848.

Causey, Donna R. *Biographies of Notable and Not-so-Notable Alabama Pioneers*, vol. 3. Calera AL: Donway Publishing, 2014.

———, ed. *Some Descendants of Charles Abercrombie (1742–1819)*. Calera AL: Donway Publishing, 2012.

Cayton, Frank M. *Landings on All the Western and Southern Rivers and Bayous, Showing Location, Post-Offices, Distances, &c., Also, Tariff of Premiums on Insurance to All Points*. St. Louis: Woodward, Tiernan and Hale, 1881.

Chaillé, Stanford E. *Historical Sketch of the Medical Department of the University of Louisiana: Its Professors and Alumni, from 1835 to 1862*. New Orleans: Bulletin Book and Job Office, 1861.

Chance, Joseph E., ed. *My Life in the Old Army: The Reminiscences of Abner Doubleday from the Collections of the New-York Historical Society*, illus. Wil Martin. Fort Worth: Texas Christian University Press, 1998.

Cherry, F. L. "The History of Opelika and Her Agricultural Tributary Territory: Embracing More Particularly Lee and Russell Counties, from the Earliest Settlement to the Present Date." *Alabama Historical Quarterly* 15, vol. 2 (1953): 176–339.

Chipley, William S. "Sitomania: Its Causes and Treatment." *American Journal of Insanity* 16, no. 1 (July 1859): 1–42.

Chittenden, Hiram Martin. *History of Early Steamboat Navigation on the Missouri River: Life and Adventures of Joseph La Barge, Pioneer Navigator and Indian Trader for Fifty Years Identified with the Commerce of the Missouri Valley*. New York: Francis P. Harper, 1903.

Christian, Shirley. *Before Lewis and Clark: The Story of the Chouteaus, the French Dynasty That Ruled America's Frontier*. New York: Farrar, Straus and Giroux, 2004.

Churchill, Franklin Hunter. *Sketch of the Life of Bvt. Brig. Gen. Sylvester Churchill, Inspector General U.S. Army, With Notes and Appendices*. New York: Willis McDonald and Company, 1888.

Claiborne, J. F. H. *Life and Times of Gen. Sam. Dale, the Mississippi Partisan*. New York: Harper and Brothers, 1860.

Clark, Willis G. "State Industrial Interests." In *Memorial Record of Alabama: A Concise Account of the State's Political, Military, Professional and Industrial Progress, Together with the Personal Memoirs of Many of Its People*, vol. 1, 217–317. Madison WI: Brant and Fuller, 1893.

Clarke, Dwight L. *Stephen Watts Kearny: Soldier of the West*. Norman: University of Oklahoma Press, 1961.

Coker, William S., and Thomas D. Watson. *Indian Traders of the Southeastern Spanish Borderlands: Panton, Leslie & Company and John Forbes & Company, 1783–1847*. Gainesville: University Press of Florida, 1986.

Collins, Robert P. "A Swiss Traveler in the Creek Nation: The Diary of Lukas Vischer, March 1824," *Alabama Review* 59, no. 4 (October 2006): 243–84.

Collum, Richard S. *History of the United States Marine Corps*. Philadelphia: L. R. Hamersly and Company, 1890.

Comte de Castelnau, Francis de Laporte. "Essay on Middle Florida, 1837–1838." Trans. Arthur R. Seymour. *Florida Historical Quarterly* 26, no. 3 (January 1948): 199–255.

Congressional Record: Containing the Proceedings and Debates of the Forty-Sixth Congress, Second Session, vol. 10. Washington DC: Government Printing Office, 1880.

Conover, Cheryl, ed. "Kentuckian in 'King Andrew's' Court: The Letters of John Waller Barry, Washington DC, 1831–1835." *Register of the Kentucky Historical Society* 81, no. 2 (Spring 1983): 168–98.

———. "'To Please Papa': The Letters of John Waller Barry, West Point Cadet, 1826–1830." *Register of the Kentucky Historical Society* 80, no. 2 (Spring 1982): 183–212.

Cooley, Eli F., William S. Cooley, and Hanna L. Cooley. *Genealogy of Early Settlers in Trenton and Ewing, "Old Hunterdon County," New Jersey*. Trenton: W. S. Sharp Printing Company, 1883.

Copeland, J. Isaac. "Eaton, John Henry." In *Dictionary of North Carolina Biography*, vol. 2: D-G, ed. William S. Powell, 130. Chapel Hill: University of North Carolina Press, 1986.

Corum, Frances Bryant. *From Whence We Came—Our McCrary Family: Treasured Ancestors and Descendants of Scotland, Ireland and America*. Published by the compilers, 2000.

Coues, Elliott. *The Expeditions of Zebulon Montgomery Pike, To Headwaters of the Mississippi River, through Louisiana Territory, and in New Spain, During the Years 1805–6–7. A New Edition, Now First Reprinted in Full From the Original of 1810, With Copious Critical Commentary, Memoir of Pike, New Map and Other Illustrations, and Complete Index*. New York: Francis P. Harper, 1895.

Cox, Mike. "Frontier Medicine: Texas Doctors Overcome Disease and Despair." *Texas Medicine* 99, no. 1 (January 2003): 19–26.

Crozier, William Armstrong, ed. *The Buckners of Virginia and the allied families of Strother and Ashby*. New York: Genealogical Association, 1907.

Cullum, George W. *Biographical Register of the Officers and Graduates of the U.S. Military Academy, at West Point, N.Y., From Its Establishment, March 16, 1802 to the Army Re-organization of 1866–67*, vol. 1: *1802–1840*. New York: D. Van Nostrand, 1868.

———. *Biographical Register of the Officers and Graduates of the U.S. Military Academy at West Point, N.Y. From Its Establishment, in 1802, to 1890 With the Early History of the United States Military Academy*, 3rd ed., revised and extended, Vol. 1: *Nos. 1 to 1000*. Boston: Houghton, Mifflin and Company, 1891.

———. *Biographical Register of the Officers and Graduates of the U.S. Military Academy, From 1802 to 1867. Revised Edition, With a Supplement Continuing the Register of Graduates to January 1, 1879*. Vol. 3. Supplement. New York: James Miller, 1879.

Current-Garcia, Eugene, and Dorothy B. Hatfield, eds. *Shem, Ham, and Japheth: The Papers of W. O. Tuggle, Comprising His Indian Diary, Sketches and Observations, Myths and Washington Journal in the Territory and at the Capital, 1879–1882*. Athens: University of Georgia Press, 1973.

Cutler, Wayne, and Robert G. Hall II, eds. *Correspondence of James K. Polk*, vol. 9, *January–June 1845*. Knoxville: University of Tennessee Press, 1996.

Cutrer, Thomas W., "Brown, Jacob." In *The Encyclopedia of the Mexican-American War: A Political, Social, and Military History*, vol. 1: *A–L*, ed. Spencer C. Tucker et al., 91. Santa Barbara CA: ABC-CLIO, 2013.

Daniel, Larry J. *Days of Glory: The Army of the Cumberland 1861–1865*. Baton Rouge: Louisiana State University Press, 2004.

Daugherty, Leo J. III. *The Marine Corps and the State Department: Enduring Partners in United States Foreign Policy, 1798–2007*. Jefferson NC: McFarland and Company, 2009.

Daughters of the Republic of Texas: Patriot Ancestor Album. Paducah KY: Turner Publishing Company, 1995.

Davidson, Alan. *The Oxford Companion to Food*. 1999; reprint, Oxford: Oxford University Press, 2014.

Davidson, Donald. *The Tennessee: The Old River: Frontier to Secession*, vol. 1. 1946; reprint, Knoxville: University of Tennessee Press, 1978.

Dawson, Joseph G. "With Fidelity and Effectiveness: Archibald Henderson's Lasting Legacy to the U.S. Marine Corps." *Journal of Military History* 62, no. 4 (October 1998): 727–53.

Debo, Angie. *The Road to Disappearance*. Norman: University of Oklahoma Press, 1941.

DeLand, T. A., and A. Davis Smith. *Northern Alabama: Historical and Biographical*. Chicago: Donohue and Henneberry, 1888.

DeRosier, Arthur H. Jr. *The Removal of the Choctaw Indians*. Knoxville: University of Tennessee Press, 1970.

Diffenderffer, Frank R., "Historical Sketch." In *The Three Earls. An Historical Sketch, and Proceedings of the Centennial Jubilee, Held at New Holland, PA., July 4, 1876*, 17–76. New Holland PA: Ranck and Sandoe, 1876.

Dodge, Andrew R., and Betty K. Koed, eds., *Biographical Directory of the United States Congress, 1774–2005: The Continental Congress, September 5, 1774, to October 21, 1788, and the Congress of the United States from the First Through the One Hundred Eighth Congresses, March 4, 1789, to January 3, 2005, Inclusive*. Washington DC: Government Printing Office, 2005.

Doliante, Sharon J. *Maryland and Virginia Colonials*. Baltimore: Genealogical Publishing Company, 1991.

Donovan, Timothy P., and Willard B. Gatewood Jr., eds. *The Governors of Arkansas: Essays in Political Biography*. Fayetteville: University of Arkansas Press, 1981.

Dorman, Lewy. *Party Politics in Alabama From 1850 Through 1860*. 1935; reprint, Tuscaloosa: University of Alabama Press, 1995.

Dormandy, Thomas. *The White Death: A History of Tuberculosis*. New York: New York University Press, 2000.

Doss, Harriet E. Amos. "Lewis, Dixon Hall." In *American National Biography*, vol. 13, ed. John A. Garraty and Mark C. Carnes, 566–68. New York: Oxford University Press, 1999.

Duckett, Alvin Laroy. *John Forsyth: Political Tactician*. Athens: University of Georgia Press, 1962.

Edwards, Richard, and M. Hopewell. *Edwards's Great West and Her Commercial Metropolis, Embracing a General View of the West, and a Complete History of St. Louis, from the Landing of Ligueste, in 1764, to the Present Time; With Portraits and Biographies of Some of the Old Settlers, and Many of the Most Prominent Business Men*. St. Louis: Published at the office of "Edwards's Monthly," 1860.

Eicher, John H., and David J. Eicher. *Civil War High Commands*. Stanford CA: Stanford University Press, 2001.

Eisenhower, John S. D. *Agent of Destiny: The Life and Times of General Winfield Scott*. New York: The Free Press, 1997.

Ellisor, John T. "Like So Many Wolves: Creek Removal in the Cherokee Country, 1835–1838." *Journal of East Tennessee History*, 71 (1999): 1–24.

———. *The Second Creek War: Interethnic Conflict and Collusion on a Collapsing Frontier*. Lincoln: University of Nebraska Press, 2010.

Ellsworth, Lucius F. "Raiford and Abercrombie: Pensacola's Premier Antebellum Manufacturer." *Florida Historical Quarterly* 52, no. 3 (January 1974): 247–60.

Ellsworth, Lucius F., and Jane E. Dysart, "West Florida's Forgotten People: The Creek Indians from 1830 until 1970." *Florida Historical Quarterly* 59, no. 4 (April 1981): 422–39.

Eno, Clara B. *History of Crawford County, Arkansas*. Van Buren AR: Press-Argus, n.d.

Ewing, Robert. "Portrait of General Robert Armstrong." *Tennessee Historical Magazine* 5, no. 2 (July 1919): 75–80.

Fagge, Charles Hilton, and Philip Henry Pye-Smith. *Text-Book of the Principles and Practice of Medicine. Third Edition*, vol. 1. London: J. & A. Churchill, 1891.

Feller, Daniel, Harold D. Moser, Laura-Eve Moss, and Thomas Coens, eds. *The Papers of Andrew Jackson*, vol. 7: 1829. Knoxville: University of Tennessee Press, 2007.

Fenner, E. D., ed. *Southern Medical Reports; Consisting of General and Special Reports, on the Medical Topography, Meteorology, and Prevalent Diseases, in the Following States: Louisiana, Alabama, Mississippi, North Carolina, South Carolina, Georgia, Florida, Arkansas, Tennessee, Texas*, vol. 1: *1849*. New Orleans: B. M. Norman, 1850.

Foley, William E., and C. David Rice. *The First Chouteaus: River Barons of Early St. Louis*. Urbana: University of Illinois Press, 1983.

Footner, Geoffrey M. USS *Constellation: From Frigate to Sloop of War*. Annapolis: Naval Institute Press, 2002.

Force, Peter. *Register of the Army and Navy of the United States. No. 1. 1830*. Washington DC: Peter Force, 1830.

Foreman, Carolyn Thomas. "The Armstrongs of Indian Territory," Parts 1– 2. *Chronicles of Oklahoma* 30, nos. 3–4 (1952): 292–308, 420–53.

———. "The Cherokee Gospel Tidings of Dwight Mission." *Chronicles of Oklahoma* 12, no. 4 (December 1934): 454–69.

———. "The Cherokee War Path." *Chronicles of Oklahoma* 9, no. 3 (September 1931): 233–63.

———. "The Choctaw Academy." *Chronicles of Oklahoma* 6, no. 4 (December 1928): 453–80.

Foreman, Grant. *Advancing the Frontier, 1830–1860*. 1933; reprint, Norman: University of Oklahoma Press, 1968.

———. "Captain John Stuart's Sketch of the Indians. *Chronicles of Oklahoma* 11, no. 1 (March 1933): 667–72.

———. *The Five Civilized Tribes*. Norman: University of Oklahoma Press, 1934.

———. *Indian Removal: The Emigration of the Five Civilized Tribes of Indians*. 1932; reprint, Norman: University of Oklahoma Press, 1974.

———. *Indians and Pioneers: The Story of the American Southwest Before 1830*. 1930; reprint, Norman: University of Oklahoma Press, 1975.

———. "Nathaniel Pryor," *Chronicles of Oklahoma* 7, no. 2 (June 1929): 152–63.

———. *Pioneer Days in the Early Southwest*. 1926; reprint, Lincoln: University of Nebraska Press, 1994.

Foreman, Grant, ed. *A Traveler in Indian Territory: The Journal of Ethan Allen Hitchcock, Late Major-General in the United States Army*. 1930; reprint, Norman: University of Oklahoma Press, 1996.

Foscue, Virginia O. *Place Names in Alabama*. Tuscaloosa: University of Alabama Press, 1989.

Fossier, A. E. *History of Medical Education in New Orleans: From Its Birth to the Civil War*, part 1. New York: Paul B. Hoeber, n.d.
Foster, H. Thomas II, ed. *The Collected Works of Benjamin Hawkins, 1796–1810*. Tuscaloosa: University of Alabama Press, 2003.
Frank, Andrew K. *Creeks and Southerners: Biculturalism on the Early American Frontier*. Lincoln: University of Nebraska Press, 2005.
———. "The Rise and Fall of William McIntosh: Authority and Identity on the Early American Frontier." *Georgia Historical Quarterly* 86, no. 1 (Spring 2002): 18–48.
Frazer, Robert W. *Forts of the West: Military Forts and Presidios and Posts Commonly Called Forts West of the Mississippi River to 1898*. Norman: University of Oklahoma Press, 1965.
Fredriksen, John C. *American Military Leaders:From Colonial Times to the Present*, vol. 1: *A-L*. Santa Barbara CA: ABC-CLIO, 1999.
Frith, John. "History of Tuberculosis, Part 1—Phthisis, consumption and the White Plague." *Journal of Military and Veterans' Health* 22, no. 2 (June 2014): 29–35.
Gamble, Robert. *The Alabama Catalog: Historic American Buildings Survey, a Guide to the Early Architecture of the State*. Tuscaloosa: University of Alabama Press, 1987.
Gardner, Charles K. *A Dictionary of All Officers, Who Have Been Commissioned, or Have Been Appointed and Served, in the Army of the United States, Since the Inauguration of Their First President, in 1789, to the First January, 1853,—With Every Commission of Each;—Including the Distinguished Officers of the Volunteers and Militia of the States, Who Have Served in Any Campaign, or Conflict With an Enemy, Since That Date; and of the Navy and Marine Corps, Who Have Served With the Land Forces: Indicating the Battle, in Which Every Such Officer Has Been Killed, or Wounded,—and the Special Words of Every Brevet Commission*. New York: G. P. Putnam and Company, 1853.
Gardner, James Henry. "The Lost Captain: J. L. Dawson of Old Fort Gibson." *Chronicles of Oklahoma* 21, no. 3 (September 1943): 217–49.
Garrett, William. *Reminiscences of Public Men in Alabama, for Thirty Years. With An Appendix*. Atlanta: Plantation Publishing Company's Press, 1872.
Geiser, S. W. "Some Frontier Naturalists." *Bios* 5, no. 4 (December 1934): 141–54.
General Orders and Circulars, War Department, 1904. Washington DC: Government Printing Office, 1905.
Gentry, Dorothy. *Life and Legend of Lawrence County, Alabama*. Tuscaloosa: Nottingham-SWS, 1962.
Gibson, Arrell M. *The Chickasaws*. Norman: University of Oklahoma Press, 1971.
Gideon, D. C. *Indian Territory: Descriptive, Biographical and Genealogical, Including the Landed Estates, County Seats, Etc., Etc. With a General History of the Territory*. New York: Lewis Publishing Company, 1901.
Giddings, Joshua R. *The Exiles of Florida: or, The Crimes Committed by Our Government Against the Maroons, Who Fled From South Carolina and Other Slave*

States, Seeking Protection Under Spanish Laws. Columbus OH: Follett, Foster and Company, 1858.

Gillett, Mary C. *The Army Medical Department 1818–1865*. Washington DC: Center of Military History, 1987.

Gilliland, C. Herbert., ed. *USS Constellation on the Dismal Coast: Willie Leonard's Journal, 1859–1861*. Columbia: University of South Carolina Press, 2013.

Gilman, Edward F., and Dennis G. Watson. "*Quercus stellate*: Post Oak." ENH-720, University of Florida, Institute of Food and Agricultural Sciences Extension, November 1993.

Goodspeed, Weston Arthur, ed. *The Province and the States: A History of the Province of Louisiana Under France and Spain, and of the Territories and States of the United States Formed Therefrom*, vol. 3. Madison WI: Western Historical Association, 1904.

Gould, E. W. *Fifty Years on the Mississippi; or, Gould's History of River Navigation. Containing a History of the Introduction of Steam as a Propelling Power on Ocean, Lakes and Rivers—The First Steamboats on the Hudson, the Delaware, and the Ohio Rivers—Navigation of Western Rivers Before the Introduction of Steam—Character of the Early Navigators—Description of First Steamboats—Steamboat New Orleans in 1811, and Sixty Consecutive Boats, When and Where Built—Their Effect Upon the Settlement of the Valley of the Mississippi—Character and Speed of Boats at Different Periods—Appropriations by Congress for the Improvement of Western Water Ways—Floods in the Mississippi Valley for 150 Years—Mississippi River Commission and Its Work. Rapid Increase and Decline of River Transportation. Causes of the Decline—Destruction of Steamboats on Western Waters—Biographies of Prominent Steamboatmen—Illustrated by Photographs and Cuts of Steamboats at Different Periods*. St. Louis: Nixon-Jones, 1889.

Graf, Leroy P., and Ralph W. Haskins, et al. *The Papers of Andrew Johnson*, vol. 1, *1822–1851*. Knoxville: University of Tennessee Press, 1967.

Graham, Thomas John. *Modern Domestic Medicine; or, A Popular Treatise, Illustrating the Character, Symptoms, Causes, Distinction, and Correct Treatment, of All Diseases Incident to the Human Frame; Embracing All the Modern Improvements in Medicine, With the Opinions of the Most Distinguished Physicians. To Which Is Added, a Domestic Materia Medica; a Description of the Virtues, and Correct Manner of Using the Different Mineral Waters of Europe, and the Cold, Warm, and Vapour Baths; a Copious Collection of Approved Prescriptions Adapted to Domestic Use; Ample Rules of Diet, and a Table of the Doses of Medicines. The Whole Intended as a Medical Guide for the Use of Clergymen, Heads of Families, and Invalids*. Third Edition. London: Simpkin and Marshall, 1827.

Grant, Ulysses S. *Personal Memoirs of U.S. Grant*, vol. 1. New York: Charles L. Webster, 1885.

Green, Michael D. *The Politics of Indian Removal: Creek Government and Society in Crisis*. Lincoln: University of Nebraska Press, 1982.

Gregory, Jack, and Rennard Strickland. *Sam Houston with the Cherokees 1829–1833*. Austin: University of Texas Press, 1967.

Griffith, Benjamin W. Jr. *McIntosh and Weatherford, Creek Indian Leaders*. Tuscaloosa: University of Alabama Press, 1988.

Gudmestad, Robert. *Steamboats and the Rise of the Cotton Kingdom*. Baton Rouge: Louisiana State University Press, 2011.

Guernsey, R. S. *New York City and Vicinity During the War of 1812–'15, Being a Military, Civic and Financial Local History of that Period, With Incidents and Anecdotes Thereof, and A Description of the Forts, Fortifications, Arsenals, Defences and Camps in and About New York City and Harbor, and Those at Harlem and on East River, and in Brooklyn, and on Long Island and Staten Island, and at Sandy Hook and Jersey City. With An Account of the Citizens' Movements, and of the Military and Naval Officers, Regiments, Companies, etc., in service there*. Vols. 1–2. New York: Charles L. Woodward, 1889, 1895.

Haecker, Charles M., and Jeffrey G. Mauck. *On the Prairie of Palo Alto: Historical Archaeology of the U.S.–Mexican War Battlefield*. College Station: Texas A&M University Press, 1997.

Hahn, Steven C. "The Cussita Migration Legend: History, Ideology, and the Politics of Mythmaking." In *Light on the Path: The Anthropology and History of the Southeastern Indians*, ed. Thomas J. Pluckhahn and Robbie Ethridge, 57–93. Tuscaloosa: University of Alabama Press, 2006.

———. "'They Look upon the Yuchis as Their Vassals': An Early History of Yuchi-Creek Political Relations." In *Yuchi Indian Histories before the Removal Era*, ed. Jason Baird Jackson, 123–53. Lincoln: University of Nebraska Press, 2012.

Hain, H. H. *History of Perry County, Pennsylvania: Including Descriptions of Indian and Pioneer Life from the Time of Earliest Settlement, Sketches of Its Noted Men and Women and Many Professional Men*. Harrisburg PA: Hain-Moore Company, 1922.

Hale, Will T., and Dixon L. Merritt. *A History of Tennessee and Tennesseans: The Leaders and Representative Men in Commerce, Industry and Modern Activities*, vol. 3. Chicago: Lewis Publishing Company, 1913.

Hallum, John. *Biographical and Pictorial History of Arkansas*, vol. 1. Albany NY: Weed, Parsons and Company, 1887.

Hamersly, Thomas H. S., ed. *Complete Regular Army Register of the United States: For One Hundred Years, (1779 to 1879). Together with the Volunteer General Staff During the War with Mexico, and a Register of All Appointments by the President of the United States in the Volunteer Service During the Rebellion, with the Official Military Record of Each Officer. Also, a Military History of the Department of War, and of Each Staff Department of the Army. With Various Tables Relating to the Army and Other Important Military Information, Compiled from the Official Records*. Washington DC: T. H. S. Hamersly, 1880.

———, ed. *General Register of the United States Navy and Marine Corps, Arranged in Alphabetical Order, for One Hundred Years, (1782 to 1882), Containing the Names of All Officers of the Navy Commissioned, Warranted, and Appointed; Including Volunteer Officers, Who Have Entered the Service Since the Establishment of the Navy Department in 1798; Showing the Dates of Their Original Entry, of Their Progressive Rank, and in What Manner They Left the Service, If Not Now in It. Together with a Sketch of the Navy from 1775 to 1798. And a List of All Midshipmen and Cadet Engineers at the Naval Academy Since Its Establishment, &c., &c. Compiled from the Original Manuscript Records of the Navy Department, by Permission of the Honorable Secretary of the Navy*. Washington DC: T. H. S. Hamersly, 1882.

Hammond, E. A. "The Spanish Fisheries of Charlotte Harbor." *Florida Historical Quarterly* 51, no. 4 (April 1973): 355–80.

Hardeman County, Tennessee: Family History, vol. 2. Paducah KY: Turner Publishing Company, 2001.

Hardeman, Nicholas Perkins, *Wilderness Calling: The Hardeman Family in the American Westward Movement, 1750–1900*. Knoxville: University of Tennessee Press, 1977.

Harlan, Louis R. "Public Career of William Berkeley Lewis." *Tennessee Historical Quarterly* 7, no. 1 (March 1948): 3–37.

Harper, Kenton N. *History of the Grand Lodge and of Freemasonry in the District of Columbia with Biographical Appendix*. Washington DC: R. Beresford, 1911.

Haskett, James N. "The Final Chapter in the Story of the First Fort Smith." *Arkansas Historical Quarterly* 25, no. 3 (Autumn 1966): 214–28.

Haveman, Christopher D. "The Indomitable Women of the Creek Removal Era: 'Some One Must Have Told Her That I Meant to Run Away With Her.'" In *Alabama Women: Their Lives and Times*, ed. Susan Youngblood Ashmore and Lisa Lindquist Dorr, 10–39. Athens: University of Georgia Press, 2017.

———. "'Last Evening I Saw the Sun Set for the Last Time': The 1832 Treaty of Washington and the Transfer of the Creeks' Alabama Land to White Ownership." *Native South* 5 (2012): 61–94.

———. *Rivers of Sand: Creek Indian Emigration, Relocation, and Ethnic Cleansing in the American South*. Lincoln: University of Nebraska Press, 2016.

———. "'With Great Difficulty and Labour': The Emigration of the McIntosh Party of Creek Indians, 1827–1828." *Chronicles of Oklahoma* 85, no. 4 (Winter 2007–8): 468–90.

Heidler, David S., and Jeanne T. Heidler. *Old Hickory's War: Andrew Jackson and the Quest for Empire*. Baton Rouge: Louisiana State University Press, 1996.

Heitman, Francis B. *Historical Register and Dictionary of the United States Army, from Its Organization, September 29, 1789, to March 2, 1903*, vol. 1. Washington DC: Government Printing Office, 1903.

Hempstead, Fay. *A Pictorial History of Arkansas: From Earliest Times to the Year 1890. A Full and Complete Account, Embracing the Indian Tribes Occupying the Country; the Early French and Spanish Explorers and Governors; the Colonial Period; the Louisiana Purchase; the Periods of the Territory, the State, the Civil War, and the Subsequent Period. Also, an Extended History of Each County in the Order of Formation, and of the Principal Cities and Towns; Together with Biographical Notices of Distinguished and Prominent Citizens. Superbly Illustrated with Rare and Valuable Maps; a Full Collection of Portraits of Governors and Other Distinguished Men; and with Numerous Sketches, Drawings, Views and Scenes.* St. Louis: N. D. Thompson, 1890.

———. *Historical Review of Arkansas: Its Commerce, Industry and Modern Affairs*, vols. 1–3. Chicago: Lewis Publishing Company, 1911.

Henderson, Harry McCorry. *Texas in the Confederacy*. San Antonio: Naylor, 1955.

Hendricks, Bonnie L. *International Encyclopedia of Horse Breeds*. 1995; reprint, Norman: University of Oklahoma Press, 2007.

Henry, Guy V. *Military Record of Civilian Appointments in the United States Army*, vol. 1. New York: Carleton, 1869.

———. *Military Record of Army and Civilian Appointments in the United States Army*, vol. 2. New York: D. Van Nostrand, 1873.

Herndon, Dallas T., ed. *Centennial History of Arkansas*, vol. 1. Chicago: S. J. Clarke, 1922.

Herr, Pamela, and Mary Lee Spence. *The Letters of Jessie Benton Frémont*. Urbana: University of Illinois Press, 1993.

Heyward, James Barnwell, ed. *The Genealogy of the Pendarvis-Bedon Families of South Carolina, 1670–1900: Together with Lineal Ancestry of Husbands and Wives Who Intermarried With Them; Also References to Many Associated Southern Families*. Atlanta: Foote and Davies, 1905.

Hightower, Michael J. *Banking in Oklahoma Before Statehood*. Norman: University of Oklahoma Press, 2013.

Hill, Luther B. *A History of the State of Oklahoma*. Vol. 2. Chicago: Lewis Publishing Co., 1910.

Hinton, Harwood Perry. "The Military Career of John Ellis Wool, 1812–1863." PhD diss., University of Wisconsin, 1960.

History of Benton, Washington, Carroll, Madison, Crawford, Franklin, and Sebastian Counties, Arkansas. From the Earliest Time to the Present, Including a Department Devoted to the Preservation of Sundry Personal, Business, Professional and Private Records; Besides a Valuable Fund of Notes, Original Observations, Etc., Etc. Chicago: Goodspeed, 1889.

History of Dearborn and Ohio Counties, Indiana. From Their Earliest Settlement. Containing a History of the Counties; Their Cities, Townships, Towns, Villages, Schools, and Churches; Reminiscences, Extracts, Etc.; Local Statistics; Portraits of Early Settlers and Prominent Men; Biographies; Preliminary Chapters on the History of the North-West Territory, the State of Indiana, and the Indians. Chicago: F. E. Weakley and Company, 1885.

History of Medicine and Surgery and Physicians and Surgeons of Chicago. Chicago: Biographical Publishing Corporation, 1922.

Hochberg, Ze'v, ed. *Vitamin D and Rickets.* Basel, Switzerland: Karger, 2003.

Hodgson, Adam. *Letters from North America, Written During a Tour in the United States and Canada*, vol. 1. London: Hurst, Robinson, and Company, 1824.

Hoig, Stan. *The Chouteaus: First Family of the Fur Trade.* Albuquerque: University of New Mexico Press, 2008.

Holmberg, James J. *Dear Brother: Letters of William Clark to Jonathan Clark.* New Haven: Yale University Press, 2002.

Hoole, W. Stanley, ed. "Echoes from the 'Trail of Tears,' 1837." *Alabama Review* 6, no. 2 (April 1953): 135–52.

———, ed. "Echoes from the 'Trail of Tears,' 1837," part 2. *Alabama Review* 6, no. 3 (July 1953): 222–32.

Hopkins, James F., and Mary W. M. Hargreaves, eds. *The Papers of Henry Clay*, vol. 3: *Presidential Candidate 1821–1824.* Lexington: University of Kentucky Press, 1963.

Huddleston, Duane, Sammie Rose, and Pat Wood. *Steamboats and Ferries on White River: A Heritage Revisited.* Conway AR: University of Central Arkansas Press, 1995.

Hudson, Angela Pulley. *Creek Paths and Federal Roads: Indians, Settlers, and Slaves and the Making of the American South.* Chapel Hill: University of North Carolina Press, 2010.

Hudson, Charles. *The Southeastern Indians.* Knoxville: University of Tennessee Press, 1976.

Hudson, Linda S. "Jane McManus Storm Cazneau and the Galveston Bay and Texas Land Company," *East Texas Historical Journal* 39, no. 1 (2001): 3–16.

Ingersoll, Thomas N. *To Intermix With Our White Brothers: Indian Mixed Bloods in the United States from Earliest Times to the Indian Removals.* Albuquerque: University of New Mexico Press, 2005.

Irons, George Vernon. "River Ferries in Alabama Before 1861." *Alabama Review* 4, no. 1 (January 1951): 22–37.

Irving, Washington. "The Conspiracy of Neamathla: An Authentic Sketch." *Knickerbocker* 16, no. 4 (October 1840): 343–47.

Ivey, Darren L. *The Texas Rangers: A Registry and History.* Jefferson NC: McFarland, 2010.

"James Hervey Simpson." *Northwest Review* 1, no. 2 (April 1883): 74–81.

James, Marquis. *The Raven: A Biography of Sam Houston.* New York: Blue Ribbon Books, 1929.

James, Russell D. "Wilson, Henry." In *The Encyclopedia of North American Indian Wars 1607–1890: A Political, Social, and Military History*, vol. 2: M-Z. ed. Spencer C. Tucker et al., 848. Santa Barbara CA: ABC-CLIO, 2011.

Jemison, E. Grace. *Historic Tales of Talladega*. Montgomery: Paragon Press, 1959.

Johnson, Boyd W. "Frederick Notrebe." *Arkansas Historical Quarterly* 21, no. 3 (Autumn 1962): 269–83.

Johnson, E. Polk. *A History of Kentucky and Kentuckians: The Leaders and Representative Men in Commerce, Industry and Modern Activities*, vol. 1. Chicago: Lewis Publishing Company, 1912.

Johnson, Frank W. *A History of Texas and Texans*, vol. 3. Ed. Eugene C. Barker and Ernest William Winkler. Chicago: American Historical Society, 1916.

Johnson, Timothy D. *Winfield Scott: The Quest for Military Glory*. Lawrence: University Press of Kansas, 1998.

Jones, Kathleen W. *Taming the Troublesome Child: American Families, Child Guidance, and the Limits of Psychiatric Authority*. Cambridge: Harvard University Press, 1999.

Jones, L. H. *Captain Roger Jones, of London and Virginia. Some of His Antecedents and Descendants. With appreciative notice of other families, viz.: Bathurst, Belfield, Browning, Carter, Catesby, Cocke, Graham, Fauntleroy, Hickman, Hoskins, Latane, Lewis, Meriwether, Skelton, Walker, Waring, Woodford, and Others*. Albany NY: Joel Munsell's Sons, 1891.

Journal of the House of Representatives of the United States, at the Third Session of the Twenty-Seventh Congress Begun and Held at the City of Washington, in the Territory of Columbia, December 5, 1842, and in the Sixty-Seventh Year of the Independence of the United States. Washington DC: Gales and Seaton, 1843.

Kakel, Carroll P. III .*The American West and the Nazi East: A Comparative and Interpretive Perspective*. Houndmills UK: Palgrave Macmillan, 2011.

Kane, Adam I. *The Western River Steamboat*. College Station: Texas A&M University Press, 2004.

Kappler, Charles J., ed. *Indian Affairs: Laws and Treaties*, vol. 2: *Treaties*. Washington DC: Government Printing Office, 1904.

Kennamer, John Robert. *History of Jackson County*. Winchester TN: Southern Printing and Publishing Company, 1935.

Kidwell, Clara Sue. *The Choctaws in Oklahoma: From Tribe to Nation, 1855–1970*. Norman: University of Oklahoma Press, 2007.

Kieffer, Chester L. *Maligned General: The Biography of Thomas Sidney Jesup*. San Rafael CA: Presidio Press, 1979.

Kiser, William S. *Dragoons in Apacheland: Conquest and Resistance in Southern New Mexico, 1846–1861*. Norman: University of Oklahoma Press, 2012.

Klunder, Willard Carl. *Lewis Cass and the Politics of Moderation*. Kent OH: Kent State University Press, 1996.

Kotar, S. L., and J. E. Gessler. *The Steamboat Era: A History of Fulton's Folly on American Rivers, 1807–1860*. Jefferson NC: McFarland and Company, 2009.

Langford, Ella Molloy. *Johnson County, Arkansas: The First Hundred Years*. Clarksville AR: Sallis, Threadgill and Sallis, 1921.

Latner, Richard B. "The Eaton Affair Reconsidered." *Tennessee Historical Quarterly* 36, no. 3 (Fall 1977): 330–51.

Laumer, Frank. *Dade's Last Command*. Gainesville: University Press of Florida, 1995.

———. *Massacre!* Gainesville: University of Florida Press, 1968.

Levasseur, A. *Lafayette in America in 1824 and 1825; or, Journal of a Voyage to the United States*, vol. 2. Philadelphia: Carey and Lea, 1829.

Lewis, Charles Lee. *Famous American Marines, An Account of the Corps: The Exploits of Officers and Men on Land, by Air and Sea from the Decks of the Bonhomme Richard to the Summit of Mount Suribachi*. Boston: L. C. Page, 1950.

Lewis, Felice Flanery. *Trailing Clouds of Glory: Zachary Taylor's Mexican War Campaign and His Emerging Civil War Leaders*. Tuscaloosa: University of Alabama Press, 2010.

Leyden, James A. *A Historical Sketch of the Fourth Infantry from 1796 to 1861*. Fort Sherman ID: Press of the Fourth United States Infantry, 1891.

Lindsey, Bobby L. *The Reason for the Tears: A History of Chambers County, Alabama, 1832–1900*. West Point GA: Hester Print. Co., 1971.

Littlefield, Daniel F., Jr. *Africans and Creeks: From the Colonial Period to the Civil War*. Westport CT: Greenwood Press, 1979.

———. *Africans and Seminoles: From Removal to Emancipation*. Jackson: University Press of Mississippi, 1977.

Littlefield, Daniel F., Jr., and Lonnie E. Underhill. "Fort Coffee and Frontier Affairs, 1834–1838." *Chronicles of Oklahoma* 54, no. 3 (Fall 1976): 314–38.

Litton, Gaston, ed. "The Journal of a Party of Emigrating Creek Indians, 1835–1836." *Journal of Southern History* 7, no. 2 (May 1941): 225–42.

Livingood, James W., Joy Bailey Dunn, and Charles W. Crawford, eds. *Hamilton County*. Memphis: Memphis State University Press, 1981.

Lomax, Edward L. *Genealogy of the Virginia Family of Lomax: With references to the Lunsford, Wormeley, Micou, Roy, Corbin, Eltonhead, Tayloe, Plater, Addison, Tasker, Burford, Wilkinson, Griffin, Gwynn, Lindsay, Payne, Presley, Thornton, Savage, Wellford, Randolph, Isham, Yates, and other prominent families of Virginia and Maryland*. Chicago: Rand, McNally & Co., 1913.

Loomis, Augustus Ward. *Scenes in the Indian Country*. Philadelphia: Presbyterian Board of Publication, 1859.

Lowe, Gabriel L., Jr. "John H. Eaton, Jackson's Campaign Manager." *Tennessee Historical Quarterly* 11, no. 2 (June 1952): 99–147.

Lowery, Charles D. *James Barbour, A Jeffersonian Republican*. Tuscaloosa: University of Alabama, 1984.

Lowry, Robert., and William H. McCardle. *A History of Mississippi, from the Discovery of the Great River by Hernando DeSoto, Including the Earliest Settlement Made by the French, Under Iberville. To the Death of Jefferson Davis*. Jackson MS: R. H. Henry and Company, 1891.

Lucas, M. Philip. "Kearny, Stephen Watts." In *The Biographical Dictionary of Iowa*, ed. David Hudson, Marvin Bergman, and Loren Horton, 276–78. Iowa City: University of Iowa Press, 2008.

Lupold, John S., and Thomas L. French Jr. *Bridging Deep South Rivers: The Life and Legend of Horace King*. Athens: University of Georgia Press, 2004.

Madley, Benjamin. "Reexamining the American Genocide Debate: Meaning, Historiography, and New Methods." *American Historical Review* 120, no. 1 (February 2015): 98–139.

Mahon, John K. *History of the Second Seminole War 1835–1842*. Gainesville: University of Florida Press, 1967.

The Marine Corps in Mexico; Setting Forth Its Conduct as Established by Testimony Before a General Court Martial, Convened at Brooklyn, N.Y., September, 1852, For the Trial of First Lieut. John S. Devlin, of the U.S. Marine Corps. Washington DC: Lemuel Towers, 1852.

Marszalek, John F. *The Petticoat Affair: Manners, Mutiny, and Sex in Andrew Jackson's White House*. Baton Rouge: Louisiana State University Press, 1997.

Marten, Benjamin. *A New Theory of Confumptions: More efpecially of a Phthisis, or Confumption of the Lungs. Wherein, After a brief Hiftory of the Diftemper, its various Symptoms throughout its feveral Degrees, and every minute Step it takes, from its firft invading the Patient, to its final Termination, Enquiry is made Concerning the Prime, Effential, and hitherto accounted Inexplicable Cause of that Difeafe, fo very Endemick to this Nation, and generally fatal to thofe it feizes on. With an Account Of the great Number of Medicines, and various Methods of Cure recommended for Confumptions; and the different Opinions of Authors concerning them. Also The Poffibility of Healing Ulcers in the Lungs afferted, the ftrongeft Objections againft it anfwered, and a different and more probable Method of Cure advanced, than commonly practifed. Likewise Directions about Eating, Drinking, Sleeping, Exercife, and way of Living in general, proper for Confumptive Perfons*. London: R. Knaplock, et al., 1720.

Martin, John H., ed. *Columbus, Geo., from Its Selection as a "Trading Town" in 1827, to Its Partial Destruction by Wilson's Raid, in 1865. History—Incident—Personality. Part 1—1827 to 1846*. Columbus: Thos. Gilbert, 1874.

The Maryland Medical and Surgical Journal, and Official Organ of the Medical Department of the Army and Navy of the United States, vol. 2. Baltimore: John Murphy, 1842.

Mathews, John Joseph. *The Osages: Children of the Middle Waters*. Norman: University of Oklahoma Press, 1961.

Maverick, Mary A., and George Madison Maverick. *Memoirs of Mary A. Maverick*, ed. Rena Maverick Green. San Antonio: Alamo Printing Company, 1921.

Mayow, John. *Ῥαχιτιδολογια: or, A Tract of the Difeafe Rhachitis Commonly called the Rickets. Shewing the Signes, Caufe, Symptoms, and Prognofticks: Together with a moft accurate and ingenious Method of Cure. Written originally in Latin, (according to a new-framed Hypothefis) by that moft learned Philofopher, and Famous Phyfician, Dr. John Mayow, late Fellow of All-Souls-Coll. in the Academy of Oxon. And now (for the Benefit of his Country-men) faithfully rendred into Englifh. By W. S. To which is fubjoyn'd a profitable Appendix, touching weights and measures us'd in the Compofition of Medicines and exhibition of Medicinal Dofes.* Oxford: Printed by L.L. for Th. Fickus, 1685.

McCall, George A. *Letters from the Frontiers*. 1868; reprint, Gainesville: University Presses of Florida, 1974.

McCoy, Isaac. *The Annual Register of Indian Affairs: In the Western (or Indian) Territory 1835–1838*. 1835–38; reprints, Springfield: Particular Baptist Press, 2000.

McGuffey, Chas. D., ed. *Standard History of Chattanooga, Tennessee: With Full Outline of the Early Settlement, Pioneer Life, Indian History, and General and Particular History of the City to the Close of the Year 1910*. Knoxville TN: Crew and Dorey, 1911.

McIntosh, James T., ed. *The Papers of Jefferson Davis*, vol. 2, *June 1841–July 1846*. Sponsored by William Marsh Rice University and the Jefferson Davis Association. Baton Rouge: Louisiana State University Press, 1974.

McKenney, Thomas L. *Memoirs, Official and Personal; with Sketches of Travels Among the Northern and Southern Indians; Embracing a War Excursion, and Descriptions of Scenes Along the Western Borders*, vol. 1. New York: Paine and Burgess, 1846.

McKenney, Thomas L., and James Hall. *History of the Indian Tribes of North America, With Biographical Sketches and Anecdotes of the Principal Chiefs. Embellished with One Hundred and Twenty Portraits, from the Indian Gallery in the Department of War, at Washington*, vols. 1–2. Philadelphia: Daniel Rice and James G. Clark, 1842.

McReynolds, Edwin C. *The Seminoles*. Norman: University of Oklahoma Press, 1957.

"The Medical Department of Tulane University of Louisiana." *Medical News* 80, no. 11 (15 March 1902): 481–89.

Meek, A. B. *Romantic Passages in Southwestern History; Including Orations, Sketches, and Essays*. Mobile: S. H. Goetzel and Company, 1857.

Mellichamp, Josephine. *Senators from Georgia*. Huntsville AL: Strode Publishers, 1976.

Melton, Maurice. *The Best Station of Them All: The Savannah Squadron, 1861–1865*. Tuscaloosa: University of Alabama Press, 2012.

A Memorial and Biographical History of Johnson and Hill Counties, Texas. Containing the Early History of this Important Section of the great State of Texas, together with Glimpses of its Future Prospects: also Biographical Mention of Many of the Pioneers and Prominent Citizens of the Present Time, and Full-page Portraits of some of the most Eminent Men of this Section. Chicago: Lewis Publishing Company, 1892.

Meserve, John Bartlett. "Chief Samuel Checote, with Sketches of Chiefs Locher Harjo and Ward Coachman," *Chronicles of Oklahoma* 16, no. 4 (December 1938): 401–9.

———. "The MacIntoshes." *Chronicles of Oklahoma* 10, no. 3 (September 1932): 310–25.

———. "The Perrymans." *Chronicles of Oklahoma* 15, no. 2 (June 1937): 166–84.

The Mexican War and Its Heroes: Being a Complete History of the Mexican War, Embracing all the Operations Under Generals Taylor and Scott, With a Biography of the Officers. Also, An Account of the Conquest of California and New Mexico, Under Gen. Kearney, Cols. Doniphan and Fremont. Together with Numerous Anecdotes of the War, and Personal Adventures of the Officers. Illustrated with Accurate Portraits and Other Beautiful Engravings. Philadelphia: Lippincott, Grambo and Company, 1850.

Miller, Edward, and Frederic P. Wells. *History of Ryegate, Vermont, From Its Settlement by the Scotch-American Company of Farmers to Present Time. With Genealogical Records of Many Families.* St. Johnsbury VT: Caledonian Company, 1913.

Millett, Allan R. *Semper Fidelis: The History of the United States Marine Corps.* New York: Macmillan, 1980.

"Miscellaneous." *New Orleans Medical and Surgical Journal* 54 (April 1902): 680–90.

Missall, John, and Mary Lou Missall. *The Seminole Wars: America's Longest Indian Conflict.* Gainesville: University Press of Florida, 2004.

Moffatt, Walter. "Transportation in Arkansas, 1819–1840." *Arkansas Historical Quarterly* 15, no. 3 (Autumn 1956): 187–201.

Mooney, James L., ed. *Dictionary of American Naval Fighting Ships.* Vol. 2. 1963; reprint. Washington DC: Office of the Chief of Naval Operations, Naval History Division, 1969.

———. *Dictionary of American Naval Fighting Ships.* Vol. 3. Washington DC: Office of the Chief of Naval Operations, Naval History Division, 1968.

Moore, Stephen L. *Savage Frontier: Rangers, Riflemen, and Indian Wars in Texas,* vol. 3: *1840–1841.* Denton: University of North Texas Press, 2007.

Morris, Larry E. *The Fate of the Corps: What Became of the Lewis and Clark Explorers After the Expedition.* New Haven: Yale University Press, 2004.

Morris, Lois Lawson. "Potts, Kirkbride." In *Arkansas Biography: A Collection of Notable Lives,* ed. Nancy A. Williams and Jeannie M. Whayne, 227–28. Fayetteville: University of Arkansas Press, 2000.

Morrison, W. B. "Fort Towson." *Chronicles of Oklahoma* 8, no. 2 (June 1930): 226–32.

Moser, Harold D., David R. Hoth, and George H. Hoemann, eds. *The Papers of Andrew Jackson,* vol. 5: *1821–1824.* Knoxville: University of Tennessee Press, 1996.

Moses, John, and Joseph Kirkland, eds. *History of Chicago, Illinois,* vol. 2. Chicago: Munsell and Company, 1895.

Motte, Jacob Rhett. *Journey into Wilderness: An Army Surgeon's Account of Life in Camp and Field during the Creek and Seminole Wars 1836–1838.* Ed. James F. Sunderman. Gainesville: University of Florida Press, 1953.

Mulroy, Kevin. *The Seminole Freedmen: A History*. Norman: University of Oklahoma Press, 2007.

The National Cyclopædia of American Biography: Being the History of the United States as Illustrated in the Lives of the Founders, Builders, and Defenders of the Republic, and of the Men and Women Who Are Doing the Work and Moulding the Thought of the Present Time, vols. 8, 11. New York: James T. White, 1898, 1901.

A Naval Encyclopædia: Comprising a Dictionary of Nautical Words and Phrases; Biographical Notices, and Records of Naval Officers; Special Articles on Naval Art and Science, Written Expressly for This Work by Officers and Others of Recognized Authority in the Branches Treated by Them. Together with Descriptions of the Principal Naval Stations and Seaports of the World, Complete in One Volume. Philadelphia: L. R. Hamersly and Company, 1881.

Nelson, Gil, Christopher J. Earle, and Richard Spellenberg. *Trees of Eastern North America*. Ed. Amy K. Hughes. Princeton NJ: Princeton University Press, 2014.

Neville, Bert. *Directory of River Packets in the Mobile-Alabama-Warrior-Tombigbee-Trades 1818–1932*. Selma: Selma Printing Service, 1967.

———. *Directory of Tennessee River Steamboats (1821–1928)*. Selma: Coffee Printing Company, 1963.

New Charter of the City of Columbus, Georgia, Declaring the Rights and Powers of Said Corporation, and for Other Purposes. Approved November 29, 1890. Together with Ordinances Adopted Since Adoption of City Code in 1888; July 1, 1888, to May 1, 1898. Columbus GA: Thos. Gilbert, 1898.

Newell, Clayton R., and Charles R. Shrader. *Of Duty Well and Faithfully Done: A History of the Regular Army in the Civil War*. Lincoln: University of Nebraska Press, 2011.

Northen, William J., and John Temple Graves, eds. *Men of Mark in Georgia: A Complete and Elaborate History of the State from its settlement to the present time, chiefly told in biographies and autobiographies of the most eminent men of each period of Georgia's progress and development*, vol. 2. Atlanta: A. B. Caldwell, 1910.

Norton, Charles D. "The Old Black Rock Ferry. Read Before the Society, December 14, 1863." In *Publications of the Buffalo Historical Society*, vol. 1, 91–109. Buffalo: Bigelow Brothers, 1870.

Nuttall, Thomas. *A Journal of Travels into the Arkansa Territory, During the Year 1819. With Occasional Observations on the Manners of the Aborigines*. Philadelphia: Thos. H. Palmer, 1821.

O'Beirne, H. F., and E. S. O'Beirne. *The Indian Territory: Its Chiefs, Legislators and Leading Men*. St. Louis: C. B. Woodward, 1892.

Ogle, John W. *On the Relief of Excessive and Dangerous Tympanites, by Puncture of the Abdomen. A Memoir*. London: J. and A. Churchill, 1888.

Omer, George E. Jr. "An Army Hospital: From Dragoons to Rough Riders—Fort Riley, 1853–1903." *Kansas Historical Quarterly* 23, no. 4 (Winter 1957): 337–67.

Owen, Thomas McAdory. *History of Alabama and Dictionary of Alabama Biography*, vol. 4. Chicago: S. J. Clarke, 1921.

Paige, Amanda L., Fuller L. Bumpers, and Daniel F. Littlefield, Jr. *Chickasaw Removal*. Ada OK: Chickasaw Press, 2010.

Paredes, J. Anthony. "Back from Disappearance: The Alabama Creek Indian Community." In *Southeastern Indians Since the Removal Era*, ed. Walter L. Williams, 123–41. Athens: University of Georgia Press, 1979.

Parker, Daisy. "John Milton, Governor of Florida: A Loyal Confederate." *Florida Historical Quarterly* 20, no. 4 (April 1942): 346–61.

Parsons, John E., ed. "Letters on the Chickasaw Removal of 1837." *New York Historical Society Quarterly* 37 (July 1953): 273–83.

Pate, James P., ed. *The Reminiscences of George Strother Gaines: Pioneer and Statesman of Early Alabama and Mississippi, 1805–1843*. Tuscaloosa: University of Alabama Press, 1998.

Patton, James. *Biography of James Patton*. Asheville NC: [s.n.], 1850.

Payne, John Howard. "The Green-Corn Dance." *Continental Monthly* (January 1862): 17–29.

Perdue, Theda. *Cherokee Women: Gender and Culture Change, 1700–1835*. Lincoln: University of Nebraska Press, 1998.

Peskin, Allan. *Winfield Scott and the Profession of Arms*. Kent OH: Kent State University Press, 2003.

Peter, Robert. *The History of the Medical Department of Transylvania University*. Louisville: John P. Morton, 1905.

Pettigrew, Thomas Joseph. *On Superstitions Connected with the History and Practice of Medicine and Surgery*. Philadelphia: Ed. Barrington and Geo. D. Haswell, 1844.

Pickett, Albert James. "The Death of McIntosh, 1825," *Arrow Points* 10, no. 2 (February 1925): 31–32.

———. *History of Alabama, and Incidentally of Georgia and Mississippi, From the Earliest Period*, vols. 1–2. Charleston: Walker and James, 1851.

Pierpaoli, Paul G. Jr. "Armstrong, Robert." In *The Encyclopedia of the War of 1812: A Political, Social, and Military History*, vol. 1: *A–K*, ed. Spencer C. Tucker et al., 21. Santa Barbara CA: ABC-CLIO, 2012.

Pittman, H. D., and R. K. Walker, eds. *Americans of Gentle Birth and Their Ancestors: A Genealogical Encyclopedia, Embracing Many Authenticated Lineages and Biographical Sketches of the Founders of the Colonies and their Descendants Found in All Parts of the United States*, vol. 1. St. Louis: Buxton and Skinner, 1903.

Pope, William F. *Early Days in Arkansas: Being for the Most Part the Personal Recollections of an Old Settler*. Ed. Dunbar H. Pope. Little Rock: Frederick W. Allsopp, 1895.

Prichard, Walter, Fred B. Kniffen, and Clair A. Brown, eds. "Southern Louisiana and Southern Alabama in 1819: The Journal of James Leander Cathcart." *Louisiana Historical Quarterly* 28, no. 3 (July 1945): 735–921.

"Proceedings of the Association of Medical Superintendents." In *American Journal of Insanity*, vol. 38, 155–262. Utica: State Lunatic Asylum, 1881–82.

Proceedings of a Court Martial Convened for the Trial of Lt. Col. Joshua B. Brant, at St. Louis, June 15, 1839, Upon Charges of Fraud, Violation of Official Trust and Neglect of Duty, and Conduct Unbecoming an Officer and a Gentleman; Containing the Charges, Specifications, and Evidence. Saint Louis: Charles and Hammond, 1850.

Prosch, Thomas W. "The United States Army in Washington Territory." *Washington Historical Quarterly* 2, no. 1 (October 1907): 28–32.

Prucha, Francis Paul. "Andrew Jackson's Indian Policy: A Reassessment." *Journal of American History* 56, no. 3 (December 1969): 527–39.

Rand, Jerry. "Samuel Morton Rutherford." *Chronicles of Oklahoma* 30, no. 2 (June 1952): 149–59.

Ratner, Lorman A. *Andrew Jackson and His Tennessee Lieutenants: A Study in Political Culture*. Westport CT: Greenwood Press, 1997.

Ray, Worth S. *Austin Colony Pioneers: Including History of Bastrop, Fayette, Grimes, Montgomery and Washington Counties, Texas*. 1940; reprint, Austin: Pemberton Press, 1970.

Register of All Officers and Agents, Civil, Military, and Naval, in the Service of the United States, on the Thirtieth September, 1835. With the Names, Force, and Condition of All Ships and Vessels Belonging to the United States, and When and Where Built; Together With a Correct List of the Presidents, Cashiers, and Directors of the United States Bank and Its Branches. To Which Is Appended the Names and Compensation of all Printers in Any Way Employed by Congress, or Any Department or Officer of Government. Washington DC: Blair and Rives, 1835.

Register of All Officers and Agents, Civil, Military, and Naval, in the Service of the United States, from the Thirtieth September, 1841, to the Thirtieth September, 1843. With the Names, Force, and Condition of All Ships and Vessels Belonging to the United States, and When and Where Built; Together with the Names and Compensation of All Printers in Any Way Employed by Congress, or Any Department or Officer of the Government. Washington DC: J. and G. S. Gideon, 1843.

Register of Commissioned Officers of the Sixth Regiment of Infantry, U.S. Army. Commanded by Colonel Melville A. Cochran. From 1808 to 1896. Fort Thomas KY: Published by the Regiment, 1896.

A Register of Officers and Agents, Civil, Military, and Naval, in the Service of the United States, on the 30th of September, 1829; Together with the Names, Force, and Condition of all the Ships and Vessels Belonging to the United States, and When and Where Built. Washington DC: William A. Davis, 1830.

Register of the Commission and Warrant Officers of the Navy of the United States; Including Officers of the Marine Corps, &c. for the Year 1825. Washington DC: Way and Gideon, 1825.

Register of the Commissioned and Warrant Officers of the Navy of the United States, Including Officers of the Marine Corps, for the Year 1835. Washington DC: Blair and Rives, 1835.

Register of the Commissioned and Warrant Officers of the Navy of the United States, Including Officers of the Marine Corps, and Others, for the Year 1847. Washington DC: C. Alexander, 1847.

Register of the Commissioned and Warrant Officers of the Navy of the United States, Including Officers of the Marine Corps, and Others, for the Year 1854. Washington DC: Robert Armstrong, 1854.

Register of the Commissioned and Warrant Officers of the Navy of the United States; Including Officers of the Marine Corps and Others, for the Year 1860. Washington DC: N.p., 1860.

Reid, John, and John Henry Eaton. *The Life of Andrew Jackson, Major General in the Service of the United States: Comprising A History of the War in the South, From the Commencement of the Creek Campaign, to the Termination of Hostilities Before New Orleans*. Philadelphia: M. Carey and Son, 1817.

Remini, Robert V. *Andrew Jackson and His Indian Wars*. New York: Viking, 2001.

———. *The Legacy of Andrew Jackson: Essays on Democracy, Indian Removal, and Slavery*. Baton Rouge: Louisiana State University Press, 1988.

Report of the American Board of Commissioners for Foreign Missions, Read at the Twenty-third Annual Meeting, Which was held in the City of New York, Oct. 3,4, and 5, 1832. Boston: Printed for the Board by Crocker and Brewster, 1832.

Reports on India Rubber Air Pontoons, and Bridges, from the United States Quarter-Master's and Ordnance Departments. New York: Daniel Fanshaw, 1849.

Reynolds, John G. *A Conclusive Exculpation of the Marine Corps in Mexico, from the Slanderous Allegations of One of Its Former Officers; with a Full Official Copy of the Record of the General Court Martial, Held at Brooklyn, New York, 1852. By Which He Was Found Guilty and Dismissed the Service; and Collateral Documents*. New York: Stringer and Townsend, 1853.

Rhees, William J. *An Account of The Smithsonian Institution, Its Founder, Building, Operations, Etc., Prepared from the Reports of Prof. Henry to the Regents, and Other Authentic Sources*. Washington: Thomas McGill, 1859.

Richard, J. Fraise. "History of Franklin County." In *History of Franklin County, Pennsylvania, Containing a History of the County, Its Townships, Towns, Villages, Schools, Churches, Industries, Etc.; Portraits of Early Settlers and Prominent Men; Biographies; History of Pennsylvania, Statistical and Miscellaneous Matter, Etc., Etc.*, 137–614. Chicago: Warner, Beers & Company, 1887.

Risch, Erna, *Quartermaster Support of the Army: A History of the Corps 1775–1939*. Washington DC: Quartermaster Historian's Office, Office of the Quartermaster General, 1962.

Rives, John C., ed. *The Congressional Globe: Containing the Debates and Proceedings of the Second Session of the Thirty-Third Congress*, vol. 30. Washington DC: John C. Rives, 1855.

Robarts, William Hugh, comp. *Mexican War Veterans: A Complete Roster of the Regular and Volunteer Troops in the War Between the United States and Mexico, from 1846 to 1848*. Washington DC: Brentano's, 1887.

Roberts, Thomas P. *Memoirs of John Bannister Gibson, Late Chief Justice of Pennsylvania. With Hon. Jeremiah S. Black's Eulogy, Notes from Hon. William A. Porter's Essay Upon His Life and Character, Etc., Etc.* Pittsburgh: Jos. Eichbaum, 1890.

Robertson, John E. L. *Paducah: Frontier to the Atomic Age*. Charleston SC: Arcadia, 2002.

Rockwell, Stephen J. *Indian Affairs and the Administrative State in the Nineteenth Century*. New York: Cambridge University Press, 2010.

Rollings, Willard H. *The Osage: An Ethnohistorical Study of Hegemony on the Prairie-Plains*. Columbia: University of Missouri Press, 1992.

Romans, Bernard. *A Concise Natural History of East and West Florida*. Ed. Kathryn E. Holland Braund. Tuscaloosa: University of Alabama Press, 1999.

Rosen, Deborah A. *Border Law: The First Seminole War and American Nationhood*. Cambridge: Harvard University Press, 2015.

Ross, Margaret Smith. "Cadron: An Early Town That Failed." *Arkansas Historical Quarterly* 16, no. 1 (Spring 1957): 3–27.

———. "Squatters Rights Part III: The Cadron Settlement Prior to 1814." *Pulaski County Historical Review* 4, no. 4 (December 1956): 51–66.

Rothman, Sheila M. *Living in the Shadow of Death: Tuberculosis and the Social Experience of Illness in American History*. 1994; reprint, Baltimore: Johns Hopkins University Press, 1995.

Rowland, Dunbar. *Mississippi: Comprising Sketches of Counties, Towns, Events, Institutions, and Persons, Arranged in Cyclopedic Form*, vol. 2. Atlanta: Southern Historical Publishing Association, 1907.

———. *The Official and Statistical Register of the State of Mississippi, 1908*. Nashville: Brandon Printing Company, 1908.

Royall, Anne. *Letters from Alabama on Various Subjects: To Which is Added, an Appendix, Containing Remarks on Sundry Members of the 20th & 21st Congress, and Other High Characters, &c. &c. at the Seat of Government. In One Volume.* Washington DC: N.p. 1830.

———. *Mrs. Royall's Southern Tour: or, Second Series of the Black Book*, vol. 2. Washington DC: N.p. 1831.

Rucker, Brian R. "In the Shadow of Jackson: Uriah Blue's Expedition Into West Florida." *Florida Historical Quarterly* 73, no. 3 (January 1995): 325–38.

———. "West Florida's Creek Indian Crisis of 1837." *Florida Historical Quarterly* 69, no. 3 (January 1991): 315–34.

Ryan, Harold W. "Matthew Arbuckle Comes to Fort Smith." *Arkansas Historical Quarterly* 19, no. 4 (Winter 1960): 287–92.

Satz, Ronald N. *American Indian Policy in the Jacksonian Era*. Lincoln: University of Nebraska Press, 1974.

———. "Carey Allen Harris 1836–38." In *The Commissioners of Indian Affairs, 1824–1977*, ed. Robert M. Kvasnicka and Herman J. Viola, 17–22. Lincoln: University of Nebraska Press, 1979.

———. *Tennessee's Indian Peoples: From White Contact to Removal, 1540–1840*. 1979; reprint, Knoxville: University of Tennessee Press, 1985.

———. "Thomas Hartley Crawford 1838–45." In *The Commissioners of Indian Affairs, 1824–1977*, ed. Robert M. Kvasnicka and Herman J. Viola, 23–27. Lincoln: University of Nebraska Press, 1979.

Saunders, James Edmonds. *Early Settlers of Alabama. With Notes and Genealogies by His Granddaughter Elizabeth Saunders Blair Stubbs, New Orleans, LA*. New Orleans: L. Graham & Son, 1899.

Saunt, Claudio. *Black, White, and Indian: Race and the Unmaking of an American Family*. New York: Oxford University Press, 2005.

Scarborough, Jewel Davis. "The Georgia Battalion in the Texas Revolution: A Critical Study." *Southwestern Historical Quarterly* 63, no. 4 (April 1960): 511–32.

Schunk, John F., ed. *1850 U.S. Census, Autauga County, Alabama*. Witchita: S-K Publications, 1987.

Schweikart, Larry. "Antebellum Southern Bankers: Origins and Mobility." *Business and Economic History* 14, no. 2 (1985): 79–103.

Sevier, Cora Bales, and Nancy S. Madden. *Sevier Family History: With the Collected Letters of Gen. John Sevier, First Governor of Tennessee and 28 Collateral Family Lineages*. Washington DC: N.p., 1961.

Shappee, Nathan D. "Fort Dallas and the Naval Depot on Key Biscayne, 1836–1926. *Tequesta: The Journal of the Historical Association of Southern Florida* 1, no. 21 (1961):13–40.

Shinn, Josiah H. *Pioneers and Makers of Arkansas*. 1908; reprint, Baltimore: Genealogical Publishing Company, 1967.

Ships' Data: U.S. Naval Vessels. Washington DC: Government Printing Office, 1921.

Sholes, A. E. *Directory of the Taxing District of Memphis, Shelby County, Tennessee*, vol. 10. Memphis: Rogers and Company, 1883.

Silver, Anna Krugovoy. *Victorian Literature and the Anorexic Body*. 2002; reprint, Cambridge: Cambridge University Press, 2004.

Silver, James W. *Edmund Pendleton Gaines: Frontier General*. Baton Rouge: Louisiana State University Press, 1949.

Simpson, Henry. *The Lives of Eminent Philadelphians, Now Deceased. Collected From Original and Authentic Sources*. Philadelphia: William Brotherhead, 1859.

Simpson, James H. *Journal of a Military Reconnaissance, from Santa Fé, New Mexico, to the Navajo Country, Made With the Troops Under Command of Brevet Lieutenant Colonel John M. Washington, Chief of Ninth Military Department, and Governor of New Mexico, in 1849*. Philadelphia: Lippincott, Grambo and Company, 1852.

———. *Report of Explorations across the Great Basin of the Territory of Utah for a Direct Wagon-Route from Camp Floyd to Genoa, in Carson Valley, in 1859*. Washington DC: Government Printing Office, 1876.

Slatta, Richard W., and Jane Lucas De Grummond. *Simón Bolívar's Quest for Glory*. College Station: Texas A&M University Press, 2003.

Sledge, John S. *The Mobile River*. Columbia: University of South Carolina Press, 2015.

Smith, H. Perry, ed. *History of the City of Buffalo and Erie County, with Illustrations and Biographical Sketches of Some of Its Prominent Men and Pioneers*, vol. 2. Syracuse NY: D. Mason, 1884.

Smith, Sol. *The Theatrical Journey-Work and Anecdotical Recollections of Sol. Smith, Comedian, Attorney at Law, Etc., Etc. Comprising a Sketch of the Second Seven Years of His Professional Life; Together with Sketches of Adventure in After Years, with a Portrait of the Author*. Philadelphia: T. B. Peterson, 1854.

Smithers, Gregory D., and Brooke N. Newman, eds. *Native Diasporas: Indigenous Identities and Settler Colonialism in the Americas*. Lincoln: University of Nebraska Press, 2014.

Snyder, Christina. "Conquered Enemies, Adopted Kin, and Owned People: The Creek Indians and Their Captives." *Journal of Southern History* 73, no. 2 (May 2007): 255–88.

———. *Great Crossings: Indians, Settlers, and Slaves in the Age of Jackson*. New York: Oxford University Press, 2017.

———. *Slavery in Indian Country: The Changing Face of Captivity in Early America*. Cambridge: Harvard University Press, 2010.

Southerland, Henry DeLeon Jr., and Jerry Elijah Brown. *The Federal Road through Georgia, the Creek Nation, and Alabama, 1806–1836*. Tuscaloosa: University of Alabama Press, 1989.

Sprague, John T. *The Origin, Progress, and Conclusion of the Florida War; To Which is Appended a Record of Officers, Non-Commissioned Officers, Musicians, and Privates of the U.S. Army, Navy, and Marine Corps, Who Were Killed in Battle or Died of Disease. As Also the Names of Officers Who Were Distinguished by Brevets, and the Names of Others Recommended. Together with the Orders For Collecting the Remains of the Dead in Florida, and the Ceremony of Interment at St. Augustine, East Florida, on the Fourteenth Day of August, 1842*. New York: D. Appleton, 1848.

Stagg, J. C. A. "Between Black Rock and a Hard Place: Peter B. Porter's Plan for an American Invasion of Canada in 1812." *Journal of the Early Republic* 19, no. 3 (Autumn 1999): 385–422.

Stanley, J. M. *Portraits of North American Indians, With Sketches of Scenery, Etc.* Washington DC: Smithsonian Institution, 1852.

Stevens, Walter B. *St. Louis, The Fourth City, 1764–1911*, vol. 2. St. Louis: S. J. Clarke, 1911.

Stouffer, Midge. "The E.W.B. Nowland Family of Fort Smith," *Journal of the Fort Smith Historical Society* 30, no. 1 (April 2006): 38–44.

Stryker's American Register and Magazine 4 (July 1850): 9–600.

Stuart, James. *Three Years in North America*, vol. 2. Edinburgh: Robert Cadell, 1833.

Supplement to Encyclopædia Brittanica. Ninth Edition. A Dictionary of Arts, Sciences, and General Literature, vol. 4. New York: J. M. Stoddart, 1889.

Swanton, John R. *Early History of the Creek Indians and Their Neighbors*. Smithsonian Institution Bureau of American Ethnology Bulletin 73. Washington DC: Government Printing Office, 1922.

Tallapoosa County: A History. Alexander City: Tallapoosa County Bicentennial Committee, 1976.

Terry, James G., ed. "Record of the Alabama State Artillery from It's [*sic*] Organization in May 1836 to the Surrender in April 1865 and from It's Re-organization Jany 1872 to Jany 1875." *Alabama Historical Quarterly* 20, no. 2 (Summer 1958): 141–447.

Thian, Raphael P. *Notes Illustrating the Military Geography of the United States, 1813–1880*. Ed. John M. Carroll. Austin: University of Texas Press, 1979.

Thompson, Jerry. *Civil War to the Bloody End: The Life and Times of Major General Samuel P. Heintzelman*. College Station: Texas A&M University Press, 2006.

———. *Fifty Miles and a Fight: Major Samuel Peter Heintzelman's Journal of Texas and the Cortina War*. Austin: Texas State Historical Society, 1998.

Thrapp, Dan L. *Encyclopedia of Frontier Biography*, vols. 1–3. 1988; reprint, Lincoln: University of Nebraska Press, 1991.

Tissot, S. A. D. *An Essay on Bilious Fevers; or, The History of a Bilious Epidemic Fever at Lausanne, in the Year MDCCLV*. London: Printed for D. Wilson and T. Durham, 1760.

Toll, Ian W. *Six Frigates: The Epic History of the Founding of the U.S. Navy*. New York: W. W. Norton, 2006.

Tomer, John S., and Michael J. Brodhead, eds. *A Naturalist in Indian Territory: The Journals of S. W. Woodhouse, 1849–50*. 1992; reprint, Norman: University of Oklahoma Press, 1996.

Trennert, Robert A. "William Medill 1845–49." In *The Commissioners of Indian Affairs, 1824–1977*, ed. Robert M. Kvasnicka and Herman J. Viola, 29–39 .Lincoln: University of Nebraska Press, 1979.

Trent, Hank, ed. *Narrative of James Williams, an American Slave: Annotated Edition*. Baton Rouge: Louisiana State University Press, 2013.

Tyler, Lyon Gardiner. *Encyclopedia of Virginia Biography*, vol. 5. New York: Lewis Historical Publishing Company, 1915.

U.S. Congress. House Document 48. *Letter from the Secretary of War, Transmitting, With a Letter from the Chief of Engineers, Reports on Preliminary Examination and Plan and Estimate of Cost of Improvement of La Grue River, Ark.* 67th Cong., 1st Sess., 1921.

———. House Document 60. *Letter from the Secretary of War, A statement of the names, situation, and pay of all persons employed in the Indian Department, &c.* 23rd Cong., 1st Sess., 1834.

———. House Document 284. *Letter from the Secretary of War, Transmitting the information required by a resolution of the House of Representatives of the 16th January last, In Relation to an Examination of the Muscle Shoals in Tennessee River, with a View to Removing the Obstructions to the Navigation thereof, and the Construction of a Canal Around the Same.* 20th Cong., 1st Sess., 1828, Serial Set 175.

———. House Document 276. *Letter from the Secretary of War, Transmitting Documents in Relation to Hostilities of Creek Indians.* 24th Cong., 1st sess., 1836.

———. House Executive Document 209. *Official Reports from General Taylor.* 29th Cong., 1st Sess., 1846.

———. House Report 2. *Case of Judge John C. Watrous.* 36th Cong., 2nd Sess., 1860.

———. House Report 30. Alexander J. Robison. 22nd Cong., 2nd Sess., 1833.

———. House Report 47. *Horatio N. Crabb and John G. Reynolds.* 22nd Cong., 2nd, Sess., 1833.

———. House Report 87. *Remove Indians Westward.* 20th Cong., 2nd Sess., 1829, Serial 190.

———. House Report 98. *Report of the Select Committee of the House of Representatives, to Which Were Referred the Messages of the President U.S. of the 5th and 8th February, and 2d March, 1827, with accompanying documents and a report and resolutions of the Legislature of Georgia.* 19th Cong., 2nd Sess., 1827, Serial 161.

———. House Report 250. *U.S. Frigate "Constellation."* 63rd Cong., 2nd Sess., 1914.

———. House Report 2561. *Virginia Taylor Randall.* 49th Cong., 1st Sess., 1886.

———. Senate Committee Report 142. *In Senate of the United States.* 31st Cong., 1st Sess., 1850.

———. Senate Committee Report 307. *In the Senate of the United States.* 32nd Cong., 1st Sess., 1852.

———. Senate Document 512. *Correspondence on the Subject of the Emigration of Indians, Between the 30th November, 1831, and 27th December, 1833, With Abstracts of Expenditures By Disbursing Agents, in the Removal and Subsistence of Indians, &c. &c.* 23rd Cong., 2nd Sess., 1834–35, Vol. 1, Serial Set 244.

———. Senate Report 641. *Priscilla Decatur Twiggs.* 47th Cong., 1st Sess., 1882.

———. Senate Report 1457. *Abner Abercrombie.* 53rd Cong., 2nd Sess., 1895.

Utley, Robert M. *Geronimo.* New Haven: Yale University Press, 2012.

Vincent, Francis. *Vincent's Semi-Annual United States Register: A Work in Which the Principal Events of Every Half-Year Occurring in the United States Are Recorded,*

Each Arranged Under the Day of Its Date. This Volume Contains the Events Transpiring Between the 1st of January and 1st of July, 1860. Philadelphia: Francis Vincent, 1860.

Vandiver, Wellington. "Pioneer Talladega, Its Minutes and Memories." *Alabama Historical Quarterly* 16, no. 1 (Spring 1954): 9–155.

Viola, Herman J. "Thomas L. McKenney 1824–30. In *The Commissioners of Indian Affairs, 1824–1977*, ed. Robert M. Kvasnicka and Herman J. Viola, 1–7. Lincoln: University of Nebraska Press, 1979.

von Gerstner, Franz Anton Ritter. *Early American Railroads: Franz Anton Ritter von Gerstner's Die innern Communicationen (1842–1843)*. Ed. Frederick C. Gamst, trans. David J. Diephouse and John C. Decker. Stanford CA: Stanford University Press, 1997.

Walz, Robert B. "Arkansas Slaveholdings and Slaveholders in 1850." *Arkansas Historical Quarterly* 12, no. 1 (Spring 1953): 38–74.

Warner, Ezra J. *Generals in Blue: Lives of the Union Commanders*. Baton Rouge: Louisiana State University Press, 1964.

———. *Generals in Gray: Lives of the Confederate Commanders*. Baton Rouge: Louisiana State University Press, 1959.

Waselkov, Gregory A. *A Conquering Spirit: Fort Mims and the Redstick War of 1813–1814*. Tuscaloosa: University of Alabama Press, 2006.

———. "Formation of the Tensaw Community." In *Red Eagle's Children: Weatherford vs. Weatherford et al.*, ed. J. Anthony Paredes and Judith Knight, 36–45. Tuscaloosa: University of Alabama Press, 2012.

Watson, Winslow Marston, ed., and Benjamin Ogle Tayloe. *In Memoriam: Benjamin Ogle Tayloe*. Washington; Philadelphia: Sherman & Company, 1872.

Whalen, Brett E. "A Vermonter on the Trail of Tears, 1830–1837." *Vermont History* 66, no. 1 (1998): 31–38.

White, Christine Schultz, and Benton R. White. *Now the Wolf Has Come: The Creek Nation in the Civil War*. College Station: Texas A&M University Press, 1996.

White, Frank L., Jr. "The Journals of Lieutenant John Pickell, 1836–1837." *Florida Historical Quarterly* 38, no. 2 (October 1959): 142–71.

Weaver, Herbert, and Wayne Cutler, eds. *Correspondence of James K. Polk*, vol. IV: *1837–1838*. Nashville: Vanderbilt University Press, 1977.

Wesley, John. *Primitive Phyfick: or, An Easy and Natural Method of Curing Moft Diseases. Ninth Edition*. London: W. Strahan, 1761.

Wilcox, Cadmus M. *History of the Mexican War*. Ed. Mary Rachel Wilcox. Washington DC: Church News Publishing Company, 1892.

Williams, John Lee. *The Territory of Florida: or Sketches of the Topography, Civil and Natural History, of the Country, the Climate, and the Indian Tribes, from the First Discovery to the Present Time, With a Map, Views, &c.* New York: A. T. Goodrich, 1837.

Williams, Joseph S. *Old Times in West Tennessee. Reminiscences—Semi-Historic—of Pioneer Life and the Early Emigrant Settlers in the Big Hatchie Country*. Memphis: W. G. Cheeney, 1873.

Williams, Thomas M. "Dixon H. Lewis." *Alabama Polytechnic Institute Historical Studies*. Fourth Series (1910): 1–33.

Wilson, Elinor. *Jim Beckwourth: Black Mountain Man and War Chief of the Crows*. Norman: University of Oklahoma Press, 1972.

Wilson, James Grant, and John Fiske, eds. *Appletons' Cyclopædia of American Biography*, vols. 2, 4, 5. New York: D. Appleton and Company, 1888–1900.

Wilson, Samuel Jr. "An Architectural History of the Royal Hospital and the Ursuline Convent of New Orleans." *Louisiana Historical Quarterly* 29, no. 3 (July 1946): 559–659.

Winn, William W. *The Triumph of the Ecunnau-Nuxulgee: Land Speculators, George M. Troup, State Rights, and the Removal of the Creek Indians from Georgia and Alabama, 1825–38*. Macon: Mercer University Press, 2015.

Woodward, Thomas S. *Woodward's Reminiscences of the Creek, or Muscogee Indians, Contained in Letters to Friends in Georgia and Alabama*. Montgomery AL: Barrett and Wimbish, 1859.

Worley, Ted R. "Arkansas and the 'Hostile' Indians, 1835–1838." *Arkansas Historical Quarterly* 6, no. 2 (Summer 1947): 155–64.

———. "Arkansas and the Money Crisis of 1836–1837. *Journal of Southern History* 15, no. 2 (May 1949): 178–91.

———. "The Arkansas State Bank: Ante-Bellum Period." *Arkansas Historical Quarterly* 23, no. 1 (Spring 1964): 65–73.

———. "The Batesville Branch of the State Bank, 1836–1839." *Arkansas Historical Quarterly* 6, no. 3 (Autumn 1947): 286–99.

Wright, J. Leitch Jr. *Creeks and Seminoles: The Destruction and Regeneration of the Muscogulge People*. Lincoln: University of Nebraska Press, 1986.

Wright, Marcus J. *Reminiscences of the Early Settlement and Early Settlers of McNairy County, Tennessee*. Washington DC: Commercial Publishing Company, 1882.

———. "Return Jonathan Meigs, 1801–1891." In *Magazine of American History with Notes and Queries*, ed Martha J. Lamb, vol. 28, July–December 1892, 125–28. New York: Historical Publication Company, 1892.

Yates, John R., Jr., and Thomas Yates. *The Boston Marine Barracks: A History, 1799–1974*. Jefferson NC: McFarland and Company, 2015.

Young, Mary Elizabeth. *Redskins, Ruffleshirts, and Rednecks: Indian Allotments in Alabama and Mississippi*. Norman: University of Oklahoma Press, 1961.

Zellar, Gary. *African Creeks: Estelvste and the Creek Nation*. Norman: University of Oklahoma Press, 2007.

INDEX

Printed in the USA
CPSIA information can be obtained
at www.ICGtesting.com
LVHW092240141023
760911LV00026B/292/J